W9-CFH-096

PEBBLES TO COMPUTERS

Minister of State
Science and Technology

Canada

Ministre d'État
Sciences et Technologie

OTTAWA, December 1985.

Dear Reader,

Hans Blohm's and Stafford Beer's personal vision is a remarkable testament to the depth and richness of humanity's technological achievements. In their book *Pebbles to Computers*, they present a convincing visual argument that high technology does indeed go back to the dawn of time. Canada represents an impressive part of that achievement, overcoming its great size and relatively small population through the genius of modern communications. It was the first country to launch its own domestic satellite and the third to put a satellite into orbit. There is more to come. Perhaps a later edition of the present book will feature the genius of space-age materials, lasers and fiber optics, as high technology in Canada continues to evolve.

Yours sincerely,

The Honourable Frank Oberle, P.C., M.P.,
Minister of State for Science and Technology.

Ottawa, Canada
K1A 1A1

PEBBLES TO COMPUTERS

The Thread

Hans Blohm
Stafford Beer
David Suzuki

OXFORD UNIVERSITY PRESS
Toronto • 1986

FROM HANS BLOHM

In memory of my father whose enquiring mind prepared me for this venture

Hans-Ludwig

FROM STAFFORD BEER

To my mother with my love for all of hers

Tony

PEBBLES TO COMPUTERS
The Thread
Original Idea and Photography by Hans Blohm
Text and Design by Stafford Beer
Special Contributions by Rudi Haas
Introduction by David Suzuki

Produced by Fortunato Aglialoro
for Boulton Publishing Services, Inc., Toronto

CANADIAN CATALOGUING IN PUBLICATION DATA

Blohm, Hans
Pebbles to computers
ISBN 0-19-540536-6
1. Science. 2. Knowledge, Theory of. 3. Numeration – History. I. Beer, Stafford. II. Suzuki, David T., 1936– III. Title.
Q172.B58 1986 500 C86-093331-8

1 2 3 4 - 9 8 7 6

Printed in Hong Kong by Scanner Art Services, Inc., Toronto

INTRODUCTION

David T. Suzuki

Human beings are remarkable creatures. We evolved out of nature itself and remain inextricably bound up in it but we have a sense of self-awareness that gives us the feeling of being special. We perceive ourselves as being different from all other life-forms and in many ways unique and superior. Yet we are not particularly gifted—an elephant can easily outrun us, a fierce dog can overwhelm us. We can't see in the ultraviolet or infrared, we don't have night vision, we can't hear low or high frequencies, we can't smell or taste minute concentrations of molecules, nor detect magnetism—yet many other organisms can. So physically there is nothing that distinguishes us. But we do have a large *brain*, an organ that has more than compensated for our deficiencies in physical prowess. With that brain we have created technology, which has enabled us to extend with machines the range of our sensory acuity and physical strength, beyond anything known in the biological world.

The survival strategy of our distant hominid ancestors was a high 'brain-to-brawn' ratio. Information flowing from peripheral sense organs into that complex brain could be processed, the potential *consequences* of different responses estimated, and then a *decision* made. Now there was *choice* and a *future* of multiple possibilities. The brain could remember, recognize problems, solve them by abstract thought and learn from experience.

Organizing the World

However long ago consciousness emerged, it was accompanied by a desire to 'make sense' of the world around, for the human brain has a need to create order out of chaos. To those early men for whom there was no causal basis for daily events, life must have been chaotic; and accompanying chaos is terror. By creating order in the surrounding environment, early man had some hope of predicting and controlling the cosmic forces impinging on his life. Those early people had to be keen observers, because for them this meant the difference between survival and death, and they must have accumulated a large body of knowledge based on their observations and beliefs. However fantastic to us their explanations for the rise and fall of tides, the seasons, day and night, animal migrations, illness or death may seem, for them the explanations worked, providing a causal basis and a significance to all events. Even earthquakes, floods, diseases and accidents could be explained by invoking supernatural forces.

The need for order resulted in 'worldviews'—complete explanations of the entire universe in which everything was intimately linked. Thus the occurrence of an extraordinary event, such as the birth of a severely defective child, an eclipse or an earthquake, marked a conjunction of all the cosmic forces. Such occurences then had to be seen as the consequences of past events or as portents of future ones. Worldviews provide explanations for everything (although gods usually are a big fudge factor). Mythology is the codification of that body of knowledge. Of course, mythology is an amalgam of superstition, close observation and a great deal of folk wisdom. North American Indians knew they should consume foxgloves for certain ailments, although it took scientists to characterize the active ingredient as *digitalis* for heart problems. South American Indians poisoned fish with extracts of plant roots that are only now known to yield curare. Ancient Chinese acupuncturists could control pain without knowing that they were stimulating the release of endorphins in the brain.

The Role of Information

The father of modern science, Francis Bacon, observed in the seventeenth century that 'knowledge is power' and so it has been ever since human brains began to process information. Information, knowledge, experience, could be stored in the brain as memory, retrieved at will and transmitted from individual to individual and from generation to generation. Special knowledge gave individuals like the *shaman* power over others, provided groups of people like priests with influence over other classes, gave one nation an advantage over another. Information has always been a vital commodity in the strategy for human survival and the existence of power élites within societies but much of it was bound up in superstition and fantasy.

> 'Once there was only god, Ymir. And from his skull, the world was created. From his hair, the plants; from his tongue, the oxen; and man came forth from his eyes.'

This incredible Norse creation-myth is no more remarkable than hundreds of myths from other societies. Here is another.

> 'Once all matter in the entire universe was contained in a point. Matter as we know it didn't exist, time had no meaning, nor was there space. Then, fifteen billion years ago, that point exploded and boiled out into

> space as hundreds of new states of matter appeared from nothing and disappeared into nowhere. And as the universe grew, gradually clots of dust coalesced into a ball that burst into flame, lumps of matter circled such fires, and life appeared on one of them where none existed before.'

Is this 'creation story', told by scientists, any less fantastic than the Norse myth? Of course not. Yet this one we 'believe' while the others we dismiss. Why?

The Rise of Modern Science

During the time of the ancient Greeks a new spirit of questioning arose, a faith in the ultimate power of the human intellect. The Greeks accepted nothing and questioned everything, laying to rest many mystical explanations of the world around them. In the process, they laid the foundations for the twentieth century. When the Renaissance breathed new life into open enquiry, the stage was ready for the explosive force of a new way of knowing—*science*. Science did not set as its goal a new worldview. Instead, scientists recognized that they couldn't explain such an immensely complex universe in its totality. Theirs was a far more modest task, to focus on a small part of nature, to isolate it from everything else, and to learn as much about it as possible. This meant *reducing* parts of nature to their smallest or simplest level. And remarkably, this reductionist approach provided powerful new insights into those isolated parts. The great success of science was in limiting its field of vision to a narrow sphere. This knowledge provided power, power to interfere, to manipulate, and ultimately to control.

Science arose within a Western worldview in which Man was seen to be the pinnacle of all life, created in the image of God. Ours was the mandate to fill the earth and dominate all of nature; and so progress came to be measured by the degree to which we controlled nature. As the power élites of religion recognized the challenge of scientific insight, they chose to fight. Galileo, Darwin, Freud and Einstein were the eventual victors over the forces of dogmatism. Having lost faith in religious doctrines, people turned increasingly to the possessors of scientific knowledge for *truth*. But science can *never* provide a worldview—by its very methodology, it is incapable of it.

Limits to Science

In this century, scientists themselves began to realize an unsettling fact, that the goal of finding absolute truth was impossible. Where Isaac Newton had once viewed the universe as a gigantic clockwork mechanism, ultimately knowable through the power of science, now relativity suggests that truth may depend on our point of view. In any scientific experiment, the act of observation perturbs the observed so that we can never 'know' it as it is in its natural state. And even at the level of subatomic particles, behaviour can only be predicted as a statistical probability, not as an absolute certainty.

Scientists also began to realize that it is not possible, by understanding properties of matter at one level, to predict or extrapolate to a more complex level. Thus information about subatomic particles informs us very poorly about how atoms behave. Knowledge about single atoms does not generate predictions about their activity in molecules. This is true at higher levels of complexity, from the components of cells, multicells and individuals, to groups and ecosystems. Our knowledge of how single neurons work in the brain is of little or no help in treating a psychotic person or coping with loneliness. In a world of human values, science is singularly incapable of answering the most important questions—about what is right or wrong, the differences between good and evil, the significance of murder or love.

Technological Power

Yet the output of our brains in the form of science and technology has taken us to a position of global dominance in a startingly short period of time. Indeed to some we seem like a feral species, newly introduced to an environment and out of biological control. We are now the most numerous large mammal on the planet and we are ubiquitous. Perhaps the most astonishing achievement of our species has been the invention of a technology, namely the computer, that has the potential to be even more creative and powerful than our own brains. To the philosopher who once suggested that the brain is too complex ever to understand itself must be added the cautionary note that it may have created something so much faster and potentially so much more powerful, that it will transcend the brain and decipher it.

Today we live in a period of social change accelerated by scientific insight and invention. Where once pottery, metal, needles or dyes heralded social revolutions many centuries apart, now multiple revolutions occur within a single lifetime. Anyone over the age of 40 has already witnessed the introduction of plastics, television, jets, satellites, computers, lasers, tranquillizers, recombinant DNA, oral contraceptives, nuclear power and organ transplants. To-day's youth will spend most of their adult lives in the *21st century* and will take for granted what we now regard as science fiction.

The key to this revolution is, as at the dawn of human consciousness, *information*, and nowhere is it more profound than in our understanding of information in genes, brains and computers. As we acquire knowledge in these areas, we will also gain in manipulative power and control. But who will have access to that knowledge, and how will it be used? Have we learned from history the limitations of scientific reductionism and the concentration of knowledge in a power élite? Can we go on applying fragmentary knowledge to affect entire groups or ecosystems?

Limits to Technology

The rapidity with which modern technology has developed now threatens all life on the planet. Powerful machines can 'harvest' natural resources like oil and gas, trees, fish, soil and water in vast quantities; but a side effect is the industrial toxins that now poison the air, water and earth and so devastate portions of the ecosystem that they may never recover. Nuclear technology has become so powerful, accurate and fast that it lies beyond the human capacity to respond. We regard the dinosaurs as losers because they suddenly disappeared, yet they flourished for 150 million years. We haven't been here for a million years, yet already we are changing the planet as explosively as in the period when the dinosaurs disappeared.

We must resist the temptation to be mesmerized by our technological success. Where once our brains served to compensate for our lack of physical strength, that ability coupled with technology can now become counter-productive. For we continue to apply technology as if we were still under the same survival imperatives as our hunter-gatherer predecessors; but it is a 'brute force' technology that is neither subtle nor cognizant of natural boundaries established by millions of years of evolution. This struck me one summer when I spent time with the San People of the Kalahari Desert, one of the last group of hunter-gatherers on the planet. I appeared suddenly in their midst with all of the paraphernalia of an industrial civilization—planes, film, canned goods, camping gear. They had never seen television, a refrigerator or a computer, yet they are the remnants of a culture that has lived in equilibrium with the environment for tens of thousands of years. Much to their amusement I wasn't able to crack open the *mongongo* nut on which they depend, nor could I read the signs that told of the *kudu* that had passed by a few hours before. They could survive easily with just their wits. I had the power to radically alter their surroundings, but wouldn't last long even with my support-technology because it and I were not in harmony with that environment. Intoxicated with our achievements, have we lost sight of what it's all for and of our own place in the natural order?

The Flaw in Science

To the San People, survival depends on an understanding of nature far more sophisticated and profound than we can ever achieve with our analytic tools of science. That is because the great strength of science is also its weakness. By looking at nature in bits and pieces, our understanding of it can only be fragmentary, for nature is not the sum of its isolated parts. Components of ecosystems interact in ways not predictable by separate knowledge of each component. Too often the history of modern science has been the derivation of insights which, when applied through technology, have unexpected and often unpredictable effects. In focussing on problems amenable to analysis and solution, we can never encompass the larger context within which that problem is important.

For people living within a different worldview, with a different perspective from the scientific and technological approach of the West, the linearity of our thinking must be puzzling. To an Amazonian Indian, our system of plant classification would be as mystifying as it is useless compared to his, which is based on seasons, habitat and edibility. To the North American Indian who asks forgiveness before taking the life of an animal, the spirit world is as real as the atom is to us. In the world of science, although its practitioners are first and foremost human, there is no equation for emotions or things spiritual, yet it may be just those aspects that are vital to prevent this great enterprise from taking us into insurmountable difficulties.

Many Realities

Like all other organisms, we have the ability to receive information about the world through our sensory apparatus. That information is far from complete. We also have the ability to filter out, from among the many inputs, the signals that we deem important. The filtering mechanisms are conditioned by handwiring (inborn neural circuitry) and learning-through-experience. Thus, we *create* reality, and that reality is highly personal. Science only knows through a restricted set of tools that provide repeatable, verifiable observations and results; but when reality is a construct of personal heredity and experience, there is much that cannot be validated by scientific methods. That is why scientific pronouncements often elicit a sense of discomfort, because they seem to deny a large part of our own spheres of reality.

The Search for Answers

Since the earliest days of human consciousness, we have sought to know who we are, how we got here, why we're here and where we're going. Now science and technology add insight to the answers, helping us to eliminate superstition and misconceptions, but also giving us a picture that is uncomfortably incomplete. We have to retain a sense of mystery, wonder and awe at the forces of nature and at the enormous variety of human perceptions. Only then can we balance the illusion that our technology is so powerful that nothing lies beyond its reach, and that all of nature, including human nature, can be wrestled under our control.

Historical Puzzles

Human beings have been gifted with the ability to communicate through systems of images, from prehistoric paintings to pictographs to abstract characters of language. You are about to embark on an adventure that continues that long tradition.

This book gives us a peek at the long history of human inventiveness in print and calculation. Many of the symbols and devices shown are still opaque to our understanding. That of course is why they fascinate. What motivated people in so many cultures in the past to invest so much time, thought and effort to construct the puzzles that remain to-day? It is a tribute to the human spirit and imagination that they should leave such artifacts for us to ponder. Some, in the chauvinism of the contemporary, seem to find it impossible to accept that people in the past could have been as clever as we, and therefore postulate visitors from outer space who must have provided the intelligence. It is the height of arrogance to think that because *we* can't figure out some things, people in the past couldn't have done so either.

We think of computers as recent inventions. While the silicon chip of a modern computer is certainly a recent arrival, the roots of this technology go back long before transistors and vacuum tubes, before electricity, indeed before recorded history. Now, when the scientists living today comprise over ninety percent of all the scientists who have ever lived, there is a tendency to think that our own generation has a virtual monopoly in the history of intelligence. In terms simply of population numbers, there may be more 'smart people' around today than at any time before but, in terms of creative imagination and the quality of thought, many ancient cultures were fully as perceptive as our own. Their philosophers and scientists were every bit as 'smart' as ours.

Today there is so much information available that a budding scientist must focus early and intensely to reach the cutting edge of research. Too often that will be at the expense of a historical appreciation. This book should help to correct that deficiency, giving us an inspiring view of the vast sweep of human creativity, and putting modern science into perspective, as we consider the reach of a long and wonder-woven story.

D.T.S.

Pebbles...

Everyone picks up and examines pebbles from time to time. Perhaps the fascination lies in the smoothness, or in beautiful markings. But there is something else about a pebble, which maybe stirs us more profoundly.

A pebble is an entity. It is one of the simplest, most familiar things that demonstrate a unity. After all, if we had a pebble that was rather flat or worn down at one end, it would not be tempting to say: this is *really* only nine-tenths of a pebble. No, a pebble marks itself off from everything else—to be ITSELF. In that case, it is remarkable that no two pebbles out of billions are alike. This apparently simplest and most familiar of things turns out to be quite an abstract concept!

The abstraction derives from ignoring the specific shape, the peculiar colouring, of any particular pebble. We pass from that physical unity, to the notion of a unit—any unit, as typified by any pebble. But that unit still constitutes a mark that makes a distinction.

All computing is based on this idea.

There was an early start to it all. For example, let's go back to the early years of Athenian democracy. That is a journey in time of roughly two-and-a-half thousand years. The meeting of the people, the *ecclesia*, held ballots. As the voters passed by the tellers, each person cast a pebble into the pot that indicated his preference. So now the pebble, the mark that draws a distinction, stands for the voter's preference itself—and the pebbles may be counted.

The ballots were called ψήφοι, the very word for 'pebbles'. Any subsequent democratic decree drew on that root again, to be called ψήφισμα. Transliterating the Greek to Roman letters, we get *psephoi* and *psephisma*.Small wonder then that academic commentators who appear on television at election time to talk of 'swings' this way and that are called 'psephologists'. They are students of the way the pebbles are falling. They need computers to do it.

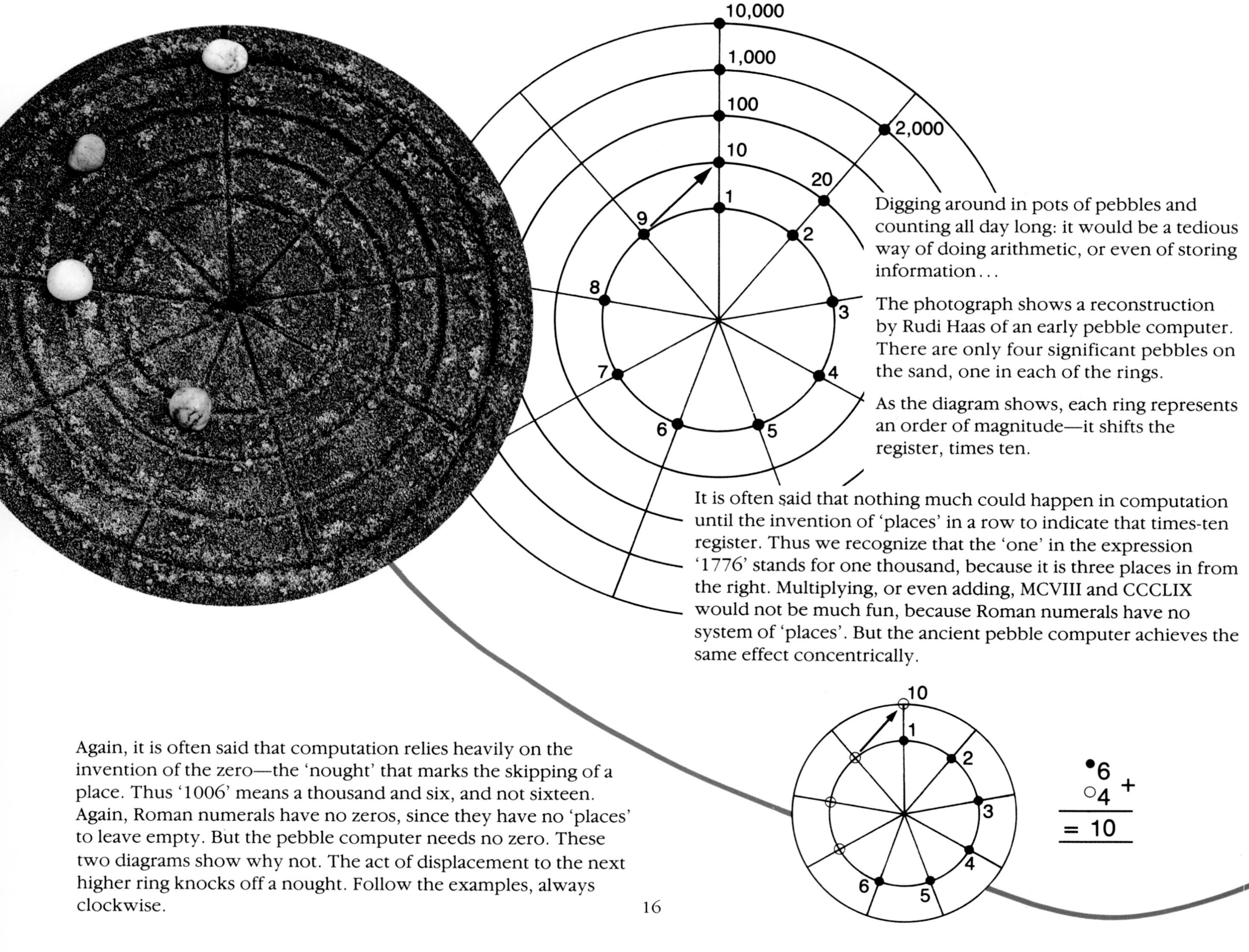

Digging around in pots of pebbles and counting all day long: it would be a tedious way of doing arithmetic, or even of storing information...

The photograph shows a reconstruction by Rudi Haas of an early pebble computer. There are only four significant pebbles on the sand, one in each of the rings.

As the diagram shows, each ring represents an order of magnitude—it shifts the register, times ten.

It is often said that nothing much could happen in computation until the invention of 'places' in a row to indicate that times-ten register. Thus we recognize that the 'one' in the expression '1776' stands for one thousand, because it is three places in from the right. Multiplying, or even adding, MCVIII and CCCLIX would not be much fun, because Roman numerals have no system of 'places'. But the ancient pebble computer achieves the same effect concentrically.

Again, it is often said that computation relies heavily on the invention of the zero—the 'nought' that marks the skipping of a place. Thus '1006' means a thousand and six, and not sixteen. Again, Roman numerals have no zeros, since they have no 'places' to leave empty. But the pebble computer needs no zero. These two diagrams show why not. The act of displacement to the next higher ring knocks off a nought. Follow the examples, always clockwise.

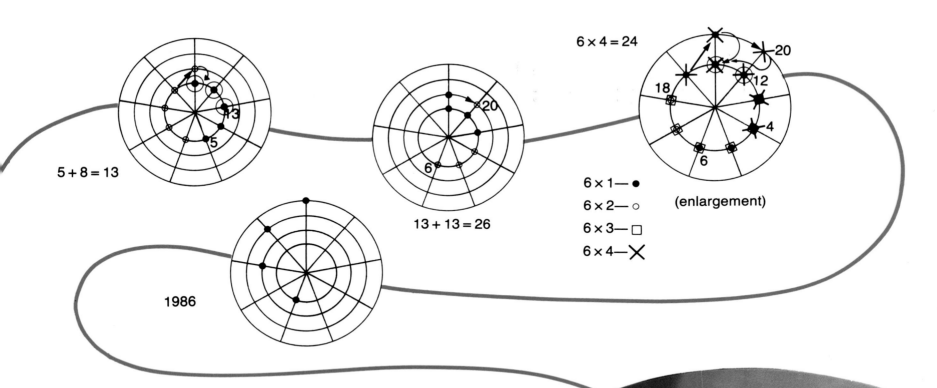

5 + 8 = 13

13 + 13 = 26

6 × 4 = 24

6 × 1— ●
6 × 2— ○
6 × 3— □
6 × 4— ✕

(enlargement)

1986

The Red Thread That Connects the pebble computer to this modern disc-storage device travels far through space and time—and technological distance too. Yet always we are dealing with the same fundamental ideas. If you worked at the 6x4 multiplication example, you will have realized that pebble computers did not 'know their tables'. Was it disappointing to find that six was being *added* to six, four times over? It should not be—for that is exactly how your pocket calculator does the trick! The computer disc records its 'pebbles' in a spiral space. It reads its record by radial as well as spiral movements of its tracking arm. It has a memory made accessible in two dimensions. So has the pebble computer: you can read '1986' above without counting nearly two thousand positions to see what is in each one. We continue to use the disc idea for exactly the reason that the man we imagined did not want to sift through pots of pebbles all day long. Mind you, this shining disc records the equivalent of thirty million pebbles —which is just as well.

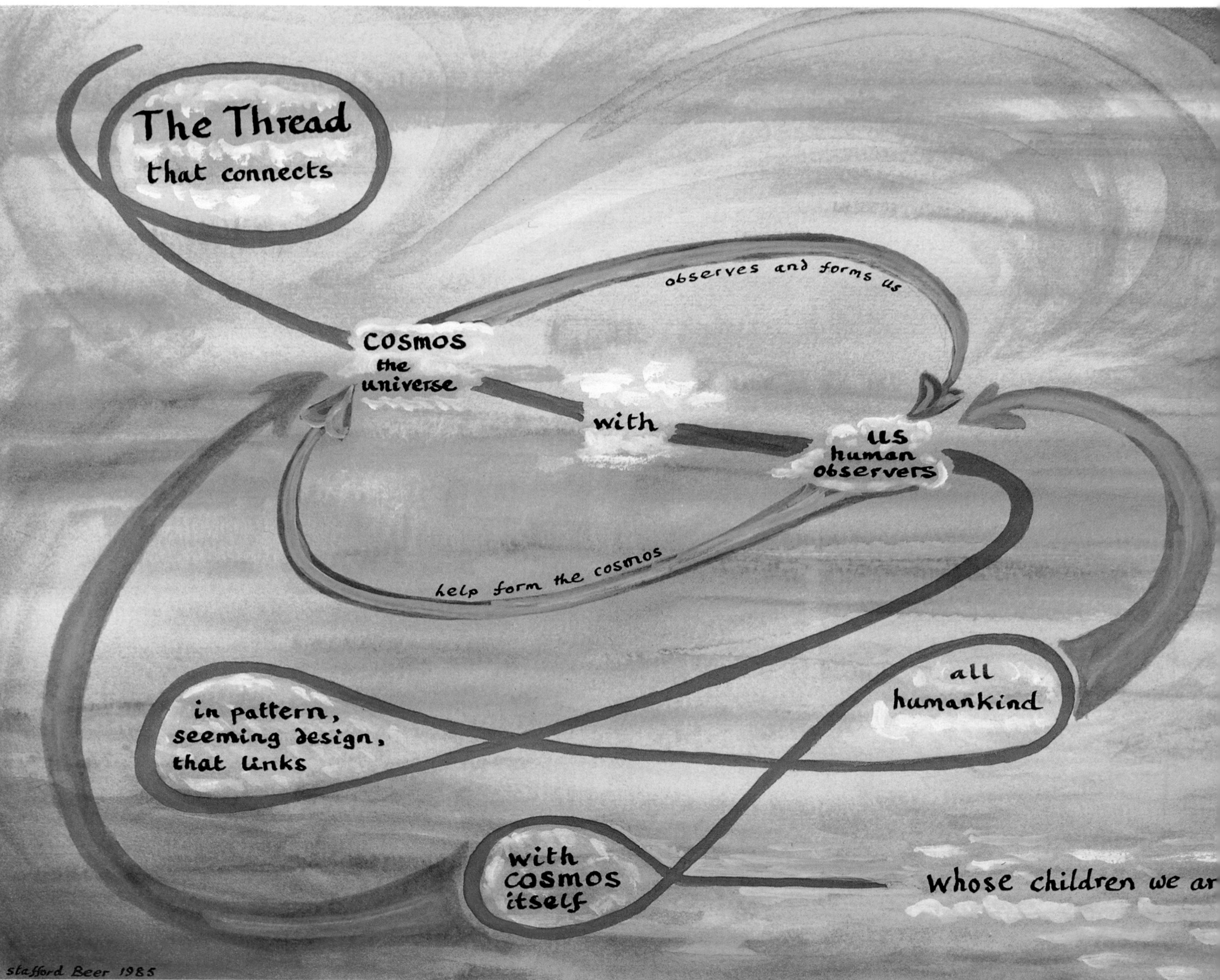
The Thread
that connects
observes and forms us
cosmos
the
universe
with
us
human
observers
help form the cosmos
all
humankind
in pattern,
seeming design,
that links
with
cosmos
itself
whose children we ar
stafford Beer 1985

The Thread

proposes clear links between the pebble and the computer. The pebble is a discrete unit—a self-contained entity. As soon as we begin to compute with it, the point is simply whether or not the pebble is there in a given position and, if so, how to find it. Is it in the voting pot, or not? Is it in the sand or magnetic disc, just *here*, or not?

But there are other links; and this thread cannot claim to be unique. Threads connote *connexion*, a concept that is nearly lost to our neatly packaged existence . . .

- We have packaged physics and packaged chemistry, just as if God knows the difference between them. We have packaged health and packaged education, as if it were not the same person who is well and literate, ill and illiterate, or any other combination between those two.
- We packaged genes into well-favoured food plants, the nutrients to go with them, the pesticides to protect them . . . and lost sight of the multiple connexions to the rest of life. So there are dust-bowls, depleted gene-pools, and strains of pests that can survive almost anything—even to the radiation of nuclear war, the scenarios for which have lost all track of *their* connecting threads. For example, when the world's leaders crawl out of their bunkers, who will they find to bury all those dead?

Large thoughts have soon invoked a purpose belied by so small a book. The idea of connexion is central to it, and that is exemplified by a Thread. And since there is not one thread, but a thousand, some choices have to be made. The book's coherence its thread that connects, derives from the *selection* of photographs and the relationships *recognized* between them. These in their turn are no more than exemplifications of the hidden thread drawn forth in the facing picture. The picture is meant as some kind of antidote to the dis-ease resulting from packaging: it puts connexion back—and in an overriding role—as a guide to the book itself.

There is a thread, the picture says, that links the cosmos—the whole of everything, whatever that may be—to us humans who partake of it. We 'live' the cosmos in various ways; surely one way is by observing it. Our observations help make the cosmos what it is: we select and direct and magnify and distort and suppress all our perceptions of it. In turn we become what it declares, because we have 'observed' the cosmos to contain, not to exclude us. Then we may recognize the patterns, the design, that we have put there: the picture shows the double reinforcement of that basic loop. A view that once was 'mystical' is now centred in contemporary science.

- These ideas are firmly set in modern physics, in leading discoveries of the neurosciences, in arcane areas of epistemological research.

This basis lends high credence to the attitude to life that flows from this picture, and this account of it. Our age often complains about 'alienation'. Workers are supposedly alienated from the product of their labour, and children from their parents. People are alienated from the society of which they are supposedly a part. Some are audacious enough to count themselves alienated from God: the audacity springs from adding 'if there is one'. But, says the picture, we CANNOT be alienated from the cosmos whose children we are.

- Amen to that. Let's get on with the book.

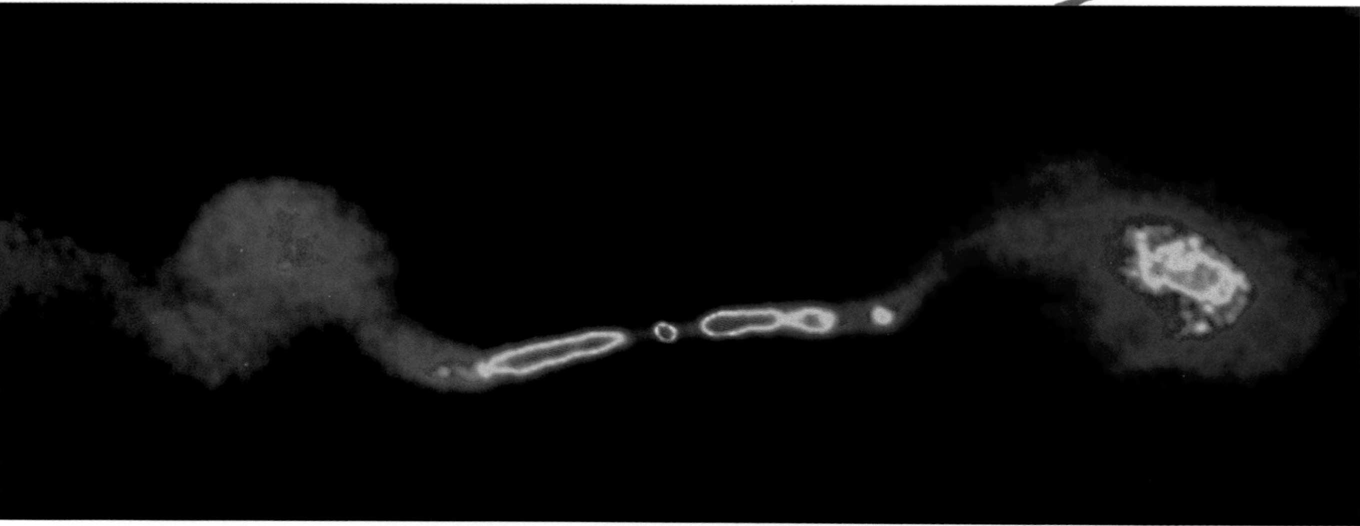

COURTESY NRAO/AUI Observers: Richard A. Perley and Anthony G. Willis

this is SPACE RADIATION— power exploding in distant darkness

No optical telescope ever saw this image. The photons that generated it had to be collected by radio telescope, the measurements obtained being enhanced and composed into a picture by computer. Photons are small particles of energy, travelling with the speed of light. But they are measured as waves, and these are perhaps three centimeters long. They take some catching! The wavelength does not belong in the visible spectrum, and it is much shorter than most of the wavelengths belonging to the radio frequencies that broadcast to our homes. But the radio telescope can operate all the time, not just at night.

. . . everything begins with transmissions of Energy . . .

And this? Some might agree to call it
GODHEAD RADIATION—
power transmitted in creating man.
Whether for you it represents myth or reality, this mighty image is well-known. It shows God and Adam, painted on the vault of the Sistine Chapel in Rome. Michelangelo was a sculptor first, perhaps, so that his paintings look as though they were wrought by chisels: monumental.

In any case, the resemblance to the facing page is there; resembles too
HEALING RADIATION—
power transmitted by LOVE.
—whether we think
of miracles or medicine,
nurture or nursing,
the touch of loving hands—

or of Steven Spielberg's
Extra-Terrestrial E.T.
the fascinating 'alien'
with the healing touch
whom children will remember.

And now this...

CANADARM RADIATION—
power transmitted in nearer space.

This is a photograph of a painting depicting the manipulative system made in Canada for the U.S. Space Shuttle. The 'radiation' in this case is the artist's way of showing how the joints move—to handle satellites for instance in and out of the shuttle's cargo bay: a transmission of energy indeed. There are four 'spaces' indicated on these pages... and always one outstanding image.

Courtesy Canadian National Research Council

ourtesy Canadian National Research Council
anada/France/Hawaii telescope on Mauna Kea, Hawaii
bserver Laird Thompson, Univ. of Hawaii

thus we find ourselves

joined

For those who find computer-composed images somewhat unreal, here is a 'proper' photograph! It was taken from an optical telescope at the Mauna Kea observatory in the clear thin air of an Hawaiian mountain top—exposure time: one whole hour.

This shows the famous spiral galaxy M51, called 'The Whirlpool' Here is the debris of a mighty celestial explosion—bridged by the interaction of their gravitational fields to another, attendant, galaxy. Despite the immense distance involved, it is possible to see this galaxy with field-glasses. The red spots in the spiral arms are emission nebulae; the blue spots are clusters of brilliant blue stars.

Spiral patterns such as this are everywhere in nature—

down to snails
and fircones
and the molecules of DNA
that carry our genetic codes.

Just now we spoke of *radio* telescopes, however. We noted that they work around the clock 'catching photons' from the wavelengths that the eye cannot see...

by a Thread *to the Cosmos*

Here is the Algonquin radio-telescope at Lake Traverse, Ontario, that does just that. The film exposure this time was short enough, but it took all day to capture the image of *these* spiral arms.

The spirals here are absolutely NOT visual images of the galaxy! They are artefacts caused by the shape of the dish aerial, reflecting local light. So why are these reflections also spiral?

The reason is that the dish's shape is paraboloid—quite like an average bowl, and the 'arms' we see are therefore parabolas. It is easy enough to understand the nature and purpose of the paraboloid. . . .

The telescope's job is to collect photons, and they are arriving in parallel streams. Then they have to be *concentrated* on a single point. Think of these particles as tennis balls. Those hitting the dish at the bottom will bounce straight upward; those hitting the side will bounce into the centre at an increasing angle. The paraboloid is the curve on the bowl for which this is true.

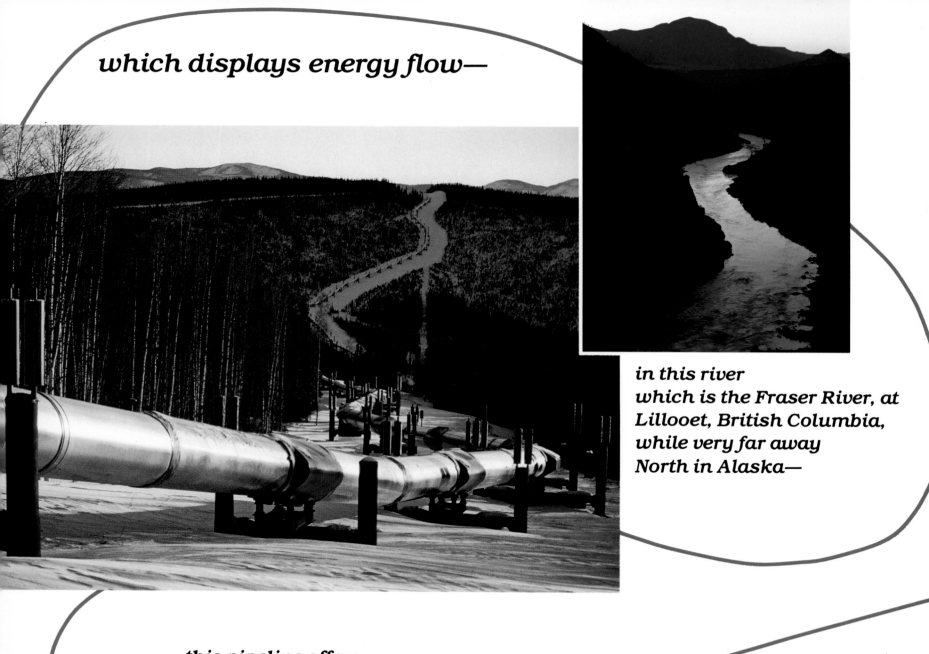

which displays energy flow—

in this river
which is the Fraser River, at Lillooet, British Columbia, while very far away North in Alaska—

—this pipeline offers manmade mimicry

the Thread follows a coincidence of images…

…and the thrust of both energy and information into and out of the sky

the Algonquin telescope undergoes the metamorphosis of night

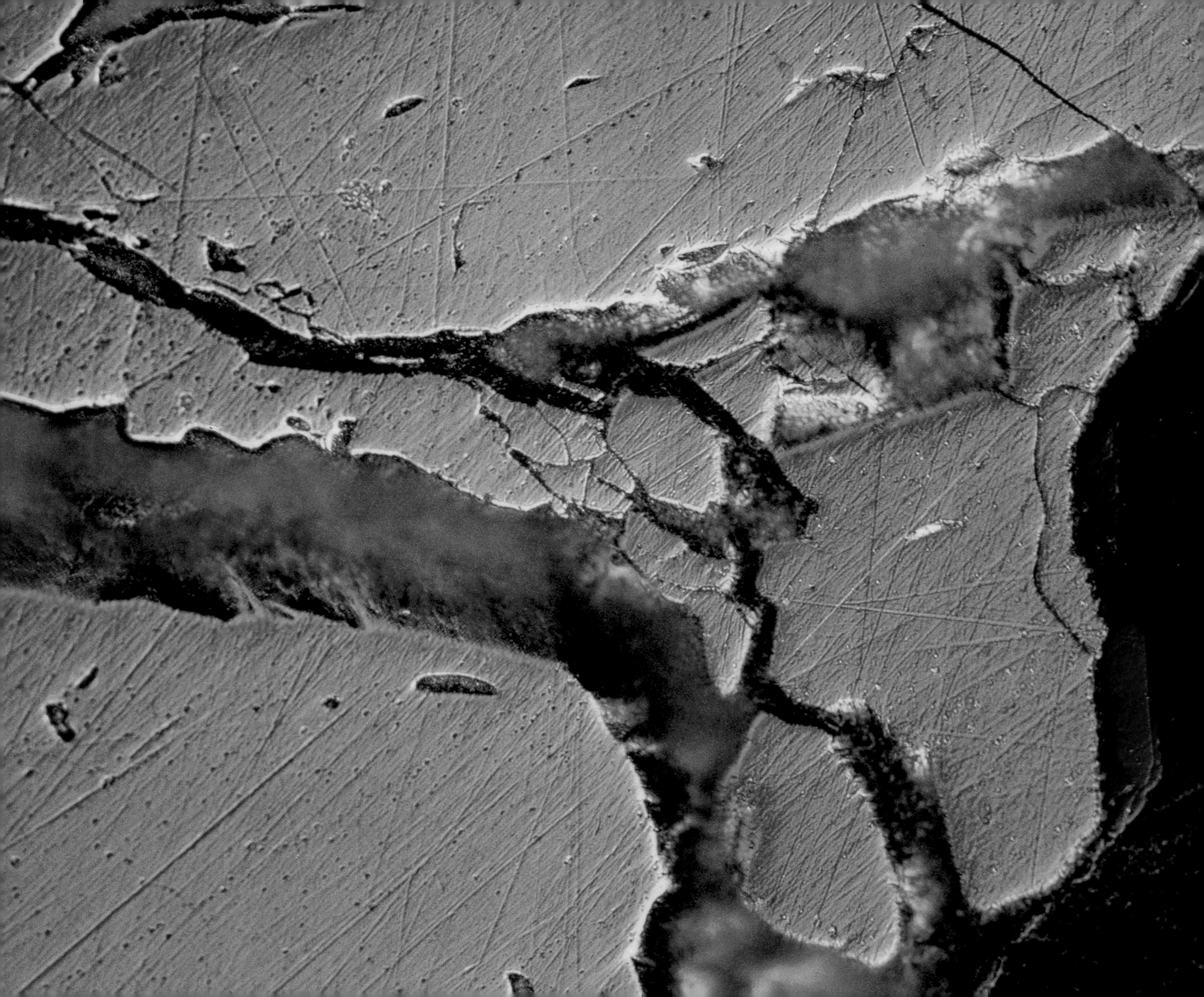

pause for reflection...

With what temerity did the previous page aver: *the Thread follows a coincidence of images*. What does 'coincidence' really mean? Literally it means 'happening together.' Well, obviously the pictures do that much, because they are printed adjacently—as a result (we said it before) of deliberate selection. But when we say 'coincidence' we usually mean that something strange seems to lie behind the literal happenstance. How strange does such a *WOW!* coincidence have to be? The ancient computer distributed its pebbles over a disc of sand, just as the modern computer stores its bits over a magnetic disc, where 'just as' means that information retrieval is made easier. So there is 'an explanation'. Next we saw energy being transmitted through a pivotal point: but is it so surprising that this happens in four kinds of space? Two of these are distance-spaces. We made the hundred miles or so orbit of the shuttle seem relatively near by speaking first of galactic distance, and reinforcing that immensity with the image of the spiral nebula. The *inner* spaces of identity, in creation, and of love, in healing, are perhaps fancifully portrayed as matching arms and pivots. But if these are 'merely' fanciful, why do they so commonly occur? The example of energy flow is surely the easiest to handle.

'coincidence' may be the inability to see what really matters

The Fraser River flows downhill, following the path of least resistance. Although men built the Alaska Pipeline, they were not so stupid as to do anything else. Thus we had the pleasing mirror-image of the two on the preceding page. Was that a *WOW!* coincidence or not? Does the explanation eliminate the *WOW!* or not? It does not seem to be a matter of what can be explained away, which is the usual treatment for disposing of coincidences. Perhaps it *is* a matter of what can be explained: the magic may evaporate from the *WOW!* somewhat, but the explanation always points to the coherence of the cosmos itself—and that is magical in its turn. The status of an explanation is therefore more mysterious than we usually think. Whether the coincidences found in the images of this book are *WOW!* coincidences is dependent on the reader's imagination—but whether the explanations explain or explain away is a matter for deep thought. When we cannot see any explanation at all, the statement in the centre of this page may yield some fruit.

Meanwhile, here is a picture of a river delta, taken from a satellite; or perhaps it is a hair follicle; it could be a micrograph of a polished section of nickel ore; or how about a nerve process at a synapse? Let us not take our coincidences too lightly... In fact, it is number three.

Light reflecting from the turbine blades that transmit the immense power of the jet engine.

images of Energy and Information... aspects of the same thing...

That pause for reflection may have been worthwhile. Because what comes now is surely a *WOW!* coincidence.

The Thread of energy transmission and flow that we have been following leads straight into the world of computation through the connexion of **information**. This is because energy and information are aspects of the same thing—the name of which is entropy. One way of expressing the shared law of entropy mathematically is this:

$$H = -\Sigma p_i \log_2 p_i.$$

There goes the only mathematical statement in this book. It is given simply to show that the law is quite precise and succinct. The residual value of H measures the energy that is available to achieve work in a given system. Its negative is exactly the amount of information that this same system contains. This is notoriously difficult to understand—and therefore worth the effort!

Information

Light reflecting from the tiny microchips of a silicon wafer, which comprise the integrated circuits that transmit vast amounts of information inside the modern computer.

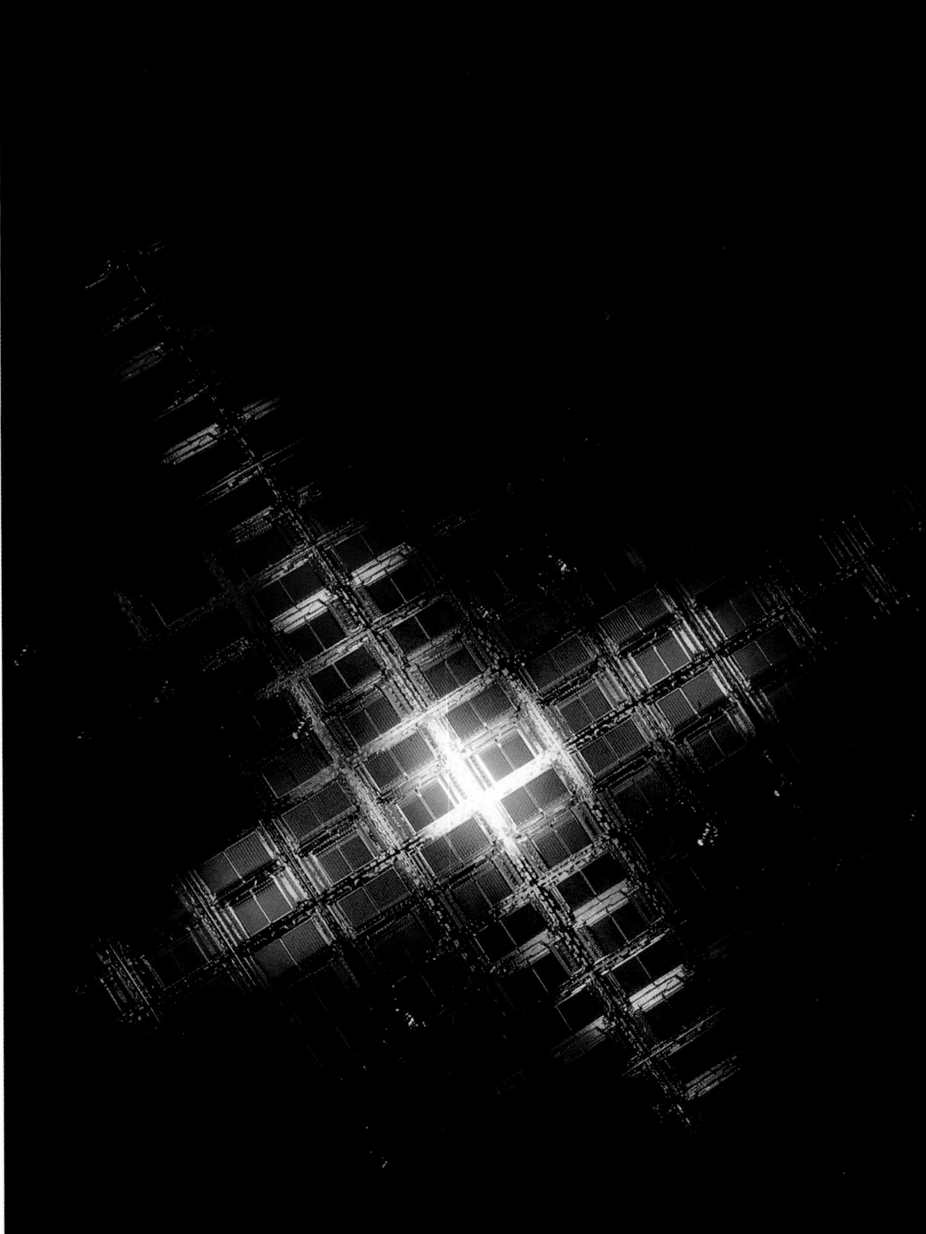

Take energy first. The formula prescribes a way of calculating the probability (those P_i's) that a total system (that's the Σ) is in the state that it is. The cosmic system itself, and all the systems it contains, are recognizable because their elements are in some special order. The Whirlpool galaxy and the Crab nebula look different because they are ordered differently. The same goes for an oak leaf and a sycamore leaf; that sort of order is called 'shape.' A cup of hot coffee and a bowl of ice-cream are differently ordered in terms of their heat. But the orderliness of each example tends to disappear. The galaxies are exploding—one day their debris will be spread out evenly everywhere, and there will be no galaxy left to recognize. Both leaves will rot, and become indistinguishable in the compost. The coffee will go cold, and the ice-cream will melt.

All this is because the amount of energy available to keep the orderliness is being gradually used up in so doing. The warmth we put into the coffee and the cold into the ice-cream were both forms of energy (we got it from the electricity supply) which inevitably dissipates into the surrounding atmosphere, until there is no more energy left to maintain the order that characterizes the system. The galaxies have vanished; the coffee is cold; the ice-cream is runny; the system is dead.

Information flows

To reach the twin topic of information, we sum up first on energy like this: Entropy H expresses the amount of energy still available in the system by saying how much has been *used up*. Eventually, that figure becomes **one**: 100% entropy is the death of the system.
Well, the orderliness that the energy has been needed to maintain is the mark of whatever is distinctive about a system. The oak and the sycamore leaves are different because of their 'shape', we said. To know the shape is to enjoy the information it embodies. When the entropy is low, and energy is therefore available, the leaves remain distinctive. Descriptive information is high. But when the leaves are brown and decaying for lack of energy, their shapes become ambiguous—soon to be indistinguishable. *Lukewarm* 'hot' coffee and 'ice' cream are losing the information that identifies them.

It turns out like this: processes gaining in entropy are losing information, and vice versa. To maintain high definition of differences, we need a great deal of information. Therefore the entropy must be low—meaning that energy available to maintain orderliness must be high. And this is not just a *general* outcome. It is as precise as the H formula shows it to be.

So the '$\log_2$' element of the H expression has, unsurprisingly, an informational meaning. It is a measure of the number of 'bits' (the pebbles!) required to specify the distinctive pattern of the system in question.

Information informs us; it in-forms the cosmos we know.

using Energy

at Frobisher Bay, on Baffin Island, in the Canadian Arctic, a satellite-signal receives and relays

messages...

bringing close
loved voices
or the news of war

spelling out
financial gain and loss
from distant markets

telling
the lives of people
laughing...
...dying

in coded streams
of neutral data

from the dark side
of the Earth

...messages...

... to be recorded and computed with...

carved in stone

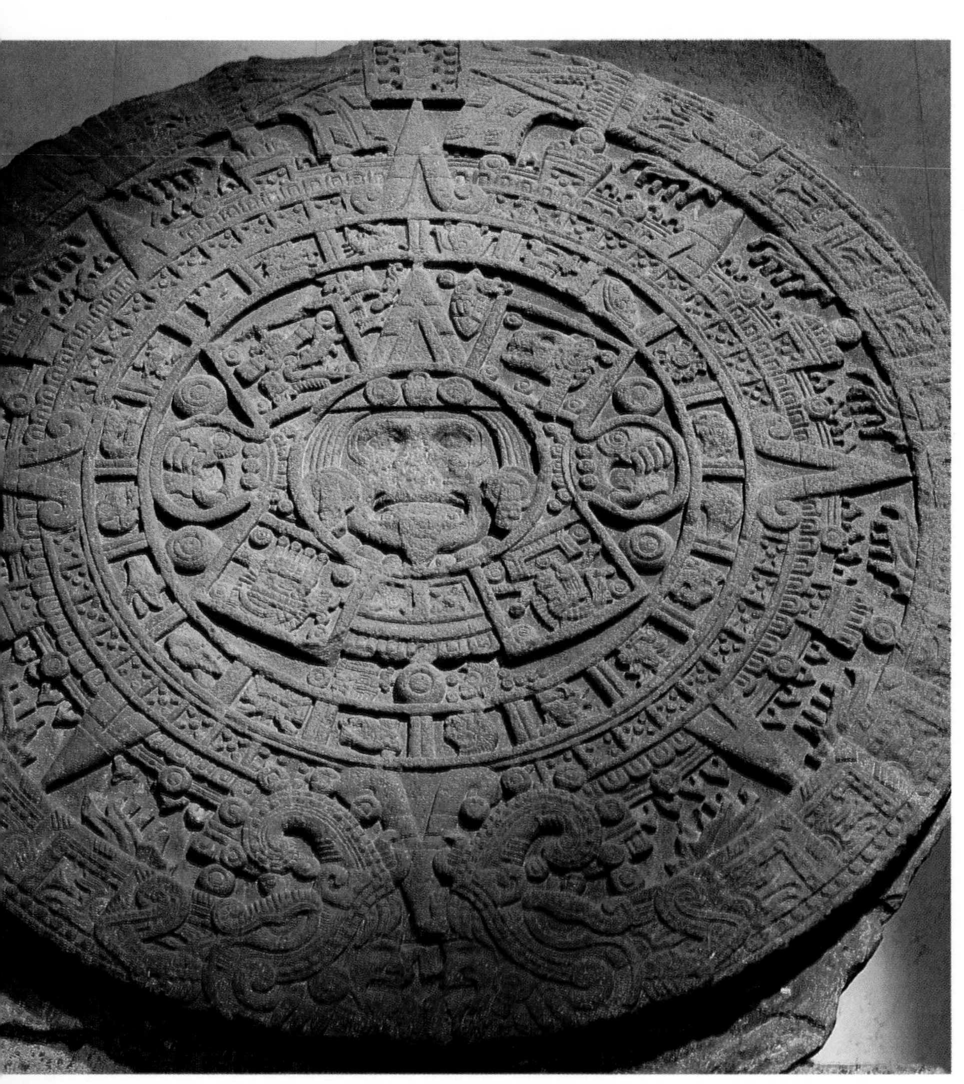

Here are our circular storage patterns once again. The stone one is just over five hundred years old, and weighs twenty-four tons. The other is only a tenth of an inch thick, and four inches across—see the facing page.

The Stone of the Sun, now in the Anthropological Museum in Mexico City, records the creation and destruction of four worlds—or earlier eras, called 'suns'—and both celebrates and determines the current era, or Fifth Sun, due for destruction by earthquake. Or so it was when dedicated as a sacrificial stone by Axayacatl, ruler of the Aztecs, in the Mexico of the late fifteenth century.

Here is a representation of the cosmos, and of the battle between good and evil; a record of the perceived history of the world, and a prophecy of final disaster.

The face of the Sun God Tonatiuh, with his open mouth, is carved in the centre. His voracious appetite for human hearts would keep him burning to the end. Such seems to have been the fatalistic philosophy of the Aztecs—one necessarily embraced by many thousands of their prisoners of war: Tonatiuh has the tongue of a voluptuary...

or silicon

Everyone by now has surely heard of 'chips,' the circuit boards that run modern computers. Well, 'boards' is too large a sounding term. A chip is about the size of a little-toe nail. It is almost impossible to believe that a chip may contain *thousands* of electrical circuits—even a whole micro-computer. So how is it done?

Manufacture starts from a very small and pure crystal of silicon. The commonest form of silicon is the stuff on the seashore that we know as **sand**. Very pure silicon is a very poor conductor of electricity. A good start, you might think! Conductivity is introduced by the imposition of impurities. How big they are determines their electrical function—to be resistors or capacitors or whatever.

Micro-electronics this may be: but no one could get a computer circuit onto a grain of sand. The pure crystal is processed at very high temperatures to *grow*—quite large. Then its rough edges are smoothed. We end up with a cylinder, some four inches in diameter, that can be sliced up like a salami. The slices are called **wafers**, and those are the four-inch circles on the right.

About two hundred and fifty **chips** are imprinted on each wafer. 'Imprinted' is a good word, because the thousands of circuits are *photographed* onto the crystal—using chemicals, and masks, and ultraviolet light. The chemicals maintain the non-conductivity of the silicon where it is needed, for layer upon layer of circuits imposed.

the Thread meanders...

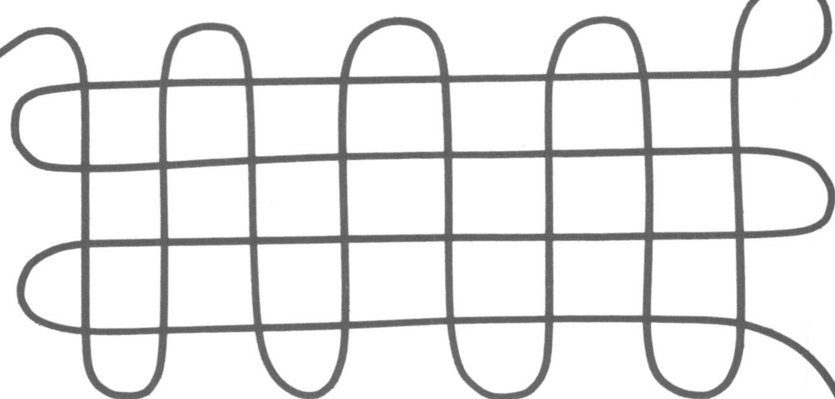

... then makes this basic mark to recognize flat space:

the up-and-down
slashed
by the across

Until we met the 'chip' on the previous page, our Thread was moving in a *linear* way: that is to say, like a line. It achieved area—two dimensionality—essentially by *continuing the line* as a spiral. Although we saw concentric rings, we made little leaps to get onto the next circle: and there was the linear spiral once again.

The chip uncompromisingly slashed up the area, two ways: a mathematician would say 'orthogonally', meaning 'at right angles'. This concept is enormously important in approaching our universe, our cosmos. With *orthogonal* dimensions, you may proceed in one direction, without moving in another dimension at all.

For example, take a high-rise office block: beautifully described in this night-image as the jewelry it looks less like by day. Step into an elevator; ascend for thirty floors. You will step out, and *you have prefigured the floor plan in your mind because the building has orthogonal design.*

What any self-respecting Thread-watcher would like to know is this. How is it that the Thread can move about orthogonally in **space**—across any one of three dimensions, in fact, without invading either of the other two—but must in the process necessarily take up **time**? This fourth dimension seems not to be orthogonal at all. The elevator needs time to go directly up. These are tricky but not irrelevant thoughts.

Look first above, at the wiring of an early computer. It reduplicates the dancing, slashing Thread. Those shining copper wires are connected in highly complicated but orthogonal ways. And if anything went wrong with the circuitry, it sometimes took *days* to disentangle the knitting.

Now to the chip again: on the right, a micro-circuit magnified five hundred times. The orthogonality is still in evidence—the jewelry too, perhaps, to the eye of our 'coincidence'.

But whereas the unit of non-orthogonal time in that early computer was a millisecond, we work in terms of nanoseconds, at the most, today. Well, in 1950 a millisecond, as a thousandth of a second, seemed a fast response. But a nanosecond is a thousand millionth—a billionth—of a second. If that is the measure, what can we do 'in time'? The consequences of all this are astonishing: turn the page . . .

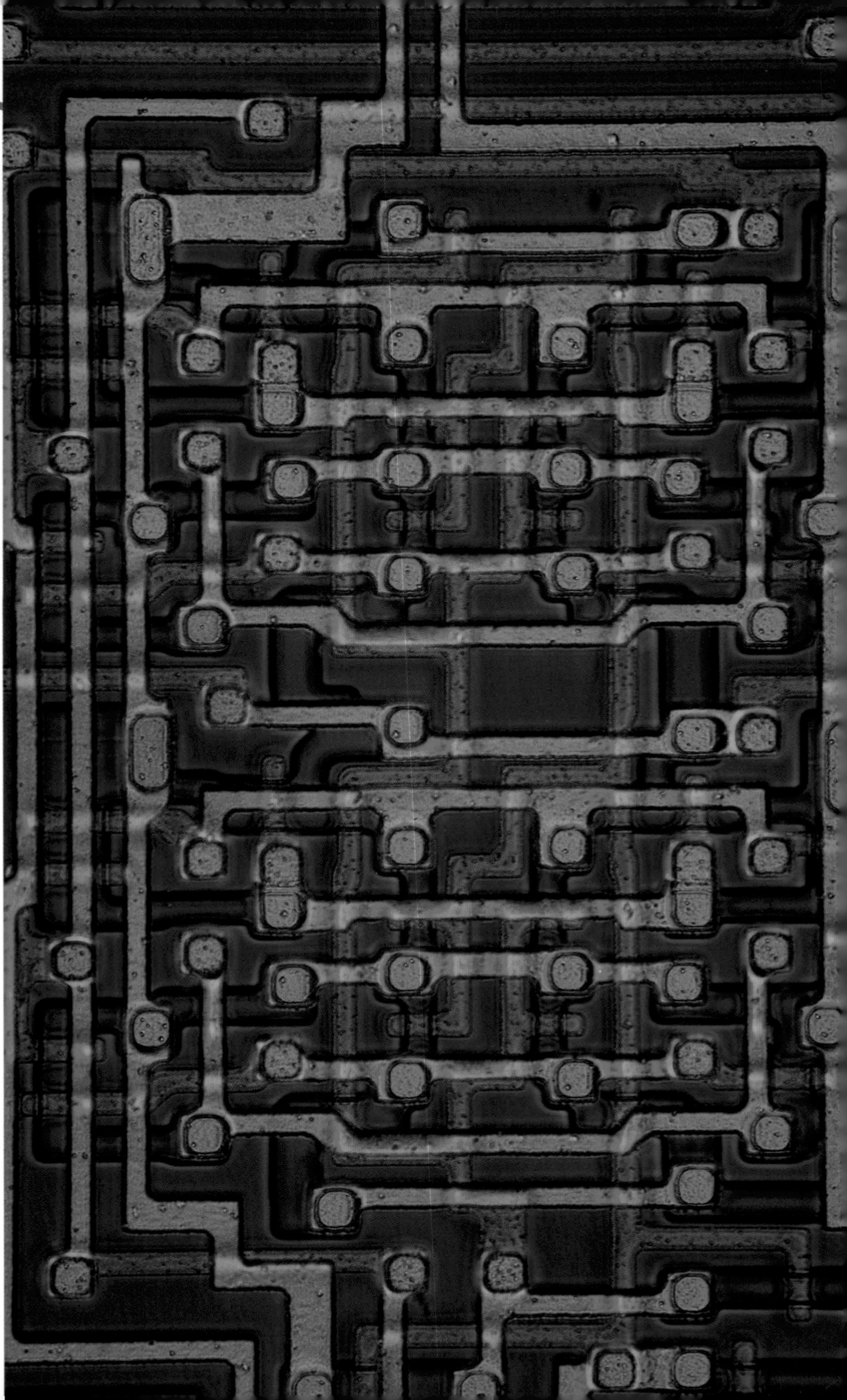

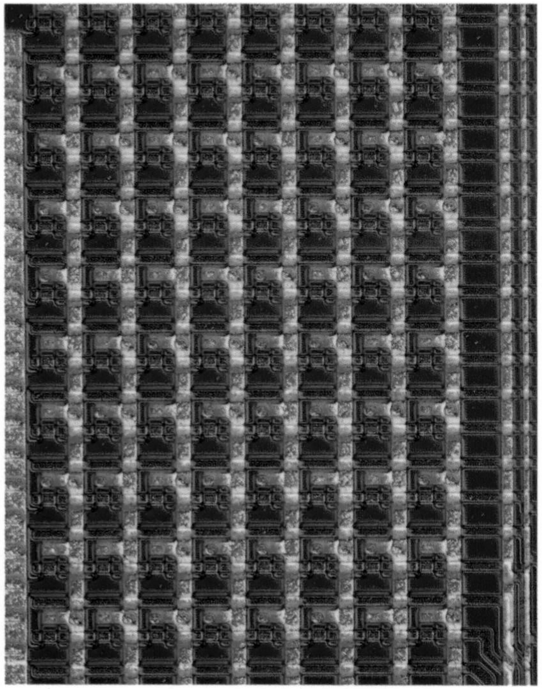

the last page says:

a nanosecond is a thousand millionth of a second

another chip...

Why should anyone bother about so inaccessible a concept? There are serious reasons.

Nothing can travel faster than light. At the very moment when a particle of matter attains that speed, it *turns into* light. That's what happens in the cosmos as understood by Albert Einstein. The speed of light is a limiting factor in that universe.

Consider then:

- in a nanosecond *light itself* moves less than a single foot;
- today we compute in *fractions* of nanoseconds.

So that is exactly why microprocessors became inevitable. Were they not minuscule, light could not traverse the chip 'in time'. Chips will necessarily grow smaller yet.

This in turn explains why, as long ago as thirty years ago, some scientists began to think that *biological* computers might be constructed to outpace even electronic achievement. At that time it was not clear that transistors themselves would become reliable! Attempts were made to implicate living cells—micro-organisms—in computations. In England in the 'fifties, one such computer solved an equation in four hours that a bright school girl or boy could solve in (maximum) four minutes. Its time had not yet come!

Today, biotechnology is taking us into the ultimately small in computation. Called genetic engineering, it recombines long molecules that constitute the stuff of life. And frightening it is.

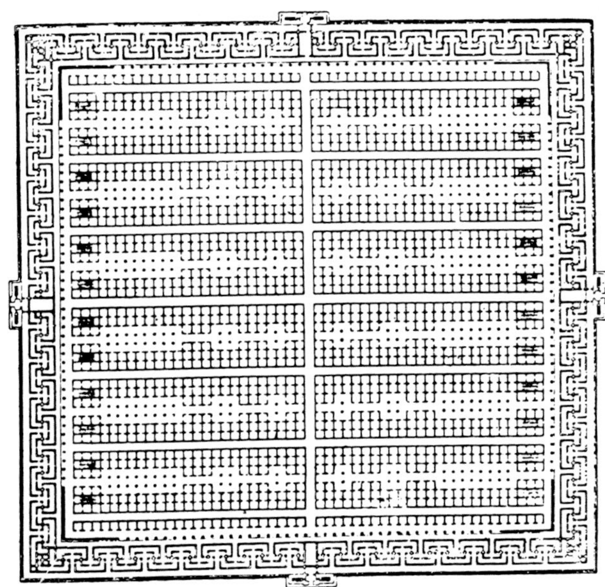

not another chip, at all...

Here is another 'coincidence' of form, the sides of which are not chip-sized as a toenail. The sides are probably two hundred and fifty *metres* long. As to the incursion of this spatial array into time: what is left of this construction is about four thousand years old...

This is the plan of a temple labyrinth at Lake Moeris in Egypt that was built by King Amenemhet III (1842–1797 B.C.). The plan was drawn in 1840 by the Italian archaeologist Camina. He based it on descriptions left to us by the Greek historian Herodotus, who went to see it in the fifth century BC, and by others—including the Roman Pliny, who got there five hundred years later. Nearly fifty years after the plan was drawn, the British archaeologist Flinders Petrie discovered and disclosed the actual site.

We see twelve courts, and the designations of three thousand rooms—half of which were above and half below the ground. The tombs of kings were here, and sacred crocodiles...

But there are drawings similar to this, never transformed to massive architecture. In India there are mandalas—pictures conveying sacred insights not expressed in words. Our modern chips may not be sacramentals, but they use no form of words. Come now (someone might protest), we know what the chip does, the functions it performs. So (it should be replied) did the yogis of India, the lamas of Tibet, also understand their own mandalas.

Then what did Amenemhet himself understand by his labyrinthine temple? Surely it was not made like this just to confuse Herodotus and Pliny, late-comers as they were. That would be like saying that chips are *really* made to fool archaeologists two thousand years from now into thinking that we wore such things as costume jewelry...

the Thread explores a little...

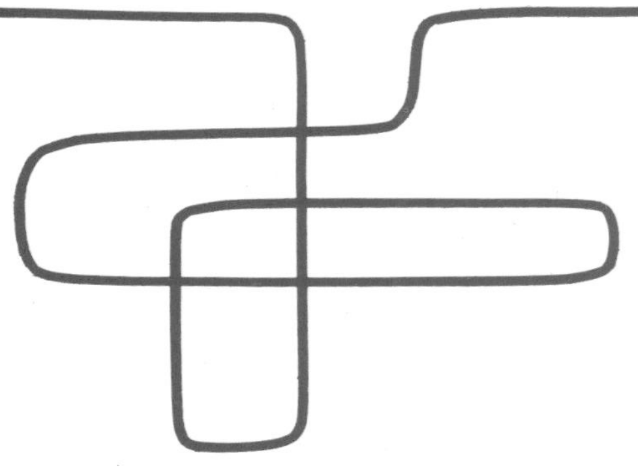

The simplest version of the up-down-and-across investigation of flat space is the cross itself, which marks out two dimensions.

The pattern on the left suggests why the mathematical consequences of exploring a flat space by making crosses tend to create 'courts' and 'squares'—as we saw in palaces and chips, and see in towns.

The Cross, and variants upon it such as the Swastika, were powerful symbols of antiquity—long before they acquired the particular potency that each holds for contemporary culture.

There is another way of cutting space in two, of demarcating the up-down-and-across, whereby the across becomes a lintel upheld by two supports—just like a doorway.

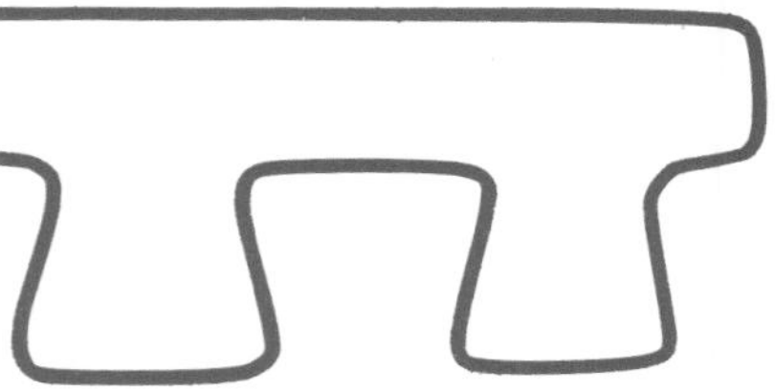

Instead of staying with the minimum division of space by two components, we now acknowledge three. This one is a **trilithon**, meaning (from Greek) 'three-stones'.

This element too had potency—and retains it too. For here, on a lonely moor in Western England, folk arrive each year to celebrate

five thousand years of lonely mystery and people-populated magic...

...of course it is Stonehenge

Older than Amenemhet's temple by a thousand years, and much more visible today, Stonehenge receives the better part of a million tourists a year. As a result, it is widely known that the axis of Stonehenge pointed to the rising sun on the horizon at the summer solstice—which is the furthest sunrise to the North.

'The Druids', so people vaguely think, worshipped this phenomenon. Certainly, moderns clad in white robes, together with many strangers who are mystically inclined, attend Stonehenge (police permitting) on the 21st day of June each year. However, the historical Druids were actually Celts, who did not appear on the scene for two-and-a-half thousand years after the first circles (starting with a ditch and bank) were begun.

The fact seems to be that Stonehenge was both a solar and a lunar observatory. Wonderful scientific work has been carried out, not only by archaeologists but by mathematicians too, on these megalithic remains. It took some calculating to prove that when the sun rose over the Heel Stone four thousand years ago, exactly half the solar disc would be visible! Professor Thom demonstrated this, and also that four (of five) sets of the trilithons are precisely contained within two significant ellipses. There is an error of only an inch or two after all these years...

When the whole geometry was in position, covering not only the trilithons but the major ring, the only stones that did not fit perfectly were those that had been 'straightened' in the last hundred years or so.

Taking both age and complexity into account, Stonehenge is probably the most venerable computer still extant. It is difficult to contemplate, surely—everything is so stolid and so static. The 'pebbles' of this computer are massive: the trilithon supports weigh fifty tons apiece!

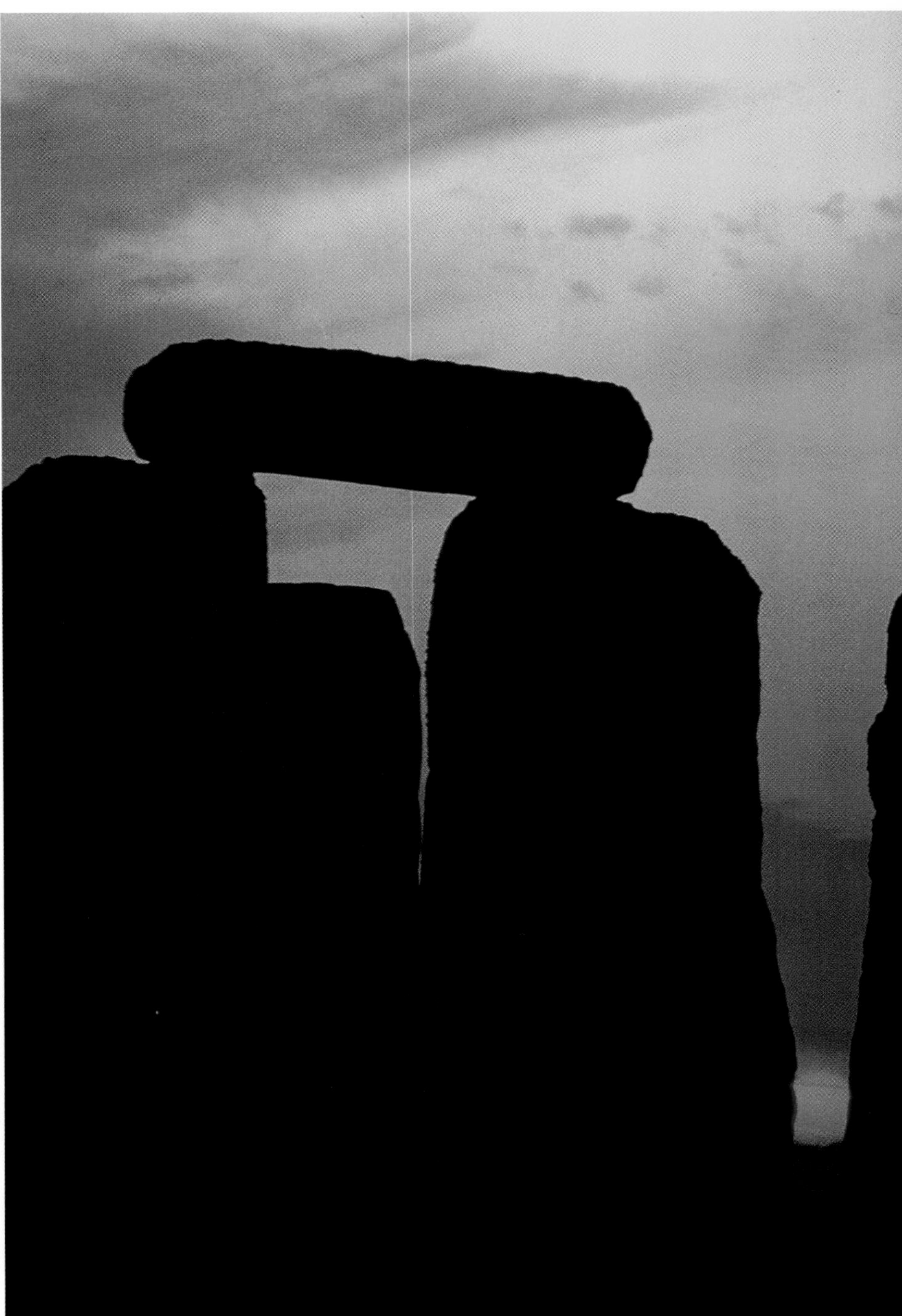

Stonehenge...

Computer 'pebbles' weighing fifty tons apiece... Let's think, though, why this should be strange. They do not move. Yet neither does the chip have moving parts. This has become a tale of **Relativity**.

Clocks, and music boxes, and the early kinds of computing machines, have moving parts. They are seen to be 'computing'. The chip has moving parts we do not see. They are called electrons. These fundamental particles are moving like mad (as we saw, it's at the speed of light) to change negative flows to positive and back again—thereby churning out the logic they sustain. This is the *micro* computer, after all.

So what moves at Stonehenge? Ah—Stonehenge is a *macro* computer. What is moving relatively is the sky. That much is understood. But computers are supposed to be accurate...?

The answer is exciting. The critical faces of those gigantic stones, the megaliths, were precisely finished. They were polished. Then, from an exact spot, one might align two polished surfaces across the ring. The sun, when it arose would flash across a tiny chink—at a moment to be recorded with great accuracy.

More: the 'ray' of the sun that registered this moment would cross the land that stretches to the horizon. This ray would 'graze' a mound or hillock on the way. Thom calls these markers 'foresights' and 'backsights': he has identified points in front and to the rear that might have served. The farthest is nine miles away.

—it can hardly be left at that...

Hence one may think of Stonehenge as a **computer**, maybe twenty miles across—on its major axis.

This computer is fixed against the Earth. But it is moved in relation to the sky like a giant telescope—steered by the Earth's rotation. Some contemporary radio-telescopes work just like this: they have an array of fixed aerials, spread across some miles of terrain.

An image of Stonehenge according to this understanding, seen from the air, would look much like the picture on this page.

The central portion with the dark surround stands for the monument we know. Foresights and backsights, and sideways-on-sights (measured from the surrounding ditch and bank) would align features on the local landscape, and on the horizon, with the sun's rays at critical times.

You will know well enough by now that this is **not** an artist's impression of Stonehenge. It is a photograph of an integrated circuit—a chip—with attachments leading to its carrier frame.

At Nazca in Peru gigantic birds and beasts are marked into the ground: they cover more than one hundred square miles. No one can be sure what they mean; but it is not inconceivable that they also constituted a celestial computer. If so, then they record stellar events older than the two-thousand-year-old ceramic relics found in that place.

Incredibly, the ancient lines are so straight that even modern air-survey techniques cannot detect deviations—which are no more than two metres in each kilometre.

Below is a section of a standard photograph of one of the Nazca birds, colour enhanced by Hans Blohm—while on the right is a massive enlargement of the integrated circuit's carrier frame...

evidently

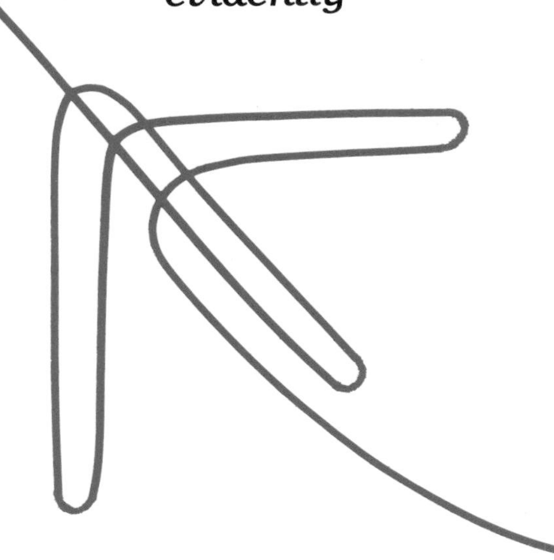

there are other kinds of THREESOME...

This is Stonehenge's larger ring, outside the trilithons, part of a whole circle. It is a **foursome**—because lintels are missing from the adjacent stones.

The ones we see in place are held together by mortice and tenon joints—still, to this day, bracketing arcs of the compass, telling the time (and how much more?) within this celestial computer.

There were thirty uprights and thirty lintels, in a ring of a hundred-foot diameter. It made an immensely strong structure.

The breaking-up of spaces for engineering use thus becomes the problem of

functional design

we started with a single line—
threading,
spiralling...

then we came to
two-fold space
thence

to trilithons,
arrow-heads—

now FOURS, and ...

Why foursomes? Each design has its own rationality behind its own aesthetic. Trilithons share the lintel's weight between two supports. Four props will nearly halve its weight (nearly, because of course there are now three lintel stones instead of two) on each.

The gardener below distributes his foot's thrust over four tines: perhaps he finds this the most effective way of breaking up the soil.

Who guessed the chip-carrier frame on the right? (And who said: 'Chips with Everything'?!) This is the carrier frame.

There is nothing magical about this number four—beyond the magic that we may discern in any number whatsoever...

Humankind has always delighted in the properties of number. If it were not so, we should never have done much with quantities at all—as we shall shortly see.

Meantime, let's take another pause to spend a final moment at Stonehenge...

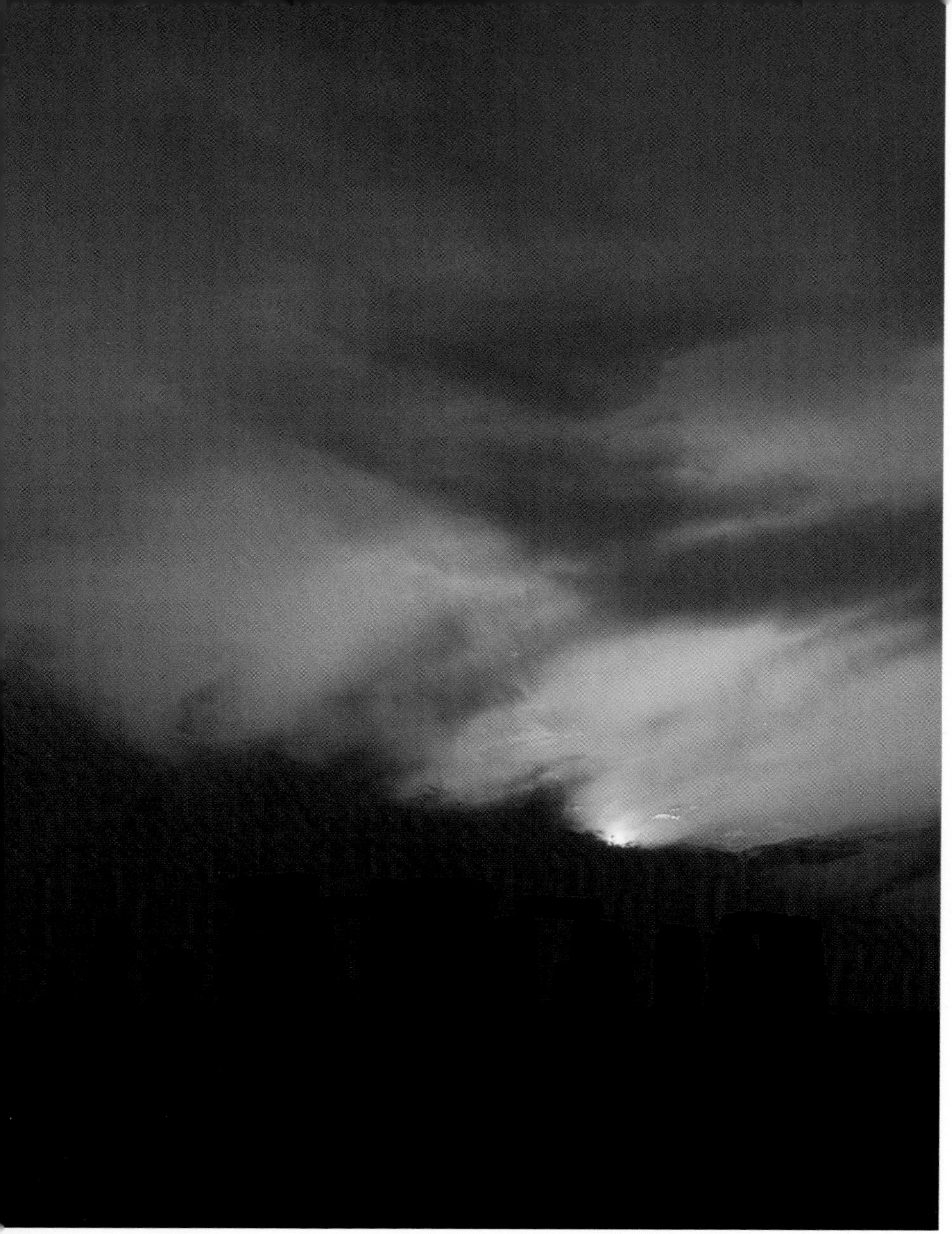

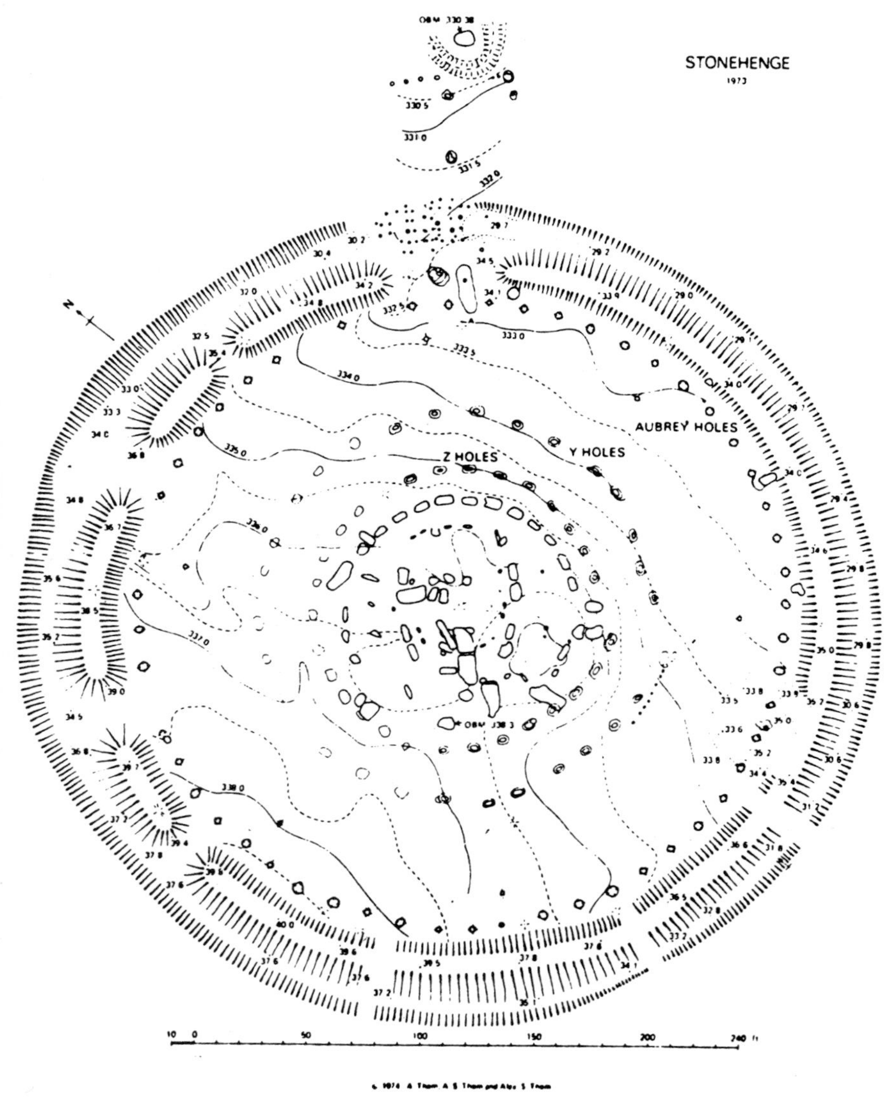

one, two, three, four...

calculating lasts...

counting continues...

the Thread meanders on

Pausing with mystery, it is well to contemplate the understanding of the cosmos that may have disappeared within a single, stereotyped, scientific vision, the pursuit of power over nature, and the reckless following of our own technological nose . . .

We mused at the start about pebbles: how each marks off a distinction. Whether we assemble them to be computers or they assemble themselves by 'coincidence' they stand for distinctions that **contain**—that are the boundaries, then—of spaces that map out the world.

'Continent' in this piece of poem has its old usage of 'containing.'

'here was the knowledge
lost from gnostics
alchemists
that continent distinction builds
the universe
in a plane space make a mark
the world will follow from this'

—'One Person Metagame' 1974, from *Transit*.

meanders . . . and falls downstairs

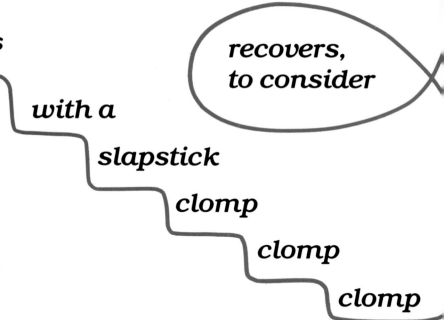

recovers, to consider

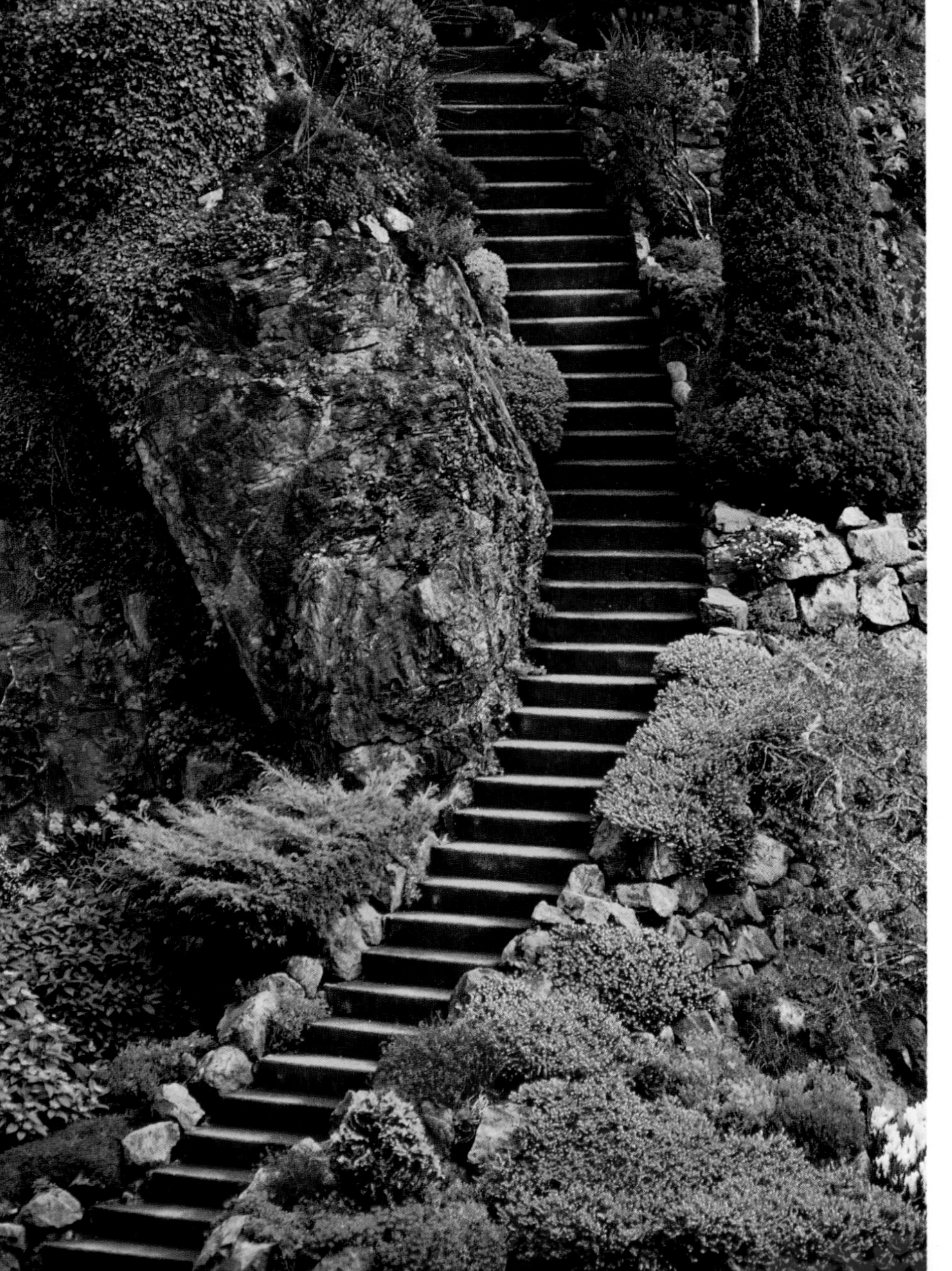

with a

slapstick

clomp

clomp

clomp

To do so, in the magnificent Butchard Gardens at Victoria, British Columbia, would (as you see) result in a bruising succession of clomps. Let us hope that the red dot that traces the Thread's descent, bouncing on each step, would manage to stop, before falling all the way down.

The whole point is that the tumbling red dot would have to land on a particular step: the seventh or the twentieth, or the thirty-third. No pebble, no red dot, can fall down *half* a step.

Likewise: although the average number of children per family may be (say) 2.3, no parents manage to beget a fraction of a child.

These activities, then, signify

digital operations.

When we speak of 'digital' computers, we mean just this—that the measurements work in quantum jumps: a fixed quantity at a time. A digital watch has hours, minutes, seconds; and nothing is registered in between each.

Bits

Some people can remember when children were amazed to hear that computers were so stupid that they could not count beyond one! Today it is the children who know most about bits. Some of their parents know that **bit** is a pleasing contraction of 'binary digit', and that those digits in turn read either 0 or 1.

They can imagine that this is a convenient notation for an electrical machine full of on-off switches (such as relays), or an electronic one that can stop and start streams of electrons. Even so, many folk look at tables purporting to show the equivalence between decimal and binary notations, and give up. What if 101 *is* the binary form of 5? Perhaps the tables remind them of the fiendishly difficult 'perms and combs' that they confronted in school algebra lessons.

Let us not give up. It is very easy to master binary notation if it is treated as a **process** instead of a table. Ordinary arithmetic has a *modulus* of ten. That means simply that counting stops there. So if you add one to nine, you cannot write down the answer—not in that column. We say: 'Write down nought and carry one.' Binary, as the name says, has a modulus of two. Write down one, by all means. But if you now add one, you cannot put the answer in that column. The same old rule applies: 'Write down nought and carry one.' So 1 + 1 in binary equals 10. Please do not call this 'ten' (because it is actually two!). Call it 'one-nought' or 'one-0'. Add one to this, and you get 11—one-one. In going from this binary three to four, you will need to add another one. Add one, then, to the right-hand one. Write 0, carry 1. Add the carry figure to the next column: it already contains a one. Write 0, carry 1. So four becomes 100—and obviously that is why five becomes 101—as we said at the start.

Perfectly straightforward then, is it not? It comes to this. We are used to counting columns of figures from the right, and calling the columns in turn: units, tens, hundreds, thousands, and so on—multiplying each time by the modulus ten. In binary, we multiply each column by the modulus two, and the column's names become: units, twos, fours, eights, sixteens, and so on. So, for example, seventeen is 10001—*not* to be referred to as 'ten thousand and one'!

Binary numbers are longer than decimal numbers. It is a matter of entropy again. They use up the available 'places' faster, because the information content of a 'place' is five times less.

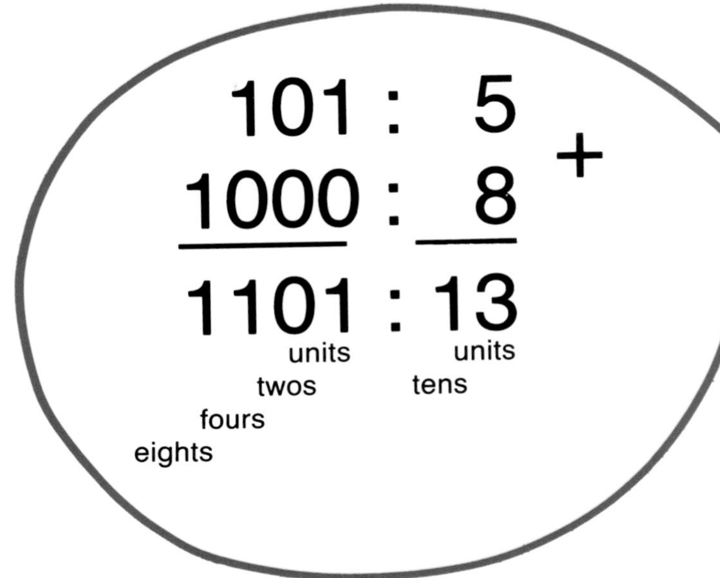

changing an outlook... ...as the Thread just changed direction

Down, upwards, and across, it is far from easy for the human mind—and makes all innovation difficult...

Pursue for a moment, and for interest's sake, the question of computers and arithmetic. 'Arithmetic' has seemed to be (for most of us) the manipulation of the numbers 0 to 9. As we shall see, even the greatest minds of the Western world, a few centuries ago, used decimal notation. After the last few pages though, it should be easier to understand that arithmetic is a particular *language* for 'doing logic'. Logic supplies a set of formal rules for making inferences—in this case deductions. Arithmetic has a language to speak, whereby it floats numbers around on the underlying rules. The binary language demonstrates quite clearly that the language 0 to 9 can be translated into 0 to 1—without any loss of deductive power. As we saw, the modulus does not matter. The rules matter, such as 'carry one'. After a schooling spent in decimal, however, it is hard to change.

As many tourists still remember, the British currency used to be duodecimal. Its arithmetic had a modulus of twelve. There were twelve pence in a shilling, and two hundred and forty to the pound sterling. This was grossly inconvenient—since there were no decimal points to shift. People needed to know the 'twelve times' table: some did not! Attempts were made over several hundred years to get the system changed to decimal. By the time that the political machinery moved, calculating machinery had moved too. Because 12 has so many factors (2,3,4, and 6) the duodecimal system became quite attractive. This was just the moment for the country to 'go decimal'—clearly. And it did!

The point here is to emphasize that numbers are a linguistic convention, while the logic of their manipulation is fixed. Computers, then, are best regarded as **logical engines**. Internally, they use the most convenient modulus, which is two. Arithmetic can be floated on the logic, using whatever modulus you choose—so alphabets can be handled easily as well (which folk did not believe, thanks to their schooling, when computers first were launched in business and industry). The term 'logical engine' was used by early inventors. Charles Babbage, whom we shall meet later, wanted to drive his by steam! Had we stuck to the term, maybe the enormous logical power of computers in their first twenty years of industrial use would not have been largely frivolled away on... *payrolls*.

and at last

the Abacus

The abacus, thousands of years old, and used worldwide, is the most ancient of the **digital computers**.

Some obvious questions:

- What happened to the pebble computer, then?
  — it was a form of abacus, but it did not survive on sand.
- Why 'digital'? It sounds essentially electronic.
  — no; remember the garden steps. This, like the steps, moves in a quantum jump, one bead at a time.
- does that mean the abacus is binary?
  — oh no. It is a *digital* machine that operates in the *decimal* mode.

It is notorious that a far Eastern clerk, using an abacus, won a competition against a U.S. Army sergeant using the latest (end of WW II) electro-mechanical calculator of its day.

- how does it work?

It is simplicity itself. In the photograph, the calculator is standing up. To use it, lay the frame flat on its back, and move *all* the beads away from the central bar. This registers nothing whatever, and we are ready to start.

The columns are the standard decimal columns. A bead becomes operational—it 'counts'—when it is moved towards the middle bar. The five lower beads are the units of each column; the two upper beads count as 5 each. Evidently it is possible to set any number from 1 to 10 in each column. Addition and subtraction are child's play.

That is that. You can even do square roots on an abacus. But if this is your desire, that is definitely *not* that!

tired of digital constraints —the quantum jumps— the Thread

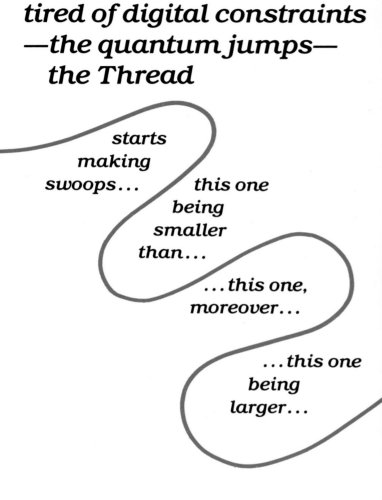

starts making swoops... this one being smaller than...

...this one, moreover...

...this one being larger...

Evidently, not all kinds of measure are digital. Something else is going on when we make comparative quantitative judgements—

make no mistake though—
quantitative.

Who, knitting a garment, has not 'tried it on' as work proceeds...?

These activities, then, signify ***...analogue operations.***

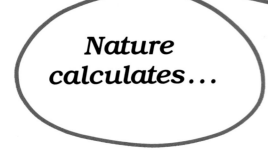

Nature calculates...

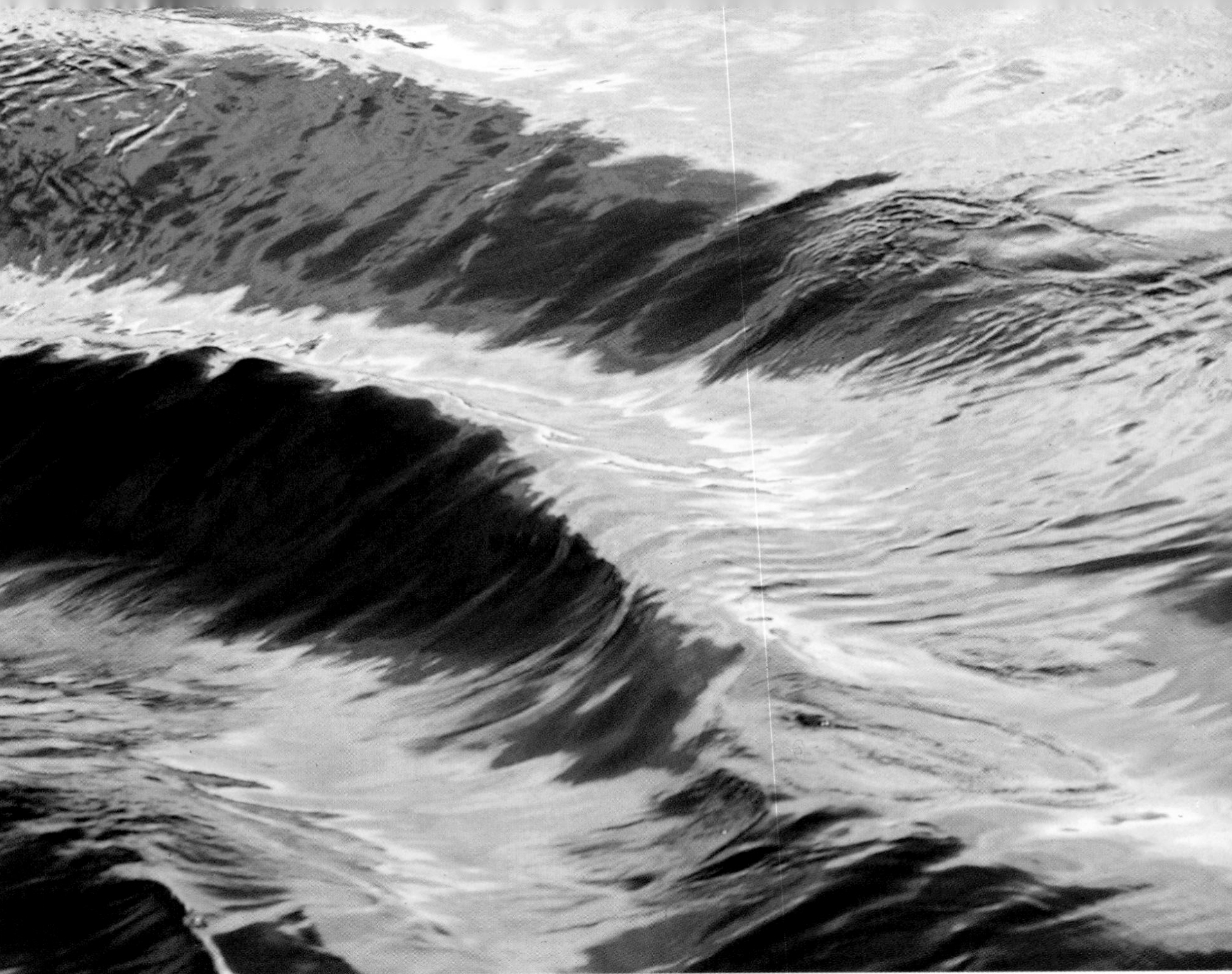

without using digital tricks, but **measuring** for sure—else why do we say:

'Nature is profligate'
(think of semen)
'Nature is parsimonious'
(the numbers in a litter)?

Above all, and despite these pejorative (and contradictory) judgments of nature's estimating, how does the cosmos mostly get things right?

This exquisite photograph of water in movement—it is the Gatineau River in Quebec—has a very subtle message for us. It is that nature's computers *are* that which they compute.

If one were to take intricate details of wind and tide and so on, and use them as (it's called) 'input' to some computer simulating water—what computer would one use, and how express the 'output'?

Water itself: that answers both those questions.

On the next page is a poem that struggles to express this same idea. These are **analogue** computations: we cannot read off the numbers, because nature does not put labels on its solutions—it *becomes* them.

Have you seen a better map of some piece of countryside than that actual terrain itself?

Examples of cosmic **analogue** computation are everywhere one looks.

If you had been shelling garden peas just before coming to this page (and guess who was!), might it have occurred to you to wonder (guess who did) how nature calculates when to stop the pod growing? No one has seen a pea pod ten miles long. Why not? Because nature *is* an analogue computer.

'Computers: the Irish Sea' ... and...

'That green computer sea
with all its molecular logic
to the system's square inch,
a bigger brain than mine,
writes out foamy equations from the bow
across the bland blackboard water.

Accounting for variables
which navigators cannot even list,
a bigger sum than theirs,
getting the answer continuously right
without fail and without anguish
integrals white on green.

Cursively writes recursively computes
that green computer sea
on a scale so shocking
that all the people sit dumbfounded
throwing indigestible peel at seagulls
not uttering an equation between them.

All this liquid diophantine stuff
of order umpteen million
is its own analogue. Take a turn
around the deck and understand
the mystery by which what happens
writes out its explanation as it goes.'

'Computers: The Irish Sea, 1964,
from *Transit*.

The waves are breaking for evermore at Long Beach on Vancouver Island, as they do on coastlines all around the world.

Look at the close-up sketch (at upper right) and compare it to the water just two pages back.

We know this basic shape, from early on. It is the shape of the *parabola* once more. The smooth curve is gradually made into a peak. At the point when the subtended arc at the top of the wave reaches 120°—exactly then—the wave 'breaks', as we say.

The wave is in catastrophe. Its days are over; and beautiful it looks as it runs all spent into the shore.

Science knows the hydrodynamics of all this, and science makes the measurements, using its digital operations to do so.

How does nature know? Can you be sure the question makes no sense?

the Calculating Waves

. . . to

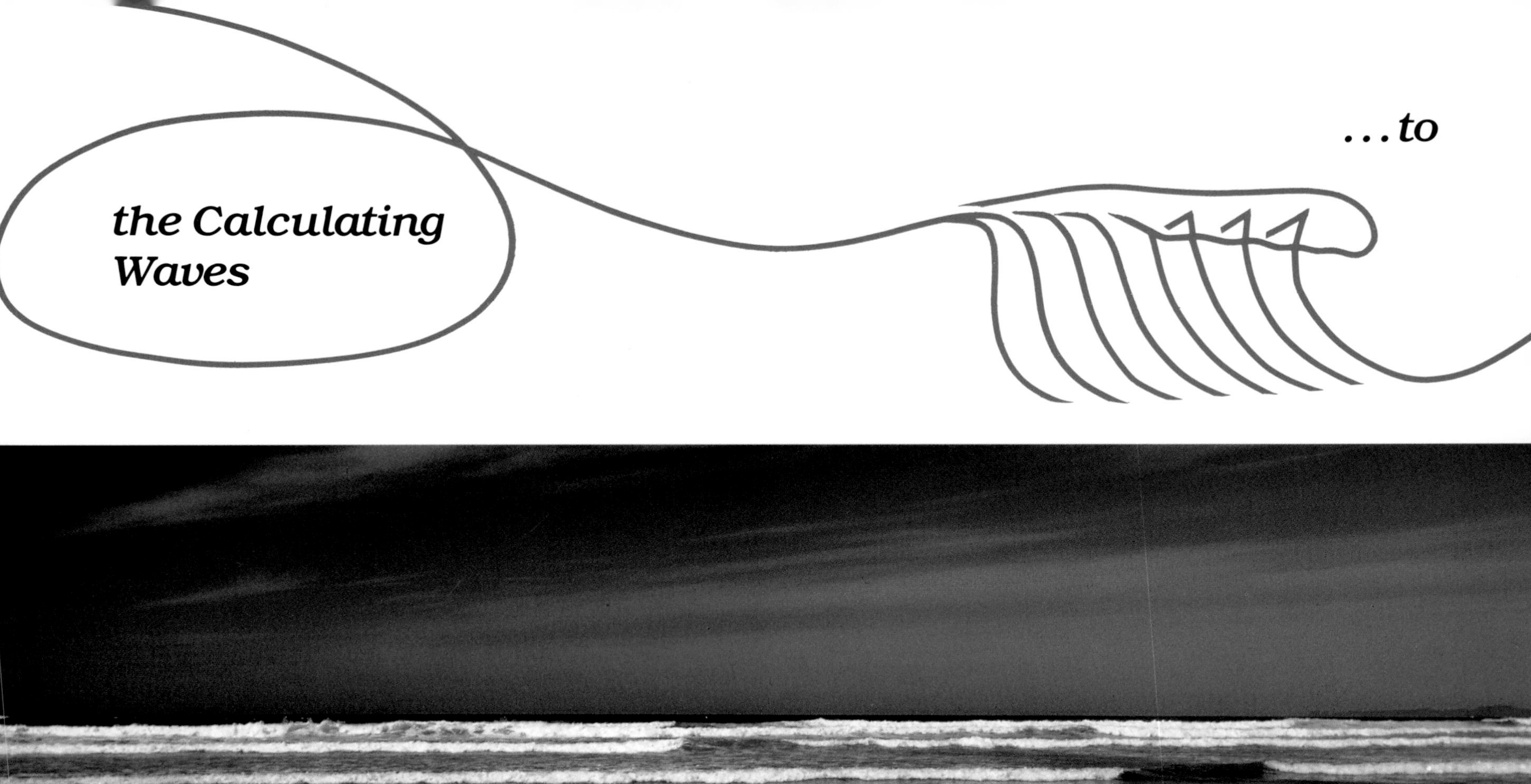

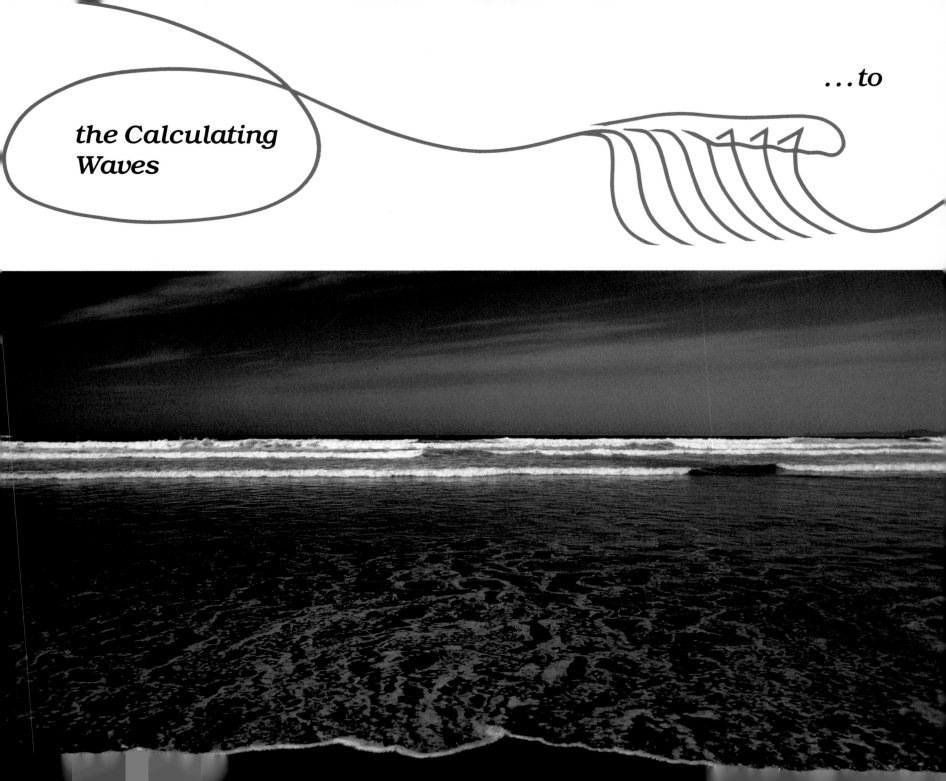

Balance...

The uneasy feeling that the last page may have caused derives, perhaps, from insecurity as to who is supposed to be in charge.

Science (surely?) 'knows the score'. Science does the measuring, after all. But if art is often said to imitate nature, so does science. Parabolas are *there*: science works out how to describe them, and how to calculate the consequences—such as waves—that nature was producing all along.

But nature's measurements are **analogue**-inspired. We are not used to this, although we know for instance that water does not flow uphill—'finds its own level', we say. Who will realize when the bathroom cistern has been filled—someone with a ruler and a button to press, or the ballcock that floats up to switch the water off?

Nature is (let it be clear that) **nature** is in charge.

And nature's analogue measurements revolve essentially about *balance*. Here is a picture of a mechanical artefact that invokes the very name. The right-hand pan contains scraps of metal—they could be lead or gold. What should we put in the left-hand pan? It could be a pile of grain, or a glass of grain's gold—whisky! If so, then this would surely be an analogue computer. Someone could exchange his drinker's draft for gold—without any measurement's being made on either side. **Balance** is measurement itself.

Weights are artefacts too. They are digital devices set to compute 'the scale' of analogue involvements. The digits here are used to *account* for nature's analogue. So we might call this balance a computational **hybrid**.

Hybrids

are fascinating, since they make no gross pretense that nature can count. This pleasing old thermometer carries our Thread for just a page to make this yet more clear. The column of alcohol **balances** the ambient temperature against its height.

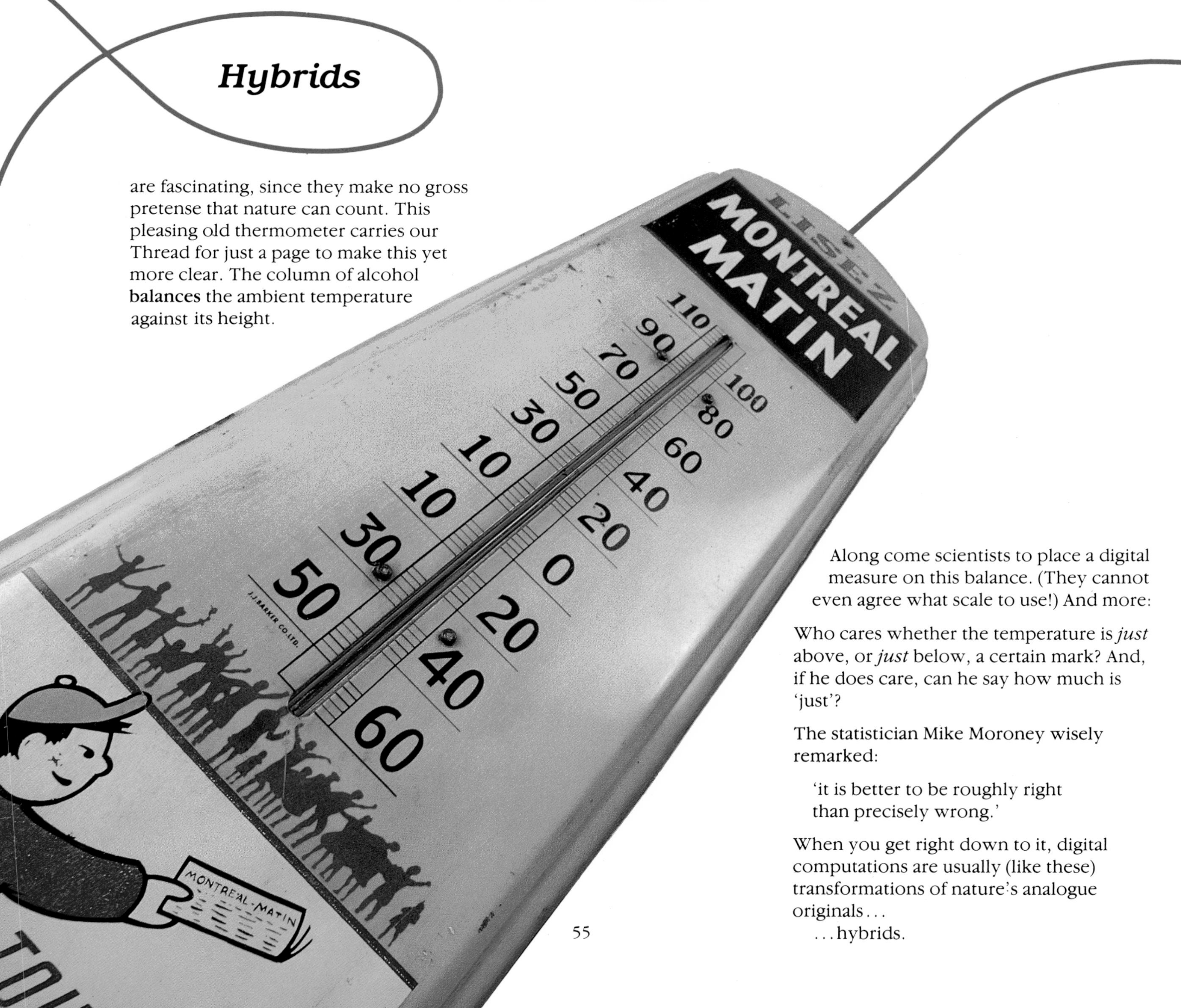

Along come scientists to place a digital measure on this balance. (They cannot even agree what scale to use!) And more:

Who cares whether the temperature is *just* above, or *just* below, a certain mark? And, if he does care, can he say how much is 'just'?

The statistician Mike Moroney wisely remarked:

> 'it is better to be roughly right than precisely wrong.'

When you get right down to it, digital computations are usually (like these) transformations of nature's analogue originals . . .
. . . hybrids.

and...

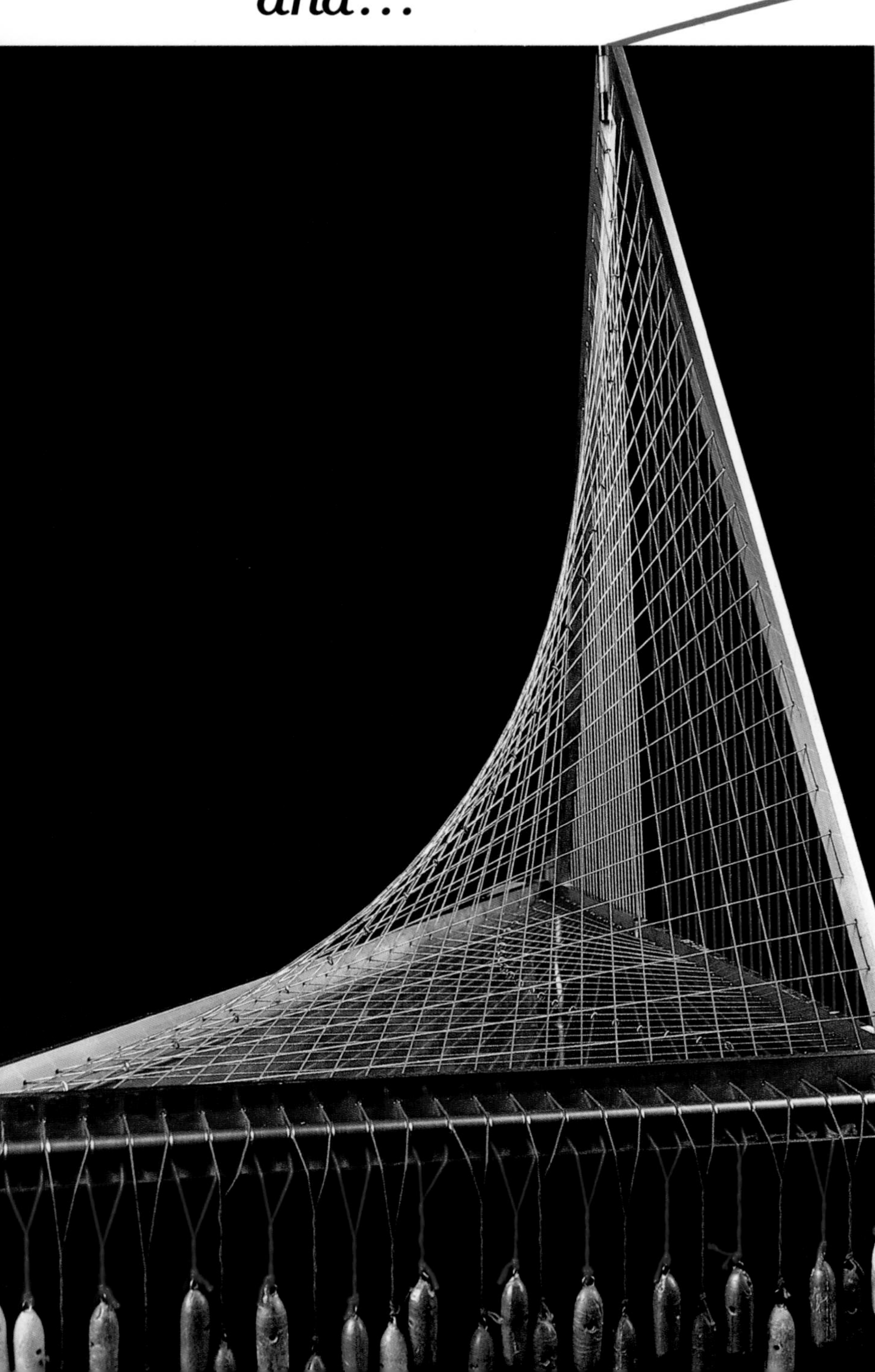

...Conversion

Probably the simplest way to remember the important distinction between digital and analogue operations is to think of the car's dashboard. The odometer measures the mileage digitally, while the speedometer is an analogue device. But as the 'hybrid' notion indicates, we can always turn one system into another.

Nature's own devices, like the waves, are normally analogue in form. The medieval philosophers used to say '*natura non facit saltus*': nature does not make jumps. But this is not completely true. Fertilization is a definite act, and so is the fall of a leaf when it breaks from the tree...

The device on the left is interesting too. We keep encountering parabolas in this book, and they are very smooth waves. There are smooth curves visible here, but they are generated by a wholly digital piece of equipment, made by De Lagrange of Paris. The brass frame has equal sides, which are pierced with holes at equal distances. The threads are drawn tight by lead weights. But the frame is *twisted*, with the effect you see. The surface is a 'hyperbolic paraboloid', and looks continuous to the eye. A typical parabola is traced out by the rings, and again the eye readily smoothes the curve.

So this is a digital-to-analogue hybrid device. And what does it tell us about the eye-and-brain activity that is the observing part of the total system which declares: 'smooth curves'?

The Slide Rule

on the other hand, is an analogue-to-digital device. To work it, you move the slide in or out against the fixed stock. Since there are no gears to click into place, no switches to throw, the position of the slide is infinitely variable. But the reading of the scales is possible in fairly accurate digital terms, because the scales are finely divided, and a slide carrying a hair-line is moved to connect the moving scale with the fixed one.

An English country parson, William Oughtred, invented the slide-rule in 1632—and it was the constant companion of engineers everywhere for the next three hundred years. None was ever seen without his 'guessing stick'! The pocket calculator has made the slide rule virtually extinct in one short generation.

You can clearly see that the intervals on the scales become steadily shorter as you move to the right. This is because the distances reflect the *logarithm* of the number shown. It means that the hair-line will find the answers to multiplication and division sums, instead of just adding the marks on two adjacent scales—which would be easy, and not too useful.

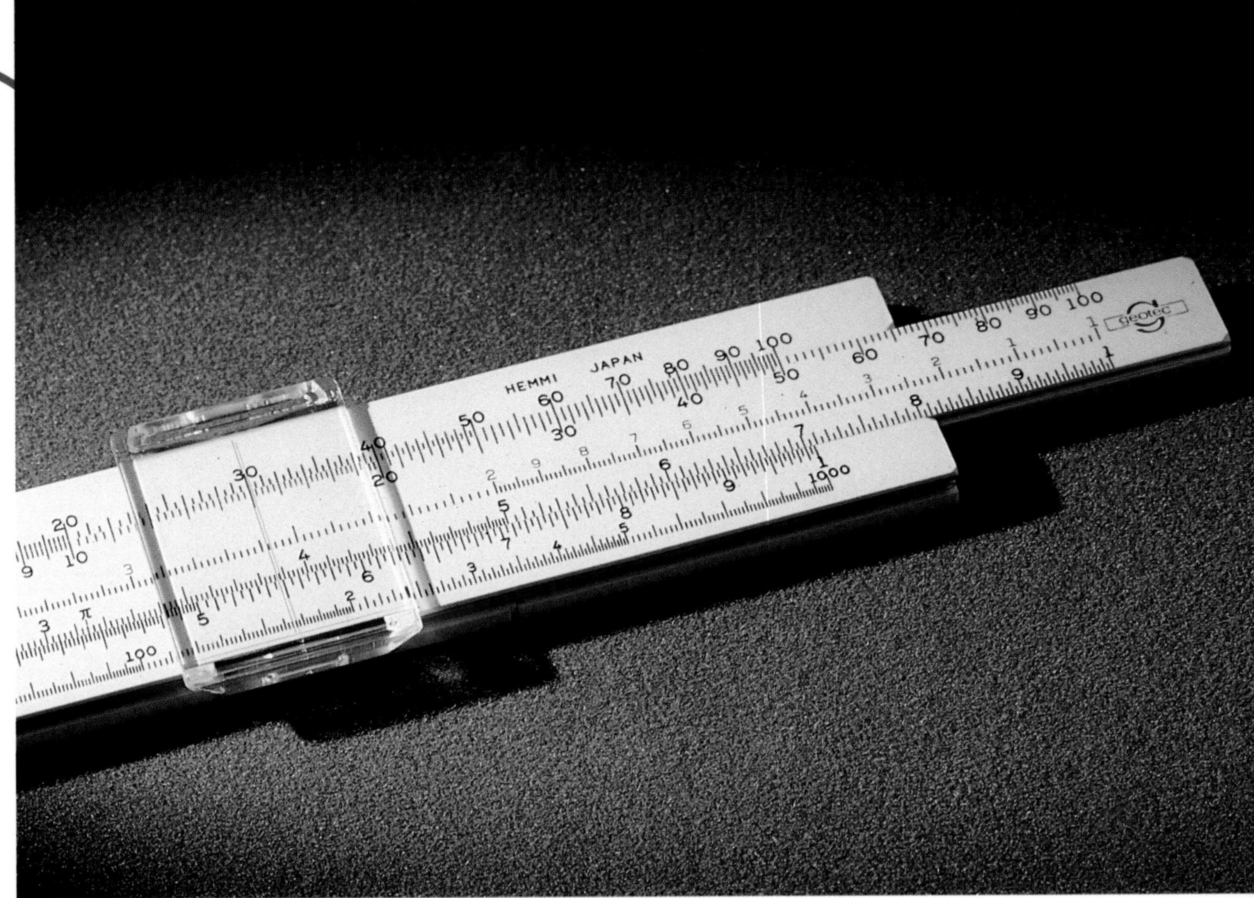

In the early days of automation, much attention had to be given to the problem of **analogue-digital** conversion. Industrial processes tend to *flow*, and not to go in jerks; and to measure what was happening often involved keeping watch on a variable voltage or a fluctuating source of light, and converting it to a stream of bits. Electronic means used nowadays make this much easier to do.

Interestingly enough, inside the body, and despite the medieval philosophers, information *does* proceed in jumps. Electrical pulses move down the nerves in little spikes. The conduction is absolutely *digital*. Well, this is counter to intuition, after all. Things seem to get hotter, more painful—in short, more or less intense—on a continuous (analogue) scale. So one might expect a wave of variable amplitude to be moving along a nerve. It is not so. Nor do the spikes get taller, as the next guess might be. They are uniform spikes. What happens is that they become **more frequent**. So if the brain is to detect a smooth curve on the facing page, it has to be a **digital-analogue** converter.

At Lascaux, in the Dordogne, Southwestern France, an incredible discovery was made in 1940. Five young boys, in rescuing their dog, fell into an underground passageway inside a hill above the town of Montignac. The passage led into the Great Hall of Bulls—a vast cave, sixty by thirty feet, with a ceiling painting dominated by four black bulls, one of which is as long as eighteen feet. There were other finds: more passages, more caves, more paintings of more animals—and signs galore.

We thought that at five thousand years Stonehenge was rather old (Egyptian archaeology as well), but here at Lascaux we are in the Upper Paleolithic age: these pictures have been preserved for *fifteen thousand* years. The date rests upon the evidence of lamps and

the Thread returns to Origins of counting

spears, and above all, charcoal, since that yields a radiocarbon date. There seem to have been at least three periods involved in the stylistic development, but all are referred in general to this age—the brilliance of the paintings well preserved by a thin calcite film deposited as water seeped through rock, year after thousand year.

Intuition suggests that counting originated with the numbering off of items by the digits on the hands—then by extension to 'pebbles' of whatever sort.

Here for the first time we see what certainly appears to be numerical recording. There are dots and dashes all over Lascaux's caves. Note particularly (for later reference) the set just below the horse's face at bottom center.

in widely

separated sites— and times...

Once again, history and sanctity merge to produce some unknown mixture of what *happened* with what *mattered*.The Chief Myeegun was also a shaman—a medicine-man. He ventured across the lake in five war-canoes, and did battle at Agawa Rock. The pictogram is thought to commemorate this feat—though to what extent it flattered the chief no one knows! There he is, at least, riding a horse (top left). To his immediate right is the vestigial remnant of Mikenok the turtle—a magical protector, 'ally' from the spiritual world. The five canoes are over on the right.

It is the meaning of the lower symbol that most interests us. The interpretors say it counts the *four suns over water* that the journey took. Mikenok may symbolize 'reaching land'. The Ojibways, anyway, seem to be recording numbers here.

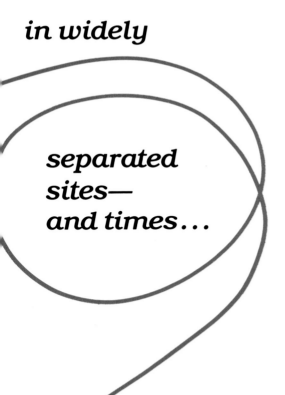

In this other case, we are thousands of miles from Lascaux and thousands of years away as well. But these are aboriginal paintings just the same...

This is the Agawa Rock at Lake Superior, Ontario, in Canada—the pictographs were made on the perpendicular face of a cliff, by the Ojibway Indians, about three or four hundred years ago.

recording numbers?

These Mexican artefacts (the first is Mayan) both reproduce the 'dot-and-dash' pattern of the cave and cliff artists . . .

. . . is *this* coincidence? —or were the Mexicans also 'counting the suns across the water'?

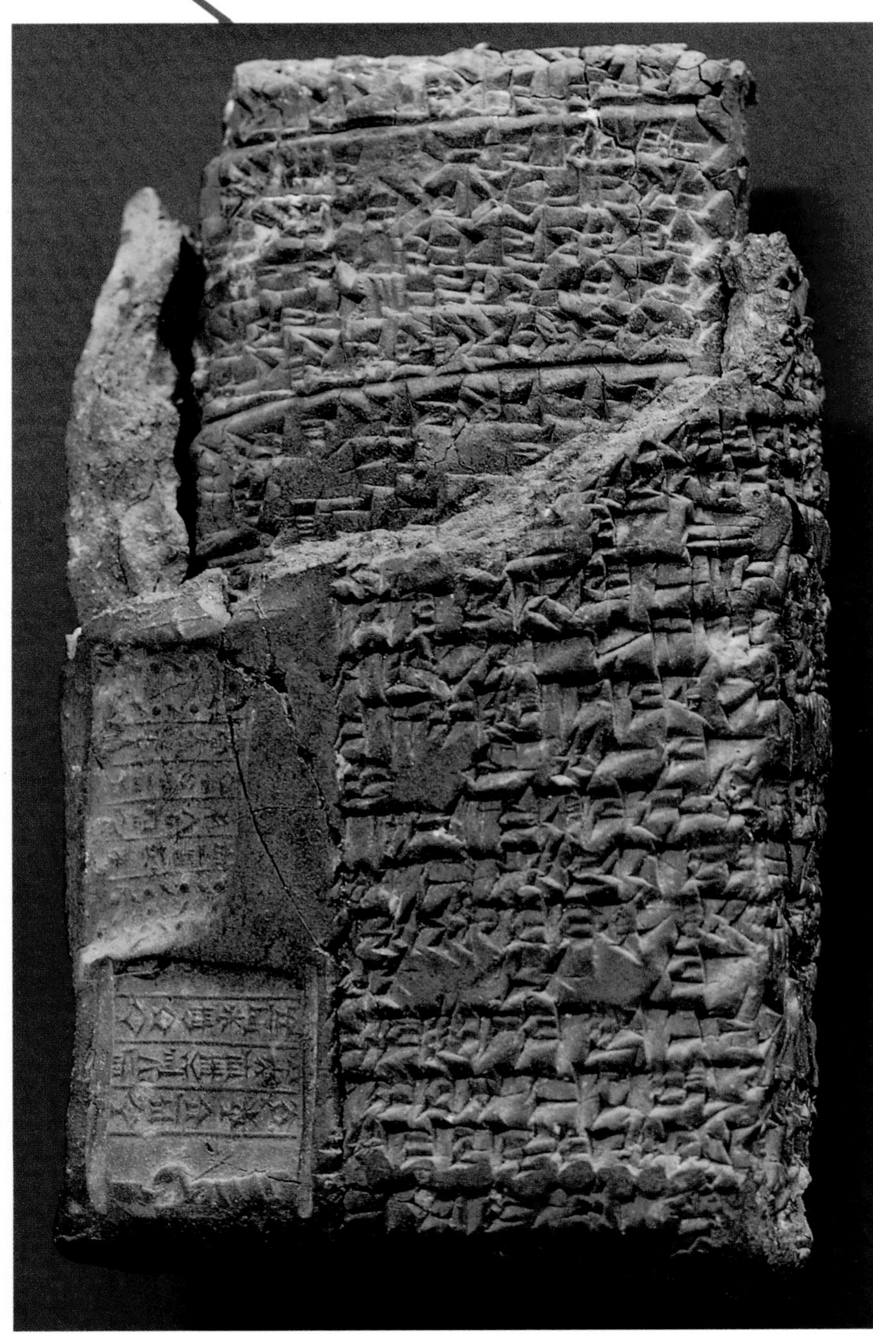

...this clay tablet too...
the
earliest
'legal file'?

This clay tablet was stored—for filing or for mailing?—in an envelope...

The time is roughly 1700 BC.

It concerns a legal case between the King of Aleppo, Abbai'l, and his sister, Bittati, about the division of property belonging to Amurabi.

Niqmeba heard the case, and five witnesses sealed the envelope.

still 3500 years ago

the Phaistos disc

Many have heard of the bull-like monster called the Minotaur, who inhabited the labyrinth of Crete. We speak again of roughly 1700 BC.

Like other civilizations, the Minoan vanished quite suddenly (in this case more than three thousand years ago). No one can be quite sure how the ancient Greek culture and the Minoan interacted. It is a 'chicken-and-egg' problem—made no less mysterious by the linguistic discoveries of Michael Ventris, who solved the problem of decoding the manuscript called 'Linear B'. Minoan or not, Linear B turned out to be (a very) ancient Greek.

That leaves the disc of Phaistos.

The Minoan palace of Phaistos gave up its relic—shown here in approximately actual size—in 1908. It is a clay disc, baked by accident or design: but in either case, why only one? Ventris had hundreds of examples of Linear B on which to work.

The first thing to be said is beyond controversy, but still surprising. Here is an example of movable type, thousands of years before Gutenberg and Caxton. The clay is cut with a die.

The Phaistos disc has markings on both sides, and as you see it makes a spiral statement that can be unwound. Many scholars have tried to 'decode' the messages.

In a boldly adventurous piece of yet unpublished work, Rudi Haas interprets the disc at several levels. He finds it to be a calendrical device, on which daily activities in the palace were scheduled for two months ahead. He also finds an exact sequence of stellar events which actually happened between 21 December and 19 February for a year in that era (1700 BC). Further yet, he finds a code that predicts the site plan of the palace erected on the site of the ruins in which the disc was found!

Detective puzzles of this kind are difficult indeed—and it is fortunate that dedicated scholars work on them. For gradually we uncover more of our origins; and as this book repeatedly attests, we need a deeper understanding of the cosmos than the mere 'mastery of nature' will allow . . .

Even so, take a look with twentieth-century pride at a contemporary 'Phaistos disc':

a plasma etching tunnel to process Integrated Circuits.

Bright spots around the wafer boat result from deactivating excited molecules of nitrogen . . .

Is there perhaps an echo anywhere that says: 'technical chauvinism'?

Marking and counting endlessly continue…

Egyptian hieroglyphs

on clay,
on papyrus,

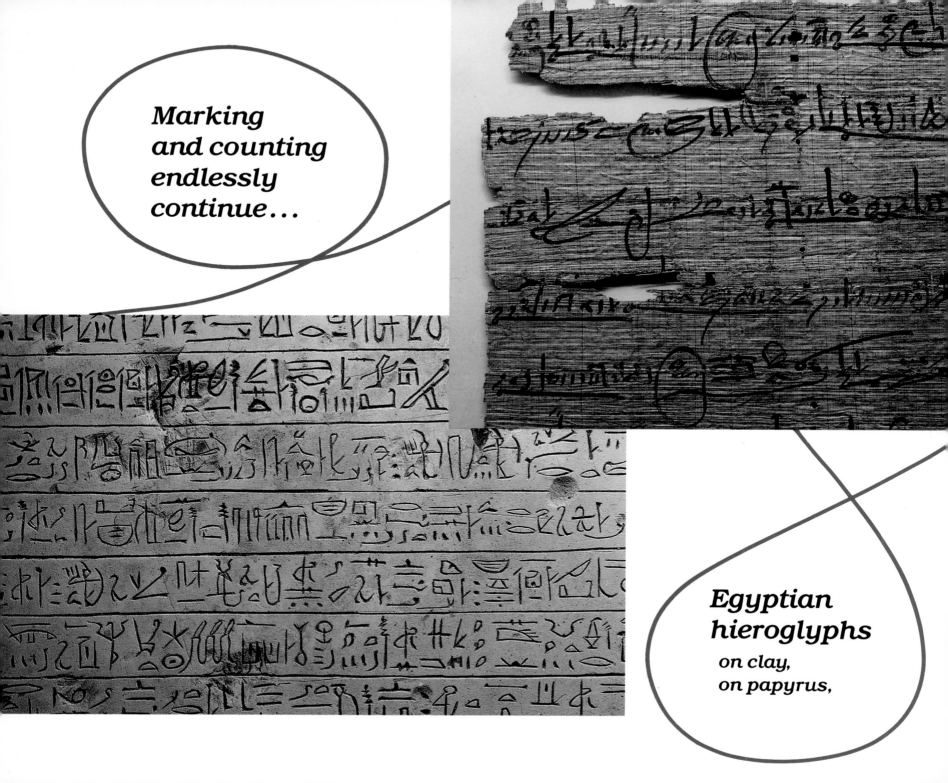

take us through thousands of years to RUNIC writing...

Textures are lovely.

And the development of man's calligraphy is lovely too. Three examples will have to suffice.

Egyptian writing is well known. The runic stone is a Viking monument: that is now AD 1000—comparatively modern, and yet still a whole millenium old.

This stone, near Schleswig in Germany, comes from the southernmost Viking settlement of its time.

It commemorates the death of Skarthi, liege-man of King Sven. The inscription is in Old Danish—written in the Runic alphabet.

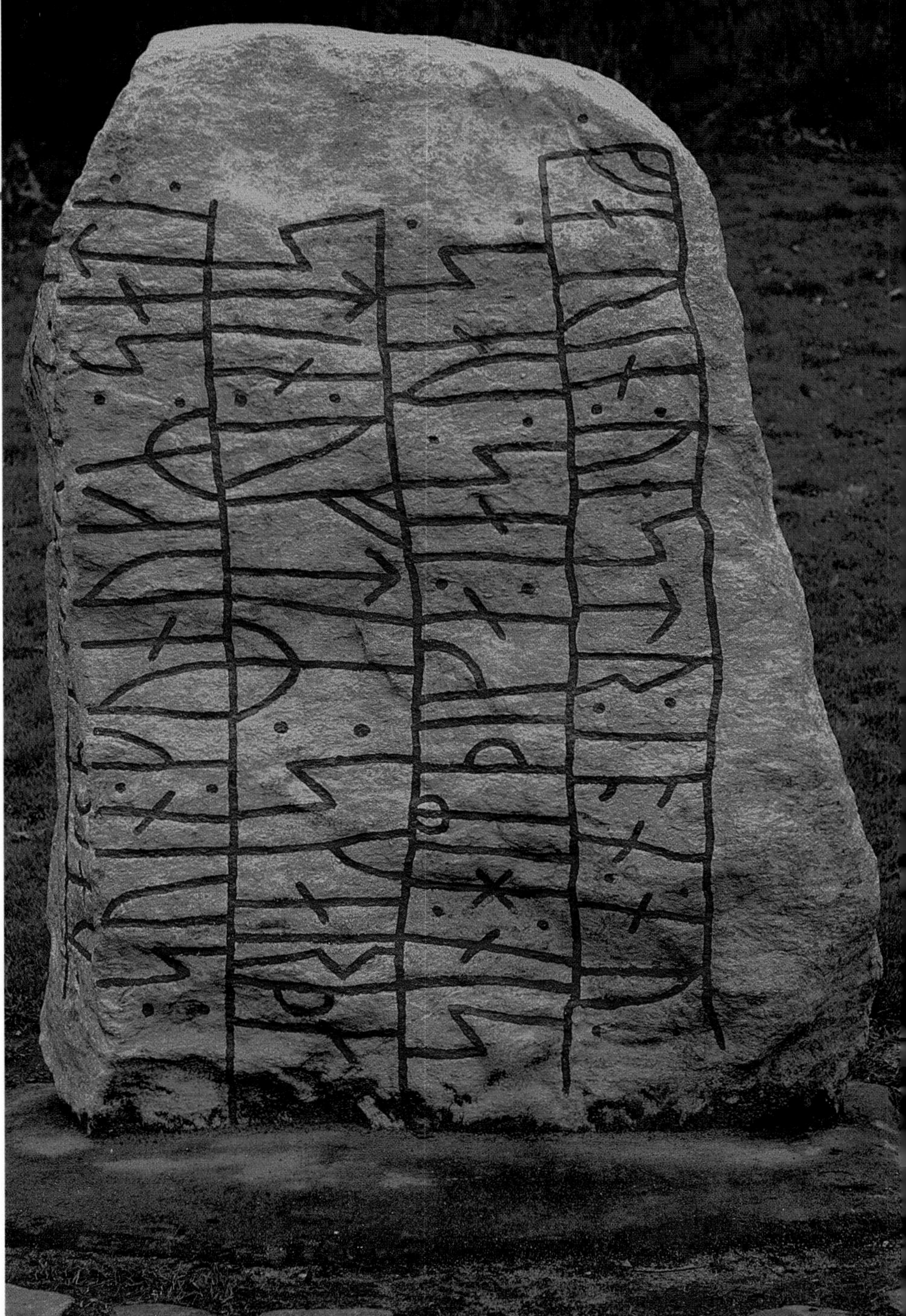

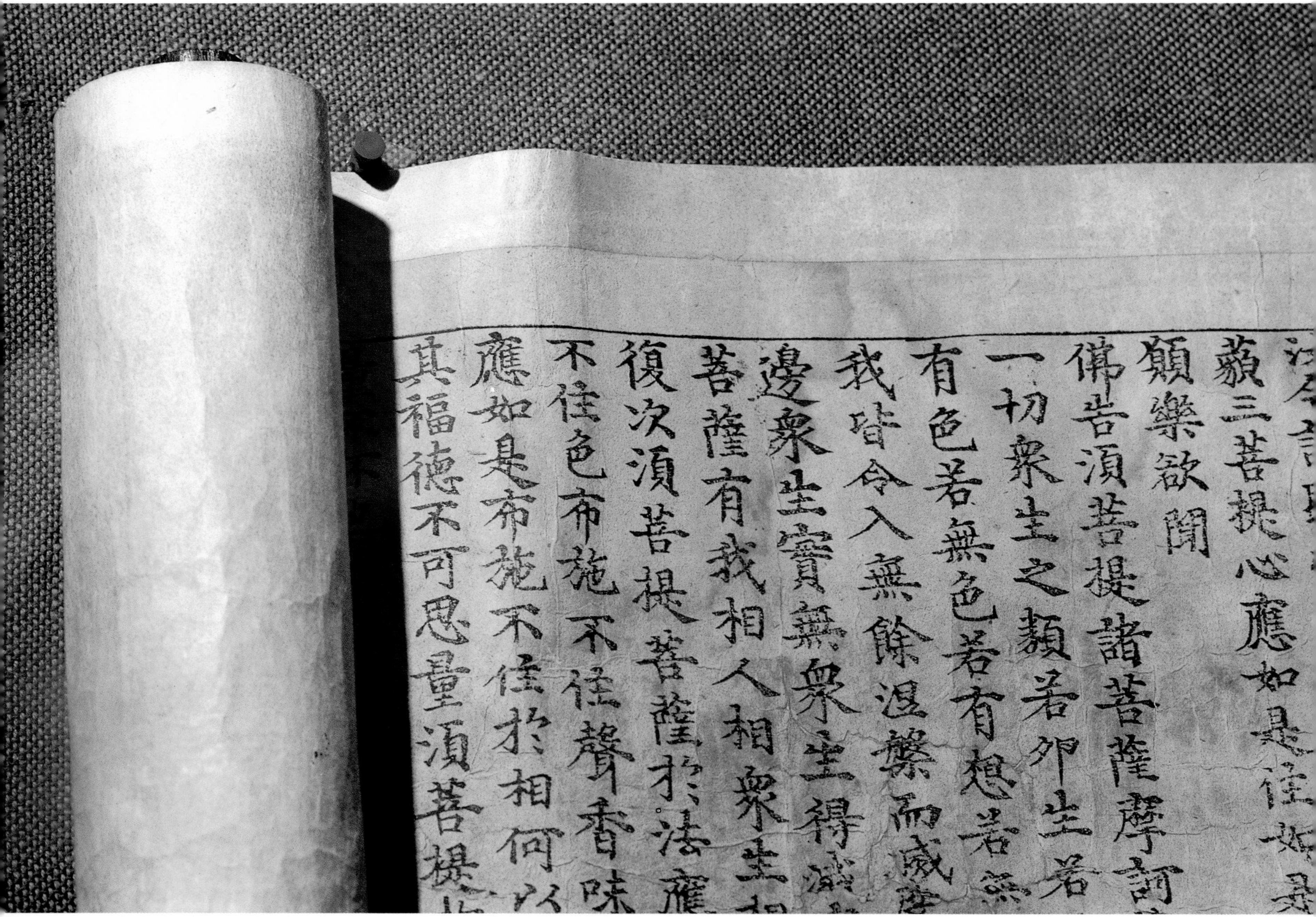

汝今諦聽
藐三菩提心應如是住如是
願樂欲聞
佛告須菩提諸菩薩摩訶
一切眾生之類若卵生若
有色若無色若有想若無
我皆令入無餘涅槃而滅度
邊眾生實無眾生得滅
菩薩有我相人相眾生相
復次須菩提菩薩於法應
不住色布施不住聲香味
應如是布施不住於相何以
其福德不可思量須菩提

and to the print we know...

The cast-lead letters of the Gutenberg Press—shown below—mark the 'official' beginning of the printed word. But China was in advance of that; and the Phaistos disc was two thousand years earlier still. Whatever the details, though, humankind began to handle its distinctions—to make them, write them, record them; to *compute* with them.

Here on the left is the world's earliest dated printed book—'reverently made' for his two parents by Wang Jie. The date is AD 868

This is block printing, which had already been in existence for a hundred years by then.

The Buddhist text is the famous *Diamond Sutra*. Here is a notion from that text, to stand beside the powerful and ancient images...

Think a thought, it says, 'unsupported by sights, sounds, smells, tastes, touchables, or any objects of the mind.'

Can you do that?

about Gears...

So printing evolved, and it is not the present task to follow that story further. Even so, here is a beautiful picture of an 'old-fashioned' Canadian printing press—its gear train, to introduce the subject of gearing. It looks like a digital operation—those countable teeth! But they can be made to intermesh so smoothly that the operation is analogue instead. Well, a clock's hands move smoothly round... But is that movement analogue? The escapement and the pendulum are digital converters, no less.

In all of this lies considerable informational potency, and not just mechanical amplification—which may be the way we normally think of gears. When did all that start?

Archimedes, that profligate inventor and wise man, invented a planetarium (sun, moon and five planets) in the third century BC. The Roman historians Cicero and Ovid both described it later on. In fact Cicero was at Rhodes in 78 BC. In that very year, a ship went down in the Aegean Sea near the island of Antikythera. On board was a mysterious mechanism brought up from the sea-bed when a sponge diver found the wreck in 1900.

The object had visible signs of gearing, and scholars thought it might have been an astrolabe. We see two more of these over the page, and they are *early* examples. So the Antikytheran device was most surprising.

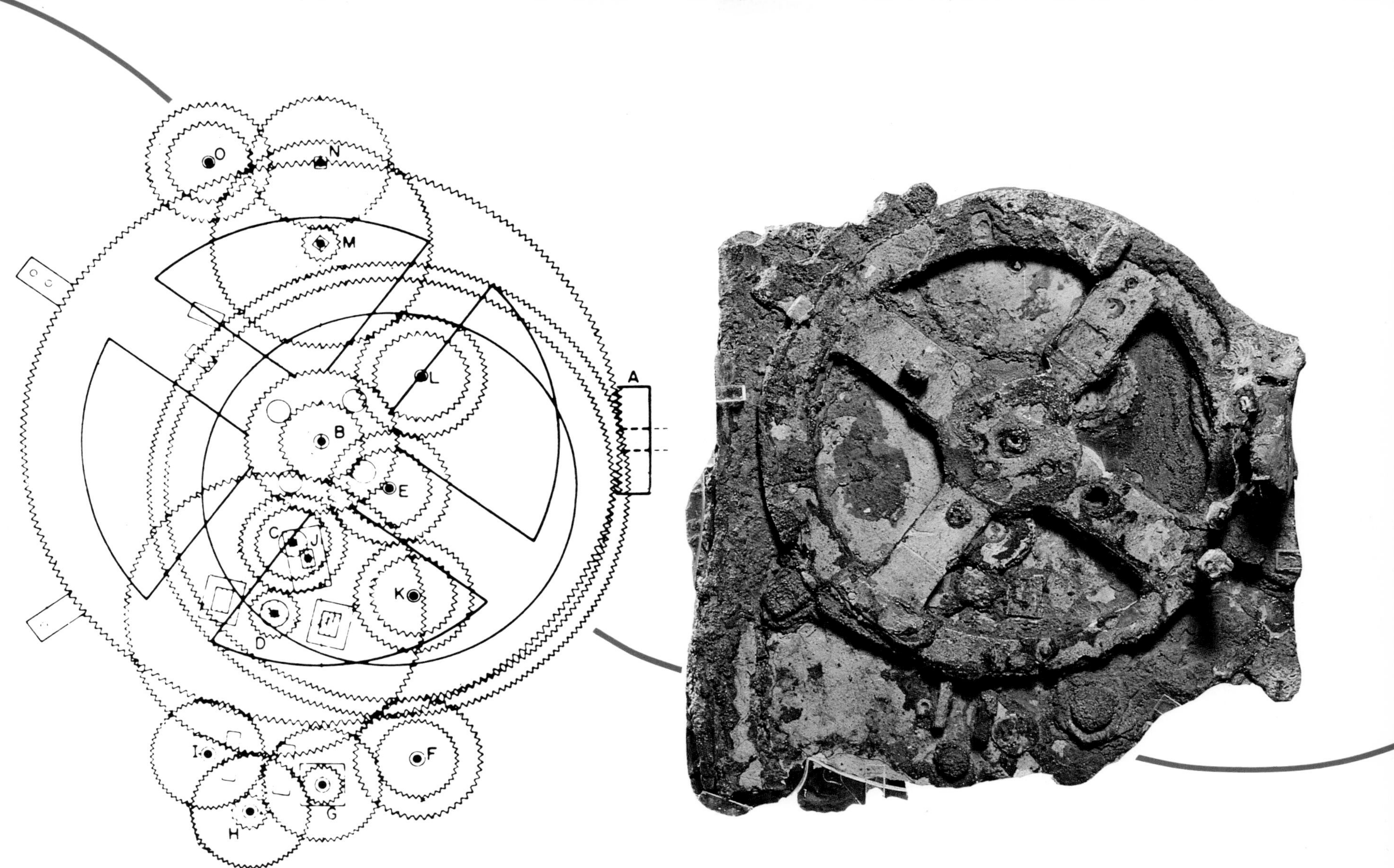

As can be seen above, however, further surprises were in store. Derek de Solla Price of Yale spent twenty-three years trying to understand the mechanism. Eventually, with the help of gamma rays, he was able to 'see inside' the parts that had solidified, melded together. The graphic diagram shows his findings—and the gear ratios relate to relevant astronomical data. Price has not hesitated to call this a *computer*, built, it seems, in 65 BC—and so not Archimede's own! The most astonishing feature of these gear trains is a differential gear, such as allows a car's rear wheels to turn at different speeds. As we noted before, much knowledge seems to have been lost. Nothing like this was found before or since.

and Astrolabes

'Mathematical' gearing is so called because the relative rates of rotation of the wheels are an exact computing device. In ordinary gearing, used for transmitting energy, the exact number of teeth does not matter. Here, on the contrary, we see a working model of the solar system—and the gears are transmitting information.

This Byzantine machine is a sundial-calendar, the pieces of which were handed in to the Science Museum in London as recently as 1983. The instrument is dated at AD 500, which makes it the oldest known geared calendrical device after the Antikytheran example. The photograph on the left is of a reconstruction made at the Museum. Of course, the gears are inside.

The instrument is basically a sundial, which has to be set correctly according to the latitude, after which the day of the week is set on the small dial. This is connected to a ratchet and gear mechanism that leads a wheel having fifty-nine teeth. This is the moon disc, rotating once in two lunations, giving alternately twenty-nine and thirty days in the lunar month.

Replica by Michael Wright, courtesy Science Museum, London, England

Further gears however position the sun in the Zodiac, and then the moon—whose phases appear in apertures on the reverse side of the device. The conjectured gearing in the reconstruction then shows the sun as making one circuit every 366.42 days, and the moon as making one circuit every 27.3 days.

What use could have been made of this 'automated sundial'? The Museum can suggest two possibilities. One could predict whether, on a given date, there would be a large enough moon to make a night-time journey practicable. (But the instrument says nothing about the clouds!) Secondly, it would be possible to convert the lunar calendar used by peasant folk into the Julian calendar used by the upper classes... The Museum does not suggest that the machine might simply have been a conversation piece among the latter set. But in our own time many artefacts have just that social function.

The pleasing astrolabe pictured to the right is Arabian (from Spain) and is dated 1086. It seems strange, given that such advanced computational devices did exist so long ago, that so few have survived. But metal was expensive, and it seems that many precious objects were recycled.

'Celestial Computers'

From the Hellenistic origins we have seen, 'mathematical gearing' moved through several extant Islamic examples to the West. A French astrolabe with calendrical gearing, for instance, dates back to about 1300—and the astrolabe was the major technical prop of observational astronomy.

But all of these instruments were driven by hand. It seems that the origins of the *clock* were in astronomy: that is, the gearing of the solar system would be somehow powered—for preference at the pace the real solar system works.

Richard of Wallingford, who died in 1336, made a clock for St Alban's Abbey which has been reconstructed. It was not a good timekeeper, but it showed the apparent motions of the sun, the moon, and the stars—and also managed to portray lunar eclipses.

Many early clocks had elaborate astronomical dials: they were 'celestial computers'. Later, of course, the art and science of clockmaking devoted itself to 'telling the time'.

But beautiful and functional astronomical clocks, such as this huge machine in Strasbourg, were made for centuries in the geared traditions of the astrolabes. This one bears mid-nineteenth century dates.

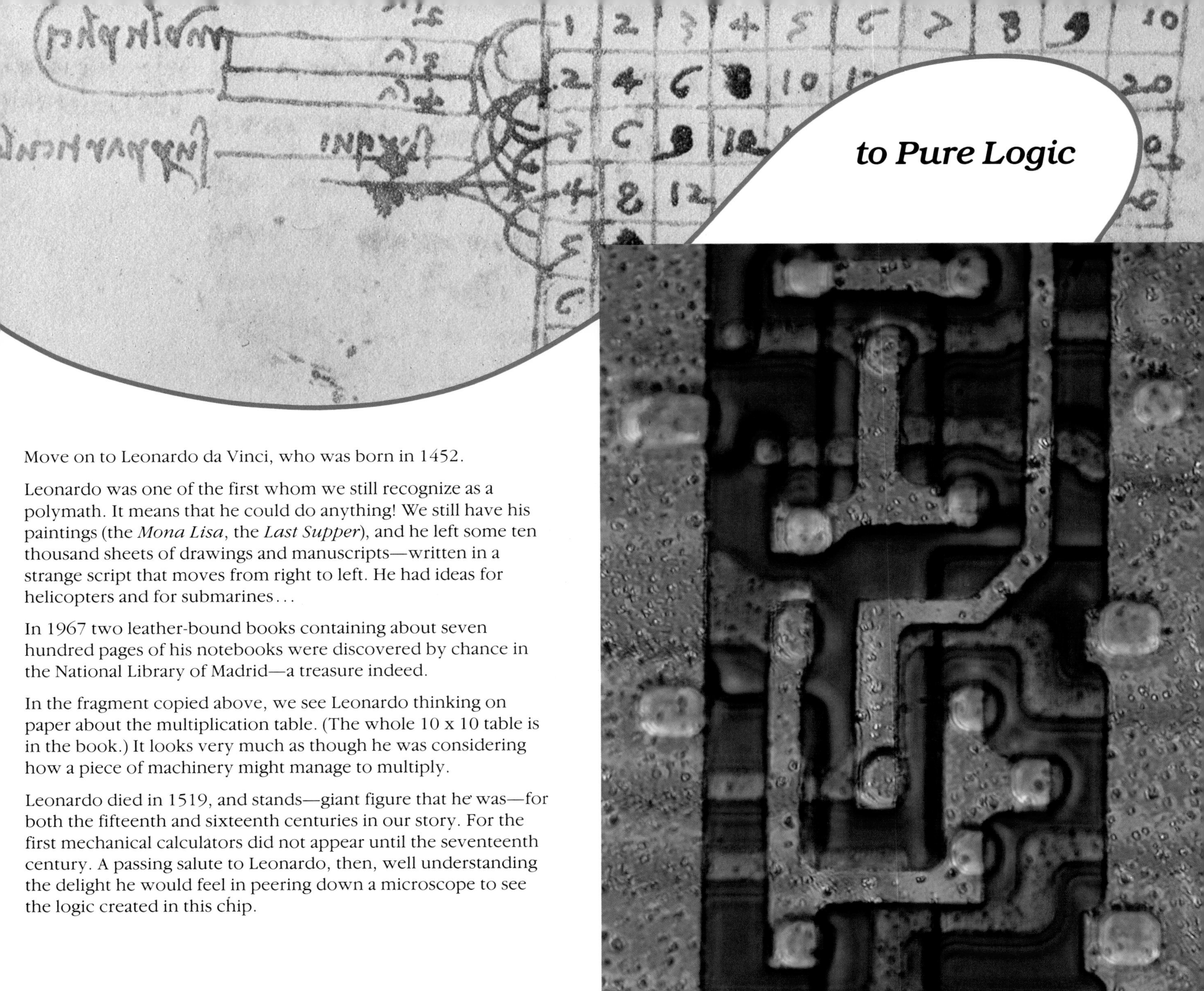

to Pure Logic

Move on to Leonardo da Vinci, who was born in 1452.

Leonardo was one of the first whom we still recognize as a polymath. It means that he could do anything! We still have his paintings (the *Mona Lisa*, the *Last Supper*), and he left some ten thousand sheets of drawings and manuscripts—written in a strange script that moves from right to left. He had ideas for helicopters and for submarines...

In 1967 two leather-bound books containing about seven hundred pages of his notebooks were discovered by chance in the National Library of Madrid—a treasure indeed.

In the fragment copied above, we see Leonardo thinking on paper about the multiplication table. (The whole 10 x 10 table is in the book.) It looks very much as though he was considering how a piece of machinery might manage to multiply.

Leonardo died in 1519, and stands—giant figure that he was—for both the fifteenth and sixteenth centuries in our story. For the first mechanical calculators did not appear until the seventeenth century. A passing salute to Leonardo, then, well understanding the delight he would feel in peering down a microscope to see the logic created in this chip.

Wilhelm Schickard

Pascal (next page) was for three hundred years accepted as the inventor of the first mechanical calculator. And then another of those 'finds' was made...

Wilhelm Schickard—yes, another polymath—became a protégé of the astronomer Kepler in 1617. As an outcome of their discussions, he reported to Kepler in 1623 that he had invented a 'calculating clock'. He described it in Latin, and enclosed a sketch. In 1624 he explained in another letter to Kepler that the workshop in which the machine was being constructed had burned down, and everything had been lost. Meanwhile the Thirty Years' War was being fought. Half of Europe, especially Germany, was ravaged by fighting and disease. Schickard died of bubonic plague in 1635—and none of his family survived. No wonder people never heard about the Calculating Clock.

It was not until the 1930s that Schickard's two letters to Kepler were discovered in Kepler's papers, which were being prepared for publication in a complete edition. But the sketch referred to in them was missing. One day in 1935, Franz Hammer (one of the editors of Kepler's works) stumbled on a sketch—the one on the left below. He realized that it related to Schickard's letters, but nothing happened about the matter, and then there came the Second World War...

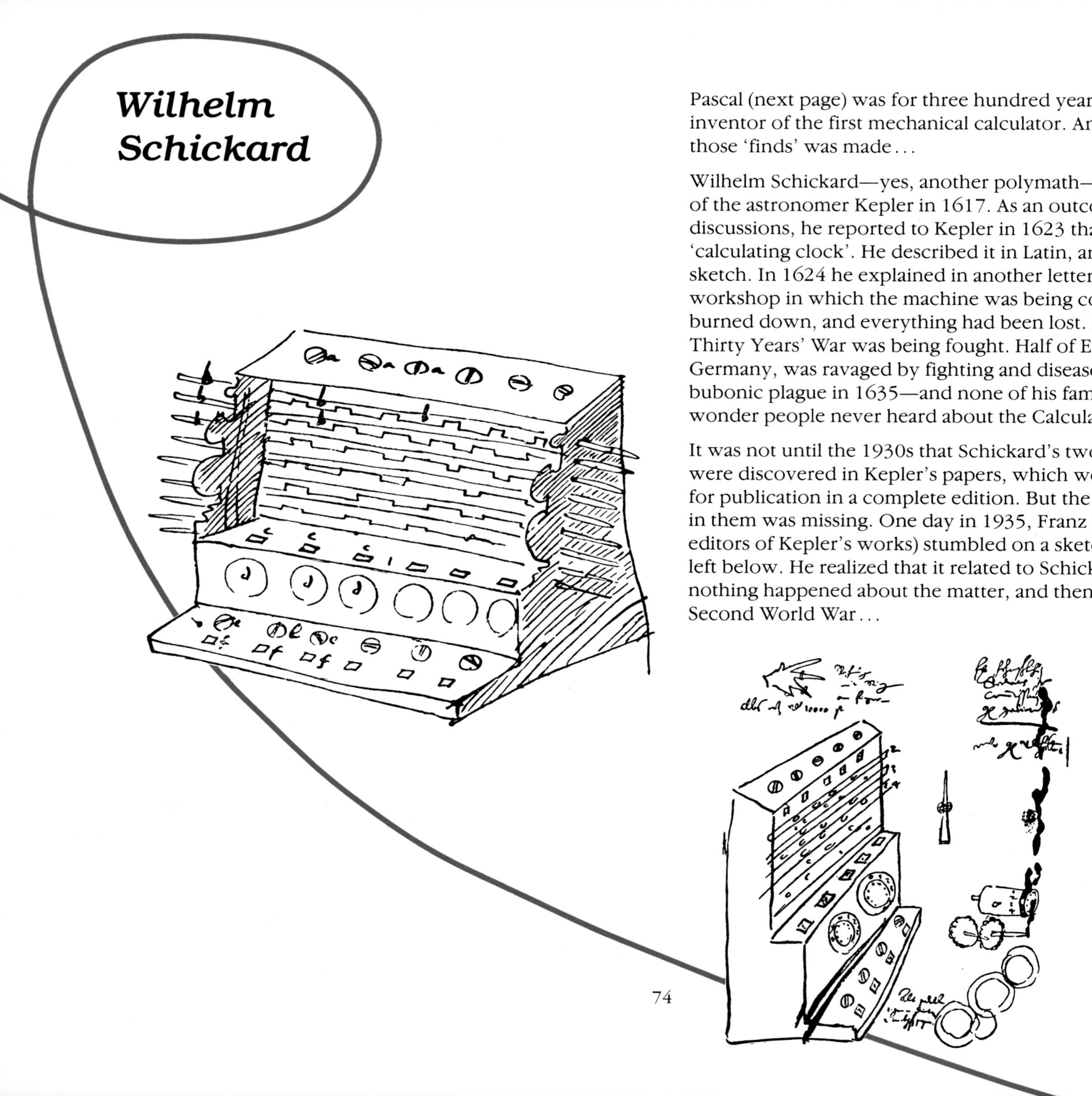

Twenty-one years later, Franz Hammer was going through Schickard's own papers in Stuttgart when he found the second drawing, together with some instructions for a mechanic. He remembered what it was. And so it happened that Professor von Freytag, at Schickard's old university at Tübingen, came to reconstruct the machine: here is its photograph.

The background to this invention hinges on the invention of logarithms in 1614 by John Napier, a Scottish baron. These make it possible to multiply and divide by adding and subtracting exponents of numbers instead of doing long sums with the numbers themselves. You need to know what the exponents are—hence the publication of sets of 'log tables'. Napier went on to devise his numbered sticks, or rods, which did the same job by moving one rod in relation to another—and some versions of Napier's rods were cylindrical.

It seems that Kepler and Schickard had been discussing Napier's methods, and that the Calculating Clock was the result. The top half of the machine is simply a set of Napier's logs. The slots on the left allow the setting of a multiplier, and the logarithmic answers appear in the little windows. These must now be added up. So the box with the numbered dials is essentially an adding machine, which could also subtract. The numerical scale across the bottom of the device is the earliest 'memory': you set numbers in there that you wanted to remember.

The innovative part of Schickard's calculator was the 'carrying' mechanism—an ingenious piece of gearing which meant that when a register passed from 9 to 0, the next gear would notch up one tooth. Schickard told Kepler that when he saw this working, he would laugh. Alas, he never did.

Blaise Pascal

As we said just now, Pascal was for centuries thought to have invented the mechanical calculator—and here it is: the 'Pascaline'.

Well, it turns out that Blaise Pascal was born in precisely the year, 1623, that saw Schickard announcing his Calculating Clock to Kepler. However, Pascal was no plagiarist—he knew nothing of Schickard's work—and indeed he was troubled by imitations and patent processes himself.

The fact is, moreover, that the Pascaline is not nearly such a good device as Schickard's. It did not have an inbuilt multiplication system, such as Napier's cylindrical logs. Worse still, since its crown gears needed an elaborate ratchet system, they could not move in reverse. We have addition, but no (straightforward) subtraction. A complicated method of subtraction known as 'nines complements', permitted the operation. It involves subtracting the number to be subtracted from a row of nines, which the machine was pre-programmed to do, and then *adding* this complement. Then the highest figure must be carried round behind into the units column.

Example:
387 – 245 = 142

Pascaline Method:

$$\begin{array}{r} 999 \text{ (stored)} \\ -\ 245 \\ \hline 754 \\ +\ 387 \\ \hline (1)\,141 \end{array} = 142$$

(1) carry

Blaise invented the machine for his father Etienne—who was the tax-man. So one might have expected that the Pascaline would have concentrated on getting subtraction rather than addition right . . .

Pascal invented many other devices and mathematical theorems before he died in great pain of stomach cancer at the age of thirty-nine. But he was only twenty-one when the Pascaline was ready to be marketed (though it seems not many were sold). His later life, young as he was, was marred by religious mania in a Jansenist monastery. His scientific work was cut off but his machine was a sensation. It has stood as an emblem of computational reform. But the France of Cardinal Richelieu—its high society—was uninstructed in science and mathematics: that held things up. It might be emblematic too of how the upper echelons, even today, are often heard to boast (in a self-deprecating way) of their innumeracy. It is not healthy for society.

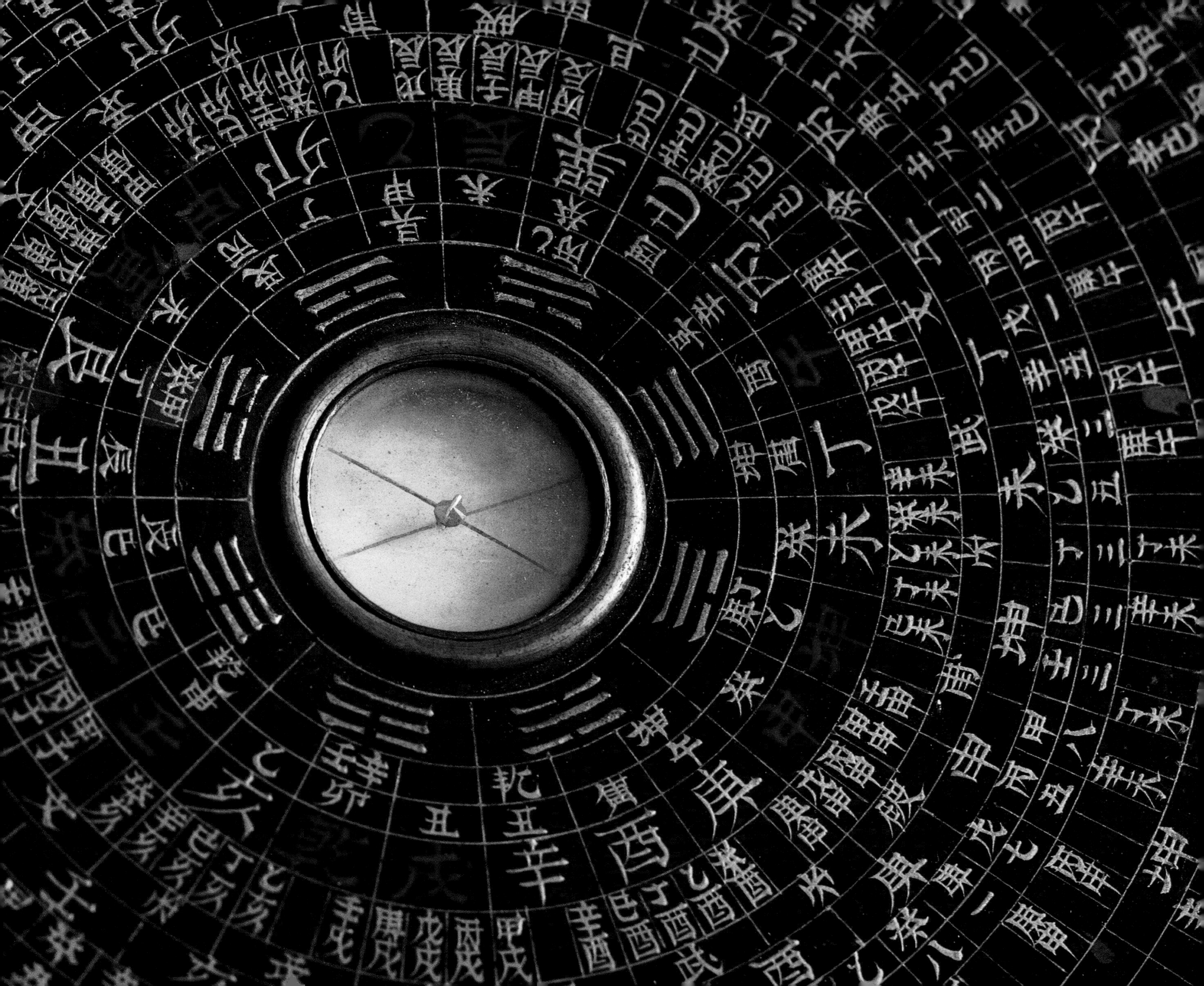

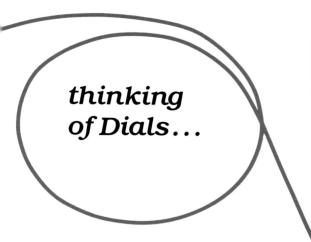

thinking of Dials...

Dials were the method for reading whatever machines had to tell us from earliest times—witness the sundial, and the compass.

The Chinese are credited with the invention of the compass—and here is a superb example.

In England, as you may see above, Sir Samuel Morland—following Pascal's lead—produced this mechanical calculator for addition and subtraction.

The date it gives is 1666, the year of the Great Fire of London. What may interest us the more is the duodecimal scale of Morland's money dials. As was mentioned earlier, there were until recent times twelve pence in a shilling, and two hundred and forty pence in a pound—making twenty shillings on the largest dial. There were moreover four farthings to the penny—and so remained within living memory.

Both photographs here display unusual dials... But lately dials have been virtually replaced by digital displays, to which electronic technology lends itself. Only the clocks and watches seem to be fighting back!

on to the Stepped Reckoner...

If Pascal was a polymath, then Leibniz was one whose name almost defines the word. He was one of the world's outstanding philosophers—his system (called the Monadology) has been influential since his own day (his dates were 1646 to 1716), and may well become more so in the future as Eastern and Western ways of thinking tend to coalesce. Not that Leibniz himself was an Oriental master, but his Western thoughts are none the less compatible with those of Vedantic philosophy. He was a famous mathematician—who invented the differential calculus. This seems to have been independently of Isaac Newton, and probably a good many years later; even so it is Leibniz's notation, and not Newton's, that we use today. He was a logician, and interested in binary notation...

Leibniz must have come very close to inventing the kind of computer we know, but he did not transfer his understanding of binary logic back into arithmetic. And so he stayed with the decimal system of counting. Here we see his Stepped Reckoner, dated from about 1674. It was specifically based on the Pascaline, which he read about in Pascal's posthumously published book, the *Pensées*. However, Leibniz's special gear could multiply mechanically; but the carrying mechanism for addition and subtraction needed human intervention! Probably the machine never really worked. But the 'Leibniz wheel' became an important device. So too was the moving carriage: you shifted one place to the left for every decimal place, and turned the multiplier handle once for every digit. Electric calculators were still using both devices in the mid-twentieth century. Like so many great men, and despite his spectacular career, Leibniz died in penury and disregarded.

of Gottfried Leibniz

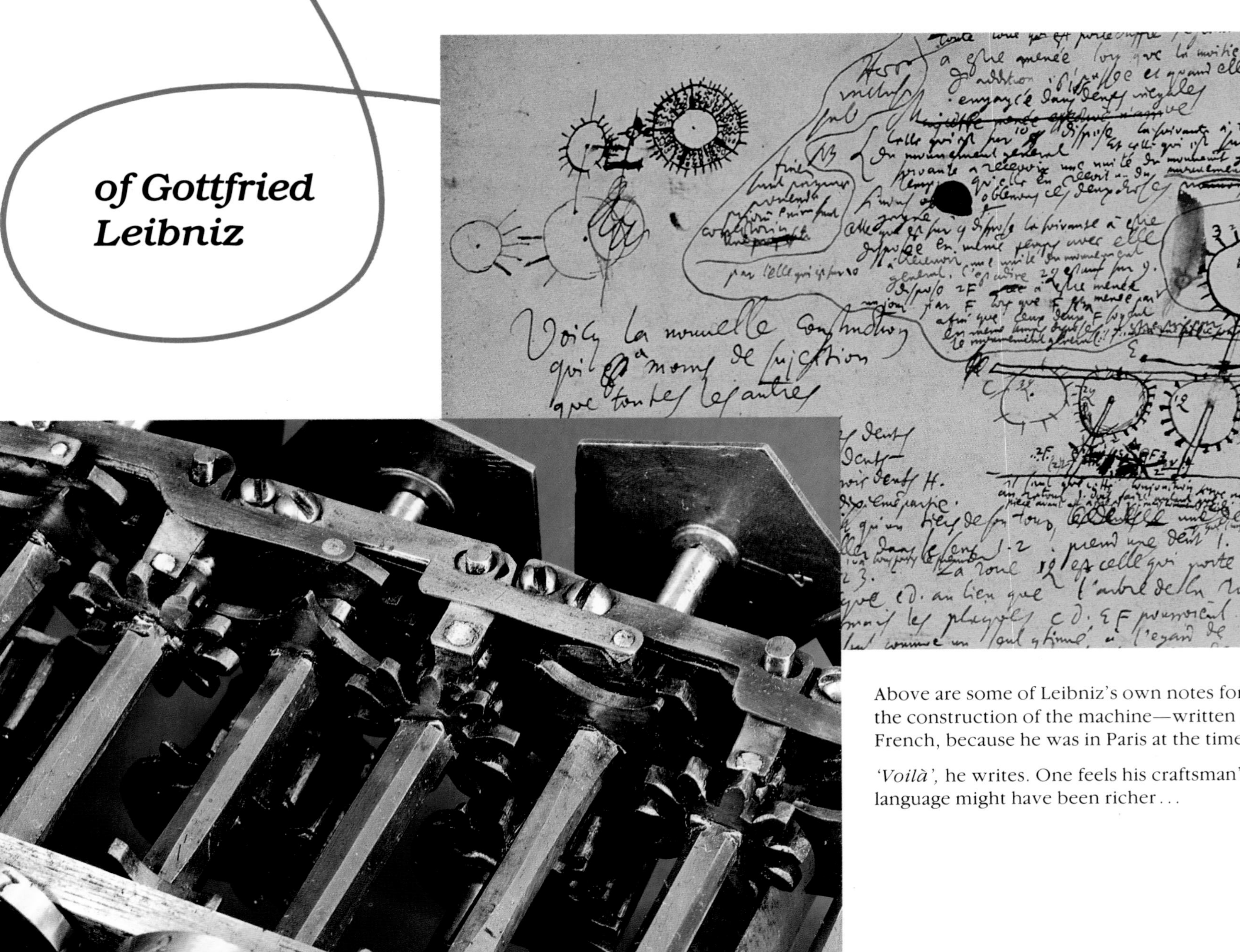

Above are some of Leibniz's own notes for the construction of the machine—written in French, because he was in Paris at the time.

'Voilà', he writes. One feels his craftsman's language might have been richer . . .

Hunderttausender
Zehentausender
Tausender

first thoughts on Storage

Pushing forward to the late eighteenth century, we find the problems of calculating mechanisms being investigated by watchmakers. In this German example, by a watchmaker named Sauter, we see star-shaped gearwheels in the upper row—which are of a kind often found in repeating watches.

But computational devices will not now make much progress without considering the problem of **storage**. If you enter numbers into a machine, and then operate upon them, you will lose the original numbers. Of course, it is possible to enter them onto a special set of dials: recall that Schickard's machine had just such a provision. The real problem arises when the machine needs to remember its own half-way calculations, for later use.

The problem may best be typified by jumping ahead in time to one of its solutions. If you have a grid of wires, and try to record information in the squares thereby created (as is done on a map), or at the intersections of the wires, then everything will simply be electrified—and all discrimination will be lost.

Jay W. Forrester, a modern-day genius, is best known nowadays for his work on World Dynamics—the mechanisms by which a finite planet shuffles and depletes its resources. But in 1949 it was Forrester who invented the **ferrite core memory**, pictured here.

What happens is that tiny rings (the picture is greatly enlarged) of highly magnetic ferrite are fitted across the intersections of a grid, and are given north or south magnetic polarity by the receipt of charges from one direction or the other. They thus become binary recorders—since the magnets hold their 0 or 1 state after the current is switched off. A string of say sixteen bits (making up a 'word') would then be written *through* a stack of sixteen grids—one bit at the same intersection on each grid.

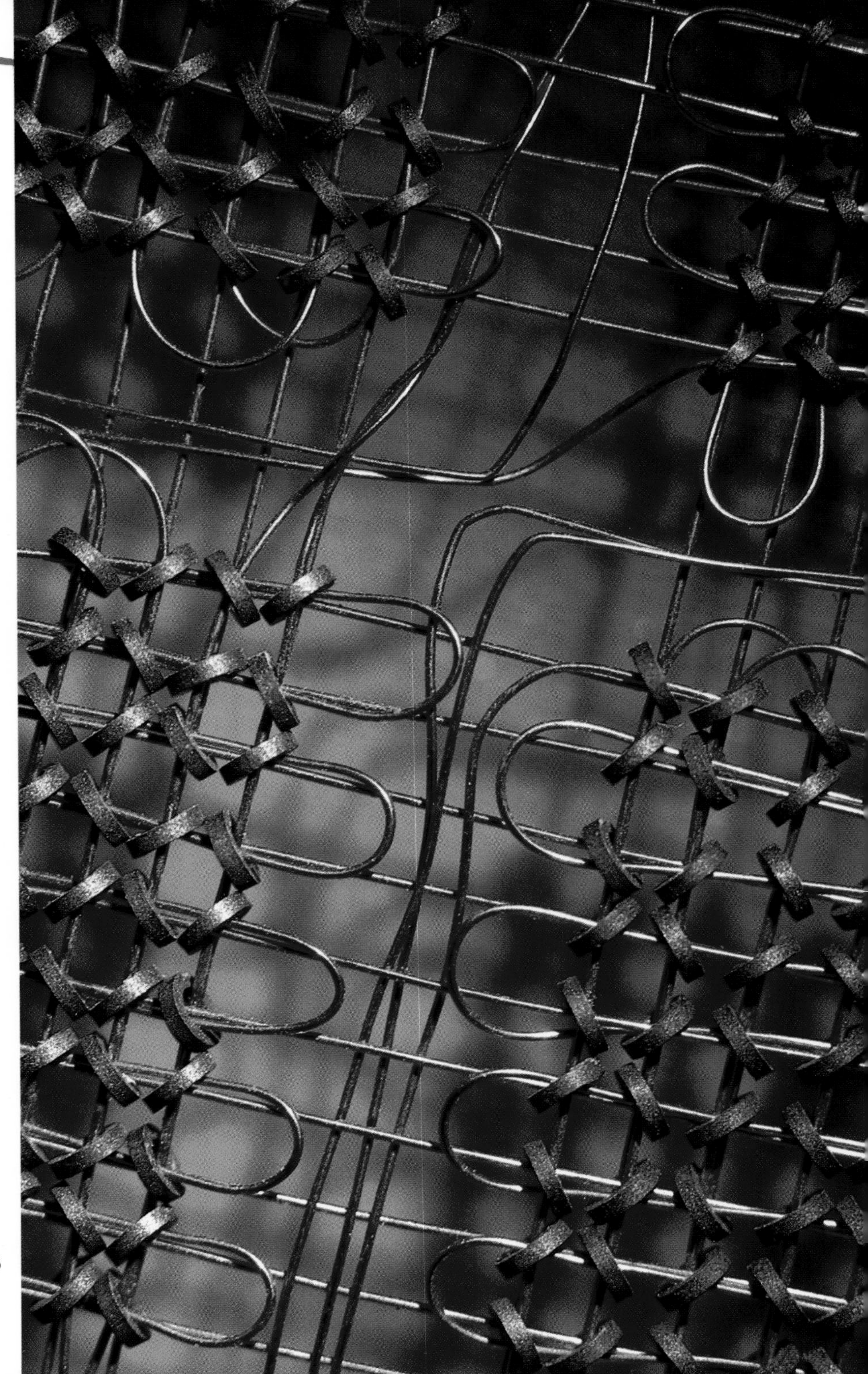

Joseph Marie Jacquard

...amazingly ahead...

Storage inside a machine, to retain half-way results, is one problem.

A far more subtle problem is to store the information that will **tell a machine what to do**. This is known as a machine *program*.

In the late nineteen forties, when electronic computation was in gestation, there was much confusion on this point.

As it happened, two hundred years earlier, weavers had grappled with the problem. Looms are not calculating machines, no indeed. But they are *very* complicated mechanisms. So anyone wishing to control the movements of shuttles, the behaviour of the threads called 'warp' and 'woof', in pursuit of elaborately woven designs, had problems that if solved by human skills took many hours of work to undertake.

...the Programmable Machine...

The weavers—or some of them—throughout the eighteenth century developed the use of the very punched cards that we associate with Hollerith a hundred years further on, to store information.

This information was of the kind that held data—in this case a woven pattern—that would be needed later, but **also the instructions** as to how the loom should use those data.

Jacquard himself perfected the mechanism that took the whole century to evolve, and Jacquard's loom took over in the year 1801. It resulted in mass unemployment: there were 11,000 Jacquard looms in use by 1812 in France alone. The lesson of automation had still not been learned by 1950—maybe not even today.

It is not that scientific progress should be stopped, but that inexorable consequences should not be ignored. They always have been, and perhaps they always will be, ignored.

At any rate: Jacquard (look at his punched cards revolving on the left, and take in the intricate design shown on the right) used **binary logic** to make a **fixed program** that would operate in **real time**—150 years ahead of the game. And people outside textiles hardly noticed.

Thomas de Colmar

The 'Leibniz wheel' was cylindrical—so the gears followed the *axle* (1,2,3 . . .) several places, and then stopped. It is easy to see how this gear was transformed into a slide—it travelled up the gear's axis.

It took about a century and a half of 'Leibnizian' machines before any major new development took place. After a hundred of those years, the German Mathieus Hahn and the Englishman Lord Stanhope produced effective machines. But the nineteenth century was under way before mass production made the mechanical calculator an inevitable adjunct to the age of industry and numerical significance.

About 1820, the Arithometer (shown on the left) began to reap the harvest that its intellectual ancestors had sown. It was invented by a Frenchman, Thomas de Colmar. There was nothing sensationally new about this machine—except that it actually worked!

The Arithometer dominated the scene until the twentieth century dawned, when it was made obsolete, quite quickly, by the innovation of the **keyboard**. So: dials, to slides, to keys—it is an interesting progression.

and

George Boole

George Boole is another of our astonishing characters. He was five years old when the Arithometer became a reality—and must have lived with it all his life. He died before he was fifty, in 1864.

Boole did not meddle with machines. He was a simple schoolteacher, in Lincolnshire, England—and had no university education at all.

But soon he invented Boolean Algebra. This took off from the very point where Leibniz had left off—so many years before. It is a **binary** logic: Things either are or they are not. 'Not' expresses the 0 as against the 1. 'Or' expresses that they are alternatives. But 'and' could say that they are not alternatives at all: both might be true together.

With these three notions—'and,' 'or' and 'not'—anything at all can be expressed.

Out of these three binary notions can be generated $2^3 = 8$ Boolean functions. Boole's two books, notably the *Laws of Thought*—published in 1854—became the logico-mathematical foundations of the business of computing to this day. Remember this?

This is a pebble.
No pebble is here.

Then follows: This pebble *and* this pebble
This pebble *or* this pebble

Contemplate the 'pebbles' once again in an interference contrast control microphoto of an integrated circuit (magnified 500 times, above). It would have delighted Boole!

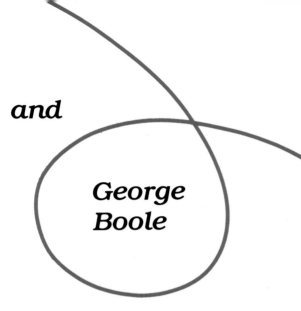

and so to Babbage...

Despite his humble origins, George Boole was not our typically disregarded genius. He was made a fellow of the Royal Society, and a Professor of Trinity College, Dublin. The famous Babbage, regarded as the modern father of computing, was born twenty-four years *before* Boole—but he lived seven years *longer*... Moreover, Babbage had read, and highly regarded, Boole's work.

We are left with a mystery. Why did Charles Babbage, wonder-worker that he was in many ways, not switch from decimal to binary notation? Do not say, well, that was a matter of style. As we see from the photographs, Babbage's massive machines (of which these experimental versions were just sample *parts*) were rigid with their own inertia. As we recounted earlier, Babbage proposed to drive the things by steam...

Much has been written in praise of Babbage's work, and rightly so. That is because he was the first to solve a crucial puzzle (facing page). None the less, the mystery remains: with Leibniz and Boole to work on, why did he not break through? People say: technology had not yet come of age. But logic *had*.

Babbage was another polymath—a real genius. Marx quoted him in *Das Capital* many times, so did John Stuart Mill in *Political Economy*. But he became involved in the Newton-Leibniz controversy over calculus while still at Cambridge, spent all his inherited fortune (and some government grants) on two machines—the Difference Engine, and the Analytical Engine—and died at eighty, still seeking subsidies, but still a famous man.

Something of what we know about him as a man is derived from his relationship (and their letters) with Lady Lovelace: a brilliant mathematician—and devoted admirer, at the least. Augusta Ada, Countess of Lovelace, was the poet Byron's daughter—who understood, perhaps better than Babbage himself, where all of this (what you see here) would finally lead.

If Babbage did not see quite far enough, perhaps it was because his image of computing lay in TABLES. Tables of every kind were needed in his day. He designed machines to work to the sixth order of difference, and to *print out* forty-four digits a minute—on numbers calculated to the *twentieth* place. In the process he used *punched cards*...he owned a black and white silk portrait of Jacquard himself, woven from a *fixed program* of ten thousand cards. Two forty-digit numbers could be added or subtracted in *three seconds* on the Analytical Engine...

In this process Babbage designed a computer that could be programmed, and could organize itself. It had a store. The particular puzzle it solved was to distinguish the **controller** (his 'barrel') and the **CPU—Central Processing Unit** (his 'mill'). Wonderful Babbage: he was a hundred years ahead.

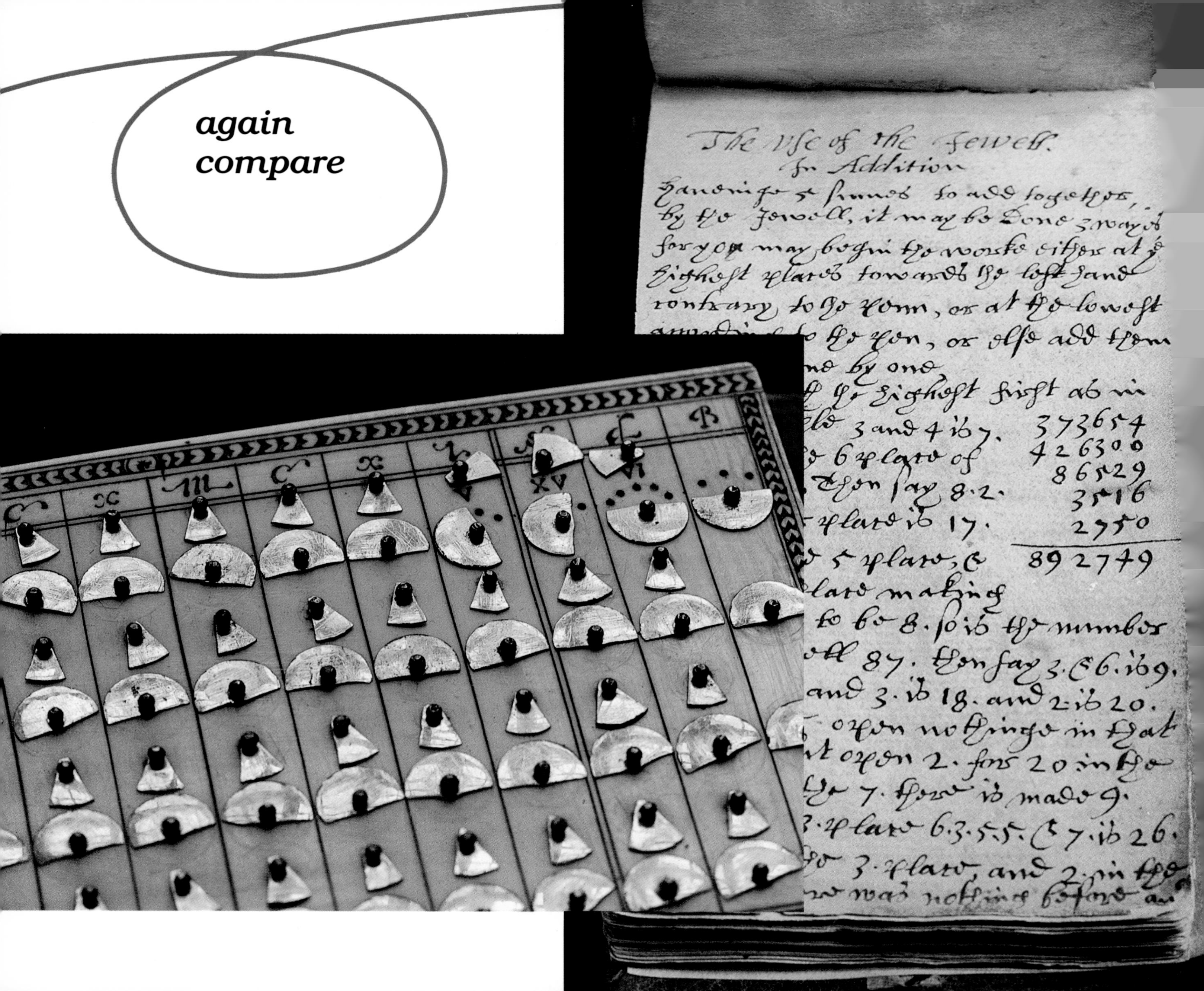
again
compare
The Use of the Jewell.
In Addition
373654
426300
86529
3516
2750
892749

some 'coincidental' dials...

We entered the nineteenth century with Jacquard and Babbage...

By 1880, Herman Hollerith had begun to study the system required to do the calculations involved in the United States census. He was twenty years old. His system of punched cards was tested against the orthodox system, and by the 1890 census he was in real business. Above we see how his counters, driven by punched cards, kept count of each category in the official statistics. 'Hollerith' was to dominate the collection and storage of data in government and (shortly) industry, until computers became practicable in business in the mid-nineteen-fifties. The sensing component of the system was electrical—an approach that Babbage had considered, but had necessarily (state-of-the-art at the time) rejected.

On the left is **The Jewel**, now in the British Science Museum, together with a page from its incorporated instruction manual—which purports to explain how it adds. No one quite knows how it actually works. But this very example was painted in a contemporary portrait of an Elizabethan gentleman.

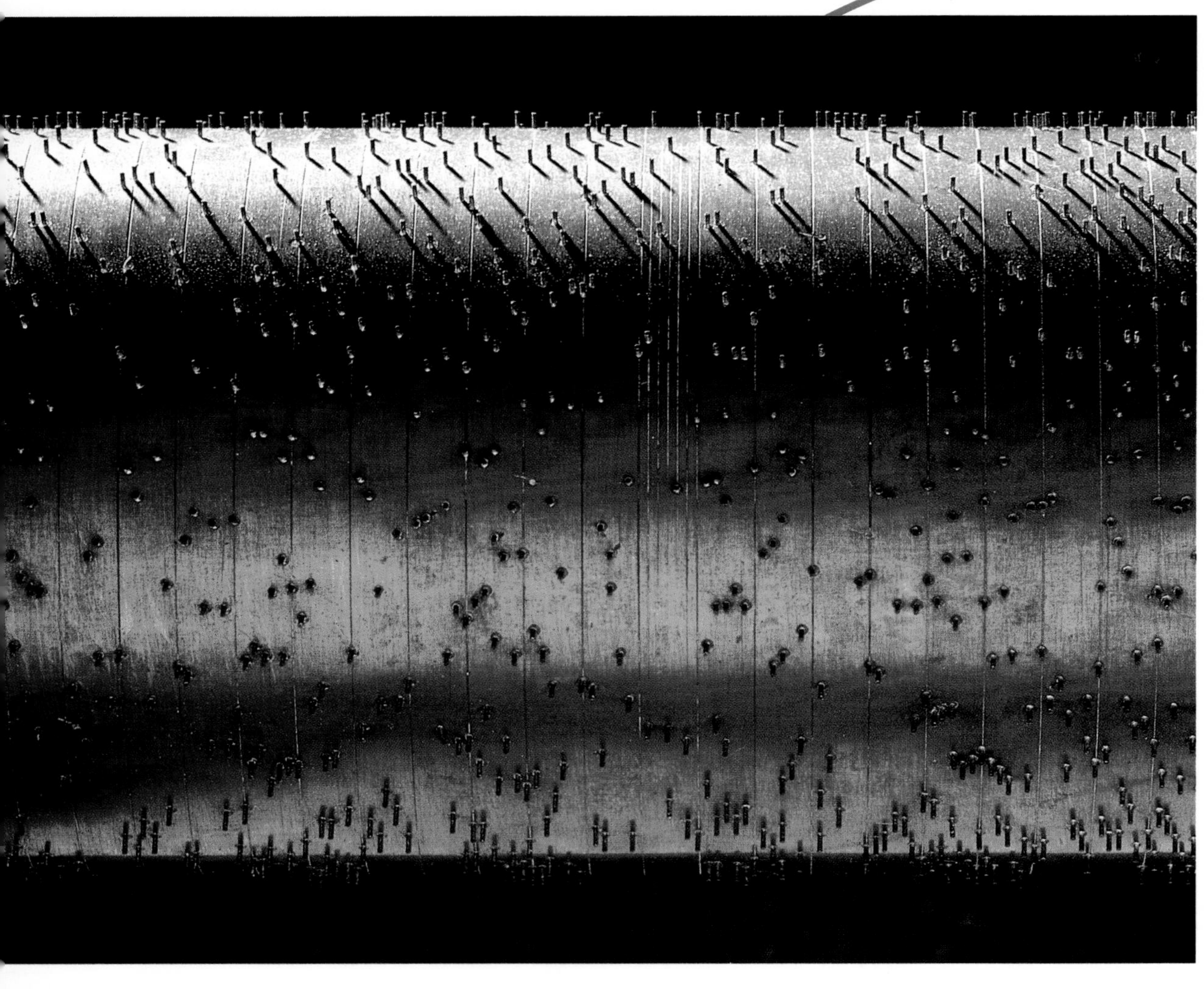

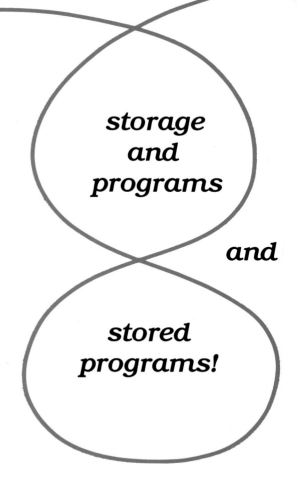

storage and programs

and

stored programs!

By the late nineteenth century, the idea of programmed machines was incorporated into the culture. This elaborate musical box, like the Jacquard loom, has a program that can be changed—by changing the cylinder: but once in place, the program is inflexible. Imagine trying to change a note on the cylinder photographed here!

Well, the birth of computers was attended by a great deal of confusion over the same question as to the flexibility of the program. The important distinction to understand in reviewing any history of those years is that between a **program** which makes a machine perform a set of operations (like the music box) and a **stored** program, whereby the computer holds all its instructions and all its data *inside*. It comes down to this: there is no 'setting-up time' (like changing the cylinder) with a stored program. And the setting-up time for the precursors of the modern computer was prodigious.

'ENIAC'...

The world's first electronic programmable calculator was built at the University of Pennsylvania. It was part of the war effort, but did not run until November 1945 (just after the atom bomb fell). It was nonetheless in time to do critical calculations for the hydrogen bomb...

However, the machine did not have a stored program—although its inventors J. Prosper Eckert and John W. Mauchly conceived of such a machine. ENIAC had to be programmed from outside—by plugging in cables, setting switches, feeding in punched cards in relays—all this on a machine weighing thirty tons, and consuming 174,000 watts of power. This much energy was needed to run seventeen and a half thousand tubes! Before the invention of the transistor, all the early machines were veritable space-heaters...

The Manchester Mark I...

was the world's first electronic *stored program* computer. Built at Manchester University, by a team under F.C. Williams, the Mark I first ran on 21 June 1948. Its principles were quite different from the American machine, and it used cathode-ray tubes (as in the television set) for internal storage.

The next stored program computer to run—a year later—was the EDSAC at Cambridge University, closely followed by the first stored program machine in America—called BINAC.

Looking back today at the monstrosities that the first computers were, by comparison with the astrological clocks and musical boxes we see here in all their elegance, it is just possible to understand why computer pioneers (like all other pioneers) were forced to fight their way...

SAGE... but was it? —and other critical ideas...

'Space heaters' was the term we used for these arrays of tubes (or thermionic valves). Not only did they generate colossal heat: they were immensely prone to accident. Failures will occur with tubes, though not too often. The trouble was that using tens of thousands of them at once meant that failures would occur almost continuously. The tubes had special tests, and they were run at less stressful levels than their theoretical limits. Even so... the picture gives quite a good idea of what was involved. This photograph of SAGE, operational in 1958, shows another in the growing generation of computers that had very special new features—not to mention fifty-five thousand tubes!

SAGE means 'Semi-Automatic Ground Environment'. Evidently, then, it was (like its American predecessors) a military device. It is fairly safe to say that the computer industry would not have taken its contemporary shape without its military funding: business was very slow indeed to see the benefits or take the risks. Twenty-six SAGE centres were however built to monitor air security across the United States; and each of them weighed two hundred and fifty tons.

Apart from these mammoth proportions though, two very special features here emerged. First was Forrester's invention, explained earlier, of the **ferrite core memory**. Necessity as the mother of invention is well brought out—for Jay W. Forrester himself was the engineer in charge of Project SAGE!

The second issue was this. For reasons of state security, the SAGE computers had to work for twenty-four hours a day, and they **must not** be in error. Look at all these racks of all these tubes... how could this be even possible in an imperfect world?

The answer lay in **duplexed** engineering. Each SAGE computer contained two central processors and memories, but shared peripheral devices—and bulk storage.

The principle of *redundancy* that this design reflects was already well known to cybernetic science, which deals with the laws of control. John von Neumann (among others) had published papers on the **logic** of reliability—and he was on centre stage in the development of American computers at this time, as a mathematician of world renown.

But there are more powerful ways to protect machines from failure than simply to duplex the main components. The logics of redundancy have been in use for thirty years—but not exploited fully to this day.

so on to further generations ...two are here...

Below we see the first **transistorized** computer built in Canada. No longer weighing hundreds of tons, and yet commissioned only two years after SAGE—in 1960—this machine was known as 'Dirty Gertie', a somewhat less grandiose name than SAGE! It was used in the development and control of Canada's first satellite, *Alouette I*. The cards in the 'filing drawers', four hundred of them, each contained **fifty thousand** circuit elements.

And what do you suppose is the familiar-looking little package sitting in Gertie's lap? A pocket calculator, obviously enough, yet not quite so familiar as you may suppose—because it is *programmable*. But yes, they are around. And each of those can equal Gertie's power—in information handling, that is. On the right is an Integrated Circuit carrier frame, looking again like ancient jewelry—and—gold-plated, no less.

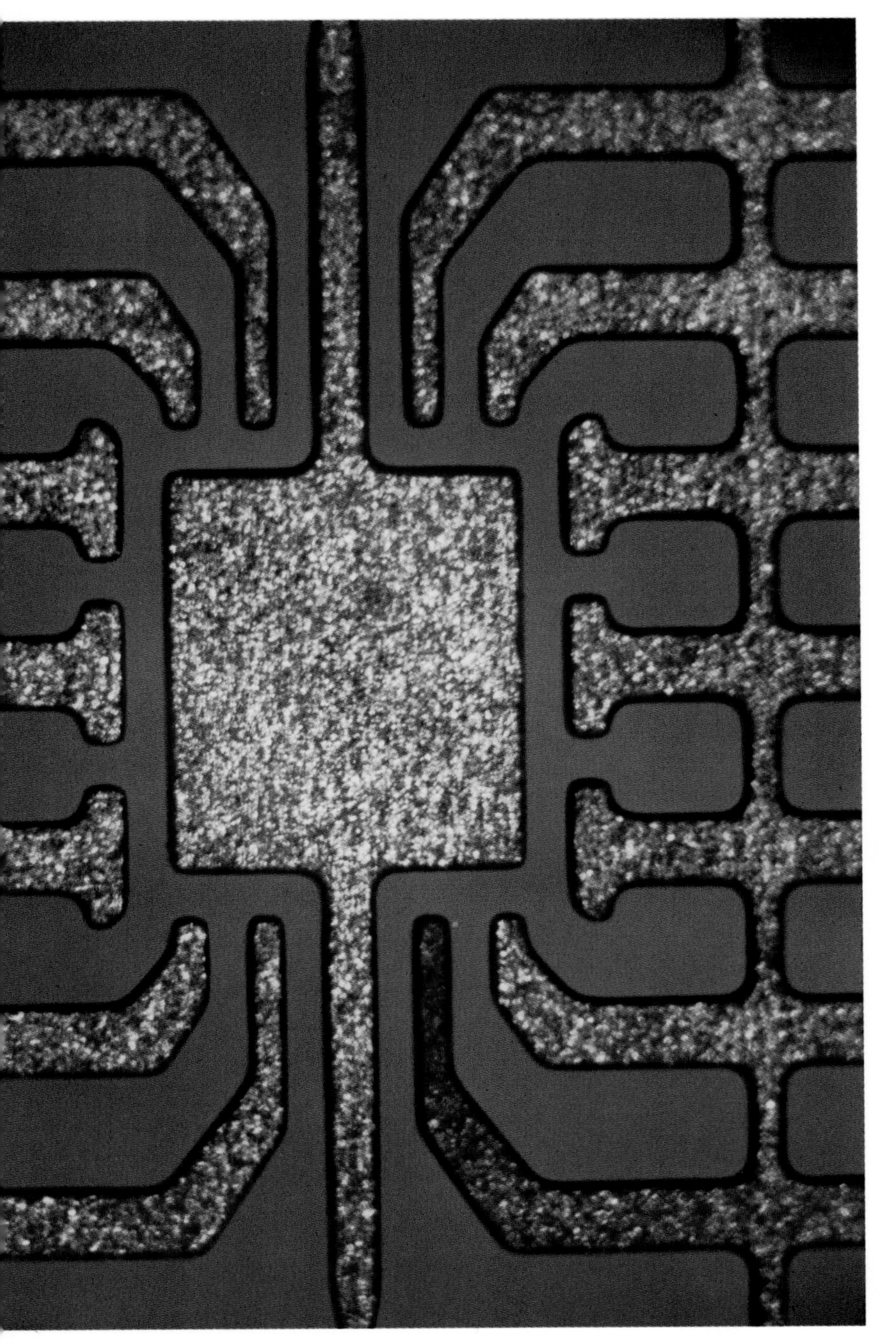

remembering Alan Turing...

This book did not set out to be a history of computers, but it *has* tried to isolate some critical issues, and to mention many of the outstanding names. Alan Turing, difficult, tormented man, who took his life when only forty-two, deeply merits the Thread's red ring above.

Hilbert, a great German mathematician born in 1863, posed the *Entscheidungsproblem* in 1928. This had to do with the question whether logic is complete—whether *any* logical problem could in principle be solved. Gödel had shown, with his 'Incompleteness Theorem', that the answer was 'no'. But it fell to Turing to demonstrate to the London Mathematical Society in 1937 the formal answer to Hilbert's *problem*.

Turing's paper, *On Computable Numbers*, when published, contained a totally astonishing footnote. It gave a precise and simple mathematical definition of a **universal machine**. The 'Turing machine' defined the modern computer: in 1937.

Many serious workers—Zuse in Germany, and the ENIAC builders—had not read this paper. Von Neumann, on the other hand, knew Turing personally... At all events his work was seminal, and is cogent to this day.

The Thread emerges from burrowing through the story of machines to make a few last linkages...

In short, we are back with a few visual 'coincidences' again. The left side of this montage is a *quipu*, a means of calculating—and perhaps computing—that comes from Peru. The Chimú people seem to have developed this device before they were overtaken by the Incas, who had similar methods of recording of their own. Improvements were made...

The cords hanging from the ring of cord represent units, tens, and so on, and the knots mark off the decimal digits once again. Different colours of cord would indicate tribute, lands, ceremonies, marriages and so forth in the imperial accounting.

All this was happening between the twelfth and fifteenth centuries. Village teachers were appointed to instruct in *quipu* recording, so that what we should call a data-base could be maintained, and village headmen kept informed. The 'Chief Accountant' was accordingly called the *Quipucamoyoc*.

There is, however, no knowing how elaborate this information system by **knots** may have become. There are after all many *kinds* of knot. The *quipu* might have had a mystical significance too.

No reader will have been surprised by now to recognize a chip in the centre of the page! What is happening here is a testing procedure, and the radial arms are no longer knotted strings but probes.

All the integrated circuits and their carrier frames featured in this book belong to the telecommunications industry, and are manufactured by Mitel of Canada. And, you may think, this is a 'fun' montage. Certainly it was tempting to make these two halves merely thirds of the montage—so as to include *another* third. It would have been a segment of an internal surgical operation, and surely the visual image would have matched...

But to the extent that this book concerns itself with 'coincidence', remember the suggestion at the start? It said:

Coincidence may be the inability to see what really matters.

The surgical radii would perhaps be suction tubes and clamps. What the montage in two halves actually shows is the **flow of information outwards from a centre**.

today, in Teotihuacan, are

desolated courts...

The dominant god was Tlaloc, god of rain; but very present too was mighty

QUETZALCOATL—

the feathered serpent. He was dominant in turn in Toltec times (say AD 1000): master of the pantheon entire.

The powerful images of those two gods are everywhere in Teotihuacan, together with —entangled with, indeed—the fierce face of the jaguar,

whose cult was founded
in animal power—
just as was Tlaloc's
in fertility.

Incidentally... the Street of the Dead and its adjacent temples are oriented at a seventeen degree angle to the meridian. Thus, when the avenue was laid out in AD 200, the whole symbolic axis of the place pointed to the setting sun twice a year... yes—at the equinoxes.

Recall the Aztec calendar? That was in the fifteenth century—and the Aztec civilization had appeared only a hundred or so years before. But the Aztecs themselves believed that *their* world was created in the ancient City of Teotihuacan. Still visible today, some thirty miles east of modern Mexico City, it was founded round about the time of Christ. It grew to cover eight square miles of ground. Some quarter of a million people, of many and specific social ranks, lived in the city centre—where there were great markets, imperial monuments, and overwhelming displays of religious fervour in ceremonies and artefacts alike...

The famous Pyramids of the Sun and the Moon still dominate the Street of the Dead. The ruins of courts and shrines and temples shown above are photographed from the Pyramid of the Sun.

Quetzalcoatl, Lord of the Universe, left Mexico in dubious circumstances. Many legends talk about his going—and part of the dubiety concerns the date. Some stories say he left at the foundation of Teotihuacan; others say he left at its demise. At any rate, he left; but Quetzalcoatl was expected by the Aztecs to return.

Now according to the Franciscan scholar Fray Bernardino de Sahagun, who came to Mexico in 1529 and wrote the critical history of the Spanish Conquest, when Cortes arrived King Moctezuma thought that he was 'Quetzalcoatl who had come to land. For it was in their hearts that he would come, that he would come to land, just to find his mat, his seat.' Moctezuma continued to receive Cortes in this guise until close up to the end. The collapse came quickly, and Moctezuma died. The Spanish Conquest, appalled as it had been by the brutality—and especially large-scale human sacrifice—of the Aztecs, then set about butchery itself. In the name of the Christian God, and Christian saints, it wiped out a pagan civilization—beyond all but fanciful recall. It took the gold.

Alternatively to the Quetzalcoatl legend, and to that theory of King Moctezuma's fall, computer simulations commissioned in recent times (by a Mexican bank) say that the Aztec civilization had reached a point where an overloaded economy, intent on building monuments to its own virility, collapsed—under its own weight. And that report might well reflect the state of Mexico and many others among our societies today...

Was Quetzalcoatl Cortes himself, or the burdensome force of power and wealth—then as now?

converted to these

verdant-seeming courts...

the simulating Integrated Circuits...

... so

Science advances...

In the University of Tübingen, in Germany, hangs a portrait of Wilhelm Schickard (whom we have met before, with the first computer). The time... it is about the time of William Shakespeare. In his right hand Schickard holds a model planetarium. Here is a replica.

Of course it shows how the sun, the Earth, and the moon spin in relation to each other—and how the light must fall. The ratios of sizes, distances, are not correct; but that could not have been the point. Schickard was not that stupid!

It took some four hundred years for humankind to get out there in space, to see the Earth, to land upon the moon...

Across the page, looking out into the solar system, seeing the Earth much as Schickard visualized it all that time ago, is (among others)...

Marc Garneau—the first Canadian in space. He is on board Space Shuttle *Challenger*, launched on 5 October 1984.

There she goes...

Replica by Professor Dr Ludolf von Mackensen of Kassel, Germany.
Theodor Haering House, Tübingen, Germany

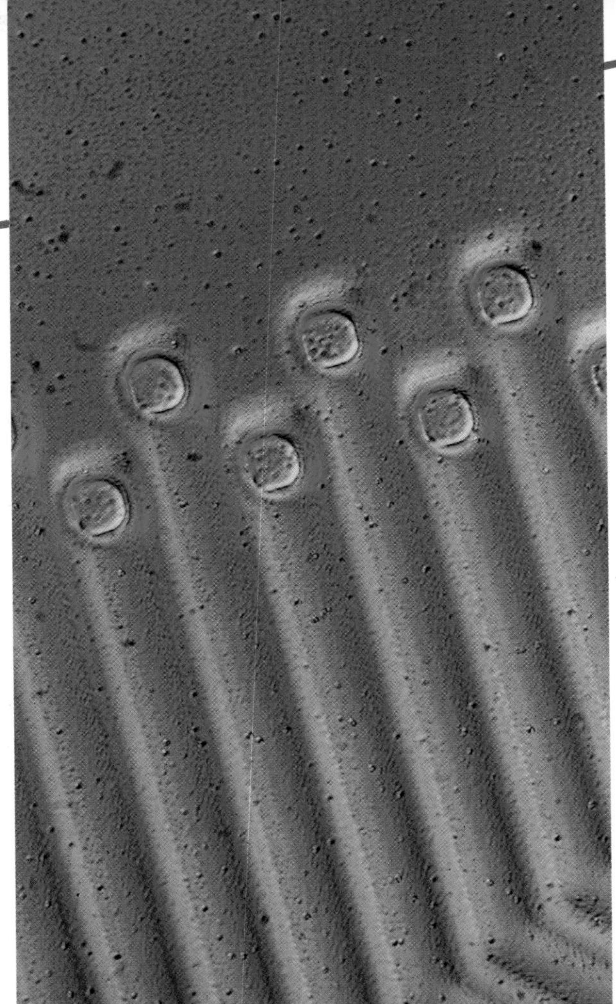

Behind the *Challenger*, TWO THINGS:

- Energy, the enormous power of rockets measured as energy-still-available, or **entropy**, and its negative—
- Information, *negative* entropy, exemplified by this hugely magnified Integrated Circuit —looking (coincidentally) just like a rocket barrage too . . .

will there be an end?...

'Make the smallest distinction... and heaven and earth are set infinitely apart.' The words are those of Sengstan, third Zen patriarch, writing in Chinese in the seventh century—but this was the very premise of this book, when we took a pebble as the mark of distinction. In its more abstract form, the pebble is the 'bit' with which we compute, the nought-or-one distinction marked in computers with magnetic signs.

The cosmos, viewed under the physics of Relativity, cannot support movement faster than light—and we saw that (since light travels no more than a foot in a nanosecond) this has a truly practical bearing on the design of computers. There is a second major aspect of modern physics that bears on the business of nought-or-one distinction, and that is Quantum Theory. According to this, there is a physical limit on the rate at which this switchover, 0 to 1, which is the 'creation' of a bit, can happen. This limit is not directly threatening to computing practice, because Planck's constant, which determines it, is so very small. It is interesting, however, that such a limit actually exists—that at a measurable level of 'fineness' in the physical components of the universe, the distinction (*any* distinction, therefore) must be lost.

This has been understood by thinkers for a very long time, and long before the models of the cosmos in vogue through twentieth century physics came to the forefront of our minds. The basic thought is this: having drawn a distinction, which our perceptual apparatus linked with the logic of our brains dictates that we continuously do, then it is wise to put the two parts back together—to form the larger unity again. We find this notion, that distinctions are illusory and misleading, in the Vedantic philosophy of India—which goes back five thousand years. It moved across to China and Japan with the spread of Buddhism, as the quotation opposite shows. *Except the two be one...* we find it in the aprocryphal gospels of Jesus, in the Christian gnosticism of the Dead Sea Scrolls, in the papyri found in Upper Egypt. We find it echoed in the recent works of C.G. Jung, for whom the unity of emptiness and the unity of fullness were expressions of the selfsame unity.

The computers will not stop. And although there are limits that must be understood, science will not stop either. Remember how young is modern science. Most of the scientists who have ever lived—almost all in fact—are living now. We could well guess that science has only just begun: its growth financed, almost entirely, by military needs or fantasies.

Then bear in mind the other wisdom too. The pebble in this photograph is not a mark of distinction, but the subject of a yogic meditation. Yoga, in Sanskrit, means union so, *finally*...

the Knower and the Known are one.

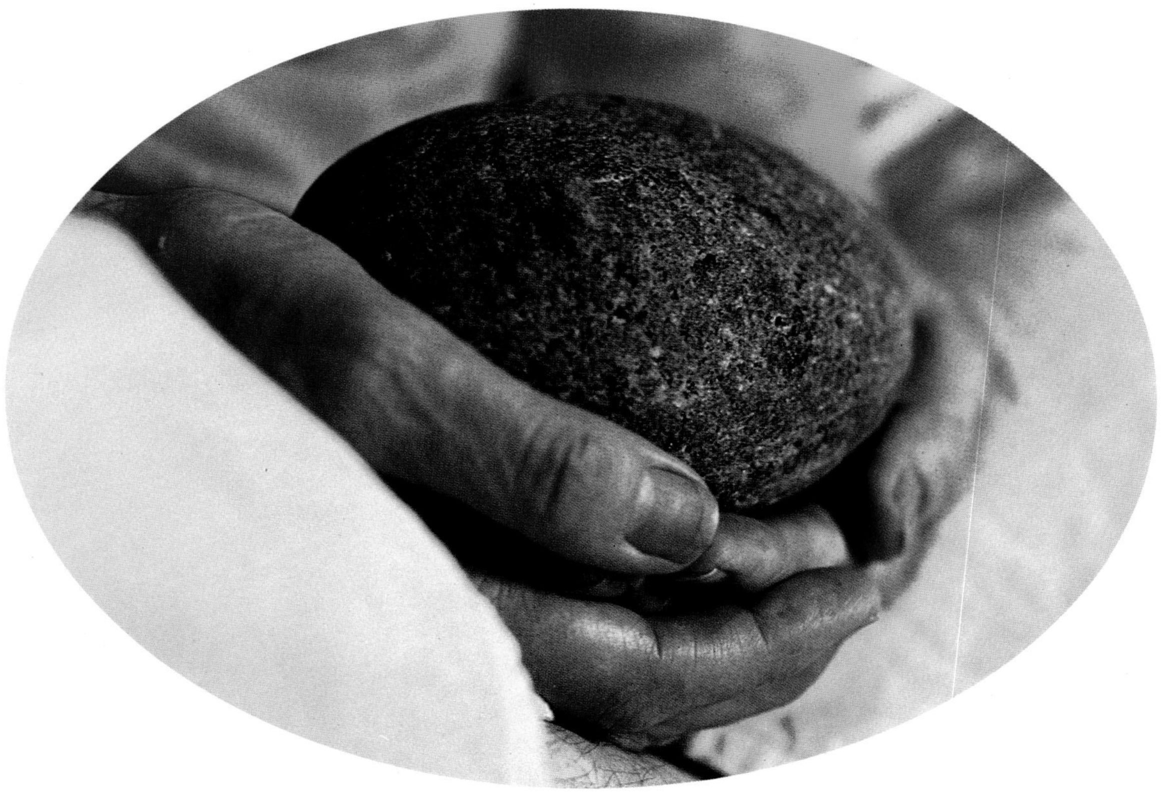

Things are objects because of the mind;
The mind is such because of things.
Understand the relativity of these two
and the basic reality: the unity of emptiness.

In this emptiness the two are indistinguishable
and each contains in itself the whole world.

from *hsin hsin ming*
by Sengstan
third Zen patriarch – died 606.

EPILOGUE

Hans-L. Blohm

It is with a profound sense of satisfaction and relief that I see *Pebbles to Computers* take its final form, both emotions being in response to the long and often difficult process of its making. It was six years ago that I began to discover the beauty of microchips as I photographed them through a microscope. I felt as though I stood upon a mountain top, marvelling at the beauty all around, humbled and elated at the same time.

Shortly thereafter I produced my first photo-micro-mural for the lobby of Mitel Corporation. It was backlit and enlarged sixteen million times in area, to 10 feet by 14. Eight more murals followed, for locations as far apart as Puerto Rico and Ireland, Washington, D.C. and Wales. Three travelling exhibitions came into being for External Affairs, Canada, and are concurrently on show in Japan, Central and South America and Australia.

I envisioned a catalogue to accompany these exhibitions—an idea that expanded in discussions with my good friend Rudi Haas. I knew of his research into ancient devices for information storage. The disk of Phaistos from the Island of Crete, the ground design on the Plains of Nasca in Peru, and other such 'instruments' of the ancient world... A new vision began to unfold, suggesting the relationship between the prehistoric and antique technologies and the so-called 'high-technologies' of today.

It was then that *Pebbles to Computers* was conceived. There was no holding back; nothing would prevent the realization of the idea. The search for background material, the taking of countless photographs, these became a hunt that led me over continents. I travelled through many countries, exploring sites and visiting museums. The more I ventured forth, the broader the spectrum became, the wider the horizon. Unexpected finds and connexions emerged. Special permits were needed to photograph national treasures. Unusual situations, logistic challenges, technical difficulties, all these were encountered and had to be overcome, with the help of many thoughtful and enthusiastic people. It was a journey into time, an encounter with mystery.

Stonehenge alone was worth a book. There, at the summer solstice of 1983, I was present when thousands of people from many countries and of all ages occupied the circle of megaliths. I too was gripped by a sense of awe as the sun rose and a vast collective sigh went up from the multitude. An absolute silence followed. A magical moment indeed!

Standing atop the Pyramid of the Sun in Mexico, driving through the Andes, looking and marvelling at Leonardo's inventions in Milan, touching Leibniz' calculator in Hanover, looking at the faces of people studying the disk of Phaistos in the Museum of Heraklion, pondering the meaning of the Rosetta Stone—all these were great experiences for me.

Putting it all together and shaping the project in collaboration with writers, designers and publishers—this was an experience in itself.

The final version of *Pebbles to Computers*, with the powerful yet gentle text, and the beautiful design, of my friend Stafford Beer, will convey to the reader 'the thread' that connects all the efforts of mankind to record time and memory, to *'create order out of chaos'*, as the Nobel laureate François Jacob put it.

With the exception of a small, partial grant from the Public Awareness Program of the Federal Department of Science and Technology, all financing came from my own resources; but I acknowledge with gratitude the superb cooperation of many individuals, corporations, institutions, and embassies that helped me in my quest with encouragement, with ideas, with advice and with logistics.

In particular I am grateful to the Mitel Corporation, to the British High Commission in Canada and Mr Charles Chadwick of the British Council, to the Embassy of the People's Republic of China, the Embassy of France, the Embassy of the Federal Republic of Germany, the Embassy of Greece and His Excellency Mr E.M. Megalokonomos, the Embassy of Italy, the Embassy of Mexico, the Embassy of Peru, External Affairs Canada, Mr James O'Hara, the Canadian Embassies in Athens, Bonn, Paris, Rome, and the Canadian High Commission in London. In the United Kingdom I must especially thank the Science Museum, London and Dame Margaret Weston, the British Museum and Mr Andrew Hamilton, Kings Library, London and the UK Department of the Environment; in France the Musée de l'Homme and Al. Leroi-Gourham; in Italy the Museo Leonardo da Vinci, Milan; in Germany the Landes Biblioteck, Hanover and Dr Albert Heinekamp, the Staatliche Kunstsammlungen, Kassel and Dr Ludolf von Mackensen, the Gutenberg Museum, Mainz, the Deutsches Museum, Munich, the Theodor Haering Haus, Tubingen; in Greece the National Museum, Athens and the Museum at Heraklion, Crete; in Mexico the Science Museum and the Museum of Anthropology; in the USA the National Radio Astronomy Observatory, Sorocco, New Mexico, Dr R.A. Perley, Dr A.G. Willis, Dr J.S. Scott, and the Computer

Museum, Boston; in Canada the Museum of Science and Technology, Dr J. William McGowan and Ted Paull, the Department of Science and Technology, Public Awareness Program, the National Research Council, Dr Norman Broten, Dr Wally Cherwinski; the Canada-France-Hawaii Telescope Corporation, Hawaii and Dr Laird Thompson.

Thank you, Ingeborg, my wife. *I always knew the book would be!*

H-L.B.

Selected References

A. Thom and A.S. Thom: *Megalithic Remains in Britain and Brittany*, Clarendon Press, Oxford, 1978
Stafford Beer: *Transit*, Mitchell Communications, Charlottetown, 1983
Stan Augarten: *Bit by Bit*, Ticknor and Fields, New York, 1984
J.V. Field and M.T. Wright: *Early Gearing*, Science Museum, London, 1985

List of Plates

44–45 Stonehenge.
46 Butchart Gardens Victoria, British Columbia.
49 Chinese abacus, National Museum of Science and Technology, Ottawa.
51 Flowing water on top of falls in the Gatineau River, Quebec.
53 Breaking waves on Long Beach, Vancouver Island, British Columbia.
54 Gold scale, Pete Erickson's cabin, Hunter Creek, Yukon.
55 Antique thermometer.
56 Parabolic parabaloid, National Museum of Science and Technology, Ottawa.
57 Slide-rule.
58 Cro-Magnon cave painting, Lascaux, France.
59 Canadian-Indian drawing at Agawa Bay, Ontario.
60 Mayan codex and stone, Museum of Anthropology, Mexico City.
61 Clay tablet, British Museum.
62 Disk of Phaistos, Museum of Heraklion.
63 Plasma etching-tunnel, Mitel Corporation.
64 Egyptian hieroglyphs, British Museum.
65 Viking Runic Stone, near Schleswig, Germany.
66 Earliest dated printed book, from China; Kings Library, British Museum.
67 Cast-lead letters from the Gutenberg Press, Gutenberg Museum, Mainz.
68 Gears of an early printing press, National Museum of Science and Technology, Ottawa.
69 Antikythera Device, National Museum of Greece.
70 Replica of a Byzantine sundial-calendar, by Michael Wright, Science Museum, London.
71 Arabian Astrolabe from Spain, Staatliche Kunstsammlungen, Kassel.
72 Astronomical clock, Strasbourg.
73 Silicon chip, Mitel Corporation, Ontario.
75 Wilhelm Schikard's computer; replica by Professor von Freytag, Theodor Haering House, Tubingen.
76–77 Pascaline, National Museum of Science and Technology, Ottawa.
78 Chinese compass, British Museum.
79 Pocket calculator by Samuel Morland, Science Museum, London.
80–81 Leibniz calculator, Landes Bibliothek, Hanover.
82 Desk calculator by Sauter of Germany, Science Museum, London.
83 Ferrite-core memory of early Canadian computer, National Museum of Science and Technology, Ottawa.
84–85 Jaquard loom, Science Centre, Toronto.
86 Arithmometer by Thomas de Colmar, National Museum of Science and Technology, Ottawa.
87 Silicon chip; detail.
88–89 Babbage differential engine, Science Museum, London.
90 'The Jewel', an Elizabethan pocket calculator, Science Museum, London.
91 Multiple dial on the Hollerith tabulating machine, the Computer Museum, Boston.
92–93 Canadian musical box, National Museum of Science and Technology, Ottawa.
94 Vacuum tubes, Sage Computer, the Computer Museum, Boston.
96 'Dirty Gertie', Canadian Computer c. 1960, National Museum

of Science & Technology, Ottawa.
97 Silicon chip carrier-frame.
98 Left half of composite: replica by Ted Paull of a Peruvian 'Quipu' counting and calculating device, National Museum of Science and Technology, Ottawa.
Right half of composite: testing device for silicon wafers, Mitel Corporation, Quebec.
100 Ruins of courts at Teotihuacan, near Mexico City.
101 Silicon chip as part of a total wafer; photomicrograph in interference contrast, Mitel Corporation, Ontario.
102 Schikard's hand planetarium; replica by Professor Dr Ludolf von Mackensen of Kassel, Theodor Haering House, Tubingen.
103 *Left:* Space shuttle 'Challenger', 5 October 1984, courtesy NASA.
Right: High-magnification interference-contrast photomicrograph of silicon chip, Mitel Corporation, Ontario.
105 Pebble in human hand.

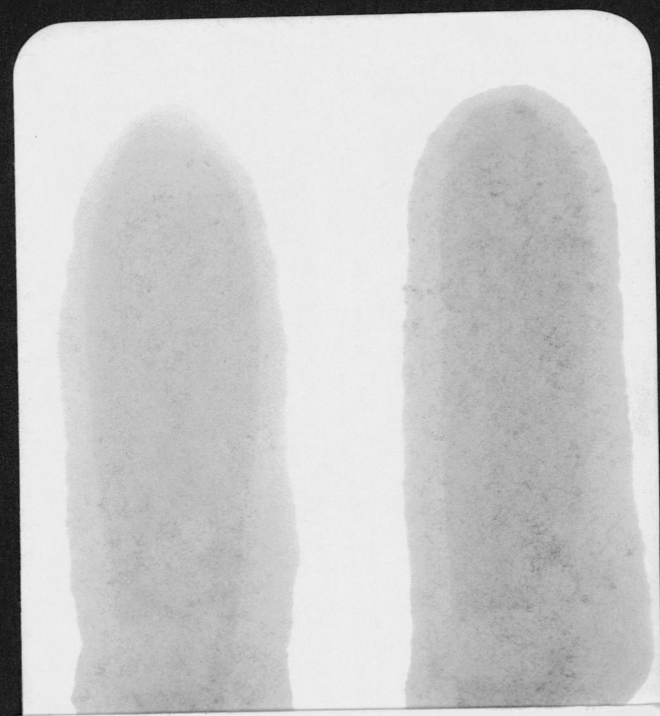

The *Mystery* of *MIGRATION*

The *Mystery* of *MIGRATION*

Chief Contributing Editor **Dr Robin Baker**

A Studio Book
The Viking Press · New York

Contributors

First published in 1981 by
The Viking Press
625 Madison Avenue
New York, N.Y., 10022

ISBN 0 354 04197 5

Edited, designed and produced by
Harrow House Editions Limited,
7a Langley Street, Covent Garden, London WC2H 9JA

Editors	Lionel Bender James Somerville
Art Editor	John Pallot
Picture Editor	Celia Dearing
Art Director	Nicholas Eddison
Production Manager	Kenneth Cowan
Production Editor	Fred Gill
Managing Editor (Natural History)	Lionel Bender
Consultant Editor for Macdonald Futura	Felix Brenner

Filmset in Plantin 110 by
Tameside Filmsetting Ltd, Ashton-under-Lyne, England
Illustrations originated by
Reprocolor Llovet S.A, Barcelona, Spain
Printed and bound by Brepols S.A., Turnhout, Belgium

Library of Congress Cataloging in Publication Data
Main entry under title:
The Mystery of migration.
(A Studio book)
Includes index.
1. Animal migration. 2. Plants—Migration.
3. Man—Migrations. I. Baker, Robin, 1944-
QL754.M9 591.52′5 80-16839
ISBN 0-670-50286-3

Chief Contributing Editor
Dr Robin Baker
Lecturer in Zoology,
University of Manchester, England

Heather Angel MSc
Biologist and Natural History
Photographer, England

Dr Martin Angel
Research Oceanographer,
England

Dr Jeremy Cherfas
Biological Sciences Editor,
New Scientist, England

Janice G Mather BSc
Researcher in Migration,
University of Manchester, England

Dr Pat Morris
Lecturer in Zoology,
Royal Holloway College, England

Contents

Introduction

Every year, as the summer wanes, willow warblers weighing only a few grams undertake a journey of 8000 kilometres (5000 miles) to escape winter's rigours. In human terms this is equivalent to travelling ten times the distance from the earth to the moon or 38,625,000 kilometres (24,140,000 miles).

It is an extraordinary fact that all eels dwelling in the rivers of Europe and North America are adults. Yet as larvae, they were all spawned in one particular area of the tropical Atlantic and took several years of travelling to complete their development in fresh water.

These are but two examples of the migratory feats that have captured man's imagination over the centuries. Migration has always had an aura of mystery about it: how could it *not* seem supernatural when journeys of such an extent and of such precision are repeatedly accomplished despite many hazardous obstacles.

Why do many animals undertake such journeys? How do they find their destination with such accuracy when they may have been there only once before? In fact why, in the first place, do they move at all? What is it that motivates animal movement?

The study of this phenomenon, which occurs in every living being, be it plant, invertebrate, fish, reptile, bird, or indeed man, reveals a comprehensive picture of migration. In each case the whole range of movement seen within the group, the obscure as well as the spectacular, is examined and an overall, if not complete, explanation emerges.

For most people the word migration conjures up the sight of flocks of birds returning or leaving our own familiar area. These flights are the most conspicuous migratory events and were the first to be described by natural historians. In fact the study of migration could well be said to have begun with Aristotle's speculation about what happened to swallows in winter.

We have certainly come a long way since Aristotle, but we are still far from knowing all the answers. Careful scientific investigation has solved some of the more puzzling mysteries, but like the Hydra of Greek mythology, questions about migration generate new ones each time one is resolved. It is impossible to predict what future developments may reveal. For example, recent discoveries concerning the relevance of the earth's magnetic field to animal behaviour could completely alter present notions of how animals navigate and might cause a radical change in our understanding of migration.

From time immemorial people have noted, and wondered about, the comings and goings of animals. Perhaps because the members of "the feathered tribe" conspicuously move furthest and seemingly with least effort, they have attracted most attention and speculation.

The author of the Book of Job, written at least two thousand years ago, knew something of migration. God, showing his power to Job, asks "doth the hawk fly by thy wisdom and stretch her wings towards the south?" (Job 39:26). Birds of prey do regularly fly south in autumn, especially in the Middle Eastern lands. Jeremiah too, alludes to migratory birds, though he seems concerned with arrivals in spring. Complaining of the impious conduct of his people, the prophet says: "Yea, the stork in the heaven knoweth her appointed times; and the turtle [turtledove] and the crane and the swallow observe the time of their coming; but my people know not the judgement of the Lord" (Jeremiah 8:7).

Other writers also refer to the movements of birds, usually in a way that makes it clear that they expected their readers to be fully aware of the facts. Around the 8th century BC Homer, in the *Iliad*, describes the Trojan army as being "like the cranes which flee from the coming winter and sudden rain". Four hundred years later another Greek poet, Anacreon, celebrated the return of the swallows in poetry. Anacreon also suggested that the swallows spend the winter along the banks of the Nile, a shrewd guess but a bit doubtful.

Classical ideas

Many other examples tell us that even at the dawn of history people were aware of migrations. They knew that some birds disappeared at certain times of the year and returned again at other times. But literary allusions do not tell us whether people understood what was happening. The first evidence we have of anyone trying to explain migration is in the works of Aristotle, the natural philosopher. Aristotle lived from 384 BC to 322 BC, and as well as his philosophical works he wrote a remarkable work of natural history, the *Historia Animalium*.

Book Eight of the *Historia* contains Aristotle's thoughts on migration. He wrote that some creatures stay put for the winter, while others move south after the autumn equinox to avoid the cold. These species move north again after the spring equinox, this time to avoid the coming heat. Aristotle also realized that some creatures migrate locally, while others, such as the cranes "may be said to come from the ends of the world". He knew that in the autumn the cranes flew in from Scythia (north of the Black Sea) and moved on to "the marshlands south of Egypt, where the Nile has its source".

Pelicans, Aristotle said, migrated from the Strymon (the Struma) to the Ister (the Danube), where they bred. "The birds in front wait for those in the rear, owing to the fact that when the flock is passing over the intervening mountain range, the birds in the rear lose sight of their companions in the van." This might explain how the flock sticks together, but it doesn't tell us how the birds in the van know where they are going, or find their way.

Aristotle also made a very astute observation. "All creatures are fatter in migrating," he writes. This is indeed the case, as has been confirmed in several scientific studies. Hormonal changes induce the bird to lay down fat, and to ensure that the bird has sufficient energy for the journey. Migration begins only if the fat content exceeds a critical level.

Not all Aristotle's observations are as sound as this. He was the first authority to suggest that birds might hibernate through the winter. Some birds, he said, "decline the trouble of migration, and simply hide themselves where they are. Swallows, for instance, have often been found in holes, quite denuded of their feathers, and the kite on its first emergence from torpidity has been seen to fly from out some such hiding-place." Not just swallows and kites either; storks, ousels, turtledoves and larks are also said to hibernate on occasion, as are wood-pigeons, ring-doves, starlings and owls.

In fact, no bird that Aristotle would have ever heard of hibernates (though at least one American species does). Birds found "asleep" in holes were almost certainly dead, perhaps after seeking shelter during a storm. This explains why they could not be revived from their torpor. Despite the lack of evidence in support, Aristotle's theory of hibernation survived for over two thousand years and was still prominent in the enlightened eighteenth century.

Another mistaken theory that Aristotle was responsible for is "transmutation". Some species, he believed, changed into others with the seasons. The redstart, for example, changed into the Eurasian robin as winter approached. The two species look very similar, except for the colouring of their feathers. The same applies to the bird that Aristotle called the beccafico (probably the garden warbler) and the blackcap; these birds differ chiefly in song and coloration, and Aristotle believed that the former changed into the latter as autumn progressed. Interestingly, the blackcap is known as beccafico in Cyprus today. His belief was supported by observations he made during autumn that, he said, were of birds in which the change was not yet complete.

Almost four hundred years later we find the Roman naturalist Pliny (AD 20–AD 79) repeating much of Aristotle's work. He supported the theory of transmutation, and that of hibernation. Indeed, Pliny tells us that hibernation and wakening are precisely determined by the stars. The wheatear goes into hibernation on the first day that Sirius is visible above the horizon, and it emerges from its hiding-place on the day that Sirius sets.

Insight and ignorance

After Pliny there is, with one notable exception, not much development of ideas about migration until the middle of the sixteenth century. Frederick II of Germany, who lived from 1194 to 1250 and was Holy Roman Emperor from 1220, provides the exception.

Frederick was a fowler and falconer. His first-hand knowledge of birds and their habits led him to views that we now recognize as a good deal more enlightened than those of some scientists who flourished six hundred years later. Frederick knew that in autumn birds migrate from colder to warmer regions. He knew that not all do so by moving great distances; some come down from the mountains into the valleys as winter approaches and climb again in the spring. He was aware of the vast congregations that gather before migrations, and that, in some cases, the exodus might be delayed if food is plentiful and the weather good. He described the V-shaped formation of the high-flying geese and cranes. He also realized that the bird at the forward point of the skein had to work hardest and was relieved from time to time by another leader. All this, and more, Emperor Frederick II put in his book *De Arte Venandi cum Avibus* (*On the art of hunting with birds*), one of the first books on falconry. An edition was printed in 1596, but unfortunately the latter part of the manuscript was missing and it is not known if his insights went even further.

Frederick's manual of falconry contained much natural wisdom, and his enlightened thought on migration is exceptional for the period. In 1555 the Archbishop of Uppsala, one Olaus Magnus, swore that swallows spent the winter under water!

The birds roll themselves up into a ball and drop into the water. Magnus knew this because fishermen told him so, and added that they often caught these underwater swallows as lumps in their nets. He wrote: "If that lump be drawn out by ignorant young men (for old and expert fishermen put it back) and carried to a warm place, the swallows, loosened by the access of heat, begin to fly about, but live only a short time, giving proof that premature birth is to be guarded against."

Olaus Magnus even gives a picture. Two fishermen are standing at the edge of the ice and hauling in a net; the net contains a mixed bag of fish and birds.

An improbable story but with some foundation in fact. With the sudden onset of cold weather, swallows do huddle together in a heap, or in what could loosely be called a ball, to conserve heat. Also, when swallows drink, they skim over the water surface, often making a splash that could possibly be interpreted as a dive.

Many great minds accepted the notion unquestioningly. Linnaeus, the Swedish naturalist who did so much to create a framework within which to place the natural world, believed the story. John Reinhold Forster, in 1735, claimed to have seen swallows taken from a river in winter. Baron Cuvier, the distinguished French scientist, said of the theory: "That it [the martin] passes the cold season under water at the bottom of marshes appears to be certain." Geoffroy de St Hilaire – a pioneer naturalist who made very careful studies of animal behaviour – believed in hibernation. In 1772 he claimed to have seen sleeping swallows; these were almost certainly bats, which do hibernate.

The Honourable Daines Barrington, a prominent naturalist of the eighteenth century, was a fervent believer in the immersion theory, and in Aristotle's ideas of hibernation. He published his beliefs in the *Philosophical Transactions of the Royal Society*, and somehow persuaded almost every naturalist of the time that he was correct. Even Gilbert White came under Barrington's influence. At first the author of *A Natural History of Selborne* thought that swallows flew south in winter, as he said in a letter to Thomas Pennant on 4 August, 1767. But eventually, while still holding on to his ideas of migration, White acknowledged that hibernation did occur, a fact that embarrasses ornithologists even today.

The notion that swallows hibernated under water survived long after this fanciful illustration was published in Olaus Magnus's book, *Historia de Gentibus Septentrionalibus*, in 1555.

A frieze of migrating fowl from *De Arte Venandi cum Avibus.*

Frederick's hunting manual was published in 1596.

De Arte Venandi cum Avibus became a standard work on the art of falconry and the manuscript has been republished in many editions right up to the present. The illustration shows Frederick II receiving gifts of falcons.

Despite the influence of Barrington, and the general acceptance of his ideas, there were a few people who questioned the ludicrous theories he propounded. One sceptic was John Hunter, the anatomist, who lived from 1728 to 1793. He approached the problem scientifically, and did experiments to determine whether or not a swallow could survive underwater. They could not. He even went so far as to capture a number of swallows and put them in a greenhouse containing large tubs full of water and weeds. None of the birds even attempted to enter the water, and needless to say Hunter could not convince himself that the myth was true.

Earlier, Francis Willughby had been very cautious, and correct. In *The Ornithology of Francis Willughby*, published in 1678, he writes: "What becomes of the swallows in winter time, whether they fly into other countries, or lie torpid in hollow trees and like places, neither are natural historians agreed, nor indeed can we certainly determine. To us it seems more probable that they fly away into hot countries, viz. Egypt, Ethiopia, etc., than that they lurk in hollow trees, or holes in rocks and ancient buildings, or lie in water under ice in northern countries."

And even as late as 1824 Edward Jenner, the man credited with developing vaccination, had to argue against the hibernation theory. Perhaps surprisingly, one of the strongest statements against the immersion theory came at a time when Barrington was at his strongest. George Edwards, in his *Natural History of Birds and Gleanings of Natural History*, published between 1743 and 1760, wrote, of the immersion theory: "It is enough to raise one's indignation, to see so many vouchers from so many assertors of this foolish and erroneous conjecture, which is not only repugnant to reason, but to all known laws of nature."

It is not easy to pinpoint the disappearance of the belief in bird hibernation. Although dying much earlier its demise was helped by the general burgeoning of scientific awareness and early experiments with rings in the late nineteenth century. A small lightweight ring on a bird's leg contains enough information to tell a scientist much of what he wants to know about migration.

One of the first rings that we know about was put on a swallow by a nobleman hiding from the mob in the years after the French Revolution. He put a copper ring on the leg of one of a pair of swallows that nested in his château in the Lorraine, and discovered that the marked swallow returned on three consecutive years to the same nest. There is also an earlier, less reliable record of a heron caught in Germany in 1770, that carried rings, put on in Turkey several years earlier.

The myth of the barnacle goose

In the days before ringing and record-keeping it is not hard to see that the various myths that accounted for migration were very plausible. But even allowing for the pervading total lack of understanding it is difficult for the modern mind to comprehend the widespread acceptance of possibly the strangest myth of all; the myth of the barnacle goose. There are many variants of the myth, but in essence it says that barnacle or brent geese (people probably did not distinguish the two) develop from the shellfish whose name they share. The little birds cling to driftwood by the beak, as barnacles, and then, when large enough, fly free, as geese. An alternative version has the birds growing as fruit on trees by the waterside; those that drop on land die, while those that drop in the water become geese.

In reality, of course, the barnacle goose is a perfectly ordinary bird that visits Europe only in the winter, breeding far north in Russia, Spitsbergen and Greenland. No one ever saw it court, copulate, or lay and brood eggs, so it was assumed to have a fabulous origin. The barnacle itself is a crustacean, related to lobsters and crabs, that has evolved over the eons so that it now lies on its back and kicks food into its mouth. The modified feet, or cirri, do look a bit like feathers, and without the benefit of a good dissecting microscope (and a knowledge of embryology and comparative anatomy) the little crustacean does look like an undeveloped bird.

The myth was handy, too. For as the goose was not "flesh" nor was it of "flesh", it could happily be eaten during fasts. Not all popes agreed that the goose was, in fact, a fish. In 1215 at the fourth General Lateran Council, Innocent III issued a Bull that forbade people to eat barnacle goose during Lent. But the myth was too convenient to be quashed by a mere Papal Bull, and goose continued to provide a welcome addition to the fast menu for many centuries. Nor was its anomalous position confined to the Christian church.

Many learned rabbis discussed the matter, and decided that even if the birds did grow on trees they were still birds and could be eaten by Jews provided that they were slaughtered in the correct manner. Later on, at the end of the thirteenth century, opinions changed. The geese were not geese but shellfish, and so were forbidden to Jews.

The truth of the matter was first recorded by one Albertus Magnus, who lived in southern Germany between 1193 and 1280. He thought the myth absurd because he and his friends had often seen the goose sitting on its egg and had seen the chicks hatch from eggs in a perfectly ordinary manner. What the barnacle or brent geese were doing breeding in Bavaria is a mystery, but it was enough to satisfy Albertus. Strangely the same man also believed that birds could grow from the putrefying leaves of the sage plant!

After Albertus there is a gap of three hundred years

G. Edwards
Delin et Sculp
1752
Undescribed small Birds, taken Novem.r 1.st 1751 on the Coast of Hispaniola, about ten Leagues from
by Tho.s Stack M.D. & F.R.S. in a Voyage from London to Jamaica: Now first Drawn of their Natural
252

George Edwards (1694–1773) has sometimes been called the father of British ornithology. Edwards illustrated many of his books himself and was responsible for this beautifully tinted engraving of the golden crowned thrush and blue fly catcher that appeared in *Gleanings of Natural History* in 1758. The engraving of these hitherto unrecorded birds was made from specimens sent to Edwards from the West Indies.

until the next true observation of the barnacle goose's origins. A group of Dutchmen set sail from Amsterdam in 1596 in search of a north-east passage to China. At a latitude of 80°N they came to two little islands in the Barents Sea, on one of which was a large number of barnacle geese, sitting on their eggs. The sailors collected sixty eggs, and killed and ate one of the geese. When they returned to Holland the captain wrote an account of the voyage that included all these details. This should have been the end of the matter, but it was not.

Several authorities, in presenting their version of the myth, quoted both Albertus Magnus and the Dutch sailors, only to dismiss them in favour of "more reliable" sources. Linnaeus, who believed that swallows passed the winter under water, also believed in the myth of the barnacle goose. He called the barnacle *Lepas anatifera* (the goose bearer) and the goose we now call the brent goose, *Anser bernicla* (the goose from barnacles). Both species have, however, now been reclassified.

Early scientific investigations

In the nineteenth century people began to study migration seriously and scientifically. Like their predecessors, they concentrated on birds because their movements were obvious and familiar, although they also began to take notice of the migratory feats of other species. Several specific questions emerged from the vague seekings of earlier times. What species migrate? Why do they do so? How do migrants find their way? What sets them off on their journey? Experiments and speculations abounded, often as foolish as the ignorant superstitions of earlier times.

In 1905, Otto Herman, a noted Hungarian ornithologist who began that country's pathfinding investigation of ringed swallows, drew up a list of some of the differences of opinion for the IVth International Ornithological Congress in London. These he posed as simple alternatives,

There are definite routes of migration.
There are no definite routes of migration.
and
The birds learn how to migrate.
The birds act by instinct.

This was very much the way in which science viewed the problem. There were correct answers to each of these points, and each eminent investigator argued for his own preferred singular interpretation.

On the part played by instinct, for instance, people tended to take a definite position. Young birds often migrate quite alone, with no guidance from their parents. They must, therefore, have an inborn knowledge, not only of when to migrate but also of where they must go. Alfred Newton, the first professor of Zoology at Cambridge in the 1870s, rejected the idea of instinct. He preferred to think that birds "act unconsciously in a manner suited to a certain purpose", which might sound suspiciously like an instinct to you or me. Others believed that birds migrated as a result of "practice" and

GEESE FROM BARNACLES

In the Middle Ages many strange myths were current asserting the unnatural generation of birds. Some, it was believed, sprang from trees; others from shellfish. The Chinese have an ancient story about a small colourful bird growing from the flowers it was frequently seen hovering above. In Europe some birds were believed to develop from rotting pinewood by virtue of its "vitreous humour". Although these myths were repeated in contemporary writings, many authors chose not to vouch for them personally.

A complete scheme of development from goose to barnacle appeared in Ulisse Aldrovandi's ornithology of 1639. The barnacle goose myth may be attributable to the goose barnacle's feathery appearance and to its presence on driftwood washed up on shores where the geese were commonly found. It was even believed that the barnacles grew on trees overhanging water, the goose embryos dropping into the sea when fully developed.

"experience", although they admitted that knowledge might be handed down through the ages so that young birds could take advantage of the experiences of preceding generations.

The truth, as it appears today, is somewhere between the two. If one catches migrating birds and displaces them from their normal flight path, young birds, that have not migrated before, will keep going in the particular direction that ought to get them to the wintering grounds. Older birds, who have experienced migration, will change course and navigate correctly to the wintering grounds, rather than using a single preferred direction. Instinct and experience both play a part.

Some people argued that birds, quite simply, could see where they were going. They flew high enough to keep an eye on their destination. This could not be so for species that migrate at night or across large expanses of water with no land along the route. But it might be possible for some species, as American naturalist and writer Henry David Thoreau noted after climbing a mountain in 1863: "The bird whose eye takes in the Green Mountains on the one side, and the ocean on the other, need not be at a loss to find its way." Then, in 1974, homing pigeons wearing frosted contact lenses were released; most flew back the twenty kilometres (12 miles) to their loft in a more or less straight line. Even if birds do use sight, some do not have to.

Other experiments have shown that birds have a whole set of very sophisticated guidance systems. They can navigate by the sun, by the stars, or they can use landmarks and some can recognize the smell of home. They can also hear the sound of surf on the shore and fly along the coast on an overcast night assuming it leads them in the right direction.

Experiments have convinced us that birds can, and do, use all these systems to find their way about, although it is far from certain that every migratory species can do so. But back in the nineteenth century the favoured popular explanation was a "sixth sense", which enabled birds and other animals to navigate unerringly, but was denied to man. The prime candidate for the sixth sense was magnetism, a theory first propounded by a Dr von Middendorff.

Supporters of the sixth sense collected anecdotes about animals finding their way home by a direct route across unknown terrain, and the pages of *Nature*, the scientific periodical, were full of stories of homing dogs, sheep, cats and even cattle. In general, however, the idea of a magnetic sense was ridiculed, and Professor Newton, when accused of believing in von Middendorff's theory, felt compelled to reply that, "I had no need to declare my disbelief in Dr von Middendorff's magnetic hypothesis, for I never met with any man that held it." Newton could not offer an alternative, though he did think that the solution was "simple in the extreme". Even ten years ago there were plenty of experts who agreed with Newton.

We now know that many species can indeed detect the Earth's magnetism and therefore presumably use it to navigate. Sceptics were especially shocked when, in 1979, James Gould and Charles Walcott found what could be the compass – a crystal of a material that appeared to be magnetite – inside the head of a homing pigeon. But we still don't know how the bird uses it.

We now see that each of Otto Herman's list of controversies does not, even now, have a definite answer. For each bird, and other migrants too, there are a series of options, each of which plays its part at the correct time. Indeed, such is the complexity of migration that it is a wonder that people today can still use the term bird brain as an insult.

The mystery of migration is an absorbing and continuing one. We have come a long way from the fanciful theories of early experts on the subject. But don't imagine that we understand the whole story. There are still countless questions awaiting answers and many species whose migratory behaviour is completely unexplained.

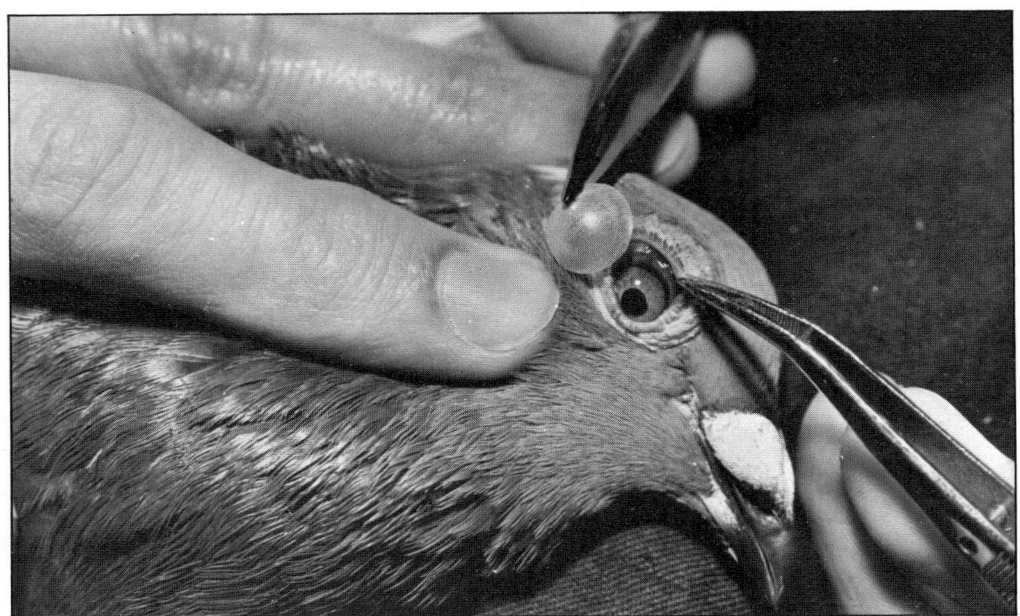

Pigeons can find their way home even when they can see no further away than a few metres. When homing pigeons, *Columba livia*, were fitted with frosted contact lenses made of gelatin, it was found that the lenses did not interfere with the pigeons' ability to orientate homeward and that a large proportion eventually found their way back to their home loft. This experiment is typical of the way in which problems in the field of migration are currently tackled.

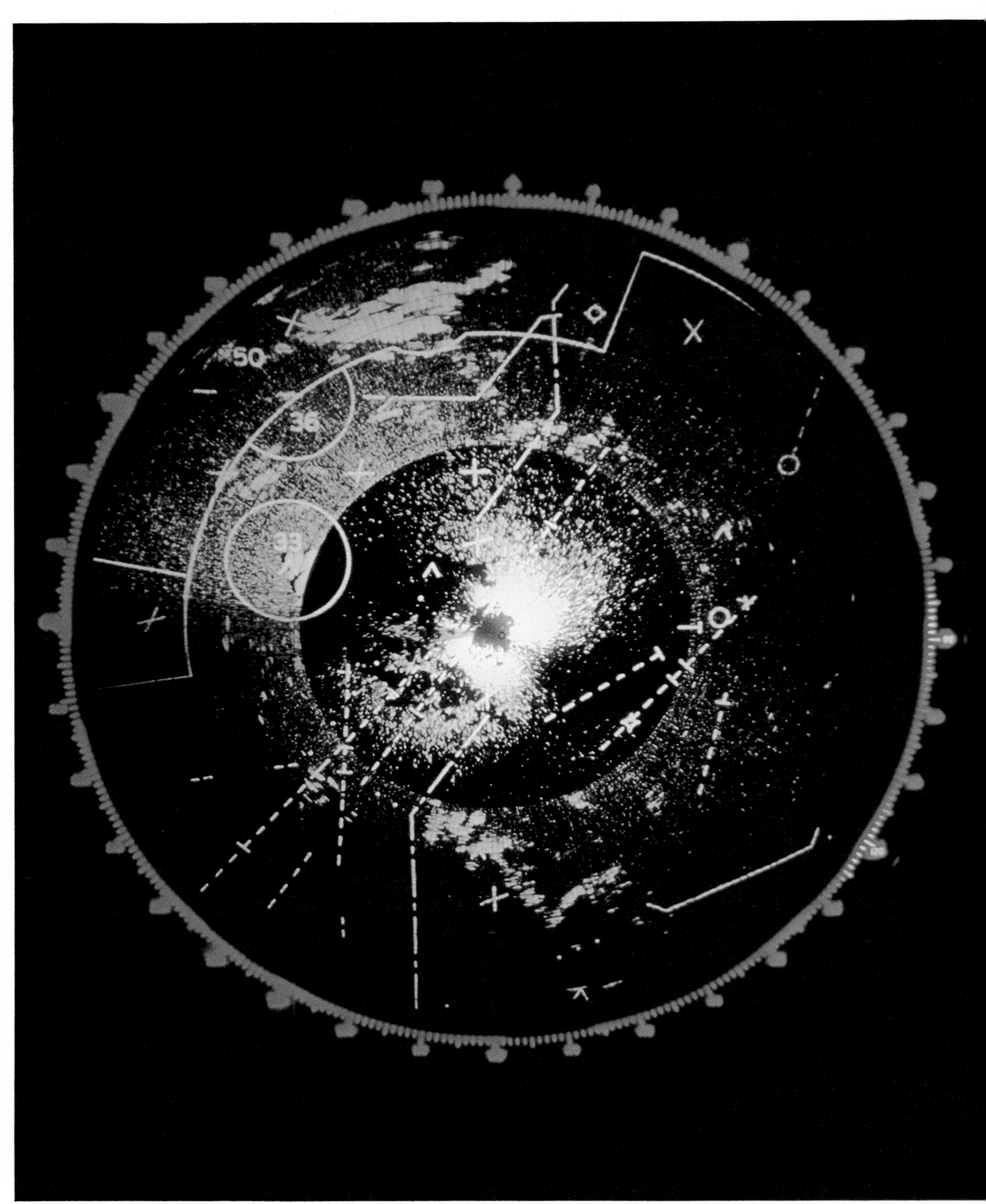
50
36
33

What is Migration?

In many books published in the past a distinction was made between migration and other forms of movement. But in recent years it has become increasingly accepted that this distinction is artificial and that movement and migration are one and the same thing. One might think that a definition that is as broad as this would provide a poor basis for scientific inquiry. On the contrary it has increased our understanding. By examining the seemingly trivial movements of creatures such as mice and lizards, scientists have amassed a store of detailed information that has justified the width of definition by shining light on the questions of how and why animals migrate.

There is also a bonus. Because migration is equated with all movement and not just movement made under one's own power, all plants may be included within the field of study. Plants, in the same way as animals, are adapted for movement, but instead of legs and fins they have adaptations, such as wings and floats, to carry them away from their parents, enabling them to reach a new site and to establish a separate existence.

By looking at each form of life in turn it is possible to clearly see the similarities and the differences between them. The most striking similarity is that basically all animals and plants migrate for the same reasons. However, the framework within which they move varies considerably from one type of organism to another. All vertebrates, including fish, reptiles, birds, and mammals and many invertebrates, typically the social insects, such as ants and bees, and some crustaceans such as lobsters, spend time learning their surroundings and for the most part migrate within these familiar areas. On the other hand, all plants and all other invertebrates, including butterflies, locusts, beetles and aphids, are always travelling on into the unknown, though not, as one might suppose, randomly or haphazardly. Their migratory strategy is different but equally effective in ensuring the organisms' optimum chance of survival.

Before describing the migrations of different forms of life, there are some fundamental concepts that need explanation. Migration means so many different things to different people that the basic principles must be clearly stated before proceeding any further. It is particularly important in this case, where a new approach to the subject is being made.

Radar allows man to see in the dark. Not until biologists applied the technique was it discovered that so many species of bird migrated at night. The radar screen displays the overall migration pattern.

What is migration? This seems to be a question that reasonably a scientist could answer simply and clearly in a few words. Many attempts have been made to formulate a simple definition that divides animals and plants into those that migrate and those that do not. All have failed. Nature refuses to be seen in absolute terms but rather exists in every imaginable variation, each merging into the next, yet remaining subtly different. Infinite variety is part of the natural world, no less in migration than in any other aspect of biology.

There are some patterns of movement that everybody would call migration. Animals such as swallows, whales, salmon and some butterflies are automatically thought of as migrants. In each case their journeys have an unusually spectacular element which has brought them to general attention. Consequently migration has a fabulous connotation and is popularly thought to be an event outside the general run of things. Stripping off this veneer and asking why animals migrate, we arrive at a set of conditions that governs the movements of all living things; plants, earthworms, ladybirds, bats, field mice and even man is seen to migrate. The best way to examine this surprising statement is by looking at some accepted examples of migration.

The barn swallow, *Hirundo rustica*, breeding in the Northern and wintering in the Southern Hemisphere is the classic migrant. Its migrations are highly conspicuous and its seasonal reappearance has been known to man for centuries. Perhaps for this reason it has become the popular model of migration. The large whales make similar seasonal journeys, but being outside everyday experience, only careful compilation of observations over the centuries has shed light on their remarkable journeys.

Atlantic salmon, *Salmo salar*, spawn in the rivers of North America and Europe. As they develop the fish drift down with the current towards the sea, where they feed for most of their adult life. When they are ready to spawn they swim back to fresh water to breed, often spawning in the same tributary in which they were born.

The monarch butterfly, *Danaus plexippus*, found in North America, heads south each year to winter in the states bordering the Gulf of Mexico, and in Southern California. In spring it flies north again, mating and laying eggs as it goes. Few, if any, make it back to where their journey started, the final leg being completed by their offspring.

These journeys contain an element of similarity; they are all made over long distances between breeding and feeding or wintering grounds. Although they are universally accepted as migration there are still important differences between them. The salmon's migration does not share the regularity or the seasonal nature of the others; the vast majority make the journey once only, dying soon after spawning. Like the salmon, the monarch's migration is a lifetime's journey, but, unlike it, the monarch does not make a round trip. In spring some fly west or east or even continue south instead of returning north.

It would appear that an animal need not move seasonally or make a return journey for it to be termed migratory. Is distance then an essential criterion? Floating in the surface layers of the sea are myriad small animals

Barn swallows, *Hirundo rustica*, feed on the wing. As they live entirely on insects, they can only survive in areas where the temperature is high enough for insects to fly. Their northward journey in autumn therefore keeps pace with the 9°C (48°F) isotherm. Swallows breed during summer in the Northern Hemisphere and are commonly found throughout Europe, Asia and North America.

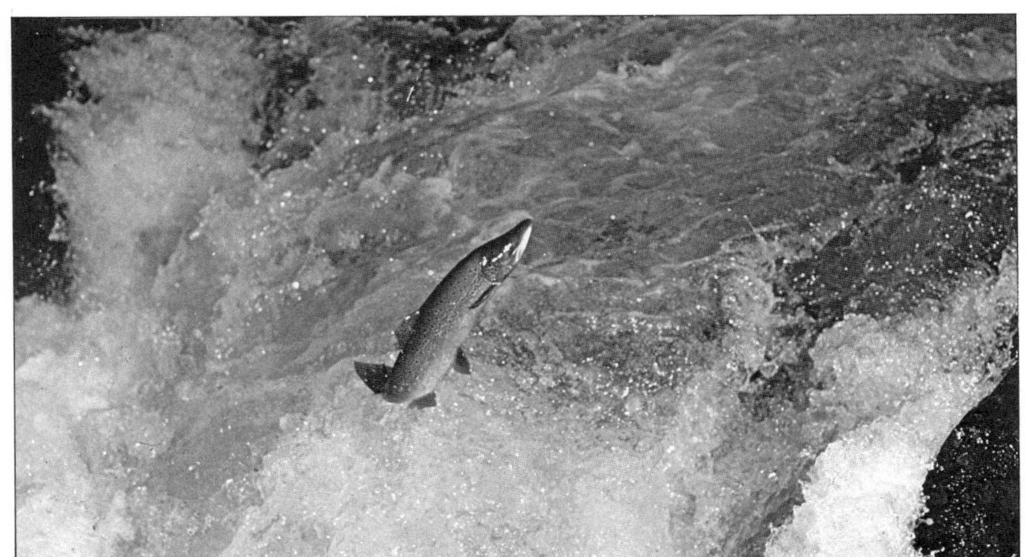

Although adult salmon live in the sea, they migrate to spawn in fresh water, where there is less risk of predation. Their preference for spawning where they were hatched themselves is an evolutionary adaptation.

The monarch butterfly, *Danaus plexippus*, found commonly in North America, is the most famous butterfly migrant. From the north of its summer range in Canada to the south of its winter range in Mexico is about 3000 kilometres (1850 miles). It is occasionally found in the British Isles and the evidence available seems to indicate that it flies across the Atlantic rather than being brought across aboard boats as was once thought.

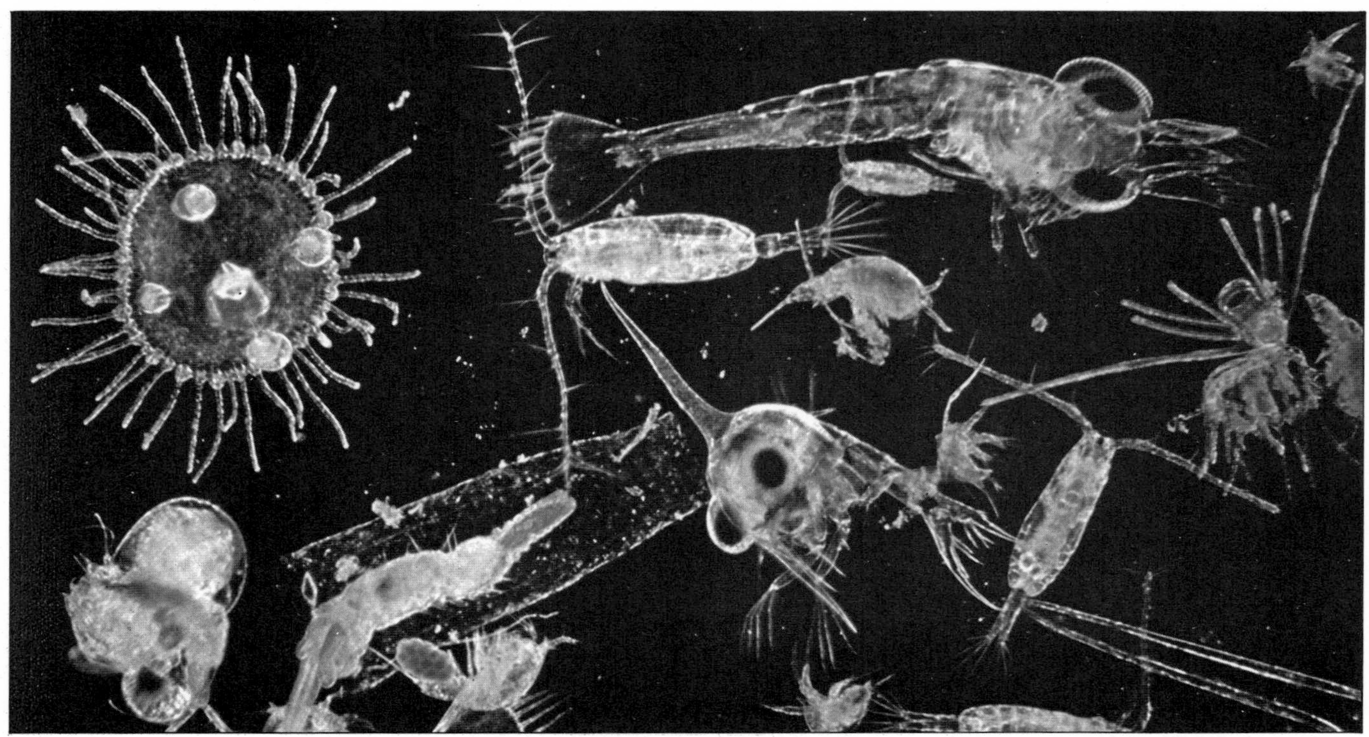

Zooplankton consist of microscopic animals such as copepods and the larvae of many fish and invertebrates. Most are herbivorous and feed on the minute plants that make up the phytoplankton. Some, however, are carnivorous and feed on other zooplankton.

known as zooplankton. These tiny creatures lie near the base of the oceanic food chain and provide nourishment for a multitude of fish and other marine animals. Plankton make seasonal movements that are widely accepted as migration. The zooplankton spend the summer breeding in the surface layers of the ocean and feeding on small plants known as the phytoplankton. In winter they descend to much deeper, colder water and do not feed at all. These to-and-fro movements are comparable in every way with the migrations of birds and whales, except that the plankton move over hundreds of metres instead of hundreds of kilometres. If we were to adopt distance as a criterion, where should we draw the line? A hundred kilometres, ten kilometres, ten metres. There is no satisfactory solution.

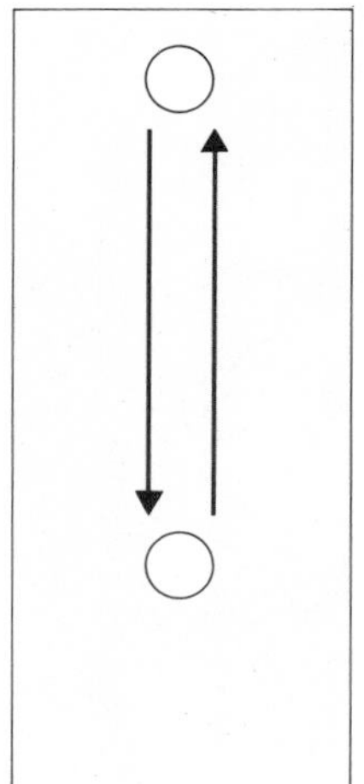

Return migration is a to-and-fro movement made by a single individual.

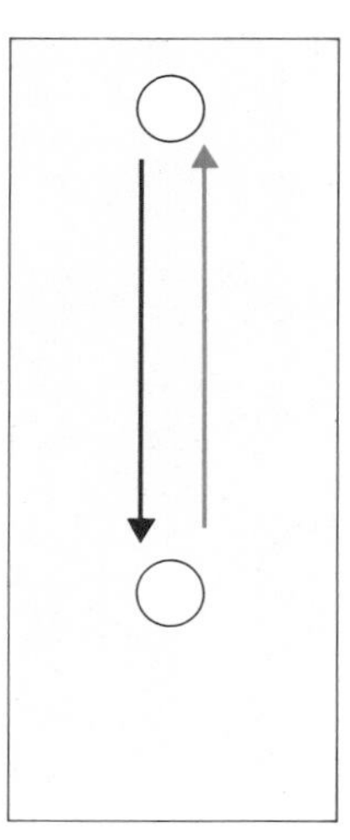

Re-migration is a return movement, completed by later generations.

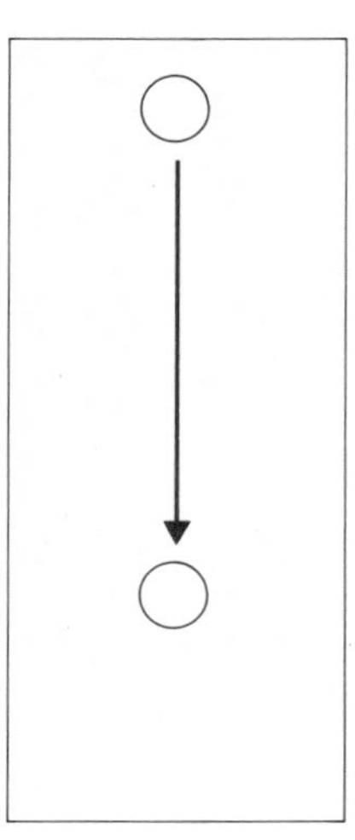

Removal migration is a one-way movement made without any intention of returning.

As we can neither use the form nor the length of an animal's journey to decide whether it is migratory, or say that this movement is migratory while that is not, the study of migration must embrace all movements that animals make from birth to death.

The path that an individual animal takes during its life, through time and space, is its lifetime track and it is this that we are attempting to understand in the study of migration. The only definition of migration we can confidently use is the general one given in most dictionaries, that migration is simply the act of moving from one place to another.

The lifetime track

An animal's lifetime track consists of all the migrations that it makes from birth to death. The pattern varies enormously from one animal to another. Some animals' lifetime tracks are cyclic and consist of a series of seasonal return migrations between wintering or feeding ranges and breeding ranges. The lifetime tracks of the barn swallow and the blue whale, *Balaenoptera musculus*, fit into this pattern. The migrations of the monarch butterfly are not in a strict sense return because their migration cycle is completed by their offspring, a pattern that is given the name re-migration.

Many forms of migration totally lack any cyclic element and are purely one-way movements. In its most familiar form this is exemplified by the emigration of a human from one country to another. This pattern is called removal migration.

THE HABITAT THEORY

Attempts have been made to define migration as movement from one habitat to another. A habitat can be defined as the minimum area required by an animal to supply it with all that is necessary for existence. However, this definition of a habitat rests on discovering what is strictly necessary for an animal's continued survival and so far no satisfactory method has been devised that distinguishes between necessary and unnecessary factors.

On the other hand a habitat could be defined as the area that is within an animal's sensory limit; in other words within its range of sight, hearing or sense of smell. Migration would therefore be any movement outside this range. However, this definition excludes some movements that are universally accepted as migration. The migration of the salmon is a typical instance. When a salmon swims upstream from the mouth of a river to its spawning ground, perhaps thousands of kilometres away, it may, from the outset, detect the chemical characteristics of its spawning ground. In this case the spawning ground is within its sensory range and, according to this definition, part of the same habitat. The salmon's journey upstream is therefore not migration.

The arbitrary nature of the habitat concept is neatly illustrated by looking at the movements of a hypothetical insect in a woodland. Depending purely on which movements we wish to study, the insect's habitat could be defined as a leaf, a branch, a tree or the entire woodland. Because the habitat can only be defined subjectively, it makes any definition of migration that relies on this concept subjective and not universally applicable.

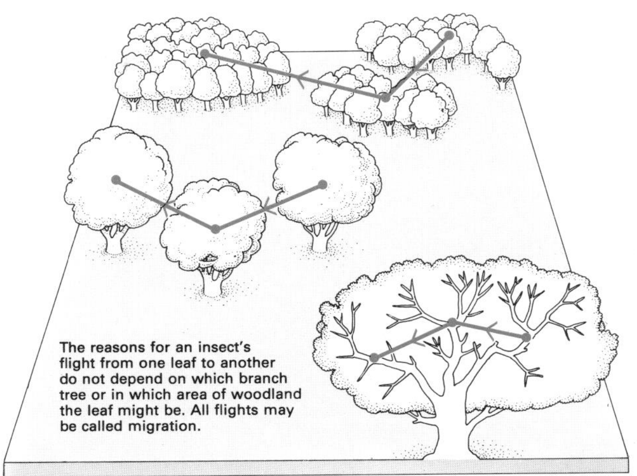

The reasons for an insect's flight from one leaf to another do not depend on which branch tree or in which area of woodland the leaf might be. All flights may be called migration.

It is possible to break down all lifetime tracks into a series of removal and return migrations. Re-migration can be seen as a series of removal migrations made by different generations.

The familiar area

Our own lifetime track as humans takes place largely in familiar surroundings and between places we have visited before. Taken together these places form a familiar area. If our memory were perfect our familiar area would consist of all the places we have ever visited.

A familiar area is a tremendous asset. If we want something, we know where to go, how to get there, and how long it will take. For this reason many animals but not all spend time learning their surroundings at an early age. However, only animals that are sufficiently long-lived or, in the case of invertebrates, mobile for long enough to take full advantage of the information ultimately, will find it worth while to invest the time initially.

It is also possible to apply the familiar area concept to nomadic animals. Returning to our human model, Australian Aborigines living within huge territories know where to find water holes and where fruit and seeds can be collected at different seasons. Their territory is just as familiar to them as city streets are to urban dwellers. Other nomadic peoples' familiar areas consist of separate areas, visited at different seasons. The Laplander's familiar area consists of his summer range along the shores of the Arctic Ocean, his winter range in the coniferous forest and the route he takes to travel between them.

This analogy is applicable to all vertebrates. A caribou, *Rangifer tarandus*, lives in a familiar area whether it spends all year in a small part of a forest or migrates thousands of kilometres between its summer and winter

To survive in the arid conditions that prevail over much of Australia, Aborigines must have familiar areas that are large enough to provide them with sufficient food and water to support them at all times of the year. As urban man does not need to search so far for food, he does not need such a large familiar area. However, both he and the Aborigine must know their familiar areas intimately to utilize them effectively.

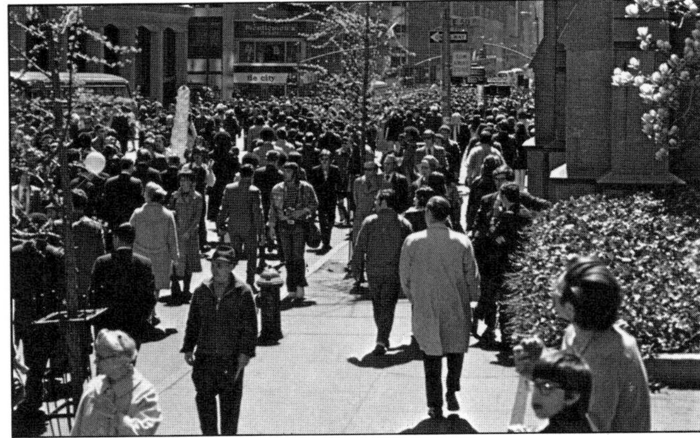

quarters. The same is true for birds, whether they are sedentary, like the house sparrow, or global migrants like the Arctic Tern, *Sterna paradisea*. No matter how far they travel, all vertebrates know where they are and where they are going, and all live within a familiar area.

Exploration

This leaves the question of how an animal acquires its familiar area. Looking at our own behaviour, we extend our own familiar area each time we visit a new place. This activity is essentially exploration. Our main phase of exploration occurs during adolescence and early adulthood, before we start to raise a family. At this age we have an inbuilt restlessness, an urge to investigate and travel, just for the satisfaction it brings.

We can see the same behaviour in other vertebrates. Most exploration occurs between the time animals become independent of their parents and the point at which they become sexually mature. Exploratory individuals travel further afield and are more restless than the others. Their tracks do not have the regularity so characteristic of adult animals.

The area through which an animal moves is its range. When the range is part of a familiar area it is described as a home range. We can recognize the different home ranges that animals occupy on separate days, at different seasons and at different times in their lives. As a young animal begins to restrict its visits to those parts of its familiar area that are useful, the home range that the animal will use as an adult begins to take shape.

The form of the adult home range depends on both the animal and its environment. Some animals such as the house sparrow have a home range that always consists of a restricted area and does not shift with the seasons. Others, like chimpanzees, *Pan troglodytes*, occupy a home range that usually remains the same all year, but may, in marginal conditions, consist of separate seasonal ranges between which they migrate. Others like the barn swallow have an adult home range that always constitutes a number of seasonal home ranges joined in the form of a seasonal circuit.

The greater the familiar area an animal builds up during adolescence, the larger its adult home range is likely to be. Not only the size of the adult home range but also its form is influenced by the size of the familiar area. A large familiar area is more likely to contain a variety of habitats and provide food and shelter at different times

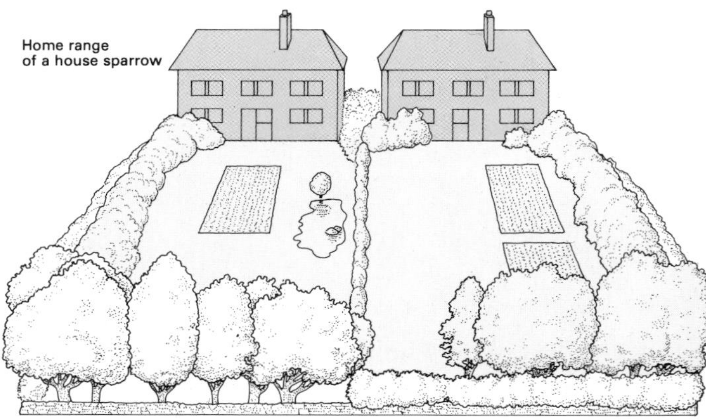

The home range of a house sparrow, *Passer domesticus*, may be no more than the size of two domestic gardens. Its familiar area probably covers several square kilometres.

The whooper swan, *Cygnus cygnus*, has a home range that consists of a northerly breeding ground, a southerly wintering area and a migration route. Its familiar area encompasses thousands of square kilometres.

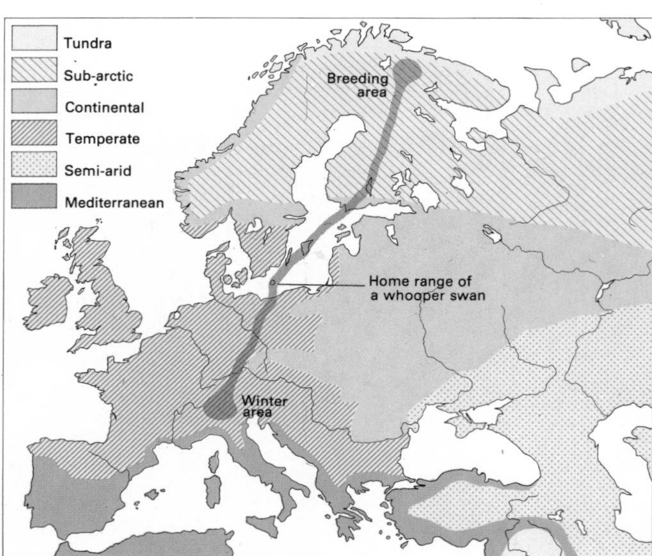

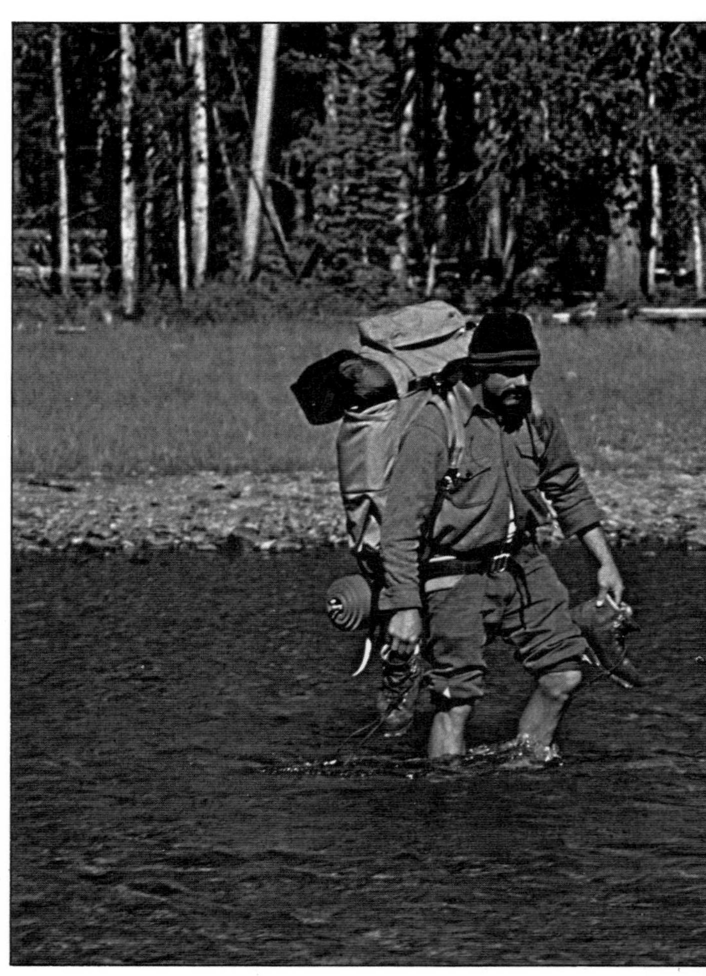

of the year. It is also true that an animal possessing a large home range is more likely to migrate seasonally. In a large home range extending between different climatic regions, the optimum places to feed and breed are bound to change with the seasons.

The age at which an animal becomes independent of its parents and begins exploration varies a great deal. Humans, like most mammals, do not really become independent until puberty, by which time they have built up a sizeable familiar area in the company of their parents that will serve as a basis for their own explorations. Many bats and some seals and sea lions, on the other hand, become independent so soon after weaning that there is little opportunity for the young to build up a basic familiar area before they begin to explore independently.

The apparent stability of a migration route does not affect exploration. Birds such as geese and swans remain with their parents for the first year of their lives and complete the yearly migration circuit before becoming independent. On independence they explore in the same way as any other animal and will change their migratory pattern if they find more suitable conditions elsewhere.

The exploratory instinct

Environment is largely responsible for the range of lifetime-track types. If a Laplander were born in New York he would develop a lifetime track indistinguishable from that of the native city dweller. If a Parisian were born among desert-living Australian Aborigines he would adopt a nomadic way of life. If there is any difference at all between the nomad and the urban dweller, it might possibly be that under the same conditions the nomad would tend to be more restless during adolescence.

This restlessness may be an expression of the desire to explore. Over the past 200 generations or so Western man has become settled. As he no longer hunts and forages there is now less advantage in having a large familiar area. His exploratory desire therefore may have decreased. In the deserts of Australia, on the other hand, those Aborigines with the largest familiar areas are best able to survive.

Restless behaviour has been investigated with caged birds and animals divorced from their natural surroundings. It has been found that they are more active at the same time and under the same seasonal and environmental conditions that they would be in exploring in the wild. Young birds are more restless than adults. Seasonal migrant birds are more active in the spring and autumn and long-distance migrants are more restless than short-distance migrants.

Breeding experiments have shown that restlessness is instinctive. When rats from a normal population are bred so that those that are more active in adolescence are

LEARNING THE ROUTE

The first migration of a young bird, from the breeding ground to its wintering area, is exploratory. Normally the journey is made in the company of adults. The young bird learns the position of leading lines, which help it to accommodate for wind drift, and also the position of intermediate resource sites. The young bird's migration is characterized by episodes of flight at right angles to the migration direction and by back-tracking.

Juvenile bird

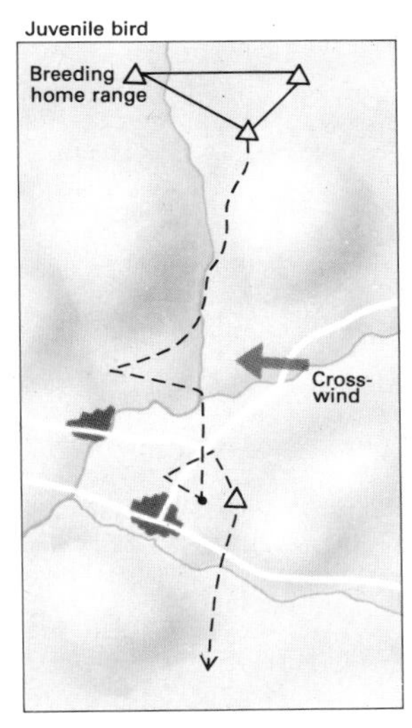

Adult bird

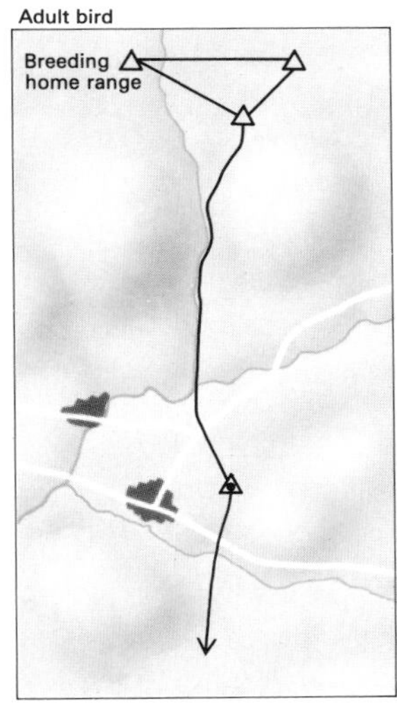

△ Resource site
• Landing site
- - → Exploratory migration
⟶ Migration in a learned direction

A familiar area is acquired by exploration, and exploratory migration is a feature of all vertebrate behaviour. The impulse is instinctive and is as prevalent in young humans as it is in any other species.

ORIENTATING BY INSTINCT

Outdoor experiments conducted with indigo buntings, *Passerina cyanea*, using funnel cages of the type in the photograph showed that the birds hopped north in the spring and south in the autumn.

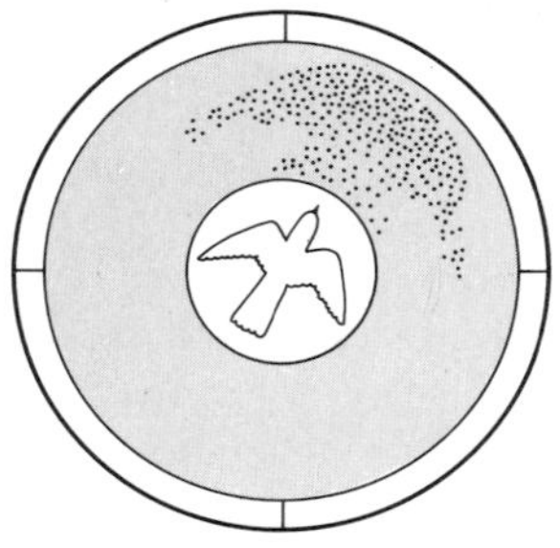

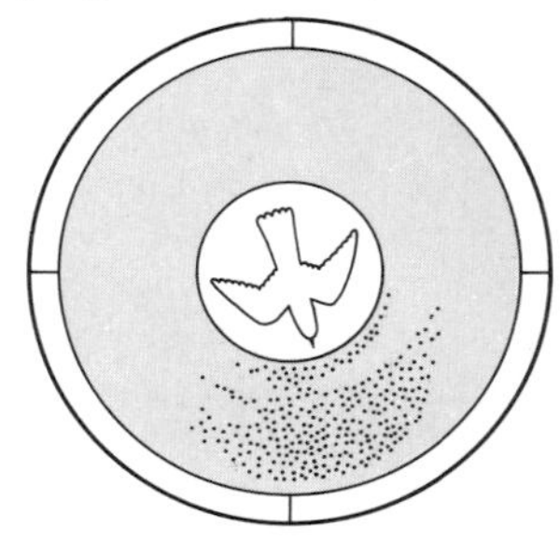

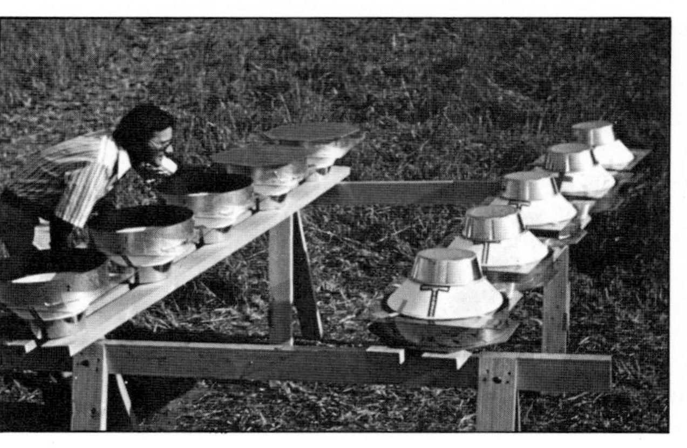

Migration direction can be expressed in percentages of animals moving in the four principal directions relative to the mean direction. The percentages may be written as a ratio or shown diagrammatically.

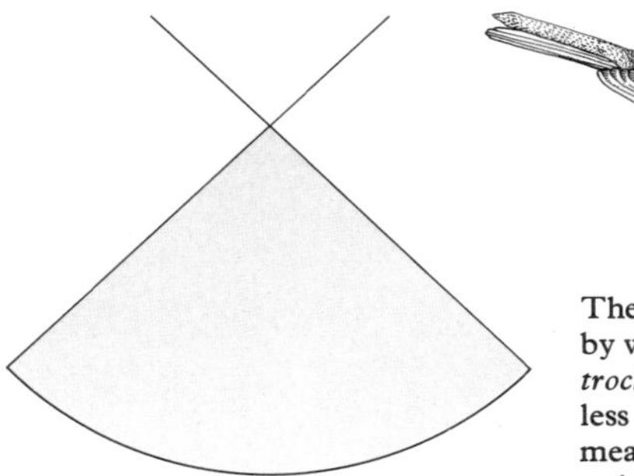

The spread of directions taken by willow warblers, *Phylloscopus trochilus*, on their migrations is less than 45° on either side of the mean. The direction ratio is written 100:0:0:0.

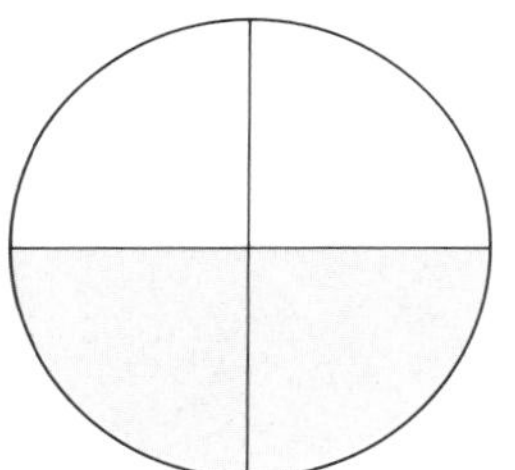

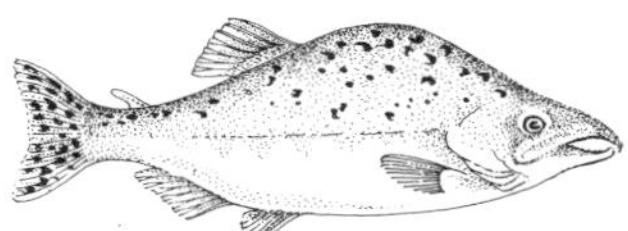

The pink salmon, *Oncorhynchus gorbuscha*, feeding in the North Pacific, fan out through 180° to reach their spawning rivers.

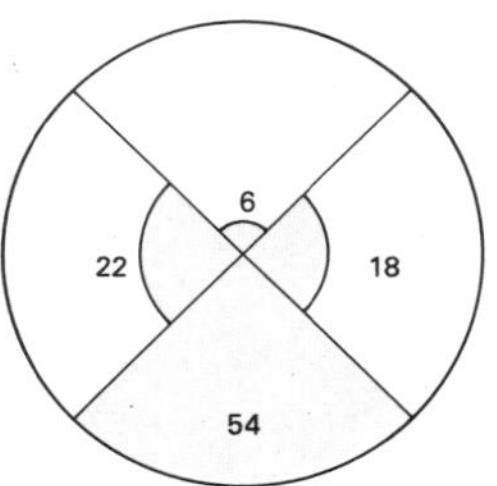

The painted lady, *Cynthia cardui*, has a direction ratio of 54:18:22:6. The numbers on the diagram indicate the order that the ratio is conventionally written.

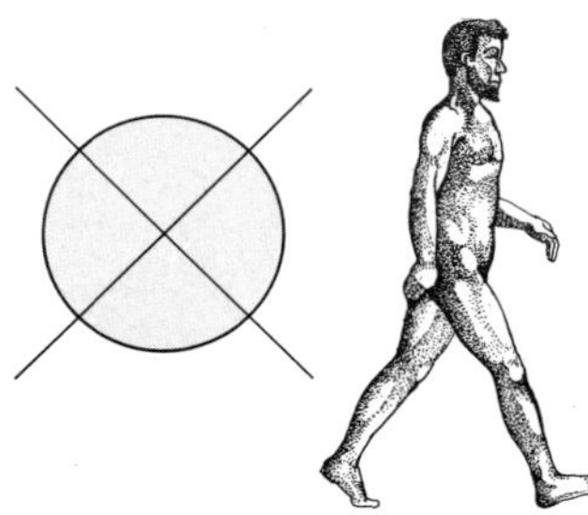

Man has no preferred migration direction and has a direction ratio that is at the opposite extremity of the range of direction ratios seen in nature. As his geographical range is so extensive, and his life style varies so much depending on the environment, all directions have equal weight. Man's direction ratio is written 25:25:25:25.

mated with each other and those that are less active in adolescence are mated with each other, two separate strains of rat are produced; an active strain and a less active strain. It seems that as well as being learnt from example, the urge to explore and its duration are passed on genetically from one generation to the next. Because the exploratory urge is inherent and not learned, it is subject to the effects of natural selection. If an animal does not show the necessary exploratory drive it will probably not survive. As most other aspects of migratory behaviour are learned, evolution acts mainly on the desire to explore.

Preferred direction

Most animals explore in all directions, but some, especially birds, have a preference for a particular one. During evolution many birds have acquired the instinct to build up large familiar areas in which there is a climatic difference between one end and the other. For these birds it is an advantage to spend winter in the part of their familiar area nearer to the equator and summer in the end nearer the poles. In this situation, the young birds that by chance prefer to fly towards the equator in autumn and away from it in spring will have a greater chance of survival. The result is that birds that make long-distance migrations, even though for historical reasons they may also make long east-west journeys, have preferred compass directions for exploration towards the poles in spring and towards the equator in autumn.

This information is programmed into the bird's genetic make-up. Hand-raised birds that have been kept caged are found to spend more time in certain parts of their cage at different times of the year. Birds from the Northern Hemisphere prefer the southern part of their cage in autumn and the northern part in spring.

Although flying broadly in a preferred direction birds often fly back along their flight path or to and fro at right angles to it, so that although flying in a general north-south direction they visit a wide range of potential roosting and feeding sites to the east and west. The river fish's preference for exploring downstream when young and migrating back upstream to spawn when adult has been produced by the same pressures of habitat suitability that determine the exploratory behaviour of birds. Deep water downstream has a richer food supply and therefore favours growth. Shallow water upstream contains fewer predators and is therefore better for breeding.

During evolution, many river fish came in contact with the sea on their downstream explorations. Some found the greater supply of food and space in the sea gave them an advantage, and, in the course of evolution, overcame the physiological problems associated with transferring from fresh to salt water. The migratory phase of fish, such as salmon, down river into the sea is comparable with the first migrations of young birds in that both are extending their familiar areas. A young salmon heading downstream to the sea knows instinctively what it is looking for. The fish is aware of how the sea should taste and feel, in the same way that a young bird, exploring southwards for the first time, has an inbuilt image of what its winter range should be like.

The young bird probably knows instinctively the day length and temperature that its winter range should possess. Some birds have an innate preference for particular types of vegetation and probably also for specific kinds of countryside. During its first autumn the young bird pushes its familiar area further and further in its preferred compass direction until it comes across an area that corresponds to its notion of what a good winter habitat should be.

Although exploratory behaviour is instinctive it is still flexible. When young birds see adults flying in a direction in autumn that is different from their preferred compass direction they may follow the adults rather than continue on their own. Similarly, if over the years the climate changes the best place to spend the winter, succeeding generations of young birds will go to the better area rather than the destination dictated by habit.

In the last few decades lesser black-backed gulls, *Larus fuscus*, born in Britain have spent the winter months further north than ever before. In the 1960s the adults of this species wintered almost entirely along the coasts of Iberia and Northwest Africa. In the 1970s most adults overwintered in Britain and only a small proportion were found further south. The pattern of exploration, however, has not changed. The young birds still spend their first winter exploring the coasts of Iberia and Northwest Africa and their second winter exploring Britain and the coasts of France. The difference is that, when they are mature, the gulls elect to spend the winter in the northern part of their familiar area, whereas previously they spent it in the southern part. The reason for changing their wintering site is unknown, but it may be connected with the massive increase in gull population during this century and the resulting greater competition for breeding space.

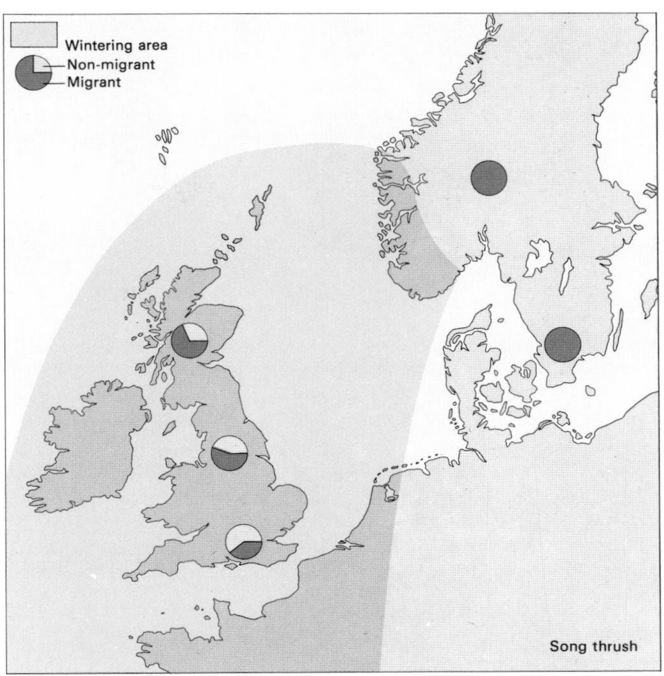

Partial migration is a form of behaviour adopted by species breeding in areas that are only marginally suitable for overwintering. In the Northern Hemisphere, the more northerly an individual's breeding home range, the more likely it is to migrate. Song thrushes, *Turdus philomelos*, breeding in the British Isles are partially migrant, while those breeding in Scandinavia are entirely migrant.

The migratory patterns of animals are not fixed. Many lesser black-backed gulls, *Larus fuscus*, now winter in Britain instead of flying south.

Partial migration

Competition is also the key to what is known as partial migration. In some cases two different forms of behaviour have evolved within a single animal population. Some members migrate long distances while others remain near their breeding site all year. Examples of partial migrants are most commonly found among birds. At one time it was thought that partial migration was a stage in the evolution towards long-distance migration, but because natural selection affects exploratory behaviour rather than the final migratory pattern, partial migration is now thought to be a pattern of behaviour in its own right. The difference between the individuals that migrate and those that remain is simply that the migrant individuals have found a more suitable site for wintering or breeding elsewhere during their exploratory phase.

In many instances the question of autumn migration depends on the situation in the breeding range. If increased competition for food or space in particular years is greater, a greater proportion than normal will migrate. Depending upon conditions it is not uncommon for some individuals to switch from migrant to non-migrant several times in a lifetime. In species with a global distribution it is found that the proportion

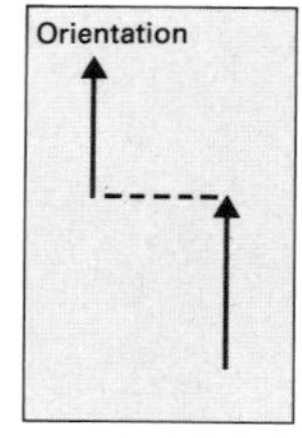

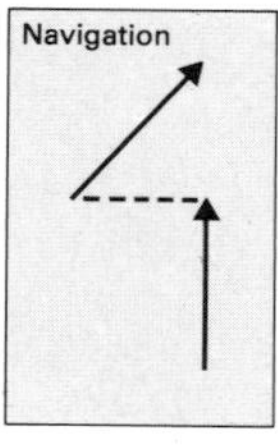

Orientation is simply pointing in a particular direction, but navigation is travelling towards a definite destination. If a migrating animal is orientating it will carry straight on as before after being displaced; if navigating, it compensates for the displacement.

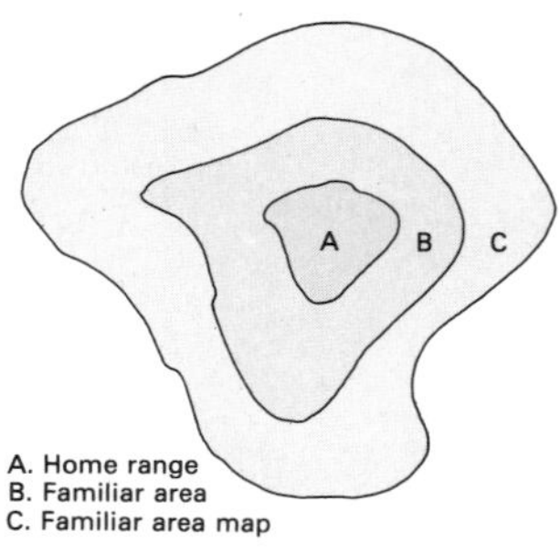

The familiar area map is always larger than the familiar area. The home range is the part of the area most used.

of birds migrating increases as the distance of their breeding ground from the poles decreases. For example, all blackbirds, *Turdus merula*, breeding in Scandinavia migrate south in autumn, whereas nearly all blackbirds breeding in Great Britain are resident.

In a highly territorial partial-migrant species, like the Eurasian robin, *Erithacus rubecula*, a young bird will not migrate in search of winter quarters if it can find a winter territory within its breeding range during its first summer and autumn. Robins that migrate long distances are usually those that are unable to find a winter territory close to their breeding area.

Navigation, orientation and pilotage

As we have seen, the factors affecting animal migration are all things which fall within the realm of human experience. It may be a little difficult to imagine what it is like to have a preferred compass direction, but it could be comparable to the feeling that some people have of always being drawn to a particular area.

Accepting the fact that animals amass a store of information about a large number of places, how do they find their way from one to another? It is easy to understand how animals find their way around within a familiar area, but how do they first learn its geography.

An animal finds its way to a known destination across unfamiliar terrain by navigation. It should not be confused with orientation, which is simply travelling in a particular direction, or pilotage, which is finding the way to a known destination across familiar terrain. Young birds orientate on the outward leg of their exploratory autumn migration. Animals employ pilotage when they are moving around within their familiar area, but navigation is a vital part of exploration.

When an animal explores, it navigates to find its way back to its familiar area and, if it has found a site that it wants to visit again, it uses navigation to find it a second time. There are two forms of navigation: route-based and location-based. In route-based navigation an animal exploring outside its familiar area collects information about its route and uses it to navigate back home. An animal does this in several ways. The simplest is by laying a trail or memorizing the exploratory route. To return home the animal must follow its route exactly and cannot take a short cut. If, instead, the animal continually notes the positions of large, distant features, such as mountains or even the sun, it is possible for it to return by estimating the direction of home, relative to these features. This is still route-based navigation, for the information used for the homeward journey is gathered along the exploratory route. Location-based navigation is quite different. The animal makes no reference to its exploratory journey, but returns by estimating the position of home from where it finds itself.

Maps and navigation

To use location-based navigation an animal must have some sort of "map". This map may take two forms, a familiar area map or a grid-map. Humans use both these map-types. A familiar-area map is, as its name implies, the learned map we have of our surroundings based on personal experience.

A familiar area map is always larger than a familiar area. When we visit a village, it becomes part of our familiar area. The hills or mountains that we can see to the east of the village become part of our familiar area map, but as we have not visited them they do not become part of the familiar area itself. Using information stored in our mental map to find a particular place is one form of location-based navigation and, inside the limits of their familiar-area maps, all vertebrates probably use this method to navigate outside their familiar areas.

Outside the familiar area map it has been suggested, but not as yet proved, that long-distance migrants such as birds, turtles and perhaps fish may use a grid-map. The grid-map best known to humans is the one based on latitude and longitude.

Some scientists think that birds can locate themselves in the same way that mariners calculate their position at sea. A mariner works out his latitude from the height of the sun above the horizon at midday and his longitude from the difference between local time and the time at Greenwich. Birds can certainly tell the height of the sun above the horizon, but it is not at all certain that they have the internal biological clocks necessary to relate local time to home time. Others think that birds may use a grid-map based on the earth's magnetic field. Birds can detect both the inclination of the magnetic field, the angle that a compass needle makes to the horizontal, and the declination, the difference between magnetic north and geographical north. Together these two pieces of information are sufficient to construct a grid-map.

Navigation – study techniques

Navigation is investigated by observing an animal's behaviour when removed from its home range. There are two commonly used methods: displacement-release, in which an animal is set free and the direction in which it makes off is noted, and displacement-orientation, in which an animal is held in a cage at the "release" point and the parts of the cage it occupies most frequently are recorded.

Few experiments are now based on homing success; that is the proportion of released animals that return home and the time it takes for them to arrive. Homing experiments are unreliable as they take no account of animals that fail to return for reasons other than failure to navigate. The animals may be killed by predators *en*

The topographic map provides man with a grid of information that he can use to locate himself in his surroundings. Apart from printed maps there are several other types of grid map, notably the guidance systems used by shipping and aircraft; shore-based transmitters provide a co-ordinate system of radio signals that can be interpreted by a navigator in terms of latitude and longitude.

route or distracted for any number of reasons. Nor does this method distinguish animals that have found their way home purely by chance.

The most important finding of recent years has been that many animals, particularly amphibians, birds and surprisingly enough humans, are able to employ route-based navigation, even though they are unable to see where they are going during the outward journey. Scientists initially overlooked this possibility and interpreted the results in terms of location-based navigation.

Two forms of grid map have been postulated as a basis of bird migration outside the familiar area. One, based on the movement of the sun, corresponds to lines of latitude and longitude. The other is based on the angles that a compass makes with true north (declination) and with the horizontal (inclination).

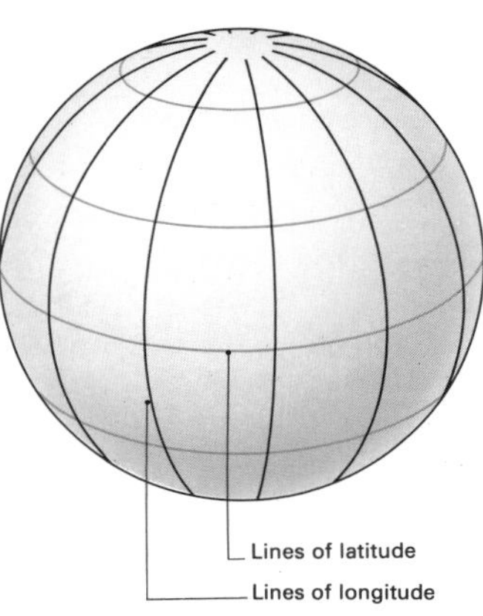

Solar map

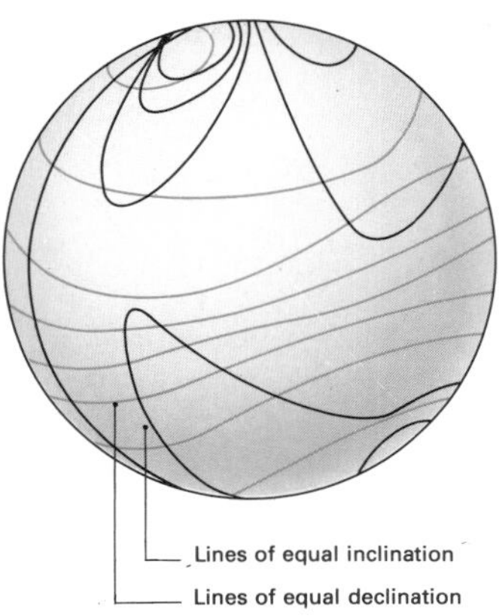

Magnetic map

BIRD NAVIGATION

Until recently it was thought that, when birds were released in unfamiliar territory, they orientated initially according to clues present at the point of release and therefore found their way home primarily by map-based navigation. However, in experiments in which homing pigeons, *Columba livia*, were taken from their home along a circuitous route before being released, it was found that they flew off in a direction that was opposite to that of the first leg of the outward journey. This implies that the birds orientated with reference to information picked up on the route and therefore found their way home by route-based navigation.

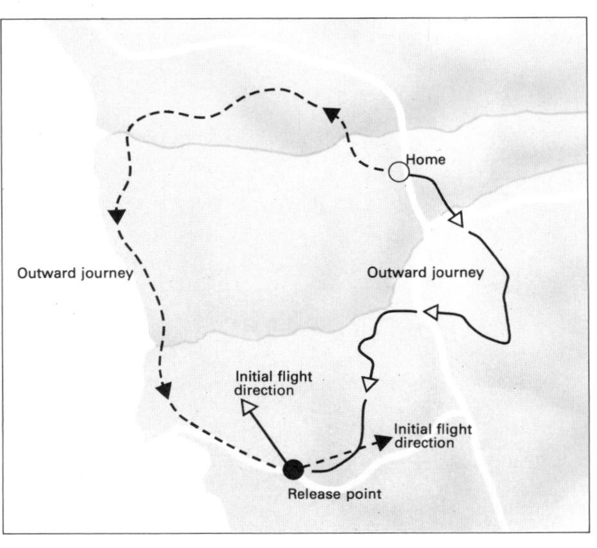

This casts doubt on past experiments in the field of location-based navigation. It is quite possible in some experiments that, despite precautions taken to prevent the animals seeing the outward route, the animals solved the navigational problems by route-based navigation using non-visual clues.

As a result, we know very little for sure about location-based navigation. What little evidence we have suggests that animals use only location-based navigation within the limits of their familiar area map and do not have access to a grid-map that can be read from anywhere on the earth's surface.

Landmarks, visible and invisible

We do know a little more about the features that animals use as landmarks in their familiar area map.

As humans we tend to think of landmarks as visible topographical features, such as rivers and mountains. However, there are also a number of sounds and smells that are as characteristic of location as anything we can see. Blind people find their way around by a combination of touch and a crude form of echolocation – detecting variation in the echoes of their footsteps as they pass different obstacles. Polynesians knew their position at sea from the taste of the water and from the type of fish and plants. The Vikings are said to have been able to tell where they were from the colour of the water.

Although some mammals probably make use of visual landmarks in the same way that humans do, many, notably dogs, deer and mice, rely heavily on familiar smells or "olfactory landmarks". Other mammals, particularly bats and toothed whales, use a system of

The Polynesian inhabitants of the South Pacific have, of necessity, acquired an intimate knowledge of the ocean. Without the aid of nautical charts and the magnetic compass, they had in the past, instead, to rely on their own innate senses. Apart from being able to navigate by the stars they could also tell their position at sea from the taste of the water and the pattern of the ocean swell.

echolocation. They send out highly structured sounds and, from the echoes, are able to interpret the topography of their surroundings. Over short distances the information gathered is thought to be very similar to that obtained by vision. Birds rely mainly on sight, but have been shown to include smells in their familiar area map and to use them in route-based navigation.

It has been found that pigeons can detect very low-frequency sounds emanating from mountain ranges and coasts. It is possible that these sounds, below the range of human hearing, may be detected by the pigeons thousands of kilometres away. If pigeons can also detect the direction from which the sounds come, then noise may form an important part of their familiar area map.

Reptiles and amphibians also make use of a mixture of visual and olfactory landmarks. Amphibians, like fish, however, place more reliance on their sense of smell. Fish can detect and discriminate between the chemical signatures of different waters. They can also tell the temperature of the water and detect its depth from the hydrostatic pressure. As no two areas of a river or an ocean have an identical combination of chemical signature, temperature and depth, a fish can establish a map of its watery world similar to a terrestrial mammal's familiar area map.

Orientation

To travel in a straight line an animal must orientate to some fixed distant feature, such as a large hill. Animals such as the monarch and the small white butterfly, *Pieris rapae*, which travel straight across country in a series of removal migrations, orientate primarily to the sun. As they rarely visit the same place twice they have little use for a sense of location.

Nocturnal insects such as moths orientate at an angle to the moon, or to the stars when the moon is not visible. Moths still seem able to orientate themselves even when the sky is completely overcast – perhaps they can detect the earth's magnetic field. Many other animals, including beetles, snails, fish, salamanders and some birds and mammals, have been shown to be sensitive to magnetic fields. Indeed, it has become such a common phenomenon that future investigations may concentrate on looking for an animal that cannot detect it.

Sun, moon, stars and the earth's magnetic field are all used by animals as compass cues during exploration and pilotage within the familiar area. Route-based navigation during exploration, when it does not rely on memorized landmarks, is based on continual reference to one of these compasses during the outward journey. Amphibians displaced experimentally in open boxes, so they can see the sun, can easily set off towards home when released. Pigeons, displaced in aluminium boxes, are able to find their way home using route-based navigation with reference to the earth's magnetic field, but cannot do so when displaced in iron boxes which disrupt the earth's magnetic field.

Young birds on their first autumn exploration pursue their preferred compass direction with reference to the sun, if they migrate during daylight, or to the moon and stars, if they migrate at night. Under thick cloud they may use magnetic cues, but many seem strangely reluctant to do this, preferring instead to settle and wait for the skies to clear.

Orientation to celestial bodies must be much more accurate when used for exploration or pilotage or to assist in navigation than when used in removal migration. Invertebrates, such as many butterflies and moths, which

All animals rely on two or more senses to form a mental picture of their environment, but in every case one sense seems to dominate. In addition to these all animals have a sense of touch, and it is becoming increasingly accepted that many, if not all, can also detect the earth's magnetic field to some extent.

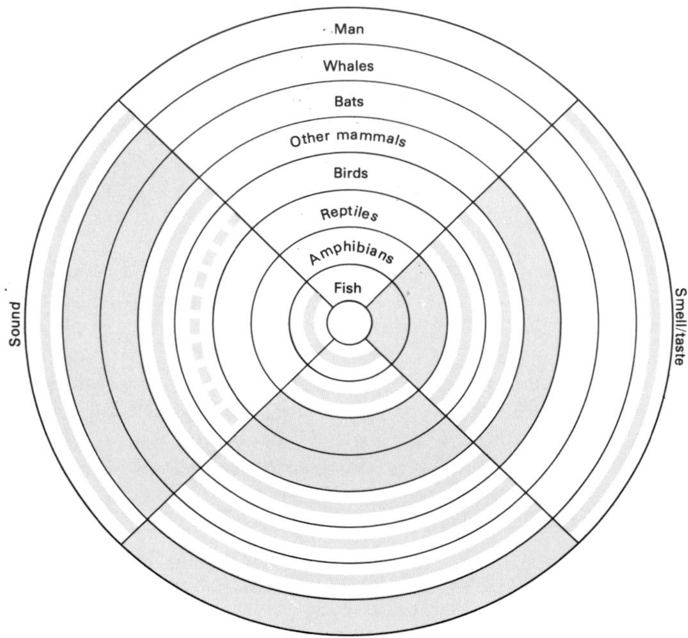

When an animal uses the position of the sun to navigate within its familiar area it must compensate for the sun's apparent motion in the sky. If, for example, a bird flies from its roosting site to its breeding site by flying directly towards the sun's azimuth (the direction of the point on the horizon apparently lying directly below the sun) and does not compensate for the change in the sun's position on the return journey, it will miss the target by a margin proportional to the length of the journey.

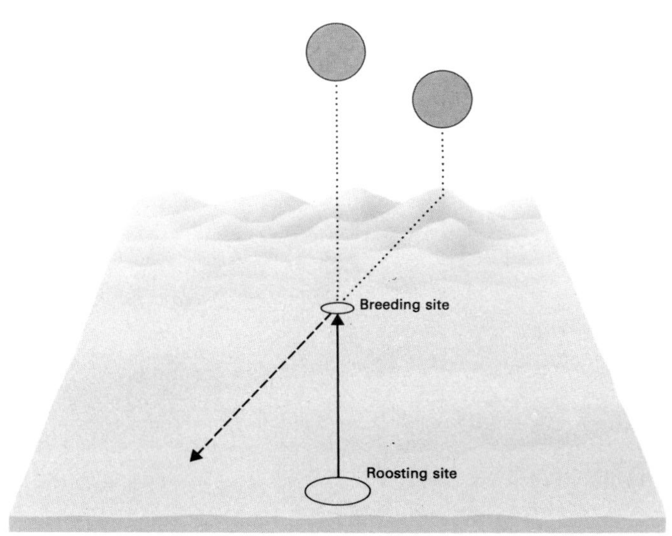

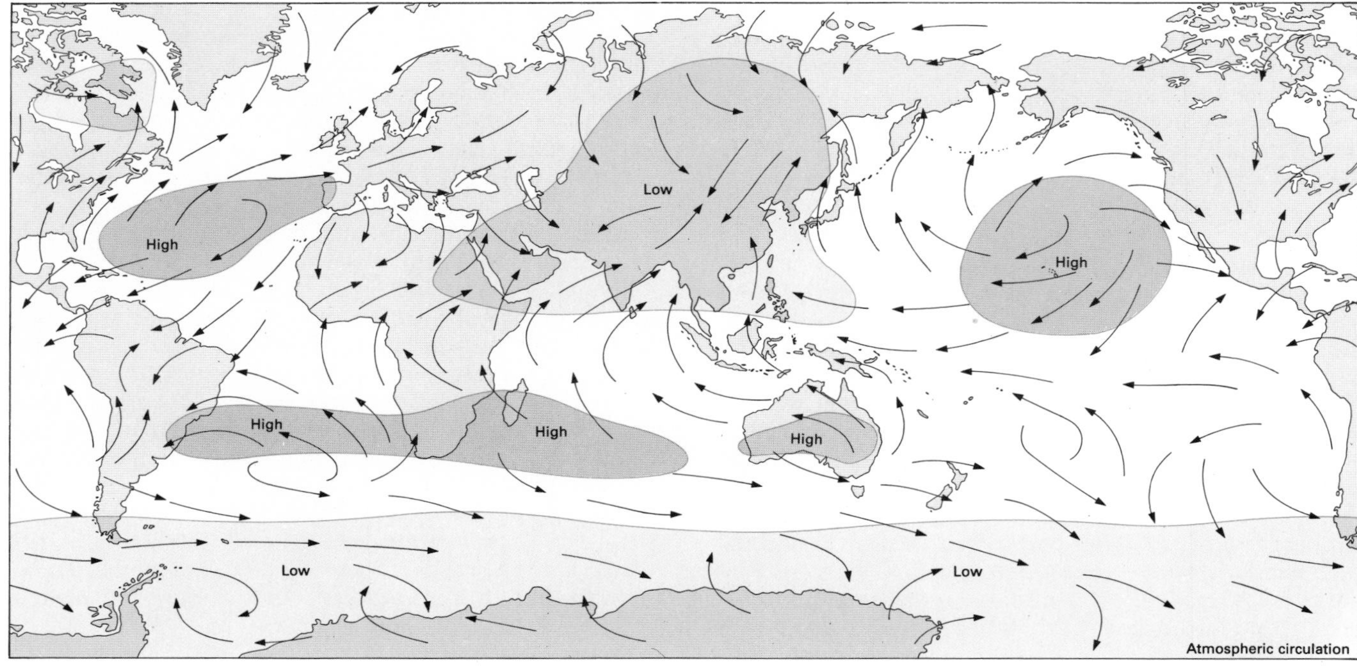

The pattern of atmospheric currents is of major importance to birds, bats and insects, and in many parts of the world it has a significant effect on their migratory behaviour.

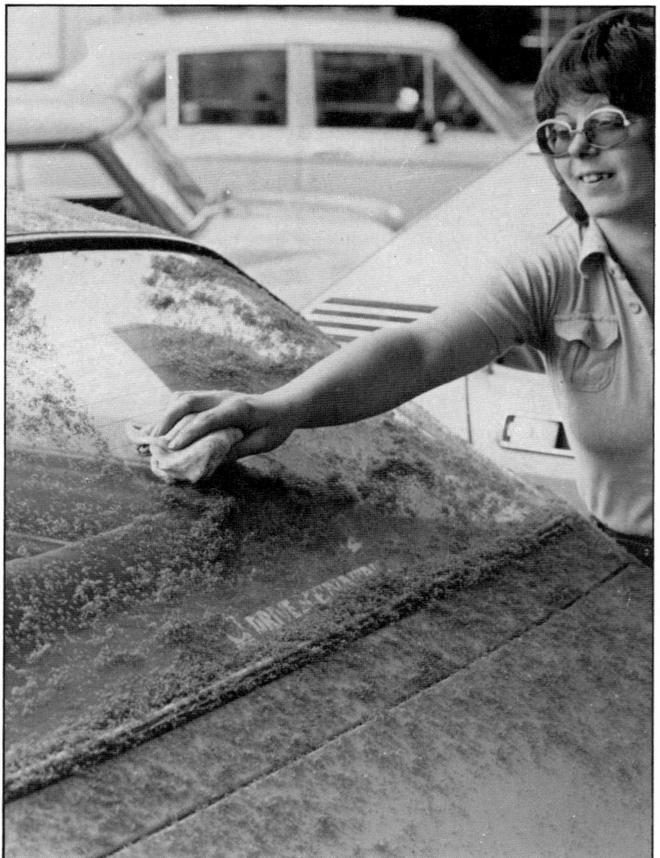

The summer of 1979 saw a vast explosion in the aphid population in parts of western Europe. Masses of these tiny planktonic creatures were deposited by the wind over much of southern England.

are constantly moving on to new territories have no necessity to fly in a precise direction and do not compensate for the apparent motion of the sun, moon and stars across the sky.

Animals living within a familiar area must allow for the sun's movements. If a bird flies from its nest to a feeding site in the morning by heading directly towards the sun, it cannot return to its nest in the afternoon simply by flying away from the sun; it must compensate for the sun's movement. The situation is highly critical for long-distance migrants, the slightest error in orientation will cause a bird to miss its target by several kilometres. All animals living within a familiar area have to learn how to compensate for the sun's movements, none is actually born with the ability. Even so, under the simulated conditions of a planetarium it has been found that pigeons find it easier to learn compass direction from an artificial sun moving across an artificial sky than they do from a fixed artificial sun, implying that the birds are at least instinctively predisposed to a moving sun.

Aids to migration

Birds back up compass information wherever possible by learning which rivers, coastlines, and ranges of hills or mountains run parallel to their preferred direction. These leading lines, as they are called, enable the bird to correct for any displacement from their track by cross winds.

As birds can detect air temperature, wind speed and direction, and are also sensitive to atmospheric pressure, they are, to some extent able to anticipate the weather conditions further along their migration track. Adults and young birds differ in the use they make of wind. Adults know where they are going and will wait for a tail wind to help them on their way. Young, exploratory birds, however, will change their course according to the prevailing winds, taking the opportunity to explore in

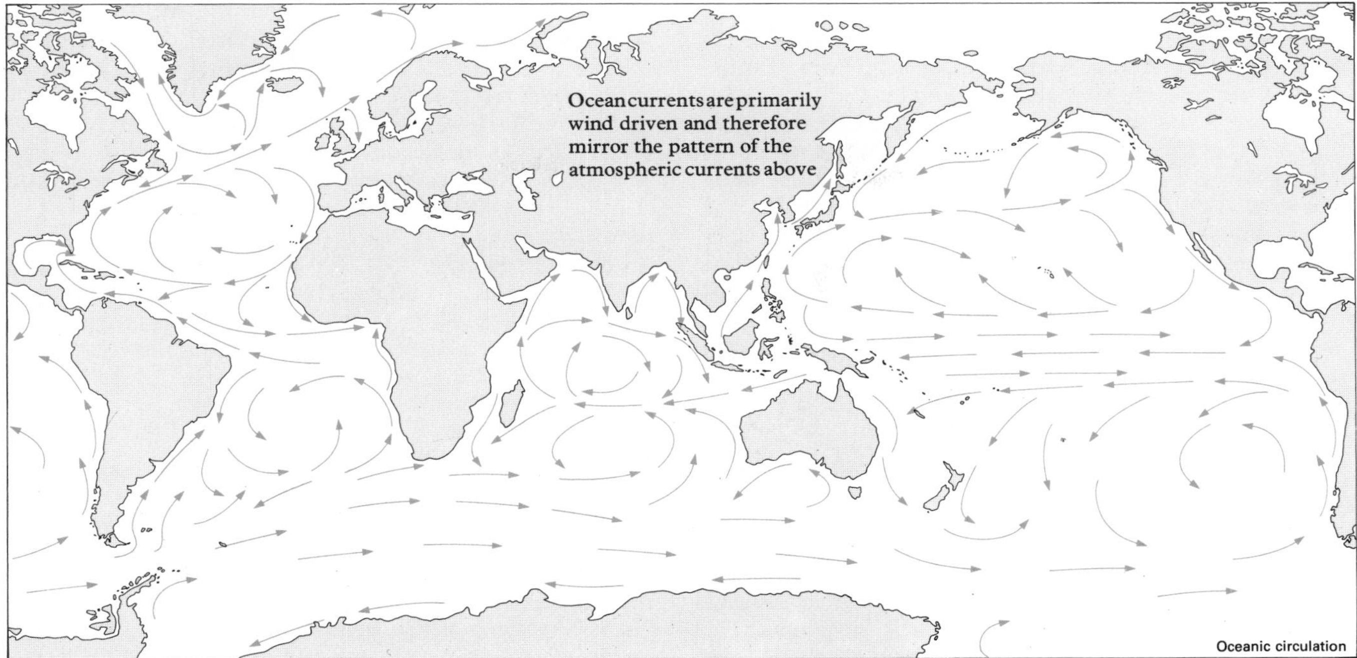

Ocean currents are primarily wind driven and therefore mirror the pattern of the atmospheric currents above

the direction they are blowing. It is for this reason that young birds sometimes appear hundreds or even thousands of kilometres beyond their normal range. The evidence we have suggests that these vagrants are not lost but are long-distance explorers, and will return eventually to their normal range.

In parts of the world where winds and ocean currents are relatively constant in direction, many birds and aquatic animals exploit the prevailing pattern of atmospheric and oceanic circulation to travel with an economy of effort over long sections of their migration circuits. This is not to say that if during exploration the young animals find a useful site which can only be reached by migrating across or against the current, that they will ignore it. Wind and water currents are only exploited when they take the animal where it wants to go, they do not determine the migration pattern.

For insects with preferred compass directions, such as tropical butterflies and locusts, speed is all-important. They will often rise high in the air to take advantage of a wind blowing in their preferred direction. When the wind is against them, however, they will drop down low close to the ground, where it is weaker.

Some insects, for example aphids and small beetles, are such weak fliers that they are unable to prevent themselves being blown downwind whenever they take to the air. These insects have no preferred direction and normally migrate by flight only once in their lifetime. They are often referred to as aerial plankton and may be carried by the wind to a height of several kilometres.

Some aerial plankton have no wings. Small, hairy caterpillars and spiders, suspended from lengths of gossamer, are found high in the air. Like airborne seeds and spores they rely on the wind to carry them to new sites, where they will have a better chance of reproducing successfully. These movements may be classed as removal migrations and are similar to those made by a whole range of water-borne plants and animals that are carried downstream in rivers and streams and to those of the real plankton found in the sea and large lakes.

Stimuli, benefits and cost

The reason an animal has for migrating is the same whether it lives in a familiar area or is always on the move; whether it can control its journey or is at the mercy of wind or water currents. When it abandons its present site it has learned, or knows instinctively, that its requirements can be found in greater abundance, or

When the percentage of prairie dogs, *Cynomys ludovicianus*, migrating each month is graphed together with the cost of migration, it is found that most migration occurs when the cost is least.

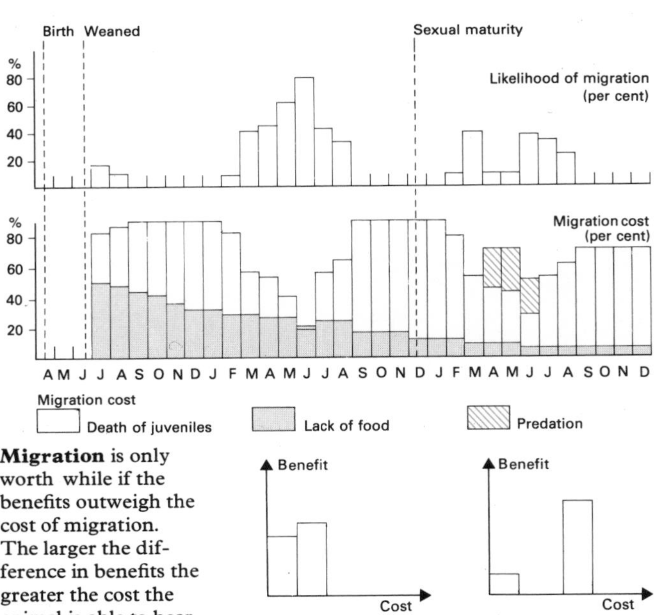

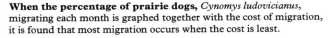

Migration is only worth while if the benefits outweigh the cost of migration. The larger the difference in benefits the greater the cost the animal is able to bear.

more easily, elsewhere. Food may be in short supply because of overcrowding; the site may be only suitable for one activity, such as feeding, and the animal must of necessity migrate to breed and find rest.

In a sense the stimuli to migrate and the benefits of migration are the opposite sides of the same coin; an animal migrating to avoid poor conditions is at the same time searching for better ones elsewhere. However, the gains cannot be enjoyed without paying the cost. Migration takes time, uses energy, and is dangerous. Before migrating, all animals, whether consciously or instinctively, weigh up the costs against the benefits and on that basis decide upon which route to take and when to leave. On average animals make the right decisions, for otherwise migration behaviour would not have evolved.

Tracking and trapping

The techniques used to study migration fall broadly into two categories, analysis of sightings and marking/release-capture. In analysis of sightings the movements of individual animals are deduced from the movements of large groups. This method is frequently used in the study of seasonally migrant birds. When a particular species, like the barn swallow, appears in the Northern Hemisphere during summer, is then seen to pass overhead in certain tropical regions in spring and autumn, and appears in the Southern Hemisphere during the northern winter, it seems likely that all individuals of the species migrate between northern breeding grounds and southern wintering grounds. The same technique has been applied to whale migration.

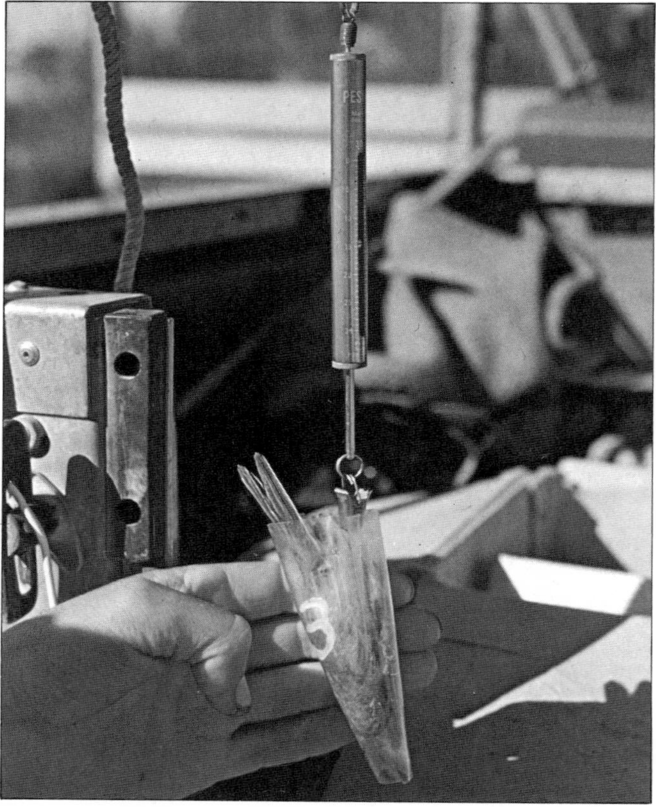

Migrant birds are often weighed as part of a ringing programme. After migration, birds recover remarkably quickly from their exertions. Experiments with wrynecks, *Jynx torquilla*, in Jordan showed that they could increase in weight by twenty-five per cent in three or four days.

The method is less successful when used to study inconspicuous species such as the tree bats, *Lasiurus* spp., of North America. As they are difficult to observe and there is a possibility that some may hibernate in winter; their disappearance is no proof of migration.

Analysis of sightings has provided our picture of aphid migration. At certain times aphids disappear from their host plants. They are caught in suction traps and in "plankton" nets suspended from aircraft and later reappear on other host plants. It is reasonable to assume from these sightings that aphids migrate aerially from one host to another even though no aphid has ever been followed over its entire journey.

Marking/release-capture is a much more thorough method of examining animal movements. As individual animals are marked before release and can be identified when subsequently caught, there is absolute proof that the animals really do travel the distances supposed. Not until an individual had been marked in the Great Lakes region of Canada and recovered in Mexico was the true extent of the monarch butterfly's journey proved beyond doubt.

Tagging the migrants

There are a great many ingenious methods of marking animals. The best known are probably those used to mark birds and bats by placing rings and bands on their legs and wings. The rings and bands are marked with a unique number and an address to which the find should be reported. Large mammals are sometimes marked in a similar way by fitting tags to their ears. Small mammals, such as mice, are marked by a system of toe clipping, which provides a unique identification within a particular experimental area. Snakes, lizards and turtles can be marked by clipping the tips of their scales, and large insects, such as the monarch butterfly, are usually tagged with discs or by clipping small notches out of the wings.

Colour ringing and tagging can be used to mark animal groups. In one famous experiment in Florida, large numbers of great southern white butterflies, *Ascia monuste*, were sprayed with red dye as they fed by the roadside, enabling observers on the ground to plot their migration along the Florida peninsula. Animals such as badgers can be tracked by mixing small coloured plastic beads with an attractive bait like honey or peanuts and then examining the badgers' faeces. By feeding different social groups different coloured beads it is possible to see how far they travel and how much interchange there is between neighbouring groups.

Radio and radar tracking

Most marking methods provide only two points in an animal's track, the point of release and the point of recapture. In recent years, however, there has been a tremendous increase in the use and sophistication of radio-tracking. Normally an individual is fitted with a radio-transmitter which gives out a unique signal that can be picked up by a receiver. The receiver may be

Before the development of sophisticated tracking methods, most information about migration patterns was collected by analysis of sightings. As many seasonally migrant birds, such as the snow goose, *Anser caerulescens*, travel in large flocks, most of the early data refers to species such as this. Flocks of snow geese may number as many as 60,000 during the spring and autumn migrations.

TRACKING BY RADIO AND RADAR

The development of radio and radar has revolutionized the study of migration and, in particular, the study of bird migration. The suitability of radar as a tool for examining bird migration was realized during the Second World War. Operators using high-powered equipment noticed that, even in clear air conditions, their radar was subject to a large amount of interference from a host of point sources. After careful investigation these "angels" as they were dubbed were found to be birds.

The FPS-16 radar at Wallops Island, Virginia, can track a bird for distances up to sixteen kilometres (10 miles).

The breakthrough in radio tracking occurred with the development of the transistor, enabling transmitters to be built compact enough to be carried by a small animal. Two or more separate receivers are needed to establish an animal's location.

THE RANGE OF LIFETIME TRACKS

The different forms of lifetime track can be grouped according to the number of times an animal migrates between separate feeding and breeding sites and the point on the track that breeding occurs. In (A) reproduction occurs evenly along the track. In (B) reproduction is concentrated towards the latter end. The animals in type (C) remain longer at each suitable site and therefore visit fewer sites during their life. Animals with type (D) tracks are typically aquatic invertebrates that have a short free-swimming phase before becoming fixed to one spot as adults. In (E) the organism migrates once only from its birthplace to a new site, where it lives and dies. Track types (F) and (G) belong to animals that live within familiar areas. They do not make a series of straight-line migrations between successive feeding and breeding sites, but migrate repeatedly between sites lying within the familiar area. The difference between (F) and (G) depends on whether or not the animal migrates away from its birthplace to form its familiar area. This can vary from one individual to another and does not depend on the species.

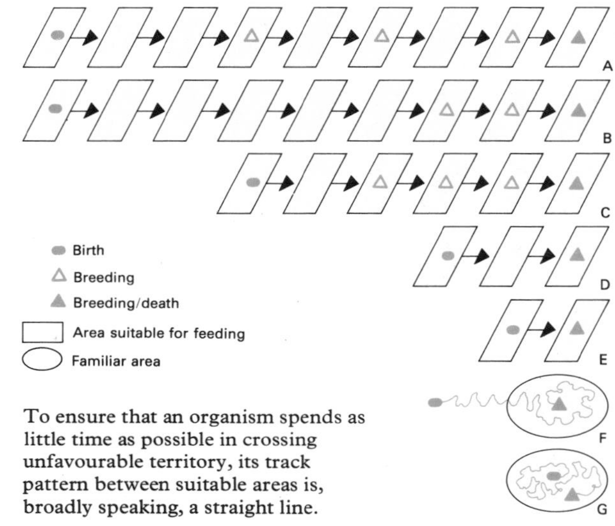

To ensure that an organism spends as little time as possible in crossing unfavourable territory, its track pattern between suitable areas is, broadly speaking, a straight line.

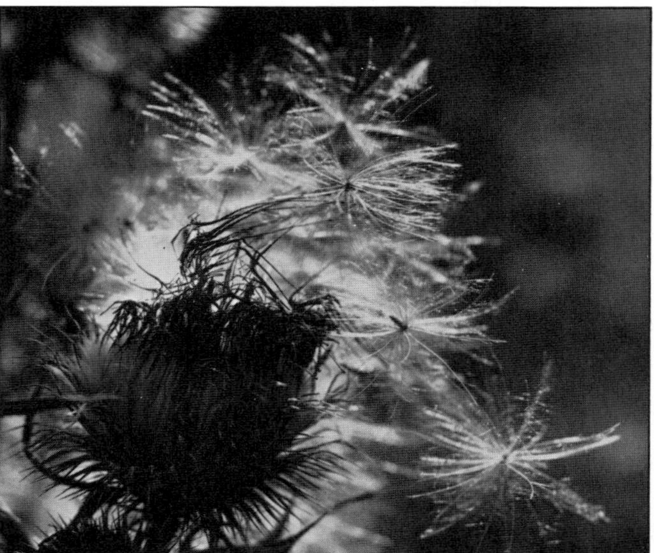

The seeds of the spear-head thistle, *Cirsium vulgare*, are carried by the wind on their single episode of migration, before being deposited where they will grow into mature plants.

either hand-held or fixed. Several receivers strategically placed enable the animal to be tracked automatically and continuously. Animals as diverse as snails and polar bears have been tracked this way. Radio-tracking has the advantage that it allows an individual to be followed along its entire track.

Over the past few years radar has been increasingly used to study bird migration and recently it has also been applied to insects. Conventional radar is only able to pick up large numbers of birds and insects. However, the development of tracking radar, which uses a pencil beam, allows a fix to be made on an individual, which can then be followed over a distance of several kilometres. Using this technique to track insects it is sometimes possible, by examining the wingbeat characteristics, to identify the species and even the sex of the subject on the radar screen. Sonar is less precise than radar, but has been used successfully to follow animals under water.

Despite the array of available techniques we are still a long way from being able to follow a single individual throughout its entire life. Nevertheless, we now have a reasonably clear picture of the range of lifetime tracks displayed by plants and animals.

Diversity of lifetime tracks

Plants have the simplest of all lifetime tracks, when as a seed or spore they are shed by the parent plant, they have one brief phase of removal migration before taking root and beginning to grow.

Superficially, many invertebrates have a similar pattern. The larvae of barnacles are carried around by sea water for a period of time before being deposited on the shore, never to move again. There is, however, a difference. By making daily vertical migrations the barnacle larvae are able to vary their depth in the water to find the best level for feeding and growing. Furthermore, when the young larvae arrive at the shore they are actually capable of selecting the best place to settle, something a plant cannot do.

Many invertebrates spend their entire adult life in removal migration from one temporary familiar area to another. In many cases removal migration results in animals becoming scattered or dispersed. This happens when winged king and queen ants or termites fly away from the parent colony in search of a new site. In other cases removal migration leads to convergence, as seen when adult ladybirds head towards the same mountain or hillside to spend the summer or winter. The term dispersal is often used to mean the same as removal migration, but unless we are certain that the animals are actually scattering and by migrating are intending to disperse, it would be more appropriate always to use the term removal migration.

Another group of invertebrates, including winged ants and aphids, begin life with a brief phase of removal migration followed by a period searching for a place to settle. When they have selected a site, many seem to have a sense of location and build up a familiar area by exploration. After a planktonic larval phase similar to the barnacle, many crabs and lobsters acquire large familiar areas containing winter and summer, breeding and feeding home ranges that are quite as complex as those of any vertebrate. Some invertebrates such as snails or the honey bee, *Apis melifera*, probably start to build up a familiar area from the moment they hatch, without an initial burst of removal migration.

Among invertebrates we find the entire range of lifetime tracks, from those scarcely different from that of a plant to those similar to that of a vertebrate. Vertebrate lifetime tracks are much less varied. All live within a familiar area and all seem to build up their familiar area more or less from the moment of birth. Removal migrations do occur, but normally only under special circumstances, as in the case of lemmings.

Even so, within the familiar area the range of lifetime tracks is enormous and varies considerably within each vertebrate group. The lifetime tracks of fish, for instance, range from the small-scale movements of those living on coral reefs or in small ponds to the huge migration circuits made by salmon and tuna. Amphibians and reptiles, on the whole, travel only short distances within a small territory or between separate sites on land and in water. Sea turtles, however, make huge migration circuits comparable with those of oceanic fish.

Birds show every variation from the house sparrow, visiting places no further than a few kilometres apart, to the barn swallow, *Hirundo rustica*, or arctic tern, *Sterna paradisea*, that migrate thousands of kilometres.

The lifetime tracks of mammals are equally diverse and vary even within a single species, as typified by the caribou. Looking at ourselves, the lifetime tracks of man range from the daily to-and-fro commuting of the city dweller to the nomadic wanderings of the Bedouin.

The lifetime track lies at the heart of migratory behaviour and their variety is the factor that makes the subject fascinating. The contrast and similarity existing within animal and plant groups is striking and sometimes surprising, and sheds light on the whole field of migration.

The arctic tern, *Sterna paradisea*, is probably the most extreme example of a seasonally migrant bird. Most terns travel immense distances from their breeding grounds in northern latitudes to winter in the tropics. The arctic tern, however, travels virtually twice this distance, spending six months of the year in the Antarctic; a yearly round trip of about 40,000 kilometres (25,000 miles).

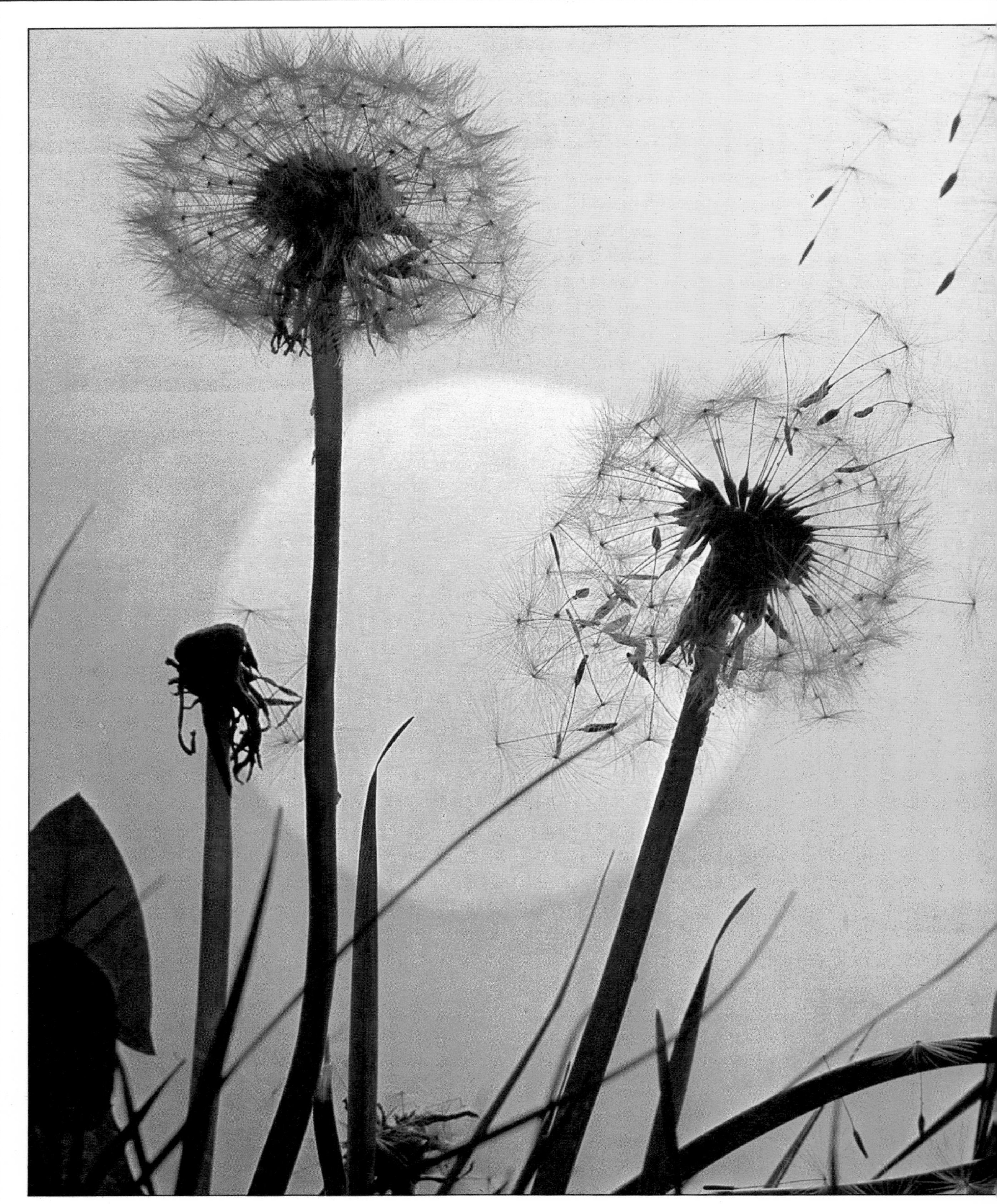

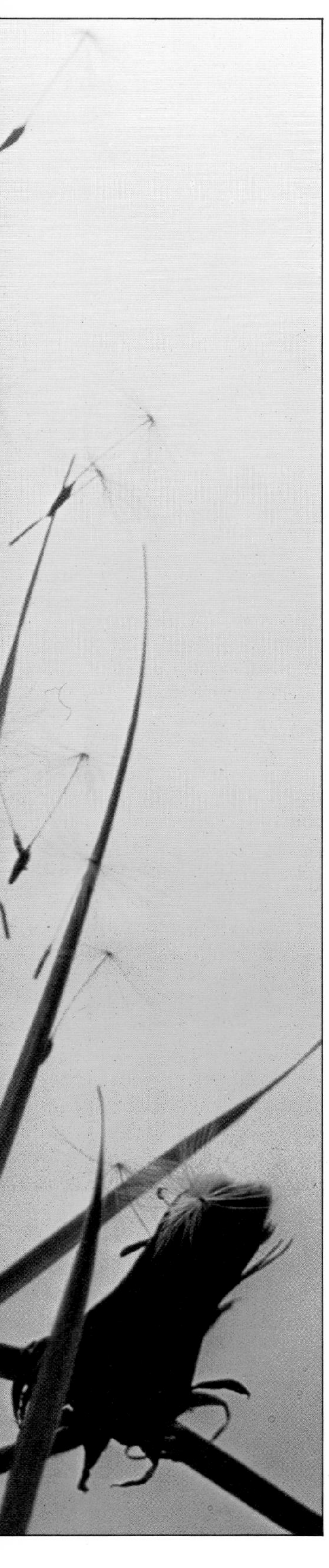

Plants

Plants have the simplest of all lifetime tracks. As a spore or seed, they have a usually brief period of travel. This is followed by a period when they remain rooted in the ground or attached to some other substratum such as a rock or perhaps another plant. Only a few fully-formed plants move from their home, as when tumbleweeds roll across deserts. The major exception to this rule of immobility is the myriad minute plants that live suspended in the fresh and sea waters of the world. These, the phytoplankton, are forever on the move with the water currents.

During their period of travel the majority of plants migrate with the wind and water currents or exploit animals for transportation of their spores or seeds; their movements invariably involve passive displacement. The function of their migration is, by using mechanisms that are the products of millennia of evolution, to escape from their birthplace and land in a place suitable for germination and growth. The distances involved range from only a few metres to many thousands of kilometres and depend on the size of the spore or seed and the method of displacement.

When many spores or seeds are produced by a single plant one consequence of their displacement is that they disperse. But whether dispersal is a function or an unavoidable consequence of migration can rarely be determined. Furthermore, a single spore or seed cannot disperse (except by exploding). For these reasons it is best to refer to the mechanism of all plant movement as displacement.

Parachute-like seeds being blown from a dandelion "blow ball" – wind displacement such as this is the major mechanism of migration of plants which invade and rapidly colonize newly cleared ground.

WANTED

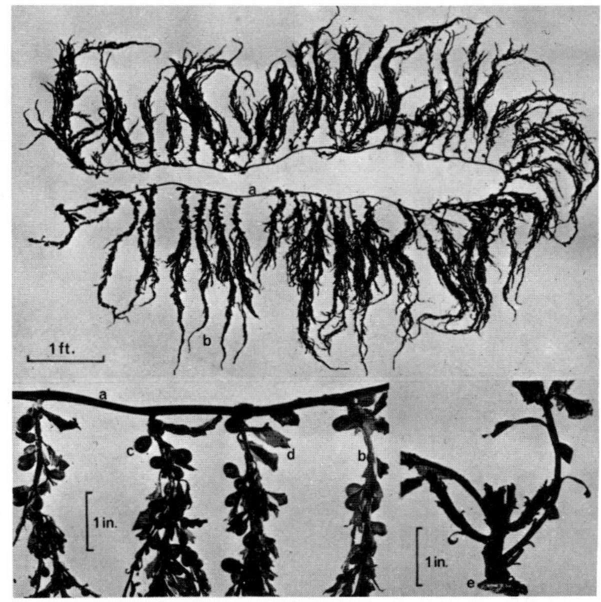

JAPANESE SEAWEED *SARGASSUM MUTICUM* IS AN UNDESIRABLE ALIEN ON BRITISH SHORES. IT CAN BE RECOGNISED BY THE LONG, ROUND MAIN AXIS (a) AND LATERALS (b), WHICH HANG LIKE WASHING FROM A LINE. LATERAL BRANCHES SUPPORT SMALL AIR BLADDERS (c) AND LEAF-LIKE STRUCTURES (d). IF FOUND REMOVE THE ENTIRE PLANT INCLUDING ATTACHING HOLDFAST (e), AND DESTROY WELL AWAY FROM THE SEA-SHORE. URGENT HELP IS REQUIRED WITH THE ERADICATION OF THIS SEAWEED. NEW RECORDS FOR ATTACHED PLANTS SHOULD BE SENT TO ONE OF THE FOLLOWING WHO CAN HELP WITH THE IDENTIFICATION OF *SARGASSUM*.

In the mid-1970s in coastal waters of southern England the spread of japweed, *Sargassum muticum*, occurred at such an alarming rate that the authorities were moved to introduce control measures. Posters describing the appearance, likely habitats and methods of reproduction of the seaweed were distributed in the hope that along the length of the coast people would destroy these plants before they spread further.

Mosses and liverworts commonly reproduce asexually by flattened groups of cells, or gemmae, breaking away from the parent plant and growing into new plants. The gemma cups of the liverwort *Marchantia polymorpha* are shown, below. Raindrops splashing on these cups help further to displace individual gemma.

Migration of algae and aquatic fungi

Water currents are essential for the migration of many of the non-flowering plants, notably freshwater and marine algae such as seaweeds and water moulds, stoneworts, liverworts and mosses. This reflects the aquatic beginnings of the plant kingdom.

The simplest way for seaweeds to migrate is by the fragmentation of parts of the adult plant, which are then carried away by water currents. This is the basis of the rapid spread in British waters of japweed, *Sargassum muticum*, which originates from the Pacific and may have been introduced to Britain accidentally along with Japanese oysters. It bears long, brittle, brown fronds, portions of which are kept buoyant at the water surface by means of tiny air bladders. The fronds are easily broken by the movement among them of waves and animals, including humans; they also get caught up in boat propellers, which accelerates their displacement from the parent plant. Since its first appearance in the Solent in 1973, japweed has spread throughout the coastal waters of much of southern England. It is now also present in the waters of northern France, Belgium and the Netherlands.

Similarly the fragmentation of *Spirogyra*, a filamentous freshwater alga, helps its spread within ponds and reservoirs. Migration of *Spirogyra* from one body of water to another, however, is effected only by the small spores produced by a form of sexual reproduction known as conjugation. This takes place in midsummer, when each of the cells of two adjacent filaments develop swellings which meet and fuse to form a tube, through which the contents of the cells of one filament pass to the corresponding cells in the neighbouring filament. After the contents of each pair of cells are combined, a thick-walled spore is formed. As the "mother" filament breaks down, the individual spores are released. They are displaced primarily by water, but they can also be transported by wind or by being trapped in the feet of water birds. Migration in this manner is responsible for the sudden appearance of blooms of *Spirogyra* in artificial ponds and water pools.

Seaweeds reproduce sexually by forming sperm- and egg-like cells which fuse and, by subsequent division and multiplication, give rise to a new plant. The sexual reproductive bodies of these plants, which take the form of thickened parts of the fronds, can be most easily seen on such species as bladder wrack, *Fucus vesiculosus*, and egg wrack, *Ascophyllum nodosum*, which inhabit the intertidal zone of rocky shore lines. Inside each of the frond swellings thousands of sex cells develop. At low tide, as the exposed fronds dry out, the sex cells become squeezed out on to the frond surface. As the tide flows up the shore, the water washes the cells from the fronds and mixes them together. Sperm fuse with eggs to produce fertilized ova which, since they are scattered by the motion of the waves, act as important agents for migration.

Aquatic algae can also reproduce asexually. They do so by forming spores of various kinds, the majority of which are readily displaced by water currents. For example, *Chlamydomonas* spp., which are freshwater, motile, single-celled algae, reproduce in normal conditions by growing to a certain size then dividing to form two, four or eight motile spores. So rapid is this method of reproduction that a single *Chlamydomonas* can give rise to as many as two million individuals in only a week, so "turning the water green". In adverse conditions, however, species such as *C. nivalis*, the cause of "red snow", lose their motility and form thick-walled resting spores. When favourable conditions return, these give rise to one or two normal motile cells. Green and brown seaweeds also produce motile spores, while many red seaweeds produce spores that are non-motile and which are displaced not only by water but also by wind.

Among aquatic fungi there is a group of moulds, the Saprolegniales, which live on damaged fish and any submerged dead animals. The moulds characteristically develop into white tufts, which, when viewed with a hand lens or microscope, can be seen to comprise individual filaments that are swollen at their free ends. The swollen tips are reproductive structures which produce asexually many tiny free-swimming spores. These are released into the water and are displaced by the currents. On contact with a suitable food source, the spores germinate and grow into new fungi.

Saprolegniales also migrate by means of water-borne spores produced by sexual reproduction involving male and female sex cells that are released into the water in a manner similar to that of seaweeds. This is also the migration method of the few completely aquatic species of mosses and liverworts. The most important stage of the life cycle for migration in stoneworts – green plants that grow completely submerged in fresh or slightly brackish water – is the sexual spore.

Seeds and fruits displaced by water

In the migration of flowering plants, water plays a less important role. However, as a means of displacement many seashore plants have evolved seeds which float on water, are protected from salt water by an impermeable coat and which germinate only on coming to rest on a warm, sandy shore. One such plant, the beach morning glory, *Ipomoea pes-caprae*, which grows in a continuous belt along the high-tide line, has achieved a widespread pan-tropical distribution by this method. Found in similar habitats is the well-known coconut palm, *Cocos nucifera*. This produces huge nuts covered with a fibrous husk, which helps both to protect the nut, which is really a giant seed, and to buoy it up in sea water. But even if a coconut survives a long immersion in the sea, its chances of being washed up on a shore in a position where it can germinate and grow successfully are extremely slight. Yet the coconut palm has also spread almost throughout the tropics.

While ocean currents clearly help to accelerate the migration of a plant species from one island or continent to another, they can, in specific circumstances, also prevent colonization from taking place. This seems to have been the case with the coconut palm on Hawaii. For seeds to travel across the Pacific to the Hawaiian archipelago they would have to cross three currents – the north and south equatorial currents flowing to the west, and in between the counter-current running to the east. There is no positive proof, but it seems probable that the coconut palm was brought to Hawaii by the Polynesians rather than by water currents.

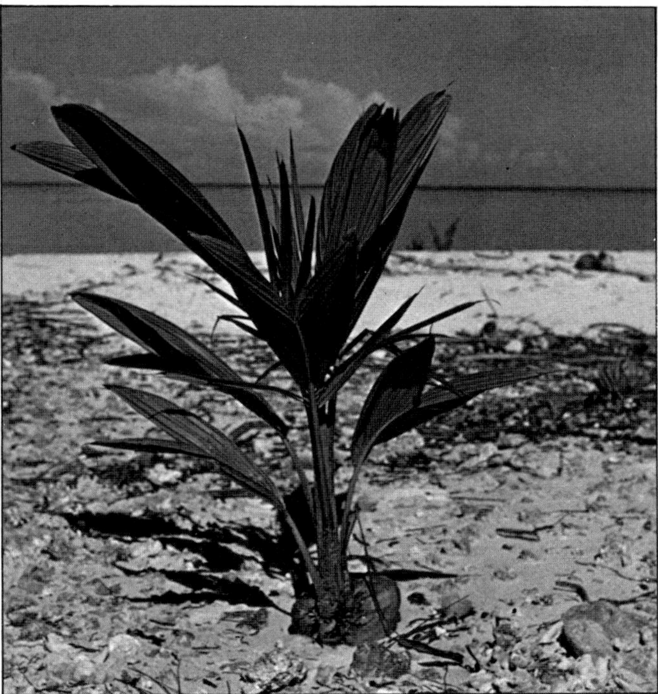

Colonizing a tropical beach is a coconut palm, *Cocos nucifera*. Originating in southeastern Asia, this palm has been displaced widely and is now one of the world's most important crop trees.

The currents in the Pacific Ocean may also be responsible for the limited distribution of the coco-de-mer palm, *Lodoicea maldivica*. This produces curious bilobed nuts which contain the largest seed of any living plant, weighing between thirteen and eighteen kilograms (30 and 40 pounds). These nuts, which have a remarkable resemblance to the lower half of the female human torso, were highly prized as fertility symbols in the Maldives, India and Indonesia, where they occasionally became washed ashore. No one knew where the nuts originated, and it was believed they were the fruits of large submarine trees – hence their name today. It was in 1768 that their true origin was found. In that year, a French botanist, Pierre Sonnerat, saw the coco-de-mer nuts growing on palms on the island of Praslin in the Seychelles. To this day, Praslin is the only place in the world where the coco-de-mer palms occur naturally.

Plants that have seeds or fruits which do not naturally float may be transported across oceans by rafting on natural vegetation mats. Such mats often take the form of huge rafts of reeds or water hyacinth, *Eichhornia crassipes*, which are occasionally discharged from tropical rivers in spate. In 1975, in the Caribbean, the US Navy followed the drift of just such a floating island, which was carrying six young palm trees. The raft remained afloat for nearly three weeks.

Special adaptations to displacement by water

It is estimated that of the seeds and fruits produced by aquatic and marshland plants of the British Isles, sixty per cent sink either immediately or within a week, twenty-five per cent float for up to a month, and fifteen per cent float for more than six months. But for successful displacement of a plant by water, whether freshwater or seawater, it is essential not only that the seeds or fruits are buoyant for a time, but also that they remain viable if they should sink. The white water lily, *Nymphaea alba*, produces berries which ripen under water. They then split to release a mass of seeds. Being rendered buoyant by an outer coat filled with air bubbles, the seeds float to the surface, where they become scattered. As the air bubbles disappear, the seeds sink to the bottom of the pond or stream. Here, after a dormant period, they germinate. As the new plants develop, they rise to the surface.

A more novel adaptation has evolved in the frogbit plant, *Hydrocharis morsus-ranae*. This is a freshwater plant with small rounded leaves which resemble those of the water lily. In northern temperate regions the frogbit rarely produces seeds. Instead it develops at the ends of stolons (trailing branches which tend to take root), overwintering buds, or turions, which serve both as a means of surviving the cold weather and of displacement by water. When fully formed in autumn, the turions break off, become scattered and then sink to the bottom of the pond. There they remain quite dormant until the following spring. Then, as the embryo plant begins to use up the food reserves, the turions become lighter and float to the surface. Within a few days the first leaves of the new plant begin to form.

Displacement by wind

Localized air currents, as well as large-scale updraughts, are important agents aiding the migration of plants, particularly those that produce extremely fine spores or seeds. Evidence of this came, indirectly, from an experiment in which nets were set up on Barbados, in the Caribbean, in the hope of catching dust generated by the break-up of meteorites falling through the earth's atmosphere. Instead of trapping cosmic dust, scientists found fine dust particles with a mineral content which proved they had originated in the Sahara Desert. More conclusive proof of wind displacement of spores and seeds has come from experiments in which mechanical traps were exposed from aeroplanes flying at different altitudes. The traps contained glass microscope slides smeared with Vaseline so as to catch any floating particles. Among the specimens that were collected were the spores of various fungi and the glumes of grasses, some of which were caught at altitudes of more than 5000 metres (16,400 feet).

A water droplet landing on top of an earth star fungus, *Geastrum triplex*, displaces many millions of air-borne spores, each of which measures only 0.0001 centimetre (0.00004 in) in diameter.

Terrestrial algae, fungi, mosses and ferns all produce fine dust-like spores, which enable them to achieve the highest degree of circumglobal distribution among all plants. In fact, there are always spores of these plants present in the air. This is why, when making jam, it is so essential to seal the pots immediately they are filled. If the jam is allowed to cool first, fungal spores will inevitably land on it, germinate and grow. Indeed, all fungi produce extremely large numbers of microscopic spores. For example, it has been estimated that a ten-centimetre (4-inch) edible mushroom produces about 16,000 million spores and these are discharged at a rate of more than 100 million an hour over a period of five or six days. The giant puff ball, *Langermannia gigantea*, produces even more spores – as many as seven million million. These are contained in a sac which, when the fungus matures, opens at the top. The spores are displaced by raindrops splashing on the sac, by wind blowing across its top and also by small foraging mammals crawling over and knocking the puff ball.

Lichens, which are plants formed by a close association of a green alga with a fungus, migrate either as spores produced by the fungal partner or as mini-packets of algal cells and fungal threads, known as soredia, which form on the surface of the plant. Both spores and soredia are wind-displaced, although rain can also wash them off the parent plant. It is the migration of soredia that is believed to be responsible for colonization by lichen of newly formed volcanic lava flows, such as those on the island of Réunion in the Indian Ocean. The first colonizer of these flows is in fact the same species of lichen as occurs on the lava flows of Hawaii, several thousand kilometres away.

The wind-borne spores of mosses and ferns

The minute spores of mosses are formed in capsules which are set on stalks projecting up from the surface of the plants. Each capsule is topped by a lid which drops off as the capsule ripens. But surrounding the opening of the capsule are one or two rings of cells which function like jaws to control the release of the spores. It is beneficial to a plant to shed its spores only in dry weather, for when the atmosphere is humid the spores would tend to clump together and to fall to the ground close to the parent plant. The cells around the rim of the opening are water-sensitive so that they swell in a damp atmosphere, sealing the opening. As conditions become drier, the cells contract and part, and the spores are shot out

The dust-like spores of plants ranging from fungi to orchids are carried great distances by winds. Where conditions are ideal the spores germinate and rapidly grow. On the island of Maui in the South Pacific an early colonizer of the rim of the 3300-metre (10,000-ft) high volcano Haleakala was the flowering plant kupaoa, *Railliardia meniziesii*; below.

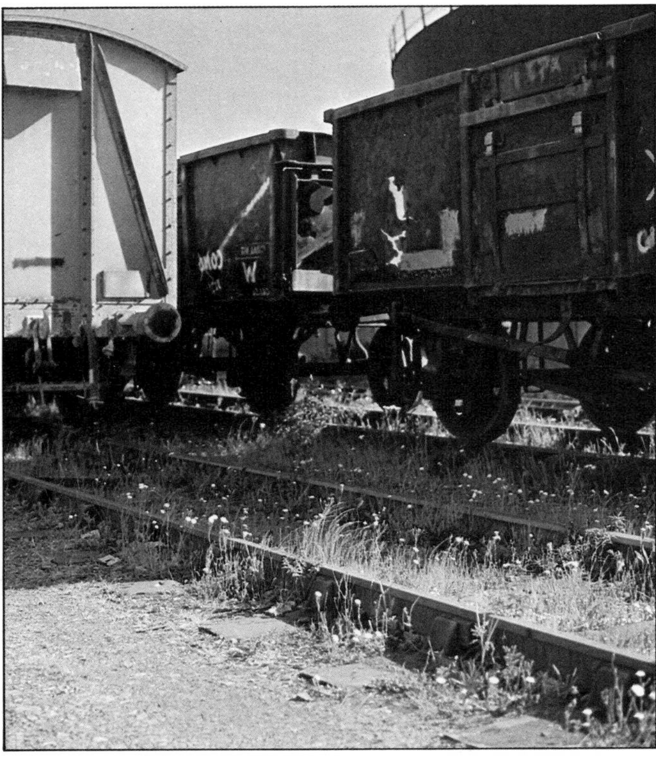

Development of waste ground has led to the near extinction of many weeds. But seeds from vestiges found in derelict areas such as railway sidings have the potential for rapidly colonizing suitable new habitats.

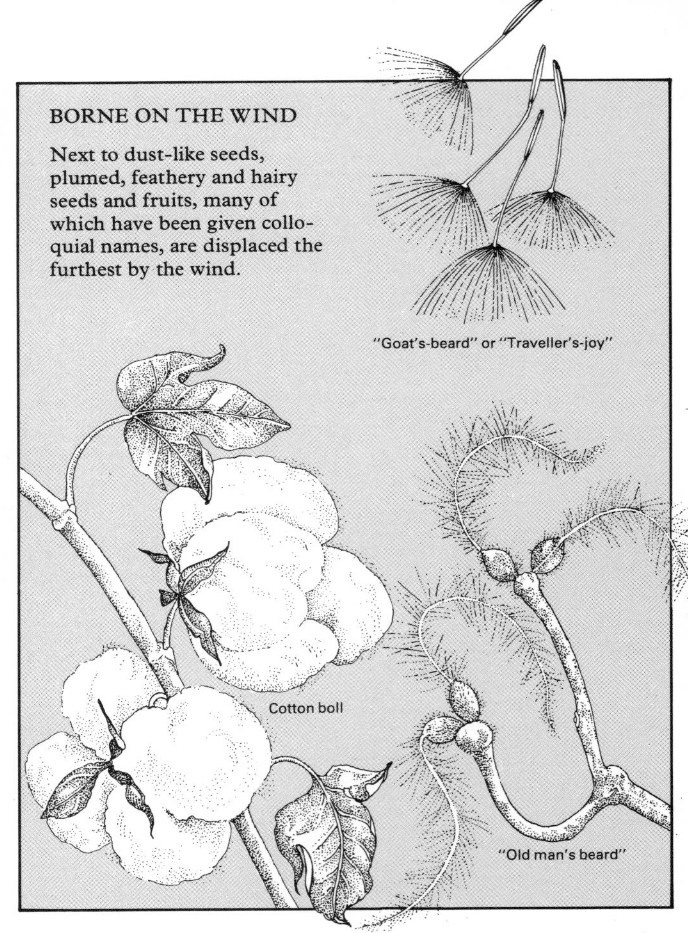

BORNE ON THE WIND

Next to dust-like seeds, plumed, feathery and hairy seeds and fruits, many of which have been given colloquial names, are displaced the furthest by the wind.

of the capsule as it is blown in the wind. A ripe moss capsule under these conditions, if shaken into the hand, can be seen to release its spores as a fine brown powder.

Ferns produce spores from sacs called sporangia, which, like the capsules of moss plants, are able to control the release of the spores to suit the prevailing conditions. The sporangia are aggregated in clusters known as sori which are positioned on the backs or along the margins of the fronds and are clearly visible as brown dots or lines. It has been found that the number of spores produced by sporangia varies from thirty or less to more than 15,000, depending on the species of fern, but that the degree of success of a fern's migration bears little or no relation to the output of spores. This may be due to variations in the size, and hence distance of displacement, of the spores, but also to differences in their viability. In general, fern spores are larger than those of fungi and mosses, which tends to make them less able to migrate long distances and to colonize new habitats. For example, on the Hawaiian Islands the fern flora comprises 168 species. Of these, 119 are endemic and grow nowhere else in the world. However, this may simply be a reflection of the relatively calm weather system that has existed in the Pacific area in recent times, for fern spores can be displaced over great distances. Evidence for this argument is based on the fact that of the 168 Hawaiian species, 135 are probably original immigrant colonizing species that must have arrived on the islands as wind-borne spores. Provided that the size of the fern spores has remained constant, this could only have taken place when the world weather system was more turbulent. It is thought that this may have occurred during a major glaciation period, when meteorologists believe strong winds were considerably more prevalent.

Feathery and hairy seeds and fruits

Flowering plants have evolved a variety of winged, hairy and plumed seeds and fruits to improve wind-displacement. Many so-called weed species, for example, are able to rapidly invade newly cleared ground by producing masses of tiny seeds that resemble parachutes. These plants are opportunists, and by peppering the locality with their tiny seeds they increase the chances of at least one of their progeny finding a suitable piece of ground on which to grow.

A century ago, rosebay willowherb, *Epilobium angustifolium*, was a local plant scattered throughout Britain. In the London blitz during the Second World War, many of the bombed areas were invaded by its light feathery seeds. Because of its liking for burnt ground, it soon became known as fireweed. Recurring fires, caused not only by bombing but also by the spontaneous ignition of vegetation on waste land during hot summers, contributed to the phenomenal spread of this plant. Further migrations occurred during the prolonged hot summer of 1976, when forest and heathland fires were a particular feature of southern Britain. Two years later, in the summer of 1978, these areas were carpeted with the bright pink fireweed spikes, which were observed subsequently to produce clouds of seeds. Fireweed has also spread rapidly in the USA wherever fire has been used for forest clearance; around Seattle it is called fireweed honey. In Sweden they go one better, calling it Himmelgrass, or herb of heaven.

Coltsfoot, *Tussilago farfara*, and Oxford ragwort, *Senecio squalidus*, are weeds that also produce copious seeds and habitually colonize waste ground. The spread in Britain of the Oxford ragwort is particularly interesting. This plant was introduced from Sicily to the Oxford Botanic Garden, where it became established on the walls of the garden in 1794. There the population remained confined until the development of the railways in the early 1800s. As its hairy seeds were wafted by the wind into railway carriages and then floated out again, the plant rapidly spread, its early distribution following the layout of the railway network of that time. It has since become a common plant of waste ground, roadsides and similar places in much of England, Wales and southern Scotland.

Other plants which migrate by means of feathery or hairy seeds or fruits are *Clematis* spp., poplars, sallows, planes, thistles and dandelions. It is the seeds of the dandelion, *Taraxacum officinale*, that are perhaps the most well known. Seeding dandelion heads are known as blow balls, and one head is often called a clock, since, according to folklore, it would tell the time from the number of puffs required to blow off the parachute-like seeds. In commercial terms the most important hairy seeds are those of kapok, *Bombax ceiba*, and cotton plants, *Gossypium* spp. The former produce capsules containing smooth seeds with long fibres, which are the source of the kapok used for stuffing cushions and mattresses. In the case of cotton plants, after the petals of the flowers die, the seed pods, or bolls, form. At first green, these turn to brown as they ripen, and each splits into three portions to reveal a mass of seeds with fluffy white fibres. When dry, the fibres become transformed to twisted filaments of almost pure cellulose. These become more and more bulky, finally splitting open the ovary to release the seeds to the wind.

Dust-like seeds

Many plants whose seeds will germinate and grow only in very specialized environments are adapted to produce vast numbers of minute seeds which can be transported over great distances by the wind. Among those species which fall into this category are orchids of the genera *Cynorchis* and *Anguloa* and broomrapes, *Orobanche* spp. Within a single fruit capsule these orchids may produce more than four million seeds, the total weight of which is a little over one gram (0.03 ounce). Such seeds have no room to contain a well-developed embryo plant, nor do they contain any food reserves to give the tiny embryo a start in life. For orchid seeds of this type to germinate successfully they must meet up with the right sort of fungus with which to form an association, which is called a mycorrhiza. Even if the association is established, growth is extremely slow and it may be three years before the first leaf is produced. The specific requirement of broomrapes, on the other hand, is chlorophyll, the green plant pigment essential for photosynthesis. These plants are parasitic, and since each species of broomrape is host specific, the chances of its seeds reaching the right plant are most remote.

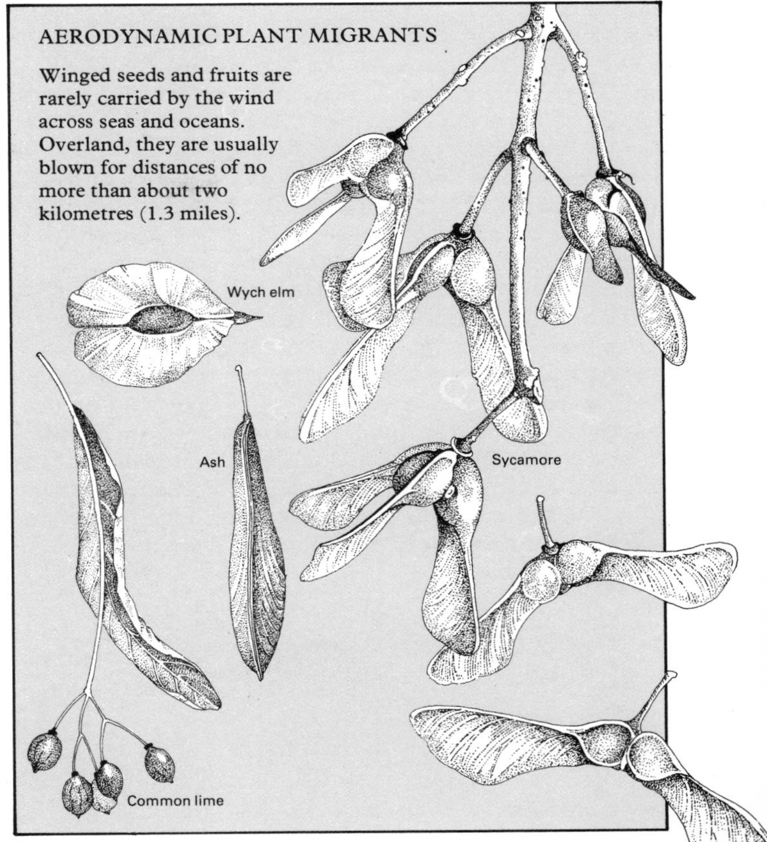

AERODYNAMIC PLANT MIGRANTS

Winged seeds and fruits are rarely carried by the wind across seas and oceans. Overland, they are usually blown for distances of no more than about two kilometres (1.3 miles).

A number of other plants that produce tiny wind-borne seeds have evolved a censor, or pepper-pot, method of displacement. As they ripen, their fruits, carried on the end of a long, flexible stalk, develop small holes in the outer casing. As the wind blows, the fruit sways to and fro and the whippiness of the stalk helps to flick the seeds out of the holes. The older flower heads of poppies, *Papaver* spp., so valued by flower arrangers, are typical of plants using this technique.

Winged seeds or "helicopters"

In temperate regions many forest trees produce winged seeds or fruits which are displaced by wind. The function of the wings is to slow down the fall of the seed, causing it to spin, so that swirling wind eddies are more likely to displace it sideways. This is essential if overcrowding and competition for light and water are to be prevented.

Coniferous trees form cones containing winged seeds, which are released on warm, dry days as the cones open. The cones close up when the atmosphere is damp, only to reopen as the sun breaks through again. In the winged seeds of elm, *Ulmus procera*, and ash, *Fraxinus excelsior*, which are popularly referred to as keys, the wings are an extension of the seed coat. Sycamore, *Acer pseudoplatanus*, and field maple, *Acer campestre*, produce winged seeds joined together in pairs. Hornbeam, *Carpinus betulus*, and lime, *Tilia vulgaris*, produce seeds in which persistent bracts form the wings. The distances from the parent tree travelled by such seeds when blown by a relatively strong, but not violent, wind have been shown to range from 80 metres (90 yards) in the case of the Corsican pine, *Pinus nigra maritima*, to more than 800 metres (880 yards) in the Scots pine, *P. sylvestris*, and from 40 metres (45 yards) in sycamores to 150 metres (165 yards) in ash trees. It is interesting to note that in all these species the distance travelled by the seeds is greater than 30 metres (33 yards) which, for such large trees, appears to be the minimum distance necessary to avoid overcrowding. Any seed which is displaced a distance less than this, and which subsequently germinates and grows, will both fail to reach full size and to produce seeds.

As well as growing from seed, many plants can grow vegetatively from pieces broken off them. Gardeners exploit this ability of plants for the purpose of propagation, but in the natural environment such pieces blown off and displaced by high winds can successfully effect migration. *Bryophyllum* spp. for example, many of which are grown as houseplants, produce new plantlets round the edges of the leaves, and these, having been knocked or blown off, will readily root. Tornadoes and whirlwinds may suck plantlets or potential cuttings high into the air and carry them over great distances. Tumbleweeds, *Psoralea* spp., and steppe-witches, *Anastatica* spp., are often displaced in this manner. These are plants which, when dry, form great balls that are blown across prairies and deserts, either shedding their seeds as they roll along or recovering to root again when they are wetted. Finally, strong winds can also displace whole fruits, such as those of the bitter gourd, *Citrullus colocynthis*. Although some ten centimetres (4 inches) in diameter, the gourds are quite light and are blown along the ground until, in the heat of the sun, they burst open, scattering their seeds.

Animal displacement of seeds and fruit

From fossil records we know that the earliest vertebrates to have displaced seeds and fruits were reptiles. Today, reptiles play a relatively insignificant part in plant migration, although seeds from a total of twenty-eight

SEEDS AND FRUITS DISPLACED BY ANIMALS

Many plants have, during the course of evolution, developed seeds and fruits which are attractive to, and thereby eaten by, animals, and in this way displaced over great distances.

Cherries

Akees

Pears

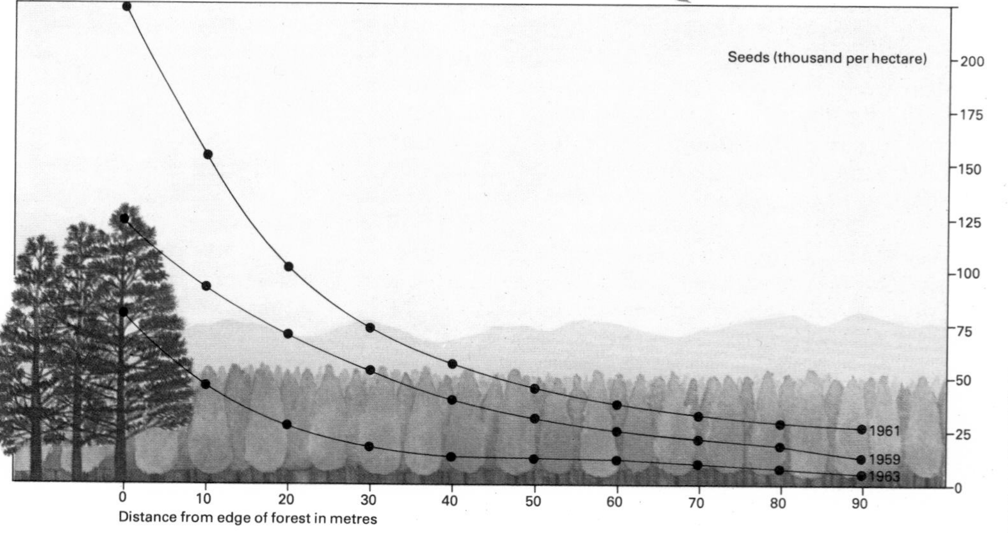

SEED DISTRIBUTION

Displacement of the winged seeds of Engelmann spruce, *Picea engelmannii*, was analysed for three years in each of which seed production was high. Measuring the number of seeds on the ground at various distances from the edge of a spruce forest it was found that, even with a following wind, only about fifty per cent of the seeds were displaced from the parent trees more than 30 metres (100 ft) and only about ten per cent more than 100 metres (330 ft).

species of plants have been found in the faeces of a giant tortoise on the island of Aldabra in the Indian Ocean. These tortoises are thought to have originated from Madagascar. Since it takes much longer for a giant tortoise to pass the remains of a meal than it takes the animal to float, at least in the present current system, from Madagascar to Aldabra, it is possible that this reptile could have introduced plants to the atoll. More important agents in plant migration today, however, are birds and mammals. These are effective in two ways: fruits are eaten, digested and then deposited some distance from the parent plants, or they are transported for many kilometres on the outside of the animals.

The close relationship which has evolved between a plant and the bird or mammal which displaces it is an example of co-evolution. In order to attract potential hosts, plants have evolved fruits and seeds which contain some form of food and which are attractive in terms of smell or colour. This colour may be external, as in the red arils of yews, *Taxus* spp., the single-stoned fruits of cherry trees, *Prunus* spp., and the berries of hedgerow plants. In many tropical fruits which split when they ripen, the seeds are attractively coloured. Carilla, *Momordica charantia*, for example, is a pan-tropical vine which produces orange hanging fruits containing bright red seeds, and akee, *Blighia sapida*, has red fruits which split open to expose black and white seeds. All these seeds have also evolved a protective outer coat which keeps them intact as they are chewed by the animals and pass through their gut. Some seeds, in fact, will germinate only when their coats have been soaked in digestive juices.

Small dry seeds and fruits, such as the grain of grasses, are displaced almost exclusively by birds. Viable seeds have been recovered from bird droppings more than five days after the seeds have been eaten. In five days, a migrant bird can fly many thousands of kilometres. Seeds of water plants such as rushes can also be displaced by birds, by getting stranded on the mud and then sticking to the birds' feet.

Many small rodents such as squirrels, bank voles and field-mice displace nuts, berries and soft fruits. They frequently bury these in the ground some distance from the parent trees or bushes. Having been suitably planted in the soil, those seeds that are not subsequently eaten by the rodents may germinate and grow.

HOOKED FRUITS

Fruits such as those of *Xanthium* spp., burdock, agrimony and wood aven, which adhere to animals' fur or feathers by means of hooks, can be carried many kilometres before they are knocked off the animal. This method of migration is perhaps more unreliable, but no less successful, than displacement by wind or water.

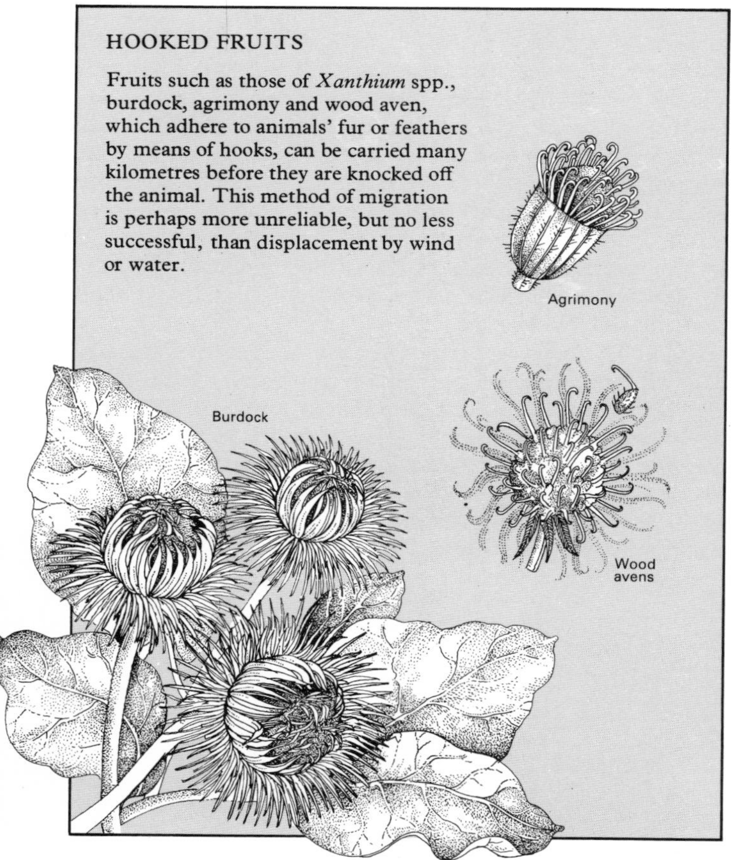

Squirting cucumbers, *Ecballium elaterium*, are one of a small group of plants that migrate actively. They bear fruits which eject their seeds by an explosive mechanism.

Fruits displaced by mammals generally tend to be larger than those transported by birds and are sometimes hard-shelled. Acorns, hazel nuts and beech masts are all collected and displaced by squirrels and mice. Some of the nuts are eaten in the autumn, but many are stored in nests or buried in the ground to be consumed during winter. In the tropics, mammals also play an important part in the displacement of large fruits, which begin to rot as they fall to the ground. These include the fruits of the avocado, *Persea americana*, cacao, *Theobrama cacao*, and date palm, *Phoenix dactylifera*. Plants belonging to the family Sapotaceae have their fruits displaced by bats, but even more extraordinary is the displacement of the fruits of the Malaysian plant *Rafflesia arnoldi*. This grows as a parasite on the roots of certain vines. It produces one of the largest flowers in the world, and its fruits are also very large. The latter are thought to be displaced by sticking to the feet of elephants, which are the only animals heavy enough to press the fruits sufficiently deep into the ground for the seeds to come into contact with the vine roots.

A third group of animals involved in plant migration is ants. These displace the seeds of many plants over distances of perhaps a few metres in temperate woodlands and tropical forests. In temperate woodland there is, in fact, an ecological relationship between the method of seed displacement and the type of plant; the seeds of trees are mostly wind-displaced; many shrubs produce seeds that are displaced by birds; those of tall-growing herbs tend to be displaced by mammals; and it is the seeds of low-growing herbs in particular that are frequently displaced by ants. Plants adapted to this method of migration produce seeds with a projection which contains food or some other attractive factor. The seeds of gorse, *Ulex europaeus*, for example, having been thrown to the ground from their pods as these dry and split open, are often displaced still further by ants attracted by the seeds' brightly coloured wart-like outgrowth, or caruncle, which is filled with an oily food.

Fruits sticking to fur, feathers or clothing

Colloquial names of plants such as beggar's-ticks and stick tight for bur-marigolds, *Bidens* spp., and sticky buttons and sweethearts for burdocks, *Arctium* spp., have clearly evolved from the plants' method of seed displacement. Bur-marigolds have simple daisy-like flowers with large outer ray florets. After pollination, each ray floret forms a single-seeded fruit that develops up to four stiff, barbed bristles, which all too easily catch in fur or birds' feathers. Each bract of a pollinated burdock flower similarly develops a terminal hook so that the entire flowerhead readily becomes attached to a passing animal. Fruits with more robust hooks, such as those of plants of the genus *Tribulus*, which occur throughout the tropics, attach to the feet of ungulates.

Indirectly, man, too, aids the spread of these plants with hooked fruits, as anyone who has walked in the countryside in late summer must be only too aware. Of greater importance to long-distance plant migration, however, is man's introduction to a country of alien plants by the accidental importation of their seeds with bird food, cereals, vegetable seeds or even packaging materials. In parts of Britain, for example, scrap wool, or shoddy, is used as a fertilizer and mulch for fruit trees, and a large number of exotic "shoddy aliens", originating from as far afield as South America and New Zealand, have appeared in apple orchards. In New Zealand itself, a red-topped grass was introduced in hay-filled mattresses brought in by immigrants from Nova Scotia.

Self-displacement by vegetative methods

Although not usually replacing migration by seeds or fruit, vegetative spread is a method of self-displacement that has evolved in a number of species. *Opuntia* cacti, for example, commonly known as prickly pear and chollas, spread chiefly by portions of the stem breaking off and sprouting. In Queensland, Australia, *Opuntia inermis* has spread at a rate of 400,000 hectares (one million acres) a year by this method. Strawberry plants, *Fragaria* spp., and the creeping buttercup, *Ranunculus repens*, migrate by sending out long tillers, or runners, at the end of which new plantlets grow. Many succulent plants, like cacti, grow secondary plants or offsets, which will root freely if they get knocked off and fall to the ground. Other plants spread vegetatively, as well as over-winter, by producing subterranean foodstorage organs, which are often important vegetables utilized by man. Potato tubers are the best-known example of these. Each of these storage organs can also be displaced short distances by foraging mammals, or long distances by man.

Active displacement by explosive methods

Plants producing fruits which displace their seeds by active ejection do so by mechanisms involving the up-take or loss of water. A Mediterranean plant known as the squirting cucumber, *Ecballium elaterium*, has evolved perhaps the most spectacular mechanism. Each of its five-centimetre (2-inch) long green, berry-like fruits is attached at its base to a stalk which projects into the fruit like a cork into a bottle. As the fruit ripens, the cells which surround the "cork" break down, so that when the fruit is knocked by an animal it is suddenly shot away from the stalk. The black seeds and a juicy pulp inside the fruit, which are under pressure, get ejected violently. The seeds have been known to travel as far as six metres (20 feet) from the fruit. Since the squirting cucumber commonly grows in waste places beside the road, the fruits are often triggered by people unwittingly brushing against them.

A different explosive mechanism has evolved in Himalayan balsam and jewelweed, which are plants belonging to the genus *Impatiens*. These produce seed capsules, the outer cell layers of which are very turgid and therefore under considerable tension. When ripe, the capsules can be induced to explode simply by touch. When the fruit of the sandbox tree, *Hura crepitans*, is ripe, it falls from the tree and, on hitting the ground, explodes like a hand granade showering seeds all around. In *Geranium* spp., ejection of seeds is effected by a catapult mechanism and in *Viola* spp., by a sudden contortion of the walls of the fruit. Such explosive mechanisms are, however, relatively uncommon among the 300,000 or more species comprising the plant kingdom.

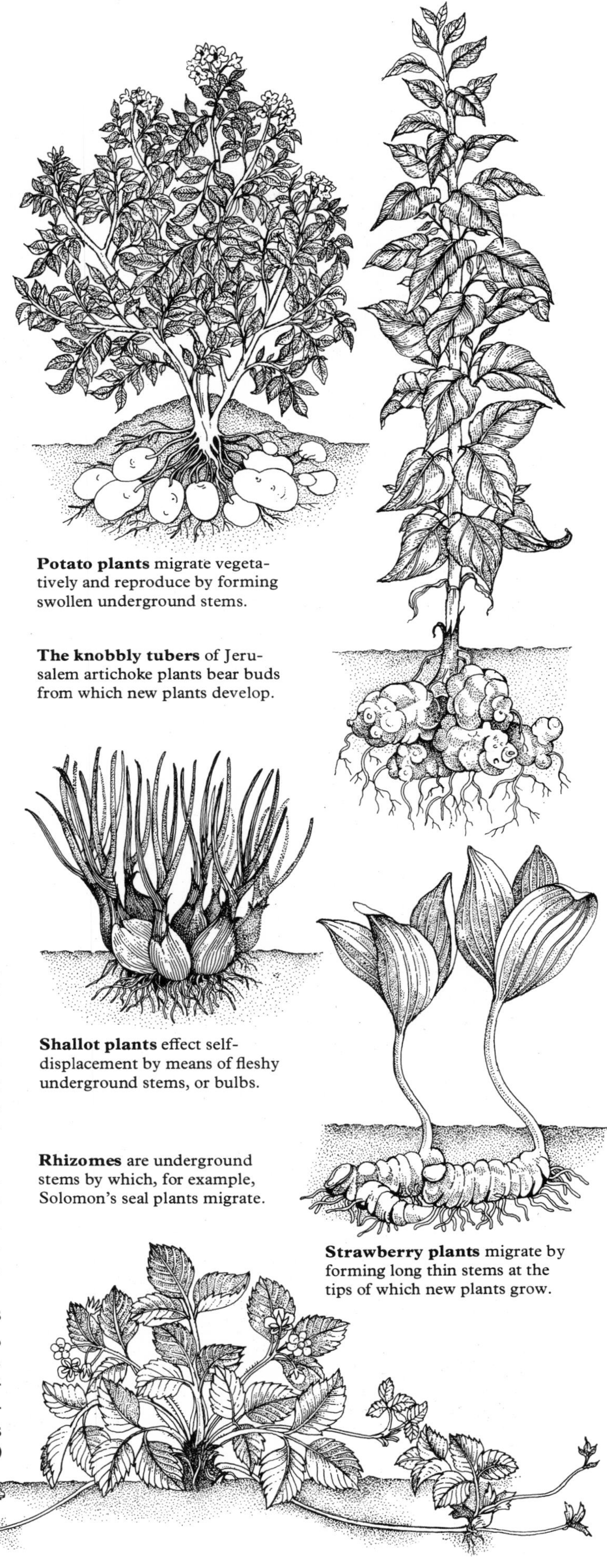

Potato plants migrate vegetatively and reproduce by forming swollen underground stems.

The knobbly tubers of Jerusalem artichoke plants bear buds from which new plants develop.

Shallot plants effect self-displacement by means of fleshy underground stems, or bulbs.

Rhizomes are underground stems by which, for example, Solomon's seal plants migrate.

Strawberry plants migrate by forming long thin stems at the tips of which new plants grow.

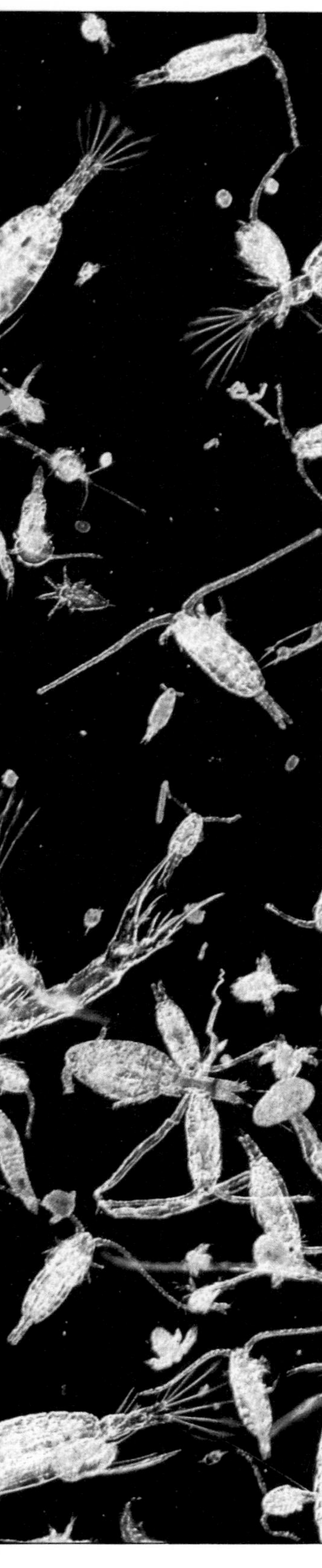

Invertebrates

Invertebrates show a range of body forms more varied than the rest of the animal kingdom put together. In the sea there are, at one extreme, small crustaceans, jellyfish, arrow-worms, comb-jellies and other members of the plankton and inhabitants of the sea bottom and, at the other extreme, giant squids, true invertebrate monsters of the deep. On land there are the earthworms that burrow in the soil, spring-tails that scramble among the leaf-litter, scorpions and harvestmen that scamper over the soil surface and small aeronaut spiders that balloon their way into the air.

The nature of their lifetime tracks is equally as varied. Barnacles have lifetime tracks little different from those of plants – a brief phase of mobility as a microscopic planktonic larva, during which the barnacle performs a once-only trip from its birthplace, followed by a prolonged period of immobility anchored to some rocky surface. Plankton migrate vertically with a rhythm that is both daily and seasonal. So, too, do earthworms and small land creatures such as false scorpions. Some squid may perform huge annual migration circuits within oceans. In terms of distance, snails may die within a few tens of metres of the place where they were born, while gossamer spiders may migrate thousands of kilometres before they die. Finally, octopuses, lobsters, snails and, perhaps, scorpions, all of which develop familiarity with an area, have lifetime tracks as sophisticated as those of any vertebrate. And for each form of lifetime track there is a different strategy for feeding and reproduction. Variability and adaptability are the key words for invertebrates.

The migrations of zooplankton – tiny animals which drift almost passively in seas and oceans – range from one-way journeys in surface waters to return movements vertically through the water.

Displacement of planktonic larvae

Marine invertebrates lead a very precarious life. Some swim actively against the water currents and chase after their food, others just drift, but many live a stationary life, catching food as the water flows past. These sedentary creatures are to be found attached to rocks or floating objects or embedded in sand or mud under the sea or on beaches. But this can lead to overcrowding or to an inability to escape unfavourable conditions. The vast majority of them have therefore evolved a life-cycle in which they produce free-swimming larvae that function as the migratory stage of the animal. The larvae may spend weeks or even months moving in a communal plankton before coming into contact with a suitable habitat and developing into adults. During this time they may drift long distances in the ocean currents. Most of the larvae, however, get eaten, die of starvation or fail to find an ideal place in which to settle.

The life cycle of the goose barnacle, *Lepas fasicularis*, is a good example of the need for displacement. The adults of this species live attached to a great range of flotsam and jetsam; pieces of wood, lumps of fuel oil, feathers, pumice and fishing floats all serve as platforms for these animals. Many of these objects remain afloat for only short periods of time. The barnacle larvae, having found such a habitat, thus have to reach maturity in perhaps only two or three weeks, and then, as adults, to invest all their energy in reproduction. To compensate for the high odds against the survival and successful mating of their offspring, goose barnacles produce vast numbers of eggs. Each of these contains very little yolk, so that once the larvae hatch, they have to feed ravenously on the microscopic plant life in the water. In some other species of barnacles, release of larvae from the parents occurs when this food source is most abundant, which in northern temperate waters is early spring.

Studying the distribution in the Atlantic of many shallow-water species of invertebrates, biologists have

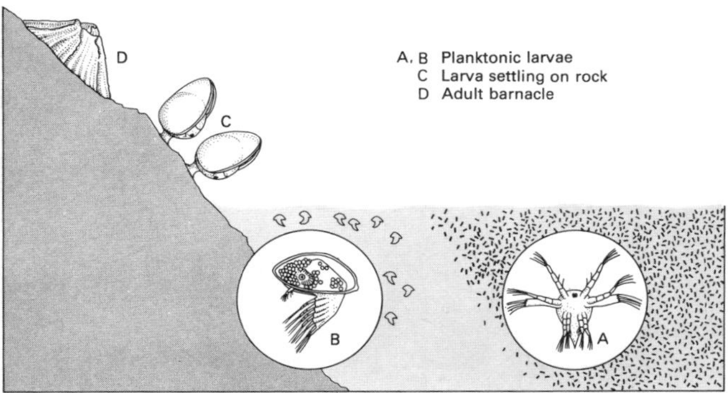

A female of the barnacle, *Balanus balanoides*, may each year produce upward of 10,000 planktonic larvae. But of these, less than one per cent will survive to reach a suitable habitat and develop into an adult. The rate of wastage during development of a group of 1000 newly hatched larvae is shown, left.

Larvae of goose barnacles, *Lepas fasicularis*, tend to settle where adults are already present. This promotes successful mating.

found a considerable number that occur on both the western and the eastern side. Among these are the worm *Laonice cirrata*, the mollusc, *Cynatina parthenopeum*, and several colonial sea anemones, *Polythoa* spp. Examination of plankton samples collected at points all the way across between North America and Europe and Africa soon revealed that larvae of these species released on the American side are initially carried across in the Gulf Stream, which joins a slower, less well-defined current, the North Atlantic Drift. Alternatively, they can travel in the fast-flowing equatorial undercurrent. Larvae released on the African coast cross the Atlantic westward in the surface equatorial current. Such ocean crossings, in either direction, are estimated to take between 150 and 300 days.

Off the coast of Western Australia the use of surface-drifting buoys tracked by satellites has similarly given scientists a useful insight into the distribution patterns of the commercially exploited rock lobsters, *Panulirus longipes cygnus*. This crustacean starts life as a flattened, leaf-like, highly transparent planktonic larva, or phyllosoma. The larvae spend between seven and nine months in the plankton, and only when they move into coastal waters do they start to develop into adults. The buoys have revealed that an enormous current eddy exists off the coast and that larvae caught up in the current will be carried inshore every few weeks. Some of the buoys have spun out of the eddy and have then been quickly carried in a surface current across the Indian Ocean and close to the northern tip of Madagascar and up the eastern coast of Africa. The rock lobsters that occur off eastern Africa are therefore derived, at least in part, from the larvae of Australian lobsters.

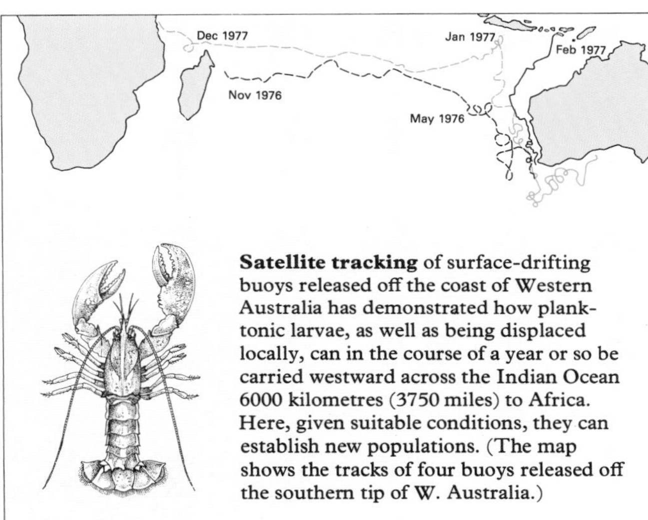

Satellite tracking of surface-drifting buoys released off the coast of Western Australia has demonstrated how planktonic larvae, as well as being displaced locally, can in the course of a year or so be carried westward across the Indian Ocean 6000 kilometres (3750 miles) to Africa. Here, given suitable conditions, they can establish new populations. (The map shows the tracks of four buoys released off the southern tip of W. Australia.)

The total mass of egg yolk produced by marine invertebrates of the same genus tends to be similar. But those species living in arctic waters invariably produce fewer, much larger-yolked eggs than those which inhabit temperate waters, as is shown below. In temperate waters food for the newly hatched young is more abundant and there is less need to produce eggs with large food reserves.

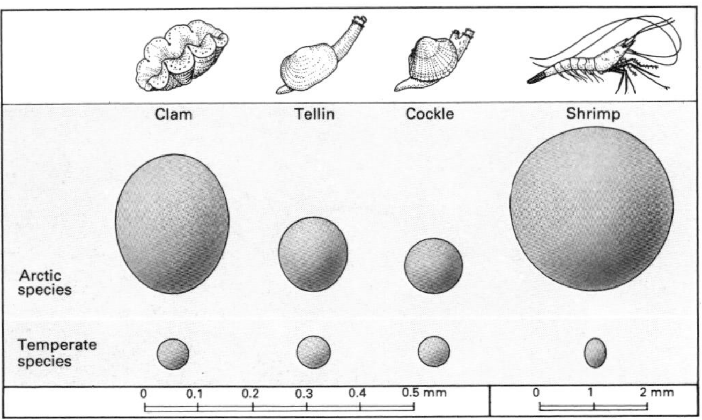

Not all sedentary marine invertebrate species produce massive numbers of larvae that live for a relatively long time in the plankton. In the Arctic, because the summers are short and the winters long and cold, the growth of marine flora is minimal, and the worms and shellfish that live on the sea bed get very little food. In order to endure the winter, when food is scarce, their larvae have to be provided with sufficient food reserves to survive until the next summer. The result is twofold; firstly, the female adults are forced to invest a considerable amount of energy in each egg they produce and, secondly, the risky planktonic stage is kept to a minimum and may last only a day or so. The bivalve mollusc *Nucula nitida*, for example, an inhabitant of arctic waters, each year produces about 100 large, yolky eggs which hatch into larvae that have a very short planktonic existence, whereas closely related species in temperate waters, such as *Abra* spp. and *Corbula* spp., produce about a million tiny eggs and the larvae feed and grow as plankton for several weeks. In consequence, the larvae of invertebrates such as *Nucula* are capable of travelling only short distances and often are insufficiently long-lived to be able to traverse barriers created by unsuitable habitats; they may not get past a region of cliffs and rock, yet there may be plenty of suitable habitats further along the coast.

Animals living on the sea bed at great depths in the ocean face a similar problem. They are dependent for food on the rain of detritus from surface waters. Throughout its long fall thousands of metres down through the water, the detritus progressively diminishes in quantity because it is either broken down by bacteria or eaten by midwater animals. Compared with the near-surface layer, at a depth of 2000 metres (6600 feet) there is only one hundredth the amount of food available. At depths of 5000 metres (16,400 feet), there is only a thousandth. A bottom-living animal therefore gets only a minute quantity of food, most of which is needed just to keep itself alive. Thus it can afford to expend only a tiny amount of energy on reproduction. The shallower its larvae can float up in the water, the greater the quantity of food they will be able to garner, but at the same time the greater will be the chances that they will be eaten by predators. So the majority of deep-living animals produce very few well-provisioned eggs that hatch into larvae that are free-living for only a day or so. Their migrations, too, can be over only short distances.

Seasonal vertical migrations

In the deep ocean at high latitudes large numbers of planktonic species perform seasonal vertical migrations, swimming up to the surface in spring and down into

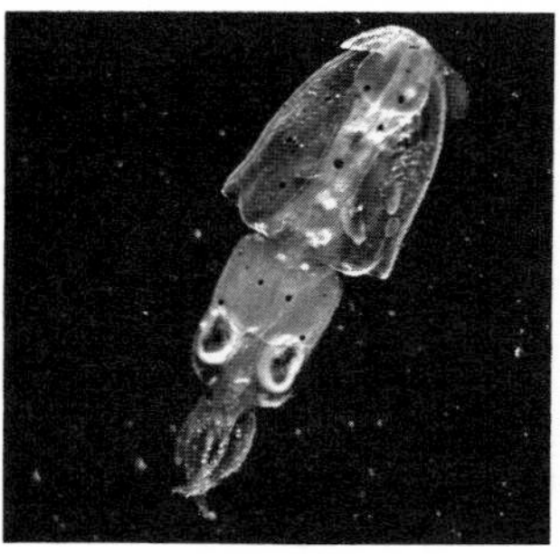

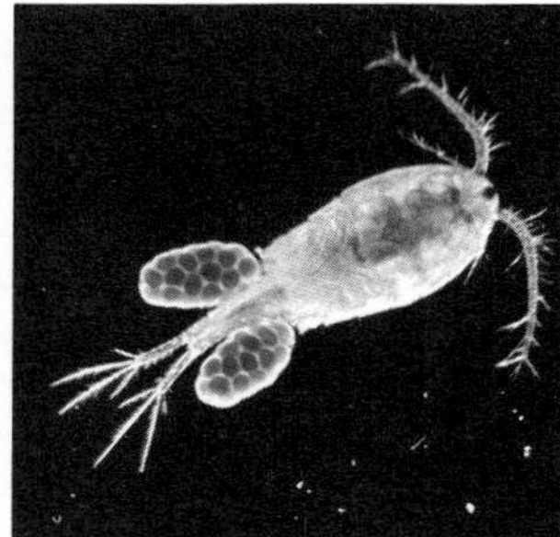

Young squid *Loligo* sp.
Female *Cyclops* with egg sacs
Adult *Calanus finmarchicus*

Marine invertebrates range from tiny planktonic creatures to large squid and octopuses. Among the zooplankton there are two main groups; those that spend their lives as permanent members of the plankton, such as the copepods *Calanus* spp., and those which are only temporarily planktonic. The latter includes the larvae of barnacles, *Lepas* and *Balanus* spp., and of sea anemones and molluscs. Each of these larvae, after drifting in the sea and reaching a suitable habitat, settle and develop into adults. But whether planktonic larvae or adult squid, most marine invertebrates perform vertical migrations in response to changes in the quantity of food available and the number of predators present at different depths in the sea or ocean.

In seas and oceans food chains are based on plankton. For example, one lumpsucker (A) will eat three gobies (B) in one meal. These in turn during their lifetime will probably have consumed several thousand sea gooseberries (C). The latter will have eaten some 100,000 tiny copepods (D), which will have consumed many millions of diatoms (E).

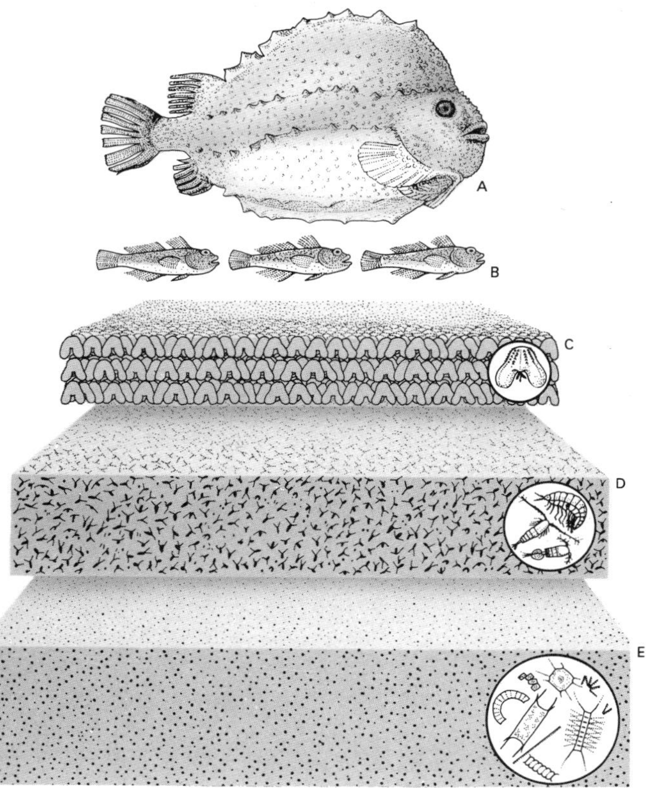

deep waters in autumn. During the long winter there is, as we have seen, a paucity of minute plants in the water, the phytoplankton. Also, because storms churn up the water to depths of 400 metres (1300 feet) or more, any plants that are in the water will soon get carried beyond the depth to which sufficient sunlight penetrates for photosynthesis to be possible. In the winter in the North Atlantic, at depths of between 500 and 1000 metres (1650 and 3300 feet), the whole population of the copepod *Calanus finmarchicus* is to be found. All the individuals are juveniles ready to mature into adults. They are very oily; sixty to seventy per cent of the animals' body weight consists of lipid. This acts both as a food reserve and as a way of keeping the animals neutrally buoyant such that they hang suspended in midwater; they do not have to expend energy swimming either up or down in order to maintain their position. In the spring, once the surface water begins to warm a little, the ocean becomes stratified and the warmer surface waters no longer mix with the deeper, cool water. The phytoplankton cells are now no longer continually being carried down into the dark depths, and they start to grow rapidly. This produces a "spring bloom" of phytoplankton on the surface. The onset of the bloom is the signal for all the larval copepods in deep water to break their period of delayed development and to migrate up towards the surface. Here they undergo a maturation moult and immediately start to breed, using their fat reserves to fuel their reproductive effort. The eggs they produce hatch into the tiny nauplial larvae just as the phytoplankton becomes really abundant, so that there is ample food for them to grow rapidly. In the autumn, these larvae migrate, as juveniles, to deep water, so maintaining the cycle.

In the North Pacific the timing of the spring bloom is much more predictable. It has been found that the overwintering juveniles of the locally dominant copepod species *Calanus plumchrus* do not migrate back to the surface but mature and spawn at depth, and it is their eggs that float upward. These hatch as soon as they reach the surface, which coincides with the start of the spring bloom. In other respects, the life cycle of the two copepods is much the same.

Daily vertical migrations

Zooplankton in the open ocean make a similar, but daily, vertical migration, moving up towards the surface at dusk and down again at dawn. The source of food for the herbivores among them is the phytoplankton that grows only in the near-surface sunlit layers, so these species have to feed in this zone. But here the concentration of predators is much higher. By swimming downward the herbivores may be able to reduce the chances of encountering a predator. If they swim down at daybreak they can avoid in particular those predators that hunt by sight, such as fish and squid. Some herbivores, however, do not migrate; instead they camouflage themselves by being as transparent as possible. There is a tendency for larger species to migrate to greater depths than smaller ones, and this may be because the former are still visible in the low light intensities at which small animals are no longer detectable.

The deeper the descent in the ocean the darker it gets, until at a depth of about 1000 metres (3300 feet) daylight can no longer penetrate and a world of permanent darkness is reached. This, too, may in part be the reason for some species performing daily vertical migrations during only certain stages of their life cycle. Newly hatched larvae are very small, possibly too small to be seen by visually-hunting predators, so they have no need to migrate and usually remain in the surface layers. It is indeed doubtful if they are either strong enough or carry sufficient energy supplies to make a migration. As the larvae grow so they begin to migrate, and the extent of their migration progressively increases until they reach maturity.

This picture of the daily vertical migration of plankton being merely a method of minimizing predation while still allowing the animals as long as possible at shallow depths where food is plentiful, is deceptively simple. Firstly, it is not only the herbivores that perform these migrations but also their predators, the carnivores, or at any rate the smaller carnivores. Decapod prawns and lantern fish make some of the most extensive migrations. The lantern fish, *Notoscopelus elongatus*, in the Bay of Biscay, migrates each morning from the surface down to depths of between 1000 and 1250 metres (3300 and 5700 feet), only to return to the surface again at dusk. Some of the large red prawns, *Acanthephyra* spp., make regular migrations in the early spring when few of the planktonic species are migrating. Secondly, at high latitudes the daily migration in some planktonic species and in shrimps such as *Eucopia hanseni*, which travels between layers of water several hundred metres apart, occurs only in summer and early autumn. Finally, it is not immediately clear why, during the spring bloom, the vertical migration is not undertaken by a large number of species, unless at such times the abundance of food and the need to get on with breeding makes the risk of predation of less importance to the animals.

There are other consequences of vertical migrations in oceans. The conditions in the surface layers are notoriously patchy. Nets fished in quick succession near the surface will bear catches that are very different in composition and which vary in quantity by a factor of up to ten. Clearly, survival for a herbivore depends on locating a patch where phytoplankton is abundant, and a carnivore to find where its prey is most plentiful. But the range of the migrations is controlled to some extent by light intensity; the brighter the sunlight and the clearer the surface waters the deeper the migrants descend. One effect of migrating deeper is that when the animals swim up again they come up into a totally different parcel of water. This is because the sea is rather like a multi-layered cake, with each layer sliding over the next. The more layers the animal swims down through the greater the distance it will be displaced from its original surface position. Beneath a patch of dense phytoplankton the light will penetrate to a shallower depth because the plant cells absorb or scatter a large proportion of it. As a result, the migrants will not move so deep and will tend to stay close to the patch where the feeding is good. They will tend to aggregate into the parcels of water where more food is available.

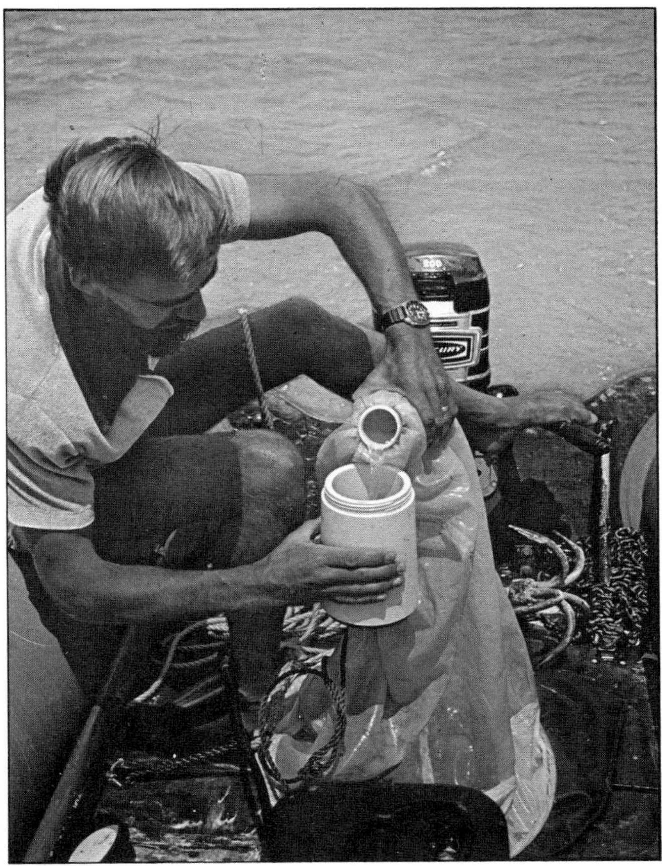

Plankton are collected using fine-mesh nets suspended in the water from slow-moving boats. The samples are stored in labelled jars to be taken back to the laboratory for identification of the plankton and chemical analysis of the water. Comparison of samples from different locations in terms of the types and numbers of planktonic larvae present tells us much about the migrations of many marine invertebrates.

MIGRANTS OF A SANDY BEACH

Invertebrates that live on sandy shores, such as the worms and hydrozoan illustrated, below, invariably also perform seasonal vertical migrations, moving towards the surface in summer and away from it in winter. Diagrams representing the summer and winter distribution (dashed and solid lines respectively) on a sandy shore of populations of a polychaete worm (A), a flatworm (B), a hydrozoan (C) and a gastrotriche (D) are shown.

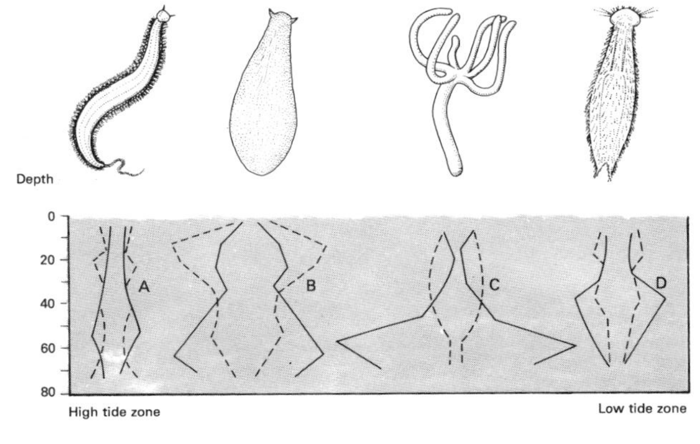

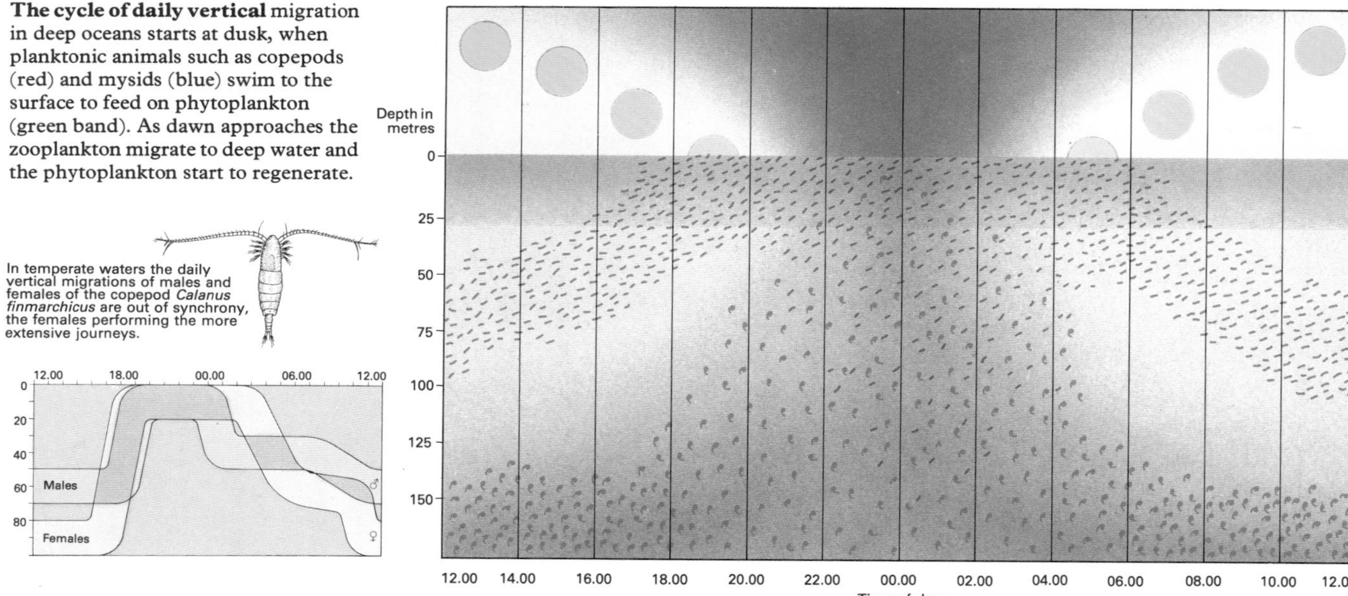

The cycle of daily vertical migration in deep oceans starts at dusk, when planktonic animals such as copepods (red) and mysids (blue) swim to the surface to feed on phytoplankton (green band). As dawn approaches the zooplankton migrate to deep water and the phytoplankton start to regenerate.

In temperate waters the daily vertical migrations of males and females of the copepod *Calanus finmarchicus* are out of synchrony, the females performing the more extensive journeys.

The effects of vertical migrations

The pattern of growth in phytoplankton is for the plant cells to photosynthesize during the day and then at night to use the food they have produced for growth. The plant cells tend to divide at about dawn so that their number increases, and may even double, each morning. To crop the phytoplankton most efficiently the animals should start feeding at, or just before, dusk, when the phytoplankton is numerous and most nutritious. As the plant population is grazed down so the energy expended by the animals in filtering the tiny cells out of the water becomes almost as much as that obtained by eating them. So if the phytoplankton is left untouched from the early hours of morning until dusk, the number of cells will increase again at dawn and they will receive a whole day's sunlight with which to build up their nutrient reserves. Hence one effect of vertical migration is to optimize the efficiency by which the phytoplankton is cropped.

Another effect of the migrations may be to increase the flow of genetic material, by means of cross-breeding, within the population. Any lack of synchronization in the migrations of males and females of a species will result in the population spreading out. This will, in turn, reduce the chances of matings between closely related individuals and prevent inbreeding which would otherwise reduce the vigour of their offspring. In adults of many species one sex, usually the male, is either more restricted in its range of vertical migration or may not migrate at all, often staying in deep water.

A further advantage has been postulated arising from the fact that in most parts of the ocean the deeper an animal swims the cooler the water it encounters. Cooling an animal has two effects. One is that it slows metabolism and, two, it tends to make females produce fewer, larger and more viable eggs. Slowing the metabolism when the animal is resting and not feeding will mean that it is expending less energy on maintaining itself, and it has more available for growth or for investing in reproduction. Although there are examples of vertical migration resulting in a metabolic bonus to the migrants, two factors prevent this from being a universal benefit. Firstly, the temperature range over which many migrants move is not sufficiently large to result in the metabolic bonus. Secondly, physiological experiments have shown that in many, but not all, migrants the slowing effect of the cooler temperatures is counteracted by an accelerating effect of the increasing pressure of the body of water above. Each additional 10 metres (33 feet) of depth increases the pressure by an atmosphere, so at a depth of 1000 metres (3300 feet) the pressure is a hundred times that of the atmosphere at the surface.

What is clear, however, is that daily vertical migration is mostly restricted to depths to which detectable daylight penetrates. Indeed, very few animals migrate from depths greater than 1000 metres (3300 feet). This must be because either the energy expended in swimming up is greater than the benefit derived from the more abundant resources of foods, or alternatively no advantage accrues from swimming any deeper. Many deep-living animals do undergo very extensive vertical migrations during their life cycle. For example, some of the large, deep-living squid, such as the species *Lepidoteuthis grimaldi*, are known as adults only from specimens found in the stomachs of sperm whales. Sperm whales feed extensively on squid and can feed close to the sea bed at depths of 1000 metres (3300 feet) or more. The big squid are probably too active to be caught by the trawls which biologists use to study the deep-living fauna, but the small larvae of these invertebrates are caught in plankton nets fished quite near the surface. The identification of these larvae is often a problem because they look totally unlike the adults. Only by laboriously accumulating series of larvae showing each stage of their development can they eventually be related to their adult form. One curious piece of side information is that the routes taken by migrating whales have been established by identifying the squid remains in their stomachs. Whales caught off South Africa have been found to have in their stomachs the beaks of Antarctic species of squid.

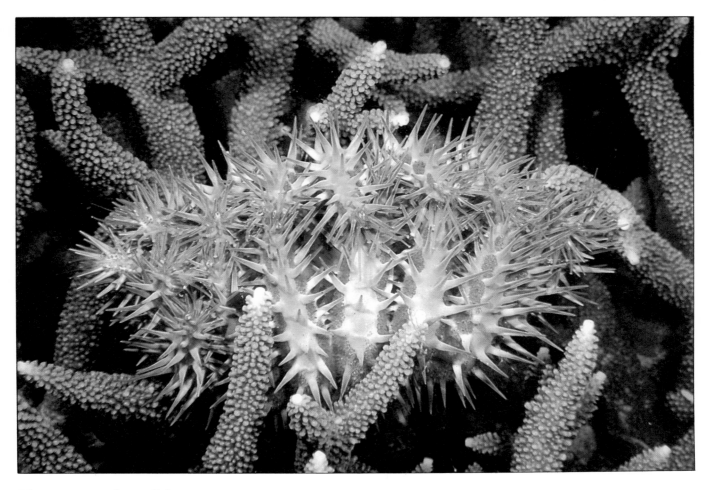

Flatworms and starfish

Vertical migrations occur over a great variety of ranges, but perhaps the tiniest are those made by the flatworm *Convoluta roscoffensis*. This lives on sandy shores in Normandy and Brittany in France. When the tide ebbs these little flatworms move on to the wet surface of the sand and then burrow down to a depth of about ten centimetres (4 inches) as the tide rises again. Within the tissues of the flatworm live, symbiotically, green single-celled flagellates. For the flagellates to photosynthesize they need sunlight, and this is why the flatworms migrate up to the sand surface. But if the flatworms stayed on the surface, the rising tide would sweep them away. Their migration has been shown to be related to the tidal cycle, because flatworms kept in an aquarium maintain their migration rhythm in time with the tides of their natural environment.

There are many appearances and disappearances of animals that are totally unexplained and may well result from migrations. The best example among marine invertebrates was the sudden appearance in the early 1970s of the crown-of-thorns starfish, *Acanthaster planci*, on many coral reefs in the Indo-Pacific. Divers suddenly noticed that over large areas of reef the coral had been killed. It was soon discovered that at the edge of each of these areas, large numbers of these very spiny starfish emerged at night from under the coral overhangs and continued to eat their way along the reef. The

The crown-of-thorns starfish, *Acanthaster planci*, feeds on corals. Following a population explosion (or mass immigration) of the starfish, coral reefs become desolate save for weeds.

Flatworms, *Convoluta roscoffensis*, as they migrate in vast numbers on to the surface of a beach, colour sand green. A close-up photograph of the worms reveals the agents responsible – within each worm is a multitude of green plant cells. These are the worms' food suppliers.

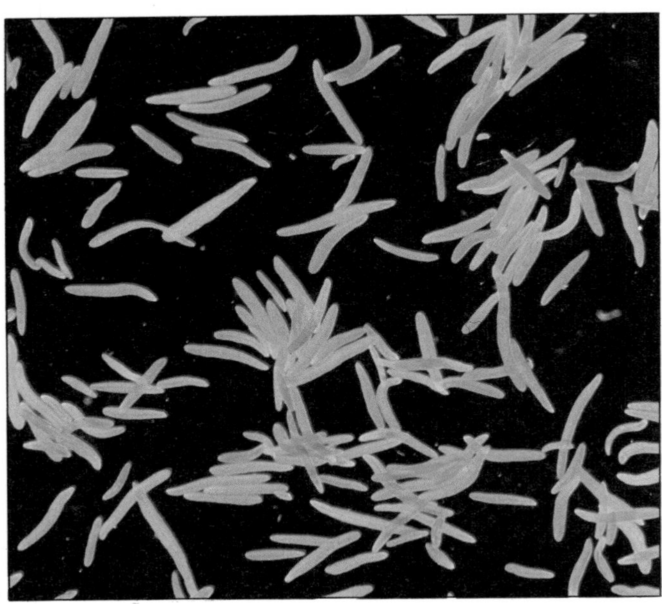

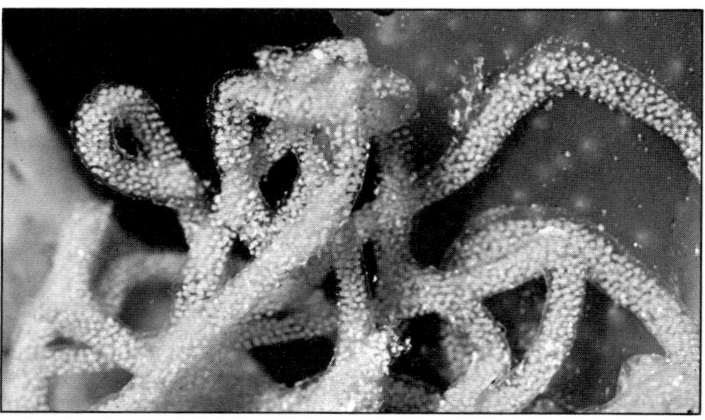

The mass of jelly (above) produced by a spawning sea hare, *Aplysia* sp., contains some 40,000 eggs. But of the larvae emerging from these eggs only one or two will survive to become adults (below).

devastation was so complete that many people feared that the reefs would be destroyed and that the coasts of many tropical countries would become vulnerable to erosion by the waves. On the Great Barrier Reef of Australia groups of divers tried to stem the tide of starfish, but despite killing many tens of thousands, they were unable to halt the destruction of the reefs. Panic set in. Yet within two years or so, throughout the Indo-Pacific, the starfish numbers began to dwindle and the reefs recovered unexpectedly quickly. Examination of sandy deposits has yielded sub-fossil remains of the starfish that show that every one or two centuries they have a similar population outburst. Whether man's dredging and blasting of the coral reefs make conditions ideal for the starfish or, as is believed, a mass migration is involved, and if so, from and to where do the starfish travel, remains a mystery.

Spawning migrations – sea hares and crabs

Many animals migrate at spawning time. The aim of this migration is to find areas either of greater safety or areas in which the right kind of food is most abundant for the hatching larvae. In the spring, in many places throughout the world, sea hares, *Aplysia* spp., migrate high up on to the shore from deep water. Sea hares are snails that have very tiny, reduced shells and produce a purple dye if they are attacked. Normally they live below the low-tide mark, browsing on the seaweeds. At spawning time they congregate in great masses. Each animal is a hermaphrodite, being capable both of laying eggs and of fertilizing other sea hares with sperm packed in a special love dart. The fertilized eggs, which are laid in masses that resemble balls of pink wool, are usually deposited among green seaweeds on sandy mud beaches. Once they have spawned, the adult sea hares die. The eggs encased in a jelly are safer on the beach because while the tide is out the many and varied potential predators are inactive. Below the low-tide mark not only are these more numerous but also they are continually on the prowl. After a week or so the eggs hatch into tiny "hairy" larvae that live and disperse in the plankton for up to a month or two.

Even more extraordinary than the aggregations of sea hares is the sight on British shores of huge piles of spider crabs, *Maia squinando*, exposed at low tide in early summer. These big crabs, with their very hard carapaces, can mate only immediately after moulting, when the new carapace is still soft. Since as adults they are unable to moult, the females can mate just once in their lives, namely within moments of the moult at which they become mature. As the female crabs sense they are about to undergo a maturation moult they move inshore and congregate in groups. The scent emanating from these groups of females attracts large numbers of males, who join the groups and wait to mate with the newly moulted mature females. As more and more crabs congregate together, so the pile grows. Clearly, this type of migration helps every female to ensure that she is successfully mated. After mating, both males and females, the latter carrying the fertilized eggs under their abdomen, migrate back to deep water, where they spend the winter. The planktonic larvae that hatch from the eggs the following spring also carry out further migrations, but these are related to finding a place to settle down and grow into adults.

Fantasies of the early settlers on the eastern seaboard of the USA concerning monsters emerging from the deep must have been reinforced when they first saw the spawning migration of the horseshoe, or king, crabs, *Limulus polyphemus*. These weird, primitive crustaceans are the only living relatives of a very ancient fossil group. They have a large domed head-shield that is hinged to a large rectangular body plate, which bears a long tail-spike. Beneath the body are five pairs of walking legs and a small pair of pincers. A fully grown female may be sixty centimetres (24 inches) long and thirty centimetres (12 inches) across. King crabs usually live in deep waters, but every spring they migrate inshore. When spring tides coincide with a full moon, they congregate on sandy beaches and estuaries at the edge of the sea. Each male clambers on to the back of a female and hooks himself on. The female then scoops out a hollow in the sand and proceeds to lay between 200 and 300 eggs, which the male fertilizes. The mating pair subsequently crawl away back into deep water, leaving the eggs to develop buried in the sand. The eggs hatch at the next spring tide and the larvae are washed out into the shallows, where they mature.

King crabs, *Limulus polyphemus*, whose larvae resemble, and are named after, the now-extinct trilobites, reach sexual maturity at about three years, after which they annually perform spawning migrations.

The life history of spider crabs, *Maia squinando*, involves three larval stages, each of which grows in size with moulting of the carapace. But moulting ceases as sexual maturity is reached and the crabs' one and only spawning migration and mating is therefore timed to coincide with this. As adults the crabs may live for several years.

The migrations of squid and palolo worms

Another remarkable spawning migration occurs on the Pacific coast of North America, where once a year huge numbers of the squid *Loligo opalescens* enter Monterey Bay, California. So many animals cram into a small area that the ground is literally carpeted with them. This great aggregation of squid is reminiscent of the great herds of wildebeeste that congregate on the Serengeti Plains at the time of calving. The wildebeeste are surrounded by prides of lions and packs of hunting dogs, both of which take a heavy toll of the parents and their calves, partic-

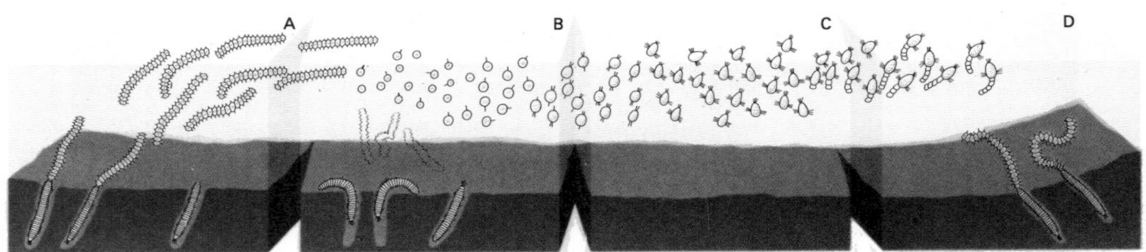

The breeding cycle of palolo worms, *Lysidice* spp., involves shedding of the tails (A), the release of eggs and sperm from the tail segments (B), the fusion of sperm and eggs to produce larvae (C) and growth of the larvae and the start of the next breeding phase (D) by the adults.

For South Pacific islanders, collection of the tails of spawning palolo worms, which is performed at night, is a festive event.

ularly round the edges of herds. Similarly, the great congregation of squid is attended by numerous carnivores, ranging from fish to sea birds and sea lions. So abundant are the squid that the carnage inflicted by these predators has little effect on their overall numbers. The squid spawn and then die. The young hatch from the eggs as recognizable squid-like creatures, which migrate out of the bay before the onset of winter.

One of the most dramatic spawning migrations among marine invertebrates is that of the palolo worm, *Lysidice oele* – a relative of ragworms and catworms – which lives in the reefs around Fiji and Samoa. The extraordinary element of these migrations is that it is only the tail end of each worm that takes part. During the moon's last quarter in October or November, the millions of worms living in the reefs synchronously shed their tails into the water. The tails, which have grown special paddle-like lobes on each segment, are packed with eggs and sperm. They migrate up to the surface in amazing numbers and shed their contents into the water, thus ensuring maximum success in fertilizing the eggs. (The eggs hatch into planktonic larvae and are scattered by the water currents.) However, the arrival of the tails at the surface is awaited by a seething host of predators. Even the local natives collect the tails assiduously, as they are considered to be a great delicacy. The vast number of worm tails satiates the greed of the predators and still leaves enough to breed. Meanwhile, the head-ends of the worms in their burrows on the reefs get on with the task of regenerating a new tail in preparation for the next breeding season.

In many parts of the world other species of worms produce similar mating swarms. Among these are Pacific and Atlantic palolo worms, *Eunice viridis* and *E. schemacephala*, the ragworm, *Nereis succinea*, an inhabitant of the Atlantic seaboard of North America, and the worm *Odontosyllis enopla*, which swarms off Bermuda, and *O. phosphorea*, which gathers near Vancouver in Canada. Their migrations are also precisely synchronized with the lunar cycle, but none are quite as dramatic as the swarming of *Lysidice*.

Sandhoppers, *Talitrus saltator*, possess a sun compass regulated by an internal clock. This is itself influenced by changes in the day/night length of the environment; sandhoppers kept in an artificial environment in which the daytime was twelve hours behind that experienced by a second group of sandhoppers, moved in almost the opposite direction.

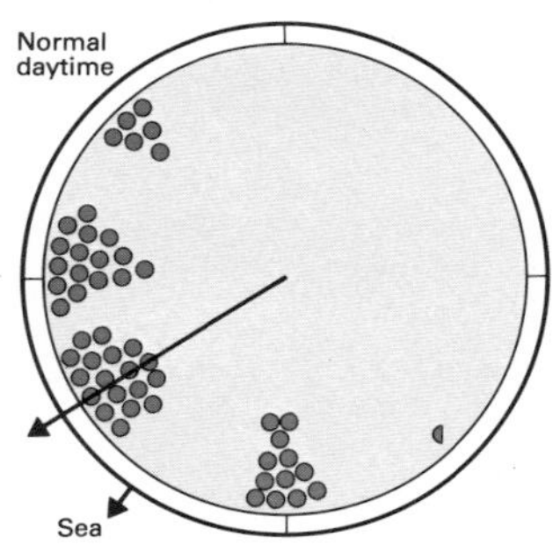

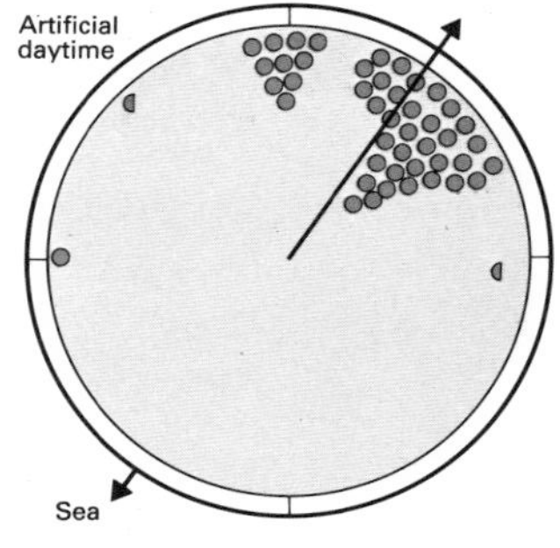

The migrations of sandhoppers

Sandhoppers, *Talitrus saltator*, are small crustaceans that are found in their millions on sandy beaches throughout Europe. They spend the daytime buried in the sand high up on the beach. At night they migrate down the beach to forage on the areas exposed by the retreating tide. When the tide turns or day breaks, whichever is first, the sandhoppers migrate back up the beach to their daytime shelters. This is a beguilingly simple piece of behaviour, but how do the hoppers know in which direction to hop to escape from the advancing sea? Hoppers that have been displaced from one side of a bay to the other set off in the wrong direction, unaware that they have been moved. Obviously they are not just moving down the slope of the beach, but are navigating, choosing a direction that takes them back to their resting places.

In an experiment performed in Italy, hoppers displaced from the Adriatic to the Mediterranean coast set off inland. Similarly, it was found that hoppers flown from one side of the USA to the other set off at an angle to the sun which measured the same as the number of degrees of longitude through which they had been moved. The tiny hoppers were suffering from a form of jet-lag. They clearly use the sun as a compass and compensate for its movements across the sky during the day. Other experiments have shown that they can also learn to use the moon as a compass and to compensate for its movement across the sky.

Journeying in search of food

Migrations towards sources of food are often initiated in response to some sort of chemical or mechanical stimulus. For example, inhabiting the surf-pounded beaches of

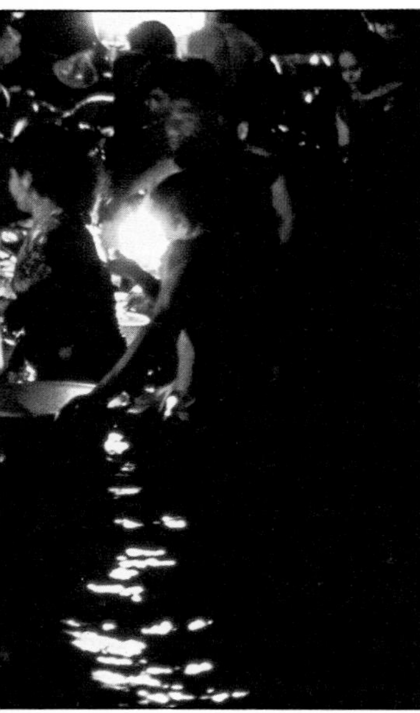

The distribution of the snail *Bullia rhodostoma* on the beaches of Natal is closely linked with the tide cycle. The snails tend to congregate at the water's edge, where their food is most abundant. This is shown on the profile, below, of a beach during the spring tide period. The distribution of a sample of ten snails is indicated. (There are two low and two high tides each day.)

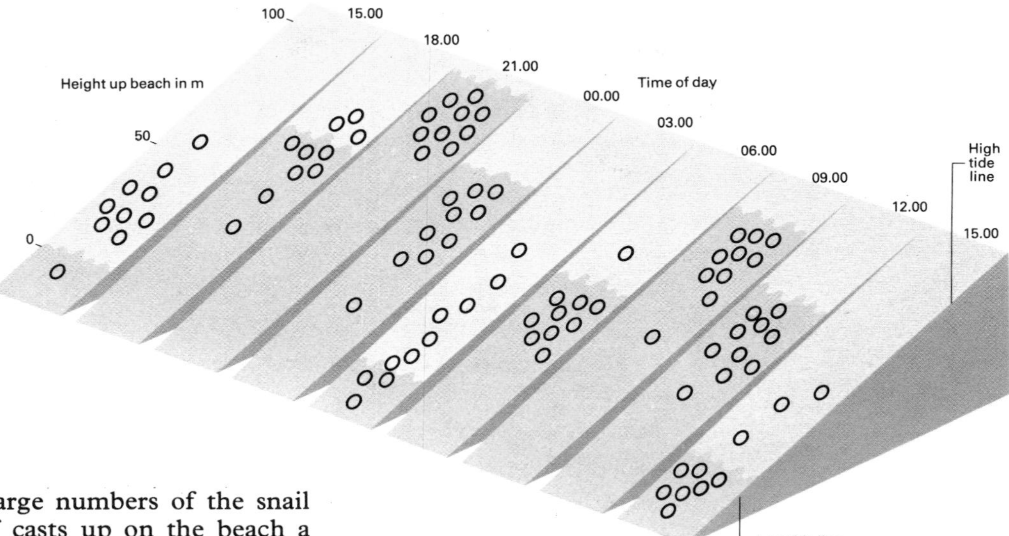

Natal in South Africa are large numbers of the snail *Bullia rhodostoma*. The surf casts up on the beach a whole gamut of dead and dying animals. As the surge drags the bodies over the sand, a faint trail of body fluid is left behind. Buried in the sand, the snails are constantly scenting water at the surface. At the faintest hint of food they emerge from the sand and march unerringly towards the food. Within a matter of a few minutes a large jellyfish will be fringed with hundreds of snails attracted to the bonanza.

On the bed of the deep ocean surprisingly large populations of scavenging carnivores have recently been discovered by means of dropping into the water tethered cameras focused on a bait. Within a few hours, vast numbers of animals are attracted to the bait. The largest among them are fish such as sharks, but crabs, large prawns, brittle stars and sometimes immense hordes of amphipods – relatives of sandhoppers – are attracted. Some of the pictures taken in the deep trenches of the west coast of South America show seething swarms of amphipods that resemble great swarms of bluebottles around a corpse. Since these amphipods are rarely caught by deep trawls fished by oceanographers, it seems likely that they converge on the bait from some distance away.

Scientists proposed a similar explanation for the curious outcome of an experiment performed in Plymouth Sound in southwest England, in which researchers attempted to keep conger eels alive in submerged enclosures. The congers were put into long lengths of drain-pipe closed at each end with wire mesh, which were marked with a buoy and left for a week on the sea bed. When the pipes were retrieved it was found that the congers had gone, yet the wire mesh at the ends of each pipe was still in place and undamaged. A repeat experiment in which the pipes were retrieved after only two days showed the answer to be elementary. The congers had indeed left through the meshes of the wire, but inside the stomachs of numerous migrant isopod carnivores, which had eaten them alive.

Bullia **snails** (right) are particularly partial to jellyfish. On detecting the scent of a jellyfish on the beach, the snails migrate rapidly towards it; their trails are clearly visible in the sand (below). Meanwhile, the tide has receded and the snails, being stranded on the beach and in danger of drying out (and of being eaten by predators), burrow into the sand. They emerge when the tide returns.

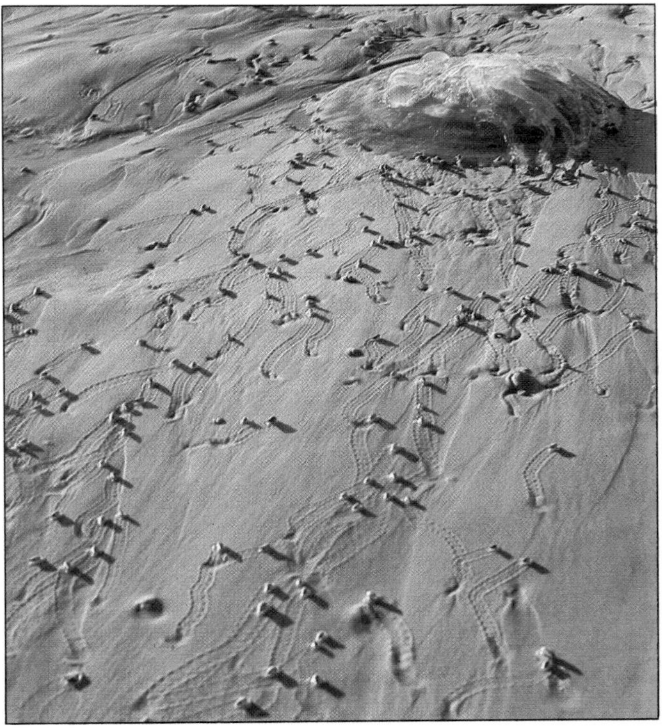

Retreating to a place of safety

Feeding migrations are often followed by migration to a place of safety. Anyone who regularly goes crabbing on a rocky shore soon gets to know good holes in which big crabs can always be found at low tide. The crabs feed during the night and then migrate to a hideaway, where they spend the day. The number of deep holes on a beach is limited, and the best holes are taken by the biggest crabs. Once a hole becomes vacant it is re-occupied by another crab. The areas around the holes are then defended vigorously and the occupant learns its way around its territory, building up a familiar area. The crab can then quickly home in on its refuge when danger threatens.

On a much smaller scale, male fiddler crabs, *Uca* spp., in mangrove swamps defend an area around their burrow against other males. Young immature crabs are tolerated, and females are courted by means of ostentatious semaphore signals with one of the pincers, which is greatly enlarged. Because the males defend a territory, their burrows tend to be evenly distributed, but the females' burrows are randomly scattered. Each crab feeds on the algae and detritus on the mud surface close to its burrow while it is exposed during low tide. The incoming tide or any slight movement by an observer is enough to send all the crabs within sight scuttling for the safety of their burrow.

Fiddler crabs aggressively defend their burrows, and it is to these that each crab migrates as the returning tide approaches. Here they remain buried in the sand until it is safe for them to emerge.

All over the world there are many types of limpets living on rocky shores. Each individual limpet migrates, after feeding, to the safety of its own home position. If the rock is hard, the limpet's shell becomes shaped so that it forms a watertight seal between itself and the rock surface. If the rock is soft, the shuffling movement of the limpet as it clamps itself into position wears a circular groove in the rock, which is known as a limpet scar. Limpets spend low tide during the day securely clamped to a rock face so that they are neither easily knocked off by waves or predators nor dried up by the heat of the sun. At night, or during high tide, provided the sea is not too rough, they crawl away to rasp microscopic seaweeds off the rock surface. As the tide falls, or when dawn comes, they return to their original position.

The migrations of limpets cover no more than about one metre (3 feet), but any animal that can home on one among possibly many hundreds of scars on a rock must have an ability to navigate and be familiar with at least part of its surroundings. It appears that limpets find

Along the edge of the mangrove swamps and sandy beaches some species of fiddler crab congregate in large numbers to feed. Here they are particularly prone to attack by predatory birds and small carnivores.

their way back each time by building up a tactile and chemical map of their area. A limpet displaced from its familiar area rarely manages to return home; it appears unable to navigate from outside this area. An interesting consequence of this homing ability concerns the species *Patella cochlear*. On the shores of South Africa this limpet feeds on the calcareous alga *Lithothamnion*. Its continuous grazing of this alga removes the competition for another, red, alga, which grows in a garden around the limpet's territory. If the limpet did not home, the garden would not develop.

The migration of octopuses and spiny lobsters

In the Mediterranean, on the muddy sea bed off the aquarium at Monaco, every ten metres (33 feet) or so one finds a little collection of stones, pieces of shard or bottles. Each of these is the home of an octopus. At night the octopuses emerge to hunt out the prawns and crabs, which they eat. Learning experiments have shown that octopuses, too, are able to distinguish quite complex shapes and patterns, and that each octopus is able to build up a mental map of its territory. Probably this map is based on touch and taste signals as well as visual landmarks.

Migrations to places of safety do not always involve homing. Off the coast of Florida, in the autumn, soon after the first storms that signal the onset of winter, the spiny lobsters, *Panulirus argus*, begin to get restless. They leave the holes in the reef in which they have spent the summer and spawned and begin to aggregate together. They then line up, each lobster touching the tail of the one in front. Queues may consist of more than

Limpets, *Patella* spp., as adults living on rocks perform short-distance migrations within their familiar area. Limpet larvae, however, migrate over much greater distances, and are responsible for extending the range of the species. Common limpets, *Patella vulgata*, breed in winter and shed their eggs into the water. Larvae hatching from the eggs may travel thousands of kilometres before settling on a rock.

THE LIFE CYCLE OF THE GREENTAIL PRAWN

In Brisbane River in eastern Australia, greentail prawn larvae migrate some eighty kilometres (50 miles) upstream. Having developed into adults, they migrate back downstream, attaining maturity and spawning on reaching the mouth of the river. Prawn length at stages in the cycle is shown.

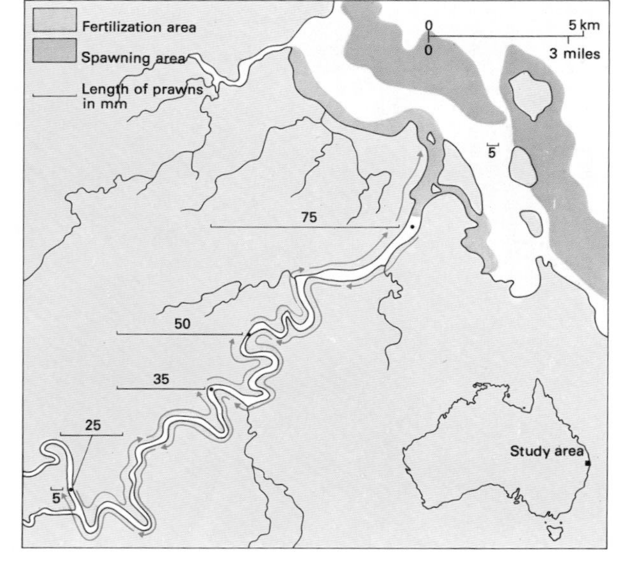

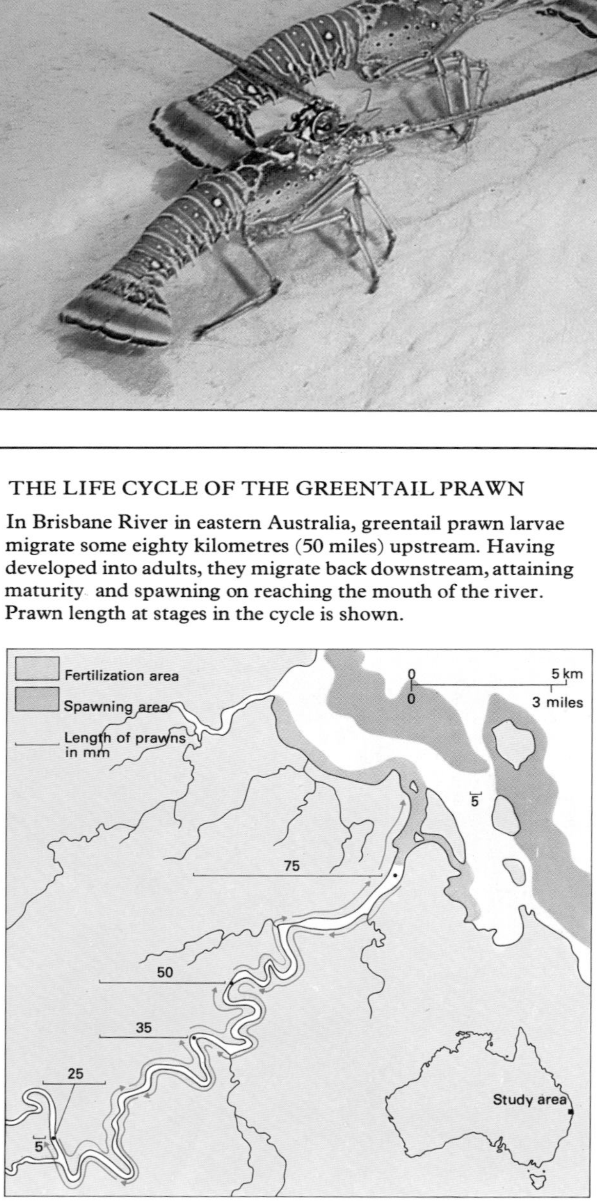

Spiny lobsters, *Panulirus* spp., perform return migrations between offshore winter haunts and spring and summer residences in reefs close to the shore. They produce larvae that live in the zooplankton and which are displaced by the water currents.

fifty animals, which, in this formation, set off at a spanking pace for deep water. The reasons for migrating to deep water are to get below the buffeting effects of the wave surge caused by the winter storms, to move into depths where there are fewer predators and to find colder conditions. During the winter, when food is short or even unavailable, animals want to use their food reserves as slowly as possible. The cooler an animal the slower its metabolism, and so the less energy it expends just to stay alive. This is the same reason why certain land mammals hibernate in winter.

Travels into estuaries and up and down streams

Near to the mouth of a river, some invertebrates migrate upstream by making use of the currents generated by the flooding tide. Often such invertebrates are the newly metamorphosed young of large crustaceans such as prawns and crabs that have spawned in the river estuary or even just offshore in shallow water in the sea. The young of the greentail prawn, *Metapenaeus mastersii*, of Australia, may travel several kilometres upstream by this method. Then, as the young grow, they gradually move downstream, arriving back at the spawning grounds just as they reach maturity. The mitten crab, *Eriocheir*

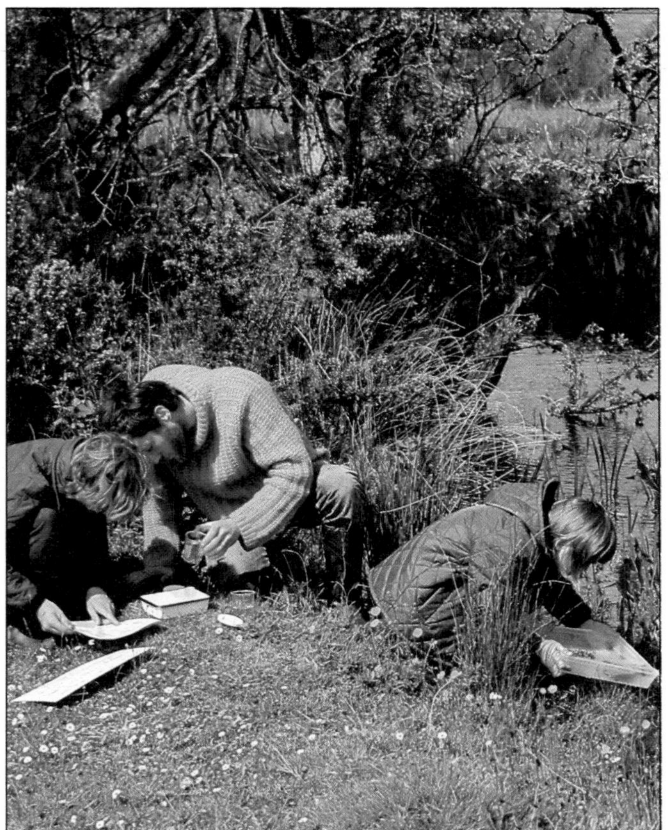

Examination of water samples taken from rivers and streams at various times of the day has revealed that most downstream drift takes place at night when the majority of freshwater invertebrates feed.

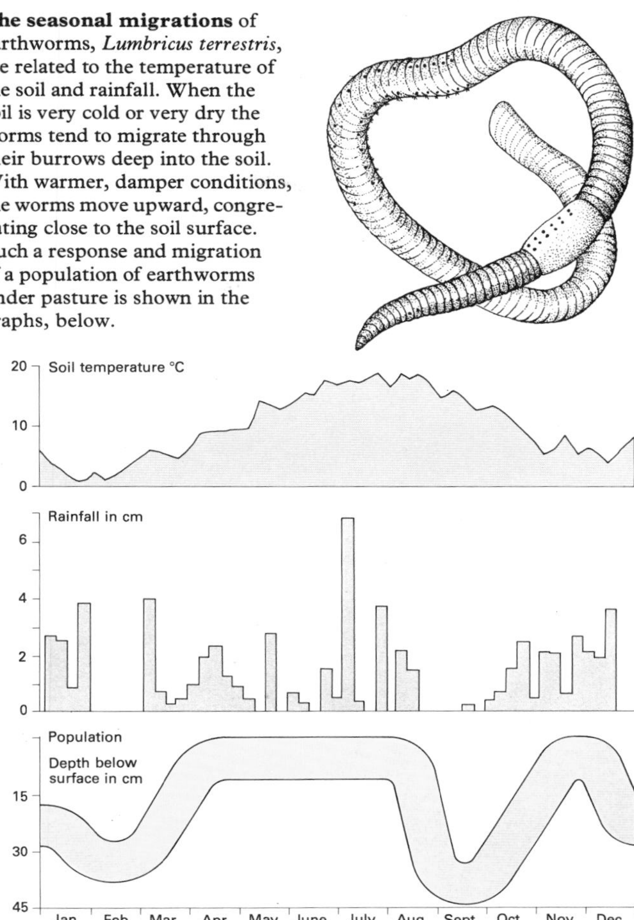

The seasonal migrations of earthworms, *Lumbricus terrestris*, are related to the temperature of the soil and rainfall. When the soil is very cold or very dry the worms tend to migrate through their burrows deep into the soil. With warmer, damper conditions, the worms move upward, congregating close to the soil surface. Such a response and migration of a population of earthworms under pasture is shown in the graphs, below.

sinensis, behaves similarly. This species has recently also performed a migration of a different type; via rivers and seas it has dramatically extended its range from its Asian homeland to occupy many of the countries of central and northern Europe, the rivers of which feed into the Black and Mediterranean seas.

The great variety of invertebrates that live in running water have only to release their hold on the stones or plants on which they are crawling and they are rapidly transported by the water current. In this way they are able to travel distances that would take them a long time to cover by their own locomotion. A fine mesh net suspended in a fast-flowing stream soon catches an assortment of insect larvae, such as those of mayflies, caddis flies and beetles, and, also, flatworms, small crustaceans (mostly amphipods and isopods), small snails and even some roundworms. These are all members of the so-called downstream drift. Zoologists still argue over what proportion of the animals present in the downstream drift are there by accident and what proportion are there because they are actively making use of the water current to migrate from one place to another. Most people believe that both explanations are correct, and that some animals are drifting purposefully, and others accidentally.

Although convenient, water transport creates a problem because it is always in the same direction, namely downstream. If all members of a population were to join the downstream drift, there would soon be no animals left upstream. However, this does not occur, and there is some evidence that even those individuals that do join the drift may migrate back up the stream some time later. Some caddis flies, for example, drift downstream as aquatic larvae and then, when they emerge into the air as adults, fly back upstream, perhaps several kilometres, before laying their eggs in the water. In Sweden, some stoneflies that emerge as adults into the cold Scandinavian winter migrate back upstream by walking along the bank over the snow. Similarly, non-insect members of the drift, such as flatworms and snails, may alternate periods of downstream displacement with periods of upstream walking. Certainly some small crustaceans, such as *Gammarus* spp., when introduced into a stream not previously supporting that species, have been recaptured more than a kilometre (0.6 mile) upstream from the point of release.

The migrations of land invertebrates

Naturally, most attention is drawn to those movements of invertebrates that involve long distances or unusual mechanisms. Yet many land invertebrates are continually on the move, performing daily and seasonal return migrations that in all respects, save that of distance, are both spectacular and equivalent to the migrations performed by, say, birds. For example, the larger earthworms, such as *Lumbricus terrestris*, during the hot, dry days of summer spend the day in the soil at depths of up to several metres, but in winter spend the day much nearer the surface. Superimposed on this seasonal return migration is a daily return migration. The worms climb through their complex burrow system to the surface at night to feed, mate and defecate and then migrate down beneath the surface again to spend the day. On the forest floor other invertebrates, such as pseudoscorpions and millipedes, may migrate up into the leaf-litter layer for the summer and then migrate down into the soil again for the winter. It is possible that they also perform daily vertical migrations.

Because land invertebrates' only method of locomotion is walking, they are very limited in the distances they can travel. It would need a lot of time and energy for an animal such as a spider, scorpion, slug or snail to travel a kilometre or more, and these are precious commodities they can ill-afford. It is not surprising, therefore, that whenever relatively long-distance migration becomes advantageous, land invertebrates make use of the free energy available to them through, as we have seen, water currents or through wind currents or the migration of other, more mobile, animals.

Most members of the aerial plankton, that largely unseen suspension of small animals high up in the air that is the food of swifts and swallows, are small winged insects such as aphids. Others, however, do not have wings. For example, some caterpillars, when small, are very hairy and light and they allow themselves to be blown off their foodplants (usually trees) and up into the air. After a brief membership of the aerial plankton, the caterpillars are deposited by the wind back near the ground, hopefully (for the caterpillar) on a suitable foodplant. Many of these hairy caterpillars are of moth species in which the adult females are wingless and cannot fly around to find suitable places to lay their eggs.

Aeronaut spiders

Other caterpillars that become airborne do so not because they are light and hairy but because they produce long threads of silk that are caught by the wind. The best example, however, of the use of silk to get up into the aerial plankton and thus to make use of wind-borne transport to migrate from place to place, is that of the gossamer or aeronaut spiders. The many species of small spiders that migrate in this way are usually species adapted to temporary habitats, such as straw and other debris, rather than those adapted to permanent habitats such as trees. The spider starts its migration by climbing to the top of a grass stem or other projection and sticking its abdomen up into the air. It then extrudes a length of silk from its spinnerets and waits for this to be taken up by the wind. As the wind tugs at the silk the spider pays out more and more. Eventually, there is enough silk to support the spider's weight, whereupon it lets go of the grass stem and is blown up into the air suspended by its silken thread. Gossamer spiders can travel long distances by this method; some have been caught at sea thousands of kilometres from land. Nobody knows whether the spider simply waits for the wind to deposit it back to earth or whether it has some control over how quickly it returns by adjusting the length of its silken thread.

Hitching a ride

There is one way that land invertebrates, too smooth or too heavy to be blown by the wind, can travel long distances across country. In just the same way as humans climb on to more mobile animals, such as horses, camels or donkeys, when they want to travel long distances, so too do many invertebrates. The best known of these so-called phoretic animals are pseudoscorpions, which attach themselves to the leg of an insect when they are ready to move to a new site. House flies are favourite hosts. Many other insects, particularly those that feed on dung or carrion, harbour heavy infestations of mites. Most often these mites are probably parasitic on their host, but the situation is not always as straightforward. Some scarabid dung beetles carry large numbers of mites around with them when they fly. When the beetle lands on dung to feed, mate or lay eggs, the mites leave their host and scatter across the dung surface. The mites then eat the eggs of various beetles, particularly those of staphylinids, the larvae of which are predatory upon the eggs and larvae of the host beetle species. Many of the mites aggregate on the scarab again before it flies off to search for more dung. The scarab actually benefits, therefore, from transporting these mites from place to place.

One final type of, albeit, short-distance migration by land invertebrates that often attracts attention is the occasional movement of large numbers of a single species all in one direction. Most often such movements result from overpopulation and the denudation of feeding areas, as when plagues of caterpillars are seen crawling across the road or other areas of bare ground. Sometimes, though, the reason for the migration is as yet unknown. But the best known invertebrates that crawl across the ground in large numbers are the nomadic driver or army ants of tropical regions, and these are discussed in the next chapter.

SPIDERS STAGE A MASS MIGRATION

When filter beds at a sewage works in Minworth, England, dried out, the millions of money spiders – notably, *Leptorhoptrum robustum* (below) – that inhabited the beds started to migrate in search of a new home. Having spun silken threads, some floated away, but others failed to gain lift and remained; the interweaving of their trail lines produced a silk sheet which enveloped the site (right).

Phoretic creatures migrate by attaching themselves to other animals, which carry them from place to place. Although some invertebrates, such as the mites on this harvestman (above), appear to behave more as parasites than as phoretic animals, pseudoscorpions (below) do just simply tag on to a host when they want to move and release themselves on being brought in contact with a suitable habitat.

Insects

Of all animals insects are the most supreme opportunists. Equipped with wings, they are able not only to rise up into the air but also to control the distance and direction of their journey. They can fly up away from the vegetation that hampers the movements of animals on the ground and thus search for new habitats from above. In consequence, they are able rapidly to find and exploit even those ephemeral habitats that appear unpredictably, flourish briefly and then disappear.

As for their migrations, to most of us this conjures up pictures of bees swarming to hives or of locusts or columns of army ants moving across country, devouring any animal in their path. The flutterings of butterflies and moths and the flights of tiny aphids and delicate damselflies, on the other hand, appear quite aimless and little to do with migration. Yet their whirls and girations are not haphazard but are a part of migrations more subtle in form. Like the movements of bees, locusts and ants, they have to do with a life cycle of emergence, feeding, mating, laying eggs and dying.

Many strong-flying insects, such as butterflies, moths and locusts, migrate across country in a preferred direction throughout their adult lives, with a number of long-lived species travelling more than 1000 kilometres (620 miles) from their place of birth to their place of death. In some, the preferred direction, taken from the sun, moon or stars, changes with the seasons. Other opportunists, the weaker fliers, such as aphids, may perform only one migration by flight during their entire adult life. Many of these seem to have no preferred direction, delegating the course of cross-country movement entirely to the wind.

The cross-country migrations of the opportunists are journeys to destinations that are unknown when the insects set out. In between such migrations, these insects may each establish a temporary familiar area at the site where it feeds, sleeps and reproduces. Some insects, among them the social bees, wasps, ants and termites, spend their entire lives within a familiar area that is as sophisticated as that of any mammal. In many ways, the migrations of these relatively stationary insects are even more remarkable than those of insects that travel thousands of kilometres during their lifetime.

Monarch butterflies, *Danaus plexippus*, overwinter in their hundreds of millions in forests in Mexico and southern USA. Here they remain until spring, when they migrate north.

Insects and wing development

If one could plot on a map the track of an individual insect throughout its life, it would be apparent that for most species movement over any appreciable distance was performed while the insect was an adult. The explanation of this is simply that nearly all adult insects bear wings and can fly, whereas not a single young insect has wings and most are forced to travel from one place to another by walking. This basic difference seems to be a consequence of the way in which insects grow.

One of the great assets of the insect body is that it is encased in a hard external skeleton, or cuticle. But this poses problems. In order to bend and move, sections of stiff armour have to be joined by more flexible membranes. These membranes are softer, more vulnerable to damage and piercing and, although protected by flaps of harder cuticle, they are definite chinks in the insect armour. As well as allowing movement, however, these membranes allow the insect to grow. But only so far. Eventually, the developing insect grows to a size beyond which its skeleton will stretch no further. The encasing cuticle must then be shed and replaced with a looser one to allow another phase of growth.

Insects moult several times between emerging from the egg and reaching adult size, and this seems to be the reason for the absence of wings in young insects. Moulting is a complex and difficult process, and the mechanical problems raised by laying down a replacement cuticle are immense. Nevertheless, all of these problems were solved during the course of evolution. All, that is, except the problem of how to moult large, functional wings in a growing animal. As a result, insects delay the formation of functional wings until they have moulted for the last time.

In all insects the rudiments of the wings, the wing buds, appear at a very early stage, and at each moult they become slightly larger. In some insects the wing buds are outside the body and appear as small, functionless wings lying flat on the body. The young of these "exopterygote" insects resemble small adults with vestigial wings and, except for being unable to fly, their life style is similar to that of the adults. In contrast, the young of "endopterygote" insects differ from the adults in both appearance and life style. Their wing buds are invaginated, protruding inside the body like a close-ended sleeve pulled inside a coat. The streamlined body surface that results from this allows a differentiation between young and adults and a colonization of habitats, such as dung, corpses and soil, that is closed to most exopterygotes. Eventually, however, via a special body form, the pupa, the wings of an endopterygote form outside the body. When the adult breaks out of its pupal casing it is complete.

The remainder of this chapter is concerned with the way that the possession of wings influences the movements of insects. Except for the awe-inspiring driver and army ants, which migrate by walking, descriptions are confined to the migration of adults by flight.

THE LIFE CYCLE OF EXOPTERYGOTE INSECTS

Exopterygotes produce young, or nymphs, with wing buds outside the body. Nymphs gradually acquire the adult form by passing through a series of moults, with the wings becoming fully functional only after the last moult. In most exopterygotes, nymphs and adults appear quite similar, as illustrated here by those of the harlequin cabbage bug, *Murgantia histrionica.* When they are similar, adults and nymphs are often found living side by side on the same plant. Even so, only one group, the termites, have evolved sociality. In some exopterygotes adults and nymphs look different and live in different places. For example, the nymphs of such insects as stoneflies and mayflies are aquatic and, unlike the adults, bear gill-like structures for breathing in water.

In addition to mayflies, stoneflies and bugs, there are more than five hundred thousand other species of exopterygote insects, among them dragonflies, locusts and aphids, of which representatives are shown here.

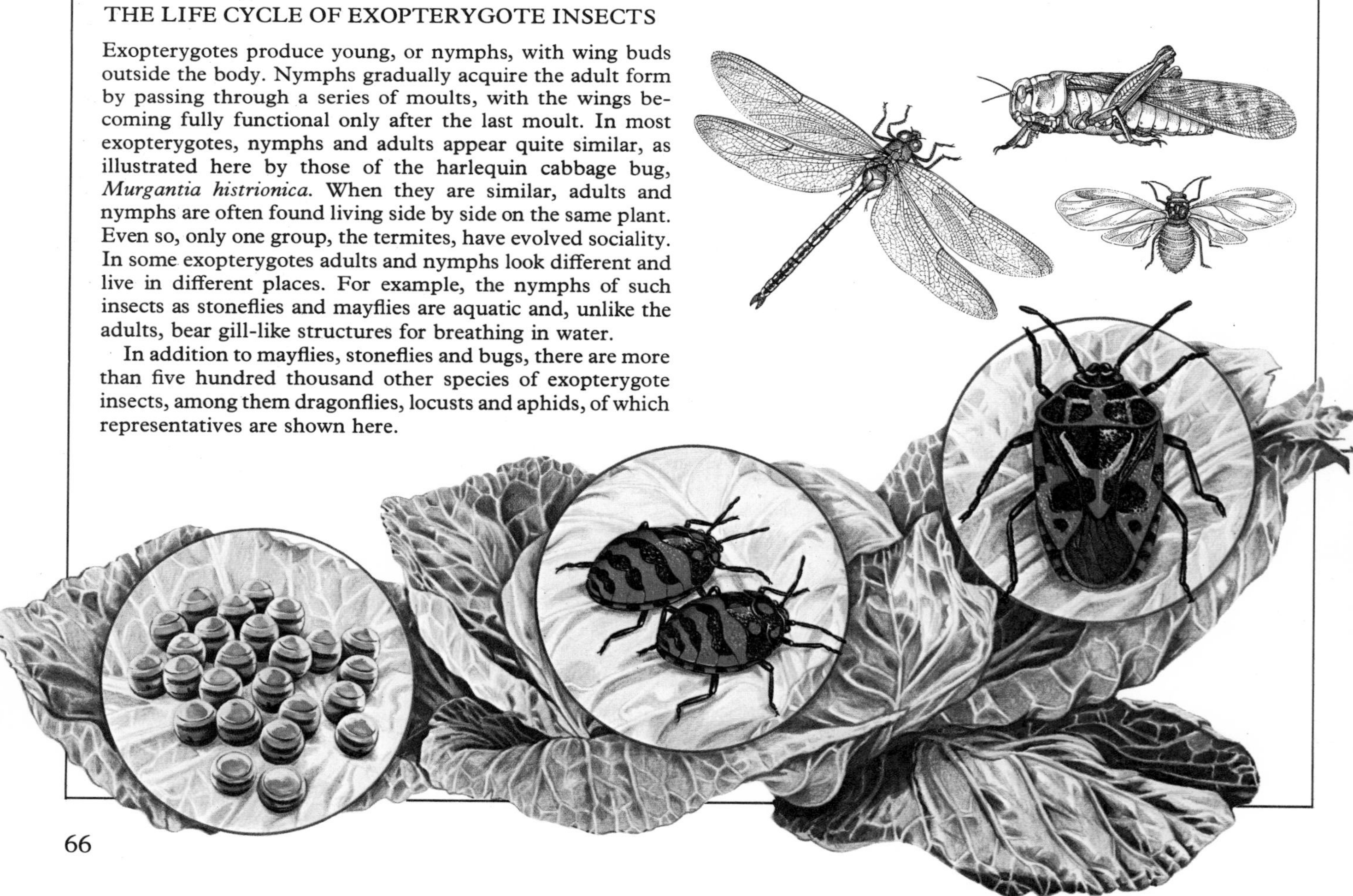

THE LIFE CYCLE OF ENDOPTERYGOTE INSECTS

The young, or larvae, of endopterygotes bear wing buds inside the body. The transformation from larva to adult of these insects is spectacular, and the mechanical problems involved are so great that the transition always occurs in four stages, as illustrated here by the life cycle of the small cabbage white butterfly, *Pieris rapae*.

First is the egg. In the small white, eggs are laid on the underside of cabbage leaves, the preferred food of the young. Then follows the larval stage, the caterpillar. During this stage the insect feeds voraciously and grows considerably in size. Next, the caterpillar develops into a chrysalis, the third, or pupal, stage. The appearance of this intermediate stage is unique to endopterygotes, and produces a life cycle involving a complete transformation of the insect. Within the outer casing of the pupa the larval tissues break down into a soup of living cells that then re-form. Thus the pupa acts as a mould for the developing adult. The life cycle is completed with the emergence from the pupa of the butterfly, the adult stage.

Although all endopterygotes undergo the same form of life cycle, the shape and structure of the individual stages differ depending on the species of insect. The larvae of many flies, for example, are without legs, while the larvae of butterflies, moths and sawflies bear three pairs of true legs and a number of pairs of additional motile structures, the prolegs, which are absent in the adult. Similarly, the pupae of many butterflies are suspended in the open from an upright such as a twig, unprotected save by camouflage, while those of many moths are each enclosed in a silken cocoon spun round itself by the larva before pupating. Silken cocoons may be spun among leaves or deep in the ground; many moth larvae that feed on the leaves of trees climb down onto the ground and then dig into the leaf litter or soil before pupating. Blowfly larvae, emerging from some hapless corpse that they have helped to consume, may also burrow into the soil. These, however, do not spin a cocoon, instead the skin of the last larval stage, rather than splitting and detaching itself from the underlying pupa, remains and hardens, forming a protective chamber within which the pupal stage is passed. Finally, aquatic larvae, such as those of caddis flies, mosquitoes and some beetles, usually pupate under water.

Among the many hundreds of thousands of species of endopterygotes, each of which share this four-stage life cycle, are the lacewing, fly, beetle, wasp and ladybird species shown here.

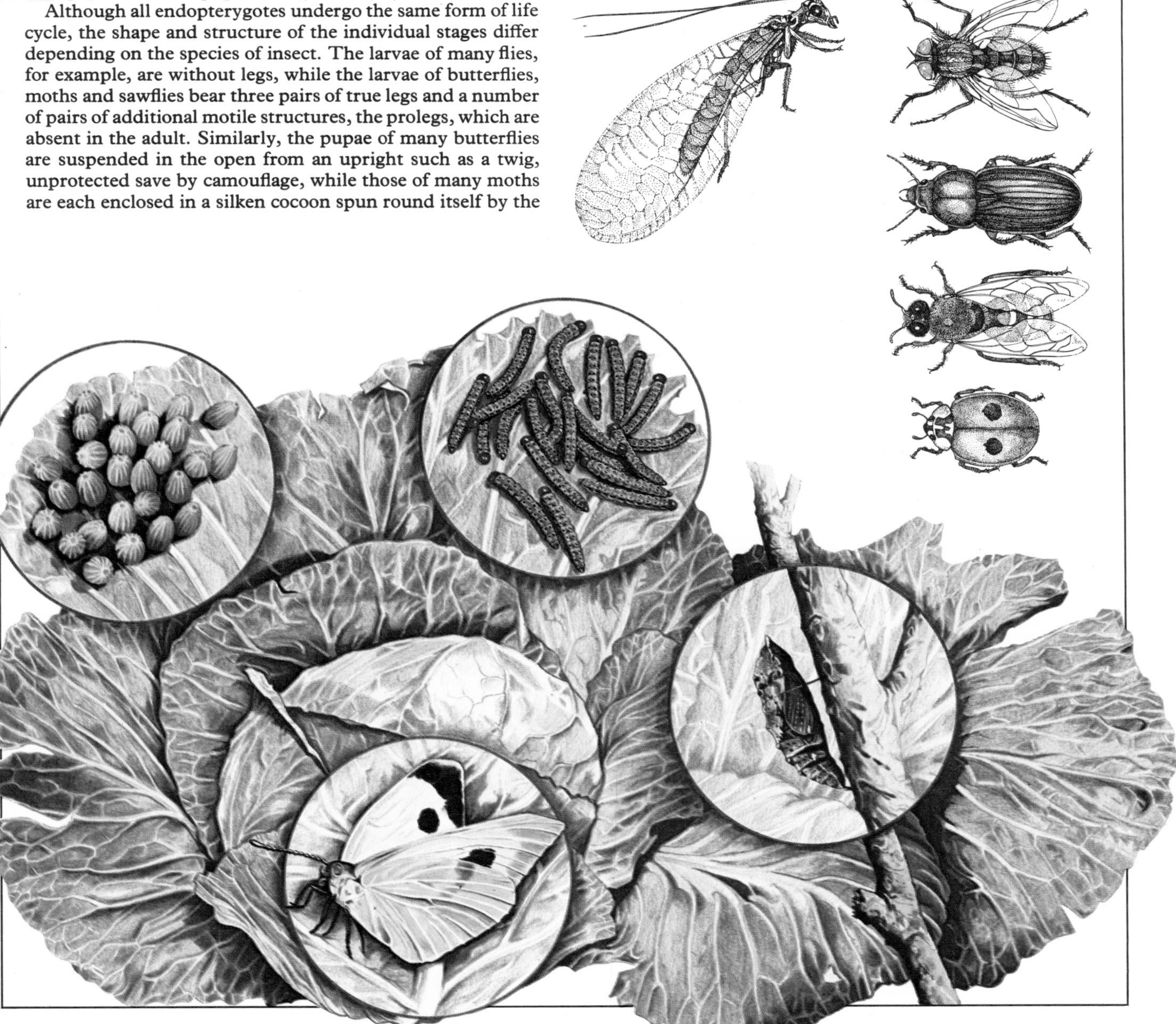

The painted lady, or thistle, butterfly, *Cynthia cardui*, is a regular spring and summer visitor to temperate regions of North America and western Europe. Here eggs are laid on the leaves of thistle or heather, the preferred food of the caterpillars. Transformation from caterpillar to adult butterfly usually takes about three weeks.

Butterflies of temperate regions

We know more about the migrations of butterflies of temperate regions than about those of any other group of insects. Yet their migrations are seldom conspicuous, and rarely as spectacular as those of butterflies in tropical regions. It is only very careful observations that have revealed that migrations are taking place at all. For many of the more common temperate butterflies, migration is neither infrequent nor sporadic, but rather a normal episode of life.

A simple experiment could illustrate the point. Anywhere in the temperate zones, if an observer were to choose a large grassy field well grazed by sheep or cattle so that the grass is short and there are few flowers from which adult butterflies could feed, in general he might expect to see two types of butterfly, the "anticipated" one and the "surprise" one. Our observer would expect to see the first of these because all its requirements are to be found in such a field. A typical example of this is the meadow brown, *Maniola jurtina*, of Europe and Asia. Female meadow browns lay their eggs on short grass and, because they are there, males come searching for mates. Both sexes also feed from available flowers and can roost in, or beneath, the hedgerows that surround the field. Butterflies of this type have a flight pattern that, while not random, involves a great many changes of direction and frequent stops to feed, roost or court. If the meadow brown butterfly does fly over the surrounding hedge, it soon reverses direction and comes back into the field, where it may stay for several hours, perhaps even several days.

The second, or "surprise", type would not be expected to visit the field. Taking Northern and Southern Hemisphere temperate regions as a whole, the most common of these surprise visitors is likely to be the small cabbage white butterfly, *Pieris rapae.* This species will behave quite differently from the meadow brown, for the field has little to offer it. There are no cabbages on which to lay eggs, few flowers from which to feed, and no tall, broad-leaved plants on which to roost, so it will not stay in the field long. Having entered by flying over a hedge on one side of the field, it is likely to fly in a more or less straight line across it and over the opposite hedge.

Some distance beyond, there may be a field of cabbages. Here one would find the roles of the meadow brown and small white reversed. In the cabbage field it is the small white that changes direction frequently, often stops, reverses direction if it crosses the field boundary, staying probably for up to an hour or so. The meadow brown, however, would fly straight across.

Another observer in the shopping centre of a nearby town may also see individuals of the small white and meadow brown. But here both butterflies fly straight through. Neither has any use for concrete.

Thus temperate butterflies respond to unsuitable habitats by flying straight across, but react to suitable ones with a flight pattern that may keep them within the habitat for hours, days, or, in some species, for an entire lifetime.

Migrant or resident?

For many years, entomologists thought that only those butterflies seen flying across country were migrants, while those seen flying around within suitable habitats were residents. This explanation has now been discarded. An observer, fit and agile enough to run across fields at a steady ten kilometres (6 miles) an hour or so, to jump gates and to crawl through hedges, will find, if he follows, say, an individual small white as it flies across country, that as soon as the butterfly encounters a field of cabbages or flowers it changes its behaviour. It stops flying in a straight line and displays a resident-type behaviour. It will stay in the field for a period and perhaps feed from flowers. A male will search for, and court, females and may even succeed in copulation and the latter may lay eggs.

Eventually, provided the sun is still shining, it will leave the field, but the direction in which it leaves will not be random. If our fit and agile observer has managed to keep his eye on the same individual small white from the moment it entered the cabbage field, he will find that when it eventually leaves, it will once more fly in a straight line, taking the same compass direction it was following when it entered the field.

By the simple, but energetic, procedure of following individual butterflies it is possible to piece together the form of their lifetime track – the track in space made by each individual animal from its place of birth to its place of death. The lifetime track of a butterfly such as

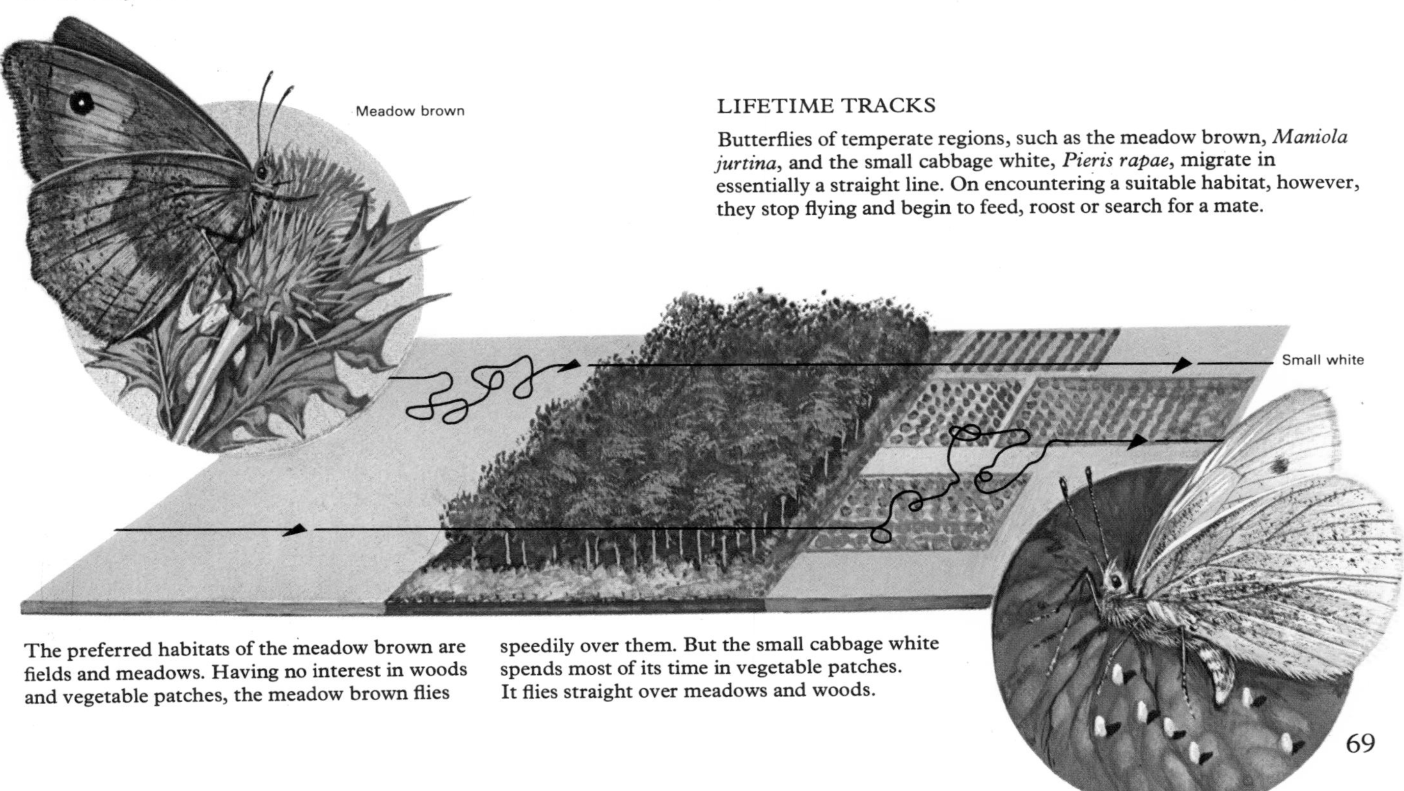

LIFETIME TRACKS

Butterflies of temperate regions, such as the meadow brown, *Maniola jurtina*, and the small cabbage white, *Pieris rapae*, migrate in essentially a straight line. On encountering a suitable habitat, however, they stop flying and begin to feed, roost or search for a mate.

The preferred habitats of the meadow brown are fields and meadows. Having no interest in woods and vegetable patches, the meadow brown flies speedily over them. But the small cabbage white spends most of its time in vegetable patches. It flies straight over meadows and woods.

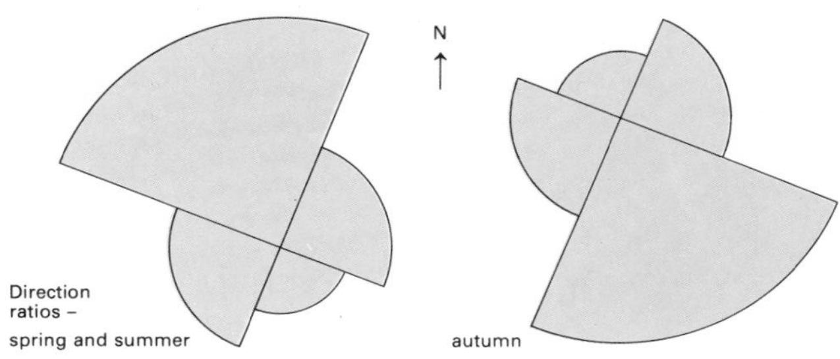

The seasonal migrations of temperate butterflies show a movement towards the poles in spring and summer and towards the tropics in autumn. Diagrams of the distribution of migration directions of the large cabbage white butterfly, *Pieris brassicae*, in western Europe, therefore, show a major movement of the population to the north in spring and summer and to the south in autumn. The stimulus for such seasonal movements is usually a change in the length and temperature of the nights.

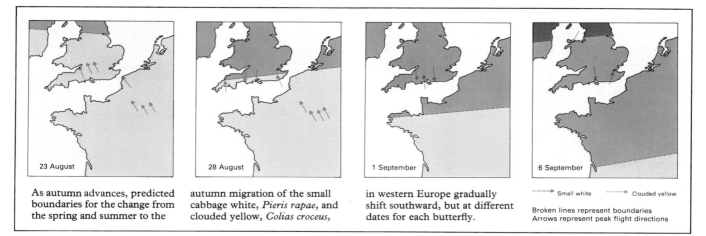

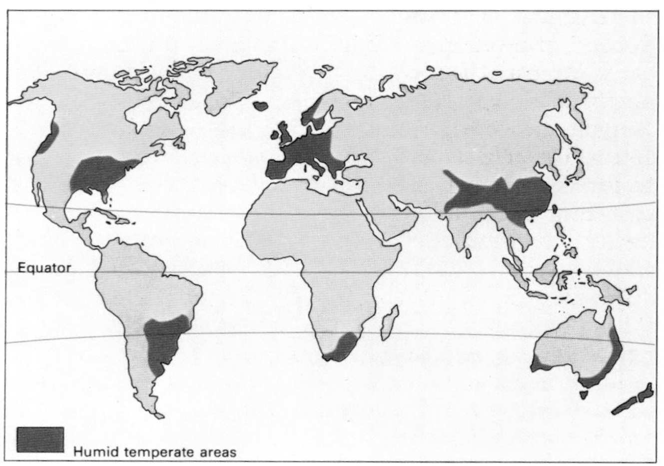

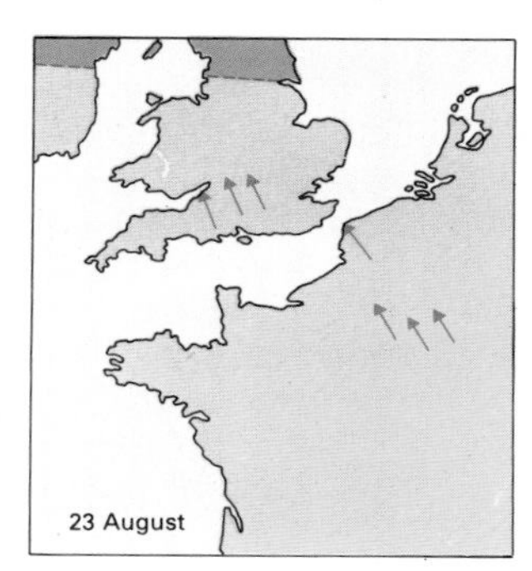

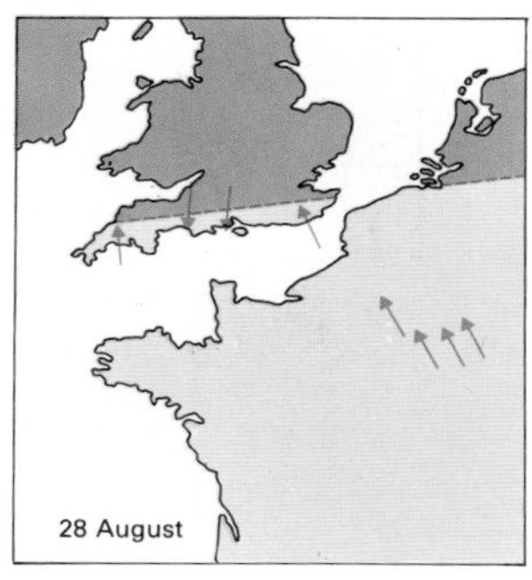

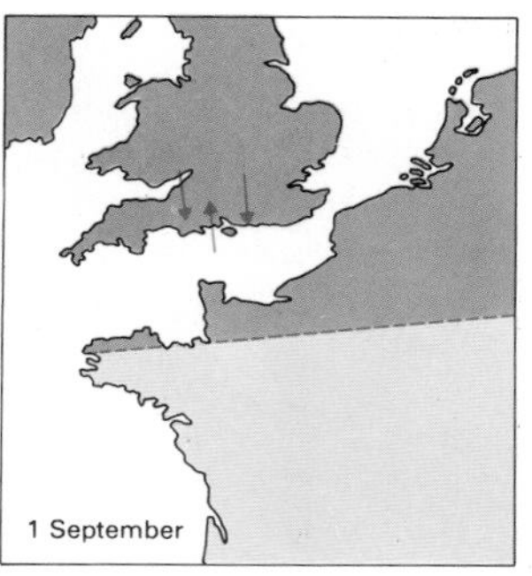

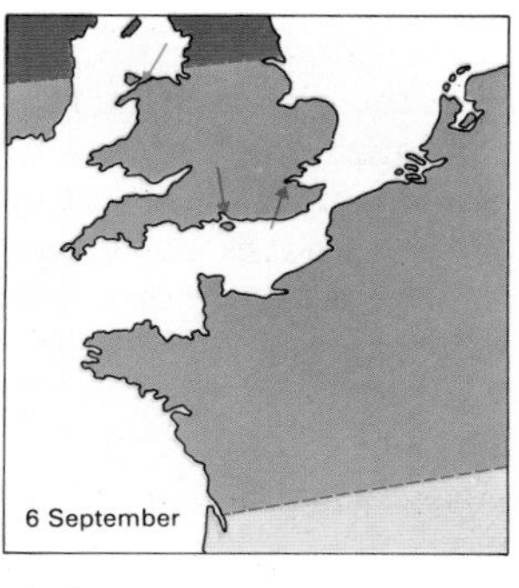

As autumn advances, predicted boundaries for the change from the spring and summer to the autumn migration of the small cabbage white, *Pieris rapae*, and clouded yellow, *Colias croceus*, in western Europe gradually shift southward, but at different dates for each butterfly.

Small white — Clouded yellow

Broken lines represent boundaries
Arrows represent peak flight directions

the small white is said to be of the linear range type. Whenever it flies in a straight line across unsuitable habitats, the individual always takes up the same geographical direction, and its lifetime track takes the form of a gradual migration across country in that particular direction.

In the various temperate regions of the world the directions in which individuals of a species fly vary, and depending on the species some flight directions occur more often than others. In western Europe, in spring and summer, more small white butterflies fly west than east. The most common flight direction – the peak direction – is north-northwest, and the distribution of directions about this is termed the "direction ratio". Forty-two per cent of all small whites fly in the peak direction or, more precisely, 159° measured clockwise from south, twenty-one per cent fly roughly west-southwest, twenty-one per cent roughly east-northeast and sixteen per cent fly roughly south-southeast. The direction ratio of the small white can therefore be expressed as 42:21:21:16, and by adding the peak flight direction, namely 159°/42:21:21:16, a more or less complete description of the migration behaviour of the species can be presented.

The peak directions and direction ratios of temperate butterflies have been studied in detail only in western Europe. Those of the painted lady, or thistle, butterfly, *Cynthia cardui*, for example, in spring and summer are found to be 162°/54:18:22:6; for the large cabbage white, *Pieris brassicae*, 159°/45:21:21:13; and for the peacock butterfly, *Inachis io*, the figures are 166°/36:22:25:17. Although both these parameters vary from species to species, it is evident that where a peak direction exists, it is generally to the north or northwest. This seems to be true for butterflies throughout the northern temperate zone, including North America. Where observations in spring exist for southern temperate butterflies, such as the small white in southeastern Australia, the peak direction is to the south. The general rule, therefore, seems to be that in spring in temperate regions butterflies have a peak migration direction towards the poles and away from the tropics.

Autumn migrations

A major change in the peak direction occurs in late summer or early autumn. In western Europe, the first butterfly to change direction is the large cabbage white, *Pieris brassicae*. Female large whites lay eggs in May and June and then die, and their offspring emerge in mid-July. These have a peak direction that is not north-northwest like that of their parents, but instead is south-southeast. Similarly, individuals of the red admiral, *Vanessa atalanta*, and the painted lady, or thistle, butterfly, *Cynthia cardui*, that emerge as adults after about mid-August, also show a peak direction to the south. Second generation small whites that appear in July and early August at first continue to show a peak direction of north-northwest. After a certain date in middle to late August, however, this peak direction changes to due south. In each instance, the change-over takes only two to three days, but occurs later further south. In north-east England, for example, small whites change their peak direction around 12 August. In southern England the change-over date is about 26 August, and in the Alsace region of France the date is about 2 September. The last species to change direction in western Europe and to show a peak direction to the south seems to be the clouded yellow, *Colias croceus*, which in each location has a change-over date that is about two weeks later than that for the small white.

What causes this change in direction? With birds, the change in direction to autumn migration is linked in some way with temperature and the hours of daylight. With temperate butterflies it is the length and temperature of the night, rather than of the day, that is important. Large numbers of second generation small whites were captured and divided into two groups, exposed to different night lengths and temperatures, then released. When their flight directions were determined, it was found that the group of butterflies exposed to two successive long, cold nights had a peak migration to the south, whereas the group exposed to two successive short, warm nights had a peak direction to the north-northwest.

Orientating to the sun's azimuth

How does a butterfly decide in which direction to migrate? How does it orientate itself? When it stops to feed in a field, how does it manage to continue on the same compass course by which it entered the field? A clue is provided by comparing the mid-morning and mid-afternoon peak flight directions. In western Europe in spring and summer, from mid-morning to mid-afternoon, the peak direction of several species shifts from west-northwest to north-northeast. Thus an individual, captured while flying west at 09.00 hours, flies north when released at 15.00 hours and another, flying east at 09.00 hours, flies south when released at 15.00 hours. Detailed study has shown that the preferred direction of each individual, as well as the peak direction of the population, changes during the day at the same rate that the sun's azimuth (the point on the horizon directly below the sun's disc) moves across the horizon. It seems reasonably certain, therefore, that each individual butterfly flies along maintaining a preferred angle to the sun's azimuth.

To this extent, the orientation of temperate butterflies during migration is the same as that of birds that migrate by day. But unlike birds, and some other insects such as bees and tropical butterflies, temperate butterflies do not compensate for the movement of the sun's azimuth across the horizon by changing their angle of orientation. Instead, their angle to the azimuth stays constant, and it is their geographical direction that changes through about ninety degrees from mid-morning to mid-afternoon. Butterflies migrate only during the warmest part of the day and if the sun is shining.

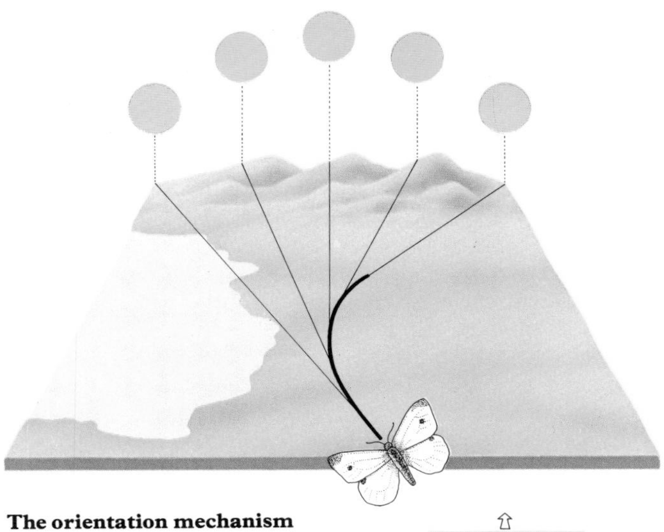

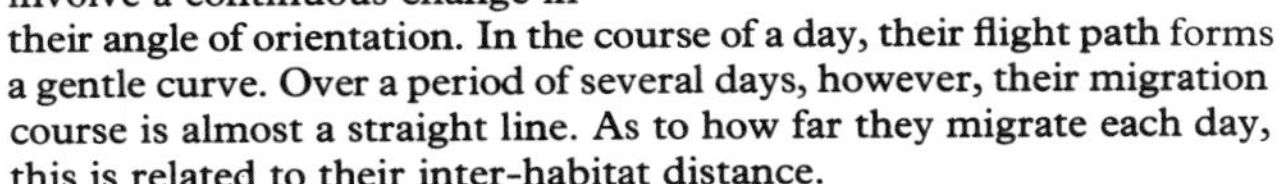

The orientation mechanism of temperate butterflies is based on maintaining a constant angle to the sun's azimuth – the point on the horizon directly below the sun. While migrating, these butterflies do not compensate for the movement of the azimuth across the horizon; this would involve a continuous change in their angle of orientation. In the course of a day, their flight path forms a gentle curve. Over a period of several days, however, their migration course is almost a straight line. As to how far they migrate each day, this is related to their inter-habitat distance.

The clouded yellow butterfly, *Colias croceus*, of western Europe, cannot survive the damp, cold northern winters, so in autumn it migrates towards the Mediterranean coast and North Africa. The following spring, the next generation returns northward.

Combating the elements

Although temperate butterflies take their primary orientation from the sun's azimuth, other mechanisms are also used, mainly to avoid displacement by the wind from their preferred direction. When there is no wind, butterflies fly straight across open spaces in their preferred direction, often relatively high – perhaps a few tens of metres above ground level. With faster wind speeds, no matter whether they are head or tail winds, the butterflies fly nearer to the ground. They also take more advantage of the shelter provided by hedgerows and rows of trees and houses. Nevertheless, they hold a course that causes them to deviate least from their preferred direction. Finally, if the wind speed increases to beyond a certain level, the butterflies no longer attempt to cross unsuitable habitats. Instead, they remain settled or flitting about and feeding within those areas that suit them.

In an extraordinary experiment on a peninsula in Florida, USA, involving large numbers of the great southern white, *Ascia monuste*, it was shown that butterflies not only maintain their flight direction independently of wind direction but also that, over a wide range of speeds of head and tail winds, they migrate across country at a more or less constant speed of ten to fifteen kilometres (6 to 9 miles) an hour. Just as they were beginning to leave the salt marshes on which they had developed, the butterflies were sprayed with red dye. Observers monitored the progress of the dyed insects at intervals along the narrow peninsula between the marking site and the next large area of suitable habitat some 100 to 150 kilometres (60 to 90 miles) away. Analysis of similar marking experiments carried out in West Germany has shown that the rate and direction of migration of the small tortoiseshell, *Aglais urticae*, is also independent of wind speed and direction.

Why should it be an advantage for temperate butterflies to fly across unsuitable habitats in a more or less constant direction at a more or less constant speed? The answer seems to be firstly that those individuals that wander haphazardly run the risk of wasting time in their search for food, mates, roosting sites or for plants on which to lay eggs by investigating such areas more than once. Secondly, butterflies that migrate too slowly will encounter fewer suitable habitats, while those that travel too fast will fail to recognize these habitats even if they pass nearby. This interpretation of the migration as searching behaviour also helps to explain why their orientation mechanism does not compensate for the movement of the sun's azimuth across the horizon. Such compensation would straighten out their track across country, but would not increase the area that the butterfly searches. (Area searched is solely the product of the distance travelled and the distance to the left and right that is within the butterfly's perceptual range.) And it is precisely this area that is important.

Lifetime track overview

Our final picture of the lifetime track of a temperate-zone butterfly is that of an individual gradually working its way across country in a relatively constant geographical direction. Each time it encounters a suitable habitat it stays there until its requirements are no longer met. Perhaps, if a male, it finds that no receptive females are present. Similarly, a female, having laid a number of eggs in one habitat, may then decide to move on and distribute eggs in several other places. Whatever the reason, whenever the current habitat becomes unsuitable the butterfly starts to fly in a straight line at its individually preferred angle to the sun's azimuth until it encounters another suitable area. This sequence is repeated throughout the individual's life.

The length, as opposed to the form, of the lifetime track depends on a number of factors, the most important of which are how frequently habitats become unsuitable, the distance between suitable habitats, and the longevity of the butterfly. Indeed, those butterflies adapted to habitats such as chalk hills and marshland, which provide all of the requirements of the species and which have a large inter-habitat distance, rarely leave their natal area and may die within a few tens of metres of the place where they first emerged. At the other extreme are species adapted as larvae to habitat-types such as cabbage and nettle patches, which contain relatively few feeding and roosting sites and which have a relatively short inter-habitat distance. Butterflies of this category may initiate a search for a new habitat many times each day.

The individual life-span of most temperate butterflies is usually no longer than three or four weeks, and may be much less. Calculations based on the observed rate of cross-country migration of butterflies such as the small white, *Pieris rapae*, suggest that over land most individuals have a lifetime track of no more than 300 kilometres (185 miles) in length. In some circumstances, however, for example, when individuals have to cross a sea or lake to reach a suitable habitat, they can fly much further.

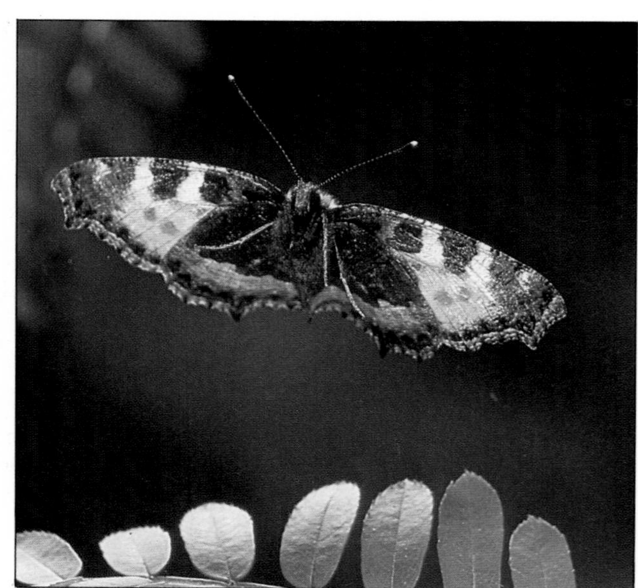

Flying downwind or against the wind, the small tortoiseshell butterfly, *Aglais urticae*, during spring and summer, migrates at an altitude of no more than about thirty metres (100 ft).

The red admiral butterfly, *Vanessa atalanta*, is a seasonal migrant of North America, Europe, North Africa and western Asia. As an adult it may live for many months, migrating hundreds of kilometres between breeding and overwintering sites.

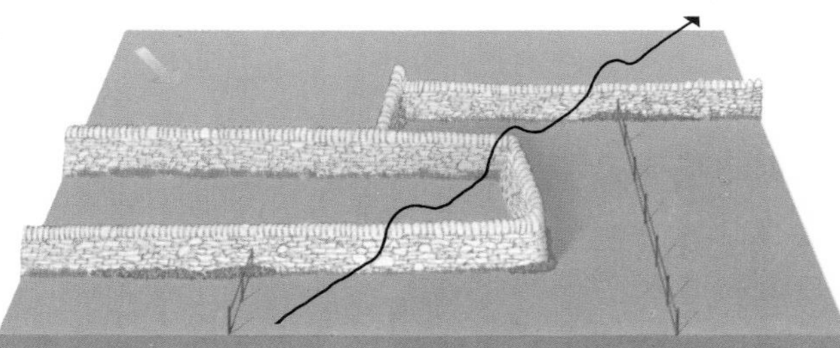

In light winds, temperate butterflies fly in a straight line across such open spaces as fields, maintaining their migration direction.

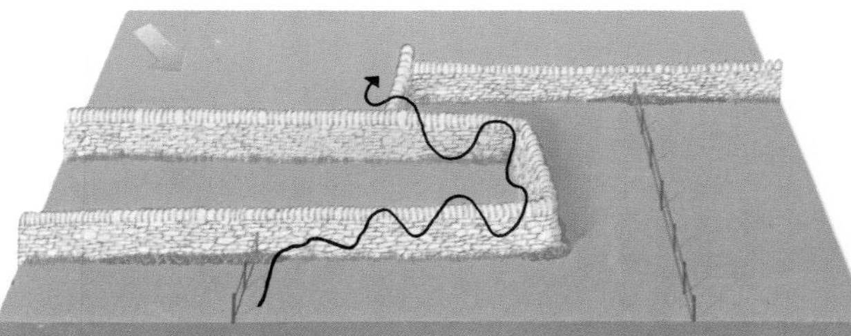

In strong winds they fly closer to the ground in the shelter of leading lines, regaining their preferred direction when possible.

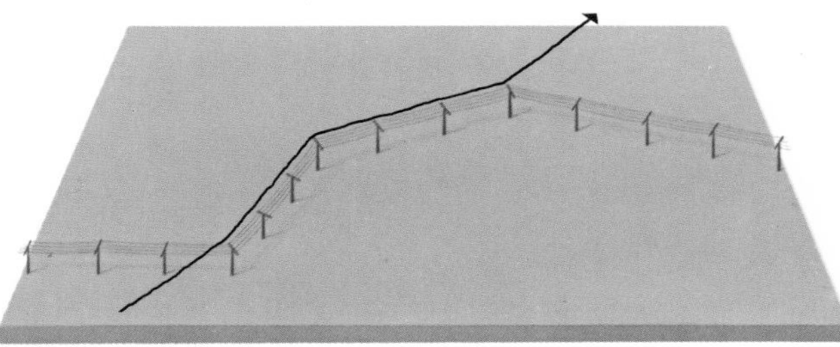

Leading lines, such as a row of telegraph poles, may be used by a migrating butterfly to maintain its preferred direction, but only until it is in danger of being led off course.

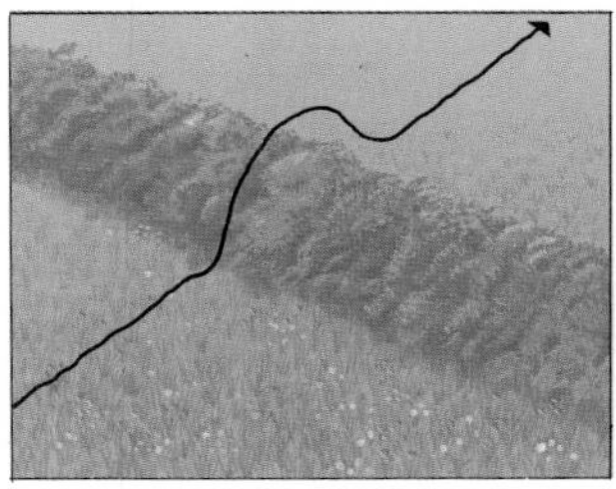

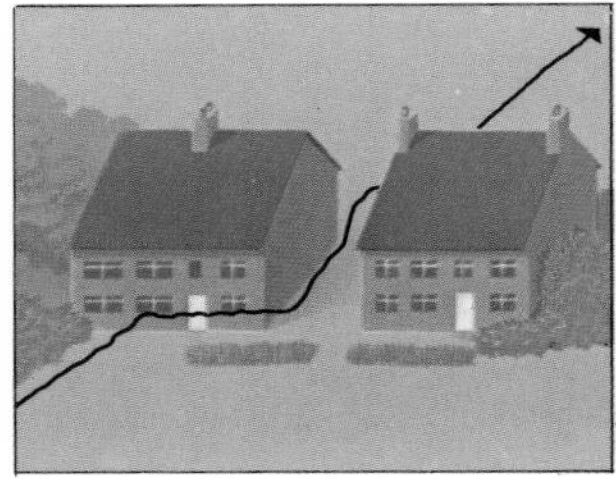

If an obstacle is encountered head on, a migrating butterfly will fly directly over it. If an obstacle lies at an angle to its migration direction, the butterfly will weave round it.

The amazing monarch butterfly

A major exception to the above rule is the monarch, or milkweed, butterfly, *Danaus plexippus*, of North America. This is perhaps the most famous of all migrant butterflies. Its life cycle is closely related to the milkweed plant – hence its alternative common name – with female monarchs laying their eggs on the underside of milkweed leaves, the principal food of the caterpillars. Each autumn, these North American monarchs – there is another population in the Americas south of the Amazon basin – migrate south in masses of many thousands. So predictable is this movement with respect to direction, time of year and the vast numbers involved, that many towns along the monarchs' flight path celebrate their arrival with festivals and carnivals. One town – Pacific Grove, California – even calls itself "Butterfly City, USA". To entomologists, however, their migration is all the more interesting and spectacular since it produces a lifetime track of a length far in excess of that of other butterflies such as the small white and meadow brown. It is thought from marking experiments that approximately two-thirds of the monarchs that emerge in the vicinity of the Great Lakes in late summer and early autumn migrate distances of between 2000 and 3000 kilometres (1250 to 1850 miles) to overwintering sites along the coast of the Gulf of Mexico or inland in Texas or Mexico. The other one-third remain there, probably hibernating in hollow trees or under the bark. They are the individuals that appear in the north the following spring.

The winter behaviour of the monarchs that fly south – referred to as the autumn generation – depends largely on how far they get. Those to the east of the Rockies that succeed in reaching Florida, Georgia or Louisiana, and those to the west that reach coastal California before being caught by the cold front from the north, form the spectacular and legendary "butterfly trees". As the polar front moves back and forth over them during the winter months, they leave their trees on warm days to feed, but return to roost at night. On cold days they remain in the trees. They do not begin to mate until the polar front starts to recede sometime towards the end of February.

The monarchs that manage to reach Texas and Mexico in autumn and thus escape the polar front altogether either climb the Mexican highlands and join butterfly trees like those on the coasts further north, or spend the winter as free-flying reproductive butterflies. They are likely to die within a few weeks of beginning to reproduce, and it will be their offspring, not they themselves, that fly north in spring.

From the beginning of March, the majority of southern monarchs fly north, laying eggs as they go. Many are the same ones that migrated south the previous autumn, and others may include their offspring. The rate of migration in spring – up to fifteen kilometres (9 miles) a day – is much slower than that in autumn, and compares with that of most other temperate species. Because they may live for four or five months after leaving their overwintering sites, some may travel more than 1000 kilometres (620 miles) before dying, but the majority do not travel so far. Even those that fly fastest and furthest are unlikely to return to the Great Lakes region from the Gulf Coast or Mexico.

Energy for migration above all else

Although at first sight the monarch appears to be quite a different class of migrant from other temperate butterflies, closer examination of its life cycle shows that for most of the year over all its range the monarch migrates in precisely the same manner. Only those two-thirds of the autumn generation produced in the northern part of

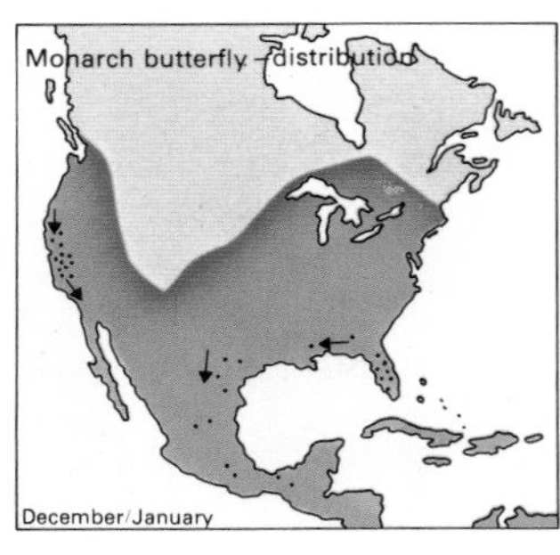

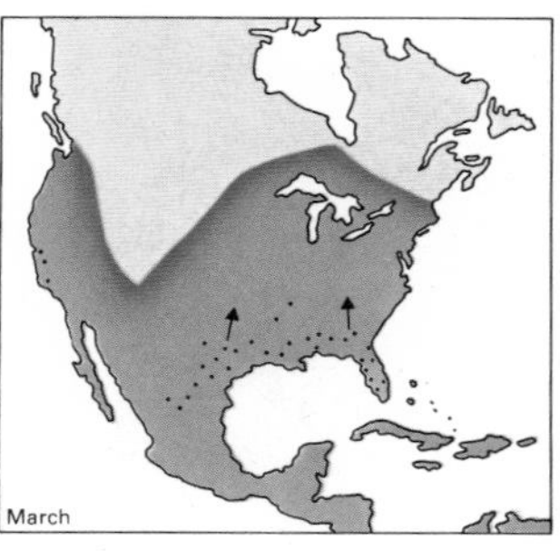

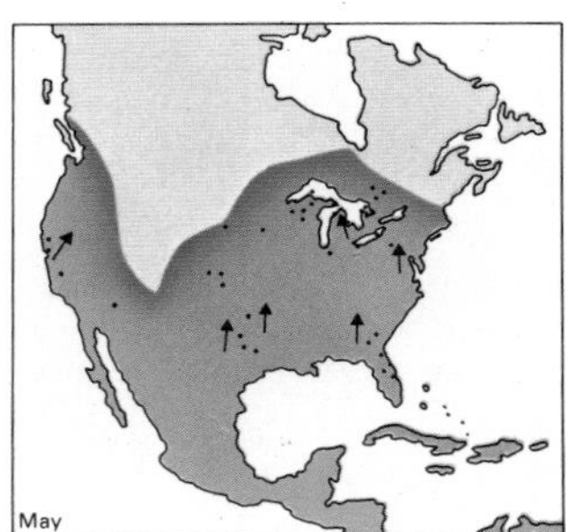

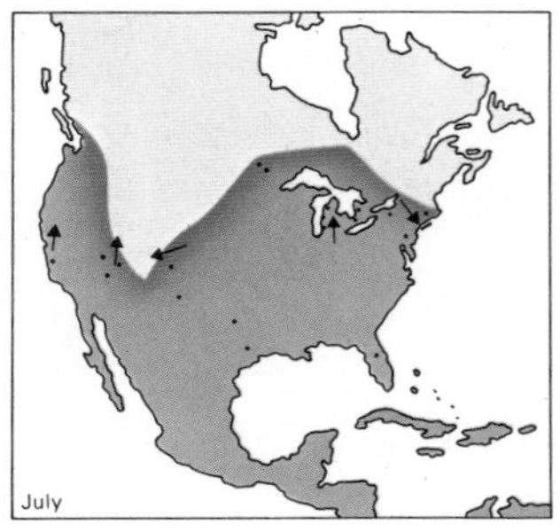

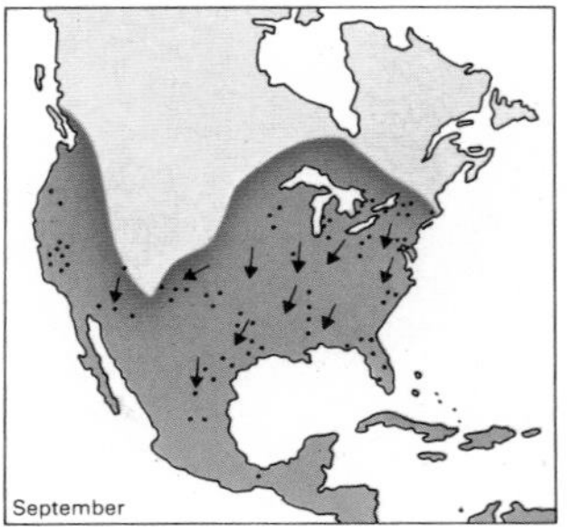

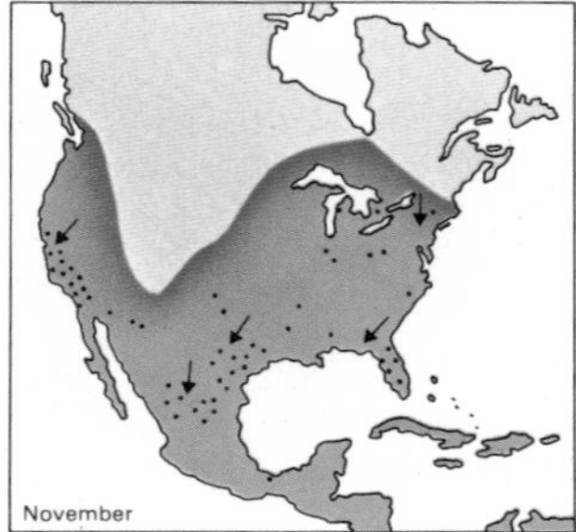

The seasonal migrations of North American monarch butterflies comprise a journey of several thousand kilometres. During December and January most individuals are to be found in California, Florida and the Gulf of Mexico. With the onset of spring, these southern monarchs migrate north, many flying towards the Great Lakes. Here they encounter those non-migrant individuals that may have hibernated over winter near the Canadian border at the northern limit of the population. As autumn fades, most monarchs reverse their migration direction and head south to much warmer regions once more. (The dots on the maps represent observed individuals.)

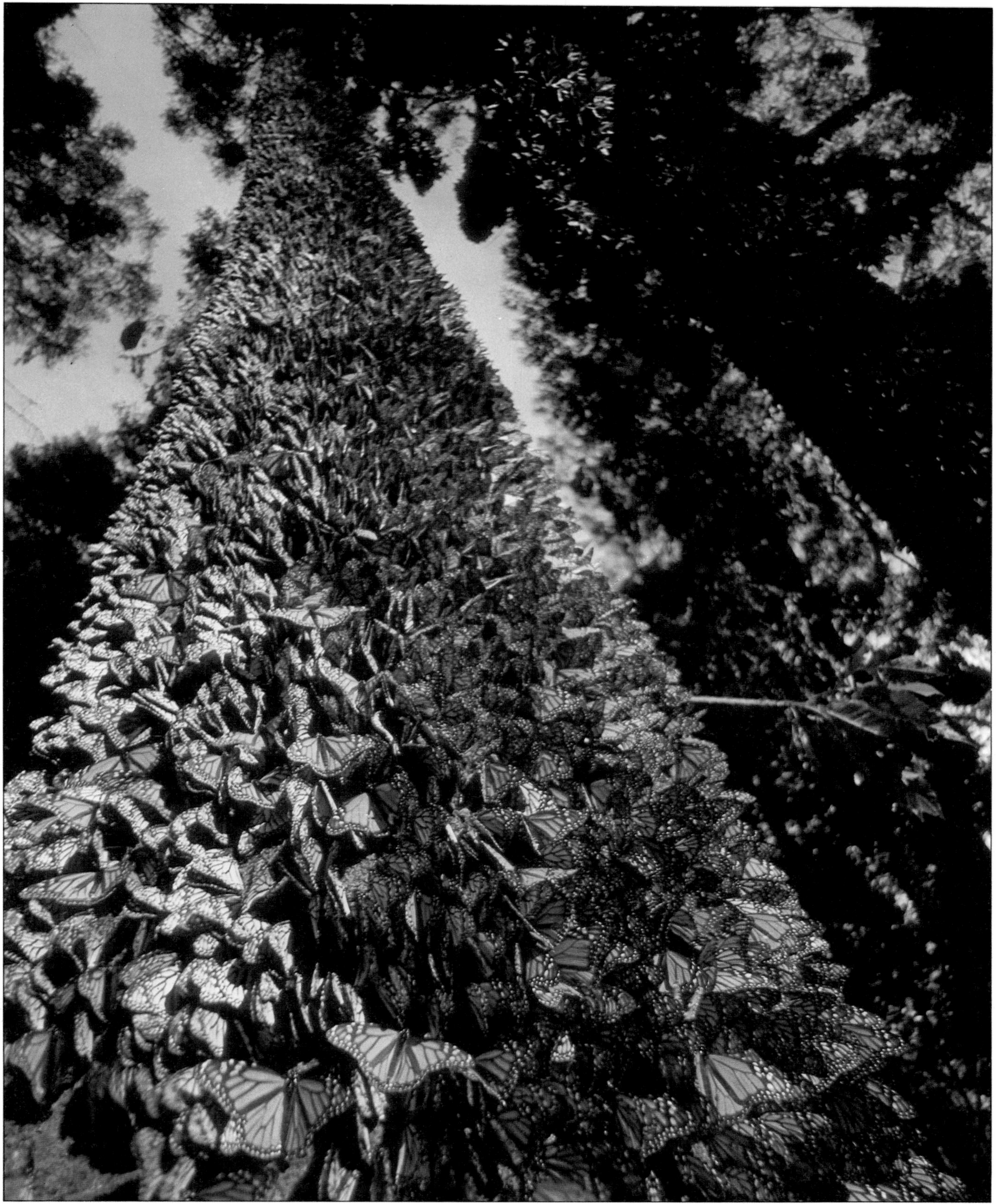

Butterfly trees appear to be literally dripping with roosting monarchs. Migrating south in autumn, most monarch butterflies overwinter relatively inactive, clustered on evergreen trees in many regions of the Gulf of Mexico and on the Californian coast. Within forests in such areas, populations of many hundreds, and sometimes even many thousands, of millions of monarchs are to be found.

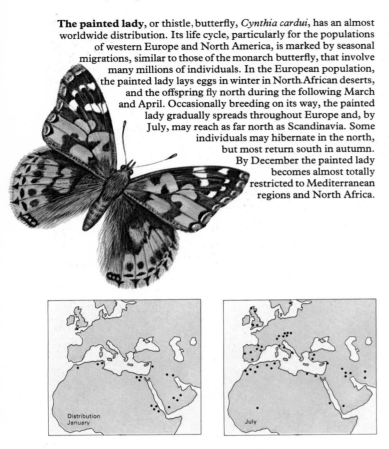

The painted lady, or thistle, butterfly, *Cynthia cardui*, has an almost worldwide distribution. Its life cycle, particularly for the populations of western Europe and North America, is marked by seasonal migrations, similar to those of the monarch butterfly, that involve many millions of individuals. In the European population, the painted lady lays eggs in winter in North African deserts, and the offspring fly north during the following March and April. Occasionally breeding on its way, the painted lady gradually spreads throughout Europe and, by July, may reach as far north as Scandinavia. Some individuals may hibernate in the north, but most return south in autumn. By December the painted lady becomes almost totally restricted to Mediterranean regions and North Africa.

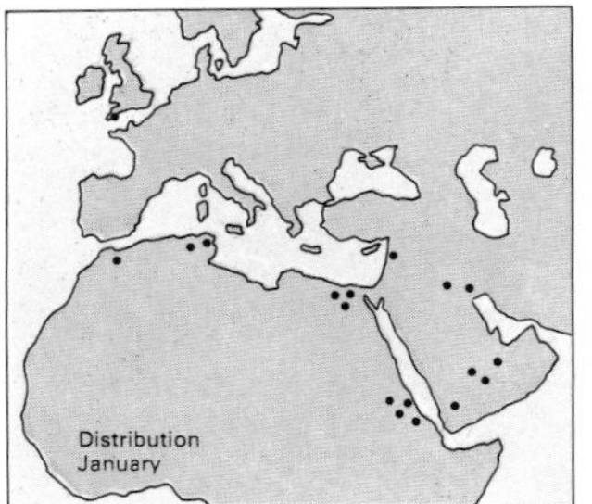

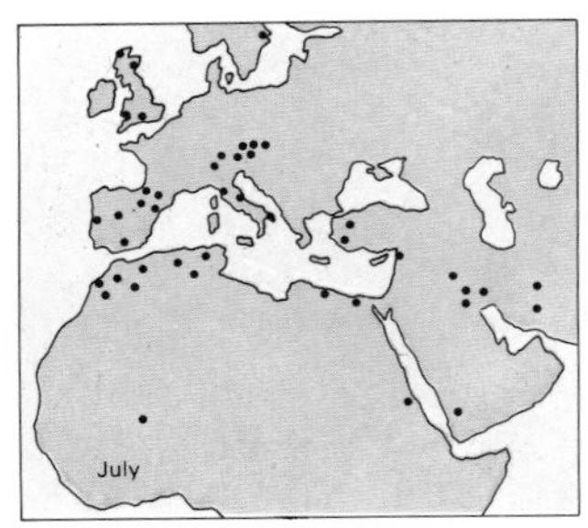

the range are different. But they are spectacularly different, migrating ten times further than most other temperate species. So what is the basis of this difference?

One important fact about the autumn generation of the monarch is that although adult, individuals are in "reproductive diapause". Not until they reach Texas or Mexico do they begin to produce sperm and eggs, and those that do not manage to get that far before being overtaken by winter do not become reproductively active until the following spring. In the autumn, therefore, monarch butterflies do not have to invest time and energy in courting or laying eggs; they need only to feed and rest. In consequence, much more time and energy is available for migration. Perhaps the evolution of reproductive diapause and the long adult life associated with it – many monarchs live nearly twelve months as adults – made long-distance migration to warmer latitudes for the winter possible. Yet the monarch is not the only species of butterfly with an autumn generation that has developed reproductive diapause.

It appears that other species with a life-history similar to that of the monarch also migrate long distances in the autumn. The red admiral butterfly, *Vanessa atalanta*, and the painted lady, or thistle, butterfly, *Cynthia cardui*, for example, in western Europe, produce an autumn generation some members of which may migrate southward for up to 3000 kilometres (1850 miles) to overwinter in the Mediterranean region.

Analysis of the autumn migration direction of the monarch and other species of butterfly that have a reproductive diapause before overwintering as adults, suggests that the critical factor for such behaviour is the length of the winter they experience, not its severity. True or not, the migration of the autumn generation of monarchs clearly has a function different from other temperate species and from the spring and summer generations of the monarch. When a monarch butterfly emerges in autumn as an adult, as soon as it has fed and stored enough energy reserves in the form of fat, its major concern is to travel south as fast as possible with the minimum expenditure of energy. For them, straight-line distance is more important than area searched.

How the autumn monarch manages to orientate we do not know, but its behaviour, with respect to wind, has been observed and found to differ from that of other temperate species and also from that of spring and summer generations of monarchs. When the wind is blowing from the south, autumn monarchs make progress against the wind by flying low and taking advantage of any shelter available. When it blows from the north, they rise high into the air and take advantage of the tail wind to travel very fast. In this respect they behave as tropical species.

Migration in the tropics

The migration of tropical butterflies is often an unforgettable sight for, unlike the temperate varieties, when it happens virtually all fly in the same direction and in such vast swarms – tens of millions have been seen in Kenya – that there is never any doubt that they are migrating.

Why do they migrate at all? The short answer is to search for food, but the underlying factor is rainfall or, rather, lack of it. In the tropics the rainfall is usually very heavy but is restricted to certain times of the year. The result is luxurious, fast-growing vegetation. The insect populations in these regions depend for their food on the blossoms produced by the rains, and the question arises as to what they should do at other times. They can choose between lying dormant, waiting for the rains to return, or migrating to where the rain is falling. Those that take the second option provide one of the great spectacles of the tropics.

These mass migrations are confined largely to great islands and to the grassland and semi-arid regions of southern Africa, South America and Asia, where rain falls either irregularly or for only a short time each year.

On the island of Sri Lanka the common crow butterfly, *Euploea core asela*, migrates from October to December during the northeast monsoons with a peak direction to the north. (Since virtually the whole population migrates together in this direction, the direction ratio of the common crow, like that of almost all other tropical butterflies, approaches 100:0:0:0.) In March and April, during the southwest monsoons, there is a second migration season. This time the butterfly shows a peak direction to the west and southwest coasts, the east coast remaining dry at this time.

The rain in Sri Lanka falls predominantly near to the coasts, and the common crow butterfly, to reach these areas, has to migrate most of the time against the wind. By contrast, in the arid regions on continental land, areas of rainfall are most often reached by flying down wind, or by flying towards high ground. The brown-veined white, *Belenois aurota*, an African migrant, feeds as a larva on caper, a bush that occurs in arid districts. Sometimes, during a really heavy migration, a caper bush standing in a particularly favourable position can be smothered with countless numbers of eggs. In South Africa, Botswana and Rhodesia, a regular seasonal migration of this species occurs in December and January. This migration is always to the east, towards an area of higher rainfall. So far, no clear return migration of this species in the regions concerned has been observed.

Movement round circuits – re-migration

The phenomenon of an apparently one-way migration is not uncommon among migrant tropical insects. The reason seems to be that an observer at any point along the route sees only one leg of the migration circuit. In order to keep pace with the areas of rainfall as they move from place to place, one generation of a species may need to migrate hundreds or thousands of kilometres to the east. The next generation may need to migrate a similar distance to the north, the next to the west, and the next to the south, so completing the circuit. (Such circuits are known for at least three species of locust, but have yet to be conclusively demonstrated for any tropical butterfly.) It is probable that this type of migration behaviour, known as re-migration, has evolved because the pattern of rainfall and the fresh vegetation that comes in its wake, in most grassland and semi-desert areas of the world, is seasonably predictable. The precise location of such rainfall and vegetation may not always be the same from one year to the next, but rain and food supply will always be more likely in one particular direction. This direction, however, will vary with time of year and geographical location.

In this sense, island and arid-zone tropical butterflies are faced with a situation similar to that faced by the autumn generation of monarch butterflies in the northern USA and Canada. Optimum migration behaviour is that which takes the butterfly from the place where it emerges both in a predictable direction and with the minimum expenditure of time and energy, to a habitat suitable for breeding and laying eggs. In the case of island and arid-zone butterflies, the favoured location is the general area in which rainfall is most likely. Like the autumn monarchs, therefore, they should compensate for the movement of the sun's azimuth across the horizon so that they fly in a straight line and take advantage of any tail wind. During their migration, they feed at intervals, settle and roost overnight or during cloudy periods or when a head wind is too strong. But, by and large, their prime strategy is to reach the rainfall area quickly and effortlessly.

Compensating for movement of the azimuth

To date, no major study has been made of the orientation mechanism of tropical butterflies during migration that tests the prediction that they will orientate by the sun's azimuth but compensate for its movement across the horizon. However, it is known that their peak migration direction does not shift during the day as does that of temperate butterflies. Brown-veined whites, *Belenois aurota*, in Botswana in January have a peak migration direction that is to the east in the morning and is still to

The African migrant butterfly, *Catopsilia florella*, migrates in vast numbers in search of vegetation blooms. Migration swarms more than twenty kilometres (12 miles) long and five kilometres (3 miles) wide have been recorded. Of the several geographical populations of whites within Africa, individuals immediately south of the Sahara Desert migrate from December to February towards rainfall areas south of the Congo basin and round Lake Tanganyika. From March to May, their migration direction leads them to rainy areas along the southeast coast and within the centre of the African continent.

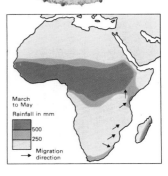

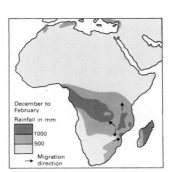

December to February
Rainfall in mm
1000
500
Migration direction

March to May
Rainfall in mm
500
250
Migration direction

Brown-veined whites, *Belenois aurota*, migrating in South Africa, regularly aggregate on bushes in small clusters to roost.

the east in the afternoon. If they are orientating to the sun's azimuth, they must also compensate for its movement. Such apparently sophisticated behaviour is not beyond the capabilities of an insect. Honey bees, *Apis mellifera*, for example, are known to do just this during their foraging trips.

As for their reaction to the wind, arid-zone butterflies react in the same way as autumn generation monarchs in North America. The great southern white, *Ascia monuste*, in the grasslands of northeastern Argentina, for example, flies close to the ground when migrating with a head wind, but rises to about 1500 metres (5000 feet) when migrating with a tail wind. The long-beaked, or snout, butterfly, *Libythea bachmani*, in the southern USA similarly migrates close to the ground unless the air is calm or has a wind component to the east or southeast, when it migrates at a height further than the eye can see.

The nocturnal migrations of moths

Moths migrate in much the same way as butterflies. At least that is what the available evidence suggests, but because they migrate at night, information about their behaviour has been very difficult to obtain. Inevitably, entomologists still cannot agree on what exactly takes place, the main argument being about whether moths, like butterflies, have a preferred migration direction or whether they simply migrate downwind.

Radar has been used, primarily in the arid tropical and sub-tropical regions of Africa and Australia, to investigate the migration of nocturnal insects in general. The majority of large nocturnal insects there – those of body length exceeding eight millimetres (0.3 inch) – take to the air about one hour after sunset. The insects then climb quite fast – over thirty centimetres (12 inches) a second – to an average height of about 400 metres (1300 feet) and a ceiling limited by temperature of 1500 metres (5000 feet). This rapid "dusk ascent" is followed by a gradual descent over a period of one to four hours for those that have flown highest. How long individual insects remain in the air and the distances covered is still unknown. Depending on the condition of the night, these insects can be in the air from one to twelve hours, and some will travel at a ground speed of between ten and eighty kilometres (6 and 50 miles) an hour depending on wind speed. These large nocturnal insects – mainly moths and solitary locusts in the areas studied – usually travel downwind, but only because their preferred direction usually coincides with the direction of the wind. If the wind shifts slightly, the insects adjust their orientation to travel on the preferred direction side of downwind.

Only one major marking experiment has been carried out on moths – in China in 1964 on the oriental armyworm moth, *Pseudaletia separata*. Many of the nation's entomologists took part, and between March and September many thousands of moths were marked and released. Only a few were recaptured and these showed that in spring and early summer a proportion, and perhaps a large proportion, of the moth population performs migrations of up to at least 1400 kilometres (900 miles) in a more or less northerly direction. Only one individual of those released in autumn was recaptured: it had flown 800 kilometres (500 miles) to the south. This suggests a north-south to-and-fro re-migration of successive generations as part of an annual migration cycle. The rate of migration can only be estimated roughly, but the moths seemed to migrate at speeds of about 150 to 200 kilometres (90 to 125 miles) a day during the first three to four days after emergence and thereafter at perhaps 30 to 50 kilometres (20 to 30 miles) a night. During those first few days not only are the moths still reproductively immature, but they may migrate by day as well as by night. The reduction in distance travelled thus coincides with the onset of reproduction, when the moths migrate only by night.

In its general pattern the armyworm moth is perhaps the nocturnal, oriental equivalent of the monarch butterfly in North America and the red admiral and painted lady butterflies in western Europe. Of a similar nature are the migrations of the silver-Y moth, *Plusia gamma*, in western Europe. Like these butterflies, the silver-Y moth has an autumn generation which

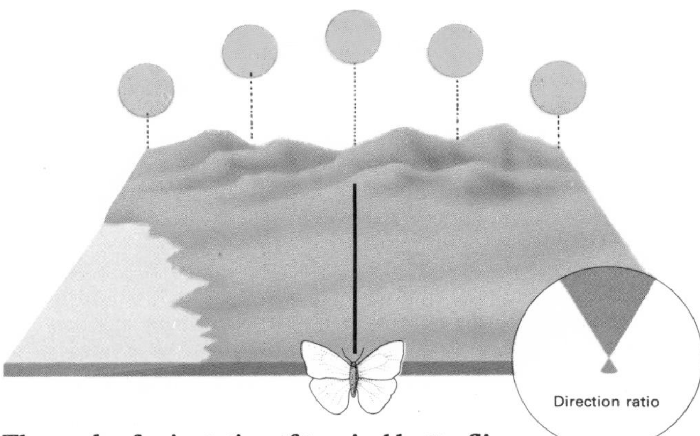

The mode of orientation of tropical butterflies is probably based on compensating for the movement of the sun's azimuth across the horizon. This enables these insects to maintain a straight-line flight path on their migrations. This ability is shared by many other tropical insect migrants, among them hunting wasps and their descendants, the ants, bees and wasps.

These white and creamy-yellow *Belenois* butterflies are inhabitants of forest and savannah regions throughout Africa. Often migrating in large numbers, they are to be seen clustered along river banks to drink.

delays the onset of sexual maturity, yet it differs in that it probably hibernates not as an adult but as a very young larva. Even so, it seems likely that in the autumn a large proportion of the population migrates to the south to reproduce at warmer latitudes. In common with the oriental armyworm moth, the silver-Y also migrates by day and by night during the first few days after emergence as an adult, but thereafter migrates only at night. This enables the immature moths to invest a greater proportion of their time in migration.

Over the past few decades, observers have collected a great many records of the flight directions of the silver-Y for spring, summer and autumn, over land and sea, by day and by night. Night observations were obtained either at dusk or by observing moths passing through the beams of lighthouses. They show quite clearly that, by day and by night, silver-Y moths have a peak migration direction to the north-northwest in spring and summer and to the south-southwest in autumn. Furthermore, analysis of the records shows

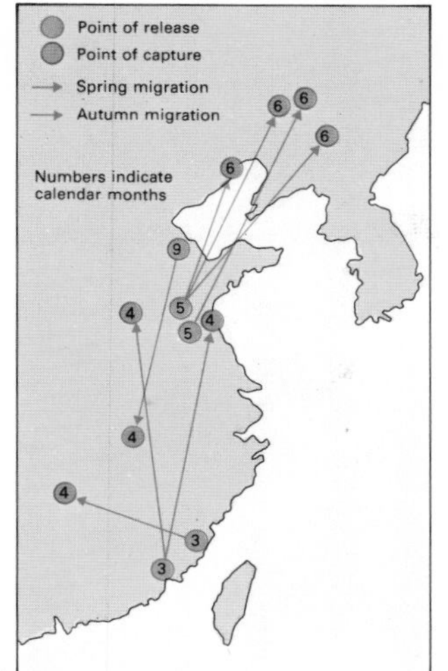

The oriental armyworm moth, *Pseudaletia separata*, was the subject of a unique marking/release and recapture experiment in eastern China. Moths were released in spring and autumn from various locations in batches over a period of several days. Although accurate time intervals between release and recapture could not be determined, it was possible to estimate the speeds of flight of migrants over the distances concerned. Since, in the laboratory, the armyworm moth is capable of flying non-stop for more than thirty hours, the somewhat astonishing migration rates of free-flying individuals of 200 kilometres (125 miles) a night seem quite feasible.

Dusk ascent is performed on warm, dry nights by a whole host of large nocturnal insects.

that, except when migrating over the sea at night, the moths show full compensation for the wind, maintaining their preferred compass direction irrespective of wind direction.

Using the stars to orientate

One interesting problem of moth migration was solved as recently as 1977. Moths migrate by night yet show a preferred compass direction. Since the sun is not visible, as it is for daytime migrants such as butterflies, how can the moths recognize and maintain their compass direction? The solution was to tether the moths but let them fly and watch what they did. In the same way that caged birds hop in the direction in which they would normally migrate, the tethered but suspended moths continue to fly in their migration direction.

Using tethered moths mainly of the large yellow underwing, *Noctua pronuba*, experiments showed that moths cannot recognize compass direction in a dark room or when their eyes are completely painted over. Thus it appears that neither the earth's magnetic field, wind, nor other non-visual cues are involved. Even when only the upper two-thirds of the moths' eyes are painted over, the insects still cannot orientate. This suggests that a visual cue more or less above the moths is involved and the night-sky is clearly implicated. Under total overcast, compass direction is not recognized by the moths and neither is it when the moon is screened off, but when the moon is visible, the moths show compass orientation. Finally, experiments at different times of night show that an individual moth's orientation shifts round as the moon's azimuth moves across the horizon. Like most temperate butterflies with respect to the sun, the yellow underwing does not compensate for movement of this azimuth. But even when the moon is below the horizon, yellow underwings show compass orientation as long as the sky is not overcast. Orientation relative to a star or star pattern when the moon is not visible is clearly implicated.

Hoppers and adult locusts

The passage of a locust swarm is a most awe-inspiring sight. The first hint is a smoky cloud on the horizon. As it approaches it darkens the sky, almost blotting out the sun and turning day to night. The noise becomes deafening and soon the landscape is engulfed in flying, hopping, devouring insects. Crops and pasture vanish in a matter of minutes, ruining farmers and causing starvation.

Swarms have been known to tower four kilometres (2.5 miles) into the sky, covering an area of 250 square kilometres (95 square miles) in flight. One observed swarm in Kenya extended to as much as 1000 square kilometres (385 square miles). Desert locusts can eat their own weight of green vegetation daily, so the devastation wreaked by swarms of tens of millions can almost defy description.

Locusts are inhabitants of tropical and sub-tropical regions of the world. There are now seven distinct species – the Rocky Mountain locust, *Melanoplus spretus*, which used to be extremely common in the arid areas of the USA, has not been seen since the end of the nineteenth century. In the arid regions of central and eastern Australia is the Australian plague locust, *Chortoicetes terminifera*, which has only recently received intensive study by migration workers. The South American locust, *Schistocerca paranensis*, is found throughout most of south and central America as far north as southern Mexico. It also occurs from time to time on some of the West Indian islands. But it is in Africa that most species, and the greatest numbers, of locusts are found.

It is the locust of the Bible, the desert locust, *Schistocerca gregaria*, which is the most widespread, and undoubtedly the most damaging, of all the species. It is found primarily in and around the desert belt of northern Africa, extending south of the equator in only Kenya and Tanzania. But it also occurs in Arabia, Iraq, Iran, Pakistan and northern India, an area that includes almost fifteen per cent of the world's land surface. Swarms of the desert locust have even been observed in the mid-Atlantic, more than 2200 kilometres (1350 miles) from the nearest possible place of origin, and it is believed that with favourable winds swarms could, in the past, have reached South America. The migratory locust, *Locusta migratoria*, which in fact is no more nor less migratory than any other locust species, also inhabits a wide area of land. Different sub-species of *L. migratoria* are found throughout most of Africa, parts of southern Europe and southern Asia, and in Madagascar, Indonesia, north Queensland and New Zealand. Finally, the Moroccan locust, *Dociostaurus maroccanus*, is found in northwest Africa and in the hilly regions of other Mediterranean countries, and the brown locust, *Locustana pardalina*, and the red locust, *Nomadocris*

The silver-Y moth, *Plusia gamma*, is found throughout Europe and North America. It performs seasonal migrations, occasionally flying across country in large numbers. Of all moth migrations, those of the silver-Y are perhaps the most carefully studied.

septemfasciata, are found in the southern half of Africa.

All locusts are short-horned grasshoppers, comprising the family of insects Acrididae, but not all short-horned grasshoppers are locusts. Throughout the arid regions of the world a handful of acridid species have evolved a very special ability. If they develop from the egg through to the adult stage in an area of abundant vegetation, where they can grow in relatively uncrowded conditions, they are indistinguishable in appearance and behaviour from conventional grasshoppers. If they develop in an area where the vegetation is scarce or becomes scarce, so that they become crowded together and have to hop long distances to find sufficient food, then their appearance and behaviour change, and they develop into a quite different creature.

As young insects, or hoppers, they join together into bands, which migrate across country, hop after hop, sometimes travelling twenty-five kilometres (16 miles) from where they were laid as eggs, before becoming adult and capable of flight. These adults are brightly coloured in yellows, pinks and reds, instead of the subdued greens and yellows of the solitary variety. They have much longer wings, delay the onset of reproduction, perhaps for as long as six months, are active by day instead of by night and, most noticeable of all, they are gregarious instead of solitary. These are the swarming locusts.

For many years the gregarious locust and its solitary, grasshopper counterpart were thought to be different species. They are now known to be different phases of the same species. By classification the desert locust is still the species *Schistocerca gregaria*, whether it develops into an adult of phase *gregaria*, the swarming type, or of phase *solitaria*, which do not. Intermediate forms also exist, which are described as phase *transiens*. It is the power to transform that merits a species being described as a locust instead of as a grasshopper. Such potential has evolved several times in different parts of the arid regions of the world to the extent that no continent, except Antarctica, is free from locusts.

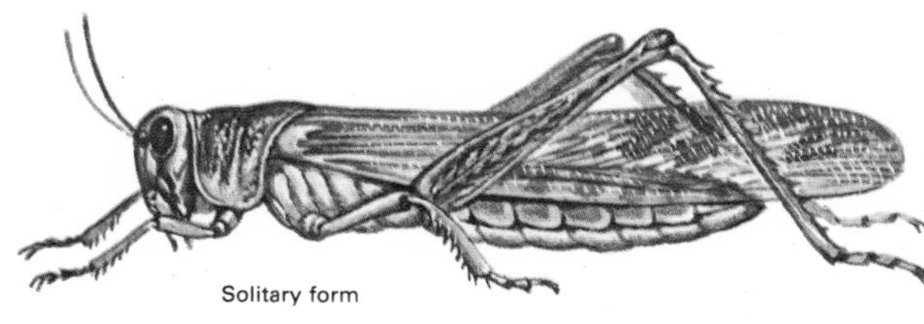

Solitary form

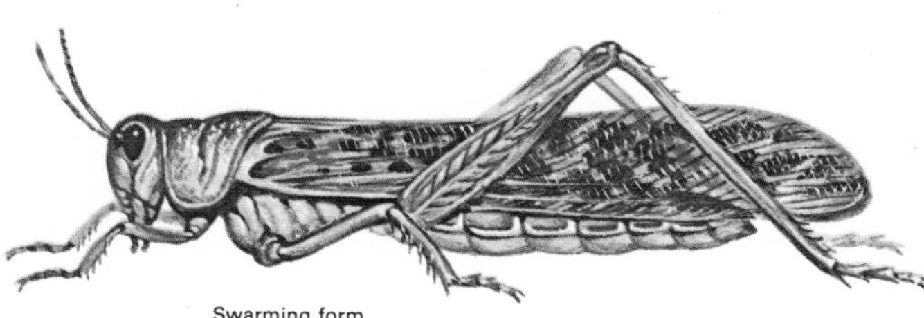

Swarming form

There are two adult forms of the desert locust, *Schistocerca gregaria* – the gregarious, or swarming, and the solitary. They differ in colour, shape, size and behaviour. In areas of sparse vegetation, emergent nymphs, or hoppers, are produced that are yellow or orange in colour with black patterning. These develop into adults that are yellow with black markings, bear long, stout wings and short bodies, and that migrate during the day in swarms of many millions. Where vegetation is abundant, the emergent hoppers are a plain green colour, as are their more grasshopper-like adults. This latter form of the desert locust migrates by night solitarily.

Whether these locust hoppers become swarming or solitary adults is determined by how crowded they are as they grow.

It seems that locusts have a more or less regular annual migration cycle adapted to the seasonal shift in zones of rainfall. In some regions this annual cycle takes the form of a migration circuit, in others it is essentially a to-and-fro migration. In both cases the migration is usually a re-migration, different stages of each cycle being performed by different generations. For example, historical evidence from the nineteenth century suggests that from July to September swarms of the Rocky Mountain locust migrated southeast from breeding grounds in the Rocky Mountains to parts of Kansas, Missouri and Texas. The following spring, in May and June, new swarms migrated northwest from these areas back to the Rockies. Swarms of the red locust from northern Zimbabwe-Rhodesia follow the major rainfall zone of Africa, the Inter Tropical Convergence Zone (ITCZ), northward in July and August. Finally, the Australian plague locust executes part of its circuit as a cohesive swarm migrating by day, but apparently completes the circuit as solitary, reproducing individuals migrating by night. In this respect it probably differs from the other species of locusts.

The swarming desert locust

Most experimental work on locust migration concerns the desert locust, *Schistocerca gregaria*. Optimally, female desert locusts lay their eggs in an area in which more than twenty millimetres (0.8 inch) of rain has recently fallen and in which, therefore, there will be an ample supply of green vegetation for the resulting hoppers. Given suitable conditions, the eggs hatch usually within a week of being laid, but they can survive embedded in dry sand for up to three months. On hatching, which occurs only as each egg absorbs its own weight in water, the young hoppers tunnel through their protective pod to the surface. Here they shed a membrane

A swarm of locusts may contain upward of 100 million individuals.

The mating of locusts takes place in areas in which rain has recently fallen, for it is only in such places that conditions are suitable both for the females to lay eggs and for the emergent hoppers to find sufficient food. Given ideal conditions, adult locusts may produce several batches of offspring before dying.

Locusts lay eggs in moist, warm, desert sand. Pushing her abdomen, which becomes greatly extended, into the sand, the female locust deposits between sixty and ninety eggs; each egg is the size of a grain of rice. She then secretes a fluid which hardens round the eggs, forming a protective pod, and then produces a quick-drying foam to seal the hole in the sand. The seal prevents loss of moisture. The eggs hatch as soon as external conditions, namely temperature and humidity, are ideal.

that encases them and start to feed. Hoppers are essentially feeding machines and they have to moult no less than five times before they reach adult size and acquire functional wings. Their daily routine comprises alternating periods of roosting in low vegetation at night and around midday, when the sun is too strong for comfort, and of hopping over ground and feeding during the morning and afternoon. It may be four or five weeks before they become flying locusts. Even then they do not mature sexually until they have encountered the corresponding zone of seasonal rainfall.

Desert locusts fall into four separate geographical populations, each with their own migration circuit or choice of migration circuits. These follow a basic pattern. The swarm of new adult locusts starts to migrate towards an area of rainfall, the direction depending on the time of year and geographical location. In May and June, the four populations choose a direction to intercept the rainfall of the ITCZ. Whichever direction is appropriate it is maintained by the swarm perhaps for several months until it brings the locusts to the rainfall zone for which they are searching. Migration in this direction is initiated each day that the sun is shining, the swarm settling late each afternoon to roost for the night.

Once the swarm reaches the rainfall area, the individuals mature and begin to mate and lay eggs. Each day, by migrating towards high ground, storm clouds or rain-in-sight, the swarm spends the maximum time possible in the precise areas where rain is falling or has fallen. Cross-country migration in a consistent direction may still continue if the rainfall zone itself persists in moving, otherwise the swarm's direction changes frequently and the locusts adopt a searching behaviour similar to that of butterflies in a suitable habitat. Eventually, as the eggs are laid and the locusts' reserves become spent, the swarm gradually dies out. By the time, some two months later, these eggs have themselves given rise to adults, the rainfall zone will have moved on, and the new swarms have to perform the next leg of the circuit, either to catch up with the same rainfall zone or to intercept a different, but nearer, zone. The annual migration cycle is finally completed when swarms arrive back in the same general area vacated by them one or two generations earlier.

Swarming behaviour related to winds

Desert locust swarms are of two types, cohesive or diffuse. The migration of a diffuse swarm is little different from that of large numbers of tropical butterflies. The locusts are widely spaced, show little if any response to other individuals, and form a swarm without a distinct edge. The topmost locusts are usually only a few metres or tens of metres above ground level. The only reason for retaining the swarm concept in such instances would seem to be because all of the locusts are orientated in the same direction.

Cohesive swarms are quite different, and have a somewhat complex structure. The top of a cohesive swarm may be four kilometres (2.5 miles) above ground level and, unlike the situation in a diffuse swarm, it is only the locusts in the uppermost layers that are orientated in the direction that the swarm is travelling. These locusts travel faster than the swarm as a whole, and eventually emerge from the swarm's leading edge. As they do so, and presumably because they no longer see locusts beneath them, they drop down and return into the swarm, either continuing to fly or settling on the ground beneath and starting to feed. (As locusts feed during migration, they can end a journey of as much as 5000 kilometres [3100 miles] weighing more than when they started.) Individuals on the ground immediately take flight when the trailing edge of the swarm passes overhead. A cohesive swarm, therefore, gradually rolls across country like a giant caterpillar track on a motor vehicle.

Much controversy surrounds the function of the two types of locust swarm. Many entomologists consider that all locust swarms of whatever type travel across country in the same direction as the wind irrespective of its source. The most likely explanation is that locusts adopt a diffuse swarm structure whenever migration direction is against the wind and a cohesive swarm structure whenever it is with the wind. Because major rainfall zones, such as the ITCZ, are actually produced by converging wind fields, migration towards such zones is invariably downwind, and is performed almost entirely by locusts in cohesive swarms.

Not all of the rainfall zones involved in the migration circuits of the desert locust can be reached in this manner. Furthermore, when the locusts arrive in the general vicinity of the rainfall zones, the precise relationship between wind direction and rain-in-sight breaks down. This also occurs when they approach storm clouds or high ground. If the wind should deviate from the direction that leads towards the rainfall zone by the shortest route, the upper layers of locusts alter their orientation slightly to compensate for the displacement. If the wind deviates by more than ninety degrees from their preferred compass direction, thus becoming a head-wind, it seems that the locusts adopt a diffuse swarm structure and fly low over the ground in the required direction.

On this interpretation, the migration mechanism of swarming locusts is little different from that of butterflies in the same arid regions; they fly low against a head wind, but rise above the ground to take advantage of a tail wind. However, if swarms pursued this policy and tried to feed as well, they would soon disperse. But locusts have evolved a mechanism to keep the swarm together; they orientate towards other individuals when they are adrift. This orientation to other individuals could well be the only major behavioural difference between migrating locusts and butterflies in the tropics.

How locusts orientate to maintain their preferred compass direction is uncertain. There is some circumstantial evidence that it is the sun's azimuth that once again provides the cue. If this is so, then locusts must also compensate for the movement of the azimuth across the horizon during the day, for individual swarms have been followed and found to migrate in the same direction in late afternoon as in mid-morning.

Almost all experiments and investigations concerning locust migration have been confined to swarming phase

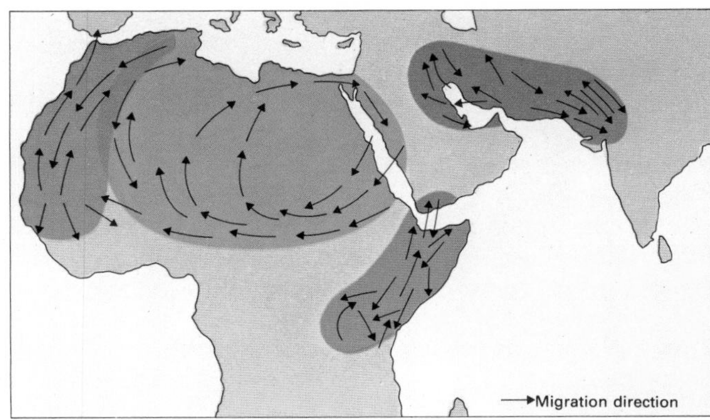

The migration circuits of the four main populations of the desert locust, *Schistocerca gregaria*, have evolved in response to the rainfall pattern in this region of the world. By flying along these routes, which are liable to change from one year to the next, locusts are most likely to reach the rainfall areas that they seek. However, desert locusts may have to migrate continuously for months on end, covering many thousands of kilometres, before such an area is found. Locusts in west Arabia and central and eastern northwest Africa, migrate in a circuit round the edge of the Sahara Desert. Those populations elsewhere in Arabia and Africa and in southwest Asia have circuits which tend to be between, or centred on, high mountains.

THE STRUCTURE OF MIGRATION SWARMS

Depending on the direction of the prevailing winds, a swarm of the desert locust, *Schistocerca gregaria*, adopts a structure that is either cohesive or diffuse. Whenever the direction of the wind coincides with the preferred direction of the swarm the locusts form a cohesive unit, but when these two directions are opposed, a diffuse swarm structure is adopted; this is less destructive.

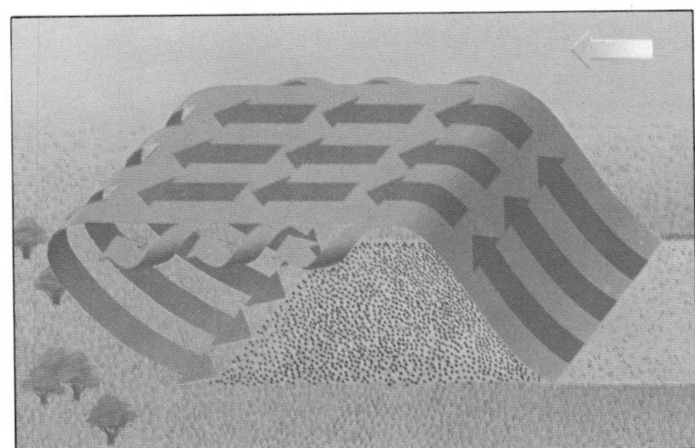

Cohesive swarm

Diffuse swarm

In a cohesive swarm it is the orientation of the uppermost locusts that determines the direction of flight of the swarm. All other locusts in the swarm show no particular orientation, though streams in any direction may develop temporarily. Any individual that emerges from the edge of the swarm immediately flies back into the centre. In a diffuse swarm (a section only is shown) all locusts fly in the migration direction; they also maintain a lower level of flight.

individuals. Solitary phase locusts also migrate, but by night, not by day. Consequently, little information is available concerning the nature of their movements. In most respects, however, their migration behaviour seems to be similar to that of tropical moths.

Since insects as diverse as locusts, butterflies and moths appear to show such strong similarity in their migration patterns and mechanisms, it might be expected that similar migration behaviour will be shown by all strong-flying insects, whether diurnal or nocturnal. There is certainly no indication that this is not the case. Marking experiments on houseflies and blowflies, for example, have indicated a straight-line lifetime track of the butterfly type that is executed by alternating periods in suitable habitats (houses in the case of houseflies) and periods of cross-country flight. Yet taken as a whole, the migrations of strong-flying insects are markedly different from those of weak-flying ones.

Insect aerial plankton

Weak-flying insects, such as aphids, fruit-flies, mosquitoes, leaf hoppers, and even quite large beetles such as ladybirds, as soon as they become airborne are more or less at the mercy of the wind by virtue of their slow speed of flight. Furthermore, their smallness tends to limit the distance that they can fly through still air. If they ever need to travel any distance across country to find a more suitable habitat, they are more or less obliged to make use of the wind for transport.

Most such insects, whenever they initiate migration, fly steeply upward until they are above the vegetation layer and then level off and migrate with the wind usually just above tree height. That way they minimize the danger of being blown into spiders' webs, but as aerial plankton they become the major source of food for such birds as swallows, martins and swifts. At this height they have the best chance of finding and dropping into the first suitable habitat they encounter. If they migrated at a greater height the wind would tend to carry them past it before they could descend.

Of course, wind often has strong up-currents as well as blowing horizontally and some small insects are temporarily carried to great heights, even several kilometres above the ground; such insects may be sampled by suspending nets from aircraft. Melon flies released from aircraft at different altitudes and then trapped on the ground beneath and aphids released in vertical wind tunnels both attempted to minimize the time spent at high altitudes. The aphids, for example, flew towards the ground as fast as possible. Small insects, like tropical butterflies, may well have to travel a fixed horizontal distance before they encounter the zone of suitable habitats, and this may force them to take advantage of the faster winds at higher altitudes. However, if the favourable habitats occur in a fixed geographical direction we might expect that the insect would only fly up into the windstream when the wind was blowing in the appropriate direction.

The beet leaf hopper, *Circulifer tenellus*, overwinters in the southern USA and in spring, on favourable winds, migrates 200 kilometres (125 miles) or so to the north. The sunn pest, *Eurygaster integriceps*, in the Middle East,

THE MIGRATION OF WEAK-FLYING INSECTS

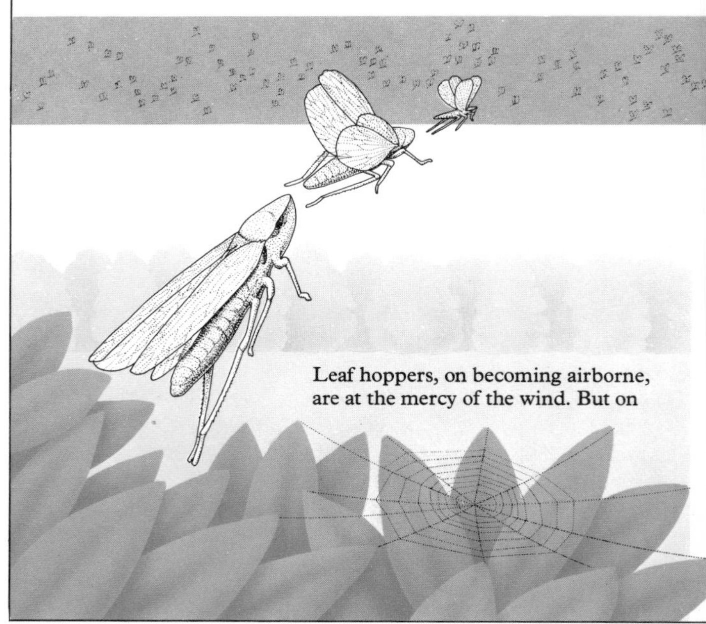

Leaf hoppers, on becoming airborne, are at the mercy of the wind. But on

and the convergent ladybird, *Hippodamia convergens*, in California, migrate from the plains to nearby mountains to pass the winter, migrating back to the plains the following spring. All of these insects are relatively weak fliers and probably make at least some use of the wind for transport. Ideally they should only initiate migration when the wind is blowing in the appropriate direction.

Wingless and winged aphids

During the summer, many species of aphids consist only of females which give birth, without fertilization by males, not to eggs but to live nymphs. These, too, are all females. Some of these nymphs will develop into winged adults and be potential migrants, others will develop into wingless adults. The proportion of nymphs that develop wings depends on the extent to which they, or their mothers before them, were crowded. Experiments were carried out on females of species whose mothers were sensitive to crowding. They were placed in test tubes, without food, for a day, at different states of crowding. They were then raised singly with abundant food and their offspring examined to see whether the proportion that developed wings was influenced in any way by their mothers' experience. It was found that mothers that were crowded in the test tube produce a higher proportion of winged individuals among their offspring than mothers that were on their own.

Although all winged aphids are potential migrants, not all actually initiate migration. The proportion that take flight depends on the degree of crowding just before and just after becoming adult and obtaining functional wings. Crowded, winged aphids are more likely to take flight than uncrowded winged aphids.

In autumn, the females of many aphid species start to produce males and females, both of which are winged.

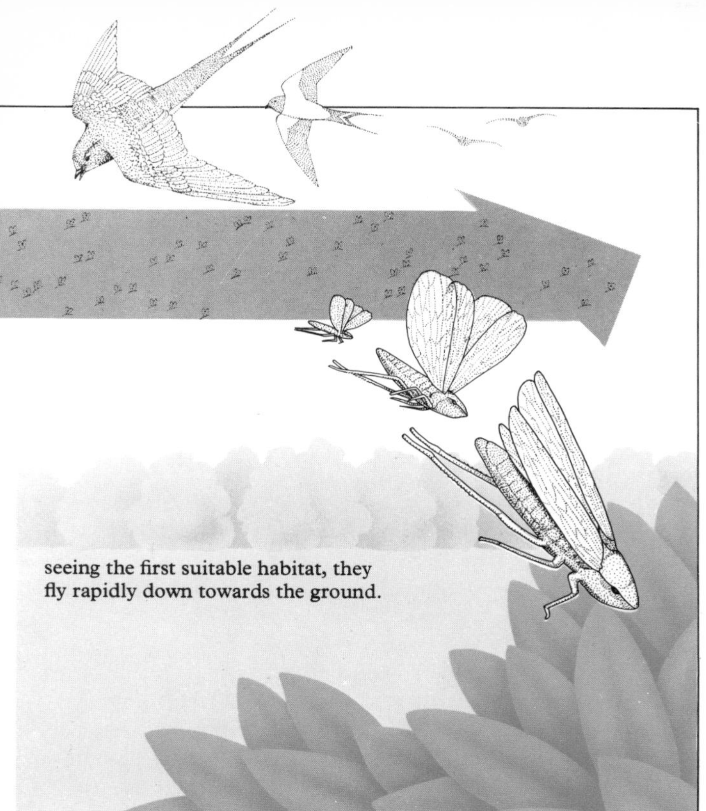

seeing the first suitable habitat, they
fly rapidly down towards the ground.

The sycamore aphid, *Drepanosiphum platanoides*, produces nymphs (A) which, in spring and summer, develop into winged adults, and in autumn develop into either winged males (B) or wingless females (C).

This generation of mixed sexes flies off and settles on a plant species, usually a tree, completely different from the plants on which the all-female summer generations lived. These sexual aphids mate and often lay eggs, in which stage the species passes the winter. The following spring, winged females migrate to plants of the first species to establish a new summer generation, so completing the life cycle.

The potato ladybird, *Epilachna dregei*, in South Africa migrates in autumn to mountains in search of warm, sheltered sites. Here it hibernates over winter in great masses. In spring it returns to the plains, often more than 100 kilometres (60 miles) away, where it spends the summer feeding and reproducing.

Establishing a familiar area

Dragonflies, which are strong fliers, in parts of western Europe often migrate in autumn to the south through the passes of the Pyrenees. Those that lay their eggs in temporary bodies of water such as cattle troughs, probably have a lifetime track similar in form and length to that of the more migrant butterflies in the same region. Those dragonflies that lay their eggs in bodies of water that are more permanent, such as rivers and large lakes, retain the ability to navigate back to that same body of water, even though they may fly several kilometres from it and stay away feeding for nearly a fortnight. With this ability they are able to establish a familiar area, learning the best places to catch insects, roost, set up territories and lay eggs. For these dragonflies this is preferable to spending time and energy migrating across country searching for a habitat that would be little, if at all, better than the one vacated. Furthermore, such habitats are often far apart so that it could take a long time and a lot of energy to find somewhere else – time that could much more safely be spent feeding or resting.

Among the first insects to evolve, there was another group, the hunting wasps, to whose advantage it was to establish a familiar area rather than migrate across country. Female hunting wasps dig themselves a burrow or construct one or more out of mud or other material.

They then fly off and catch themselves an insect or, in some species, a spider. They do not kill their prey, but paralyse it by inserting their hypodermic-like sting in just the right position to knock out the main nerve-centres. The helpless prey is then carried back and stuffed into the burrow, an egg is laid on it, and alive but immobile, it must await the emergence of the wasp's larva before it is finally eaten by the developing and voracious grub.

Some female hunting wasps finish stocking up one burrow and sealing it over before beginning the next. Others maintain several burrows at the same stage and only catch a new prey when one of the larvae has consumed the original one. The female wasp, having dug a burrow, has to be able to navigate back to it, so she must establish a familiar area.

The hunting wasp *Ammophila* hunts and paralyses the caterpillars of butterflies and moths that are too heavy to carry in flight, so the wasp has to walk back to the burrow. Before doing this the female wasp flies round the burrow exploring the area, evidently familiarizing herself with it. Once she has begun to drag a caterpillar back towards the nest it is possible to determine what clues she uses to navigate there. First, objects in the area can be moved to see if these cause the wasp to change direction. Second, the wasp, with the caterpillar, can be moved to a new position a few metres away.

When the wasp is displaced she tends at first to continue in the direction in which she was travelling before displacement, thus suggesting that she was maintaining direction by reference to some distant cue, probably the sun. After a while, she seems to realize that she is no longer heading towards the burrow and either changes to the correct direction or makes exploratory flights first and then changes to the correct direction. Experiments involving shifting or hiding landmarks have shown that at distances greater than a few tens of metres from the burrow, she uses large landmarks such as trees for navigation. When close to the burrow, she uses smaller landmarks such as patches of vegetation or large and small stones as reference points. It seems that the wasp learns during exploratory flights that the burrow is a particular compass direction from particular major landmarks and that it is located precisely within certain configurations of small landmarks.

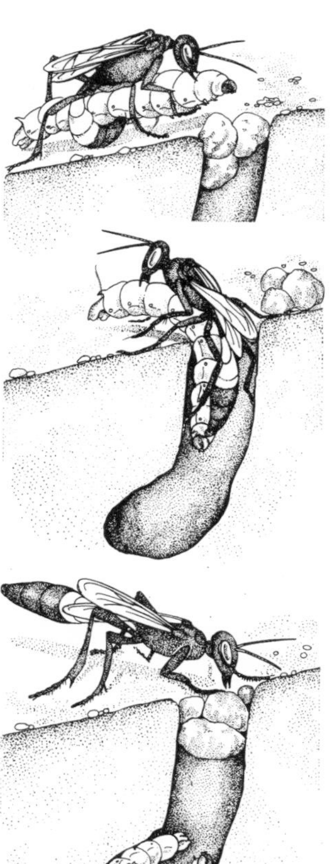

A female hunting wasp, *Ammophila pubescens*, having captured and paralysed a caterpillar that is too heavy to carry in flight, drags the prey back to its previously dug nesting hole and proceeds to stuff it into the nest. In order to relocate and return to its nesting hole, the wasp depends on an accurate sense of navigation and orientation. In an experimental area of heathland containing a few scattered clumps of heather, a female wasp, moving due west towards its nest, was displaced due south some thirty metres (100 ft) from its course. At first the wasp continued to walk in its original compass direction, but then, having made three exploratory flights, it set off due north in the home direction. Just before reaching its nest it was displaced once again, this time some twenty metres (65 ft) beyond its nest. A further series of exploratory flights was made before it located its nest. Study of the wasp's movements revealed that it navigated by having learned the location of its nest relative to the compass directions of the patches of heather. Orientation to the sun's azimuth may be involved in this behaviour.

The migrations of social insects

The habits of the female hunting wasp provide an example of an evolutionary process found in one of the most interesting groups in the animal kingdom – the social wasps, ants and bees.

Female hunting wasps tend to remain in the area of their nests, keeping contact with and provisioning their original offspring. Often they remain even longer to provision their subsequent groups of offspring as they begin to emerge as adult daughters. These can do one of two things. Either they fly away and establish burrows in an area of their own, or they remain behind and help their mothers build and provision new burrows. The latter seems to have happened many times during the course of evolution, and in the truly social insects most of the daughters are sterile. Where the daughters take over completely the role of building and provisioning burrows, they are known as workers, egg-laying remaining the sole domain of the mother, or queen. Not until the colony is a certain size and the season is favourable are daughters – and sons – produced that are capable of reproduction and of leaving the burrows to establish a new colony.

Ant and termite colonies

Most ants have a fixed nest which contains the queen, eggs, larvae, pupae and attendant workers. Workers are of different castes, ranging from small individuals that tend the larvae or forage, to fierce soldiers with large mandibles that protect the colony. All workers are wingless. It is only the male and female reproductive forms that bear wings, and these are used solely for the swarming, nuptial flight. Following this flight, male ants, having mated, die, and those females – now queens – which survive the attack of predators, lose their wings and establish new colonies. With this one important exception, therefore, ants move from place to place solely by walking.

Ants communicate with one another by scent or pheromones. When a worker is attacked, it gives off an alarm pheromone which alerts other workers to danger. When a worker ant discovers food, it lays a scent trail on the ground between the food source and the colony by dragging the tip of its abdomen over the soil. Another worker, encountering this trail, follows it to the food source. If food is still available, it too lays a scent trail as it carries food back to the colony. A worker arriving at the site and finding no food does not lay such a trail. In this way, by recruiting large numbers of workers, powerful trails are laid and maintained to good food sources while those to poor ones are weak.

Individual ants therefore have a familiar area based largely on an interpretation of the network of trails that they and other members of the colony lay down. The search for new food sources is undertaken by exploratory ants. When one discovers a new food source it finds its way back to the nest site, laying a trail as it goes by reversing the orientation to the sun's azimuth that it adopted on the outward journey. In an experiment involving placing boxes over returning ants and then removing them a few hours later, the ants no longer orientated towards home but deviated by the amount that the azimuth had moved across the horizon. This suggested that ants do not compensate for the azimuth's movement and in this they are similar to temperate butterflies. Subsequent experiments have shown, however, that ants, like bees, can perform such compensation behaviour.

Most ants have a fixed nest site from which workers go out on foraging expeditions, carrying food back to the nest and the waiting larvae. Termites, the only social insects that have not evolved from hunting wasps but are essentially social cockroaches, also have fixed nest sites. Although their nests are enclosed in impressive mounds or termitaria that project often high above ground level, termites are essentially subterranean. Their familiar area is based on a network of permanent roofed roads and less permanent scent trails.

Mass movements of army and driver ants

Although most ants and all termites have a fixed nest site, for one group of ants this is true for only part of the time. The legendary army ants of the New World tropics and driver ants of the Old World tropics move their nest site once a day, and the colony, consisting of up to half a million individuals, may travel some eight kilometres (5 miles) across country in a few months. They are voracious hunters and carnivores that kill every insect and small invertebrate in their path as well as any mammal that is unable to move out of their way.

The migration of army ants is related to the stage of development of the latest brood of offspring. When the developing larvae, of which there may be as many as 80,000, pupate and no longer need to be fed, the colony becomes stationary. The queen, pupae, and attendant workers occupy a sheltered site, such as a fallen log, and from there a single, short column of ants reaches out, collecting food for the foragers and nurse ants attending the queen and brood. Within the temporary nest the queen's body distends, and after a few days she lays a new batch of eggs. Her body then shrinks again until she is capable of walking. The emergence of the new workers from the pupae coincides with growth of the young larvae that have just hatched from the latest batch of eggs. Following this, three or four raiding columns radiate from the nest, each with a living trail of ants going out and returning with dismembered food. Raiding trails may be 100 metres (330 feet) or so in length and the quantity of food captured is enormous,

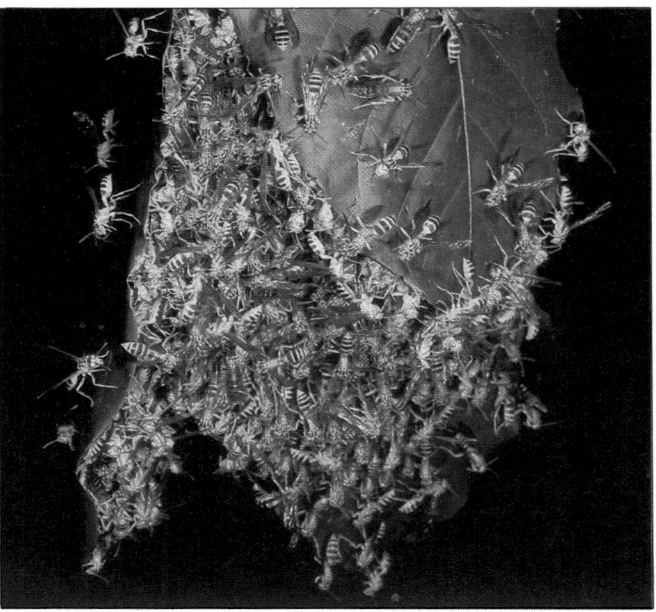

The wasp, *Stelopolybia pallipes*, has a swarming habit and, in common with other social wasps and with bees and ants, has evolved from solitary hunting wasps. Social wasps are hunting wasps that evolved sociality with only few changes in habit. Ants evolved from a hunting wasp with a subterranean habit. The ancestor of bees was a hunting wasp that became vegetarian and stored nectar and pollen in its burrow.

TERMITE COLONIES

Termites are social insects with a queen (A) and a king (B), soldiers (C) and workers (D). Unlike ants, bees and wasps, however, they have evolved not from hunting wasps but from the same ancestors as cockroaches. They feed on rotten wood and the fungi that grow upon it and on rotting vegetation and fungi in the soil. They are essentially subterranean dwellers with a familiar area comprising a network of roads and scent trails often with a mound (as shown above). The migrations of termites comprise the nuptial flight of winged males and females and the exploratory foraging trips of the workers.

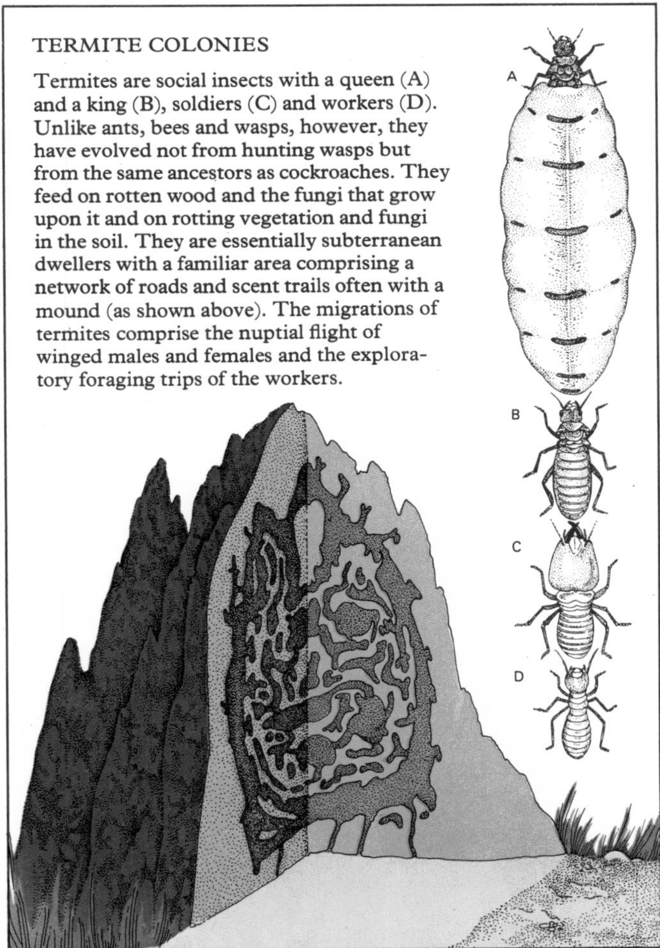

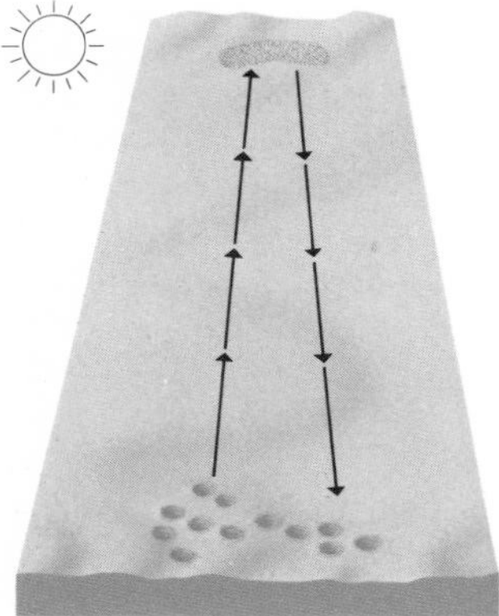

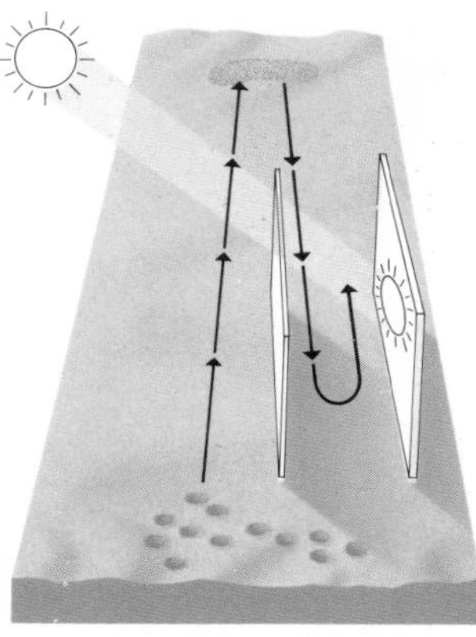

Exploratory ants navigate back to their nest from a new food source by reversing that orientation to the sun which they adopted on their outward journey. This can be shown experimentally by placing a screen that blocks out the sun's rays on one side of a returning ant and a mirror to reflect the sun's image on the other. The ant is led to believe it is travelling in the wrong direction and, in response, it immediately turns round and heads back to the food source. In a natural situation, the number of ants that lay a trail to a particular food source is related to its importance – the richer the source the greater the number of ants.

testimony to the appetite of the developing larvae. No single site can continue to support the colony and the migration phase begins.

Each night the core of the ant colony – the queen and brood – move to a new temporary nest site, or bivouac, at a location discovered by one of the raiding columns. The queen, accompanied by an entourage of workers, migrates by her own locomotion. The young larvae are carried in the mandibles of the workers. Later on in the migration phase, when the larvae are nearly fully grown, the workers store caches of food during the day along the migration route of the coming night. In this way, the larvae can be fed during migration. From initiation to completion, bivouac to bivouac, migration may take six to nine hours each night.

The flight and dance of the honey bee

Army ant migration is remarkable in the co-ordination among so many individuals. The migrations of honey bees, on the other hand, are remarkable because of the sophistication of the familiar area within which they take place, the communication between individuals that

Nomadic army ants, *Eciton* spp., migrate up to 500 metres (550 yd) each night in columns of between ten and one hundred thousand strong, on their way to a new nesting site. During their marches, most soldiers and workers forage for food while others form a protective shelter round the brood and queen. The ants' fearsome plunder consumes considerable quantities of the fauna of the forest floor.

is involved, and finally the democratic process by which the colony decides where it will migrate.

When a bee emerges from its hive for the first time it performs a series of exploratory migrations, at the end of which it has learned the position of the hive relative to surrounding landmarks. Within a day or so it has learned the pattern of movement of the sun's azimuth across the horizon and thereafter uses this knowledge for its compass to establish a familiar area. If a bee lands on a food source, such as a dish of sugar water, and the food and the bee are displaced laterally, the bee's behaviour when it leaves the food depends on whether or not it has visited that food source before. A novice bee flies straight back to the hive, thus showing that it is capable of navigation, using its surroundings to identify the direction of the hive. An experienced bee, however, flies in the direction that it has previously learned will lead back to the hive. Not until it has flown the normal distance to the hive and fails to find it does it apparently realize its mistake and navigate back to the hive.

When a bee gets back to its hive it informs other bees where it found food by means of the famous "bee dance". A "round dance" is used to announce resources discovered less than about eighty metres (260 feet) from the hive. A "waggle dance" is used to announce more distant resources and consists of the execution of a figure-of-eight with the abdomen being waggled during the oblique part of the figure. The tempo of this dance indicates the distance of the food source – the slower the dance the further away it is – and the direction of the wagging run relates to its position relative to the sun's azimuth. For example, on a vertical surface such as a bee comb, a wagging run straight upward means that the source is directly towards the azimuth, and a run, say, twenty degrees counterclockwise from the vertical means that the source is to the east of the azimuth by exactly the same angle. But the waggle dance is not only used to announce the discovery of new food sources. It is also employed to announce the discovery of a new place to live.

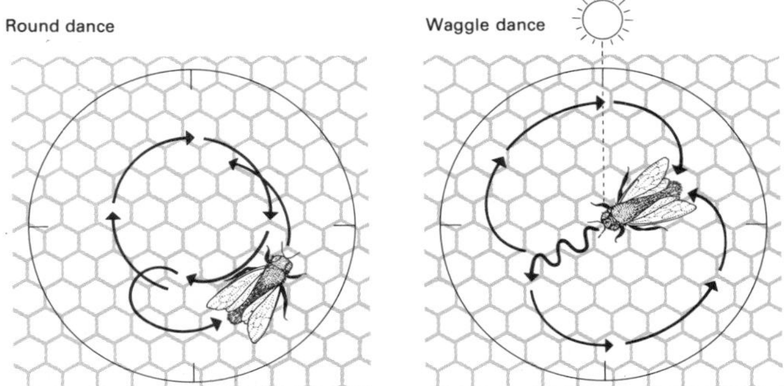

The bee's round dance is used to inform other colony members that a food source has been located close by. The waggle dance relates the source's distance (some considerable way off) and its position relative to the sun's azimuth. The dances are represented on a bee's comb.

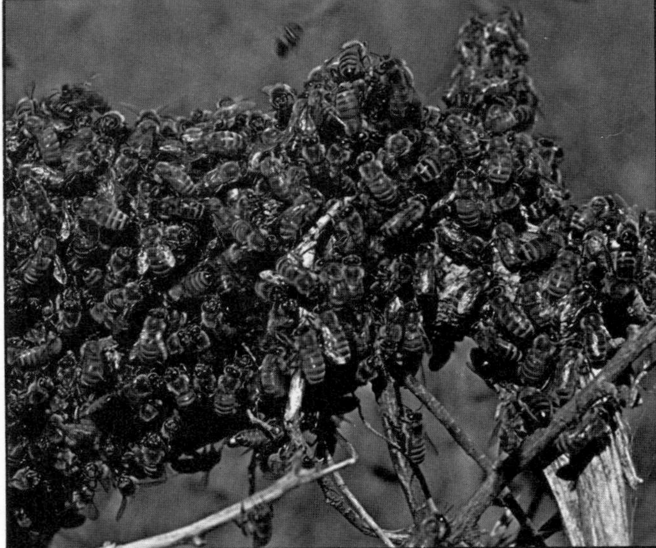

The migrations of honeybees, *Apis* spp., comprise the exploration of, and subsequent movement to and from, food sources and new potential nesting sites. Journeys to the latter are initiated by scout bees.

Scout bees start to explore for new nesting sites about three days before a swarm is due to leave the hive. When the swarm eventually leaves it consists of the old queen plus about half of the worker force; a new queen, often not yet emerged from the pupa, plus the remaining workers remain at the old site. Having left the old colony the swarm hangs from a branch or post, forming a structured, living ball of insects. There it waits until the democratic process has run its course. Within about fifteen minutes scout bees start to dance on the swarm's surface, each scout thus announcing the potential nesting place that she has discovered. Also by dancing she tries to recruit other scouts to dance in support of her site. By marking the dancing bees with a dot of paint it is possible to see how many new recruits there are dancing for each site and how many change their allegiance.

The better a bee judges its discovered site to be, the more intensely it dances in support of that site. Consequently, the more supporters it recruits to go and examine the site and to dance in support of it. A bee, dancing in support of one site, seeing another bee dancing more intensely, will fly off and examine the opposition's site. It then has to decide in support of which site it will dance when it returns to the swarm. In this way, support for different sites increases and decreases until eventually, hours or often days after the swarm first formed, only one site is being supported. Not until every single scout is dancing in support of the same site does the swarm move.

The scouts alert the rest of the swarm that a decision has been reached by performing a buzzing run over the swarm surface, and within seconds the entire swarm takes flight. Once the swarm is in the air and milling around, the scouts fly through it in a straight line in the direction of the destination. When they reach the front of the swarm they drop down, drift back, and then fly through once again. In this way they direct the swarm to the agreed destination and a new colony of bees is formed. Once the swarm is established in its new home, the queen, fertilized by a drone during the nuptial flight, starts to lay eggs. In midsummer, she may lay more than 1500 eggs a day, and the colony can eventually reach a size of more than 60,000 bees before the swarming urge arises once more.

Fish

Fish are the only animals forming a major part of our diet still hunted for food by industrialized man. Fishing makes a significant contribution to the economies of most maritime nations and in the case of Iceland the economy is largely dependent on it. Because fish populations fluctuate, the dependent fishing industries are precarious. In 1971–72 a change in the pattern of ocean currents in the Pacific Ocean caused the near disappearance of the anchovetta from the coast of Peru and a ninety per cent contraction of the fishing industry in consequence. In the early fifteenth century, for reasons that are still not clear, herring virtually disappeared from the Baltic. The north German fishery vanished, hastening the decline of the Hanseatic League.

The movement of fish is so important economically that all leading fishing nations have government-sponsored tracking programmes and many have their own research establishments. More money and effort is put into studying the migration of fish than of any other group of vertebrates.

In some ways this massive effort has been counterproductive. Although a wider knowledge of fish's movements, together with improvements in equipment, has increased catch sizes enormously, the world stock of fish has seriously declined. Overfishing has been prevalent for many years and is now a major problem with unknown ecological consequences. As far back as the 1930s unbridled exploitation was responsible for the collapse of the Californian sardine industry.

With world attention becoming increasingly focused on conservation, the emphasis in migration studies has shifted from exploitation to preservation. Before any global conservation programme can be formed, it is essential to know in detail the world pattern of fish migration. Information is needed about where fish spend the different stages of their life and most importantly where their spawning grounds and nursery areas are. In this context migration studies remain important and, if anything, need to be more comprehensive and detailed than ever before.

Investigations cannot be confined entirely to economically important species. The interdependence of fish species dictates that, to present a balanced picture, a broad perspective must be maintained. Studying the movement of fish, whether freshwater or marine, all contributes to our understanding of migration.

The movement of coral fish like the French grunt, *Haemulon flavolineatum*, over the reef to feed and breed is a response to stimuli that produce long-distance migration in other species.

Although fish are normally considered as a single group, they consist of species as far apart from one another as frogs are from rabbits. The most fundamental division is between the Agnatha, or jawless fish, and the Gnathostomata, those with jaws. The Agnatha embrace the hagfish and lampreys and are among the most primitive of all vertebrates. They have a single opening serving as both nose and mouth through which they feed by sucking and rasping the flesh of their victims.

The Gnathostomata are divided into two classes, those with cartilage skeletons – the sharks, skates and rays – and those with bony skeletons. The bony fish are evolutionarily more recent and much more numerous than either the Agnatha or the cartilaginous fish. There are over 20,000 known species and each year around another 100 new ones are discovered. They are also more diverse, ranging in size and shape from flat, bottom-dwelling species such as sole, *Solea solea*, to streamlined free-swimming species such as the bluefin tuna, *Thunnus thynnus*.

Much more is known about the movements of bony fish than of cartilaginous fish, probably because bony fish are much more important economically and have therefore been more intensively studied. The migrations of Agnatha are known to some extent and lampreys have been studied in detail.

The constant motion of a fish's watery world sets it apart from land animals. In a fish's life, movement is the natural state of affairs and remaining in one place requires effort. Perhaps because of this nearly all fish migrate to some extent – a greater proportion of fish species than species of any other animal group make seasonal migrations.

Marine fish's oceanic "atmosphere" is in many ways similar to the atmosphere of gases that constitutes the air above. It has winds in the form of currents and there are recognizable fronts between warm and cold water just as there are between air masses. As in air, circulation in the sea occurs in three dimensions. Currents do not just flow along the surface but are present at all depths. However, as ocean currents are driven primarily by the wind, they are strongest near the surface.

Sunlight does not penetrate sea water much below 200 metres (650 feet), and as nearly all life is dependent, either directly or indirectly, on it, most fish are found in this upper mobile, sunlit zone.

Freshwater fish living in rivers are also affected by currents even though these are predictably downstream. The most important thing that affects their behaviour is the strength of the current. Even fish living in lakes do not escape water movement. Currents are always present even though they are much weaker than in the sea.

The Atlantic salmon, *Salmo salar*, is an important member of that best known group of anadromous fish, the salmon. They may spend between one and eight years in fresh water before entering the sea.

Perch, *Perca fluviatilis*, are found in fresh or brackish water throughout Europe, Asia and North America. Their eggs are normally laid in shallow water in long shreds, wrapped around stones or weeds.

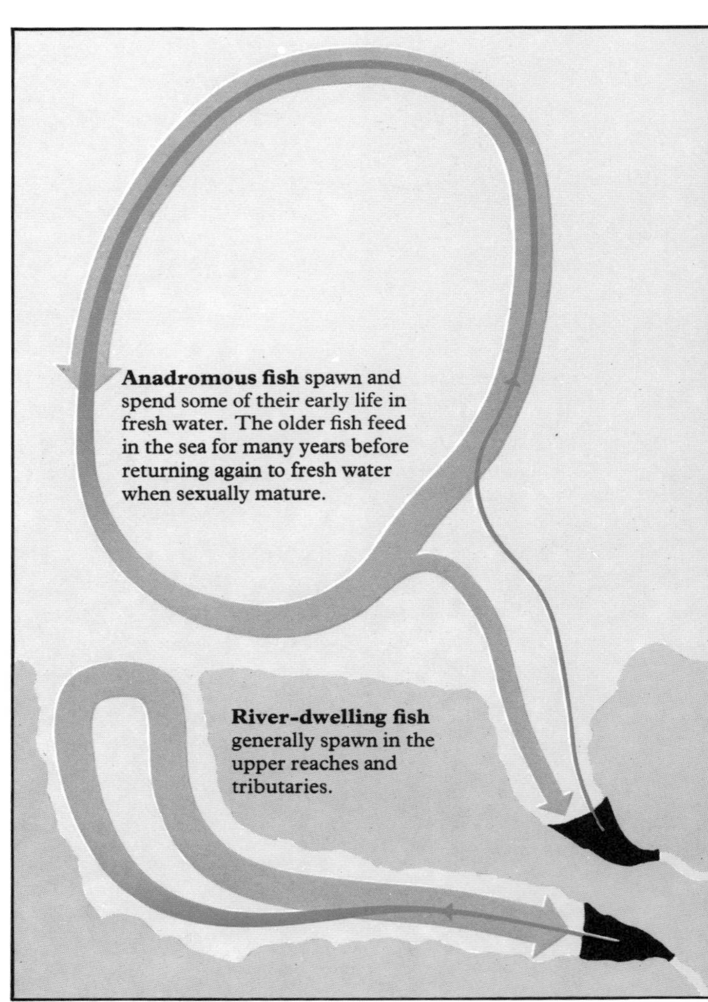

Anadromous fish spawn and spend some of their early life in fresh water. The older fish feed in the sea for many years before returning again to fresh water when sexually mature.

River-dwelling fish generally spawn in the upper reaches and tributaries.

Patterns of migration

Fish migrate for the same reasons that land animals and birds migrate; the need for food and a place to breed or spend the winter. Some migrate across thousands of kilometres of ocean – others within a single mountain stream. Some migrate only in the spawning season, others are almost constantly on the move. Some fish migrate with the tide, others with the moon and others according to the seasons. The variety of behaviour is infinite and the range enormous.

Many freshwater fish migrate primarily to spawn. Lake-dwelling fish very often spend most of the year feeding in one particular area, migrating only at the appropriate season to spawn. Their spawning grounds may be within the lake itself, or some distance upstream in one of the rivers or streams flowing into it. Some river- or stream-dwelling fish migrate seasonally, swimming downstream to deeper water in the winter or dry season, depending on the climate, and upstream again in the summer or wet season. In other freshwater fish migration is linked with development – the young fish moving from their natal site, where their parents spawned, to nursery areas further downstream, where they feed and grow to maturity. When adult, these fish will again migrate back upstream to spawn. Some river fish migrate so far downstream to feed that they find themselves in brackish, estuary water. The migration of fish that leave fresh water altogether to spend their adult life feeding in the sea, can be seen as an extension of this. They only return to fresh water when sexually mature and ready to spawn.

Fish that breed in fresh water but spend part of their lives in the sea are said to be anadromous. Of the many species behaving this way, most only travel short distances from the shore, staying within the relatively shallow water of the continental shelf. Others, including the salmon, the most celebrated anadromous fish, travel thousands of kilometres in huge migration circuits before arriving back at the coast where their native stream enters the sea. In making these enormous oceanic journeys, anadromous fish behave similarly to purely marine fish, such as herring, cod and tuna. The only major difference between them is that salmon spawn in fresh water while marine fish, described as oceanodromous, remain in the sea to spawn. Most eels perform oceanodromous migrations, but they are unusual in that they migrate towards deeper water to spawn, and towards shallower water for the major feeding and growth phase of their life. Most species spend this phase in coastal waters, but one genus, *Anguilla*, enters fresh water to feed and grow to maturity. They are the only major group of catadromous fish, that is fish

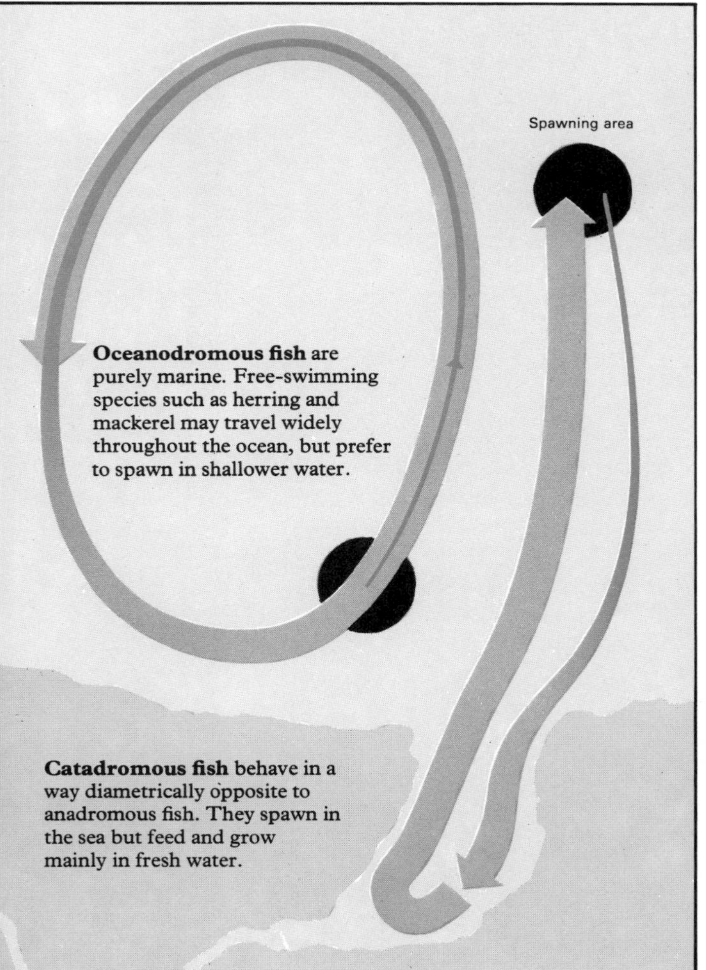

Oceanodromous fish are purely marine. Free-swimming species such as herring and mackerel may travel widely throughout the ocean, but prefer to spawn in shallower water.

Catadromous fish behave in a way diametrically opposite to anadromous fish. They spawn in the sea but feed and grow mainly in fresh water.

Mackerel, *Scomber scombrus*, are typical free-swimming oceanodromous fish. Their distribution in the North Atlantic corresponds to more nutrient-rich areas where tropical water mixes with Arctic water.

Eels of the genus *Anguilla*, such as the European and North American eel, constitute the largest group of catadromous fish. They lay their eggs, near the surface, over the deeper parts of the ocean.

spawning in the sea but spending part of their lives, usually the adult feeding phase, in fresh water.

A great many species living in coastal waters make inshore-offshore migrations, once or twice a day in relation to the tides. Others migrate when there is a change in temperature, migrating offshore for winter and inshore for summer. In yet other coastal species migration is related to a particular stage of development, the fish spending their early lives feeding and growing offshore and migrating inshore again to spawn when they are adult.

A new view of fish behaviour

There are numerous forms of fish migration and, although biologists are well aware of the gaps remaining in our knowledge of them, there are considerable difficulties standing in the way of a complete understanding of fish's behaviour. Man is very much a land animal and consequently finds it difficult to comprehend the fish's watery world. In the past most descriptions of fish migration have conveyed a picture of animals living in a virtual sensory void, having little if any appreciation of their position in space and possessing, at most, only a tenuous link with their natal or home site. Their migrations were portrayed as made by swimming with, or battling against, river and ocean currents, or simply drifting within the oceans' circulatory system until brought back to the area where their migration began a year or more earlier.

In such a view migration is a rigid, inflexible behaviour. Migration circuits were portrayed as the means whereby fish timed their arrival at spawning grounds to

If one particular place could supply all a fish's needs at all times of the year, no fish would ever migrate. But as most fish do migrate this can hardly ever be the case. The survival of the sockeye salmon's hatchlings depends largely on the parents' choice of spawning ground. The salmon is prepared to make an enormous journey from the Pacific Ocean into the rivers of western North America to meet their needs.

coincide with their breeding cycle. Those fish that did not arrive in the right place at the right time failed to reproduce and only those fish with the genes that produced the necessary instinctive behaviour survived. Therefore, in this view, the only "right" place for an anadromous fish, such as a salmon, to spawn was in the stream where it was spawned itself. Any salmon that failed to return to its natal site was considered lost.

The modern interpretation of fish migration supposes that fish know precisely where they are in the sea at any one time and where they have to travel at different times of the year to meet their various breeding, feeding and wintering requirements.

Exploration

According to this interpretation, fish learn about their surroundings during their early life and establish a familiar area in the same way as all terrestrial vertebrates, including man. Within this familiar area the locations of all their different seasonal requirements and resources, such as the best places to feed and spawn, are learned and in a way that enables the animal to travel between them with the minimum expenditure of time and energy. More often than not, therefore, these routes are down-current and it seems likely that a fish will often use one spring feeding ground rather than another, with which it is equally familiar, purely because one is down-current from its winter feeding grounds and the other is not. Fish take advantage of water currents in the same way that birds and insects take advantage of the wind to reduce the effort needed to travel to the place or in the direction they prefer.

Although the clues used by fish to learn about their surroundings naturally differ from those used by land animals, they are learned in essentially the same way. Immediately after hatching a fish begins to establish a familiar area by making a series of exploratory migrations. It may explore on its own, or as a member of a shoal of fish of similar age. It may accompany older fish on their migration, or use some combination of these methods. During the period leading up to maturity, the young fish might be expected to travel further afield than the adults, giving it the opportunity of finding fresh spawning and feeding grounds. As it approaches maturity, it will concentrate its visits on those places which it has learned are best, or most productive for a particular activity at a certain time of year. It will visit those places in the sequence and by the routes which it has learned from past experience give the maximum benefit for the minimum effort. By the time the fish begins to reproduce as an adult it will have whittled down the size of its familiar area to a much smaller home range, usually in the form of a migration circuit between the places that the fish uses for its various needs. Sometimes, as is the case with cod, the circuit takes the form of a seasonal to-and-fro migration between feeding and breeding grounds.

This is broadly the way that all vertebrates, whether terrestrial or aquatic, and some invertebrates are thought to organize their lives.

One of the corollaries of this theory is that because fish migration is flexible and based on exploration and learning, as new habitats arise or are made available they will be rapidly exploited by the fish. For instance as the waters of the northern oceans have become warmer during the present century, many oceanic fish, such as Atlantic cod and bluefin tuna, have extended their existing migration circuits northward or have developed completely new ones to take advantage of the change.

In the early 1900s immature, five-year-old cod, *Gadus morhua*, of the Icelandic-spawning population left their migration circuit between Iceland and southwest Greenland and established a completely new migration circuit and spawning ground off the west coast of Greenland. Until about 1920 the northern limit followed by the Mediterranean-spawning population of tunny, *Thunnus thynnus*, seemed to be in the region of the English Channel. It now extends as far north as Norway.

A recent development in the North Atlantic has highlighted a feature of fish behaviour that was previously unrecognized. Following a general increase in ocean temperatures in the early part of this century, cod from the Icelandic spawning population moved into the waters of western Greenland and started a completely new migration cycle. It would appear that the pattern of fish migration is much less rigid than was previously thought and that fish find no difficulty in taking up new opportunities as they arise.

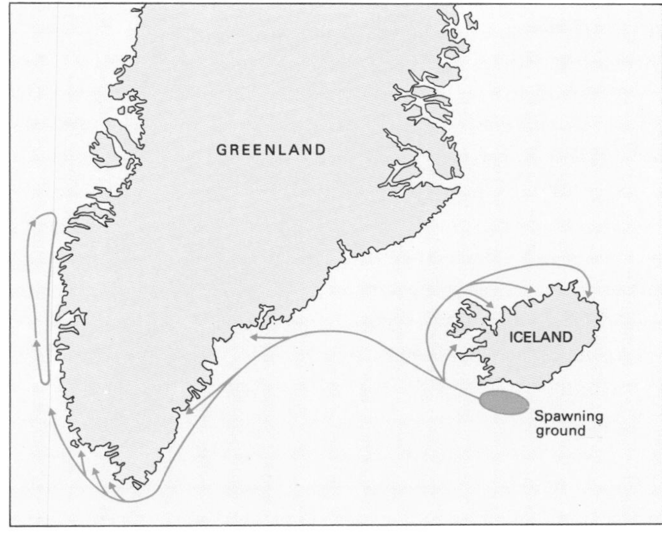

When adult salmon fail to return to their natal stream but instead spawn in another one, according to the modern view they do so not because they are lost but because they have decided that the new stream is more suitable for spawning than the old one. If salmon do in fact choose their spawning grounds, and if the level of pollution can be reduced in rivers that have not supported salmon for many years, a rapid recolonization can be expected. On the old, inflexible view, recolonization by natural means, if it occurred at all, would have been very slow.

Freshwater fish

The idea that fish migrate within a familiar area also seems to hold good for freshwater fish. It has been shown experimentally that lake-dwelling fish, which return to the same places each year to spawn, are able to recognize the direction of their spawning grounds from elsewhere in the lake. Studies of the white bass, *Roccus chrysops*, have indicated that nearly ninety per cent successfully find their way back to spawn.

Although some fish, living in lakes, remain there all their lives, many lake-fish migrate into tributary rivers to spawn. In Africa, for instance, various relatives of the carp, order Cypriniformes, such as the catfish, *Clarias* spp., and the tiger fish, *Hydrocyon* spp., behave this way. Usually they enter one or other of the inlet streams which run into the lake and then travel some distance upstream. Occasionally, individuals living very close to an outlet stream may migrate downstream to spawn, but this is unusual, and often individuals living around the mouth of an outlet stream will migrate all the way across the lake to spawn in an inlet stream.

In some lakes, particularly in tropical regions, which have neither inlet nor outlet streams, it has on occasion been noted that when man has created an artificial inlet for irrigation or other purposes, some fish have almost immediately made spawning migrations into the newly created stream. Such flexibility of behaviour is clearly consistent with the modern view of fish migration.

The life-history of fish, which spend most of their feeding life in lakes and only migrate into rivers or streams to spawn, varies from species to species, but the brown trout, *Salmo trutta*, may be taken as a typical example. The young fish live in nursery streams for between one and four years before joining the adult population in the lake. The adults become mature in the autumn or winter and swim back to the streams to spawn, the males usually arriving before the females. In turbid water, migration may take place throughout the day, but in clear water the fish will travel only at night. After spawning during the latter part of the winter and the early spring, the spent fish migrate downstream to the lake again. They often return to the feeding territory they occupied the previous year.

The migration of lake fish up inlet streams to spawn seems to follow a pattern of behaviour that is common to all freshwater fish. On the whole, fish living in rivers migrate upstream or into tributary rivers to spawn. A great variety of species behave in this way, including sturgeons, paddlefish, garpikes, shads, suckers, barbels, minnows, catfish and some darters. Even species such as carp, *Cyprinus*, normally considered to be sluggish, have been seen leaping over small obstacles such as low head-dams barring their way upstream. By swimming upstream before spawning fish reduce the risk of their eggs and larvae being eaten by larger predators. The very shallowness of the water excludes many of their natural enemies. However, the upper reaches are likely to be short of food so the adult fish will normally return downstream to feed immediately after spawning. The fish larvae left behind are well provided for by a yolk sac which will sustain them until they drift into richer waters.

It is obviously much easier for fish to migrate downstream rather than upstream and, unless they make some effort to withstand the current, they will be involuntarily carried downstream. The faster the river current the more effort the fish need to expend to stay where they are. The strength of the current influences the fish's behaviour. In fast-flowing rivers fish that are normally free-swimming take shelter in areas of slow-moving water, establishing territories in the "dead" water behind obstacles such as rocks in the river. In shallow fast-flowing water the young of the brook trout, *Salvelinus fontinalis*, become territorial, but in slow-moving water they swim freely in shoals.

The energy expended by fish to combat the current affects their development. Food that would normally contribute towards growth is used up in continual swimming. In studies of the brown trout in Germany it was found that the fish grew better in slow streams than in fast ones and better in natural rivers with lots of irregularities that slowed down the current than in artificially straightened channels.

All the return migrations mentioned above are ontogenetic, that is related to the life-history of the fish, and involve downstream migration when young and upstream migration to spawn when adult. If a species spawns many times over a period of several years these downstream and upstream migrations become essentially a seasonal return migration. A case in point is the brook trout, a commonly occurring native of eastern North America, which migrates upstream during the autumn spawning season (September-November) and

The white bass, *Roccus chrysops.*

Catfish, *Clarias* spp., are found typically in swampy or stagnant water in Africa or Asia. In common with many lake fish they prefer to swim into the shallower, flowing waters of a tributary river to spawn, where they are well out of reach of their natural predators.

The white bass, *Roccus chrysops*, of Lake Mendota in Wisconsin, spawn in May and June at two separate sites around the northeastern shores of the lake. Males were collected from spawning sites during the breeding season and attached to floats by lengths of nylon line. When they were released in the centre of the lake, it was seen from the movement of the floats that, to begin with, most fish swam northward – the arrow shows the average direction the fish swam in during the first hour. After this, however, they became more spread out as each fish made for its own spawning ground. When the fish that had returned to the spawning grounds were examined it was found that at one site ninety-six per cent had been originally collected there and at the other, eighty-nine per cent had been collected there. The fact that the fish returned almost invariably to their original point of capture seems to indicate that they were released within their own familiar area. However, as in total only fifteen per cent of all fish released were ever recaptured, it is difficult to say just how far we can go in making deductions from the results.

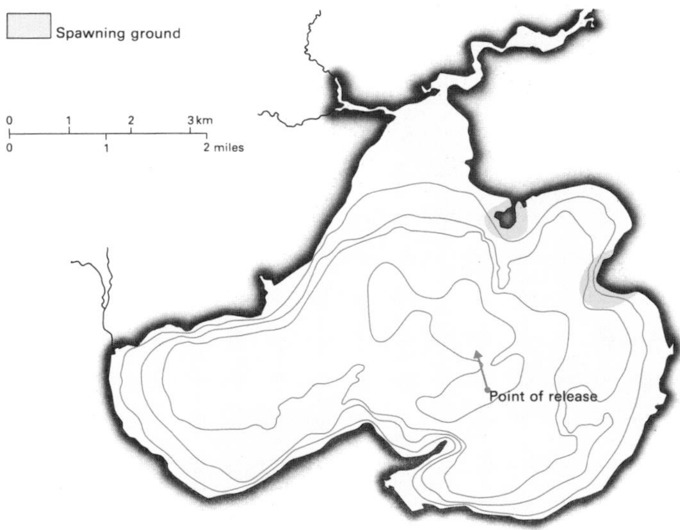

LIVING BETWEEN THE RIVER AND THE SEA

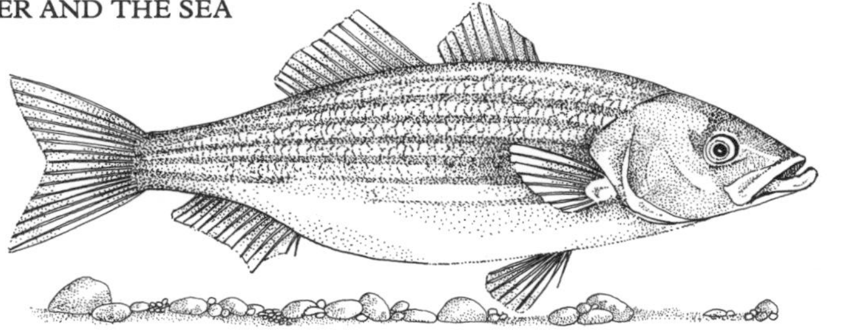

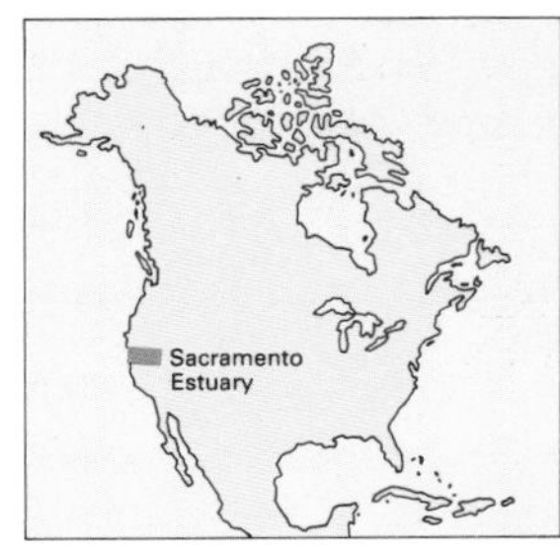

The striped bass, *Roccus saxatilis*, spawning in the tributaries of the Sacramento estuary in California, behaves in a way that is partway between a wholly freshwater fish and a truly anadromous fish, such as the salmon. Between November and March the fish are concentrated mainly in the estuary, but as the April breeding season approaches they fan out and ascend the tributary rivers. When spawning is over the fish gradually move back downstream through the estuary towards the sea. During the summer months, between June and August, the adults are found mainly in the brackish water at the mouth of the delta, but the young fish prefer to remain further upstream in fresh water. The fish, particularly the younger ones, may sometimes spawn in a different tributary each year, suggesting that their exploration of the area as juveniles was particularly thorough and extensive, and provided them with a whole range of possible spawning sites to choose from. The striped bass's adventurous nature helps to explain the fish's rapid spread along the coast of North America. The fish were introduced to the Sacramento River from the Atlantic in 1879, and had reached Oregon only twenty years later. In 1906 they were being fished in the Columbia River, 1000 kilometres (620 miles) to the north.

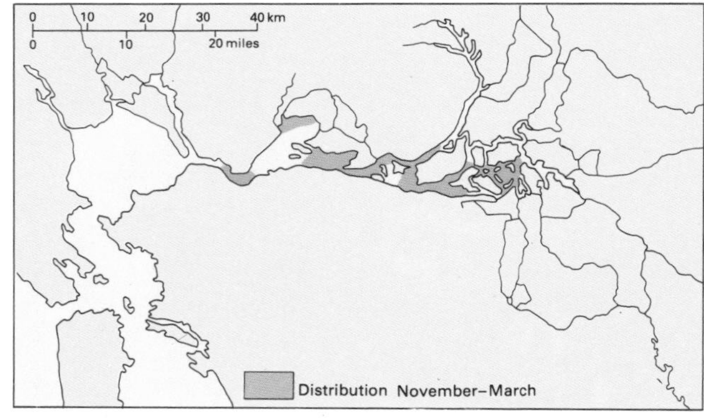

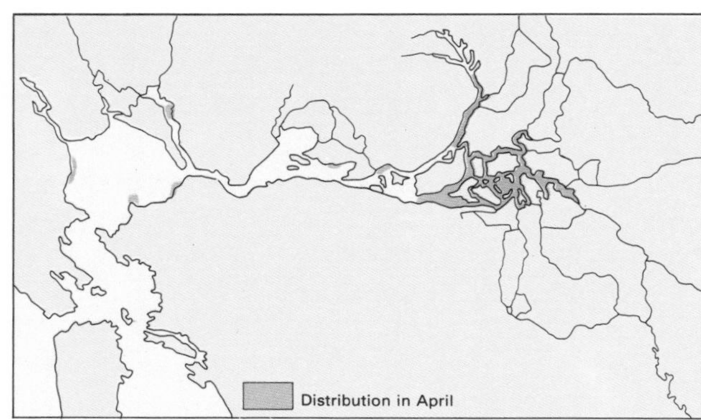

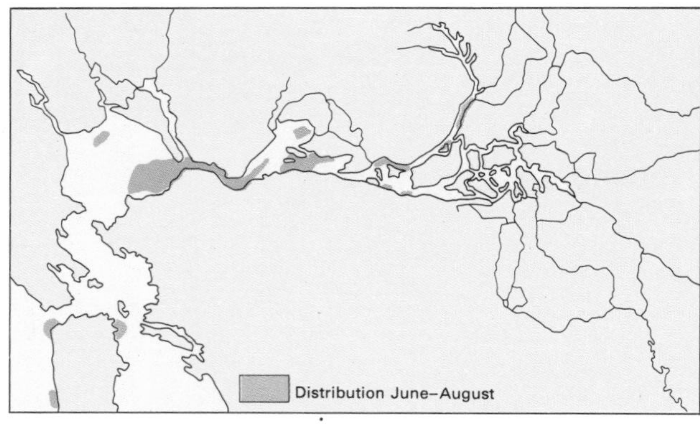

The common sturgeon, *Acipenser sturio*, migrates into the rivers of Europe to spawn between April and June. It prefers fast-flowing water no more than ten metres (32 ft) deep and may lay between 800,000 and 2,400,000 eggs at a time. They are the largest freshwater fish found in Europe, up to two metres (6.5 ft) in length. Some live to be 100 years old.

downstream again to deeper water for the colder winter months. Another is the fierce, predatory Danube salmon, *Hucho hucho*, which prefers the upper reaches of the Danube tributaries to spawn during March and April. It then returns downstream in the autumn and winter to deeper waters, where the fish upon which it feeds spend the cold season in large numbers.

Migration to deeper water for the winter is characteristic of the behaviour of many temperate fish, such as darters, minnows, trout and the sterlet, *Acipenser ruthenus*, found in the Volga. In arid climates there is usually a pronounced downstream migration during the dry season when the headwaters and swamps begin to shrink. However, the migration is purely temporary and they return later when conditions improve.

Entry into the sea

All these downstream-upstream migrations take place entirely within fresh water. The migration of some species, however, results in at least some individuals spending part of their lives in brackish or salt water. An experiment with the striped bass, *Roccus saxatilis*, carried out in the Sacramento-San Joaquin delta, California, showed that after spawning almost all the adult fish swam down into the brackish water of the estuary or into the sea.

Many species of fish are only partially anadromous, some individuals entering the sea at some stage of their migration, others migrating entirely within fresh water. In these species the sea-going individuals may look quite different from their permanent freshwater counterparts. They are usually larger and more silver in colour and are frequently referred to by different common names. In the past they were often considered to be different species. Probably the best known example is the trout, *Salmo trutta*. Originally a native of Europe, it has now been introduced into many parts of the world. Individuals that remain in fresh water are known as brown trout, whereas those that reach the sea are referred to as sea trout. The North American equivalent, *Salmo gairdneri*, is known as the rainbow trout when it stays in fresh water but the steelhead when it enters the sea. Whereas sea trout rarely travel beyond coastal waters, the steelhead migrates several hundred kilometres out into the open sea.

Within certain groups of fish some species are anadromous while other closely related ones are entirely freshwater. The most important group with this characteristic embraces the lampreys. River lampreys, *Lampetra fluviatilis*, spawn and spend their larval stage in fresh water but spend their adult life in the sea. The brook lampreys, *Lampetra planeri*, on the other hand are purely freshwater. These two groups of fish are so closely related that in most cases each anadromous river lamprey can be matched with a purely freshwater counterpart. During their larval stage lampreys are filter feeders, but on entering the sea, the river lamprey becomes parasitic, attaching itself to and feeding on the blood and body fluids of other fish. However, the brook lamprey never adopts the parasitic mode and in fact never feeds again after maturity. It is interesting to speculate why only the anadromous form has become parasitic. It may be due in part to a lack of suitable fish to act as parasitic hosts in the rivers themselves.

Many fish species spawning in fresh water, however, consist of entirely anadromous individuals. Several of the sixteen species of sturgeons, Acipenseridae, well known as the source of caviar, fit into this category. Adult sturgeons are large fish, two to three metres (6 to 10 feet) in length. Some species measure as much as seven metres (23 feet) and weigh a tonne. The European sturgeon, *Acipenser sturio*, feeds in the deep water of the North Atlantic and Mediterranean and spawns in the rivers of North America and Europe. It is rarely captured at sea and consequently its marine distribution and migrations are little known. In spring and early summer large numbers enter the rivers of continental Europe during the spawning migration and a few are found in the rivers of Britain, Denmark, Norway and Sweden. In large rivers, such as the Rhine, Elbe and Vistula,

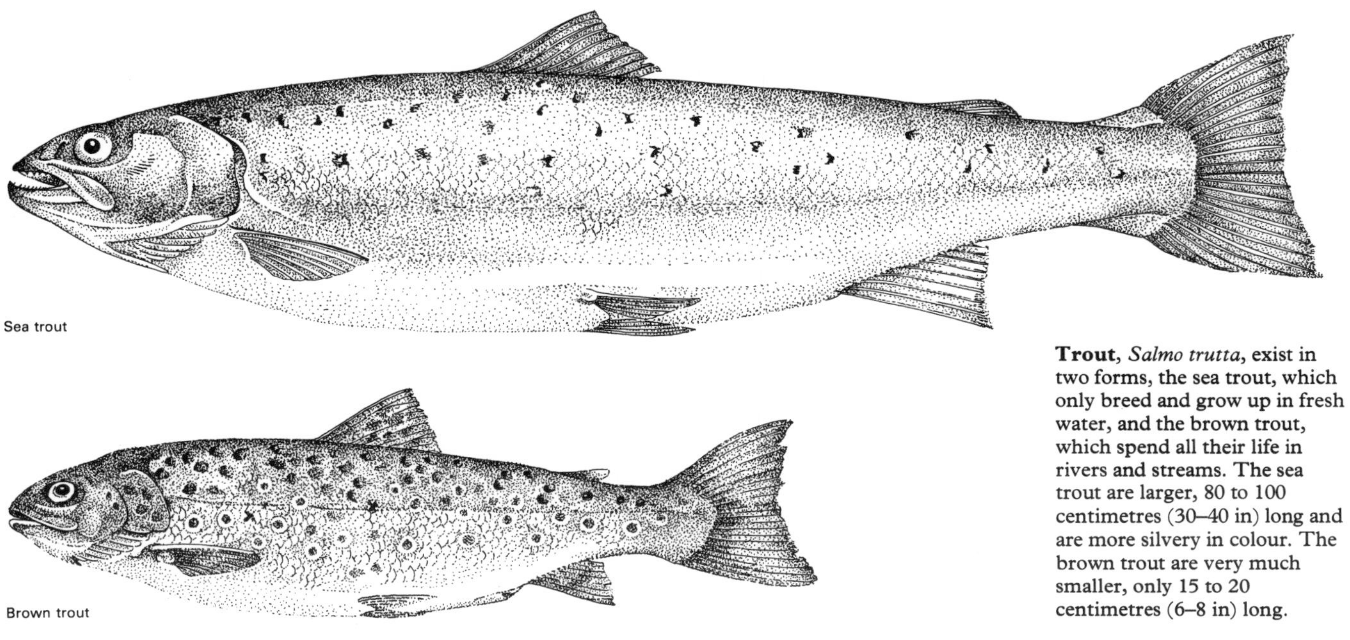

Trout, *Salmo trutta*, exist in two forms, the sea trout, which only breed and grow up in fresh water, and the brown trout, which spend all their life in rivers and streams. The sea trout are larger, 80 to 100 centimetres (30–40 in) long and are more silvery in colour. The brown trout are very much smaller, only 15 to 20 centimetres (6–8 in) long.

the fish often travel far upstream, but in others they may spawn just beyond the brackish water. The females normally migrate upstream at night in the company of a number of smaller males. The eggs, caviar, are laid and fertilized in a depression dug in the river bottom. The young migrate down to the sea in the same summer that they hatch. Those entering the Danube from the Black Sea may have a one-way migration distance of 2000 kilometres (1250 miles).

The Atlantic salmon

Undoubtedly the best known of all anadromous fish are the Atlantic Salmon, *Salmo salar*, and Pacific salmon, *Oncorhynchus* spp. The Atlantic salmon spawns in late autumn or winter, usually far upstream in gravel suitable for the construction of a "redd" or spawning pit. The fertilized eggs, which eventually become buried fifteen to thirty centimetres (6 to 12 inches) deep, hatch after a period of between 70 and 160 days. On hatching, the young fish, known as alevins, are only about one centimetre (0.5 inch) long and possess a large yolk sac attached to their underside. They remain in the gravel for about three to four weeks until the yolk sac is nearly absorbed and they are ready to feed. This stage is the riskiest period in a salmon's life. The tiny little fish, only between two and three centimetres (1 and 1.5 inches) long, must compete with thousands like them for the available food while at the same time avoid being eaten themselves. Those that survive for more than a year in these conditions are known as parr.

In many more northern areas, because food is in such short supply the fry and parr hardly grow at all during the winter months and rely on the spring and summer months to supply enough food for growth. It seems that salmon fry, like adult river fish, try to establish feeding territories and experiments have shown that when fry and parr are removed from their usual place in the river they normally try to swim back to it. Individual fish are known to have returned to their original territories from more than 200 metres (220 yards) in both upstream and downstream directions. Parr and fry that are unsuccessful in the competition for feeding space are gradually forced further and further downstream into more unsuitable waters to feed. Parr are also known to migrate downstream at other times, particularly in the spring, but it is not really known why. It is possible that they have outgrown their previous territory and are searching for a new one.

Before a parr can become a smolt – the stage at which it enters the sea – it must be at least ten centimetres (4 inches) long. The time it takes to grow to ten centimetres varies with the geographical location of the river. In the Hampshire Avon in England over ninety per cent of parr become smolts within a year, whereas in northern Scandinavia the parr may take seven to eight years to reach this stage. Some male parr never become smolts, but become sexually mature at the freshwater stage and migrate back upstream to the spawning grounds. The tiny male swims into the redd as it is being constructed by the female and fertilizes the bottom-most eggs, which have fallen into a position where they cannot be reached by sperm produced by the normal-sized, relatively huge, male who would defend the female from the attentions of other large males.

In the spring following their growth to over ten centimetres (4 inches), most parr change into smolt and migrate downstream. At first, smolt migrate only by night, but later on, in late May and early June, they travel during the middle part of the day as well. It is thought that the smolt "drop" downstream, tail first, at a rate of between 0.5 and 2.0 kilometres (0.3 and 1.2 miles) a day. Before entering the sea the smolts prefer to acclimatize themselves gradually to the saline conditions, and if an estuary is present at the mouth of the river they will pause there a short time before finally swimming out to sea.

Salmon – adult life

Little is known of the movements of Atlantic salmon smolts at sea. Marked smolts from rivers in northern Sweden have been recaptured as adults in the southern Baltic, and British smolts have been found off Greenland during their first year. Older fish from Britain, Canada and Norway are often caught off Greenland, but some salmon from Norway and the USSR and possibly Sweden may remain in the eastern part of the North Atlantic. At sea the salmon's main food is fish, particularly herring, capelin and sand eels. In their turn, salmon are eaten by various other fish and by seals, particularly the grey seal, *Halichoerus grypus*.

After a marine phase of one to four years, Atlantic salmon return to fresh water. Those that return after only one year are known as grilse. The season at which they re-enter fresh water to spawn varies from river to river. The longer the river, the earlier the salmon must enter it to arrive at the spawning ground in time to breed. Some fish re-enter fresh water as much as twelve months before spawning. During migration upstream the salmon, which are on average seventy centimetres (28 inches) long, travel for distances of from ten to twenty kilometres (6 to 12 miles) in a day without feeding. They may lose as much as twenty-five per cent of their body weight on the journey.

After spawning, the death rate in spent fish, both male and female, is very high, and on average only twenty-six per cent survive to return downstream to the sea. The spent salmon, known as kelts, spend between four and eighteen months feeding in the sea before returning again to fresh water. It is estimated that of all spawning salmon, only three to six per cent have spawned before. This figure may be very much higher for salmon spawning in short-course rivers. In some Scottish and Canadian rivers as many as thirty-four per cent have spawned at least once before. One salmon captured was thirteen years old and had spawned four times.

The Pacific salmon, *Oncorhynchus* spp., which spawn in rivers bordering the Pacific, as far south as California in the east and Korea in the west, have a broadly similar life-history. However, they differ in that they always die after spawning. The pink salmon, *O. gorbuscha*, and chum salmon, *O. keta*, spawn just above the brackish water near river mouths. They migrate as fry more or less directly to the sea within a few weeks of hatching, without passing through the parr and smolt stages.

THE SALMON LIFE CYCLE

The salmon's downstream journey towards the sea parallels its development from larva to adult. The life cycle of the Atlantic salmon, *Salmo salar*, represented here may take between three and twelve years to complete. Excepting for the pink salmon, *Oncorhynchus gorbuscha*, and the chum salmon, *O. keta*, which head straight towards the sea at the fry stage, the life cycle of Pacific salmon, *Oncorhynchus* spp., is broadly similar. Most become sexually mature and return to spawn after about four or five years, but the sockeye salmon, *O. nerka*, pictured below, may take up to eight years to reach maturity. On the way back to spawn the digestive organs degenerate and the salmon becomes a mere carrier of sperm and eggs. After spawning Pacific salmon are totally exhausted and soon become diseased and emaciated.

The female salmon digs her redd or spawning pit by washing out a small hollow in the river sediments with her tail. Both eggs and milt are deposited in the redd and covered with gravel by the female.

The appearance of salmon changes radically on their way upstream to the spawning grounds. They become highly coloured and the males develop a hooked lower jaw. Salmon do not feed at this time but rely on their own reserves of fat.

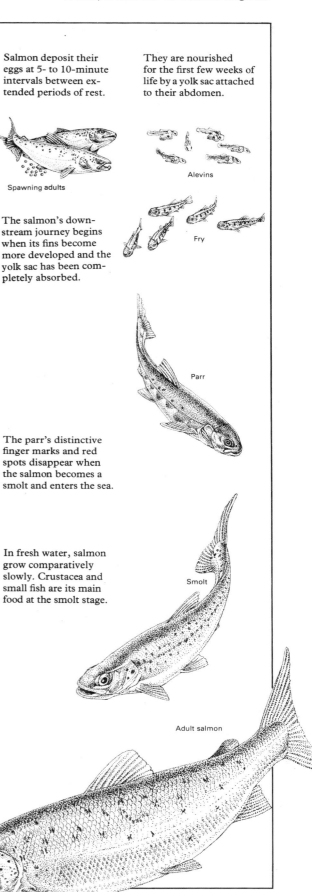

Salmon deposit their eggs at 5- to 10-minute intervals between extended periods of rest.

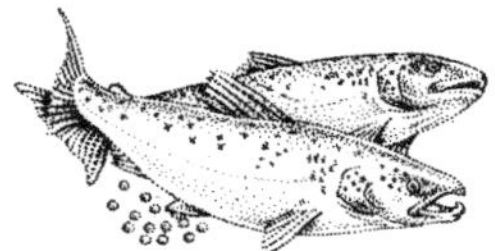

Spawning adults

They are nourished for the first few weeks of life by a yolk sac attached to their abdomen.

Alevins

The salmon's downstream journey begins when its fins become more developed and the yolk sac has been completely absorbed.

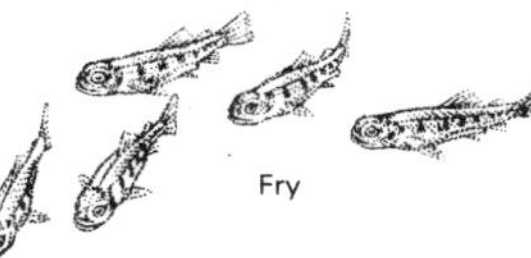

Fry

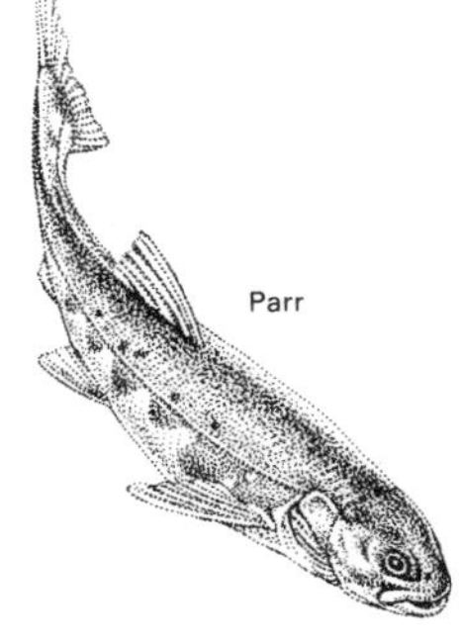

Parr

The parr's distinctive finger marks and red spots disappear when the salmon becomes a smolt and enters the sea.

In fresh water, salmon grow comparatively slowly. Crustacea and small fish are its main food at the smolt stage.

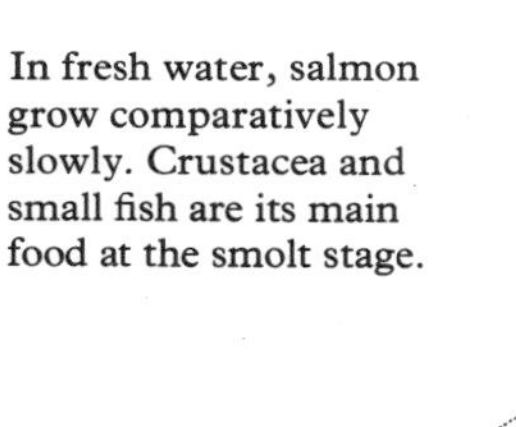

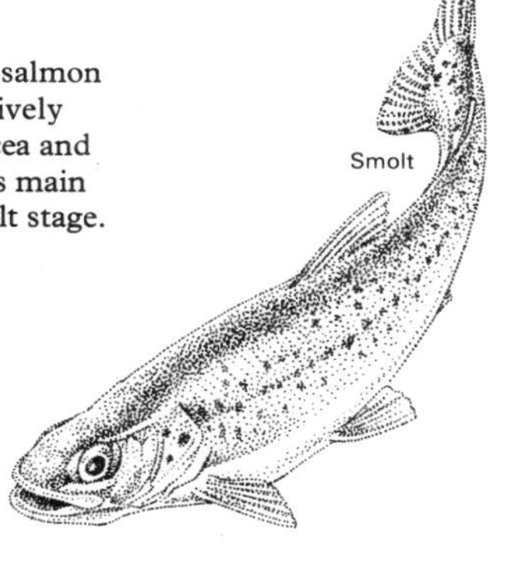

Smolt

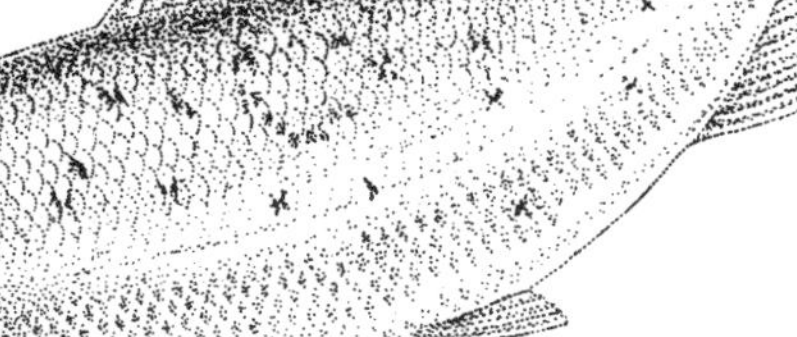

Adult salmon

THE ATLANTIC SALMON

While at sea, the Atlantic salmon, *Salmo salar*, are dark blue backed with silvery sides. They lead a free-swimming predatory life near the surface of the ocean, feeding mainly on small fish and crustaceans. Little is known of their movements, but feeding grounds have been found along the Norwegian and Greenland coasts, where they return year after year. In sea water most salmon are caught along the coast during their spawning migrations back to the rivers. Their demand for oxygen is high and they cannot tolerate polluted waters.

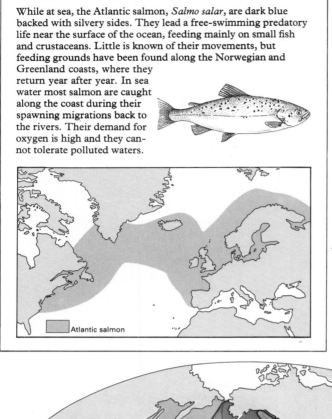

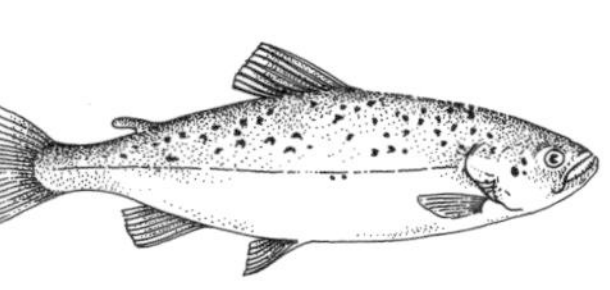

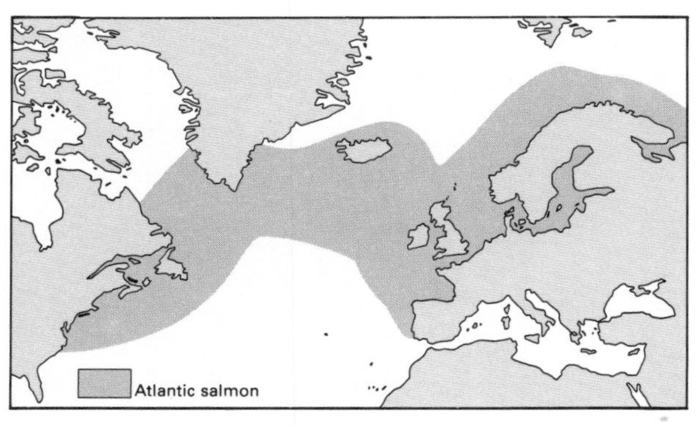

Salmon – navigation

The most absorbing aspect of the salmon is undoubtedly their ability to navigate across the sea to return to the place where they hatched, in order to spawn. This raises the important question of what proportion of salmon succeed in finding their way back and to what extent the return to the spawning site is strictly necessary for them to reproduce successfully. It was for long believed that those fish failing to return to their hatching place to spawn were lost, their navigation mechanism having failed. If this were the correct explanation, one would expect that those species spending longest in the river in which they were spawned and travelling the least distance from the coast would be more likely to return to their hatching place. In fact the converse is true. Species such as the pink salmon stay in the river for only a few weeks and migrate up to 4000 kilometres (2500 miles) from the coast. About ninety per cent of those surviving return to their hatching place to spawn. On the other hand, species such as the trout, *Salmo trutta*, which either do not leave the river at all or, as sea trout, travel only within coastal waters, spawn far less often at their hatching place.

It appears that species that spend all their lives in their native river system or on the coast round its mouth have the maximum opportunity for exploration and therefore have a greater chance of locating other suitable spawning

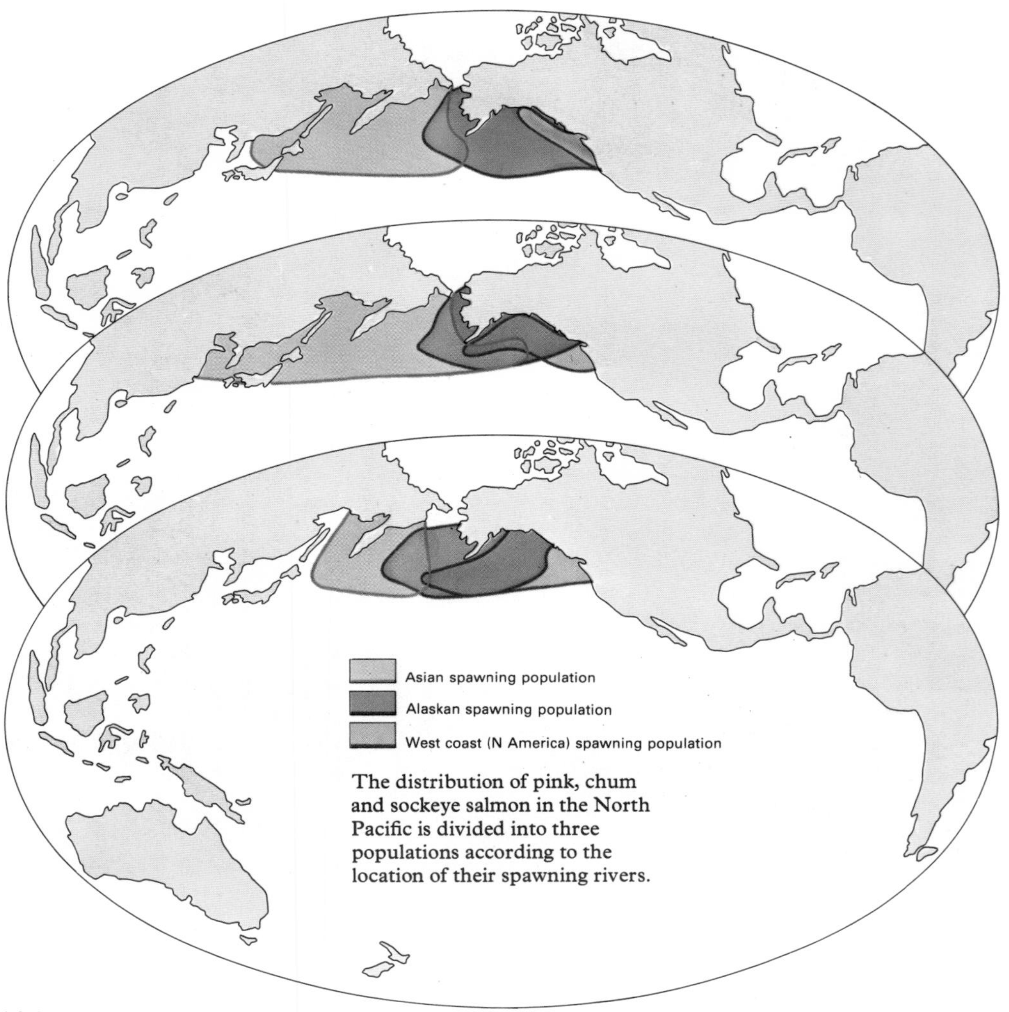

The distribution of pink, chum and sockeye salmon in the North Pacific is divided into three populations according to the location of their spawning rivers.

PACIFIC SALMON

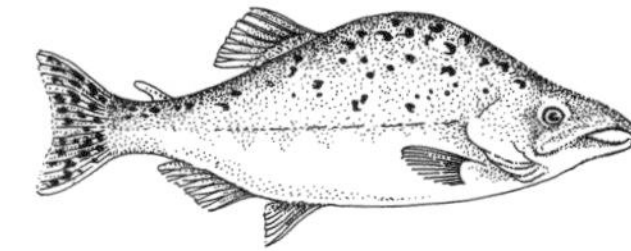

The pink salmon, *Oncorhynchus gorbuscha*, is the smallest salmon found in the northern Pacific. When they are ready to spawn, the males develop a pronounced hump and are often called humpback salmon.

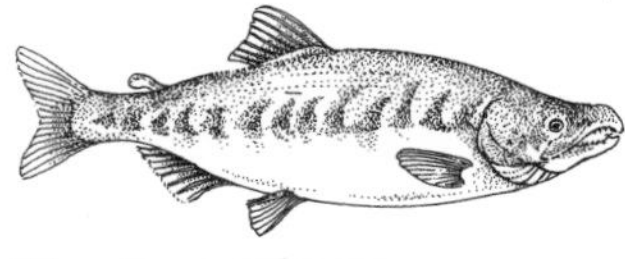

The chum salmon, *Oncorhynchus keta*, is most abundant off the coast of Alaska. They are usually two years old before they spawn and weigh between three and five kilograms (6–11 lb) when adult.

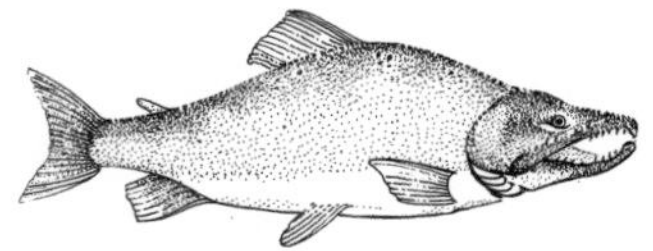

The male sockeye salmon, *Oncorhynchus nerka*, changes dramatically in the breeding season. His head becomes green and his back and sides turn to flame red. Although spawning once, he does so flamboyantly.

sites. Those that leave at an early stage and swim rapidly out to sea do not. When the time comes for spawning, the only information the offshore fish have is about their own hatching place, which must have been suitable or they would not have survived themselves. As they have no opportunity of finding another site beforehand the only way they can ensure the survival of their own larvae is to return there.

Investigations of salmon navigation have concentrated on the freshwater phase of their migration and the way in which the fish locate the area of coast where their "home" river system enters the sea. It has been found that if salmon eggs, fry or even parr are transferred from one stream to another it is to this second stream that the mature fish return to spawn. That is, where they developed as parr and subsequently became smolts. Clearly, therefore, it is at this stage that the characteristics of the "home" river are learned.

Other experiments indicate that the young fish are aware of how the chemicals carried in the water change between the upstream spawning grounds and the point of entry into the sea. The olfactory signature of river water – the characteristics that the fish recognizes through its sense of smell – are probably peculiar not only to each river system but also to each tributary and remain relatively unchanged over a number of years. When an adult salmon arrives back at the coast after its feeding and maturation phase, it locates the position where fresh water with a familiar olfactory signature enters the sea. It then swims upcurrent, passing by a familiar series of smell signposts until it reaches its spawning grounds. It literally smells or tastes its way home.

Coastal migration

Countless species of coastal-dwelling fish migrate relatively short distances, daily or seasonally, between shallow water and the shore-line. None behaves in a more spectacular manner than a particular species found on the west coast of the United States.

When the Spaniards first reached California in the eighteenth century they are said to have heard from the local Indians of a fish that danced on the shore at full moon. They were describing for the first time one of the most remarkable and dramatic events in biology – the spawning of the grunion.

The grunion, *Leuresthes tenuis*, a small fish related to the grey mullet, is found along the coast of southern California and in the northern Baja California. It migrates inshore to spawn on the three or four nights following each new and full moon in spring and summer, when the tides are at their highest. It is the precise timing related to the tides that fascinates biologists. At the peak of spawning thousands of small, shimmering

Salmon must be in prime physical condition to reach their chosen spawning ground far upstream. Swimming constantly against the current, through rapids and over waterfalls, only the fittest fish can return to spawn and transmit their genes to the next generation.

Over two or three nights, twice a month, between March and September, the beaches of southern California are covered with thousands of spawning grunion. Riding in on the waves, they wriggle onto the beach to lay their eggs before swimming back out to sea.

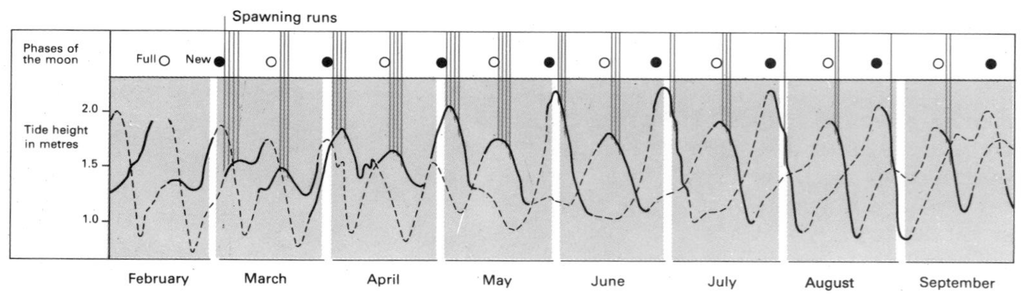

The Baja California, in common with most parts of the world, has two tidal cycles per day. If the two highest tides per day are plotted on a graph, the plotted positions can be joined together by two curves, one for each tide. The grunion's spawning runs, occurring immediately after the full and new moons, are timed to coincide with the highest tides during hours of darkness.

Mudskippers, *Periophthalmus sobrinus,* living on the tidal flats of Inhaca Island, Mozambique, know their way around their own territory so well that they can find the way back to their nests in the mud flats even when they are totally covered by water.

silver fish appear to be dancing on the beaches. The spawning "run" begins with a few lone fish, usually males, swimming on to the beach. The females arrive about twenty minutes later and spawning starts. About an hour after the first fish have appeared, thousands of fish may be on the beach at the same time. Each female, accompanied by up to eight males, swims with a breaking wave as far up onto the sand as possible. As the wave recedes, she digs herself into the sand and deposits between 1000 and 3000 eggs. The males curve round her discharging their milt near her onto the sand. Digging in and egg laying takes about thirty seconds, whereupon the spent female frees herself from the sand and is immediately washed back out to sea with the next wave to reach her. When the tide drops by about thirty centimetres (12 inches) the run suddenly stops. Females may spawn between four and eight times on consecutive nights during a season.

The eggs, deposited in about five centimetres (2 inches) of sand, soon become covered with more sand as the outgoing tide washes over them, until ultimately they lie at a depth of between twenty and forty centimetres (8 and 16 inches). Here they remain above the high-tide mark for about ten days until the next high tide washes them out of the sand. Two minutes or so later the eggs are freed and the young grunion hatch and are swept out to sea.

Countless other fish migrate with the tide. Their movements are however daily, usually made to feed, and take many forms. Some follow the tide up and down the shore so that they always stay the same distance away from the water's edge. Most, however, like the Red Sea blenny, *Alticus saliens,* and females of the European blenny, *Blennius pavo,* only follow the tide part way up and down the shore at certain times of the day. Other fish such as the woolly sculpin of California, *Clinocottus analis,* which remains in rock pools at low tide, follow the tide only to a certain point on the shore, where they wait until the sea overtakes them again.

Other species migrate inshore primarily to exploit rich food sources which are only accessible at high tide. Along the beaches of Long Island, New York, the mummichog, *Fundulus heteroclitus,* behaves this way. It moves up tidal creeks to feed on the flood tide and migrates back downstream again as it ebbs. Even where tidal movements are less marked some fish still swim inshore to feed, although normally only once a day. In Hawaii the blenny, *Entomacrodus marmoratus,* migrates upshore each night, and in the virtually tideless Mediterranean another blenny, *Blennius pavo,* also comes inshore nightly to feed.

Seasonal onshore-offshore migrations are usually related either to seasonal variations in temperature or to the timing of spawning, or to both. An analysis of the migration of the shanny, *Blennius pholis,* a yellow or greenish-coloured coastal fish living in Europe, shows a clear correlation with temperature.

Seasonal migration generally varies according to latitude. In Sweden, for example, the sandy-shore goby, *Pomatoschistus minutus,* migrates offshore in winter, whereas 1800 kilometres (1100 miles) further south at Penpoul in Brittany, it shows hardly any seasonal movement at all. The lumpfish, *Cyclopterus lumpus,* at the north of its range in Russia, remains inshore in summer and migrates offshore for winter. In the south of its range in Britain, however, the migration is reversed; the fish spends the summer in deeper water offshore and migrates inshore in winter to spawn, attaching its eggs near the low-water mark.

The fish's mental map

Although mudskippers, *Periophthalmus sobrinus,* are fish, they idiosyncratically spend much of the time out of the water foraging for food on mud flats. These fish, found along tidal channels in mangrove swamps, migrate with the tide like other coastal fish but above the tide rather than below it. At low tide they are to be found skipping around on their leg-like fins about thirty centimetres (12 inches) away from the water's edge. As the tide advances the mudskippers move up into the mangrove, often climbing into the branches to stay out of the water. Mudskippers spend the night in "nests" in the mud. Their knowledge of the mudflats is such that they can find their way back to them even when they are under water.

Some shore-fish learn the details of their territory with astonishing accuracy. For example, the frillfin goby, *Bathygobius soporator,* which lives in tidal pools along the coasts of the western Atlantic, familiarizes itself with its surroundings while swimming over its territory at high tide. The fish's spatial memory is so detailed that at low tide, when the rock pools are cut off from one another, it can jump accurately from pool to pool, hardly ever landing on the dry land in between, even though it is unable to see from one pool to another.

Deep water fish – herring

Herring occur in both the Pacific, as *Clupea pallasi*, and the Atlantic, as *C. harengus*. As adults, both species feed mainly on plankton and both produce planktonic larvae. The Pacific herring spawn only in spring, coming right inshore to lay their eggs on the seaweed lying between high and low tide, while the Atlantic herring spawn at any time of the year on shingle or gravel beds at depths of from 40 to 200 metres (130 to 650 feet).

The Atlantic herring can be divided into a number of spawning groups between which there is little interchange of individuals. Each group has its own particular migration circuit and its own particular spawning season. The migration behaviour of the Norwegian spring-spawning herring may be taken as representative of oceanic fish in general. They spawn between February and April along the coast of Norway. As spring advances they move northwest and west, entering the cyclonic system of the Norwegian Sea, probably via the western branches of the Atlantic current. This migration is presumably to keep pace with the shift in plankton production. Although they keep to the warm side of the transition area between the warm Atlantic and the cold Arctic waters during summer, they often cross it to take advantage of the larger amounts of plankton found in the more nutrient-rich upwelling waters of the Arctic. Some herring are found in the open sea within a year of hatching, but most remain within the coastal waters of the Norwegian fjords. For the next few years their migrations are restricted to seasonal inshore and offshore journeys; inshore for the summer and offshore for the winter. When they are fully grown the fish swim out into the Norwegian Sea, where they spend one or two years making exploratory migrations to find the best places to spawn and feed before reaching sexual maturity. It is during this exploratory phase that an interchange of fish between spawning groups is most likely. Recruitment to a new group may take place in any winter between the fourth and seventh year of a fish's life.

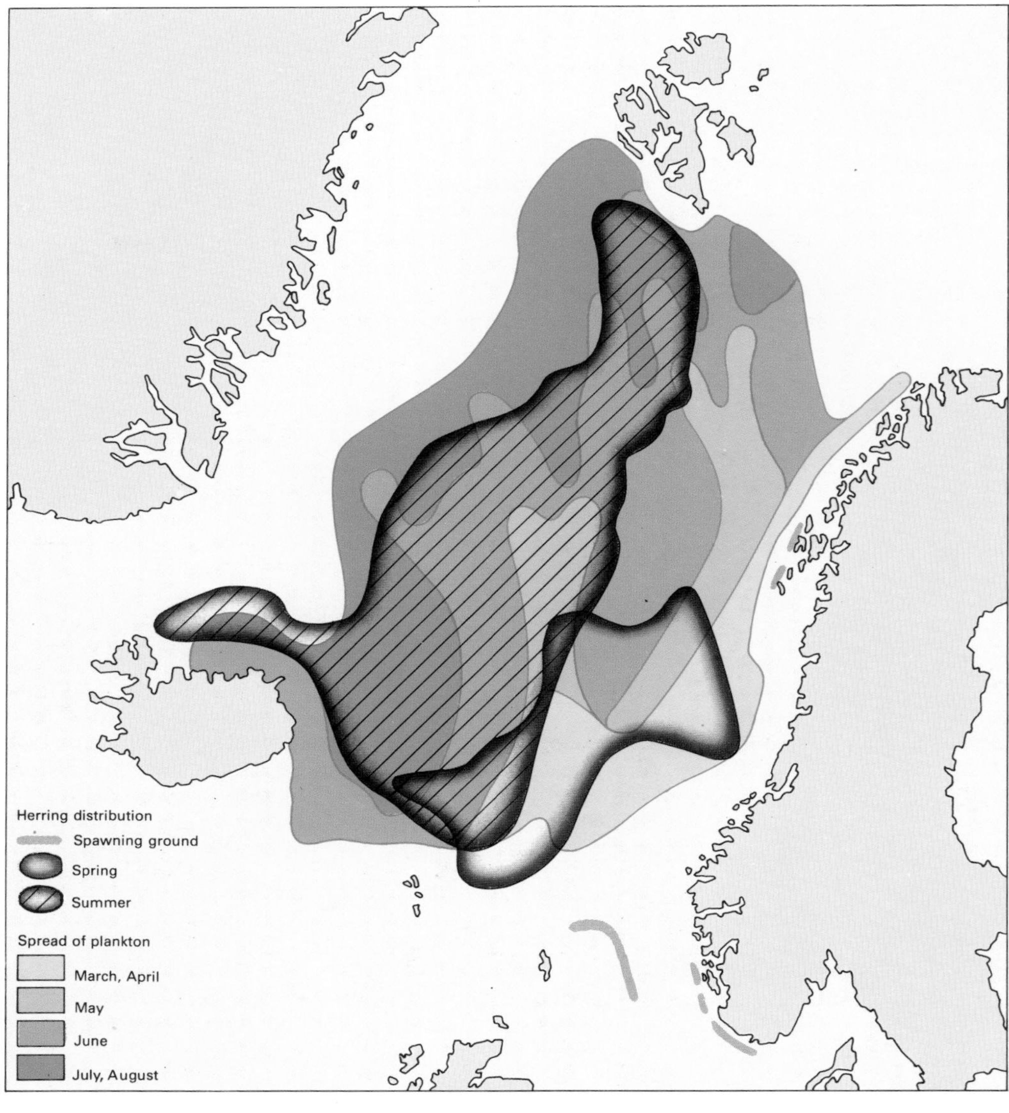

Plankton, those microscopic plants and animals living in the surface layers of the sea, form the very foundation of the marine food chain. They are the principal diet of the ocean's filter feeders, a group of animals that range from herring and sardines to baleen whales. As the amount of plankton in the ocean varies from place to place with the seasons, filter feeders are continually on the move. When spring returns to the North Atlantic, the zone of plankton production spreads gradually northwestward from the coast of Norway towards Greenland. The herring shoals fan out from their spawning grounds in the early spring to exploit these expanding feeding grounds.

Plankton feeders such as sardines, *Sardinia pilchardus*, live in shoals for the same reason that animals live in herds. Being one of a crowd reduces an individual's risk of being caught and eaten by a predator.

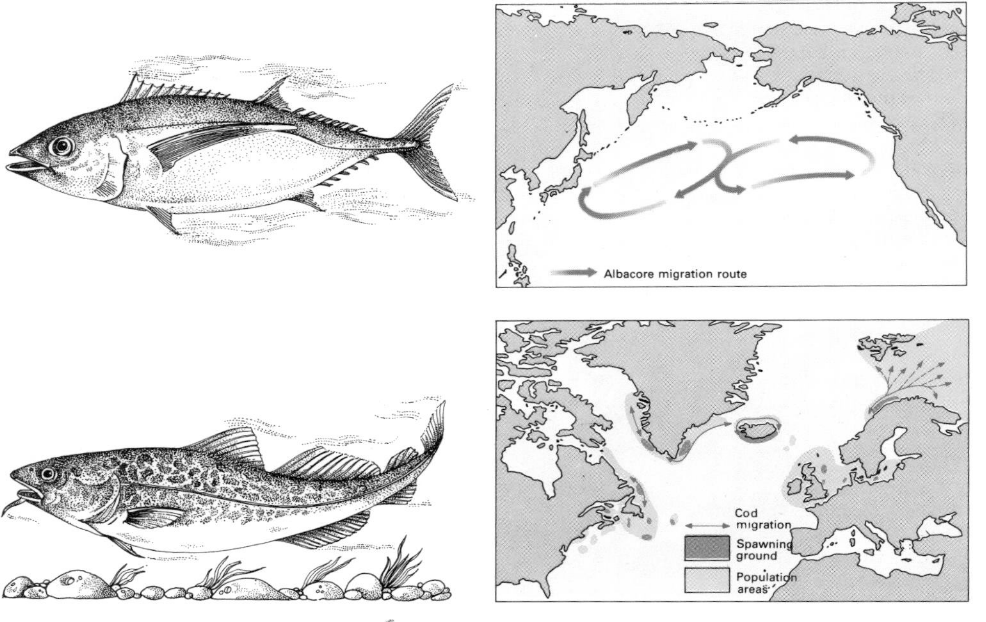

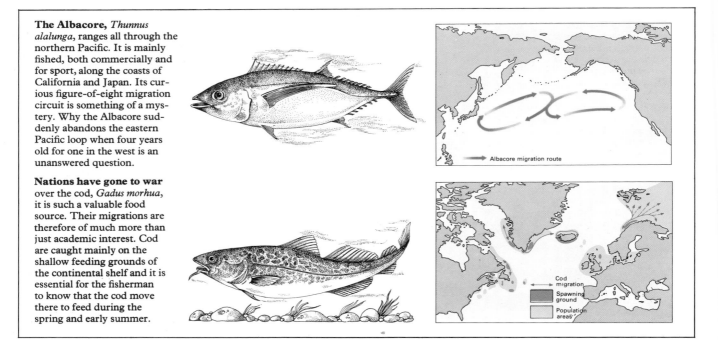

The Albacore, ***Thunnus alalunga*****, ranges all through the northern Pacific. It is mainly fished, both commercially and for sport, along the coasts of California and Japan. Its curious figure-of-eight migration circuit is something of a mystery. Why the Albacore suddenly abandons the eastern Pacific loop when four years old for one in the west is an unanswered question.**

Nations have gone to war over the cod, *Gadus morhua*, it is such a valuable food source. Their migrations are therefore of much more than just academic interest. Cod are caught mainly on the shallow feeding grounds of the continental shelf and it is essential for the fisherman to know that the cod move there to feed during the spring and early summer.

The life of the cod

Cod, *Gadus morhua*, are found throughout the North Atlantic in the shallow waters of the continental shelf. They are bottom dwellers living on or near the seabed at depths of between 200 and 300 metres (650 and 1000 feet). They feed on a wide variety of fish and crustaceans. Like herring, the world population of Atlantic cod are divided into a number of spawning groups, each with its own migration circuit. There is relatively little movement of individual fish between one group and another. Spawning groups exist in the waters round Newfoundland, the Faeroes, in the North Sea and in many other areas. The cod caught in the Barents Sea between February and September and along the Norwegian coast in the winter and early spring all appear to belong to a single group occupying one large annual migration circuit. Those spawning in the waters south of Iceland and feeding off southern Greenland are also believed to be members of a single migration circuit.

Atlantic cod generally spawn between February and June but occasionally spawn in the autumn. They prefer fairly cool water between 3°C (37°F) and 6°C (43°F). Unlike herring, which lay their eggs on the seabed, cod spawn within 100 metres (330 feet) of the surface. Over a period of several days each female spawns between 0.5 and 15 million eggs. The eggs float in the water until they hatch about fourteen days later. The young larval cod remain near the surface for the first three to six months of their lives, feeding on zooplankton, particularly on the small crustaceans known as copepods.

During this early free-swimming phase the tiny cod is to some extent at the mercy of the surface currents of the Atlantic Ocean. However, it would be a mistake to assume that the young fish has no sense of location or direction. When it eventually settles down on the sea bottom to feed, it can probably remember at least the direction in which it travelled and perhaps even some characteristics of the water it swam through. For when the time comes to reproduce, anything between five and fourteen years later, most cod are able to migrate back to the general area in which they themselves were spawned. For instance, cod feeding off southwest Greenland migrate back to Iceland to spawn, and cod feeding in the Barents Sea return to the Norwegian coast.

When the young fish first arrive on the seabed they make seasonal migrations between shallow waters in summer and deep waters in winter in the same way as coastal fish do. But one year before they spawn for the first time, the young cod join a shoal of adult fish and make a complete "trial" migration circuit. This trial circuit probably represents the final stages of learning about their surroundings and where the best places to feed and spawn are to be found.

Even though fish such as cod have a learned migration circuit and have apparently made decisions about which sites to use for feeding and breeding at an early age, their behaviour is still flexible. The same feeding and spawning grounds may be used by a particular group year after year for decades or longer. If for some reason a region becomes unsuitable, or if the fish find an even better area elsewhere, their migration circuit will change accordingly. Sometimes the entire group may change its annual circuit. On other occasions only a certain proportion, usually the younger members, adopt the new circuit.

The migration of the tuna

The bluefin tuna, or tunny, *Thunnus thynnus*, is an imposing fish with a dark blue back and silver flanks flecked with gold and opalescent spots on the fins. It may grow to a length of four metres (13 feet) and weigh up to 450 kilograms (1000 pounds), but on average a bluefin of fourteen years is about 2.5 metres (8 feet) in length,

Bluefin tuna have been caught for centuries in the Mediterranean using multi-chambered traps. The traps are set jutting out from headlands to catch the tuna as they migrate along the coast. When the fish are to be harvested they are driven through the trap into the final trap compartment, called the "death chamber". Small boats are brought alongside and the bottom netting is hauled up. The writhing tuna are gaffed onboard with vicious-looking hooked sticks. When the operation is under way the water turns blood red and "boils" with thrashing wounded and dying fish. In recent years catches have declined and the Mediterranean tuna industry, particularly in Sicily, is in some danger. At one time shoals of tuna 10,000 strong could be seen passing through the Strait of Gibraltar on their way to feed in the Atlantic off the coast of Norway. The tuna cover this distance in about a month.

longer than the height of a man. Its principal food is small schooling fish such as sardines, anchovies and young herring. It will also feed on larger fish, such as cod and on coastal species, such as eels. It spawns for the first time when three years old.

Although principally an Atlantic species, bluefins are found throughout the world. The main group in the western Atlantic spawns in the vicinity of Bermuda in April and May. During summer they migrate north and are found off the coast of Nova Scotia in late August and September. The main tuna sport-fishing events are held at this time of the year off the coasts of New England and southern Canada. The size of tuna shoals has declined sharply in recent years because of commercial exploitation on both sides of the Atlantic and the fish could very well become an endangered species if radical measures are not taken to control catch sizes. In the eastern Atlantic bluefins spawn around the Strait of Gibraltar. There are other groups in the Mediterranean, the Black Sea and in various parts of the Pacific.

The migration pattern of tunny like that of cod in the North Atlantic has recently altered. The northern limit of the group of bluefins spawning in the Mediterranean now extends as far as Norway. After spawning, in the western Mediterranean, part of this group occupies a migration circuit entirely within the Mediterranean. Between November and February, the Atlantic fish swim southward again, swimming deeper and deeper into the water. With the arrival of spring they return to the surface and, as the spawning season approaches, enter the Mediterranean once more.

A close relation of the tunny, the albacore, *Thunnus alalunga*, is undoubtedly one of the handsomest and most sought-after fish in the sea. Their dark blue backs merge into greenish blue at the tail and their undersides are creamy white. The fish has a metallic lustre, almost bronzed in appearance. They are in constant demand

The bluefin tuna, *Thunnus thynnus*, is the heavyweight of the tuna family and can swim at over eighty kilometres an hour (50 mph).

because of their very pale flesh and are often called "the chicken of the sea".

The albacore spawns in the tropical waters of both the Atlantic and Pacific Oceans. It seems that the whole of the North Pacific is populated by a single spawning group occupying one enormous migration circuit. The circuit changes, however, as the fish age. During the first three years of their life the albacore explore the eastern half of the North Pacific. In late winter they are concentrated in the central North Pacific around the Hawaiian Islands. In spring they migrate eastward and by the summer are found off the California coast. In autumn, they turn north and west, eventually arriving back in Hawaiian waters in early winter. When four years old, the young albacore no longer turn east from the Hawaiian Islands in spring but migrate to the west and southwest and spend their next three years exploring the western half of the North Pacific. With the advent of maturity at about six years of age the albacore migrate southward in spring to breed in tropical waters.

In the North Atlantic both adults and young migrate northward in February after spawning and arrive in British waters in May and in Icelandic waters in September. The fish keep pace with the northward movement of a water temperature of about 14°C (56°F). In the autumn, albacore migrate south again, gradually taking to deeper and deeper water like the bluefins, until, by winter, they reach depths of between 250 and 350 metres (820 and 1150 feet) in tropical waters.

River fish that spawn in the sea

Some sea-spawning fish spend part of their lives in fresh water. It is not possible to say exactly which species behave this way, for a great variety of marine fish throughout the world are found in rivers from time to time. Sharks, gobies and pipefish have all been recorded in the lower reaches of the Zambezi. Sting rays have been found far upstream in the rivers of Nigeria and South America. Menhaden and anchovies have been reported entering fresh water in Virginia. However, in some sea-spawning species a freshwater phase is an essential part of their life cycle. These species, termed catadromous, spend their larval and juvenile stages in the sea and their adult life feeding in fresh water.

It seems strange that catadromous fish find it favourable to spend the egg and larval stages in the sea, whereas anadromous fish – those ascending rivers to spawn – find it more favourable to spend these stages in fresh water. It is possible that the movement of both fish types between fresh and sea water to spawn was evolved to protect the larval stages from traditional predatory para-

The life cycle of the European and North American eel was a complete mystery until the beginning of the century. The adults were common enough in fresh water but no trace of their eggs or young could ever be found. Probably because they sometimes winter buried at the bottom of streams and ponds they were popularly thought to generate spontaneously from mud. However, thanks to the work of the Danish oceanographer, Johannes Schmidt, we now think that both eels spawn in the Sargasso Sea near the West Indies and that the larval stage is spent in the waters of the North Atlantic. The larvae had been discovered earlier, but were classified as a separate species, *Leptocephali brevirostris.*

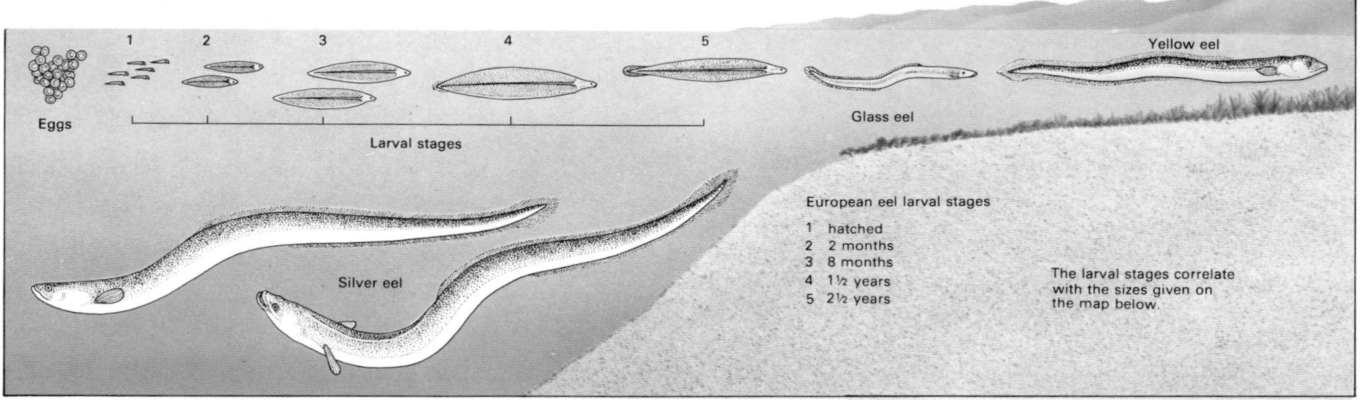

The larvae of the North American and European eel metamorphose just before they arrive in the rivers, which explains why none has ever been found in fresh water. After quite some time at sea – about one year for North American eels and three years for European eels – the larvae reach coastal waters, and change into transparent elvers, often known as glass eels. After their first summer, feeding in fresh water, the elvers become pigmented; their backs become dark and their undersides greenish yellow. At this stage they are known as yellow eels. When they are about six or seven years old the eels develop into mature silver eels, ready for the long journey back to spawn in the Sargasso Sea. The head becomes more streamlined and the eyes grow to twice their previous size.

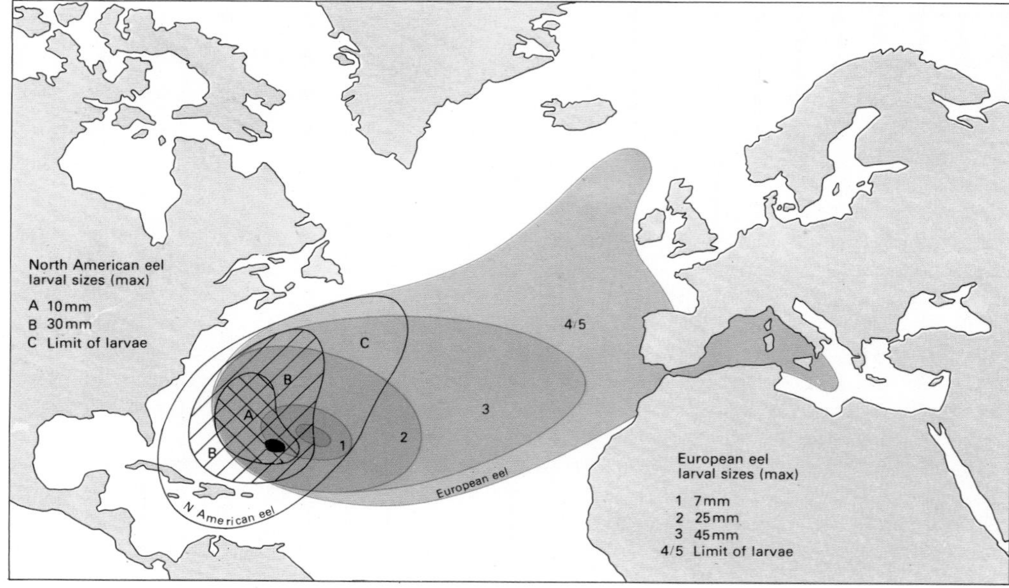

sites. If this was the only reason one would expect that anadromous and catadromous fish would be found equally all over the world. However, this is not so. Anadromous fish are found mainly in temperate and sub-polar waters whereas catadromous species are largely tropical. The implication is that water temperature or some factor closely related to it is the important element. Perhaps there is some advantage for adult fish living in the tropics to feed in fresh water and for adult fish in colder waters to feed in the sea.

The best known catadromous fish are the eels of the genus *Anguilla*. The genus consists of sixteen species, all of which are catadromous. They are all found where rivers enter the sea near deep water. Although eels spawn only at a depth of between 400 and 750 metres (1300 and 2500 feet), they prefer warm saline water overlying the deeper parts of the ocean. The eggs are released into the water, where they drift with the current and develop into leaf-like, leptocephali (small-headed) larvae. When they reach the coast the larvae metamorphose into glass eels, or elvers, and swim into the rivers.

The eels remain feeding in the rivers for several years. When they are sexually mature they migrate back, most probably to their natal site, to spawn once and die. Nothing is known for certain about the adults' return migration, for no *Anguilla* spp. has ever been caught in waters beyond the continental shelf. It is most likely that they swim back at some considerable depth. Mature eels have certain characteristics associated with deep-sea fish. Their eyes are large and some have a retinal pigmentation that helps them see in the dark.

Eels of Europe and North America – a puzzle

In the Atlantic, the northern spawning area of the Sargasso Sea has been a centre of controversy for decades. Two populations of eels spawn here; one found in North American rivers and the other found in European rivers. The argument is whether these two populations are the same species or two separate species. Most zoologists now believe that there are two species; the American eel, *A. rostrata*, spawning in the southern Sargasso Sea in early spring and summer, and the European eel, *A. anguilla*, spawning at the same time but slightly further north.

The American eel grows more rapidly than the European eel and is carried by the surface currents to the west Atlantic coasts anywhere from the Guianas in the south to southwest Greenland in the north. It arrives in coastal waters in either the first or second year of life. The European eel, growing more slowly, is carried by the Gulf Stream to the Atlantic coasts of Europe and into the Mediterranean and the Black Sea, arriving during the third or fourth year of its life. Metamorphosis to the elver stage and upstream migration therefore occurs much earlier in American eels.

The timing of the transformation seems to be dependent on certain characteristics of the water. Those larvae of the European eel which enter the Mediterranean have further to travel to reach fresh water than those entering west European rivers and change into elvers at a much later date.

Apart from differences in growth rate there are also differences in bone structure. Adult American eels have between 103 and 111 vertebrae, whereas adult European eels have on average seven or eight fewer. If the European eel and the American eel are two separate species, these differences must be genetic. If, however, they are different populations of the same species, then they must be due to environmental factors.

An experiment conducted with European eels under different temperature conditions showed that those experimentally grown in warmer water had fewer vertebrae than the others. This seems to support the idea that the differences are environmental. It has also been suggested that the distance between Europe and the Sargasso Sea that the adult European eel has to swim, against the current, to spawn is too great for it to make the journey successfully, and therefore only the American eel returns to breed in the Sargasso Sea, providing the eggs and larvae for both populations.

As eels do not spawn in fresh water, their occurrence in landlocked pools and ponds with no outlet to the sea would seem at first sight to be an impossibility. However, being almost snakelike, eels have no difficulty in wriggling short distances over wet grass from nearby rivers. The eel is also better equipped to survive out of the water than most other fish. It has a comparatively thick skin and narrow gill openings which prevent it from drying out quickly. In countries where eel fishing is economically important, eel passes are built round man-made obstacles such as dams and weirs that block the eel's progress upstream. Because eels can travel through vegetation out of the water, these passes need to be no more than a bundle of reeds and twigs placed up against the obstruction.

If this were true it would mean that the proportion of American eels spawning in the part of the Sargasso Sea that gives rise to the European population would be producing offspring that would not reproduce themselves. From what we know of evolution this seems unlikely. One would expect natural selection to suppress individuals with a genetic make-up causing them to breed in conditions that prohibit the reproduction of their offspring.

Fish tracking

Scientists have found it extremely difficult to discover what happens to eels once they leave the rivers and begin their journey back to the spawning grounds. One technique that has been tried in the last few years is radio tracking. Eels are caught as they enter the sea, and are fitted with tiny transmitters. Usually the transmitter is inserted under the skin of the fish, but sometimes it is attached to the dorsal fin or the fish may be induced to swallow the transmitter disguised in some food. The eel is released into the sea and followed by a research boat equipped with a radio receiver.

Recent investigations have shown that those entering the sea from German, Scandinavian and British rivers swim in a northwesterly direction at depths no greater than some sixty metres (200 feet) while over the continental shelf. But as soon as they pass over the edge and find deep water beneath them, they dive to 400 metres (1300 feet) or more and turn to swim west-southwest in the direction of the Sargasso Sea.

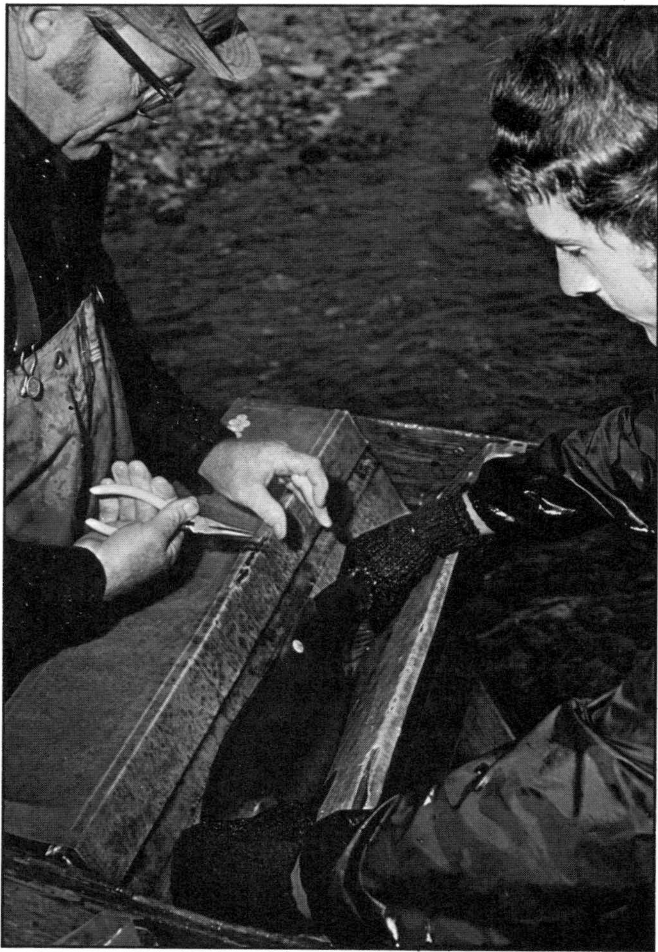

Tagging with numbered plastic discs is one of the many ways that fish can be individually identified. The recapture of marked individuals provides the basic data needed to build up a picture of a fish's movements.

Radio tracking is a highly versatile technique and can provide information about many different aspects of a fish's life. It is possible to track several fish at once by attaching transmitters that emit signals of different frequencies. Some transmitters emit signals that vary according to temperature and other conditions, giving information about the characteristics of the water through which the fish is swimming. If fed to the fish or inserted inside it, it can provide details about the way the fish's body responds to the rigours of migration. The study of fish by radio is still in its infancy but, over the next decade or so, the technique will undoubtedly reveal many insights into their behaviour.

In the past, fish migration was studied mainly by tagging, using clips or discs attached, in most cases, to the dorsal fin. Short-term studies still make use of fin clipping – cutting recognizable notches in the fish's fins. Even when these notches heal they leave a scar which can still be identified. There is always some uncertainty with this technique, however, for it is just possible that the fish could have received a similar injury accidentally. Fin clipping has been used particularly successfully in homing experiments with salmon. The fish, captured as they swim up a tributary river to spawn, are tagged and released in another. Since the salmon can be identified when recaptured it is possible to tell how long it takes them to swim back to the original tributary.

Fin clipping has also been used in longer-term experiments. Salmon fry clipped before they entered the sea in one experiment could still be identified when they returned to fresh water several years later.

Navigational landmarks

The sense of smell is probably the most important faculty a fish uses to learn about its surroundings. Experiments with salmon have shown that they learn the smell or taste of the water through which they swim. These olfactory "landmarks" are extremely important features in the fish's mental map of its familiar area, and it has been found that salmon with plugged nasal tubes cannot find their way back to their spawning sites.

Many fish have good eyesight and seem to rely on it to find their way about. Experiments in which they were prevented from seeing have shown that they must use visual landmarks, to some extent, in recognizing their home site.

Fish are somewhat unusual in having a sense that can detect pressure waves. This sense, the lateral line system, consists of a row of organs down both sides of the body which can detect the tiny waves reflected by objects in the water. The information received can probably be formed into a memorized map of landmarks in much the same way that information received from the senses of sight and smell is amassed.

At any one time of the year the pattern of ocean currents is much more predictable than the pattern of air currents found in the atmosphere. The ocean current system can be used as a reliable frame of reference in which a fish can determine its position, and the direction of particular currents probably forms an important part of the familiar area map built up by oceanic fish. As long as a fish can see the sky or the sea bottom it is able to detect the direction in which a current is flowing. Some, if not all, can also tell the current direction even without reference to a fixed point.

One of the most recent discoveries, although it was suggested as a possibility many years ago, is that cartilaginous fish, sharks, skates and rays, can determine direction from the earth's magnetic field. As the fish or the water, or perhaps both, moves through the magnetic field, small electromotive forces are set up around the fish which it can detect with an electric sense. This sense rests in certain highly specialized organs, the Ampullae of Lorenzini, which appear as small pits in the fish's snout.

In laboratory experiments it has been found that sharks and skates trained to rest in, say, the nothern part of a tank can be made to rest in the eastern part by using huge electric coils to rotate the magnetic field in the tank by ninety degrees.

THE FISH'S EXTRA SENSE

A fish can tell the position of an object that it is unable to see. To accomplish this, fish have evolved an organ that is sensitive to the small changes in pressure produced by water currents. This organ, the lateral line system, runs along both sides of the fish, from head to tail, and consists of a fluid-filled tube exposed through the fish's skin to the water outside. Changes in pressure are transmitted through the fluid to a small organ, the neuromast, lying at the base of each pore. The information is relayed through a nerve running behind the lateral line to the fish's brain. The fish is able to interpret the signals in terms of solid objects.

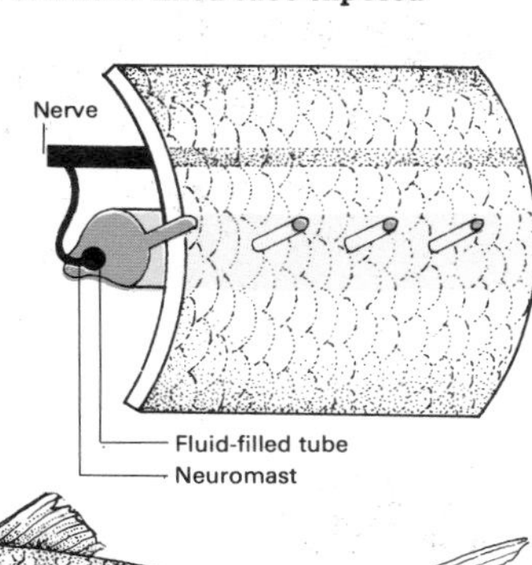

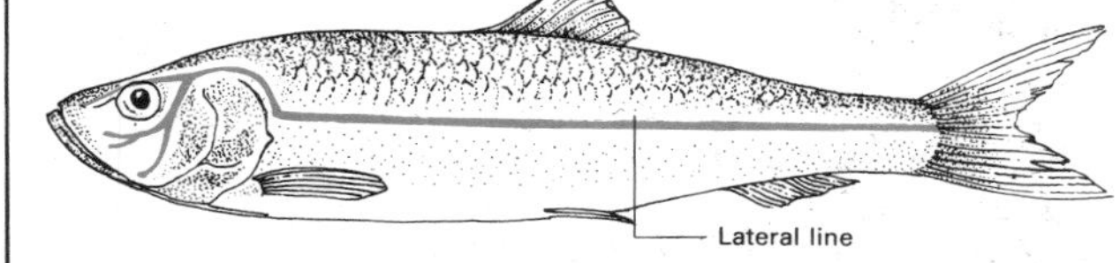

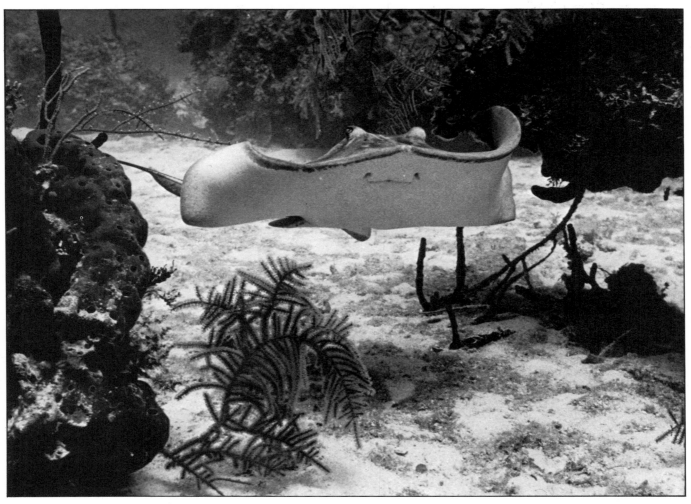

Sharks, skates and rays appear to have their own inbuilt direction finders. Many of these cartilaginous fish can detect the earth's magnetic field. The evolutionary more recent bony fish may also have this ability, but detailed experiments have not yet been carried out.

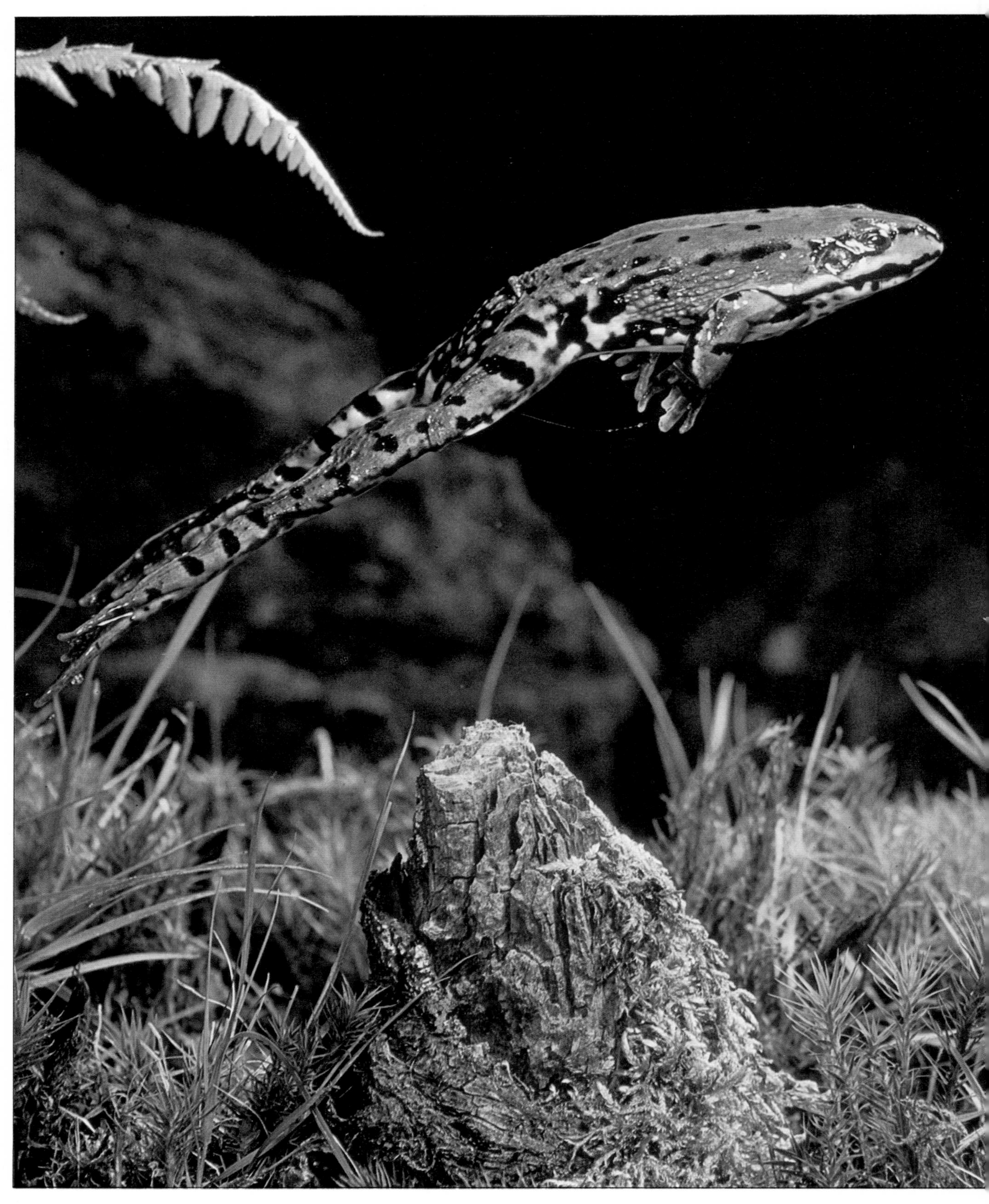

Amphibians and Reptiles

Lying between fish and mammals in the evolutionary scale, amphibians and reptiles might be expected to have lifetime tracks falling midway between them. In the case of amphibians it could be said that this in fact was true. The amphibian's larval or tadpole stage is spent in fresh water like a fish and the adult phase on land like a mammal. Water is, however, much more important to an amphibian than it is to a land mammal. As an amphibian's skin is permeable and involved in breathing it must be kept moist. Adults therefore never travel very far away from water. The latter part of an amphibian's life is punctuated by a series of return migrations to breed, often in the same place where it was hatched itself.

Some reptiles such as alligators, caimans and marine turtles are also highly dependent on water. They are highly adapted to an aquatic environment and spend nearly all their life in water, only emerging on land to breed. Others, such as snakes, lizards and land turtles, have, except for drinking, lost all contact with water and can in many cases tolerate quite arid conditions.

The migrations of most amphibians and reptiles consist of seasonal movements between feeding, breeding and in some cases hibernation sites. The distances travelled, however, are relatively short and in most cases the places an animal visits in the course of a year are no more than a few kilometres apart. However, two groups of reptiles do make huge migration circuits covering thousands of kilometres – the marine turtles and sea snakes. They are the only reptiles in existence to have colonized the sea. The journeys of sea snakes are not well documented and are based, for the most part, on isolated observations. Marine turtles have been studied in more depth and, although the precise migration circuits have not been identified, their feeding and breeding sites are well known.

The edible frog, *Rana esculenta*, spends most of its life in water. But if its pond dries up it is compelled to venture across land to find another. It hibernates during winter in mud or at the water's edge.

The ancestors of modern frogs, toads, newts and salamanders were the first vertebrate animals to clamber out of the sea on to land. The first ones appeared about 350 million years ago and were little more than fish with rudimentary lungs and leg-like fins. The fish ancestors of these primitive amphibians developed lungs in the first place so that they could breathe in air and therefore survive in stagnant pools of water lacking in oxygen. Legs gradually evolved enabling the animals to compete more effectively for food. If a pool of water became overcrowded or dried up, those fish that could crawl away on their fins to a less crowded neighbouring one would then have a greater chance of survival. In this way the basic equipment of all land vertebrates, legs and lungs, evolved.

When these creatures emerged from their pools they found a land teeming with small invertebrates such as worms and insects – a perfect food supply for any hungry predator able to get about on legs and to solve the problem of desiccation.

Life cycle of frogs, toads and newts

In common with many other animals, the amphibian's early development mirrors its evolutionary history. The eggs that amphibians lay in water are very similar in appearance to fish spawn. They go through a larval stage in the shape of tadpoles in much the same way as fish do before reaching maturity.

Apart from a little-known worm-like order, present-day amphibians are divided into two groups: those with tails – newts and salamanders – and those without – frogs and toads. The main differences between the two groups, besides appearance, are their behaviour when mating and the way in which the eggs are fertilized. Newts and salamanders are more solitary during the breeding season. A male finds and courts a female and deposits a sperm packet on a rock or piece of weed. The female picks it up and places it in the opening of her reproductive tract, thus fertilizing her eggs internally. The eggs are usually laid singly on submerged plants or stones.

Frogs and toads are much more gregarious. The males congregate in the breeding ponds at the beginning of the season and fill the night air with the sound of croaking. Each species has its own characteristic sound. The most bizarre are made by those in the tropics, beside which the sound made by temperate species seems colourless. Some belch, others whinny or groan, some even wail or mew like cats. Croaking is an important part of mating as it advertises the males' readiness to mate and guides the females to the breeding site.

It has been found that the females of the common toad, *Bufo bufo*, in Europe and Asia, prefer males with deeper voices, and with good reason. They tend to be larger and more able to protect the female before fertilization from the otherwise continuous attentions of the males. They are also more efficient mates. As they are larger and therefore capable of shedding more sperm, they can fertilize more eggs than the smaller males. When a female arrives at the pond she is seized by a male, who attempts to cling to her back until mating is over. However, competition is fierce and in the struggle to reproduce he may well be dislodged by another. Both spawn and sperm are released into the water together and, as in fish, fertilization takes place externally. In this respect frogs and toads are closer to their fish ancestors than are newts and salamanders. The young tadpoles

The life history of amphibians follows a general pattern. When the eggs are laid they swell in contact with the water, giving the embryo added protection. After a few days the eggs become elongated and it is possible to make out the shape of the tadpole inside. In frogs and toads the back legs develop first, followed in a few weeks by the front ones. At the same time the creature acquires rudimentary lungs, in preparation for its adult life on land. Tailless amphibians – frogs and toads – all have the same general appearance, but tailed amphibians vary considerably, as shown below.

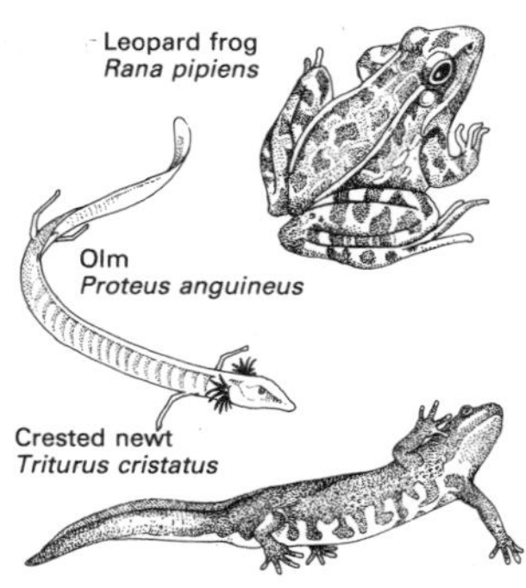

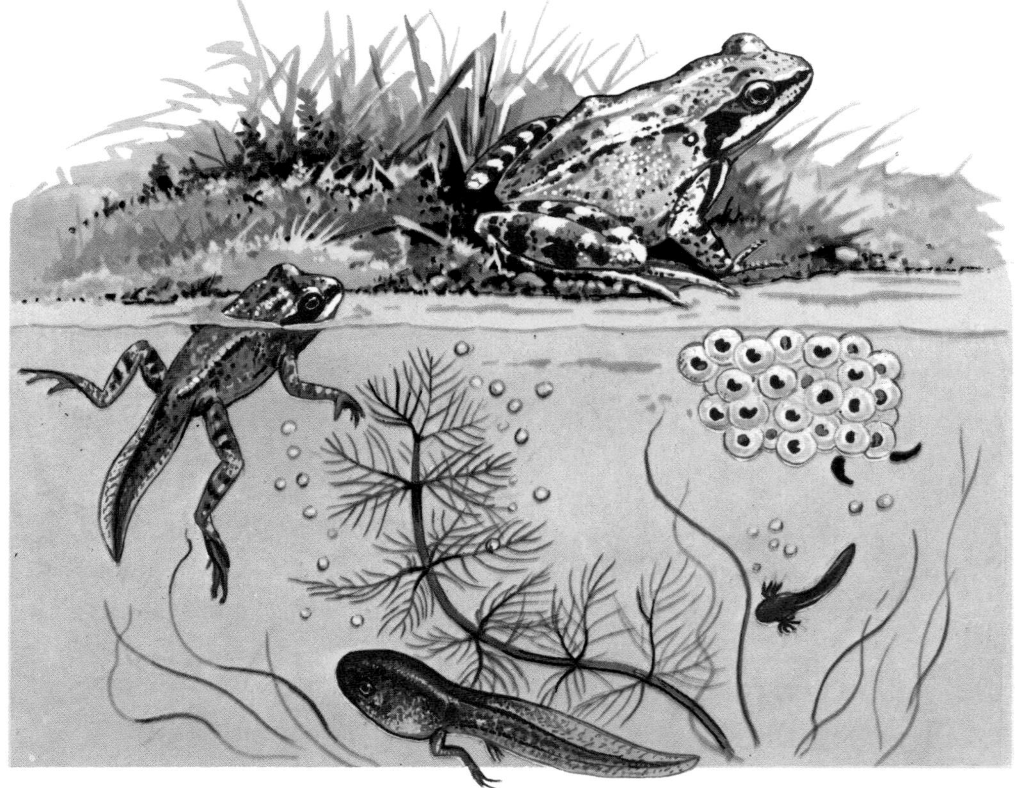

bear little resemblance to their parents; they are legless and have long tails. Instead of lungs they have external gills, looking like fringes, around their neck.

Although frogs and toads are dependent on water for breeding and while they are at the tadpole stage, some have adapted to survive in the driest conditions. In the western deserts of Australia there are species that can lie dormant for years at a time, buried in the soft mud beneath the beds of dried-up pools and streams. When eventually rain falls they suddenly reappear, and in a burst of frenzied activity cram into a brief wet period all that is necessary for life before the drought returns. They mate, lay eggs and fatten up on the insects and other animals that feed on the vegetation that springs up around them. The eggs must hatch and the tadpoles must metamorphose into frogs or toads, ready to dig themselves into the drying mud, before it is baked hard again.

Life cycle of reptiles

About 250 million years ago at least one group of amphibians began to reproduce without water altogether and gave rise to the animals we now know as reptiles. The adaptation that permitted this was an egg with a watertight skin that could be laid on land without drying out. This, and a watertight skin for the animals themselves, is the principal feature that distinguishes the reptiles from the amphibians.

As in newts and salamanders, the eggs of all reptiles are fertilized internally. This is absolutely vital, as once the egg's hard shell is formed it is as impervious to sperm as it is to water. The reptile egg can be thought of as a private pool protected from predators and from drying up by the shell.

Freed from a dependence on water, reptiles are able to colonize areas, and, what is more important, remain active in conditions that no amphibian could tolerate for long. They can stand long periods in strong sunlight and in fact most reptiles prefer warm, sunny places. At night and during cloudy weather they become torpid.

Biologists classify present-day reptiles into four orders. The largest includes the snakes and lizards which accounts for about ninety-five per cent of all existing species. The turtles and tortoises make up the next largest order, then come the crocodiles, caimans and alligators. One species alone, the tuatara, *Sphenodon punctatus*, a lizard-like creature found in New Zealand, has an order all to itself.

During the reptiles' golden age, between 225 and 65 million years ago, they were much more numerous and diverse than now and dominated the earth. The highly successful dinosaurs belong to this period.

Many reptiles such as crocodiles, turtles, terrapins and sea-snakes have an aquatic phase, but, in complete contrast to amphibians, which breed in water and feed on land, these reptiles feed in water and breed on land. Water is therefore just as important to them as it is to the amphibians and the juxtaposition of land and water plays a dominant role in forming the lifetime tracks of both groups of animals.

The lifetime track of amphibians

An amphibian, whether frog, toad, newt or salamander, has a lifetime track that can be divided into three parts. The first part consists of the movements it makes as a tadpole in the pool or stream where it was spawned. The second part covers its early life as an immature adult,

The vast majority of reptiles lay eggs, but there are some snakes and lizards that give birth to live young. In all cases the eggs are laid on dry land. The young are miniatures of their parents and do not go through a larval stage. Their diversity is indicated below.

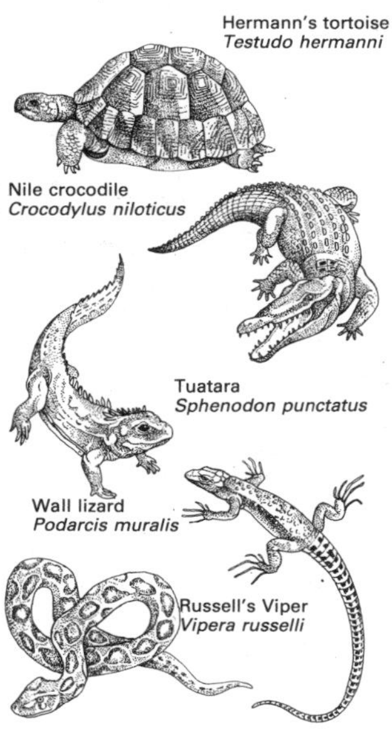

and the third part deals with its movements as a fully mature adult. The first phase has been largely ignored by researchers. The evidence that exists shows that the movement of tadpoles conforms to a definite pattern and is based on a considerable store of information about their watery environment.

Perhaps the most important thing that the tadpole learns is the direction in which it must swim to get from deep water to shallow water in the shortest space of time. Its only defence against predatory fish is to swim as quickly as possible into the shallows, where it cannot be followed. When the tadpole is larger, wading birds become the major hazard. As these birds feed near the shore the tadpole's escape strategy must take an about turn. The tadpole now seeks refuge in deep water. The escape route is still the same, only now in the opposite direction. It is thought that the tadpole learns its direction from the sun's position in the sky and can even tell it at different times of day – a feat which it accomplishes astonishingly quickly, apparently within a day of hatching from the egg.

The second phase of its lifetime track begins when the tadpole changes into an adult and emerges on to land to begin its life as a fully developed frog or newt. Although again this phase has been little investigated, it is certain that the amphibian spends much of the time exploring its new surroundings. It is important for the amphibian to find as soon as possible a succession of sites where it can find food at different times of the year. Depending on the climate it also needs to find places where it can hibernate or lie dormant during the winter or dry season. It is also probable that while still immature it discovers which sites the mature adults use to breed and is able to decide which site will offer it the greatest chance of breeding success when sexually mature.

By the time it is ready to breed, two or three years later, the amphibian will have found out enough about its surroundings to have established a stable pattern of migration between the places it has selected for each of its activities. Very often the site selected for breeding will be the stretch of water where it spent its early days as a tadpole. There is a certain advantage in returning to the native pond or stream as its suitability for breeding is borne out by the individual's own survival. This characteristic is shared with many other animals, notably fish such as the salmon. However, amphibians are not compelled to breed where they were spawned and many amphibians breed for the first time in a completely new site, a fact that anyone who builds a sizeable pond in their garden will discover; in a few years it is likely to have acquired its own breeding population of frogs or newts.

Migration between land and water

The third phase of the amphibian's lifetime track consists of a series of seasonal migrations between the feeding and breeding sites that the amphibian has chosen during its exploratory phase and it is this part that has been studied most intensively. Although the pattern is broadly similar for nearly all amphibians the details do vary considerably from species to species.

The behaviour of Fowler's toad, *Bufo fowleri*, is fairly typical of most frogs and toads. In pools bordering the southern shores of Lake Michigan breeding takes place in the spring. The males arrive first and set up croaking choruses along the shore. The females arrive a few days later. After breeding, each female immediately leaves the pools for her summer feeding site. The males on the other hand remain until all the females have arrived and have mated before moving off to feed. The distance between the breeding pools and a particular toad's feeding ground may be anything from a few metres to one and a half kilometres (1 mile), but most are unwilling to move far from water and feed within 200 metres (220 yards) of the lake shore. Even though the toads take shelter from the sun during the hottest part of the day by digging into the earth, they would soon become desiccated and die if they did not travel to the lake's edge every five days or so to sit in the water and absorb moisture. Amphibians can only take in water by absorbing it through their skin. They cannot drink like terrestrial animals.

When cooler weather arrives in the autumn the toads migrate to their hibernation sites. They remain there until the following spring, when they again migrate back to the pools round Lake Michigan. In common with most amphibians these migrations take place mainly on wet nights.

The croakings of male frogs and toads are highly specific and are made by inflating the vocal sac and passing air across resonating organs located in the throat or at the corners of the mouth.

The red-bellied newt, *Taricha rivularis*, generally returns to spawn in the same stretch of river in which it bred the previous season. An individual may return as often as six times to the same site.

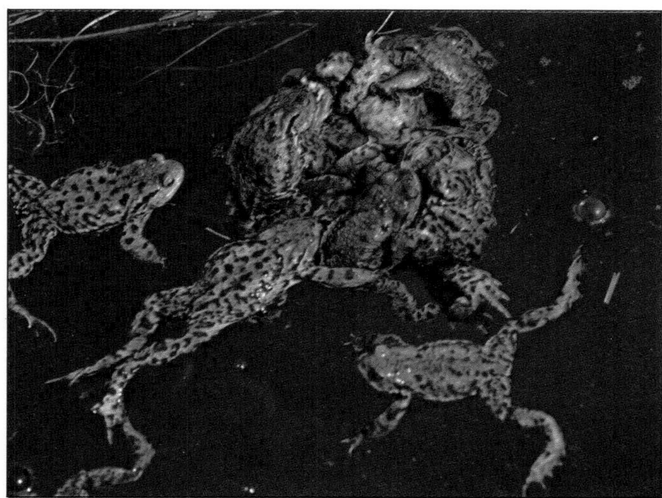

Male frogs and toads make virtually no courtship display apart from croaking. In breeding they are often indiscriminate and some may even attempt to mate with a female of a different species. As the males arrive earlier at the breeding pond, the first females are overwhelmed by the competition to mate and each female becomes a centre of frenzied activity.

Shallow, muddy ponds with plenty of vegetation to provide anchorage for the spawn make ideal breeding sites for frogs and toads. At the height of the season a single pond may contain millions of eggs, threatening a population explosion. But predation, mainly by fish, reduces the number that hatch out successfully to a tiny proportion.

Caimans differ from alligators principally in that their undersides are protected by a layer of horny plates. The spectacled caiman, *Caiman crocodilus*, gets its name from the ridge of bone between its eyes that looks like the bridge of a pair of spectacles. Caimans are entirely confined to the New World and are found in tropical and sub-tropical waters.

The painted turtle, *Chrysemys picta,* is an aquatic turtle or terrapin found in North America to the south of 51°N. They are among the most common turtle inhabitants of the United States. Barely more than fifteen centimetres (6 in) long, the dark greenish brown plates of its shell are edged with red and its underside is yellow. Although the adults feed on vegetation the young turtles are largely carnivorous.

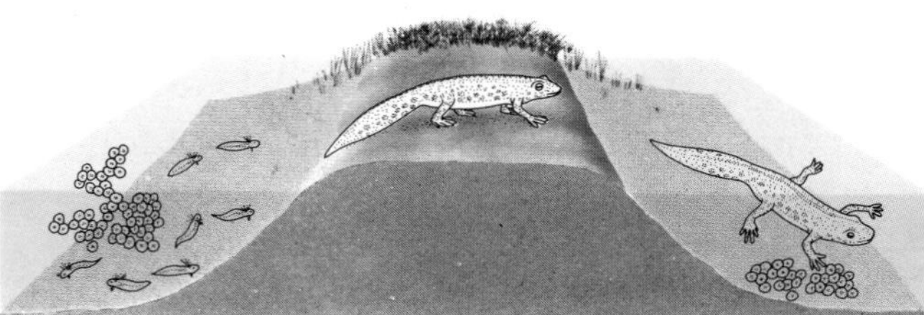

The lifetime track of an amphibian consists of an aquatic larval stage followed by a terrestrial phase as an adult. The adult phase is interrupted seasonally by return migrations to breed in water.

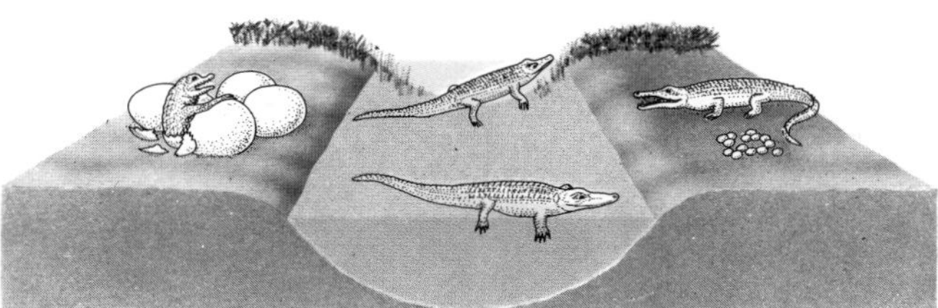

The lifetime track of aquatic reptiles also alternates between land and water, but in this case the aquatic phase occurs in adulthood. Like all other reptiles they must return to breed on land.

Many newts and salamanders spend their adult lives migrating between feeding, breeding and wintering sites in the same way as frogs and toads. The red-bellied newt, *Taricha rivularis*, breeds in the streams of the redwood belt of northwest California during the spring. In summer it migrates to its feeding ground, higher up on the heavily forested mountain slopes, where like Fowler's toad it spends the drier months buried underground. The newts emerge to forage on the vegetation of the forest floor only when the rains arrive in the autumn.

In the spring the red-bellied newt returns to the streams to spawn. It normally chooses a site in the same fifty-metre stretch of water in which it spawned the previous year. Very few newts have been recorded spawning at different sites in different years. This behaviour is common to all amphibians and is not just confined to newts. It appears that once an amphibian has chosen its breeding site, from those investigated when immature, it has virtually chosen it for life. Once fully adult it becomes fixed in its ways and will not change its habits without good cause.

When frogs and toads are removed from their breeding chorus to one nearby they almost always return to their original pond to breed. However, if they are taken some distance, perhaps several kilometres away from their own familiar area, they are compelled to adopt the new site to breed. Experiments with the red-bellied newt, where individuals were displaced four kilometres (2.5 miles) from their original site, showed that although they bred in the new site on the following two years, the impulse to return to their original site was so strong that certain individuals were found breeding back there in the third and subsequent years.

Amphibians can recognize ponds and parts of streams they have visited before and can remember how to get there, sometimes after a lapse of several years. In common with man and other vertebrates, including fish, amphibians seem to have some sort of spatial memory in which they form a mental map of their familiar area. Relatively little evidence exists for reptiles, but what there is suggests that they also build up a mental picture of their surroundings during their exploratory phase.

Reptiles – the crocodile family

The movements of the spectacled caiman, *Caiman crocodilus*, have been studied in the freshwater lagoons of Venezuela, and a pattern of exploration and return migrations has emerged similar to that of the amphibians. Caimans are members of the crocodile family, closely related to the alligators, and are found all over tropical South and Central America. Although they are popularly thought to be the smaller members of the family, some grow to more than four metres (13 feet) long and are just as ferocious as their larger relations.

The spectacled caiman – which does look as if it were wearing glasses – is small by comparison as it only grows to about 130 centimetres (50 inches). For the first eighteen months of their lives the caimans of a clutch of eggs stay together in a "pod" defended by their parents and other adults. Only when a caiman is about two years old does it set about exploring its neighbourhood and fending for itself. As the young caiman travels round looking for suitable feeding and breeding sites it inevitably meets others that have staked out their own territories, which they defend with vigour. Fierce fights are commonplace. The intruder usually comes off worst, and injuries, particularly to the tail, are frequent.

During their exploratory phase caimans are known to travel distances of at least one and a half kilometres (1 mile) over land between lagoons. Adults sometimes travel much further. Some captured in one lagoon and released in another two and a half kilometres (1.5 miles) away were found back in their home lagoon ten days later. In the dry season adults keep to the permanent stretches of water, but when the rains arrive they migrate to temporary lagoons a kilometre or so distant. They are unlikely to make such a journey speculatively and it appears that caimans know from their experience as juveniles which lagoons fill at this time.

What we know about the migration patterns of the crocodile family is largely confined to the spectacled caiman. The few scattered observations that have been made of alligators and crocodiles suggest that they behave in a similar way. In particular these giants take advantage of temporary pools during the wet season to catch unsuspecting prey.

Tortoises and terrapins

The life cycles and migrations of tortoises and terrapins are broadly similar. The painted turtle, *Chrysemys picta*, which is really a terrapin, lives in the oxbow lakes of the Elkhorn River in Nebraska and hibernates during winter in permanent pools. In spring it migrates two kilometres (1.3 miles) or so to outlying areas which have filled with water during the winter. In the early spring these pools provide a fresh and plentiful supply of the water plants on which the adults chiefly feed. When they dry out in summer the turtles migrate back to their winter quarters.

The American desert tortoise, *Gopherus agassizii*, also hibernates in cold weather. It returns each winter, year after year, to the same communal dens dug in the earth. These dens take quite a lot of effort to construct and the turtles work in relays, one taking over when another becomes exhausted. Distances travelled are not very great. The summer feeding grounds are usually no more than a few hundred metres away from the hibernation dens. The tortoises feed mainly at night, sheltering from the sun by day.

The largest of all tortoises, the giant Galapagos tortoise, *Geochelone elephantopus*, makes much longer migrations. As it lives in the tropics it has no need of hibernation dens, but uses separate sites for feeding and breeding. It grazes on the plants found in the cooler wooded highlands of the island's interior and migrates back to the coast to lay eggs where they can be buried easily in warm sand or soil.

Lizards are not great travellers and the side-blotched lizard, *Uta stansburiana*, is no exception. The adult's home range is no more than eighty metres (260 ft) from the place it was hatched.

The rock python, *Python bivittatus*, found in the Sunda Islands in Southeast Asia, begins exploring its surroundings almost from the moment of birth. For the first few weeks of life it returns each evening to sleep in the broken shell of the egg from which it hatched.

As there are virtually no rivers in the Galapagos, water holes provide the giant tortoise with their only supply of fresh water and therefore figure prominently in their migrations. The tortoise has such a detailed mental map of its own familiar area that it can remember from one drought to the next which holes always have water.

Snakes and lizards

Some snakes are enthusiastic communal hibernators. In winter large numbers have been found huddled together in crevices and holes in the ground. Precise numbers are difficult to come by, but one scientist, who specializes in the subject, described a collection of 153 prairie rattlesnakes as just a few. It is known that adult snakes return to the same sites year after year to winter, but until recently the distances they travelled were unknown. It was speculated that species such as the canebrake rattlesnake, *Crotalus horridus*, travelled more than thirty kilometres (19 miles), but it was not generally believed until a garter snake, *Thamnophis* sp., only eighteen centimetres (7 inches) long, was captured sixteen kilometres (10 miles) away from its hibernation site. It is a pity that so little is known about the movements of young snakes or we might have some clues that would tell us how they collect the enormous amount of information which allows them to find their small hibernation holes from such a great distance.

Lizards do not travel great distances at all but spend their entire adult lives within one territory containing feeding, breeding and hibernation sites. It is true that young lizards travel more extensively, but even their journeys are comparatively short.

Direction finding

We know that amphibians and reptiles build up a mental picture of their familiar area during their youthful explorations, but we are still not sure of what this picture is composed. Experiments in which amphibians and reptiles have been prevented from seeing or smelling show that they use both these senses.

It is evident from the behaviour of female frogs in the breeding season that sound must play an important part in a frog's picture of its surroundings. In an experiment, chorus frogs, *Pseudacris triseriata*, were taken out of their familiar area and kept in a cage near to an unfamiliar breeding chorus which they could hear but could not see or smell. They were then taken several kilometres further away and released. It was found that the frogs made off in a direction that would have led them back to the breeding chorus if they had been released at the site where they had been caged. It seems that the frogs learned the direction of the breeding chorus from the cage and as they had no landmarks to help them navigate from the release site, they relied instead on their remembered sense of direction.

It is still not entirely clear how frogs and toads detect compass direction. Present investigations have shown that frogs and toads can orientate by the night sky and that frogs, toads, salamanders and some terrapins can orientate by the sun in the same way as birds. It has been found that amphibians do not even have to see the sun, but can detect it through the tops of their heads.

They have a primitive eye-like organ in the pineal part of the brain, lying directly below a translucent part of the skull. In the Middle Ages it was thought that this organ was the "philosopher's stone", a substance that could change base metals into silver or gold.

Salamanders share with some fish and birds the uncanny knack of being able to tell compass direction from the earth's magnetic field. We do not even know which organ they use to detect this let alone how it works.

Marine turtles

All the migrations described so far are made over relatively short distances. There is no suggestion that, as for fish, these amphibians and reptiles are able to home in from a long way off. However, one group of reptiles, the marine turtles, does make migrations comparable with those of both birds and fish.

There are five marine genera of turtle and all of them make immense journeys of thousands of kilometres through the oceans. Sea-snakes also travel great distances, but their movements have not been investigated. At present only detailed information is available for one species, the green turtle, *Chelonia mydas*. Their lives can be divided into two phases. Phase one, from birth to maturity, and phase two, adulthood. We know nothing about the first phase. As soon as the turtle hatches it makes straight for the sea and effectively disappears. No turtle has ever been captured at sea during the first year of its life. The first phase lasts for about ten years and is prob-

In the riverless Galapagos Islands, water holes are of prime importance to the native giant tortoise, *Geochelone elephantopus*. Their ability to store large quantities of water and to remember which water holes never dry up enables them to survive drought conditions. Their survival was seriously threatened in the nineteenth century. Slow moving and weighing as much as 180 kilograms (400 lb), they were highly attractive to foraging parties from passing ships.

The moment of hatching is the most dangerous time in the life of a turtle. Its shell is still soft and it is easy prey for any carnivore.

Green turtle hatchlings, *Chelonia mydas,* in common with those of other marine turtles, are able to head straight for the sea immediately after birth, even though the water may be hidden from view by some obstacle such as a sand dune. Experiments have shown that this ability is instinctive and has something to do with the nature of light. The hatchlings are able to distinguish the appearance of light shining over water from its appearance over land and orientate themselves accordingly. Experiments in which hatchlings were taken from nesting sites in the Caribbean and released on the Pacific coast show that no compass sense is involved. The hatchlings had no difficulty in making straight for the sea even though it now lay in the opposite direction.

Green turtles are found throughout oceans of the world in a broad band straddling the tropics. They cannot tolerate the cold and the

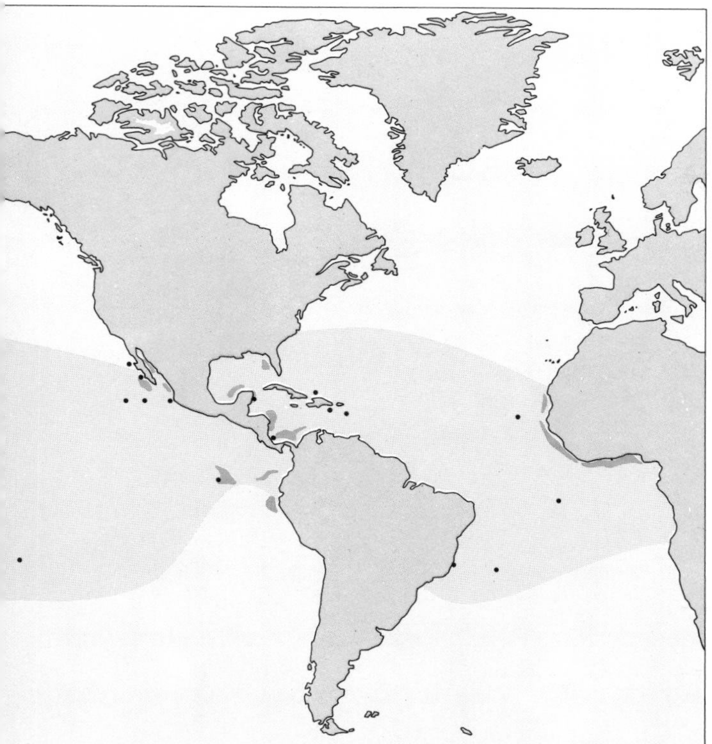

females dig their nests only on beaches that are adjacent to water which has an average temperature of at least 20°C (68°F) at all times of the year.

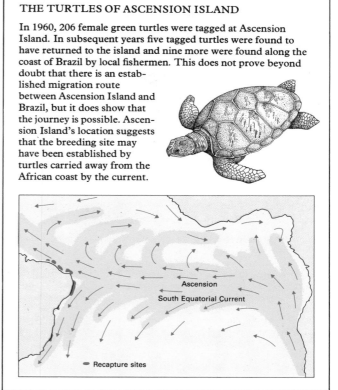

THE TURTLES OF ASCENSION ISLAND

In 1960, 206 female green turtles were tagged at Ascension Island. In subsequent years five tagged turtles were found to have returned to the island and nine more were found along the coast of Brazil by local fishermen. This does not prove beyond doubt that there is an established migration route between Ascension Island and Brazil, but it does show that the journey is possible. Ascension Island's location suggests that the breeding site may have been established by turtles carried away from the African coast by the current.

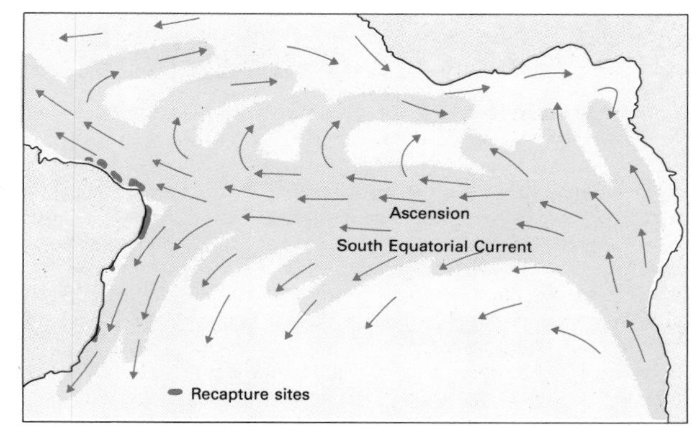

ably spent in exploration in the same way as land turtles. It appears that young turtles are always on the move and never stay in any one place for long.

We know a little more about phase two, the adult period of the turtle's life. When the turtle is about ten years old, and weighs about sixty kilograms (130 pounds), it looks for a suitable place to breed. This may be the beach where it hatched out itself, but we do not know for sure. Once a site has been established the female turtles tend to return to it every two or three years to lay eggs. As copulation occurs under water just offshore, there is no need for the males to come on to the beach at all, and it is not possible to say whether the males always breed at the same sites like the females.

Once egg laying is over, the females swim back out to sea, migrating with the surface current to their feeding ground. We know little about the turtle's migration routes or means of navigation, but each separate nesting population seems to have its own circuit.

Recently the green turtles nesting on Ascension Island in the Atlantic have been studied and the evidence uncovered seems to indicate that turtles are capable of navigating with the utmost accuracy. There are no feeding grounds around Ascension and all turtles must migrate across the Atlantic to feed. The most probable feeding site is on the coast of Brazil, 2200 kilometres (1350 miles) to the west. The South Equatorial Current flows westward past the island straight towards the coast of Brazil and so far nine females tagged at Ascension have been recovered.

The mystery is, assuming that these turtles return to Ascension to breed two or so years later, how do they find their way back to the island again. It is only eight kilometres (5 miles) across, a mere pinprick in the Atlantic. If the turtles migrated with the current as it continues down along the coast of America they would eventually be swept round with the West Wind Drift and up the coast of Africa into the South Equatorial Current again. But this route is not possible, for even assuming they were lucky enough to find Ascension again, these currents would take them through water much colder than they can tolerate. Green turtles are found only in water warmer than 20°C (68°F). The most likely explanation is that they swim back to Ascension in the equatorial counter-current that flows just beneath the surface in the opposite direction to the current that carried them away from Ascension in the first place. It may be difficult to believe that they would actually swim all that way back when there are perfectly good nesting sites much nearer in the Caribbean, but the turtles may not be aware of that. Even if they were, they might still prefer to return to Ascension because their own survival has proved its suitability for breeding.

Ascension has the added advantage that the turtles know what they are looking for. Sea water, like river water, has its own olfactory signature or "taste", which the turtles may be able to recognize. Those turtles hatched on Ascension island would be able to recognize the signature of the water in that vicinity as it drifts down with the surface current towards Brazil. Even though the turtles swim back to Ascension in the deeper counter current, they must periodically come up through the surface current to breathe and would thus be able to home in on the signature.

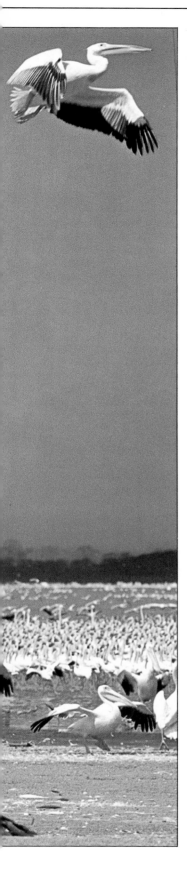

Birds

To most people, bird migration brings to mind the first swallows of summer, the interpolar odyssey of the arctic tern and pin-point feats of navigation. But species such as the swallow are generally thought quite different from the resident house sparrow that is present throughout the seasons in our gardens and parks or of the feral pigeon of the city centres that can be breeding any month of the year. Only when we examine the lifetime tracks of a wide range of bird species do we realize that migrants and residents are just two extremes of a continuous range of variation.

In some species an individual may behave like a sparrow one year but like a swallow the next, travelling to distant wintering grounds and returning the following spring. Among those species that do show seasonal migration, the winter home may be less than 100 kilometres (60 miles) or, as with the arctic tern, more than 20,000 kilometres (12,400 miles) from the breeding site. To journey between these two points, some species will cross the equator, others will not.

Not all birds migrate on a simple north–south axis. Some use different routes on their spring and autumn journeys. Others complete a large circular or figure-of-eight migration circuit. A third group, which includes species as different as the black-browed albatross of the Pacific and the budgerigar of the Australian desert, may wander over vast distances, tracing out a path with no clear pattern. Even within this group variation exists. Whereas the albatross every two years returns to the same island to breed, the budgerigar settles down to breed when and where it is able in the unpredictable desert environment. Finally, the wandering albatross migrates forever eastward, travelling the westerly winds of the southern ocean, and circumnavigates the earth many times during its lifetime. The variety is endless.

Although the navigation of birds is one mystery of migration that has not yet been completely solved, we do now know that, in addition to sight, birds use smells and the earth's magnetic field to find their way around. We also know that they can take their bearings from the stars and moon as well as from the sun, and can recognize their home after absences of up to as much as eight years.

White pelicans, *Pelecanus onocrotalus*, and lesser flamingos, *Phoeniconaias minor*, migrate in vast numbers to Lake Nakuru in Kenya to feed on the lake's rich food sources.

The patterns of bird movement

To date, about 8600 species of birds have been identified and named, but for a number of reasons it is very difficult to estimate what proportion of them are seasonal migrants. What can be said is that most species breeding in high latitudes are migratory, in temperate latitudes between a third and a half of the various breeding species may migrate, and even some of the species breeding in the tropics may make seasonal movements.

Although weather may be the proximate or immediate factor responsible for initiating seasonal migration, the ultimate or underlying reason is to ensure a continuing supply of suitable food in what would otherwise be a lean season. Conventionally, birds are regarded as belonging in the area where they breed, even though it may be their home for as little as three months in the year, and instead of regarding migration as an escape from unsuitable weather, it is possible to interpret it as a movement to an area well stocked with the food needed to raise a family.

The essence of seasonal migration, therefore, is that it is a return trip between two localities that provides the bird with suitable conditions for survival at different times of the year. This trip should be regular as to season and direction. This is the classical image of migration.

Starlings and blackbirds, *Sturnus vulgaris* and *Turdus merula*, are sedentary in the milder regions of their range. During winter they feed on any scraps of food they can find, such as these discarded fruits.

It is typified by many species of birds, among them the barn swallow, *Hirundo rustica*, which is widespread throughout the Northern Hemisphere. This is so familiar a bird that even city dwellers know it to be a species of their summer skies only, which during the northern winter is somewhere far to the south. One may describe the swallow's migration as classical or archetypal because its summer and winter homes are quite discrete, and separated by thousands of kilometres.

Members of the swallow family feed exclusively on the mass of small flying insects, which may be thought of as aerial plankton, and even the most inobservant among us will be aware that the gnats and mosquitoes which may mar our summer evenings are largely or totally absent in mid-winter. For such species it is a case of migrate or perish, but what of the many bird species whose diet comprises items like fruit, earthworms or the insects which are to be found throughout the year on the surface of the soil, the trunks of trees and in similar places? For them, too, if they migrate, it is a response to variation in food supply, but among them the position is not necessarily as clear-cut as in the case of the swallows. The swallows of temperate and northern latitudes are total migrants, the entire population leaving for the winter. In many bird species from temperate latitudes we find different patterns of movement.

Migration imposes extra physical strain and extra risk on birds. There is the possibility of being swept out to sea or falling victim to some unfamiliar enemy. Conversely, if a bird stays put it runs the risk of cold weather reducing to a critical level the food supplies on which its life depends. Thus whether or not a species migrates or is relatively sedentary depends basically on which policy offers it the best chance of survival. From this it follows that a species need not necessarily behave in the same way throughout the whole of its range. The starling, *Sturnus vulgaris*, in Europe, is an excellent example of this. In Britain and Ireland the winters are relatively mild and there the starling is almost entirely sedentary. As one moves eastward across Europe the winters get increasingly severe, with mean January temperatures of 4°C (39°F) in London, −0·5°C (31°F) in Berlin, −3°C (26°F) in Warsaw and −10°C (14°F) in Moscow. Thus the starlings of eastern Europe are total migrants, for they could not feed themselves throughout the snowbound winter months, while those in the westernmost continental countries are partial migrants. They have a less rigid migration behaviour pattern.

With partial migration some individuals from a population migrate while others stay put, or attempt to do so. Whereas for the total migrant and the sedentary species the profit and loss account of migration is clearly established, in partial migrants the balance of risks between staying put and migrating is so delicately adjusted that nature is, as it were, still undecided. Given a succession of severe winters, the advantage would start to lie increasingly with that proportion of the population which migrated, for more of them would survive to reproduce, while a succession of mild winters would tip the scales in favour of those that stayed put. With this kind of mechanism in mind seasonal migration has been defined as a shift in the centre of gravity of a bird population, for it may be that there is a considerable overlap between the areas occupied by the most northerly individuals in winter and the most southerly ones in summer.

There are two other important patterns of movement, both of which, although they may be strictly seasonal, are not strictly directional. They are dispersal/convergence and nomadism. Even the most oceanic of seabirds must come ashore to breed and their comings are regular as to season. The "shift in the centre of gravity" concept is equally applicable, but whereas the better-known migrant usually travels between two reasonably definable homes, seabirds may move in several different directions to disperse over an immense area of sea. Nomadism, too, may be seasonal, the choice of direction of movement being determined by the immediate availability of food. Such is thought to be the case with two of the Old World thrush species, the fieldfare, *Turdus pilaris*, and the redwing, *Turdus iliacus*. However, in its extreme form, met with in desert fringes of the world, nomadism is associated with the search for areas where rain has fallen. Since the rainfall is unpredictable, the timing, distance and direction of nomadic bird movement are also unpredictable.

Our growing knowledge of bird migration

It is an odd fact that although migration is the activity of live birds, the foundations of our knowledge of migration were laid down in the natural history museums of the world. In the days before the ready availability of binoculars, ornithologists worked with a gun, filling drawer after drawer with the skins of their trophies. They collected their specimens in the countryside around their homes and, on expeditions, from the savannahs and forests to the south. Then, by spreading out their collections and matching skin with skin, they were able to show, for example, that the swallows they had shot in Kenya or in Cape Province were identical with those which breed in France, The Netherlands, Germany and England. The European swallow, they were able to declare, spends the winter in the southern half of Africa. To know where a species is going was an important start.

Nowhere is one more likely to become aware of the existence of bird migration than on an island, and the smaller the isle the more apparent the basic facts of migration. One day the island may seem almost devoid of life, yet on the next every tree and bush, every sheltered gully, almost every plant, may seem to have its quota of hungry birds. A day or two later, given suitable weather, the birds will have moved on and, if others have not arrived to take a welcome rest on the stepping stone to their destination, the island will once more seem deserted.

If one lives on a tiny island, day by day one can count the numbers of grounded birds, species by species, and so record the ebb and flow of the passage. One may only guess at the birds' origins and their eventual destinations, yet it is from such counts that we have derived much basic knowledge about their migration. Obviously, these records tell us about the timing of migration, and about routes – in so far as they exist – but the numbers of grounded birds may also offer a clue to the size of migrating flocks, some species regularly occurring in large numbers, others more characteristically only a few at a time.

Birds of arid regions, such as the budgerigar, *Melapsittacus undulatus*, which inhabits the scrubland of central Australia, are invariably nomadic. They often aggregate in large numbers to drink at water holes that suddenly appear following rains.

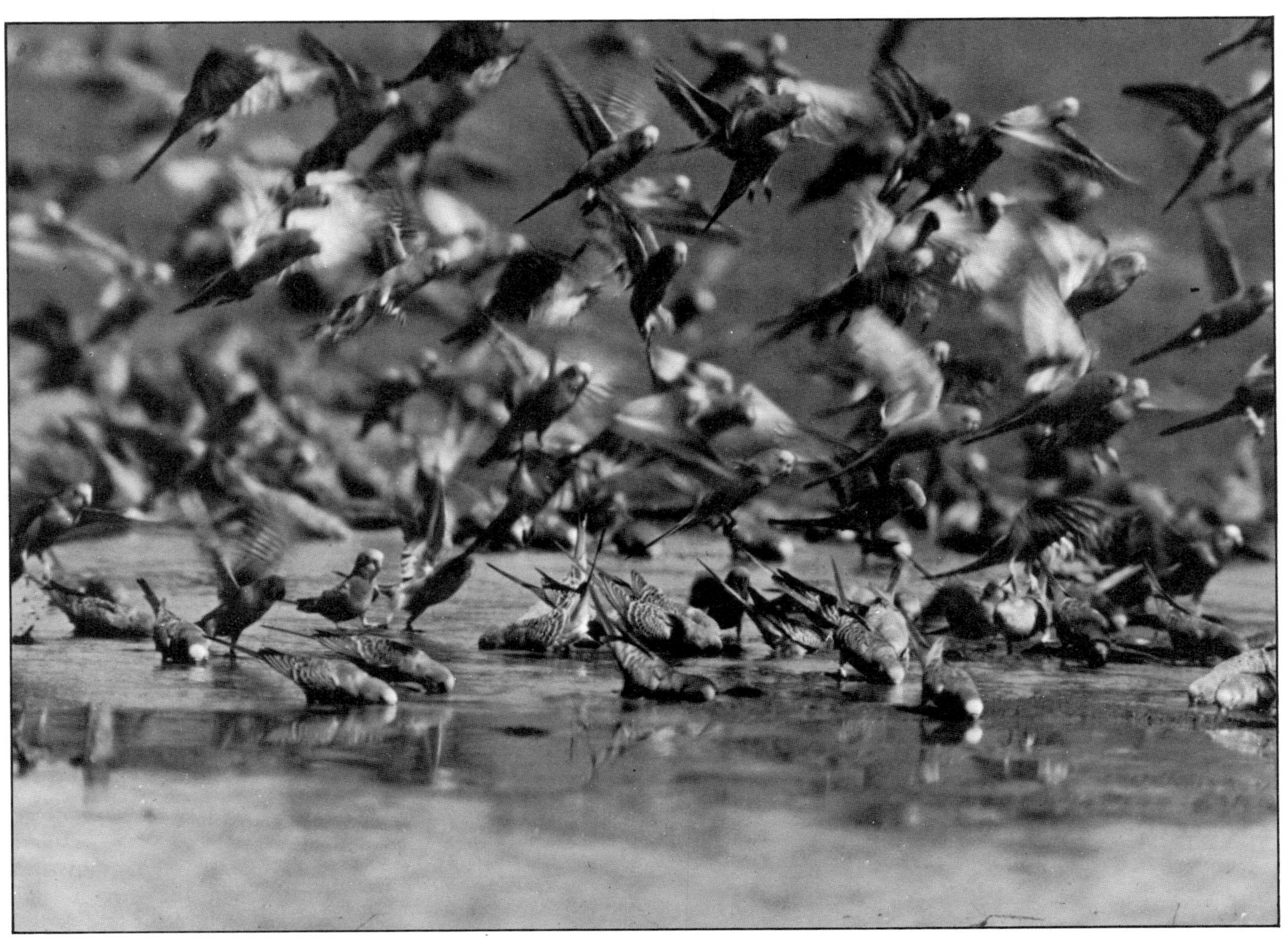

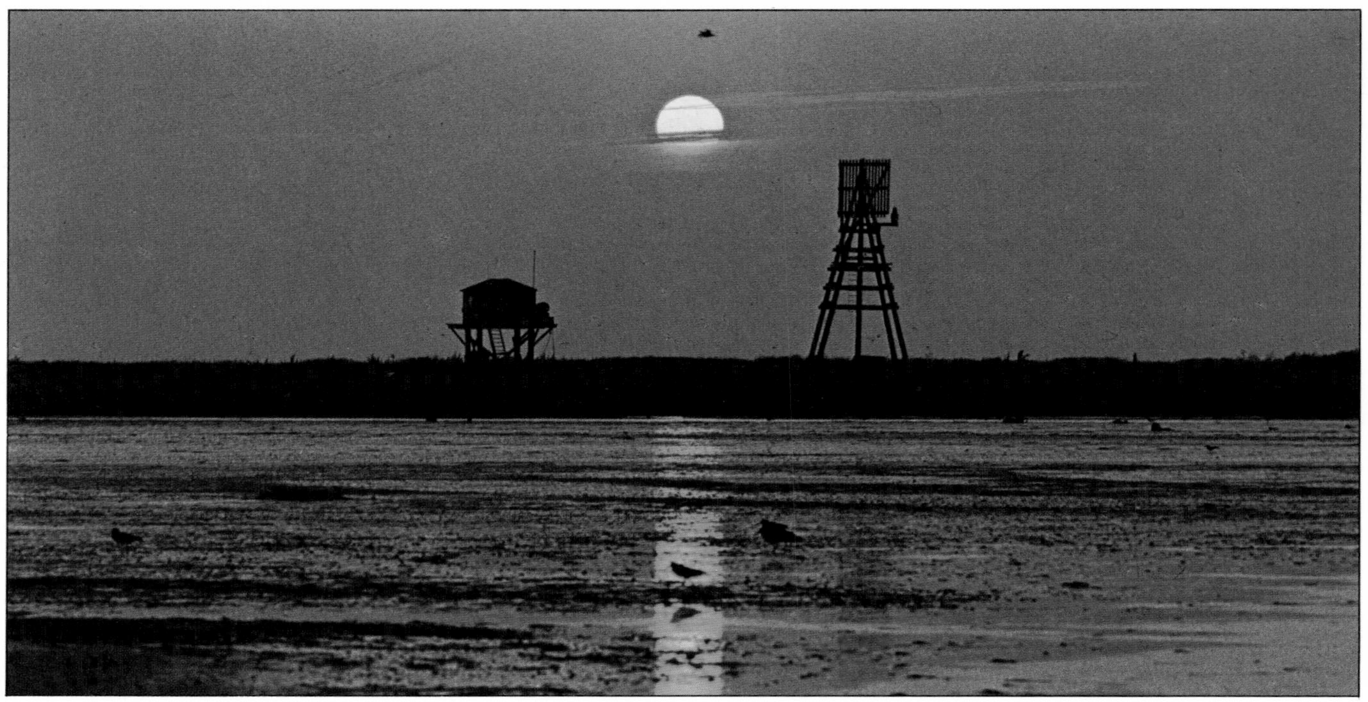

Bird observatories are often sited on the coast, particularly at points where there is a narrow sea crossing, for here birds tend to migrate in a concentrated and narrow flight path. From this observation tower at Griend in the Netherlands land birds that migrate over the North Sea towards the British Isles are monitored.

ALLURED BY THE BEACON'S BLAZE

This engraving of an early twentieth-century painting shows a swarm of birds flying round the lantern of the Eddystone Lighthouse in southwest England on the night of 12 October, 1901. Attracted to the light in bad weather, many of the birds struck the lantern time and time again, eventually beating themselves to death. Fortunately, such occurrences occur only in heavy storms and lighthouses have, and continue to be, important observation points for studying bird migration.

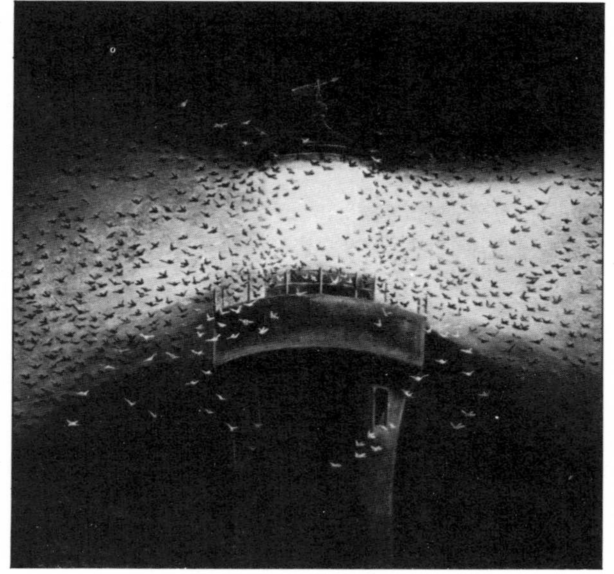

It was a German ornithologist, Heinrich Gätke, who, more than any other person, recognized the potential of small islands as bases to study migration. On the island of Heligoland, in the North Sea, he spent many years observing and recording the arrival and departure of birds. The island became, and remains, a place of pilgrimage for migration workers. Not surprisingly, researchers elsewhere sought to take up and develop his ideas, one of the most interesting and ambitious programmes being that organized by the British Association for the Advancement of Science. Throughout the decade 1881–90 they collected migration information from the keepers of the scores of lighthouses around the coasts of Britain and Ireland, organizing the data season by season and coast by coast to form a remarkably comprehensive picture.

To this day, the counting of grounded migrants is used as a basic technique for studying migration, and bird observatories are to be found in a number of countries, although they remain a particularly European phenomenon, with only few in the New World. It is, however, doubtful whether they would have persisted and multiplied in this way if they had remained primarily dedicated to the daily count, for as Gätke's work was coming to an end a new and powerful research tool was becoming available – bird ringing, or banding.

Just as new cars rolling off a production line look identical until given a registration plate, so birds of the same species cannot be distinguished one from another. But place around their leg a tiny metal ring on which is inscribed a unique serial number, and they become, to the person fitting the rings, individuals which can be recognized on future occasions. Carry the process a stage further by adding a return address, and anyone finding the bird can co-operate by reporting its locality. In short, bird ringing fixes two points in a bird's life:

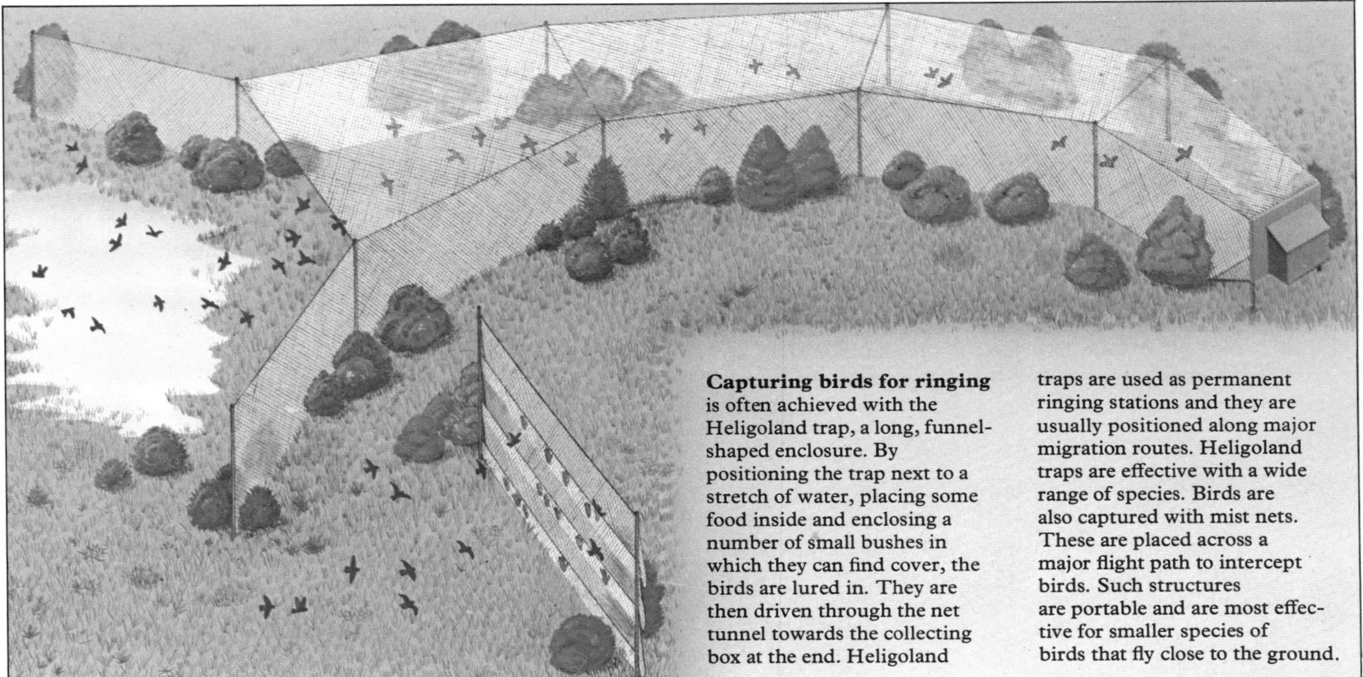

Capturing birds for ringing is often achieved with the Heligoland trap, a long, funnel-shaped enclosure. By positioning the trap next to a stretch of water, placing some food inside and enclosing a number of small bushes in which they can find cover, the birds are lured in. They are then driven through the net tunnel towards the collecting box at the end. Heligoland traps are used as permanent ringing stations and they are usually positioned along major migration routes. Heligoland traps are effective with a wide range of species. Birds are also captured with mist nets. These are placed across a major flight path to intercept birds. Such structures are portable and are most effective for smaller species of birds that fly close to the ground.

the place and date where it was originally marked and the locality and date where it was subsequently found. But ringing recoveries are of rather limited use singly. A single recovery may interest and excite the imagination, but it only tells us that the species concerned is capable of such a flight, though possibly under special circumstances. Until we have a number of such recoveries there is no means of knowing how regularly such flights occur. For example, in 1927 a ringed lapwing, *Vanellus vanellus*, a wading bird, crossed the Atlantic from Europe to America, and as there has been no similar recovery since then, one is bound to conclude that it was a freak performance; it tells us little about the migration of the lapwing.

The essence of bird ringing is that some helpful person, on finding a ringed bird, should take the trouble to write to the address on the ring. One cannot assume that this will happen in large parts of the world, including much of Africa and South America, where so many northern species spend the winter. Nor can one assume that an illiterate person will be willing to walk 300 kilometres (185 miles) to a mission station in order to hand over a ring, although a native of the Cameroons who shot a ringed cuckoo did precisely that. The fact is that when one rings large numbers of small song birds, even in closely populated parts of the world, it is unusual for more than two or three per hundred to be recovered. The recovery rate of European swallows, for example, is usually less than one per cent, so that ringing them is essentially a long-term study, to be measured in decades rather than in a few years.

There is another form of bird marking, less widely known and much less frequently employed, which nevertheless has its uses. This is colour marking, involving either the fitting of brightly coloured plastic rings or the dyeing of plumage. The latter is useful only for short-term observations, for as birds moult the dyed feathers are lost. Furthermore, as it is meaningful to only a limited number of people, a colour-marking study necessitates good publicity along the migratory pathway.

Finally, most of our knowledge of the oceanic movements of birds is derived from the accumulated observations of sailors, but what must be the most sophisticated of all migration study techniques, namely the fitting to birds of tiny radio transmitters whose signals are picked up by orbiting satellites, is also used for the study of the migrations of large seabirds such as albatrosses.

Visible migration

Many species migrate primarily by day, often taking off at first light. Sometimes they fly for a few hours, then spend the rest of the day feeding, but when conditions are ideal for migration, or when they are fleeing before advancing cold, the movement may continue all day. The overland sections of their migrations must therefore be completed in flight stages of 150 to 300 kilometres (90 to 190 miles), and perhaps because of this many of them are performed within 200 metres (660 feet) of ground level. At such heights they are clearly visible, even to the naked eye, so that one may watch migration taking place.

In the migration season, and when the weather conditions are suitable, this "visible migration" is an observational technique much used at observatories. Coasts, river valleys and escarpments all tend to canalize the passage, thus providing excellent opportunities for study. Large, featureless areas are crossed by the migrants on a broad front, so that a co-ordinated team of observers is needed, but the results of such teamwork may be very spectacular. For example, in London, in 1960, between 24 September and 13 November, a group of volunteers kept a daily early-morning watch, and their counts suggested that about four million migrating birds flew over the capital city in that period.

Watching migration, whether it be of seabirds, birds of prey or small song birds, calls for great skill in identification, for as the birds are on the move there are often only a few seconds in which to recognize the diagnostic features. Many song birds call as they fly in order to preserve flock cohesion, and so the ability to recognize the notes of each species is an enormous help. But observation does not stop with identification, for in a thorough study one will wish to record the numbers of each species, the time of day and the estimated height and the direction in which the birds are travelling. Furthermore, the very act of writing down the data means that one's attention is temporarily distracted, and to do the job thoroughly one needs an observer and a scribe. Highly skilled practitioners of this art sometimes achieve remarkable feats of identification; off the coast of southern Ireland it was established that certain migrating seabirds were being identified at a range of over six kilometres (4 miles).

Many migrants, especially among the small insectivorous song birds, choose to start their migratory flights shortly after sunset and to fly through the night. One obvious advantage of this is that they can use the daylight hours for feeding, and another likely benefit is that they escape attack by birds of prey. The existence of night migration has been known for over a century, and Gätke gives a graphic description of dazzled night migrants circling the Heligoland lighthouse – "Swarms of larks, starlings and thrushes career around in ever varying density like showers of brilliant sparks or huge snowflakes driven onward by a gale." Fortunately, from the point of view of the birds, such events occur only in bad weather and so they provide very limited opportunities of studying night migration. What was needed was a nocturnal equivalent of the technique used for studying daytime movements.

It was not until 1951 that an American ornithologist, George Lowery, announced just such a method. The system, known as moonwatching, involves observing the face of the full moon with binoculars. From time to time, perhaps no more often than once or twice in an hour, the tiny silhouette of a bird passes across the face of the moon, appearing and disappearing in a matter of seconds. There can be no question of identification, but it is possible to determine the direction of movement. This observational phase, which calls for great concentration, has to be followed by mathematical calculations. The arc of the sky, from horizon to horizon, is 180 degrees. Of that arc, the face of the moon represents a few degrees. From the numbers of birds seen crossing the face of the full moon, and assuming a reasonably uniform distribution of birds, one can calculate the approximate scale of bird movement that night.

Radar observations

What proved to be one of the most important advances in migration research came as a result of an accident. One may be sure that birds were far from the thoughts of the electronics engineers who, during the Second World War, developed radar. Indeed, history records the puzzlement of early operators, who observed on their

FLYING THROUGH THE NIGHT

Night migrants include larks, various waterfowl, thrushes and, with the exception of aerial feeders such as swifts and swallows, many small insectivorous song birds. Since many of them have to make long-distance migrations over water, where food is scarce and cover from predatory birds is absent, it makes more sense for these birds to travel under cover of darkness. Most nocturnal migrations take place on a broad front, with birds tending to fly neither in flocks nor following clearly defined flyways.

Among night migrants are such species as the great reed warbler, the well-known garden robin and the mistle thrush.

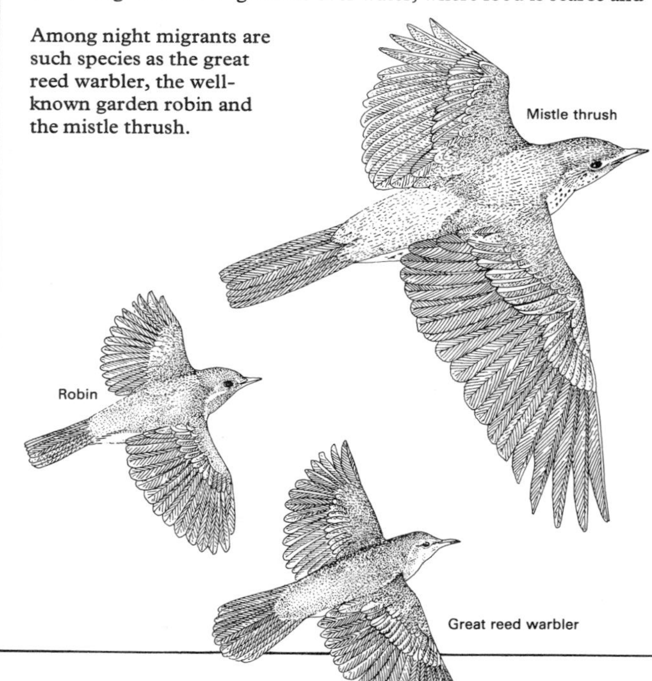

"Moonwatching" – counting birds flying across the face of the moon.

screens echoes that were far too slow moving to be aircraft. The radar beams, reaching up far beyond the range of vision, penetrating cloud and darkness with equal ease, were detecting the presence overhead of migrating birds. But it was not until peace was well established that in both Europe and North America migration research by radar really began to prove its worth.

Orthodox migration workers – those who watched birds through binoculars and telescopes – were quick to note that marvellous though radar was as an aid to research, it had serious limitations. The reflected waves indicated to the operator that birds were present, and a skilled person could learn to recognize echoes as being characteristic of small or large birds, but that was about its extent. Radar did not distinguish one species from another. Despite this, it is still a powerful research tool. It can reveal that on a morning when ground observers can see nothing moving, tens of thousands of birds are nevertheless passing directly overhead, maybe at a height of over a kilometre. On the screen the radar operator is able to follow the course of their journey for a hundred kilometres or more, observing that they are able to hold a steady course in light side winds but not in strong ones; to maintain course without deflection as they fly from darkness into dawn, or vice versa; that in fog or thick cloud they become disorientated; and that heavy rain obliges them to descend. Here, as never before, one is observing the very act of migration; observing it over great distance, and measuring it too.

Exactly how fast birds fly when migrating had long been a subject of speculation and deduction. For example, Heinrich Gätke at the end of the last century claimed that one species, the bluethroat, *Luscinia svecica*, travelled at 300 kilometres (185 miles) an hour. Bird ringers, searching through their records for evidence of rapid journeys, proved that some birds could cover as many as 1000 kilometres (620 miles) in twenty-four hours, though one could never be certain whether or not such flights had been wind assisted. Radar revealed that the still-air speed of most small migrants is no more than thirty to thirty-five kilometres (20 to 22 miles) an hour, though larger birds such as starlings and blackbirds are faster and may manage forty-five to fifty-five kilometres (30 to 35 miles) an hour. This knowledge of flight speed, when linked with information about energy reserves and consumption, enabled realistic calculations to be made about the potential flying ranges for various species.

Radar has also revealed that the bulk of migration normally takes place far beyond the range of human vision, often reaching heights of about 3000 metres (10,000 feet) and, exceptionally, up to 6500 metres (21,500 feet). Furthermore, with growing experience, and by linking radar with ground observations, it sometimes became possible to deduce which species, or at least which families, of birds one was watching. Gradually, as radar reveals the direction of flight at particular stages of the journey and ringing recoveries indicate the main stopping places, we are coming to understand something of the remarkable feats that migrating birds perform.

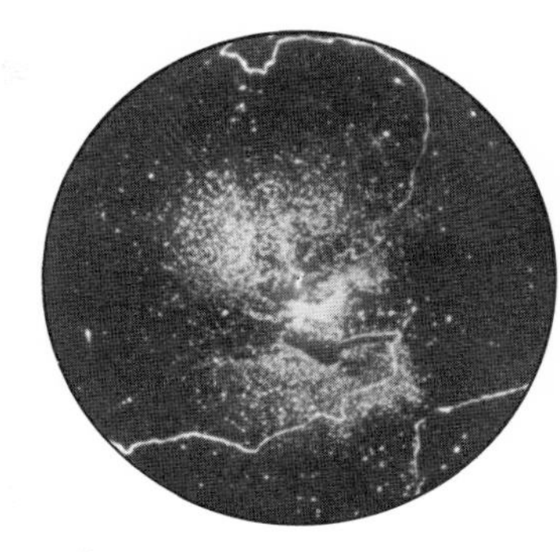

Radar ornithology is the study of the movement of birds by means of radar sets, some of which are powerful enough to detect a single bird 100 kilometres (60 miles) away. The screen shown above, from observations taken on an August evening, indicates huge numbers of birds moving across southeast England towards France and others migrating southwestward across the North Sea and along the English Channel.

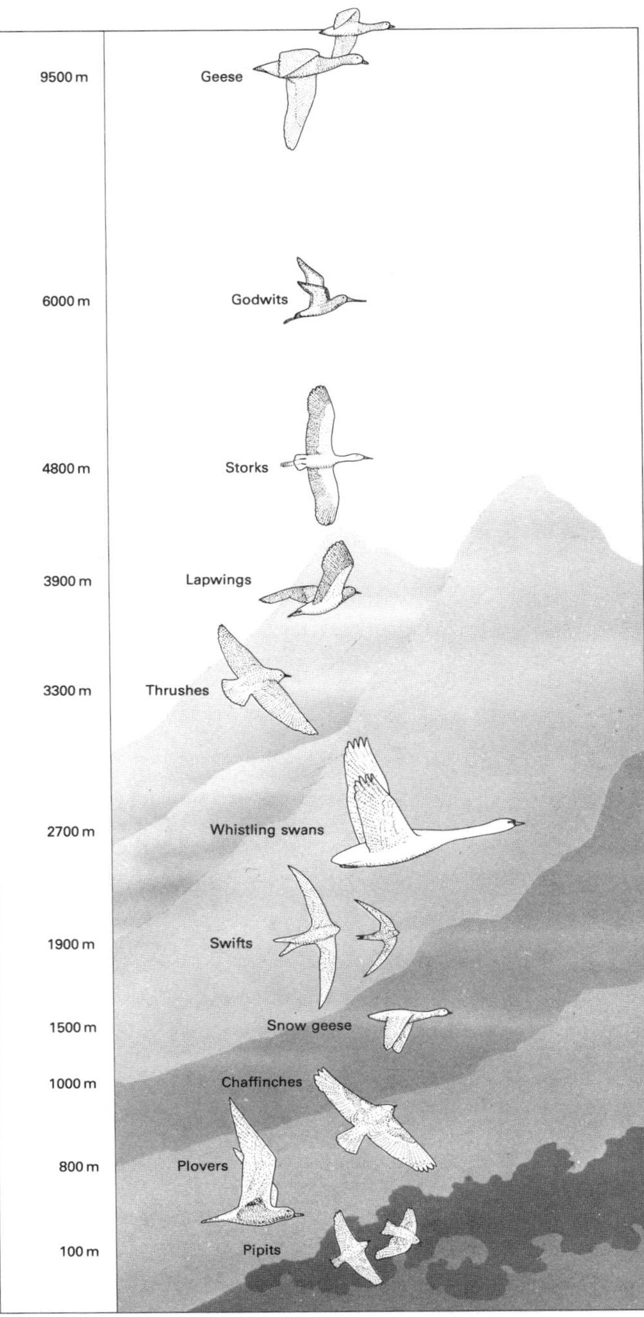

A large proportion of migrants fly at altitudes of between 100 and 1500 metres (330 and 3300 ft) above sea level. The maximum recorded height of a range of birds (not drawn to scale) is shown.

Migration in the Old World

For a long-distance migrant bird, the geography of the Old World can only be described as inconvenient. Whereas the main line of movement between breeding grounds and overwintering sites of birds is north–south, nearly all the major obstacles have an east–west axis and thus lie across the migration lanes. The four major mountain ranges – the Pyrenees, Alps, Caucasus and Himalayas – between them span several thousand kilometres across Europe and Asia. The Sahara, nowhere less than 1600 kilometres (1000 miles) across, straddles almost the entire African continent. For migrants following a more easterly course southward, there is the barrier of the desert lands that stretch from the Mediterranean to Afghanistan, as well as the great Gobi Desert north and east of the Himalayas. Finally, there are the water barriers of the Mediterranean, the Baltic, the Black and the Caspian seas.

One might suppose that this array of obstacles would largely determine the Old World patterns of bird migration, but this is not so. Certainly they are not without influence, for here and there across the continent are places such as narrow sea crossings, mountain passes and river valleys where the terrain forces the migration passage into a concentrated and narrow flight line. Yet this is the exception rather than the rule. The Baltic, the Mediterranean and the Sahara, for example, are traversed by migrants along their entire east–west ranges. Even the Himalayas do not totally deter birds, for bodies have been found in the snow by climbers at altitudes of more than 6500 metres (21,500 feet). Thus for many species there exists a broad-front migration over at least part of the journey, with here and there a stream of birds dividing to pass either side of major obstacles, rather as a river passes round a boulder.

It is perhaps for the larger birds that movement in and out of Europe is most difficult. Small birds flap their wings more frequently than larger ones. The longer and broader the wings, the more the muscular strength needed to hold them extended, let alone to flap them, increases. This in turn leads to much-increased body weight and ultimately places an upper limit on the size of flying birds. Although some large birds such as swans still use flapping flight, many others, especially storks and such birds of prey as eagles and vultures, have become specialist soarers. Naturally they can use flapping flight, but probably these birds are incapable of maintaining it for long periods. Much of the time they ride the air currents, seeking out the updraughts and thermals in which they can spiral effortlessly upward and then perform a long, gliding descent to the base of the next thermal. Thermals are rising columns of air resulting from differential heating of the land, and for this reason they seldom occur over the sea. But as we have seen, two seas, the Baltic and the Mediterranean, lie beneath the airways out of Europe. In order to cross them, the large soaring birds seek out the shortest possible sea crossings, passing over them in a narrow and spectacular stream, rather in the way that sand passes through the neck of an hour-glass.

Three such sea crossings in the Old World are famous vantage points. The most northerly is at Falsterbo, in the southwest corner of Sweden, where migrants from much of Scandinavia cross the narrow channel separating Sweden from Denmark. The two other crossing points lie at the extremities of the Mediterranean. More than 2500 kilometres (1550 miles) from west to east, and in places several hundred kilometres across, the Mediterranean is a much bigger barrier than the Baltic for migrating birds of prey, and the traffic at the crossing points is even more spectacular. One, the wider of the two, is the Strait of Gibraltar. Here, the configuration of the neighbouring land masses almost irresistibly leads the low-flying migrants towards the narrowest point. In good weather, squadrons of soaring birds make light of the journey, but when there is a head wind only the more determined among them set off, low over the choppy water, for the opposite shore.

The third, and perhaps greatest, of the major crossing points is at the Bosphorus, where on bright autumn days tens of thousands of birds of prey and storks may soar over the narrow waterway that separates Europe from Asia. A somewhat less important concentration point is the long arm of Italy, stretching southward in the central Mediterranean, and linked with the stepping stones of Sicily and Malta. This attracts large numbers of the smaller, stronger flying birds of prey, such as the honey buzzard, *Pernis apivorus*, and a number of small song birds from areas such as the British Isles and western Europe, among them several warbler species.

Near Lake Van in eastern Turkey a group of ornithologists have stopped to observe the passing of a formation of migrating white pelicans, *Pelecanus onocratalus*.

ROUTES INTO AFRICA

With information gained by ringing experiments, radar scanning and direct observations, it has been possible to build up a picture of the routes taken by migrants on their flights from the breeding grounds of Europe and western Asia to the wintering areas of Africa. The routes shown on the map opposite have been obtained primarily by superimposing the results of capture/release/recapture experiments of twenty common species of song birds, among them the blackcap, the lesser and common whitethroat, a number of other warblers, the wheatear, the nightingale and the whinchat. While these routes should not be interpreted as precise, narrow flyways, the importance as crossing points of the Strait of Gibraltar, the Bosphorus and, to a lesser extent, the short hauls to North Africa from the southern tip of Italy across Sicily and from northern Italy across Corsica and Sardinia, are evident. It is also clear that having entered Africa, many northern song birds fly directly over the Sahara Desert and the central equatorial forests.

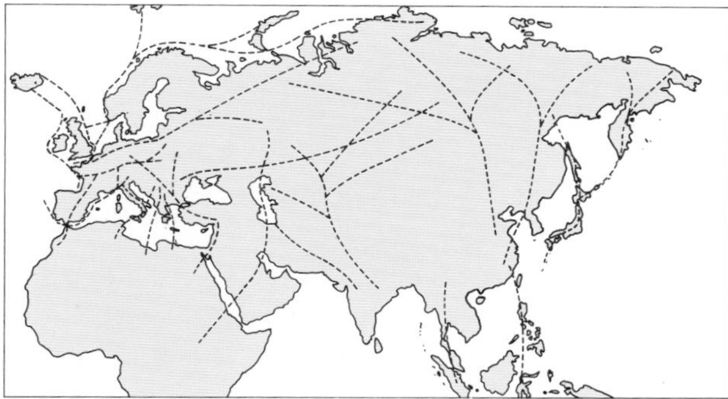

A generalized map of the main migration routes of birds travelling between breeding areas in Europe and northern Asia and wintering areas in southern Asia and Africa.

Falsterbo
Black Sea
Caspian Sea
Bosphorus
Gibraltar
Mediterranean Sea
SAHARA DESERT

The fly-past of migrant birds in autumn at the Bosphorus is one of the great spectacles of the natural world. Gilbert White, the eighteenth-century English naturalist, summarized his observation of the event as "a great and curious army of hawks and kites traversing the Thracian Bosphorus". The passage of birds across this narrow stretch of water is no less spectacular today.

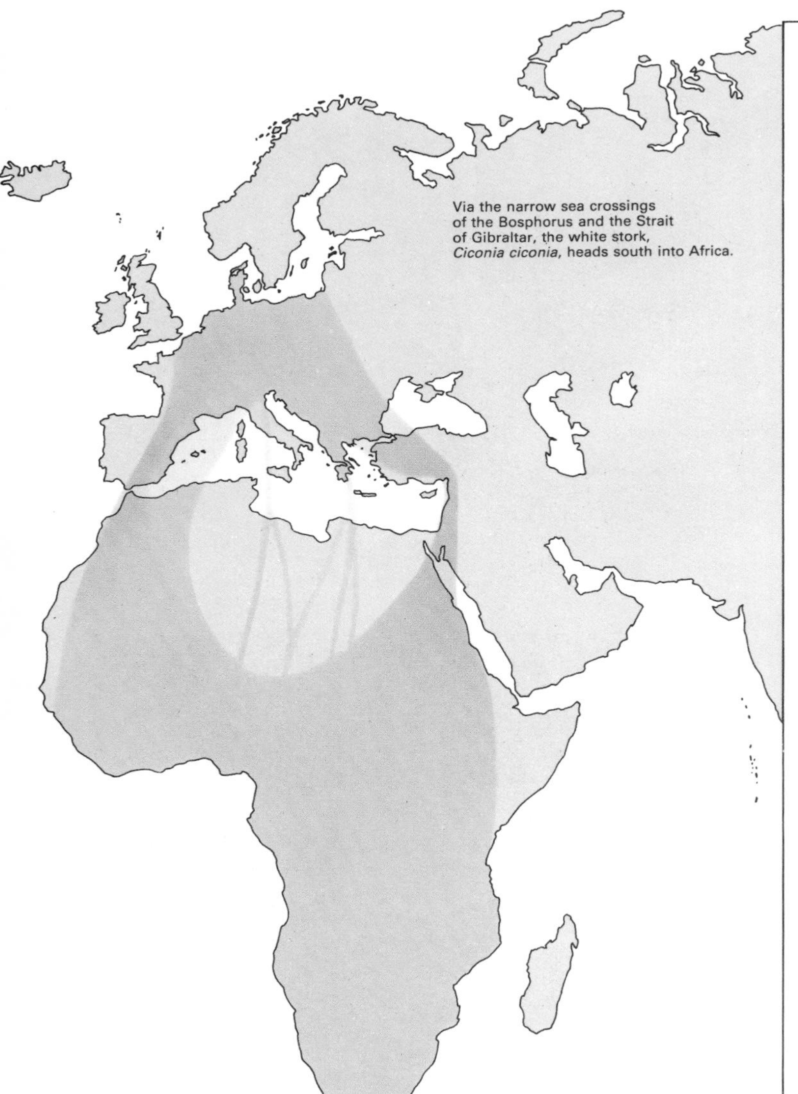

Via the narrow sea crossings of the Bosphorus and the Strait of Gibraltar, the white stork, *Ciconia ciconia*, heads south into Africa.

MAN AND BIRD LIVING IN HARMONY

The white stork breeds in the warmer regions of many countries bordering the Mediterranean. It commonly nests in trees in open ground, but in built-up areas it nests on chimneys, rooftops and church steeples. In parts of southern Germany and in the Alsace region of France, where the white stork is considered a symbol of good luck, villagers each spring renovate any remaining rooftop nests or construct new nests above their homes in order to entice the returning storks.

Major routes between Europe and Africa
Some species of bird, among them the white stork, *Ciconia ciconia*, use only two of these pathways out of Europe, and demonstrate the phenomenon of migratory divide. Birds breeding to one side of an invisible demarcation line – in the case of the stork to the west of a line running roughly north–south through the heart of Europe – move off southwestward towards the Gibraltar crossing, while the more easterly residents depart in a southeasterly direction towards the Bosphorus, later to pass south through the Levant region and into Egypt. For many small song birds, among them the warblers, chats and flycatchers, radar studies have revealed that there is north–south migration across even the widest sections of the Mediterranean, though with greater concentrations on the shorter crossings. To some degree, therefore, there is a migratory divide in the movements of many of the birds concerned.

Migratory divide apart, four main patterns of seasonal migration can be recognized in the Old World, each of which may in part owe its origins to the last ice age, when much of Europe was too cold for the insect-eating birds that now form the majority of the long-distance migrants. As the ice gradually retreated, leaving areas suitable for summer occupation, those species which survived in the southwest gradually extended their summer ranges towards the northeast, retreating annually by the route of their colonization. Thus flycatchers that nowadays breed as far east as Moscow do not set off directly south in autumn, but first head southwest to the coast of Portugal before beginning their long southward flight to Africa. If measured in terms of numbers of individuals, and probably in numbers of species too, the southwestward departure is the most important migration route in western Europe.

The converse of this situation – the second pattern of movement – is to be found in those species whose winter quarters now lie in eastern Africa or in southern Asia, and whose breeding strongholds lie in the eastern half of Europe. A number of them, the red-backed shrike, *Lanius collurio*, the lesser whitethroat, *Sylvia curruca*, and the barred warbler, *Sylvia nisoria*, for example, are believed to have spread gradually westward as breeding birds, reaching the shores of the North Sea and, in the case of the shrike and whitethroat, even the British Isles. One might expect that the westernmost populations would, in the course of time, have come to take a short cut southward into western Africa, but this is not so; they still depart southeastward crossing or skirting the Alps, traversing the Balkans, then heading south down the Nile valley.

At least two species of bird, the cuckoo, *Cuculus canorus*, and the wood warbler, *Phylloscopus sibilatrix*, seem to belong to neither of these two camps and exhibit a third pattern of migration. Evidence derived from ringing recoveries suggests that individuals from all parts of western Europe pass mainly down through Italy to cross the central Mediterranean and into Africa. Fourth, and finally, there are species that breed across most of the width of Europe and winter in a correspondingly wide area of Africa. Such species appear to move south on a broad front, corresponding to their summer distribution.

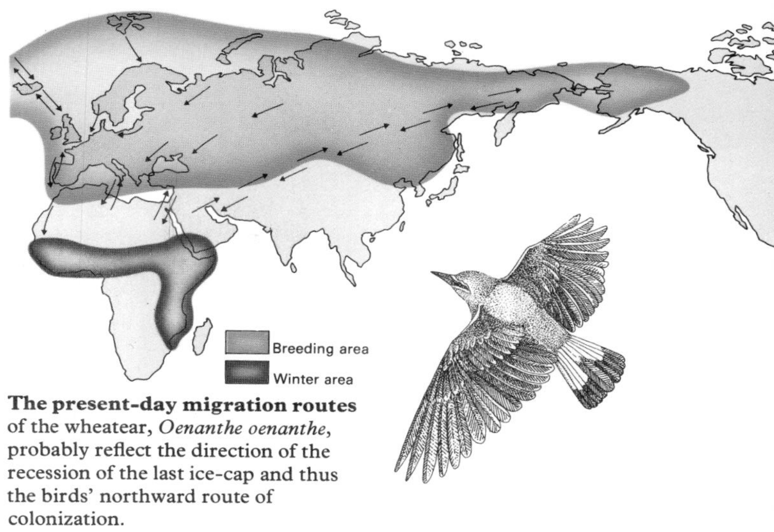

The present-day migration routes of the wheatear, *Oenanthe oenanthe*, probably reflect the direction of the recession of the last ice-cap and thus the birds' northward route of colonization.

The long-distance migrants

The extensions of range that have taken place since the last ice age have necessitated some spectacular migration journeys, particularly by small song birds. The arctic warbler, *Phylloscopus borealis*, for example, a close relative of the European willow warbler, and a bird so small as to weigh barely ten grams (0.3 ounce), is, as its name suggests, a northern species. In Europe it breeds nowhere south of Scandinavia and the northern USSR and has its homeland in the heart of Asia. From there it has gradually spread westward as far as northern Norway. Yet its winter quarters lie in southeastern Asia, with the result that those birds breeding in the far west have a transcontinental journey several thousand kilometres in length to perform twice a year. However, even this performance is outclassed by the wheatear, *Oenanthe oenanthe*.

Wheatears are birds of stony or sandy places, especially associated with hilly areas, whose winter quarters lie in the semi-desert country to the immediate south of the Sahara. Some time after the last ice age the wheatear colonized, successively, Britain, the Faeroe Islands, Iceland and Greenland. As its winter quarters have remained in Africa, each leap towards the north and west has led to a progressively longer migration, and there are few more stormy waters than those which lie between Iceland and Greenland. Yet, incredibly, the colonization has not stopped at Greenland, for from there the species has also colonized the adjacent areas of northeastern Canada and is still extending its range westward. So far as is known, at the end of the short arctic summer these pioneers must cross, via Greenland, back to northern Europe or northern Spain before facing the last long stage south across the Sahara.

Even this is not the climax of the story, for the wheatear has been equally successful in Europe and Asia. Having reached the easternmost part of Siberia, and having crossed the Bering Straits into Alaska, it has now spread so far eastward into western Canada that the gap between those entering North America via Greenland and those arriving via Alaska is thought to be less than 800 kilometres (500 miles). Again it appears that these west Canadian birds recross the Bering Straits each year to return to the ancestral winter home of their species. It would seem probable, therefore, that these wheatears spend up to eight months each year travelling; this must be migration at its ultimate development.

The red-backed shrike, *Lanius collurio*, which is commonly known as the butcherbird, in spring migrates from wintering areas in southern Africa to breeding grounds throughout Europe.

Swallows and swifts in the Old World

One of the best known species of bird, and one with an equally interesting migration, is the barn swallow, *Hirundo rustica*. This breeds over most of both the Old World and the New. The Old World swallows winter in Africa, India and Southeast Asia, and from the results of bird ringing it is possible to link a number of the breeding populations with specific winter quarters. Swallows from eastern Asia winter in southeastern Asia, occasionally reaching northern Australia, while those wintering in India apparently hail from central northern Asia. But it is on examination of the migration of swallows that winter in Africa that the complexity of their movements emerges.

Africa is the winter home of all European swallows and, judging by the results of ringing, of swallows ranging from western Asia as far as longitude 90° East, so that the easterly populations must undertake a very long southwesterly trip each autumn. Now it is possible for swallows to winter in Egypt and the Sudan – indeed, there is one race that is resident throughout the year in these countries – yet all European swallows cross the Sahara. This adds a very significant and dangerous stage to their journey; although swallows feed as they migrate, and therefore do not need to build up the large reserves of energy-rich fat found in many small migrants, there are few flying insects over the desert, so the crossing must be made largely without sustenance. (Swallows that have just completed a desert crossing are sometimes so tired that one can pick them off the twigs where they are resting.) Swallows from Germany and other parts of central Europe, for example, winter mainly in central Africa. Here, obviously, is a vast area with guaranteed safe temperatures and food supply. Swallows from Britain in the west and from Russia in the east, however, press on southward to winter in the extreme south of Africa. In so doing, they must overfly the winter homes of other European swallows, and at the same time add at least 5000 kilometres (3100 miles) to their annual round trip.

In temperate and northern parts of Europe, the swallow, together with the sand martin, or bank swallow, *Riparia riparia*, is the first migrant aerial feeder to arrive in spring. The western European population of sand martins is thought to winter mainly north of the equator, and so these birds have a shorter flight than the swallows, but in most years little separates their arrival some time in March. Presumably this is because the swallow is a bigger bird, with longer wings and a rather higher flight speed. The next aerial feeder to arrive is the house martin, *Delichon urbica*, and the difference in timing is interesting. When feeding, the house martin regularly flies higher than its two relatives, and in this way is in less direct competition with them for food. On the other hand, it is not until the air temperature starts to rise that the insects themselves fly higher and it is presumably this factor which determines the later arrival time.

The last of the four main migratory swallow and swift species to arrive in spring is the common swift, *Apus apus*. It, too, is a high flier, higher even than the house martin, and one may assume that its late arrival is correlated with the availability of adequate food supplies. Certainly it is a powerful flier, and it would have little difficulty in overtaking all the other three species if it were sensible for it to do so. It is the most aerial of them all, feeding, gathering its nesting material and even copulating on the wing, and probably never lands on the ground by design.

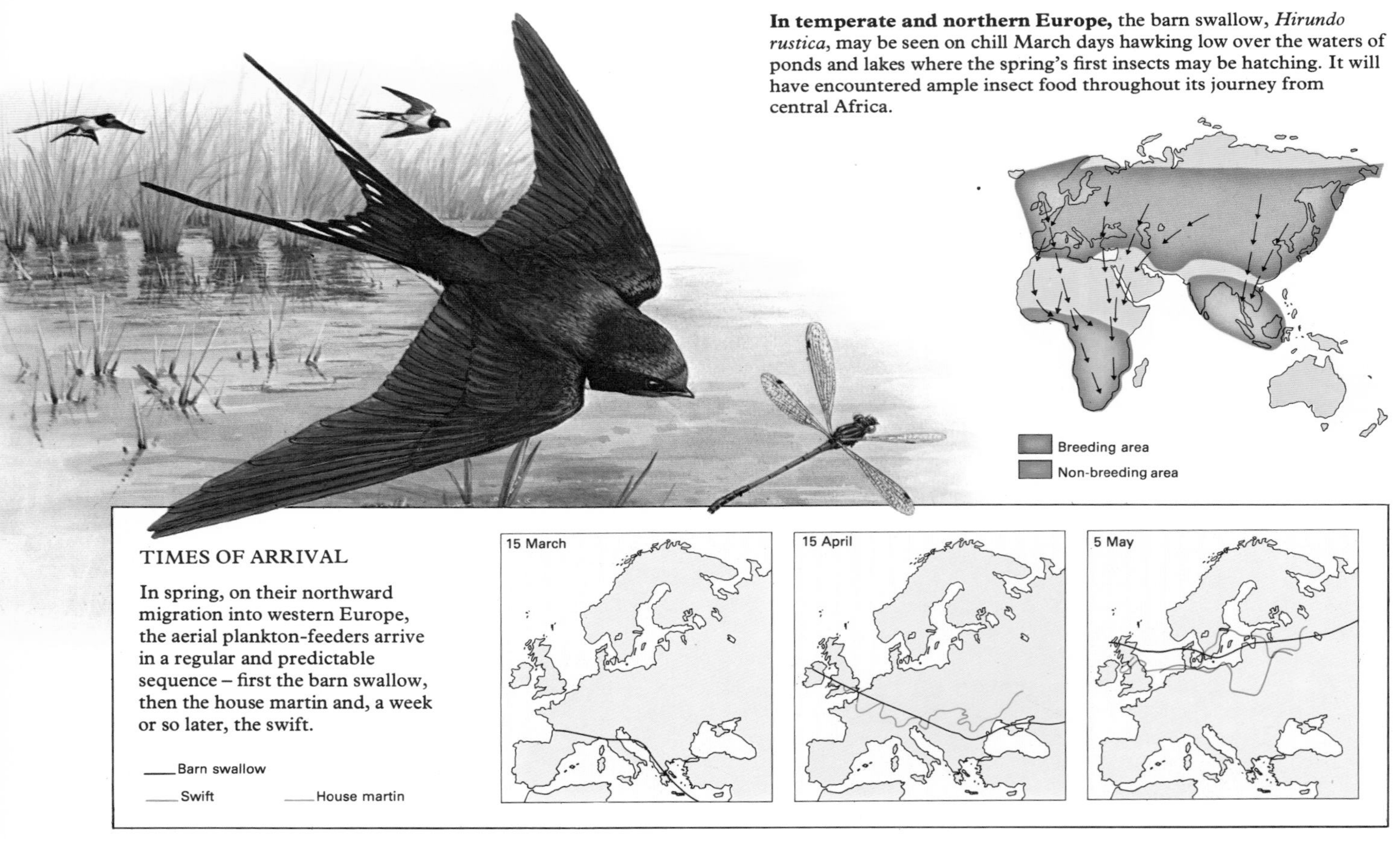

In temperate and northern Europe, the barn swallow, *Hirundo rustica*, may be seen on chill March days hawking low over the waters of ponds and lakes where the spring's first insects may be hatching. It will have encountered ample insect food throughout its journey from central Africa.

TIMES OF ARRIVAL

In spring, on their northward migration into western Europe, the aerial plankton-feeders arrive in a regular and predictable sequence – first the barn swallow, then the house martin and, a week or so later, the swift.

The swift has become so adapted to an aerial life that its legs are small and weak; on the ground it would be helpless and an easy prey to raptors and other predatory animals.

Throughout spring and summer swallows and sand martins roost communally in reed beds and osiers, sometimes forming immense congregations estimated to contain a million birds. House martins and swifts do not join them, and although they roost in their nests while they are breeding, it would hardly be possible for them to find convenient empty nests each evening while on migration. Since large roosts are not observed, perhaps these birds spend the hours of darkness aloft. As for the nests of these aerial feeders, swifts, swallows and house martins invariably nest in buildings while sand martins nest in sandy banks or pits.

Radar has shown that swifts may cover enormous distances in their quest for food, flying ahead of fronts as the turbulent air sweeps up the insect masses. When engaged in this practice they may "ride" the weather for 150 kilometres (95 miles) or more before returning to their nests. Being capable of speeds up to 100 kilometres (60 miles) an hour, such flights are a practical method of exploiting a temporary abundance of food. Indeed, their whole lives seem to be lived at speed, and in late May northerly breeders are still beating their way north, even over still-frozen lakes, to nest, raise their two young and depart. Last to arrive, they are also the first to depart, usually quitting northern latitudes by late July or early August. And their young, when eventually they fledge, must move straight into an aerial way of life, with no sitting around on perches waiting to be fed. A ringing recovery provided striking evidence of the promptness of departure after fledging. The young bird in question was ringed in Oxfordshire, England, on 22 July and was known to have fledged from its nest on the morning of 31 July. On 3 August it was picked up near Madrid in central Spain, some 1200 kilometres (750 miles) away.

Swallows congregating at sunset to roost before embarking the next day on their southward migration to Africa – a familiar autumn scene.

There is another aerial feeder, the alpine swift, *Apus melba*, whose migration is of particular interest. This is a resident of mountain country in central and southern Europe and in North Africa. Two and a half times the size of the common swift, it is perhaps the supreme flier amongst birds if speed is the criterion. Swiss experts have estimated that although when hunting for insects it flies at no greater speed than the common swift, in the wild chases in which it indulges it may reach speeds of up to 240 kilometres (150 miles) an hour. They also consider that in its feeding flights it must cover some 560 kilometres (350 miles) a day, and sometimes 1000 kilometres (620 miles). Because of its more southerly distribution, it is able to arrive much earlier from its home in the eastern Congo, usually from the end of March until early May, and stays for some six months on average.

Winter visitors from the far north

In contrast to the favourable and relatively predictable seasonal conditions of temperate and Mediterranean regions of the Old World, the high latitudes present birds with both great opportunities and great risks. Spread out round the top of Europe and Asia (and North America too) are vast areas of tundra which are totally inhospitable in winter and yet which, in the short arctic summer, offer almost unlimited living space, a profusion of insect life on which to feed, relatively few predators, and twenty-four hours of daylight each day in which to hunt. However, since trees are virtually missing from the high arctic, the species that occupy the most northern areas must nest on the ground or on cliffs. Waders and ducks and geese especially are best adapted to this way of life.

What of the risks? Firstly, the further north one goes, the more likely one is to experience bad weather during the migration season. The ocean crossings to Greenland, Bear Island and Spitsbergen, for example, may be fraught with danger, and the birds that attempt them must be strong fliers, capable of great endurance. Secondly, the arctic summers themselves are very unreliable, so that in some years, even though the migrants successfully reach their breeding grounds, either the snow never clears and birds cannot even attempt breeding or a sudden snow storm blankets the land, causing massive mortality among the newly hatched young. Thus high-arctic breeders have to be sufficiently long-lived to withstand one or two consecutive summers when they are unable to produce offspring.

Of the arctic species, most is known about the migration of the various species of geese. These birds are great traditionalists, moving to winter quarters that at times are remarkably restricted. Brent, or Brant, geese, *Branta bernicla*, from Greenland, for example, winter almost exclusively in Ireland, where they may be joined by some from Canada, while those from northern Russia winter mainly round the shores of the North Sea, especially on the southeastern coasts of England. White-fronted geese, *Anser albifrons*, from Greenland winter mainly in Ireland and southwest Scotland, while those from Russia choose a few localities in northwestern Europe. Even more restricted are the barnacle geese, *Branta leucopsis*. The Greenland population of this species winters in Ireland and on islands off the west coast of Scotland, notably Islay, while the migrants from Spitsbergen concentrate in the inner Solway, for much of the time staying within the bounds of a few parishes on the Anglo–Scottish border.

The movements of geese illustrate a type of migration generally much shorter in distance than the journeys into Africa and southern Asia. Many of the hardier species of bird, not dependent on flying insects, can winter safely within Europe. Among these are the meadow pipit, *Anthus pratensis*, and pied wagtail, *Motacilla alba yarrellii*, that live on small ground invertebrates and their larvae. They need travel no further than Iberia, and large numbers winter as far north as the British Isles. Similarly, the seed-eating linnet, *Acanthis cannabina*, and goldfinch, *Carduelis carduelis*, are as likely to be found overwintering in southern England and northern France in December as they are in Spain. The suitability of each of these relatively northerly regions is a consequence of its mild climate and this results from the presence of the warmer waters of the Gulf Stream. Western Europe, therefore, and especially Britain and Ireland, represents a very acceptable winter home at the end of a much shorter migration journey.

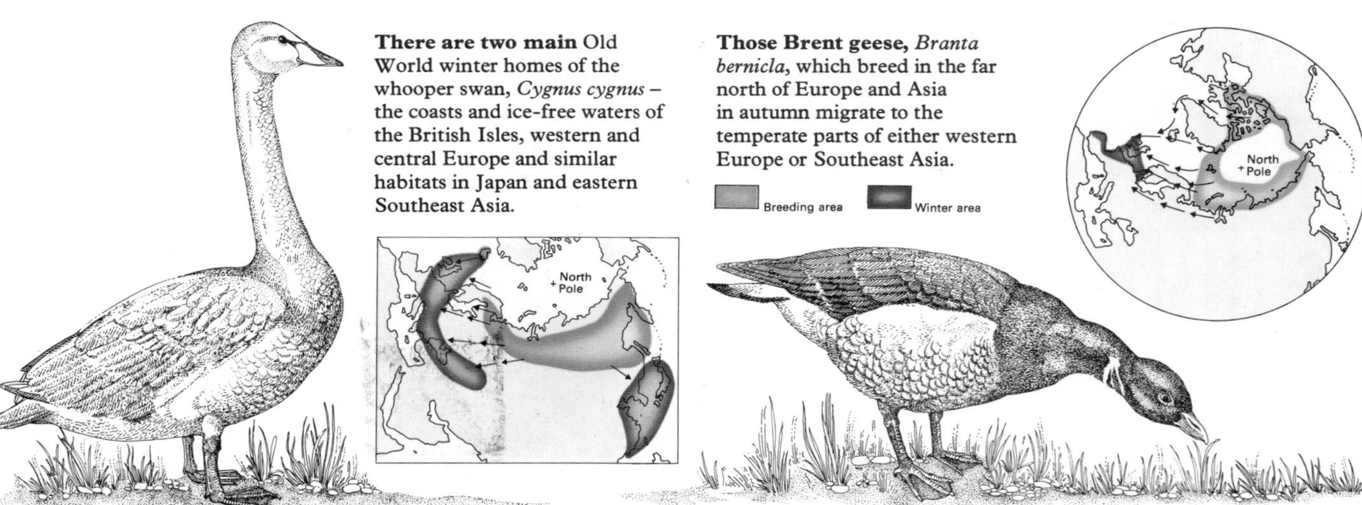

There are two main Old World winter homes of the whooper swan, *Cygnus cygnus* – the coasts and ice-free waters of the British Isles, western and central Europe and similar habitats in Japan and eastern Southeast Asia.

Those Brent geese, *Branta bernicla*, which breed in the far north of Europe and Asia in autumn migrate to the temperate parts of either western Europe or Southeast Asia.

Barnacle geese, *Branta leucopsis*, breed on islands north of the Arctic Circle and winter on coasts of the British Isles and northwest Europe.

So it comes about that after the less hardy species – warblers, swallows, chats and the like – have departed on their long flight south, a new migration starts up. This time the species are heading southwest or west-southwest into France, Britain and Ireland, or even into southwest Norway. The volume of migration is enormous, though the number of species may be few: fieldfares, redwings, song thrushes and blackbirds, all members of the genus *Turdus*, and starlings, *Sturnus vulgaris*, chaffinches, *Fringilla coelebs*, bramblings, *F. montifringilla*, and skylarks, *Alauda arvensis*, are the main song birds, though further east various members of the crow and tit families are abundant and may even predominate locally among the migrant birds. In addition, of course, there are many waterfowl and waders seeking ice-free waters and mud-flats, which support a reservoir of food throughout the winter months.

Autumn, therefore, is the time of the year when the Baltic comes to the fore, not as a barrier this time but as a major northeast–southwest highway out of northern Europe. Hundreds of thousands of duck fly over the Baltic to havens among the Danish islands or, further west, in Britain, while along its southern shores is a stream of land birds making towards the relative safety of their winter homes.

Migration in southeastern Asia

Somewhere about the line of longitude 90° East in northern Asia there is faunal divide. To the west of this imaginary line the migratory bird species mainly head southwestward to winter in Africa. To the east, many new species occur, and these mostly migrate to winter in southeastern Asia, an area stretching from southern China, through the Malay peninsula, to the countless islands of the East Indies.

Whereas migrants reaching Africa and crossing the Sahara Desert find potential winter quarters of about eighteen million square kilometres (7 million square miles), those leaving eastern Asia each autumn are heading for a reception area of about only four million square kilometres (1.5 million square miles). This contrast is even more marked when one compares the solid land masses of Africa with the mosaic of islands and peninsulas which constitute so much of the latter's winter quarters. Here, sea crossings and the attendant navigational risks abound, but since the demand for winter living room is so enormous, they do not deter the migrants. The problem is most acute for the insectivorous species, for, due to the northeast monsoons, in January cooler weather reaches almost as far south as the Tropic of Cancer, thereby confining the birds in much smaller winter quarters than would otherwise be the case.

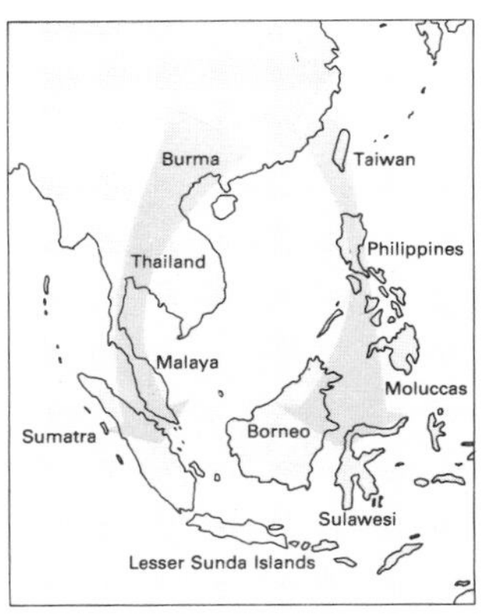

Heading south in autumn from the breeding grounds of Southeast Asia to the wintering areas of Malaya and the plethora of islands further to the south and east, the bird population demonstrates migratory divide, individuals opting for one of two main routes. Among those that take the westerly mainland route are several species of raptors and a number of warblers that breed in the high latitudes of the USSR. Birds that breed in southwestern China tend to take the hazardous, island-hopping, easterly route.

Few areas of the globe demonstrate so well the complexities of migration as does eastern Asia. It has been calculated, for example, that over 300 of the species that breed in northeastern Asia are long-distance migrants that travel towards the southeastern corner of the continent for the winter. About 180 of these species, including many of the waterfowl, larks, finches and larger thrushes, mainly winter north of the tropics, but the remainder make the long trip southward to near the equator and beyond.

There are two main routes south. Birds leaving southwestern China may travel to Taiwan and thence to the Philippines, Borneo, Sulawesi and the Moluccas. It is a course almost due south, but although along the route there are innumerable islands which the birds can use as stop-over points, the South China Sea is notorious for its hurricanes, particularly between July and November. In the 1960s an American research team revealed by ringing that among the travellers that take this route are not only endemic species but also a number of northern species, the most notable of which is the brown shrike, *Lanius cristatus*. This is a bird which breeds in the eastern Palaearctic and winters widely in Southeast Asia and the islands to the east.

For those species following the second, mainland route, there is a long journey southwestward across China, Burma and Thailand to the narrow finger of Malaya. Brown shrikes occur here too, along with many other northern species. Typical of those species that winter on the Malay peninsula itself are the Siberian thrush, *Zoothera sibirica*, and the Siberian blue robin, *Erithacus cyane* – birds whose names indicate their distant homelands. They are joined by several species of migrant warblers from the north, or the far north, and by the barn swallow, *Hirundo rustica*, which arrives from as far afield as northern Siberia.

Malaya – winter quarters and thoroughfare

Whereas the Malay peninsula is a winter destination for some migrant species, it is no more than a route south for others. There is, in fact, a considerable passage southward across the Straits of Malacca into Sumatra, with a big movement of birds of prey down the western side of the peninsula featuring prominently. Two such species, the Japanese sparrowhawk, *Accipiter gularis*, and the crested honey buzzard, *Pernis ptilorhynchus*, are the most numerous, with counts of the former sometimes exceeding 1000 individuals an hour. It has been estimated that at least 180,000 of each species pass through the peninsula each year. At Cape Rachado, they assemble in huge numbers, spiralling slowly higher before crossing the Straits of Singapore into Sumatra.

Not all the winter visitors to southeastern Asia are from the far north. Species such as the crow-billed drongo, *Dicrurus annectans*, and the hill blue flycatcher, *Cyornis banyumas*, originate from considerably further south. Individuals of the latter species actually breed on the Malay peninsula, where they are joined for the winter by populations whose homes lie rather further north. A similar situation occurs with the brown-breasted and the blue-throated bee-eaters, *Merops philippinus* and *M. viridis*, both of which breed in Malaya. In winter, more northerly populations of the same two species arrive here, but native Malay bluethroats depart to travel further south. Why one population should leave an area only to be replaced by another of the self-same species remains something of a mystery.

To and from Australia and New Zealand

South and east of the Malay peninsula, south of the Philippines, Sulawesi and the Moluccas, lies the greatest of the islands, the continent of Australia. Here the most intrepid of all the northeast Asian migrants terminate their journeys. They include about thirty species of wading birds, which reach Australia from the New and Old Worlds with some regularity. Many of these apparently follow a trans-Pacific route from eastern Siberia, a journey of some 7000 kilometres (4350 miles). They are, and need to be, powerful fliers, though most are capable of swimming for a while if necessary. This in no way detracts from their remarkable feat, but even more outstanding are the journeys of two land birds, the spine- or needle-tailed swift, *Chaetura caudacuta*, and the Pacific, or fork-tailed, swift, *Apus pacificus*. These commute seasonally between northeastern Asia and Australia, reaching as far south as Tasmania. Indeed, there have been many records of the spine-tailed swift in distant New Zealand, a round-trip migration of some 20,000 kilometres (12,400 miles).

Australia is too remote, too short of forests and too dry to act as a major reception area for migrants from the north. It thus experiences little intercontinental migration. On the other hand, it is a vast country, three-quarters the size of Europe, and recent ornithological research indicates that the regular seasonal movements of some Australian species is migration in the classical sense, and is determined by changes of temperature. The red-capped robin, *Petroica goodenovii*, and the grey fantail, *Rhipidura fuliginosa*, for example, are both migratory in the southern part of their range, while the charmingly named welcome swallow, *Hirundo neoxena*, is sedentary in western Australia but migratory in the southeast. Rufous fantails, *R. rufifrons*, from southern Australia are total migrants, retreating northward as far as New Guinea. The black-faced, or large, cuckoo-shrike, *Coracina novaehollandiae*, is a similar traveller, migrating to Indonesia and Melanesia. Even further-travelling is the rufous-tailed, or Horsefield's, bronze-cuckoo, *Chrysococcyx basalis*, which, when it vacates the colder areas of southeastern Australia, migrates to the Moluccas, western Sumatra and the Malay peninsula, reaching as far as Christmas Island in the Indian Ocean. It is, nevertheless, its close relative, the shining, or golden, bronze-cuckoo, *Chalcites lucidus*, which has earned a place in the textbooks of migration. Its reputation is based not so much on the strength of the performance of the Australian birds, which travel to New Guinea and the Lesser Sunda islands, but the remarkable transoceanic flight of the New Zealand population to winter in the Bismarck archipelago. Few species tackle so long an ocean crossing – a journey of some 4000 kilometres (2500 miles) – and it is difficult to understand the value of the practice when there appear to be other suitable winter quarters nearer at hand.

THE SHINING BRONZE-CUCKOO OF AUSTRALASIA

During the Southern Hemisphere summer this species breeds in forests and woodlands of Australasia – one population in southwestern Australia, one in Tasmania and southeastern Australia and a third in New Zealand. In late March, the southern autumn, the populations migrate to separate wintering zones on islands to the north, returning south the following August.

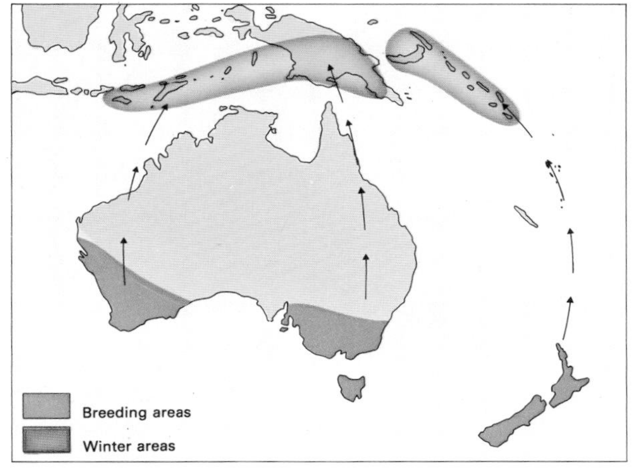

Australian avifauna contains a high percentage of nomadic species, among them Bourke's parrot, *Neophema bourkii*, the purple-crowned lorikeet, *Glossopsitta porphyrocephela*, princess parrot, *Polytelis alexandrae*, and the cockatiel, *Nymphicus hollandicus*. Such birds are to be found wherever there are flowering or fruit-bearing trees or shrubs. The birds may be absent from a given area for many years, returning only when rains produce temporary water sources and regenerate the vegetation.

Nomadic species

The brown songlark, *Cinclorhamphus cruralis*, is a widespread species in Australia, the migratory population in the cooler southern parts of the continent arriving in September and leaving in March. However, when conditions are suitable inland it probably does not migrate south. Here we come to the feature of bird movement which most typifies Australia – nomadism. The vast heart of the continent is subject to a scant and largely unpredictable rainfall regime, and many Australian bird species have during the course of their evolution become adapted to survive in such circumstances. The normal behaviour we find is that species are sedentary when circumstances permit, otherwise nomadic. This is true, for example, of the crested bellbird, *Oreoica gutturalis*, the white-fronted chat, *Ephthianura albifrons*, the grey and the brown honeyeaters, *Lacustroica whitei* and *Lichmera indistincta*, and many of the parrot-like birds. Nomadism to them means the abandonment of regular breeding and "wintering" seasons: birds wander widely until they find an area where rain has fallen. Then, with the temporary assurance of easy conditions, biological processes which are normally spread over weeks must be contracted into a few days. There is no time for the protracted courtship characteristic of temperate latitudes. In black-faced wood-swallows, *Artamus cinereus*, for example, courtship behaviour has been seen within a few minutes of the onset of rain, followed by copulation a mere two hours later. Following the rain the desert land will briefly flower: there will be insects, fruit and seeds. It is an ephemeral cornucopia and full advantage must be taken of it; a new generation must be established before the parched aridity sets in again and the nomads have to move once more in search of survival. This is often a matter of weeks rather than months.

North America, more so than Europe, is the land of the hunter. This has had a profound effect on the pattern of migration research in America and Canada with major studies having concentrated on birds of economic importance, especially ducks, geese and swans.

Migration in the New World

The total land area of North and South America is about forty-five million square kilometres (17.5 million square miles), which is only slightly larger than the combined areas of Europe and Africa. But there, at least from the point of view of migrating birds, the similarities end. In the matter of size, in the Old World the African winter quarters are much larger than the breeding grounds of Europe, whereas in the New World the breeding grounds of North America are more extensive than the potential wintering areas to the south. And while Africa spreads its welcoming arms east–west over more than 6500 kilometres (4000 miles), the Americas are like an hour-glass, narrow in the centre, constricting the passage of some migrants to a corridor a few hundred kilometres wide.

As we can see from this comparison, conditions probably favour migrants passing between Europe and Africa, but on two other important, and perhaps more major, accounts the advantage clearly lies with the New World migrants. Firstly, although the Gulf of Mexico represents a water crossing comparable to the Mediterranean at its widest point, to the west it is flanked by a sinuous land bridge, and to the east Cuba and the islands of the Greater and Lesser Antilles, in various permutations, provide stepping stones in what would otherwise be a very long overseas flight. Secondly, whereas the Old World mountain chains tend to run east–west across the flight lanes, in the Americas the ranges run parallel to them.

This ease of communication between breeding grounds and winter quarters is perhaps best exemplified by the fact that representatives of two tropical families, the tanagers, Thraupinae spp., and hummingbirds, Trochilidae spp., have been able to spread northward as far as Canada. This is in marked contrast to the Old World, where the double barriers of the Sahara and the Mediterranean have inhibited northward expansion of the African avifauna. So the very geographical features which have in the past allowed step-by-step colonization of the North American continent by southern species, each spring and autumn provide easy clearways for millions of birds on the move.

The flyway theory

Whereas European migration research has investigated a very wide range of species of bird, in North America as a whole, the major resources have always been devoted to studying the movements of birds of economic importance, especially the waterfowl. A basic tool in these studies has been bird ringing, or banding. Although each recovery of a ringed bird relates only to the travels of an individual, in aggregate such recoveries may reveal the movements of whole populations; and in North America the scale of duck and goose ringing exceeds anything found elsewhere in the world.

It was an analysis of the recoveries from such a massive banding programme that led Frederick C. Lincoln to propound his "flyway" theory in 1950. North American wildfowl, he claimed, and possibly all New World migratory bird populations, adhered more or less faithfully to one or other of four great flyways, which he named Atlantic, Mississippi, Central and Pacific. There is no doubt that migrants do traverse these tracts of land and expanses of water, and that geography leads to certain areas being more heavily used than others, but the flyway concept is nowadays thought to have little biological significance. For example, ducks sharing a common breeding ground have been found to travel south by all four flyways. A more flexible concept is therefore required; possibly that there is more

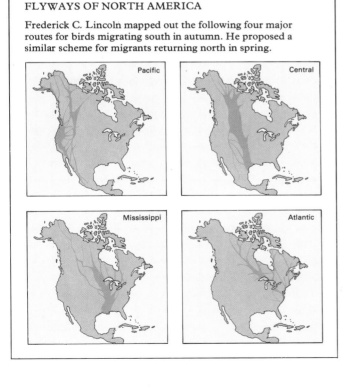

FLYWAYS OF NORTH AMERICA

Frederick C. Lincoln mapped out the following four major routes for birds migrating south in autumn. He proposed a similar scheme for migrants returning north in spring.

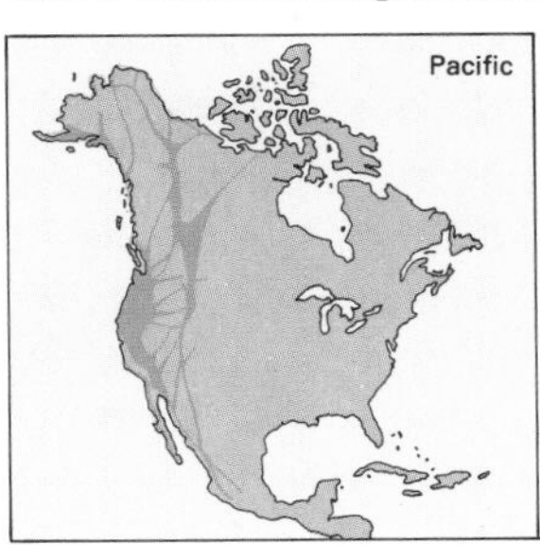

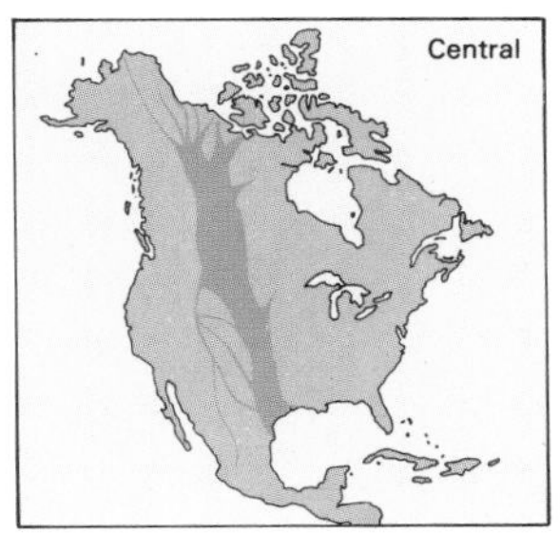

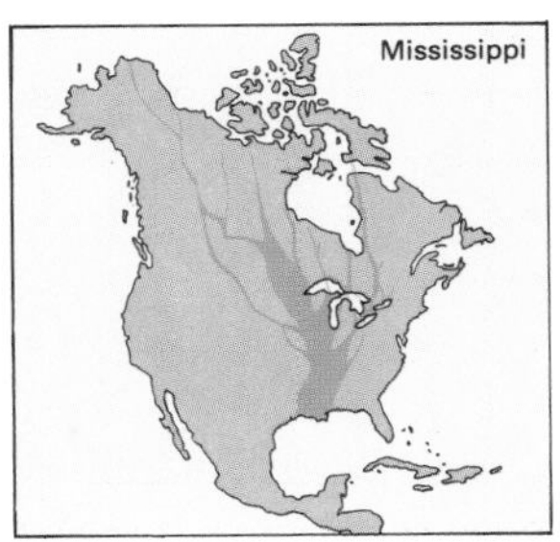

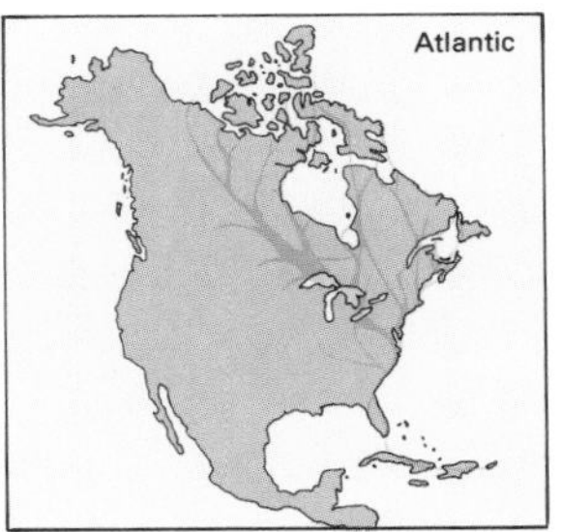

Binoculars are the birdwatcher's most valuable piece of equipment. However, "visible migration" consists not only of identifying the birds concerned – a procedure that itself requires recognition of the migrants' style of flight, their plumage and physical characteristics – but also noting in which direction the birds fly, the numbers involved, whether or not they are flying fast or slowly, in formation or singly or high or low above the ground as well as the date and time of day. By building up an accurate diary of observations over a long period of time it is possible to detect changes in migratory pattern with the seasons.

or less broad-front migration, as has been shown to be the case for so many European species, but that the configuration of land frequently tends to canalize the travellers. The broad expanse of Europe permits movement on parallel courses, but by comparison the narrowness of southern North America inevitably leads to a radiating outward of northbound migrants.

Geese from the far north

In the New World, as in the Old, goose migration has been the subject of much detailed study, and once again populations of these birds move between clearly defined, and sometimes very restricted, summer and winter homes. Here, indeed, one may think in terms of routes or flyways. For example, Ross's goose, *Anser rossii*, the smallest and rarest of the North American geese, as a breeding bird is confined to the Perry River district on the central arctic coast of Canada. The first stage of its autumn migration is across the barren lands to the Great Slave and Athabasca lakes, thence south almost to the northern boundary of Montana. Here they turn southwestward to cross the Rockies, then on to their wintering grounds in the Sacramento and San Joaquin valleys of California.

Blue geese, *Anser caerulescens caerulescens*, very close relatives of the snow goose immortalized by Paul Gallico, breed primarily in the Baffin and Southampton Island region of arctic Canada. In autumn they follow a narrow route southward to their winter home in the coastal marshes of Louisiana and Texas, but for their return route in spring they take a different flight path. This route, though equally narrow, is more westerly. Blue geese thus perform a "loop migration".

On one memorable occasion in October 1952 an unusual combination of circumstances cast a spotlight on the nature of their southward journey. Each autumn blue geese, prior to the start of their long journey, assemble in James Bay, the southward extension of Hudson Bay. At dusk on 16 October a very large flock of blue geese was seen leaving from the mouth of the Kesagami River, at the southernmost point of James Bay. Apart from the numbers involved, this observation was not particularly remarkable, but the following day airline pilots reported large flocks of geese just north of Lake Huron, flying southward at a height of 1800 to 2400 metres (6000 to 8000 feet). Indeed, one of the planes concerned was slightly damaged in a mid-air collision with a goose, and as a precautionary measure all pilots were alerted to be on their guard against migrating geese. The next day, 18 October, large flocks of blue geese were reported over southern Illinois, heading south at an altitude of about 900 metres (3000 feet): presumably these were the same birds that had been encountered over the Lake Huron area. One final observation com-

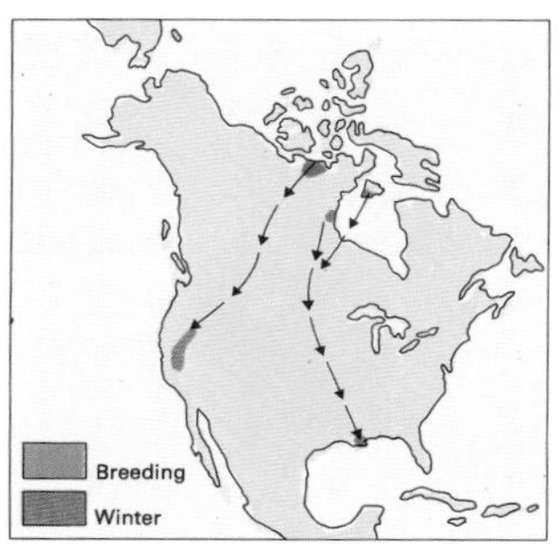

Ross's goose, *Anser rosii*, migrates south in autumn along two separate flyways.

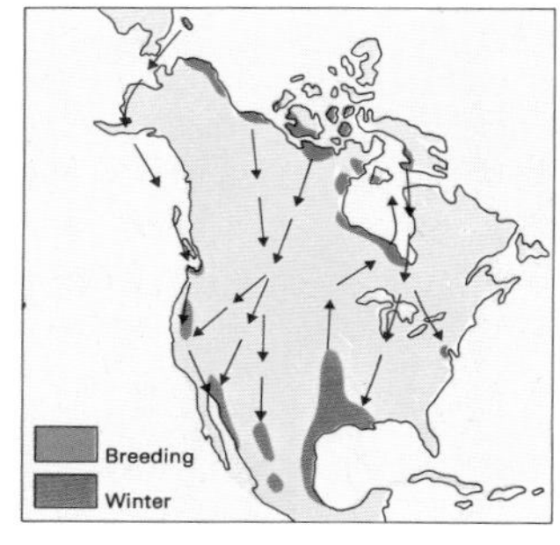

The blue goose, *Anser caerulescens caerulescens*, in the east performs a loop migration.

WATERFOWL AND WADERS OF THE FAR NORTH

pleted the story, for on the morning of 19 October large flocks of blue geese arrived in Vermilion on the Louisiana coast. If the same flocks of geese were involved in all four sightings, a not improbable assumption, then in the sixty hours that had elapsed from take-off to touchdown, the geese had covered about 2700 kilometres (1680 miles) at an average speed of almost forty-eight kilometres (30 miles) an hour.

Journeys of the waders – the golden plover

It is among birds that breed in the far north, especially in the waders, that one finds the truly long-distance migrants of the New World. For example, some sanderling, *Calidris alba*, breeding in the tundra of northern Alaska, range southward to southern Argentina, although others may be found wintering as far north as Vancouver and New York. Another, the American, or lesser, golden plover, *Pluvialis dominica dominica*, which breeds commonly on much of the tundra, has evolved a remarkable loop migration more than 20,000 kilometres (12,500 miles) in length.

As long ago as 1915 an American biologist, W. W. Cook, showed that in autumn the golden plover withdraws southeastward to the coasts of Labrador and then heads southward out over the Atlantic to the Lesser Antilles or even non-stop to the northern coast of South America, the latter representing a flight stage of about 3800 kilometres (2300 miles). From there they journey south across Brazil and Uruguay to winter on the pampas lands of Argentina. In striking contrast, the return journey is accomplished mainly overland, first to Central America and the Gulf, crossing to the coasts of Louisiana and Texas, and then up the Mississippi route to the far north. Later, it was established that the young birds avoid the long and hazardous Atlantic journey south by taking an inland route that is more or less the reverse of the spring flyway followed by adults. What is so extraordinary about the migration performance of this species, therefore, is that it changes with the age of the bird. This means that each young bird must inherit not merely the tendency and ability to follow one route on its first migration but also to switch to a quite different one in all subsequent years.

The golden plover, *Pluvialis dominica dominica*, arrives at its northerly breeding grounds in May. Here it remains for about three months, departing for South America well before the onset of winter. In so doing, the plover enjoys the summers of both Northern and Southern Hemispheres each year. (Only the loop migration of those golden plovers breeding on the Canadian tundra is shown.)

Those golden plovers that breed in coastal Alaska (and also in eastern parts of Siberia) belong to a different race, and they winter in the South Pacific, including New Zealand, Australia and Southeast Asia. To do so they carry out a vast transoceanic flight, and have been recorded on most of the Pacific islands. The weight of migrant golden plovers handled for ringing on Wake Island in the northwest Pacific showed that they were carrying sufficient fat reserves for a 6500-kilometre (4000-mile) journey. Those passing northward through Wake Island in April were still carrying sufficient reserves of fat to fly non-stop to the Aleutian islands or to Kamchatka in Russia. Clearly these fat reserves are of crucial importance; either the plovers must navigate with pinpoint accuracy between the island stepping stones, or else they must carry an extra safety margin of energy which will offer them a reasonable chance of making a landfall somewhere.

In recent years it has been established that two species of wader which breed in northeastern Canada, the ruddy turnstone, *Arenaria interpres*, and the knot, *Calidris canutus*, frequently cross the Atlantic to winter in the Old World. From rather further west a number of arctic and

sub-arctic wader species appear to leave their breeding grounds in a similar southeasterly direction before turning south on reaching the eastern seaboard. Among the species moving in this way are the Hudsonian whimbrel, *Numenius phaeopus hudsonicus*, the greater and lesser yellowlegs, *Tringa melanoleuca* and *T. flavipes*, the short-billed dowitcher, or grey snipe, *Limnodromus griseus*, and the pectoral sandpiper, *Calidris melanotos*. It is an interesting fact that these central and westerly distributed waders, rather than those that breed commonly on the much nearer east coast of North America, are the ones that most frequently occur as vagrants in Europe. Presumably they overshoot the coast on the southeasterly leg of their flight, perhaps in bad weather, and on finding themselves out over the Atlantic, continue eastward.

The remarkable feats of the warblers

Any assessment of migratory performance is inescapably linked with the size of the bird concerned. For a given journey, the smaller the bird, the more incredible its achievements appear. Of the small American migrants, the wood warblers form the largest component, with fifty-seven species. Largely insectivorous, they must pull out before the onset of the winter cold, and most of them travel to the intertropical region. Among those that remain in northern regions is the myrtle, or yellow-rumped, warbler, *Dendroica coronata*, an inhabitant of the coniferous belt that may be found wintering as far north as Maine, though most commonly in the southern USA, Mexico and Central America. Like the blackcap of Europe, *Sylvia atricapilla*, it is able to winter so far north because it supplements its winter insect diet with berries and, if necessary, even seeds.

Even more northerly in its breeding distribution is the blackpoll warbler, *Dendroica striata*, which breeds right to the northern edge of the tree-line in Canada. Since it winters in north–central South America, it has one of the longest migratory journeys of all the warblers, and for this reason has been called "the arctic tern of the warbler tribe". Its northward journey in spring has been studied in some detail. It begins late, the Gulf states being crossed about the third week in April, and spreads north and northwest at a rate of some fifty to sixty kilometres (30 to 40 miles) a day. By mid-May it has reached the Great Lakes, while those travelling on towards Alaska accelerate to a rate of some 320 kilometres (200 miles) a day, the northernmost ones reaching Alaska by the end of the month.

The blackpoll warbler study

The southward journey of this species, or, rather, of some part of the population, is the subject of one of the classical migration studies of the twentieth century. Like some of the waders mentioned earlier, blackpoll warblers set off southeastward in autumn and assemble a little inland from the coast, in Massachusetts. Most of them arrive behind air masses associated with cold fronts, and at body weights of ten to thirteen grams (0.35 to 0.45 ounce). After this first stage of their journey they rest and feed, gaining weight slowly, until after ten to twenty days they weigh sixteen to nineteen grams (0.55 to 0.65 ounce). A slowing down in the rate of fat deposition follows, then there is a very rapid weight gain, up to twenty to twenty-three grams (0.7 to 0.8 ounce), or roughly double their arrival weight. Then, on the first cool, dry evening, they leave. But to where? As in the unravelling of the blue goose migration, luck was to play a part.

In the special study area, blackpoll warblers were caught and weighed, and by 30 September really large numbers were present. However, from 1 to 3 October the numbers of birds caught fell by a half, indicating that a big departure had taken place. On the night of 1 October a nearby radar station recorded a heavy departure of migrating birds on a track some ten degrees east of south, or away from the coast and out over the Atlantic. Most of the birds were flying at a height of between 600 and 1250 metres (2000 and 4000 feet), and their average speed, aided by a light tail wind, was about forty kilometres (25 miles) an hour.

At this point the element of luck entered. Some 1200 kilometres (750 miles) to the south, research workers stationed on the island of Bermuda were attempting to catch what blackpoll warblers they could. At three o'clock on the morning of 3 October a sudden shower of rain brought some fifty warblers tumbling out of the sky, a number of which were caught and weighed. They could not have left New England on 30 September for that would have meant that they had been flying for fifty-six hours, far too long a time for the distance involved. Conversely, had they set out on 2 October they could not have reached Bermuda in a mere eight hours. But a departure on the evening of 1 October and an air speed of about forty kilometres (25 miles) an hour neatly fitted the distance covered. The Bermuda birds were still fairly heavy, averaging over sixteen grams (0.55 ounce), and since the average departure weight for the species was known, it was possible to calculate the weight loss for the journey accomplished.

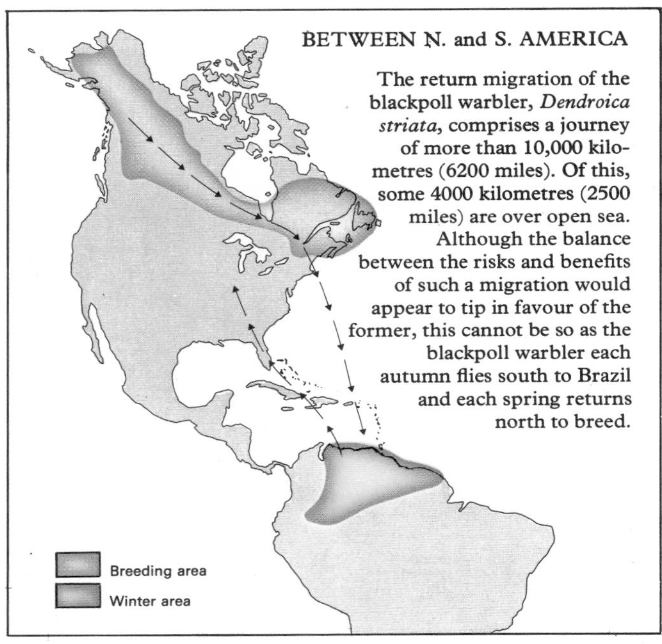

BETWEEN N. and S. AMERICA

The return migration of the blackpoll warbler, *Dendroica striata*, comprises a journey of more than 10,000 kilometres (6200 miles). Of this, some 4000 kilometres (2500 miles) are over open sea. Although the balance between the risks and benefits of such a migration would appear to tip in favour of the former, this cannot be so as the blackpoll warbler each autumn flies south to Brazil and each spring returns north to breed.

birds with the to-and-fro migration cycles of song birds. Firstly, most song birds, during the breeding season, hold and defend a territory from which they derive much of their food, and the territory system tends to bring about a roughly even distribution of the species in suitable countryside. Seabirds, however, cluster together to breed, and may defend only tiny, body-sized perimeters round their nests. In some cases this gregariousness is dictated by the shortage of suitable nesting terrain, but numbers may also give added security when it comes to driving off potential enemies. Food is less important so long as there is enough to support the colony, and is shared. Nevertheless, a large colony must make inroads into the total supply of food available, and there may be seasonal changes in the numbers and distribution of prey species. Thus, once breeding is over, it is obviously advantageous for the concentration of birds to break up and scatter widely in search of food. The movements may have a general trend, but sometimes it is a wide dispersal, like a film of oil spreading out across the surface of water.

The second point of comparison relates to age of maturity. Birds of short-lived species must necessarily start to breed at the earliest opportunity, often when they are not yet a year old. Such is the case with most small song birds. Seabirds, in contrast, tend to be long-lived. A life-span of ten years is for them probably commonplace; it is speculated that some of the large albatrosses may have a potential life-span of half a century. Such long-lived birds usually have much to learn about where and how to catch food before they are in a position to produce offspring. As a result they usually have a period of adolescence or deferred maturity. Few attempt to breed until they are two years old, and the delay may be very much longer. For example, most northern fulmars, *Fulmarus glacialis*, are about seven years old before they approach parenthood. Even then, the approach is unhurried, their first year in the colony being in the nature of a dress rehearsal.

Having become full-winged and totally independent of its parents, there is no reason for a young seabird to stay near to the colony. It is, in a sense, much freer than its parents, for they will have to be back in the colony not so many months later to start the cycle all over again. The young bird may not need to return to the colony for several years. During that time, if it is of pelagic habits – that is, a deep-sea feeder – it may roam over immense areas of ocean and never set foot on land. Once they have bred, the adults, too, disperse, but although some may travel far, it is possible that many rarely leave the waters covering the continental shelf.

Roving albatrosses

Although a few species inhabit the northern Pacific, albatrosses are predominantly birds of the Southern Hemisphere. With their long, narrow wings and economic gliding flight they are supremely well adapted to the world of the wide oceans. Long-lived, the young take many months to reach fledging age; in the large royal and wandering albatrosses, *Diomedea epomophora* and *D. exulans*, the fledging period lasts almost twelve months and the parents can thus breed only once every

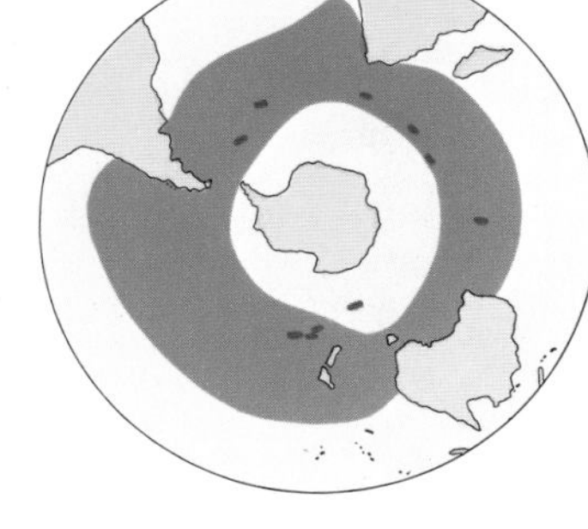

The wandering albatross, *Diomedea exulans*, with a wingspan of more than three metres (10 ft), is the largest of all seabirds. It feeds on squid, krill and occasionally fish, but will also eat floating refuse, following ships for days on end in the hope of picking up scraps. From this habit it has become known as the "seaman's companion".

Breeding sites
Range of albatross

two years. The period of adolescence is also very long, and during these early years the young travel immense distances. South of the great land masses, in the Roaring Forties, there is the possibility that some individuals circumnavigate the globe one or more times before eventually coming ashore to join a breeding colony on some remote island. There are also such records as those of the black-browed albatross, *D. melanophris*, a vagrant bird normally restricted to the Southern Hemisphere, one of which spent several summers in a colony of gannets on the Faeroe Islands, and another, which first appeared in 1967, is still associating with Scottish gannets.

That young albatrosses spend many years at sea was of prime importance in one of the saddest conflicts between man and birds. The US airforce, needing to build and operate airfields on some of the Pacific islands such as Midway, sometimes chose for their runways locations which were on the traditional nesting grounds of albatrosses. There was also the serious risk of collisions between aircraft and the birds. Attempts to solve the problem by shooting the nesting birds were destined to failure because they overlooked the existence of the rising generations still at sea. Even if one were to wipe out the entire breeding population on an island, for several years after new young birds would continue to arrive each breeding season. On Midway, at least, a policy of peaceful coexistence was accepted – "gooney birds", as they are locally called, are now treated with respect and even with affection.

Travels of shearwaters and petrels

Related to the northern fulmar and to the albatrosses are the shearwaters. These share the habit of gliding low over the water, their long, narrow wings stiffly

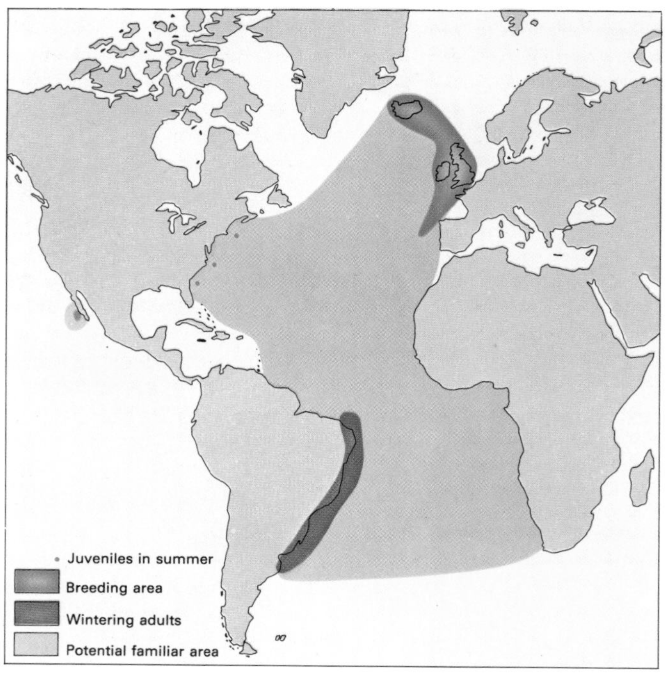

Compared to the adults, juvenile Manx shearwaters, *Puffinus puffinus*, spend more time exploring. In the Atlantic, while adults breed in western Europe juveniles often roam along the coast of North America.

The annual migration of the short-tailed shearwater, *Puffinus tenuirostris*, covers some 32,000 kilometres (20,000 miles). Leaving its breeding ground on islands north of Tasmania in early spring, it spends the next seven months on the wing searching for food. The figure-of-eight route the shearwater adopts seems both to maximize its chances of finding food as this becomes seasonally abundant in the Pacific and, since the bird can ride the prevailing winds, minimize the effort required in so doing.

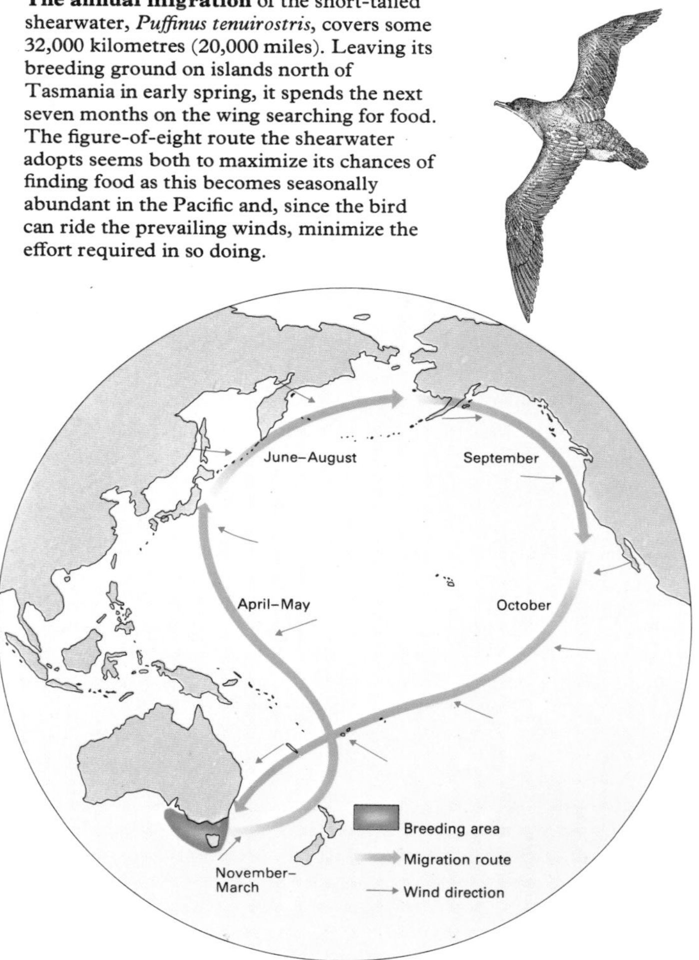

extended. Shearwaters normally come ashore only under the cover of darkness and nest in burrows, where they and their eggs and young are secure from predation by the large gulls.

One of the most intensively studied members of the family is the Manx shearwater, *Puffinus puffinus*, a major population of which breeds on islands off the west coasts of Britain and Ireland. The incubation period for these birds is very long – about fifty-one days – and is shared by both sexes. Each parent sits on the eggs for several days at a time, and the off-duty bird may, during this period, range hundreds of kilometres at sea in search of food. Just before the end of August the parents desert their young – one per brood – and head off to sea, most of them spending at least part of the winter off the east coast of South America. Meanwhile the youngsters, after waiting expectantly at the entrance to the burrow for food which never arrives, eventually make their way to the sea and set off in the tracks of their parents.

The fledglings must spend very little time indeed practising flying skills, for one young Manx shearwater was found dead on the coast of Brazil only seventeen days after it had been ringed at the entrance of its nursery burrow in far away Wales. As the straight line distance between the place of ringing and the place of recovery was about 7200 kilometres (4500 miles), even if the youngster went to sea on the day that it was ringed it must have covered the journey at an average rate of 400 kilometres (250 miles) a day. Bearing in mind that it would also need to feed as well as travel, it is clear from the speed of the journey that little if any time can have been lost through navigational errors.

As for the travels of the parent Manx shearwaters, at present there is still uncertainty about how long they remain off the coasts of South America, and about where they subsequently journey. However, round about the southern midsummer most of the population leave their temporary "winter" home. They may then travel further out to sea or migrate further north, but, whichever option they choose, they return to their European breeding haunts several months later.

There are other species of shearwater with travels even more remarkable than those of the Manx. Great shearwaters, *Puffinus gravis*, nest on the Falkland Islands and on lonely Tristan da Cunha and Gough Island, and at the end of the breeding season they head northward up the western Atlantic. By June they have reached the Grand Banks off Newfoundland, after which they turn east, wending their way past Greenland. They radiate out in the North Atlantic, but the drift is steadily eastward, and by August they are skirting the western promontories of Scotland and Ireland. They then turn south on the long return stage to their home waters. In the course of their non-breeding season they thus perform a grand tour of both the South and the North Atlantic, a journey of some 25,000 kilometres (15,500 miles).

The short-tailed, or slender-billed, shearwater, *P. tenuirostris*, performs a similar feat in the Pacific, but the distances involved are even greater. The species breeds in vast numbers on the islands in the Bass Strait between Australia and Tasmania, where it is known as the "mutton bird". After breeding, it heads eastward towards New Zealand, then north to Japan, on past Kamchatka and into the Bering Sea, before heading southward down the eastern Pacific, and finally southwest on the run home.

Considerably smaller than the shearwaters are the storm petrels, the Mother Carey's chickens of the mariners. No bigger than a European blackbird, though with longer wings, they, too, nest in burrows on rocky islands. There are many species, but two may be taken as representative. The storm petrel of Europe, *Hydrobates pelagicus*, mainly breeds in Iceland, the Faeroes, Brittany, the Canary Islands and some Mediterranean islands, though the largest numbers are perhaps to be found in Britain and Ireland. Between September and November the birds from the northeast Atlantic head south, their journey taking them past the west coast of Africa and far down into the South Atlantic, where they winter at sea. Occasionally a storm petrel ringed in Britain has been washed up dead on an African beach.

Our other representative petrel is Wilson's storm petrel, *Oceanites oceanicus*, a breeding bird of the subantarctic islands, and reputedly one of the most abundant seabirds in the world. In the southern winter it pushes northward, visiting most parts of the Indian Ocean and the Atlantic as far as latitude 50° North. Only in the Pacific does it fail to reach the equator.

Terns, and the blue riband of migration

Albatrosses, petrels and shearwaters each have a strong claim to be regarded as the greatest of travellers. Yet another family of birds – the terns – produces an even stronger claimant. Terns are an offshoot of the gulls and are fairly small, delicately structured creatures with long, narrow wings and long, forked tails that have earned them the name of sea swallows. Their flight is buoyant and graceful and they feed by plunging into the sea for small fish. The various tern species that breed along the coasts of Europe, and sometimes inland, move down the coasts of Africa for the winter, particularly to the Guinea coast. Some sandwich, or Cabot's, terns, *Sterna sandvicensis*, move further south, however, to Angola and on to South Africa, even rounding the Cape of Good Hope. But the blue riband is held by the arctic tern, *Sterna paradisea*, which, as its name implies, is a northerly species.

The breeding distribution of the arctic tern is truly circumpolar, and in Greenland it has been recorded nesting within a few hundred kilometres of the North Pole. Yet it winters in the South Atlantic, even to the very edge of the Antarctic pack ice. An individual ringed in Wales was recovered in New South Wales, representing a minimum journey of 20,000 kilometres (12,400 miles) in the first six months of its life. Even as late as June arctic terns may be seen heading due north up the middle of the Atlantic, while in autumn some of those terns nesting in the northeastern USA cross the Atlantic to western Europe before heading south. No other species spans the globe in this way.

Skuas – migrant hunters of the seas

Although there are no truly sea-going birds of prey, their nearest equivalents are the skuas, some of which are known in North America as jaegers or, literally, hunters. Part of their livelihood comes from scavenging, both on land and at sea, but the term hunter refers to their habit of chasing other species – mainly terns and small gulls –

Pattering over the water as they search for small food particles just beneath the surface, Wilson's petrels, *Oceanites oceanicus*, spend most of their lives at sea. They breed on rocky shores and islands, nesting in crevices and burrows. Although their world population is several millions, Wilson's petrels are rarely seen in large numbers, being distributed widely over the Atlantic, Indian and southern Pacific oceans. Their square-ended tail is a distinguishing feature among petrels.

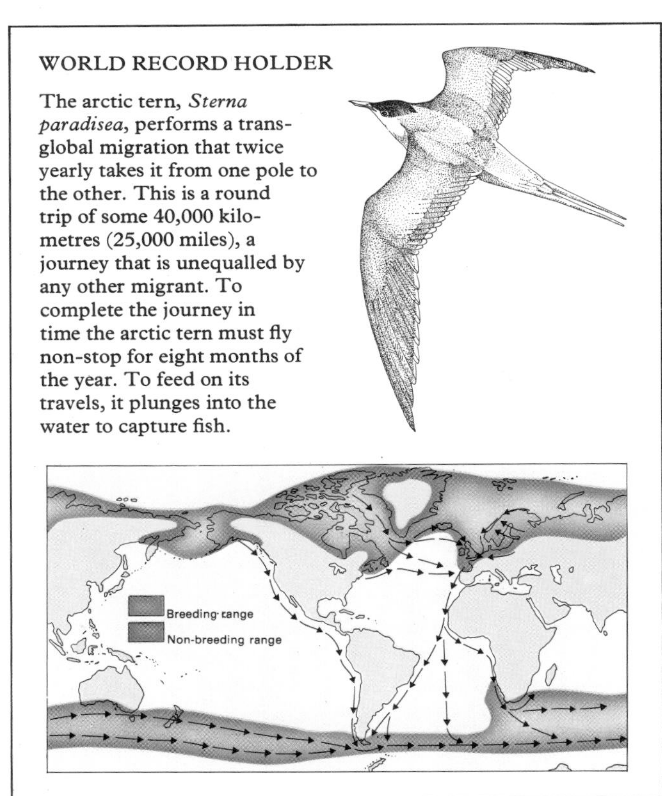

WORLD RECORD HOLDER

The arctic tern, *Sterna paradisea*, performs a transglobal migration that twice yearly takes it from one pole to the other. This is a round trip of some 40,000 kilometres (25,000 miles), a journey that is unequalled by any other migrant. To complete the journey in time the arctic tern must fly non-stop for eight months of the year. To feed on its travels, it plunges into the water to capture fish.

and forcing them to drop or disgorge the food which they have laboriously collected.

All skuas are fine, agile fliers and during a spring crossing of the Atlantic even in mid-ocean one may well see three different species – the pomarine, long-tailed and arctic, *Stercorarius pomarinus*, *S. longicaudus* and *S. parasiticus*, pressing on to their breeding grounds in the far north. During the northern winter they move steadily south, presumably partly dependent on food extorted from other birds wintering at sea. At the limit of their travels some species may pass south of the great land masses.

In some ways the most interesting member of the family is the great skua, *Catharacta skua*, a thick-set and particularly powerful bird, which is capable of killing large gulls. In the Northern Hemisphere as a breeding species it is confined to Iceland, Bear Island, the Faeroe Islands and Britain, but in the Southern Hemisphere it commonly breeds on the Antarctic peninsula and on a number of sub-antarctic islands such as South Georgia, South Orkney and the Falkland Islands. How did such a curious polar distribution come about? There is much support for the theory that the species became extinct in the north and that the present population there represents recolonization. For example, for years it had been assumed that the two populations never met, for although the northern birds are known to reach the equator, it was believed that the southern birds rarely reach as far north as the Tropic of Capricorn. Imagine, therefore, the interest when, in May 1967, two ringed great skuas were recovered in the Caribbean, well within the Northern Hemisphere. One had been marked in the Shetland Islands of Scotland, the other in the South Shetlands of Antarctica. Moreover, at the time of recovery the southern bird was at a latitude north of the northern individual. This dramatic proof that the two populations meet and mingle at sea is not evidence that colonization of the north is still continuing, and there would be physiological difficulties for any bird which changed hemisphere. Nevertheless, it suggests that the species still retains something of that degree of wanderlust that would be needed if the hypothesis of recolonization were true.

Migrations of the offshore feeders

Not all birds migrate by flight, a major exception occurring in a family of seabirds which includes the little auk, puffins, razorbills and guillemots. These have their strongholds in the northern waters of the Atlantic and Pacific, the most northerly breeding populations of some species extending beyond the 80th parallel. They feed mainly on fish, which they catch under water, descending on occasion to depths approaching sixty metres (200 feet), and their progress when hunting has been described as sub-aqueous flight. They use their wings for propulsion, the typical flying beat of half-extended wings driving them through the water.

Now a wing cannot be ideally adapted to both aerial and sub-aquatic flight. Movement through air calls for a wing with enough surface area to give lift, but large wings are an encumbrance beneath the surface. The wings of members of this family are relatively small, and although the birds can fly quite fast over short distances, for longer journeys they can move more economically by swimming on or under the sea. In consequence, their migrations are relatively modest, the journeys of most species extending less than 1800 kilometres (1100 miles).

Little auks, or dovkies, *Plautus alle*, travel down from out of the high arctic to winter in the open waters of the Atlantic, south to about 60° North in the east, but to the latitude of Newfoundland in the west. It is surprising that these small birds should winter far out to sea. The larger guillemots, or murres, and the razorbill, *Alca torda*, for example, mainly keep within 300 kilometres (185 miles) of the coasts, travelling south as far as the Mediterranean in the eastern Atlantic, and in North America south to about Massachusetts in the east and California in the west.

The three species of puffins seem to disperse widely over the ocean in winter. There is evidence from ringing of the travels of two of them. Atlantic puffins, *Fratercula arctica*, from British colonies visit the coasts of Greenland and Newfoundland, where there are breeding colonies of the species, while in the North Pacific, tufted puffins, *Lunda cirrhata*, have been recaptured as far south as about 40° North.

The migration of both little auks and puffins seems, for the most part, to involve small daily movements on the water rather than long periods of sustained flight. And why not, for the swimming bird is ideally placed to exploit the food resources it meets on its travels? This is borne out by the penguins, birds which have sacrificed flight for underwater efficiency and which are totally dependent on food from the sea.

Penguins are confined to the Southern Hemisphere. Most of them, when they leave their breeding rookeries, disperse over neighbouring seas, and they may travel considerable distances just by swimming. In the southern winter, gentoo penguins, *Pygoscelis papua*, have been seen moving on the high seas some 1000 kilometres (620 miles) from the nearest breeding place, and emperor penguins, *Aptenodytes forsteri*, breeding in the Bay of Whales in the Ross sea, were found to have in their stomachs distinctive pebbles, the nearest source of which was some 550 kilometres (340 miles) from the rookery.

SEABIRD BREEDING COLONIES

Puffins, shags, auks, cormorants and razorbills, most of which are migrants of the Northern Hemisphere, nest at different levels on cliffs. Penguins, on the other hand, nest on the ground mostly on the Antarctic wastes, with the smaller species nesting in burrows or among rocks.

Stimulus for migration

To even an only casual observer of birds, in the Northern Hemisphere the correlation between the arrival of migrants from the south and the advent of milder spring weather is obvious to appreciate, but not so the corresponding situation in the autumn. The adults of some species of bird, such as the European swift and cuckoo, *Apus apus* and *Cuculus canorus*, start to head south again in July, as soon as their short breeding season is over, and by the end of August all are gone. Yet the temperatures are still high, and there is no reason to suppose a shortage of food at this time. These are extreme cases in that the birds depart particularly early, but the fact is that in autumn, except perhaps in the very far north, most migrants depart long before falling temperatures oblige them to do so. Why? What is it about the bland late-summer landscape that triggers off the return south?

The first real insight into what happens came in the 1930s, in Edmonton, Alberta, when William Rowan, a scientist interested in the physiology of birds, captured large numbers of slate-coloured, or northern, juncos, *Junco hyemalis*, at a time when they should have been heading south. He placed his captives in two large aviaries, one of which experienced the normal weather conditions of Alberta at that time of year – shortening days and falling temperatures. The second aviary, although also exposed to the local temperatures, was equipped with powerful electric lights, which could be switched on at dusk or before dawn to give the birds a constant, or even an increasing, day length. Rowan then compared the behaviour of the two groups.

Now one of the most elegant economies of the physiology of birds is that their sexual organs – testes and ovaries – do not remain a constant size throughout the year. After all, they are needed for only a short breeding season, after which they dwindle away to a fraction of their former size and remain dormant until the approach of this season the following year. Rowan found that when the gonads – the sexual organs – were at maximum and at minimum size, namely during the breeding season and the midwinter season respectively, the birds showed little disposition to migrate, but while the gonads were diminishing or increasing, the birds exhibited migratory restlessness. He also found that if he used electric lights to subject his experimental birds to an increasing day length, he was able to bring them back into breeding conditions at a time when the birds in the control aviary, experiencing reducing day lengths, were interested in migration. In other words it looked as though shortening day length controlled the gonad cycle, with which was linked the migration cycle.

Subsequent research has shown that this was only a partial explanation, and it left too many important questions unanswered. Critics wanted to know how it was that a castrated bird was still stimulated to migrate. They also pointed out that a northern bird wintering on the equator experiences a day length which alters hardly at all from month to month. What tells it when to return? Even more confusing is the case of the northern migrant which reaches the Southern Hemisphere in October, for there the day length will be increasing. According to Rowan's findings it should quickly settle down to breed.

After much further research we now know that birds' bodies observe innate annual rhythms in which hormones regulate their behaviour throughout the year. One could liken the system to a regulator which controls a domestic boiler, switching processes on and off at predetermined times, though in the case of the birds the clock controls an annual, rather than a daily, cycle, and is itself corrected or regulated by external factors such as changing day length.

Fuel for flight

Once attention had been focused on the body of the bird and the physiology of migration, new discoveries followed. For example, it was appreciated that a bird needs reserves of energy appropriate to the flight stage it is to undertake. Before it embarks on a long uninterrupted flight, therefore, it must eat far in excess of its daily requirements, the extra food being turned into fat. Many species have been found to increase their body weights in this way by up to thirty per cent and research has shown that increases of up to 100 per cent occur in some species. While the bird is in sustained flight these reserves are converted into energy, and it has been calculated that in a small song bird the rate of consumption is about 0.8 per cent of the mean body weight per hour of flight.

The implications of these figures are awe-inspiring. Known departure weights indicate that many migrants set off with sufficient fuel reserves for a minimum non-stop flight of thirty hours, and that those species which

AN INTERNAL CLOCK

In a long-term experiment in which a hand-reared migratory garden warbler, *Sylvia borin*, was subjected to an environment of constant daylength, the bird continued to show those changes associated with migration at the normal times of the year, namely spring and autumn. This showed that an internal clock is the prime motivator of migration.

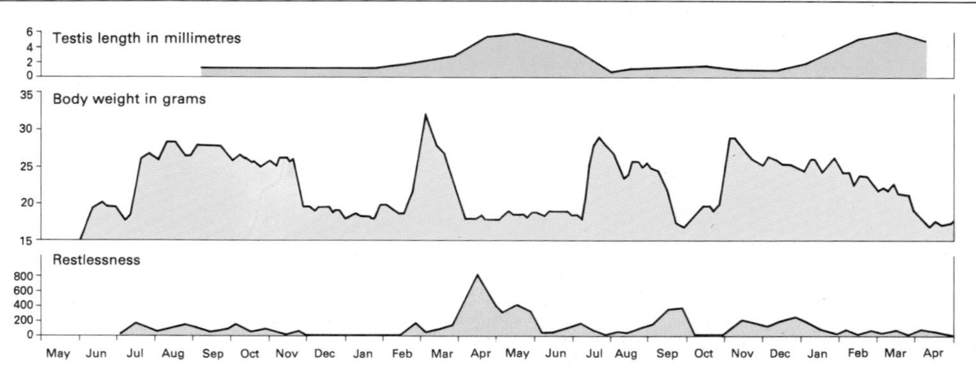

Large migratory birds, such as gulls, gannets, ducks and geese, can be followed in flight by light aircraft at distances of only a few hundred metres. These snow and blue geese were tracked as they flew low over the ground across the tundra of northern Canada.

double their body weight before departure may be capable of sustained flight for over 100 hours. Only by having such reserves can the inhospitable oceans and deserts be crossed as a matter of routine. It is worth remembering that every European bird which winters in tropical, central or southern Africa must twice-yearly face a crossing of the Sahara. This is a journey rarely less than 1500 kilometres (950 miles) and the flight is made non-stop because although a weary flyer might pause for rest, in the absence of feeding opportunities it would still be drawing upon its precious reserves of energy; not to reach its destination could be fatal.

Navigation by birds

Until as recently as thirty or forty years ago, by which time the reality of bird migration was no longer seriously in dispute, many people supposed that seasonally migrating birds found their way by a gradual process of familiarization rather than by astronomical navigation. The behaviour of homing pigeons – birds that man has used to carry messages for at least 2000 years – had much to do with this belief. These birds are more accurately rock doves, *Columba livia*, a species which, in all but the Saharan part of its distribution, shows no seasonal migration. It was therefore argued that they did not have need for the navigational gifts required by species migrating half-way across the world. Pigeons were taught their trade, being taken from their lofts and allowed to fly over progressively longer distances over ground which was partly familiar.

The hypothesis of familiarization was certainly economic in that it called for no special sensibilities on the part of birds. Indeed, the idea gained support because one could actually see birds using landmarks, as when they flew along broad river valleys. Even as late as the 1930s and 1940s experienced migration investigators were admitting to what one of them, Donald R. Griffin, called "a troubling thought". Perhaps the birds did not possess any ability for astronomical navigation at all. His response to these doubts was to learn to fly a light aircraft, and to attempt to follow birds in the air. For this exercise he required large, conspicuous birds which could be watched from a distance, and he needed some advance knowledge of where they were trying to go. Two species which met his requirements were herring gulls, *Larus argentatus*, and gannets, *Sula bassana*. He took his study birds from breeding colonies, transported them over various distances before release, then attempted to follow them. Of four gannets that eventually succeeded in homing he wrote, "The flight paths suggest

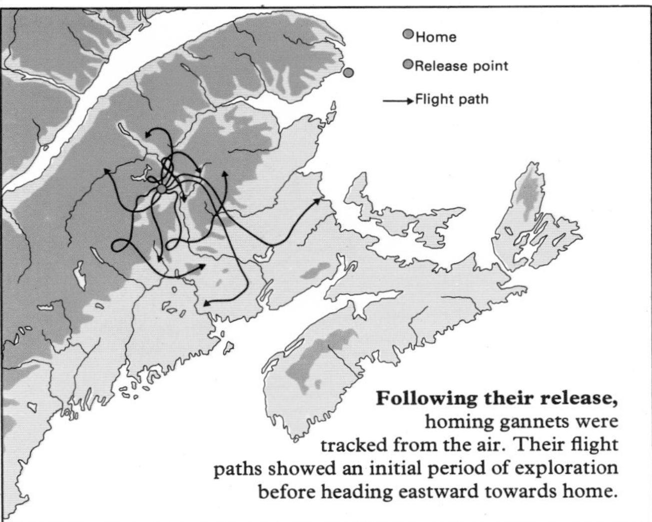

Following their release, homing gannets were tracked from the air. Their flight paths showed an initial period of exploration before heading eastward towards home.

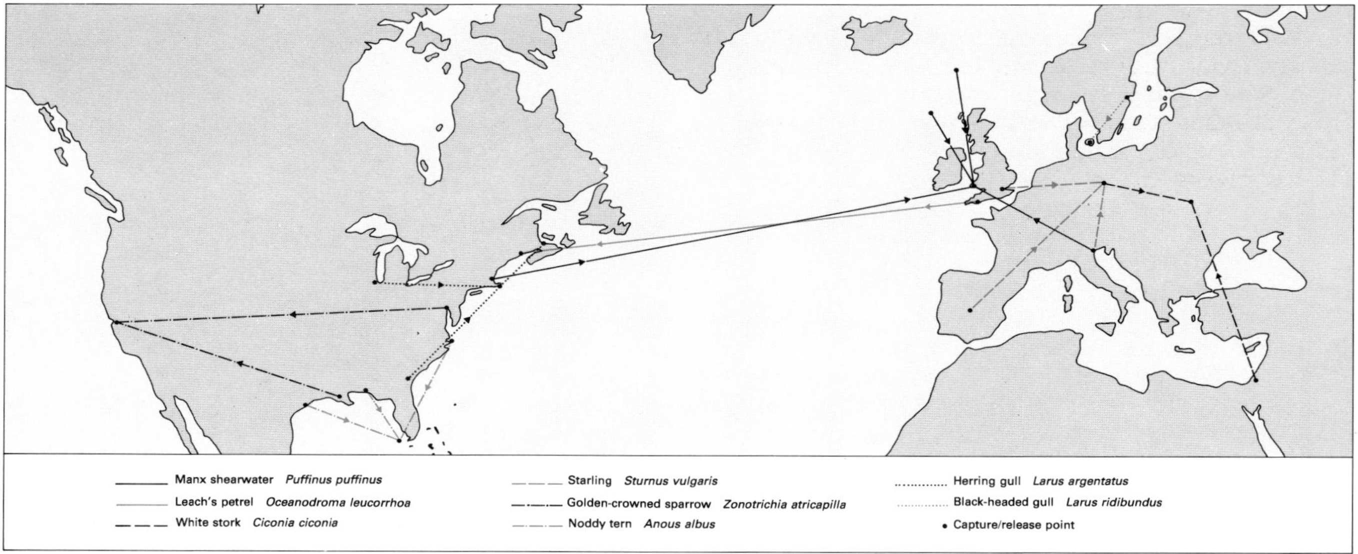

Homing experiments using ringed wild birds did much to confirm the reality of bird navigation. Although most of the birds released were never recaptured, some achieved remarkable journeys of which those outlined above are the most notable. The lines do not reflect flight paths both on account of the birds' initial exploration and because the birds were often blown off course by winds.

Homing pigeons, which are simply domestic pigeons kept for their ability to return home from a distant point, are believed to rely primarily on their sun compass to find their way home. First, however, they have to determine the compass direction of home by navigation and how they do this is still a point for debate among migration workers. The homing ability of pigeons has been exploited by man for thousands of years, using the birds both to carry messages and to race for sport. Here a message capsule is being attached to a pigeon's leg prior to its release.

no tendency to choose the correct direction . . . the behaviour . . . was consistent with the hypothesis of spiral exploration."

Griffin's work was invaluable, for it produced some firm facts about bird behaviour. Nevertheless, other facts were accumulating which did indicate the true extent of the navigational ability on the part of birds. Some of them were of a general nature. For example, as the details of seabird travels began to be known, it seemed unlikely that they could navigate solely on the basis of landmarks such as islands and differences in water temperature, colour or salinity. Then there was the undeniable fact that much migration takes place at night, and on inky black nights as well as on moonlit ones. In such conditions birds might be able to see the ground beneath them but could surely not see a distant range of mountains as a signpost on their way. Even more challenging was the case of the European cuckoo, a species in which the adults set off for Africa one or two months in advance of their offspring. Even if the adults knew the way from past experience, this could certainly not be true of the young birds travelling alone and for the first time. An inbuilt preferred direction was apparent.

Returning to the same place each year

More concrete information about the performances of individual birds was gleaned from the results of recoveries of ringed birds. For example, ringed arctic terns, *Sterna paradisea,* were found in the same breeding colony in several successive summers, having travelled during intervening winters far down into the South Atlantic, and one particular Methuselah of a swallow returned for fifteen years to the same homestead, and often to the same nest. No one doubted that long-lived individuals continue to improve their migration performance, and that recognition of localities is a part of that improvement, but since the average life expectancy of most small migrants is of the order of a year or two, only a tiny minority would survive long enough to become wise, seasoned travellers. Experience must therefore be gained quickly. Evidence from ringing of migrants returning to the precise summer home soon became commonplace. What was more remarkable were the ringing recoveries in Europe, Africa and the Americas of migrants returning in successive winters to the same, localized haunts. For such birds, it is not enough to reach Africa safely, or even the right country in Africa; they must go on to the right district and the right village. It was most likely that the birds deliberately found their way.

Evidence of birds' ability to navigate

It was an Englishman, G. V. T. Matthews, who was instrumental in proving the reality of bird navigation. From working first with homing pigeons, he went on to study wild species, including Manx shearwaters, *Puffinus puffinus*, and mallard ducks, *Anas platyrhynchos*. The former, when removed from the breeding burrows, showed remarkable homing ability, two of them having become legendary. One was released in Boston and the other in Venice, both areas where the species are rarely encountered. They returned home successfully at rates of 392 and 426 kilometres (245 and 265 miles) a day, respectively. In each case, some of the journey may have been over totally unfamiliar ocean, while the speed of the journeys allows absolutely no time for random search. In short, they displayed navigational skill of an extremely high order.

Matthews subsequently introduced various sophistications to his experiments. In particular, he took pains to release his birds in landscapes which were as featureless as possible, and to keep them in sight for as long as possible. He observed birds circling in order to pick up their bearings and then setting off in the right direction. With mallards he even released the birds at night, and by attaching small torches to their legs he was able to establish that their departures were highly directional.

One of the really significant contributions to our understanding of the respective roles of instinct and learning in bird navigation was made by a Dutchman, A. C. Perdeck. It had long been known as a result of ringing that the starlings, *Sturnus vulgaris*, which arrive in the Netherlands each October originate in countries at the eastern end of the Baltic. It was also evident that, after a brief halt in the Netherlands, many of them cross the North Sea to winter in the British Isles, while some continue to northern France. Perdeck captured and ringed 11,000 of the starlings and had them flown to various towns in Switzerland before release. In this transportation experiment he was simulating what might happen if strong gales were to blow migrating flocks far off-course into what was, at least for the immature birds, unfamiliar territory.

Now starlings migrate in flocks of anything from ten to a few hundred birds, each flock being formed of some adult – and therefore experienced – migrators and some immature birds making the journey for the first time. Perdeck upset the natural order of things by releasing the adults and the immature birds separately. The young, with no experienced adults to guide them, resumed their journey on a course parallel to their original flight path and ended up in the south of France and in Iberia. The adults, on the other hand, were shown by ringing recoveries to have reorientated, and mainly spent the winter in northern France, some actually reaching England. Perdeck thus demonstrated that young starlings do indeed inherit the tendency to orientate in a given direction and the ability to determine that direction, but that experience teaches them how to navigate accurately to a particular area.

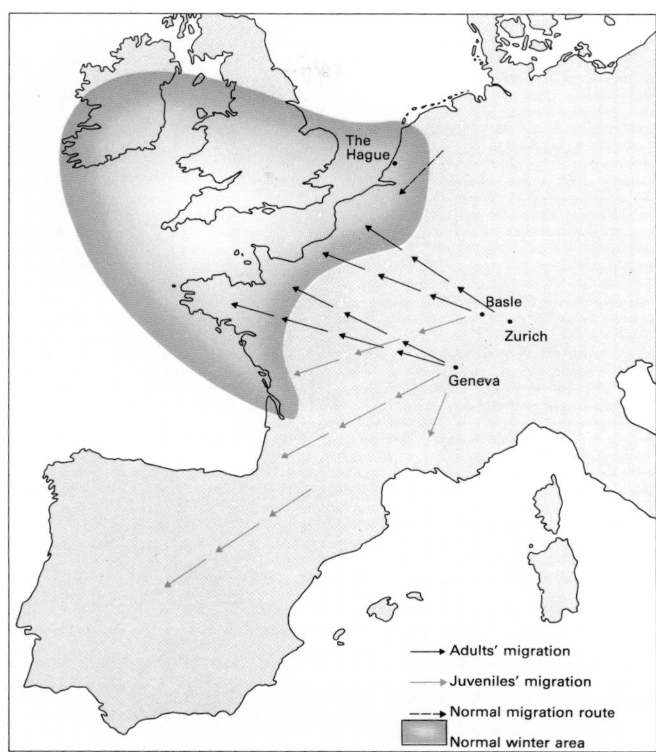

Perdeck's experiment, involving the displacement of starlings, showed that rather than inheriting an ability to home, birds acquire this through experience. Starlings migrating southwestward in autumn over the Hague were displaced to either Zurich, Geneva or Basle, distances of about 600 kilometres (375 miles). On release, the juveniles continued to fly southwestward, taking them far from the starlings' normal winter area. The adults, however, being able to home, reorientated and took a northerly direction to the wintering area in northern France and southern England and Ireland.

This transportation experiment had an interesting ending. The following spring, a number of the young birds returned successfully to the countries of their birth. This was somewhat predictable, for they were travelling to a known area. But this was not the finish, for the following winter further ringing recoveries indicated that the birds returned to the winter homes which they had been artificially induced to adopt.

How do birds navigate?

It was one thing to prove that birds have instinctive orientation ability, but an altogether more difficult problem to understand how it functions. Since birds are obviously characterized by exceptionally good eyesight, attention was first concentrated on the possibility that they use celestial cues such as the sun, moon and stars to guide them.

It was a German ornithologist, Gustav Kramer, who made the first important breakthrough by showing that if one cages a migratory bird – in this case a starling – even though it eventually adjusts itself to a life of captivity, it nevertheless becomes restive at those periods of the year when it should be migrating. What Kramer noticed was that its restlessness was directed rather than random. Thus in spring, when it should have been heading, say, northwest, most of its restless behaviour was concentrated in the northwestern sector of the cage.

How was the starling determining direction? A screen placed round the cage so that the bird could see only the sky made no difference to its ability to orientate, so it was not using landmarks. Nor did the presence of large electromagnets impair its ability to determine direction. If the bird was using the sun to determine direction, Kramer argued, at any one time it must have been calculating an angle from the position of the sun. To prove this Kramer constructed a special cage in which the bird could see the sun only through a series of mirrors, and in which he was able to alter the position of the sun as seen by the bird by altering the angle of the mirrors. As he had anticipated, the bird moved to a position which bore the same angular relationship to the image of the sun in the mirror as its former position had borne to the true bearing of the sun. The implications of these studies were far-reaching, for of course the position of the sun is constantly changing relative to any fixed point on the earth's surface. Since the starling was orientating correctly at different times of the day it was obviously making allowance for the sun's movement with the passage of time. This in turn implied that the bird had an accurate sense of the passage of time, something which has been called an internal clock. Experiments have shown the existence of this clock in many species.

With clear evidence that birds were able to determine direction from the sun, attention was turned to how this information was used. It is of limited value to be able to orientate correctly unless one knows the position of one's intended destination relative to one's present position. In other words, a bird needs map sense. An English researcher postulated that a migrating bird might adopt the following rule: If the sun is higher in the sky than seems correct for one's estimated position, fly away from the sun, but if it is too low in the sky fly towards it. Such a system would prove successful over medium distances, but it would considerably increase the flying time necessary for the bird to reach its destination, and it has been shown by ringing experiments that birds complete their journeys in times faster than would be possible using this procedure. Another explanation, put forward by Matthews, suggested that birds could determine both their latitude and longitude from observations of the sun, but this required an ability on their part to visualize, from only a glance at the sun, its noon position. However, the available evidence does not support this theory.

Meanwhile, there was the fact that many birds migrate by night, when there is no sun. Work concentrated on the possibility of navigation by reference to the star patterns. This proved easier to investigate than had sun navigation, for the special cages containing the study species could be placed in a planetarium, where the orientation of the artificial night sky overhead could be manipulated at will. Working with warblers, Franz Sauer, a German ornithologist, found that if he rotated the night sky by, say, thirty degrees, the birds adjusted their bearings by the same amount. Even birds hatched in an incubator and never allowed to see the real night sky were apparently able to determine direction from the star pattern overhead. However, when an American migration investigator, S. T. Emlen, placed hand-raised indigo buntings, *Passerina cyanea*, under a planetarium night sky he found no orientational response. But as a part of his study, Emlen exposed some birds during the summer to a night sky which rotated about a fictitious axis in which a star in the constellation Orion replaced the Pole Star. These birds, when in the autumn exposed to the planetarium sky, showed clear directional tendencies which were correct in relation to the fictitious

SUN ORIENTATION

By placing starlings in an experimental aviary in which he could alter, by means of mirrors, the position of the sun as seen by the birds, Gustav Kramer showed that birds use a sun compass to determine in which direction to fly on their migrations. The starlings maintained the same angle to the sun whether receiving its rays directly (1) or reflected by the mirrors (2). When the sky was obscured by dense clouds or by covering the windows of the aviary with translucent paper, the birds were disorientated. Similarly, in nature birds wander at random when the sun is obscured and regain their orientation when the sun reappears.

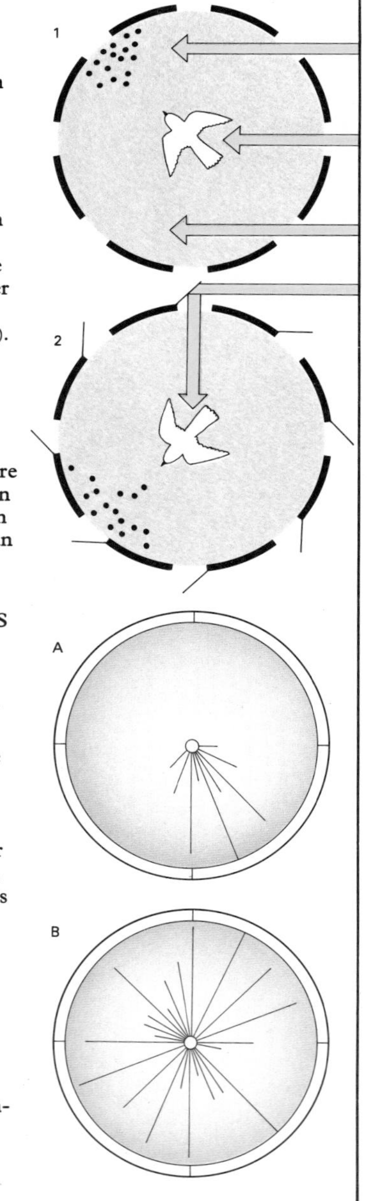

SAUER'S EXPERIMENTS

Birds' inherent ability to navigate by the stars was supposedly demonstrated by Franz Sauer in his experiment in which warblers were exposed to the night sky in a planetarium. If exposed to the star pattern normally prevailing at the time of their southerly autumn migration, the proportion of the warblers "headings" (the direction and length of time of which are indicated by the lines in the diagrams; right) was greatest in this direction (A). When exposed to a diffuse illumination the birds' headings were random (B). However, Sauer's results cannot be repeated and few now believe that birds can find their way solely by the stars.

sky. The young birds, rather than having to inherit an inborn star map, were clearly able to detect the axis round which the heavens appear to rotate.

Although much has been learned in the last twenty-five years, there is still a great deal that we do not understand about navigation. It may be that in diurnal migrants sun orientation is of overwhelming importance, yet clearly the large numbers of species which travel through night and day must be able to use both sun and stars. The most recent discovery is that when a bird is transported a hundred or more kilometres to a release point, it can follow the twists and turns of its outward journey sufficiently well to fly back in the homeward direction. This is so even if the release site is unknown to the bird or indeed even if its vision is blocked by the fitting of frosted-glass contact lenses. Various navigational clues may well be used by the bird, and it is now known that one of them is the earth's magnetic field. It has been shown that homing pigeons and European robins can indeed detect the inclination in the earth's magnetic field. Even more remarkable, since it is poorly developed in birds, is experimental evidence from Italy of pigeons being able to use their sense of smell as an aid to navigation. Evidently birds use many different cues in navigation and we still do not fully understand the mechanisms by which their remarkable migrations are achieved.

Planetaria – enclosures in which star patterns are projected on to a dome to mimic the night sky – have been used to show that night migrants use celestial cues to navigate. By studying the direction and duration of a bird's headings in a planetarium, the precise cues can be identified. It appears that birds steer by the stars and on occasion by the moon and perhaps by detecting changes in infra-red radiation, which is intense at night.

KILLING MIGRANTS BY THE THOUSAND

While in the past man killed migrant birds for food out of necessity, today he kills them largely to provide delicacies and even to preserve cultural heritage. But the number of birds killed each year is astronomical. For example, in the Paralimni district of southeast Cyprus some 285,000 birds are killed each autumn in an area of only some ten square kilometres (4 sq. miles). And there is no reason to suppose that the scale of the massacre of birds is any less in the other main catching areas of the Old World – the Landes/Gironde region of southwest France, northwest Spain, western Portugal, the Po valley in Italy and, further afield, the Lebanon, Syria and the Nile valley. The fact that bird populations have been able to sustain the heavy hunting losses during the past few hundred years cannot be taken as proof that they can continue to do so, particularly since man's destruction of the birds' breeding sites is greater than ever.

A redstart caught on a lime stick

A daily catch for one man may run into hundreds of birds

The threat to seabirds from pollution is greater than that from either disease or predation. For example, each year more than six million tons of oil are lost or discharged into the sea from tankers, and as a result thousands of seabirds are killed.

The risks of migration

The fact that a particular species is migratory means that the risk to it of associated journeys is less than that of remaining in the same locality throughout the year. For swallows in Europe, for example, the risks of attempting to overwinter in, say, Britain, or even in Iberia, are greater than those of the long migration journey to southern Africa. Yet the hazards of migration are considerable.

We have seen that in long-distance migration birds may fly non-stop for periods varying from a single night to several days and nights. We have also seen that given good visibility, migrating birds can correct for lateral drift caused by light side winds, but that in fog or complete cloud cover they may become disorientated. To be blown off course when over land may not be serious, but where migration involves a journey over water, and particularly where the intended landfall is a small island, sideways drift of only a few tens of kilometres may lead to a premature death. Even those individuals that manage an ocean crossing to a "wrong" continent may be on a one-way journey. They may find it difficult to return to their native land, while in the country of their landfall it is highly improbable that they will find a mate and breed.

For most species even the most straightforward migration flight involves risks. A bird in its home territory learns how to exploit the area to maximum effect, but all these advantages are lost when it touches down, tired and hungry, in an unfamiliar habitat. A migrant will therefore strive, against all odds, to remain within its familiar area to the extent that not only do members of a species have traditional staging posts along a migration route but that the same individuals may use them in successive years. To have survived one round trip is both an indication to the bird of the suitability of the route taken and the best guarantee that it will survive another migration. Since many species migrate in flocks, novice migrants may to some extent benefit from the accumulated experience of the older birds.

Unfortunately, the use of staging posts or traditional resting areas too often leads to the birds' undoing. Over the centuries man has discovered the advantages of hunting where the birds concentrate. In such areas various forms of snare – net, trap and bird lime – are used to harvest the passing birds. The annual toll in Europe alone runs into millions. Similarly, a study carried out by an American ornithologist immediately after the Second World War revealed that in Japan as many as twelve million birds were being netted annually.

Nowadays in many countries pressure is being applied to outlaw such practices, yet we are now placing extra, non-hunting pressures on the birds. Every time we cut down a wood, build a new town or a housing development, construct a new airport runway or a motorway, we are reducing the space available for birds. In short, we are reducing the population at source, so that in many species there are fewer birds to start out on migration.

Accidental death

Most of us rely heavily on the availability of electricity. The main links from the power stations to our homes are cables carried high in the air on pylons. On dark nights migrating birds – mostly the smaller ones – often fly into the wires and are killed. Similarly, to convey television signals we build tall, aerial-bearing towers that are supported by guys that may extend half a kilometre from each tower. Migrating birds strike these in horrifying numbers. A US government publication reports over 10,000 birds were killed at one tower on just two consecutive nights.

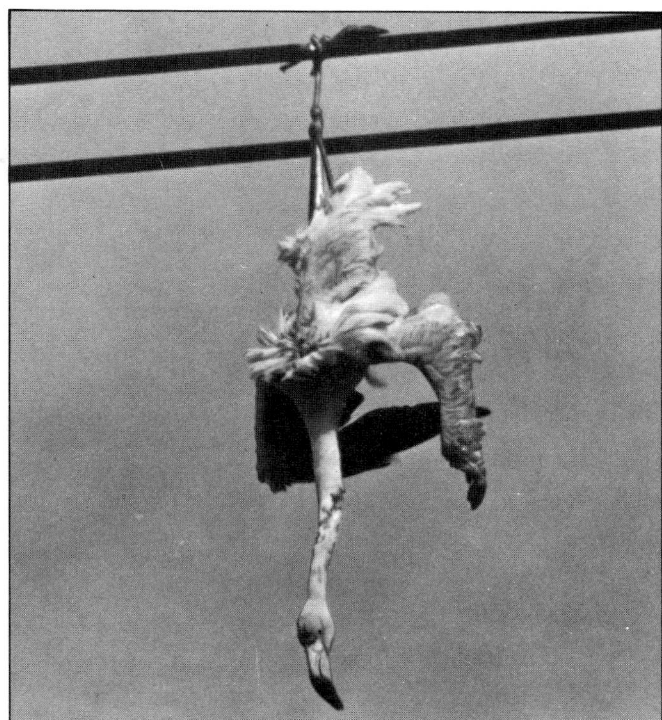

A flamingo killed on a power cable – in addition to the natural hazards migrants have to run the gauntlet of artificial obstacles.

Even lighthouses may be great killers of birds. On dark, overcast nights migrants may lose all contact with their environments, and be powerfully attracted by the beams of a lighthouse. Then, as they draw nearer, they become so dazzled that they crash into the structure and are killed. There are many reports of more than 500 migrants having met their death in this manner in a single night. A more recent and even more horrifying cause of death to migrating birds is when they fly into the gas flares on oil rigs. And oil itself is a killer, particularly of sea-birds; for example, oiled feathers make flight impossible.

One of the most frightening and widespread ways in which we have inadvertently destroyed untold numbers of birds is by the development and application of agricultural chemicals. Unfortunately, because so many bird species migrate, they can be protected effectively only if all countries co-operate to ban the use of chemicals of proved danger. Failure to do this has led to the depletion of many species of birds. Indeed, one cannot study migration without realizing the futility of attempting to protect or conserve birds solely at a national level. Without co-operation other bird species may be joining the dodo and the great auk.

Bats

Bats are flying mammals of the night. Fluttering round belfries or through caves or swooping low over the ground in pursuit of rodent prey, in their flight capabilities bats are rivalled only by birds and some insects and are surpassed by none. Their movements are thus relatively unhindered by rivers, mountains or even seas and oceans. Consequently, bats are frequently found in remote places that few terrestrial animals have reached unless aided by man. Yet despite their potential for wide dispersal, many bats seem very localized in their distribution. Whole populations may appear to be relatively static. For example, nobody has yet proved conclusively that there is an interchange of bats between Britain and the European continent, a flight of less than fifty kilometres (30 miles), which insects and birds make without difficulty. Such cross-channel flights almost certainly do take place, but probably not on a regular basis.

Mobility provided by the possession of wings offers bats the opportunity to travel widely to exploit different sources of food as they become seasonally available in different places. Equally, when food such as insects becomes scarce in the winter in temperate regions, bats have the same ability as migrant birds to go elsewhere. Yet many temperate-zone species forgo their considerable advantage and hibernate instead. The benefits of flight are abandoned in favour of physiological stress and insecurity; the most mobile of mammals opts for immobility, becoming totally vulnerable for many weeks. These bats do, at least, use their power of flight to seek out favourable hibernation sites in which to spend the winter, leading to the seasonal accumulation of large numbers (especially in caves), which disappear with the advent of warmer weather. Similarly, female bats seek a favourable place to bear and rear their young. Often huge numbers of bats gather at these nursery colonies, to disperse when the young can fly. Concentrations of bats will also be attracted to rich feeding areas or to convenient roosting sites in which to pass the daylight hours. Whether gregarious or solitary, all bats are likely to change their haunts periodically.

Most bats daily make short-distance migrations to feed. This long-tongued bat of South America, *Leptonycteris sanborni*, flies in search of plants in flower, from which it takes nectar or pollen.

Tracing the movements of bats

To discover, beyond question, precisely where bats go, when and how far they travel, and whether or not they return, a technique similar to bird banding is often employed. Bats are given an individual identity by attaching a small metal clip to their forearm. Tens of thousands of bats have been marked in this way, enabling a picture to be built up of the movements of not only single bats but also whole populations, based on the principle of capture-mark-release.

Direct observation of migration behaviour in bats is much more difficult than comparable studies with, say, birds. Bats are active under cover of darkness and it is almost impossible to follow by eye even short journeys made by the largest species of bats, let alone the small ones. Night-viewing equipment and radar tracking have proved helpful, but they do not shed much light on long-distance travel, seasonal migrations and homing abilities.

Radio tracking, which is used to study the movements of many other mammals, is now being exploited for the study of bat migration. With this technique, a small transmitter is attached to the bat, which is then released. Thereafter, at least until the transmitter's batteries run down, the animal can be located using a direction-finding radio receiver. But even the smallest transmitter weighs about 1.3 grams (0.05 ounce). Those bats big enough to carry such a burden without impediment are likely to fly beyond the transmitter's range – only a few hundred metres – in a very short time. Larger transmitters, with a range of several kilometres when carried high in the air, are suitable for the study of heavier and sturdier bats. Encouraging experiments have been performed on the relatively burly Central American leaf-nosed bat, *Phyllostomus hastatus*, and many of the larger fruit bats can be expected to carry long-lasting transmitters of over 100 grams (3.5 ounces) without unduly affecting their movements. The development of lighter and more powerful transmitters offers considerable scope for future bat migration research without the extensive use of banding, but it may never be possible to build transmitters small

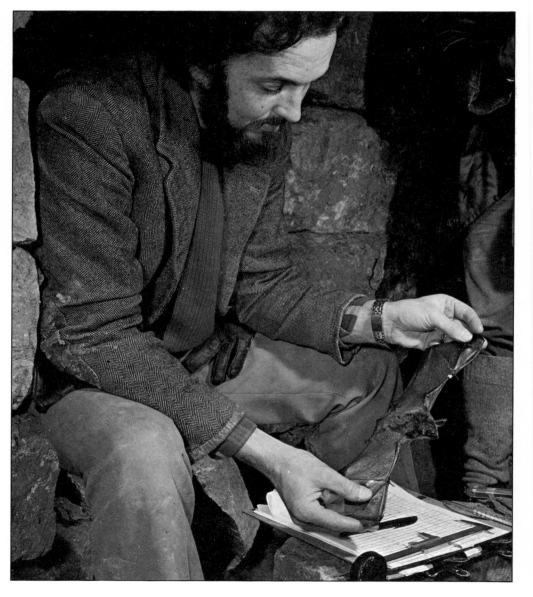

The metal clip used to mark bats is loosely referred to as a ring, but it is perhaps more accurately described by the American term band, since it is in fact C-shaped. While bird rings are attached to tough horny legs, bat bands rest on the soft wing tissue (a bat's legs and feet are too small for ringing), as can be seen on this banded greater horseshoe bat, *Rhinolophus ferrumequinum*, above. However, because bats can live twenty years or more – a long time to carry an uncomfortable object on a rapidly beating wing – and recovery rates are usually very low, with frequently less than one per cent of marked bats ever being seen again, casual banding is discouraged. When it is performed, migration workers at the same time weigh and measure the bats' wingspan and body length, right, to determine their age.

and yet powerful enough to use on the tiny bats which are most abundant in temperate latitudes.

Migrating to hibernation sites

Bats that hibernate in caves are particularly easy to study because large numbers congregate in one place in an inactive state. They can be easily handled and banded, and any that are found or caught the following summer will then indicate the animals' migrations to feeding and breeding sites. The following winter, by counting the number of marked bats in the cave, the proportion of the population that returns each year can be determined.

Using this approach, it has been shown that European bats make special journeys to and from winter hibernation sites, or hibernacula, but it seems unnecessary for them to travel far in order to find a suitable residence. In Britain, for example, few banded bats have been recovered more than eighty kilometres (50 miles) from their hibernaculum. Most probably they do not travel more than twenty kilometres (13 miles) between their winter and summer haunts. But elsewhere in the world much longer journeys may be needed; in the USA, Indiana bats, *Myotis sodalis*, banded during hibernation in the caves of Kentucky, in spring fly north 500 kilometres (310 miles) to Ohio, Indiana and Michigan to spend the summer, and in the USSR, tiny pipistrelles journey twice as far to find a suitable hibernaculum.

Certain species of bats are critically dependent on caves or mines to provide suitable conditions over winter. The greater horseshoe bat, *Rhinolophus ferrumequinum*, is a good example, and its population in many parts of Europe has declined drastically in the past twenty years largely as a result of disturbance and destruction of its subterranean haunts. In areas where caves are scarce, a single hibernaculum may be vitally important to a very large population of bats, some of whom have to migrate considerable distances to reach it. This is particularly so for the little brown bats, *Myotis lucifugus*, which hibernate in Mount Aeolus Cave in Vermont, New England, in the USA.

These little brown bats, and some other cave-hibernators that gather in large numbers in their winter quarters, migrate singly, or in small groups, during the summer. This clearly reflects seasonal needs. In winter, food is not required in quantity by a hibernator. What is needed at this time is a sheltered hibernaculum with a low, relatively constant temperature and fairly high humidity. A cave offers these and is usually spacious enough for the sheer numbers of bats not to be a problem. In summer the situation is different. The bats need insect food – a not unlimited resource – and thus disperse widely to avoid competition for it. Once out of hibernation, constancy of their immediate microclimate is no longer critical, so a wide variety of potential roosting sites, such as hollow trees, house roofs, old barns and cavity walls is available. But each of these sites can provide a home for only a small number of bats. Hence there is a seasonal pattern of migration between dispersed summer haunts and communal hibernaculum.

A number of cave hibernators, such as the greater horseshoe, the little brown bat and the similar-sized mouse-eared bat, *Myotis myotis*, of Europe, gather in clusters – at

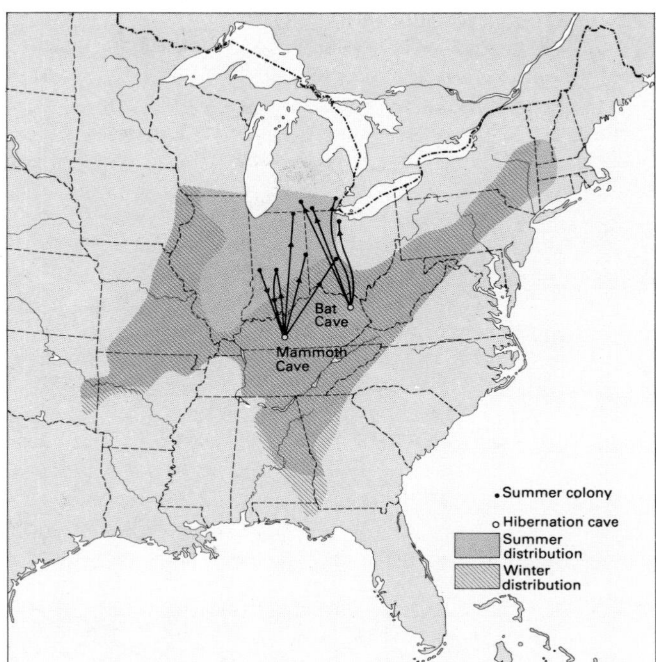

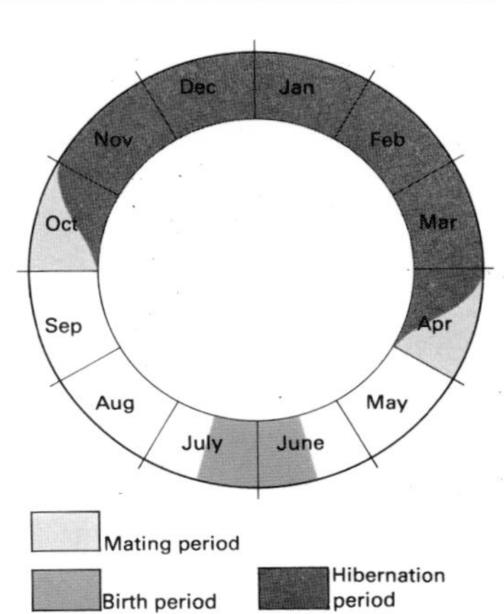

Indiana bats, *Myotis sodalis,* hibernate in limestone caves in the southeastern USA in aggregations of between 500 and 100,000 individuals. Banding experiments involving bats from Mammoth Cave and Bat Cave in Kentucky have shown that in the centre of their range Indiana bats migrate north in spring and return south in autumn. Like many bats that hibernate in winter, Indiana bats mate in their hibernation caves in late autumn, but development of the embryos is delayed until spring. Birth occurs in summer.

The distribution in Southwest England of the greater horseshoe bat, *Rhinolophus ferrumequinum,* is limited by the scarcity of caves, buildings and mines in which during summer and early autumn the females can give birth and rear their young, and during winter the bats can hibernate. This is borne out by banding experiments; the map, below, shows the direction and length of flight of banded bats migrating from around the town of Buckfastleigh in the centre of the study area and of those bats flying between other sites (solid lines and dashed lines respectively). It is evident that the seasonal migrations of the greater horseshoe form a complex pattern and are not limited to north–south journeys.

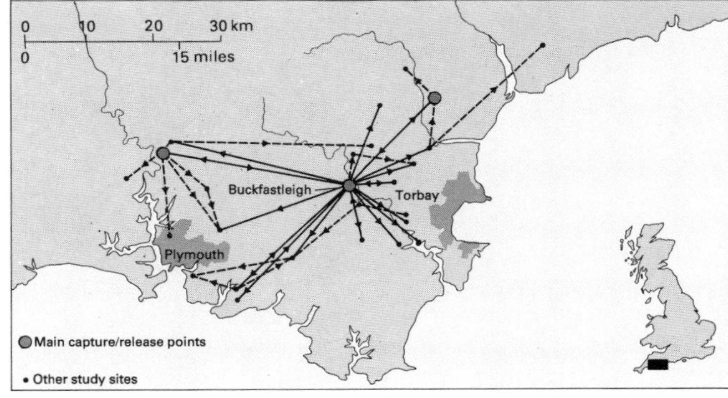

MIGRATIONS WITHIN HIBERNATION SITES

Bats such as greater horseshoes that migrate short distances within their hibernaculum to find suitable conditions, rather than moving to a location where the temperature range of the environment is the same as at the previous site, choose places of different, although specific, temperature ranges. This is shown in the graph, below. It is possible that at these locations the humidity level is the same and that the search for constancy of this factor is another stimulus for bats' midwinter migrations.

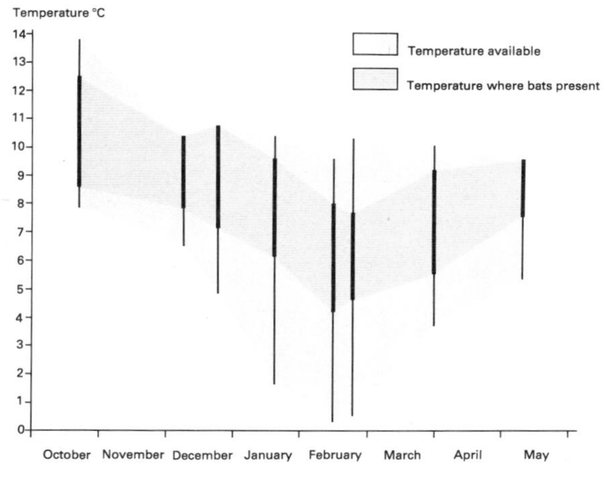

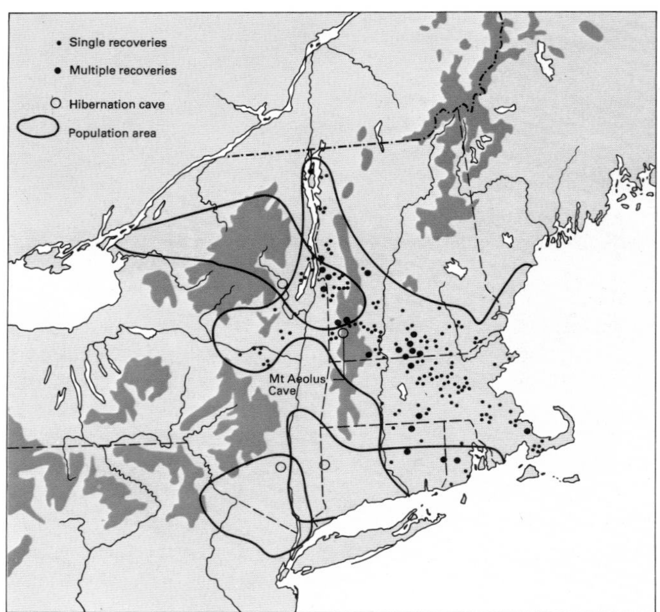

Little brown bats, *Myotis lucifugus*, in late autumn migrate from all over New England to one of four main hibernation caves. Most individuals that spend the summer in Massachusetts, New Hampshire and Vermont (see dots on map, above) hibernate in Mount Aeolus Cave. To reach this cave some little brown bats migrate from locations as far as 300 kilometres (185 miles) away. Despite the exertion of these long seasonal journeys for such small animals – little brown bats weigh no more than fourteen grams (0.5 ounce) – they do not, so to speak, wear themselves out, for individuals can live for up to twenty-five years.

Emerging from a cave are white-lined leaf-nosed bats, *Vampyrops helleri*, right. These are inhabitants of C. and S. America.

least they do in places where there are enough of them left – within their hibernacula. This behaviour may offer some advantages in maintaining a constant body temperature during hibernation. Other bats are more often solitary and tuck themselves away individually in cracks in the cave wall. In some cases each bat may return annually not just to the same cave, but to the same small cranny that it used the previous winter. After a year, and after perhaps several thousand kilometres flying about seeking food, the bat returns to precisely the same spot – in the dark!

Journeys during hibernation

It is popularly supposed that hibernators remain inactive all winter. In fact, many of them arouse intermittently and move about, resulting in short-distance migrations during the winter. Horseshoe bats, *Rhinolophus* spp., which often visit several different caves and mines during the rest of the year, may do so even during the hibernation period. These bats are highly sensitive to temperature changes during hibernation and winter journeys may result from the need to find a new cave with different air conditions as the weather changes. They also move about within the hibernaculum, choosing the optimum location. This applies particularly to male greater horseshoe bats, which tend to hibernate near cave entrances. Here, although colder conditions minimize metabolic activity and consumption of vital, energy-rich fat reserves, the more marked changes in temperature force the bats to move as the winter progresses.

Journeys to summer and breeding roosts

Some bats aggregate during the winter and disperse during the summer. Others do the reverse, migrating from their winter quarters to gather in summer in vast numbers at feeding sites and at nursery roosts, where the young will be born. These roosts may be close to, or far from, the bats' hibernacula. For example, in England, some of the greater horseshoe bats in Devon rear their young in the roof of an old barn that stands immediately outside the large cave that serves as their winter home. Bent-winged bats, *Miniopterus schreibersii*, in Australia, on the other hand, migrate more than 100 kilometres (60 miles) to the summer colony. Here they form nurseries of some 2000 females; the males form separate roosts nearby. Later in the year, the females and their offspring migrate from the roosts distances of up to 150 kilometres (90 miles). The young bats tend to fly further afield; juveniles are occasionally recovered 1000 or more kilometres (620 miles) away. The majority of the male bats do not appear to return to the communal hibernacula, instead wintering in solitary, as yet undiscovered, sites.

The American free-tailed, or guano, bat, *Tadarida brasiliensis*, provides perhaps the best example of a seasonal migrant which congregates to have its young. This bat, unlike horseshoe bats and *Myotis* spp., is adapted to fast, strong flight. It has a slim body and long, narrow wings and it is clearly suited to long-distance flying. These same adaptations, however, limit its manoeuvrability, so it often prefers large tunnels and lofty caves for breeding roosts. It may have to travel long distances to find just such a home. In fact, each summer many females of this species fly some 1500 kilometres

(930 miles) north from Mexico and gather in their millions in the caves of the southern USA.

Living in a fluttering mass of hundreds of thousands of individuals has one big advantage – warmth. The body heat of so many bats raises the air temperature of the roost, and this may be an important factor in keeping the naked young warm and enabling them to grow rapidly. But if warmth is the objective, why should the bats leave sunny Mexico in the first place? Perhaps the Mexican summer is too hot or, more likely, too dry, which would result in a diminished supply of food at the critical time. By migrating north to the humid southern USA, the bats are assured of food. Here, however, by congregating in such vast numbers – estimated at 20 million in Bracken Cave, Texas – the bats appear to risk eating themselves out of house and home, thus defeating the purpose of migrating north. But the situation is not so dire. Firstly, anyone who has ever been plagued by the whining hordes of gnats and mosquitoes that fill the warm summer air in that part of the world would doubt that any creature could ever take a significant toll of their numbers. Secondly, since the mother bats fly south in autumn as soon as the young are weaned, more food is available for the juveniles when they need it most for body growth: the young follow on later.

Curiously, not all guano bats follow the same routine. While many females migrate north to breed, a substantial part of the population remains in Mexico to have their young. Here, given a suitable climate and sufficient food,

SEPARATION OF THE SEXES

In the southern USA and Mexico most males and females of the two main populations (A and B) of guano bats, *Tadarida brasiliensis*, together perform seasonal migrations between summer roosts in the north and wintering sites in the south. During the birth period in summer, however, the sexes segregate, the females with their young living in caves in huge maternity colonies.

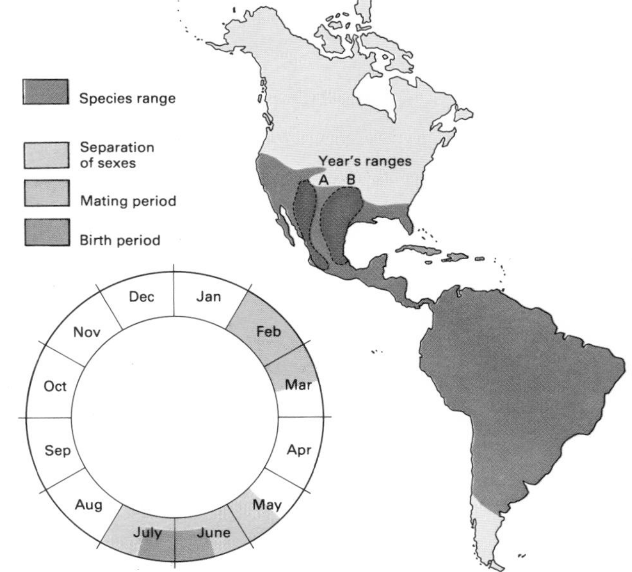

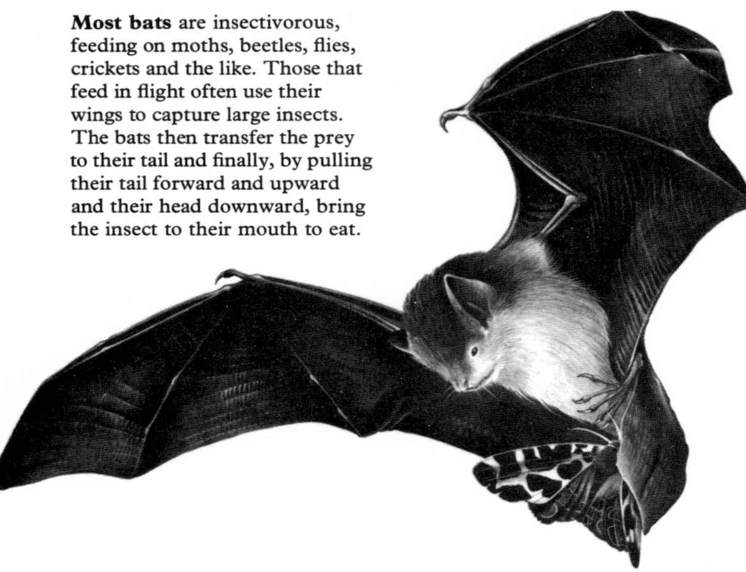

Most bats are insectivorous, feeding on moths, beetles, flies, crickets and the like. Those that feed in flight often use their wings to capture large insects. The bats then transfer the prey to their tail and finally, by pulling their tail forward and upward and their head downward, bring the insect to their mouth to eat.

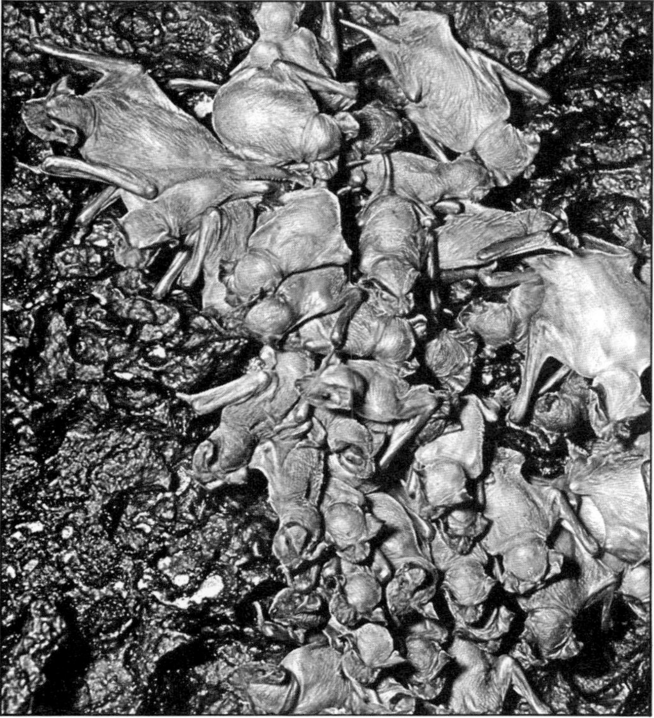

In nursery roosts in the caves of Texas and Arizona, female guano bats, *Tadarida brasiliensis*, may bear their young as late in the year as mid-July. Within only a few weeks of being born the offspring must be ready to migrate to the wintering grounds in Mexico. Their growth must accordingly be very rapid. But the baby bats are confronted with a bigger problem long before they have to embark on this journey. The mother bats leave their young hanging from the cave roof, and when the babies first try to fly they must succeed. There can be no practice sessions and no room for failure because these bats must fly fast and purposefully or not at all. If the young bat makes an error and falls to the cave floor, it will have difficulty in taking off again, and will be eagerly attacked by a host of predatory beetles living in hope of just such an accident. However, it has been shown that during their first two months of life only about one per cent of the individuals perish in this way.

the mothers and their offspring rarely migrate far from the nursery roosts; most of the male bats also remain in Mexico during the summer. When winter comes, the bats that flew north to Texas, Arizona and Oklahoma may fly south again, but some stay behind and hibernate instead. Perhaps these movements help to disperse the immense populations of guano bats, thus spreading their summer feeding pressures over as wide an area as possible. As a single colony might consume over a tonne of insects in a night, it would be disadvantageous for the whole population to be doing the same thing in the same place at the same time.

We have seen that with both guano bats in the southern USA and bent-winged bats in Australia the sexes are segregated at the time the young are born, the adult males often establishing separate summer roosts. This implies that further travelling is necessary in order to bring the sexes together for mating. This is often combined with the migration to a winter roost, where mating occurs either before hibernation or during brief periods of wakefulness in winter. This is a life-style that is common to many other species of bats that establish summer nursery roosts.

Just as some bats such as the greater horseshoes may move from one cave to another in response to a change in winter temperatures, so others, for example noctules, *Nyctalus noctula*, move between different roosts in summer. This is probably because their chosen home – a hollow tree, woodpecker hole or house roof – gets too hot. Such journeys are usually only local ones.

Fruit bats and feeding flights

Fruit bats – also known as flying foxes – comprise the sole family of the taxonomic order Megachiroptera; all other families of bats belong to the order Microchiroptera. All Megachiropterans are inhabitants of the Old World tropics and are characterized primarily by the possession of large eyes, which they use for navigation; unlike all other bats they lack the ability of echolocation. Feeding mainly on fruit and juices – some have a diet of only nectar and pollen – fruit bats also have in common a dentition specialized for crushing soft food.

Many species of fruit bats live in large colonies, or camps, in big trees, and migrate to specific traditional sites for the breeding season. The Australian flying fox, *Pteropus poliocephalus*, for example, in parts of Queensland and New South Wales, migrates in spring to congregate in nursery colonies numbering perhaps 50,000 individuals. These colonies contain both males, who establish territories in the form of sections of tree canopy or lengths of bough, and adult females, who are kept in harems. Apart from this aspect of social behaviour, the annual pilgrimage to such breeding sites is equivalent to the breeding migrations of species such as the bent-winged and guano bats.

When it comes to feeding, however, fruit bats face a problem different from that of insectivorous bats. Often the trees from which they feed are isolated and each produces fruit for only a limited period. As a food source becomes depleted, the bats must migrate to another tree, perhaps some distance away. Nevertheless, in the tropics constant warmth and sunlight ensure that something is in fruit, somewhere, throughout the year. Indeed, there is evidence that the timing of fruiting seasons in particular groups of tree species is sequential, so that fruit-eating animals such as the Megachiropterans can move from one species to the next as each crop of fruit is used up. This benefits the trees because the animals spread the seeds and often pollinate the flowers too. In fact, some tropical plants depend on fruit bats for pollination.

It is thus evident that some species of fruit bats show three patterns of movement; a seasonal return journey between the winter home and the summer breeding site; a more frequent change from one feeding site to another as a particular species of fruit becomes depleted locally; and a change, after only a few nights, from regular feeding at a single tree to feeding at another nearby tree of the same species. This may be an oversimplification of their behaviour, but fruit bats are certainly strong flyers and are easily able to make long journeys, or a great number of short migrations, to search for food. As to whether each species of fruit bat – there are about 130 – behaves in this way, there is as yet no clear evidence.

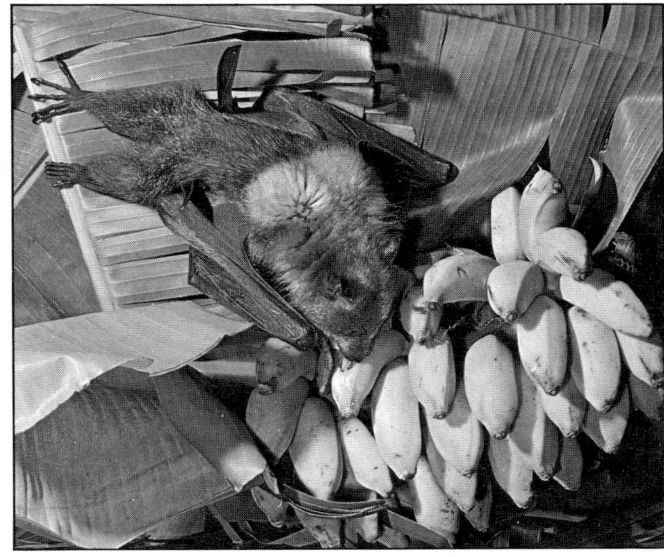

Fruit bats feed mainly on wild fruits and berries, but also eat soft, ripe figs, mangoes, guavas and other commercial fruits. Here a captive fruit bat is feeding on bananas.

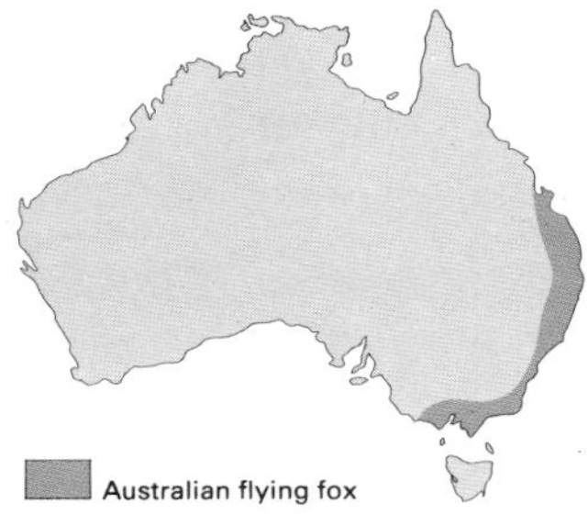

The migrations of the Australian flying fox, *Pteropus poliocephalus*, during summer comprise daily feeding flights up to twenty kilometres (12 miles) in length to and from roosting trees, and during winter, when food is less abundant, nomadic journeys of much greater distance in search of food and water.

During the day, Indian flying foxes, *Pteropus giganteus*, roost in hundreds or even thousands in trees alongside mangrove swamps and streams. At about sunset they migrate to fruiting trees to feed. Their diet comprises fruit juices and occasionally the pollen of flowers. Having eaten and digested their meal, early the following morning they return to their roosting sites. These flying foxes also appear to return to the same roosting trees each year.

ECHOLOCATION

Apart from Megachiropterans, the fruit bats, few bats rely heavily on eyesight for detecting obstacles. Instead they have evolved a system of emitting sound waves and picking up the echoes reflected from objects in their path, analogous to the way that radar sends out signals and detects the reflections from solid structures. The sounds are produced in the bat's larynx and are emitted through the mouth or nostrils. The echoes are detected by the bat's highly sensitive ears, which, via the auditory centres of the brain, can judge not only how far away an object lies but in some species can also differentiate between, say, caterpillars and the leaves on which they rest. Some bats can even detect minute insects in flight and it has been shown experimentally that they can echolocate thin wires less than a quarter of a millimetre (0.01 inch) in diameter.

Echolocation enables bats to fly without risk or hesitation, even in total darkness. They are therefore able to live in caves in the complete absence of light. Yet it is unlikely that echoes are audible and intelligible from objects very far away, severely limiting the potential of an echolocation system for orientation on long flights.

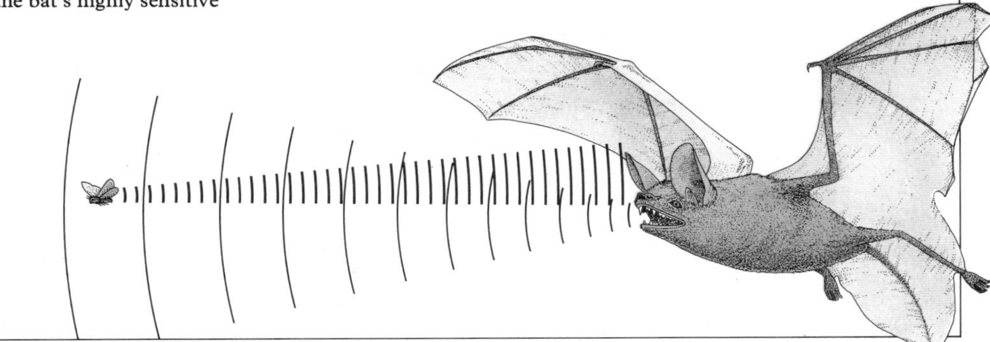

Using echolocation, bats are able to avoid bumping into each other (as seen, left) and into objects directly in their flight path, as anyone who has walked through a cave inhabited by bats can testify.

"Smooth-faced" bats, among them this long-tongued fruit bat, echolocate by emitting the sound waves through their mouth.

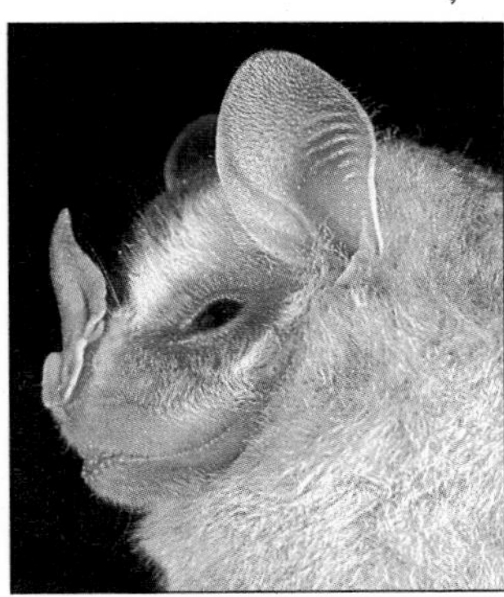

"Noseleaf" bats such as freetails emit sound waves through their nostrils – the noseleaf focuses the sound into a conical beam.

Navigation

Implicit in most of the observations of bat migration is the suggestion that bats know where they are going, or can at least find their way over long distances. They can indeed travel far, and their navigational abilities have been demonstrated through homing experiments. A number of marked bats taken from their home and released from points up to several hundred kilometres away have managed to return. Furthermore, many species are able to find their way back having been displaced laterally from their normal flight path by twenty kilometres (12 miles) or more, and some can return astonishingly fast; fifty kilometres (30 miles) in a single night is not unusual.

As expected, homing experiments generally show that fewer bats are able to navigate back to their release point the further away they are displaced. For example, in Trinidad, in an experiment involving the leaf-nosed bat *Phyllostomus hastatus*, individuals were released shortly after dusk from a number of points at varying distances from home. Of those bats released ten kilometres (6 miles) away, ninety-four per cent returned home that night, while of those bats released from the points thirty-four kilometres (21 miles) and fifty-three kilometres (33 miles) away, only fifty-seven and twenty-six per cent respectively returned home before first light. None of the bats returned that night from the release point sixty-four kilometres (40 miles) away, but during the following few days twelve per cent of these did manage to find their way back. Some may have reached home by chance, but there is considerable experimental evidence that bats possess genuine homing ability. In one study of the big brown bat, *Eptesicus fuscus*, in which three dozen individuals were released 400 kilometres (250 miles) from home, eighty-five per cent returned.

The question still remains: how do bats find their way, especially on seasonal migrations that cannot be performed often and take place in the dark? An obvious answer is that they rely on eyesight, but their system of navigation must be more sophisticated than that because some of the earliest systematic scientific experiments performed on bats – by the Italian physiologist Spallanzani in 1793 – showed that at least some of them can find their way home even when blinded. These early experiments have been confirmed many times since. However, blinding bats does seriously impair homing ability, so eyesight is certainly an important navigational aid. We might expect this for the fruit bats, which have extremely sensitive eyes, but all other bats have eyes which are neither large nor highly sensitive, although they are sufficiently adequate for the recognition of major landmarks. Studies on the Australian bent-winged bat certainly suggest that topographical features such as rivers and hills help the bats find their way to and from their nursery roosts.

It has been suggested that bats use the stars for direction finding. This is quite plausible since most bats travel by night. Moreover, it might explain how species of bats which do not normally undergo long migrations can still return home in the dark from 300 kilometres (185 miles) away when displaced experimentally.

There is also the possibility that Microchiropterans, at least, could use echolocation to guide them on long flights. We know that a bat can use echolocation to detect food and obstacles in its path, but can this be the basis of long-distance navigation? Imagine a bat setting out for its winter cave 100 kilometres (60 miles) away; it can use echolocation to avoid bumping into trees *en route*, but how can it recognize the route itself? We humans can remember a journey as sets of visual images, mental pictures that can be matched to what we actually see as we travel. But a bat depending upon echolocation is like a very short-sighted person; it can only perceive and recognize objects that are within echoing distance, namely no further away than 100 metres (330 feet) or so. Can a bat really perform such a journey based solely upon memory of echo patterns of objects encountered as it flies along?

Whether a bat uses eyesight, echolocation or, as is most probable, a combination of both, it is more likely to navigate accurately over familiar ground. An experimentally displaced bat may return from any point of the compass, so one taken anywhere within a radius of 100 kilometres (60 miles) from home would have to be familiar with the appearance and sound patterns of everything, approached from all angles, within an area of some 31,600 square kilometres (12,200 square miles)! Studies of the desert pallid bat, *Antrozous pallidus*, in Arizona, suggest that this might be possible. One adult female returned home from each of eight locations that were up to 108 kilometres (67 miles) away, implying familiarity with an area of 36,648 square kilometres (14,150 square miles)! Furthermore, young pallid bats – and the young of other species too – are less efficient in homing, as we might expect if learning familiar geographic landmarks was an important aspect of navigation.

If navigation is based only on recognition of individual landmarks, we should expect experimentally displaced bats to fly about hesitantly searching for familiar features when they are released. This does happen, but many released bats often go straight home; one Mexican cave bat, *Myotis velifer*, returned from forty-five kilometres (28 miles) away in four hours and a parti-coloured bat, *Vespertilio murinus*, has flown 360 kilometres (225 miles) home in two days. There is little sign of hesitation here.

Could it be that a bat has a kind of inbuilt gyro compass that records where the animal goes, how it twists and turns and thus always allows it to know where home lies in relation to its present position? Certainly some bats can find their way through complex cave systems in a manner that baffles humans. It is as though the bats know where they are going. Furthermore, in experiments with displaced bats in which individuals were carried by car at speeds they could not possibly attain in flight, and were imprisoned in a cloth bag from which they could not see or echolocate landmarks, some still found their way home. Perhaps bats, like many other vertebrates, are able to use the earth's magnetic field for guidance, or maybe they use some cue that has not yet been experimentally investigated. Whatever sensory input and brain analyses are used to guide and maintain a bat's flight path, the system works with the precision of an aircraft's whole electronic guidance system, yet it occupies only the volume of a single small transistor!

Our incomplete picture of bat migrations

It is clear that bats are a very mobile group and move about a great deal. But to what extent can their various journeys be classed as seasonal migration? Aggregation followed by disappearance represents circumstantial evidence for migration in bats. It is also tempting to interpret evidence of long-distance flights, such as the frequent appearance of bats on ships and oil rigs far out to sea, as a component of migration habits. Some species certainly do make long journeys: for example, the red bat, *Lasiurus borealis*, has on several occasions been found

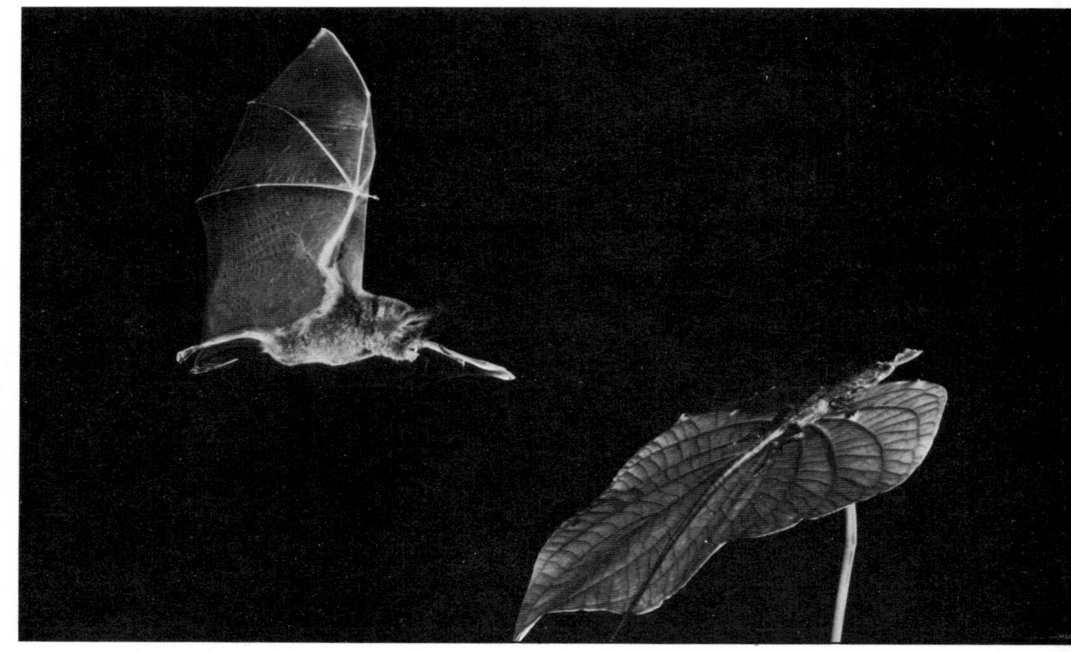

Carnivorous bats prey on small rodents and reptiles, tree frogs, fish, birds and other bats. Here a fringe-lipped bat, *Trachops cirrhosus*, an inhabitant of the island of Trinidad, southern Mexico and northern South America, has been captured on film in the process of taking a basalisc lizard resting on a leaf. (From examination of the stomach contents of a number of these bats their favourite food appears to be geckos.) The sequence shows clearly that by means of echolocation, bats are able to home in accurately on their prey. The bat's approach is quick and silent such that the victim is unaware of its impending fate and has little opportunity to escape its predator. Carnivorous bats often carry their prey to a perch, where they devour it completely save the skeleton; their homes are invariably littered with the remains of their meals.

up to 140 kilometres (85 miles) off the coast of Nova Scotia, and the European noctule, *Nyctalus noctula*, and the North American hoary bat, *Lasiurus cinereus*, are both known to have travelled distances of more than 1500 kilometres (930 miles). Such journeys are probably not accomplished without resting, though the hoary bat occasionally crosses 1200 kilometres (750 miles) of open ocean and turns up in Bermuda. This must obviously represent a non-stop flight, but the bat is probably aided by winds blowing from the American mainland.

Suggestive as these observations are, they need not be evidence for seasonal migration and might be interpreted differently. Red, noctule and hoary bats are among the very few temperate zone species that often produce twins; most bats have only one baby a year. It has been suggested that their long-distance flights might be a move to reduce the population density around breeding sites, compensating for overproduction of young. In fact, it is more likely that these species are indeed seasonal migrants: noctules in Russia are said to arrive in summer with the same predictability as swallows, and the hoary bat is only found in northern parts of its range during the summer. Occurrences of the latter in Bermuda have been mainly in spring and autumn, the very times that a summer migrant would be expected to be on the move and blown off course by strong winds.

The practical difficulties of studying small nocturnal creatures such as bats are so great that clearly the migrations of only very few species are well understood and the majority of bats have not been studied at all. To make matters worse, bats are a tropical group: only three of the eighteen families of bats occur in the temperate zones. But most bat researchers live and work in temperate countries, where the bat fauna is often rather specialized, behaving, perhaps, quite differently from its tropical counterpart. In particular, migration in response to winter food shortages is unlikely to occur in the tropics, at least among insectivorous bats, which are the very species that have to date been most intensively studied.

What we do know about bat migrations suggests that there is no general pattern. For example, some closely related species of bats of similar habits appear to differ markedly in their willingness to travel: in the Netherlands a study of four small species of *Myotis* which congregate in the limestone mines of South Limburg to hibernate, has shown that in summer three of the species may be found up to 150 kilometres (95 miles) away, but the fourth may travel twice as far. There may even be differences in migration patterns between similar species living at the same place, and members of the same species may differ in their habits if they live in dissimilar geographic regions. For example, pipistrelles in the USSR perform long-distance seasonal migrations, but there is no evidence for this in Britain. The two populations may behave differently because of local climatic conditions; in eastern Europe, which experiences a harsh mid-continental climate, pipistrelles often hibernate in caves, but they never do so in countries with a warmer oceanic climate.

There is even a degree of inconsistency among members of the same species living in the same place at the same time. Such is the case with the American free-tailed bats, *Tadarida brasiliensis*, some of which, we have seen, migrate south to Mexico for the winter while others stay behind in Texas and Arizona to spend the winter in hibernation. What determines which individual bats will migrate and which will "put their feet up" for the winter? And if some can stay behind, why not all of them; there would be little problem over competition for food as hibernating bats eat little during infrequent periods of wakefulness. Although over 100,000 guano bats have been ringed and a great many biologists have devoted their attention to this animal, we still do not know the whole story about even this abundant and accessible species.

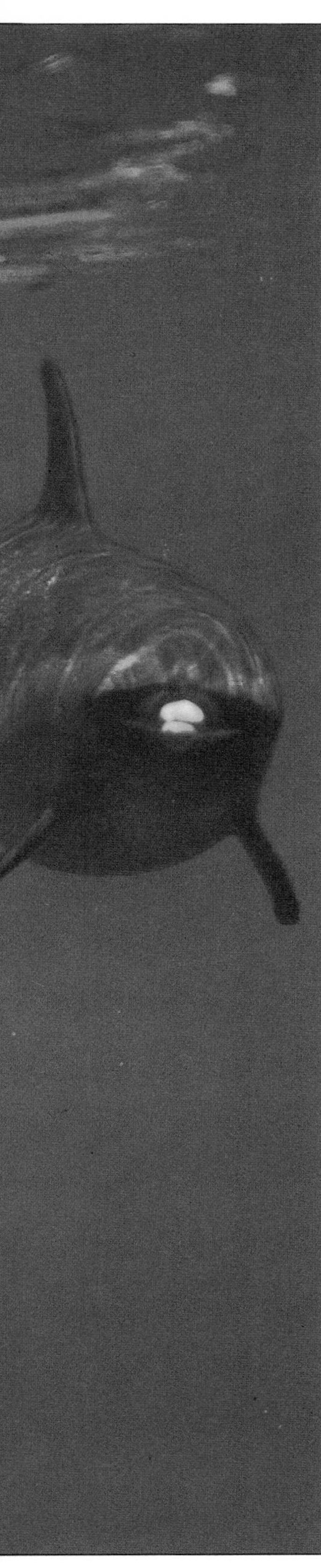

Aquatic Mammals

Only two groups of mammals are completely aquatic, the sea cows (dugongs and manatees) and the cetaceans (whales and dolphins). All other so-called aquatic mammals are more strictly speaking amphibious and return to land to give birth and sometimes to feed and sleep.

The amount of time an amphibious mammal spends in the water varies greatly from one species to another. Those animals, such as seals and sealions (pinnipeds), that are almost entirely marine, are, in general, much better equipped for an aquatic existence than those that are primarily freshwater. Most seals and sealions come ashore only to breed, and spend the rest of the time in the sea. Having flippers rather than legs they are not well equipped to travel great distances over land and all their migratory journeys are made through water. On the other hand, freshwater mammals, apart from the sea cows, are much closer to land mammals in appearance and are much better adapted for movement on land. Most of their migrations are terrestrial.

The marine mammals make the longest journeys. Many whales and pinnipeds make seasonal migrations that are thousands of kilometres in length. Some baleen whales migrate 20,000 kilometres (12,000 miles) between polar and tropical waters each year. Although the migrations of toothed whales, such as the killer whale, and the sea otter are not well known, they are probably just as seasonal and as extensive – thousands of kilometres in the case of toothed whales and up to 100 kilometres (60 miles) in the case of sea otters.

Apart from distance, the migrations of freshwater aquatic mammals are different in form from those of marine mammals. Although both groups make exploratory migrations, those of freshwater mammals often result in removal migration to a new home range, whereas marine mammals, such as pinnipeds, usually return to breed each year at the same site.

Dolphins, like other toothed whales, are flesh eaters. Their migrations have not yet been mapped out, but they are thought to be closely related to the movements of fish, which form the bulk of their diet.

The name pinniped means fin-footed and is used to describe all seals and sealions. The order Pinnipedia is divided into three families, the true seals, the eared seals and the walrus. The eared seals differ from true seals in that they have external ears and can bring their tail forward to support them on land. The walrus has no external ears, but can move its tail in the same way as the eared seals. Although these animals are all very similar in appearance they are thought to have had a quite different ancestry. True seals are probably related to the otters, whereas eared seals and the walrus are thought to be descended from a bear-like ancestor.

All pinnipeds are amphibious, living partly on land and partly in water and all spend the aquatic phase in the sea, with the exception of the Baikal seal, *Pusa sibirica*. As its name suggests the Baikal seal is found in Lake Baikal in Asiatic Russia, thousands of kilometres from the nearest sea. It is a relic of a time about eight million years ago when the Arctic Ocean extended over much of northern Asia.

All pinnipeds emerge from the water to give birth to a single pup. In all species except the harbour, or common seal, *Phoca vitulina*, the young pup stays out of the water for several weeks until nearly weaned. As the harbour seal gives birth to her pup on a sandbank or on a stretch of shore exposed only at low tide, the pup enters the sea very shortly after birth.

All eared seals and some true seals, such as the grey seal, *Halichoerus grypus*, the elephant seals, *Mirounga* spp., and the monk seals, *Monachus* spp., give birth on rocky coastal areas. The walrus and most true seals, on the other hand, give birth on ice, whether it be on ice-floes, pack-ice or on the ice-shelves that form around the coasts of polar regions in winter.

Breeding sites

Where pinnipeds breed has an important effect on their reproductive behaviour and consequently on their migration pattern. The nature of their breeding ground is a more important factor as far as migration is concerned than whether they are true or eared. As there is no shortage of ice in polar regions, those species that give birth there are normally found in small groups spread over a wide area. However, because there are very few ice-free shores available where pinnipeds can breed undisturbed, those species that give birth on rocky shores are typically found crammed together, occupying all the available space. Overcrowding is particularly severe in species such as the elephant seals, and the northern fur seal, *Callorhinus ursinus*, that give birth on oceanic islands.

After giving birth all females come into oestrous ready for mating, and therefore males always accompany females on their migrations to give birth. In pinnipeds that have their pups on ice only the females come out of the water. The males remain in the sea patrolling the waters under and around the ice and copulate with the females as they re-enter the water. In pinnipeds that give birth on rocky areas, both males and females come ashore. The males arrive first and establish territories on the breeding coast. The females, arriving a little later, are herded into harems that vary in size from about three for the South American fur seal, *Arctocephalus australis*, to around fifty for the northern fur seal. Copulation occurs a few weeks after the females have given birth. Pinnipeds have a long period of gestation, varying from nine to twelve months, depending on the species.

From the time they come ashore to the end of the breeding season, a period of about two months, the males do not feed at all. The females on the other hand alternate periods of feeding at sea with periods on shore suckling their young. A month or so after the breeding season has finished the moulting season begins. Although most species spend the moulting period out of the water the site chosen is often different from the breeding area. Males, females and young often moult at different times of the year and sometimes in different places. In many species there is a clear moult migration as there is in birds. The southern elephant seals, *Mirounga leonina*, for example, which breed on South Georgia between August and November, migrate to moult between January and March in the South Orkney Islands.

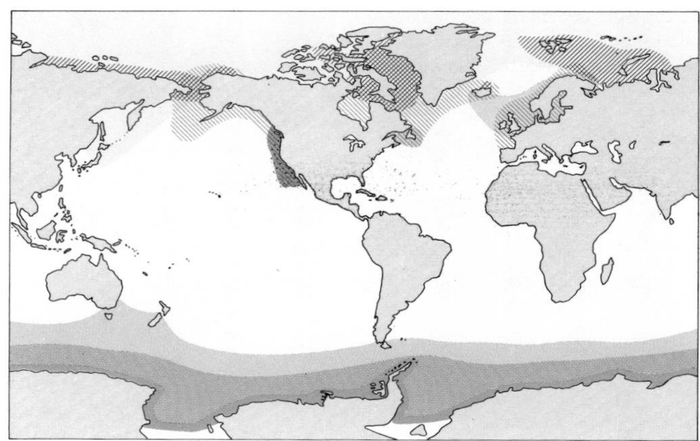

Feeding and breeding along the coasts of South Africa and Namibia, the South African fur seal, *Arctocephalus pusillus*, is probably the best known of all southern fur seals. The males come ashore to establish their harems at the end of October and the females give birth in November. When the pups are about seven months old they leave the breeding beaches and head rapidly out to sea, covering as much as 1200 kilometres (750 miles) in a few weeks. Their migration is thought to be exploratory. The pups do not return until they are two years old and the females are ready to mate for the first time.

Seals and sealions breed on islands and in coastal areas throughout the world. The walrus and most true seals breed on ice, whereas all eared seals breed on rocky coasts.

Ringed seal
Walrus
Harbour seal
Grey seal
Californian sealion
Northern elephant seal
Leopard seal
Crabeater seal
Weddell seal

After moulting is complete, all pinnipeds spend several months feeding intensively at sea. Some species use the breeding site as a shore base, alternating several weeks at sea with perhaps a week on shore. Other species leave the breeding shores entirely during the feeding phase and do not return again until the next breeding season.

When they are weaned, the young of most pinnipeds, in common with the young of many other vertebrates, enter a period of exploratory migration that lasts for about two years. Except in the case of the walrus most young pinnipeds spend this period alone. Young walrus, however, remain in the company of the adults until they are one or two years old. During this exploratory period the young pinniped seeks out a succession of places suitable for feeding at different times of the year and, in the case of rocky shore breeding species, the young animal often comes ashore on various coasts to test their suitability as potential breeding sites. Most pinnipeds return to breed on the same shore where they were born. Some, however, transfer to other established breeding grounds and a few attempt to establish a new colony on a previously unoccupied site.

Indiscriminate hunting in the late nineteenth and early twentieth centuries took many species to the brink of extinction. These species are now gradually recovering and their breeding ranges are expanding at the present time. The exploratory migrations of young animals are in most cases responsible for the extension of these ranges.

The distances that pinnipeds travel from the breeding grounds on their seasonal migrations vary considerably from species to species. It would appear from their distribution that these distances are related to the latitude at which they breed. The ringed seal, *Pusa hispida*, the most northerly of all pinniped species, travels only short distances away from its breeding territory in the pack-ice of the Arctic. After the breeding and moulting seasons, the seals remain in the surrounding waters to feed. Even in winter, when the seals are permanently in the water, they stay close to the breeding site, spending the dark months below the ice.

Arctic migrants – the walrus

Another Arctic-dwelling but more migratory species is the walrus, *Odobenus rosmarus*. Walrus feed mainly on bottom-dwelling bivalve molluscs found at depths of between 80 and 100 metres (265 and 330 feet). They normally feed only in the morning, spending the rest of the day roosting on dry land or on ice-floes. Walrus therefore only inhabit regions where land or ice is adjacent to water no deeper than 100 metres (330 feet). In the eastern Canadian Arctic, walrus are found off the west coast of Greenland, around Baffin Island and in the region of Hudson Bay. In winter they are typically found in the open water passages, called leads, produced by wind and current action on the pack-ice. In summer the walrus drift with the ice and much walrus migration can be accounted for by passive drifting while roosting on ice-

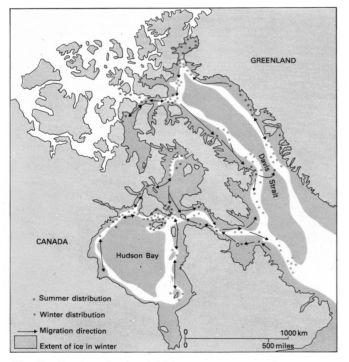

The distribution of walrus, *Odobenus rosmarus,* in the Canadian Arctic during winter corresponds to areas of open water between pack- and fast-ice. The pattern of sea ice is broadly the same from one winter to the next and the walrus are therefore usually found in the same areas. As walrus spend most of the time, between feeding expeditions, lying on drifting ice-floes, their migratory pattern is largely determined by the speed and direction of water currents. In the Davis Strait these currents result in a general counter-clockwise migration.

floes. The walrus normally adopt a particular floe as a base, abandoning it only when it drifts into deep water where the walrus cannot feed or when it approaches dry land on which the walrus may prefer to roost in preference to the ice-floe. In autumn the walrus keep to the edge of the developing pack-ice, gradually becoming concentrated in the ice-free leads once more.

Because walrus movements are largely passive, their migrations are heavily dependent on the prevailing winds and ocean currents. In some parts of the Canadian Arctic the combined influences of winds and currents have produced a pattern of seasonal return migration between wintering and breeding grounds. In the Davis Strait, the prevailing air and sea currents have produced a counter-clockwise migration circuit that takes several years to complete.

In the northern Pacific, during February and March, when the Arctic pack-ice is at its maximum extent, walrus are found throughout the Bering Sea. Males and non-pregnant females are distributed mainly in the eastern part while pregnant females gather in the west to give birth. Female walrus usually give birth during May every other year. The pups are more than a year old before they are weaned and remain with their mother for another two or more years after that. In spring the walrus follow the ice as it recedes northward and pass through the Bering Strait into the Arctic Ocean in May. The males and those females that have not given birth the previous spring head eastward towards the northern coasts of Alaska and Canada. The females that gave birth that season travel with their young westward to the northern shores of Asia. These coasts mark the most northerly limit of the walrus's annual migration. With the onset of winter the walrus move south again, passing back through the Bering Strait in November.

South of the polar pack-ice among the drift-ice of the North Atlantic is the habitat of the hooded seal, *Cystophora cristata*. This species pairs up each season and breeds in spring on the ice-floes around Newfoundland and Jan Mayen Island, each pair producing its young and mating on a separate floe. At the end of April, when the young seals are weaned, the hooded seals migrate some 2000 kilometres (1250 miles) to moulting grounds off the Greenland coast. After moulting they spend the summer months feeding among the drift-ice before returning again to their breeding grounds.

The northern fur seal

The northern fur seal, *Callorhinus ursinus*, found in the northern Pacific to the south of the pack-ice, is probably the best studied of all pinniped species. Until 1966 it bred on only three groups of oceanic islands, Robben Island, the Commander Islands and the Pribilof Islands. However, recently, seals originating from the Commander and Pribilof Islands have established a new breeding colony on San Miguel Island off the coast of California.

The male fur seals come on shore in May and establish their breeding territories. The females arrive to give

The hooded seal, *Cystophora cristata*, takes its name from the inflatable bladder-like pouch that extends along the top of its nose. Both sexes have these bladders, which are thought to have some threatening or warning function. Hooded seals breed on ice-floes in the vicinity of Newfoundland and Jan Mayen Island during March and April. The breeding unit consists of a male and a female and the female's pup of the previous season. The seals are highly territorial and will defend their ice-floe against any intruder.

A walrus family rests secure on its own ice-floe. The pups are born on the floes and are able to swim immediately from birth.

There are seven species of fur seal, one, *Callorhinus* sp., found in the Northern Hemisphere and six, *Arctocephalus* spp., found in the Southern Hemisphere. Between them they account for about half the species of eared seal in existence. The recent adoption of San Miguel Island as a breeding site by the northern fur seals, *Callorhinus ursinus*, is a lucky development for researchers in the field of seal migration. It was found that in the older, more northerly breeding sites that the young preferred to head south during their exploratory migrations. If this southerly bias is inherited, the seals born on San Miguel would be expected to explore to the south or, if the water is too warm for them to expand their range further south they might remain around the breeding site all year. If however the bias is learned then the seals will most probably explore the colder waters to the north.

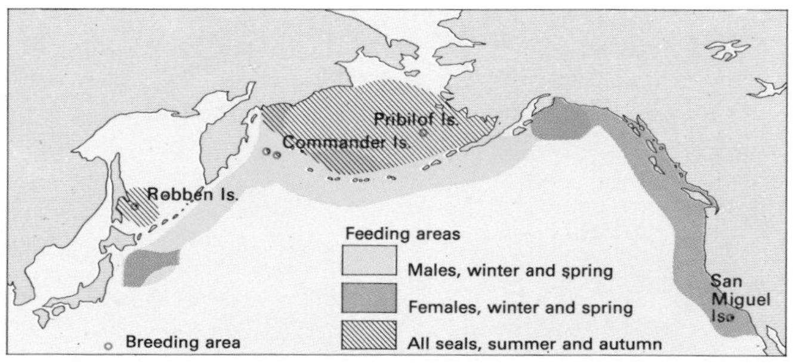

Male fur seals spend the winter and spring feeding in the waters off the Kuril and Aleutian Islands in the North Pacific. The females feed largely along the western coast of North America.

birth in June and July. After the young are weaned both young and adults spend the summer and early autumn feeding in the Barents Sea. At the beginning of October the adults leave the breeding grounds and travel south.

Fur seals migrate further from their breeding sites than any other pinniped in the Northern Hemisphere. Male fur seals migrate up to 800 kilometres (500 miles) and females may migrate as much as 2800 kilometres (1700 miles) away from the breeding grounds.

Similarly, in the southern Hemisphere, species such as the southern elephant seal, *Mirounga leonina*, and the Kerguelen fur seal, *Arctocephalus tropicalis*, that breed just north of the drift-ice region, are most migratory. Both species breed on the islands of the southern ocean in spring, migrating between 1000 and 2000 kilometres (620 and 1250 miles) northward to feed in summer.

The leopard seal, *Hydrurga leptonyx*, breeding at the edge of the Antarctic pack-ice in late spring, also travels great distances. After moulting in summer it migrates north and has been seen on the coasts of Australia, New Zealand and the Falkland Islands in winter.

Further south, well into the Antarctic pack-ice, is the breeding ground of the crabeater seal, *Lobodon carcinophagus*. After the moulting season in January and February it migrates north ahead of the advancing ice, reaching a distance of 1000 kilometres (620 miles) north of its breeding ground by mid-winter.

The most southerly seal of all, the Weddell seal, *Leptonychotes weddelli*, lives all year round on the continental coast of Antarctica. Like its northerly counterpart, the ringed seal, the Weddell seal travels only short distances from its breeding ground. Instead of travelling to warmer areas, the seals spend the winter months in the sea below the polar fast-ice. It uses cracks in the ice as breathing holes, which it keeps from freezing over by using its teeth.

The pattern of seal migration

In both the Northern and the Southern Hemispheres, the most migratory species are those such as the northern fur seal and the southern elephant seal that breed in or on the edge of the drift-ice region. Species breeding on either the polar or equatorial sides of this region migrate less far and spend shorter periods of time away from the breeding site. The migrations of temperate species such as the monk seals, *Monachus* spp., can be measured in tens rather than hundreds of kilometres. In other temperate species, such as the grey seal, which breeds around the coasts of Britain, the migration pattern is obscured by the fact that all individuals do not migrate at once and most leave the breeding beaches for only a few days, or weeks, at a time.

The males of all temperate and sub-polar breeding pinnipeds are much larger than the females. As these species all breed on rocky shores the males are territorial and assemble harems. The larger and stronger the male the more successful he will be in collecting females and defending them against rivals. Selection for breeding is therefore weighted in favour of large males. As large animals are more able to control their body temperature, this oddly enough has had an effect on the pattern of migration and in these species males and females migrate quite separately. The females of species such as the northern elephant seal, *Mirounga angustirostris*, and the California sealion, *Zalophus californianus*, breeding along the coast of California, remain in temperate waters all year while the males migrate north in summer. In the case of the northern fur seal, which breeds in much colder water, the males remain all year close to the breeding grounds, whereas the females migrate to warmer water in winter. This is a good example of how a characteristic that has been evolved through one pattern of behaviour, in this case reproduction, can influence a quite different type of behaviour, that is, migration.

Whales

Of all mammals, whales are the most perfectly adapted to an aquatic environment. Whales, together with the dugongs and manatees, are the only mammals to breed in water. Like all mammals, whales are descended from a fish-like ancestor and went through a terrestrial stage of development. This they did before returning to the water. Their adaptation is so complete that externally they bear more resemblance to their fish ancestors than they do to land-living animals.

Whales are divided into two groups, the toothed whales and the baleen whales. The toothed whales are generally much smaller than the baleen whales and feed mainly on fish. Porpoises and dolphins account for more than two-thirds of all species. The sperm whale, *Physeter catodon*, and killer whale, *Orcinus orca*, belong to this group and so does the narwhal, *Monodon monoceros*, distinguished by the male's curiously twisted tusk.

Baleen whales are plankton feeders and are so named because of the series of baleen or whalebone plates that hang down from the roof of their mouths. The plates consist of coalesced hairs which project freely on the inside of the whale's mouth, forming a fringe through which it sifts the plankton.

Because dolphins and porpoises occupy the whole of their geographical range at all times, it should not be thought that their migrations are insignificant or of only small scale. Some species have migration circuits that extend over a thousand or more kilometres. Like fish, dolphins and porpoises can be divided into demes or breeding populations, each with their own migration circuits. These circuits overlap to a considerable extent and tend to confuse the pattern of migration, reinforcing the false impression that they do not migrate very far.

The migrations of toothed whales

At present we have no overall picture of toothed whale migration. Until individuals from each population have been followed, their migration circuits will remain speculative. Although in some cases a few sections have been pieced together, so far not a single circuit has been identified in full. It is known for instance that a particular deme of killer whales, *Orcinus orca*, living in the northern Pacific, follows the walrus on its seasonal migrations between the Bering Sea and the Arctic Ocean. In the Atlantic, off eastern Canada, there is another deme that migrates in company with rorqual whales, *Balaenoptera* spp. However, these examples are a little atypical and

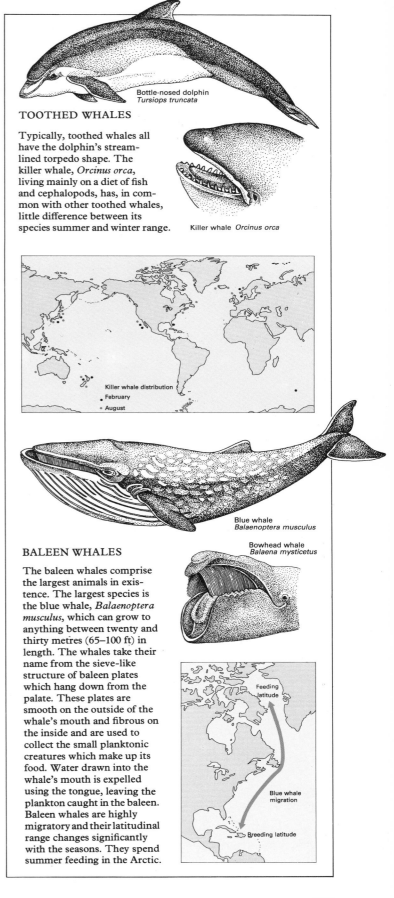

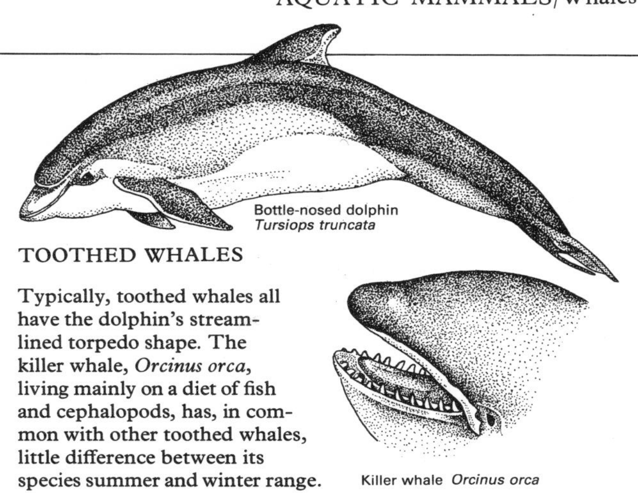

Bottle-nosed dolphin *Tursiops truncata*

TOOTHED WHALES

Typically, toothed whales all have the dolphin's streamlined torpedo shape. The killer whale, *Orcinus orca*, living mainly on a diet of fish and cephalopods, has, in common with other toothed whales, little difference between its species summer and winter range.

Killer whale *Orcinus orca*

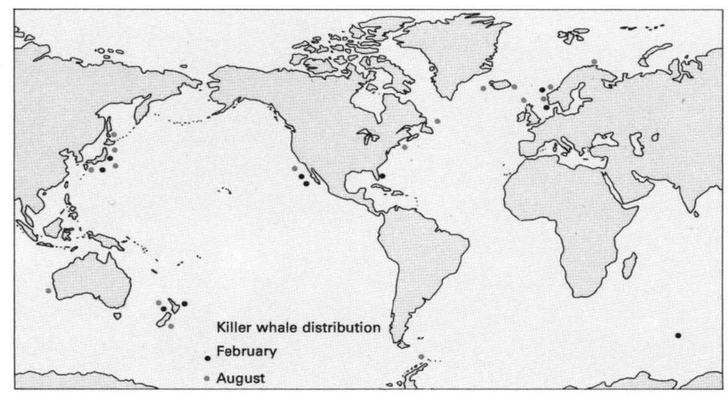

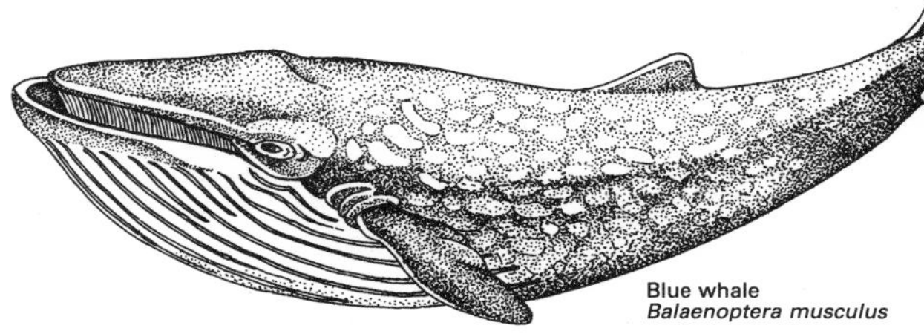

Blue whale *Balaenoptera musculus*

BALEEN WHALES

The baleen whales comprise the largest animals in existence. The largest species is the blue whale, *Balaenoptera musculus*, which can grow to anything between twenty and thirty metres (65–100 ft) in length. The whales take their name from the sieve-like structure of baleen plates which hang down from the palate. These plates are smooth on the outside of the whale's mouth and fibrous on the inside and are used to collect the small planktonic creatures which make up its food. Water drawn into the whale's mouth is expelled using the tongue, leaving the plankton caught in the baleen. Baleen whales are highly migratory and their latitudinal range changes significantly with the seasons. They spend summer feeding in the Arctic.

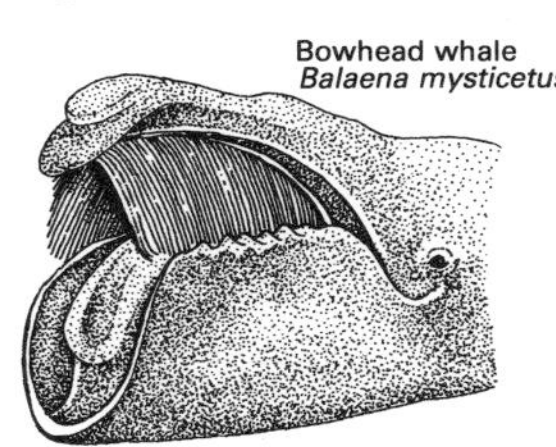

Bowhead whale *Balaena mysticetus*

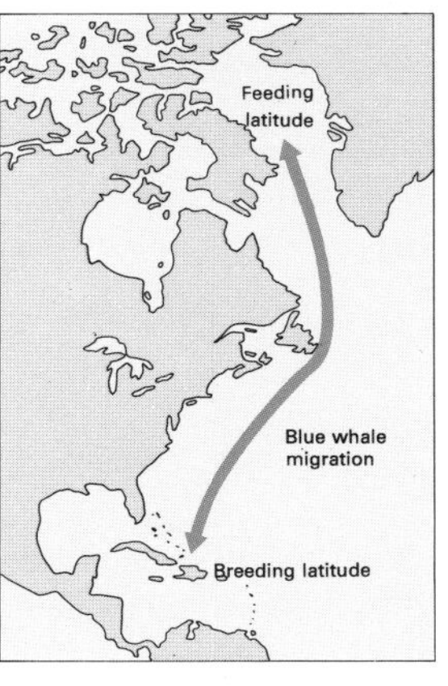

The back flip is a feature of the killer whale's repertoire. Affectionate, highly intelligent and a born acrobat, the killer whale, *Orcinus orca*, is the star performer in many oceanaria. Its reputation as a ferocious killer stems from its voracious appetite. It hunts as a member of a pack and will attack almost anything in the sea that moves – seals, penguins, porpoise, fish and squid.

in most cases the migrations of toothed whales are dependent on movements of fish. It has been found that the movement of the common porpoise, *Phocaena phocaena*, in the Bay of Fundy, Nova Scotia, closely follows the movements of the herring shoals. Off the coast of California, the white-sided, or short-beaked dolphin, *Lagenorhynchus obliquidens*, migrates according to seasonal changes in fish distribution. In winter and spring it feeds inshore on anchovies, but in spring, when the anchovies move into water too shallow for dolphins to follow, it moves offshore to feed on saury.

The distribution of some toothed whales changes seasonally. In most cases the change is one of latitude and corresponds to the expansion and contraction of the polar ice-fields. Both the beluga, or white whale, *Delphinapterus leucas*, and the narwhal, *Monodon monoceros*, living in coastal areas of the Arctic Ocean, exhibit this feature. The belugas gather at the northern tip of Alaska in October and remain there until the pack-ice forces them to migrate south through the Bering Strait. The beluga normally migrate further south than the narwhal and return northward earlier in spring, entering the Arctic Ocean again in April.

Baleen whales

Ironically the whalers, who have now reduced most species to the verge of extinction, were the first to supply information about whale migrations. They discovered that whales could only be found in certain areas at certain times of the year and that many species made enormous seasonal journeys. Later work done by marine scientists confirmed these findings. Careful studies of whales' stomach contents showed that in many cases whales caught in tropical waters had journeyed from the Antarctic. Parasites such as lice, and barnacles originating from areas thousands of kilometres apart, were found attached to the whales' skin.

TRACKING DOLPHINS

An experiment conducted off the coast of southern California has shown that dolphins, *Delphinus delphis*, can probably recognize certain features of the bottom topography and use them as navigational aids. The dolphins were fitted with radio transmitters that operated only when their antennae broke water and tracked from ships and helicopters. The dolphin tracks detected seemed to follow the alignment of submarine escarpments at depths close to the 350- and 1000-metre (1150 and 3300 ft) contours. It is thought that the dolphins may use a system of echolocation to detect the shape of the ocean bed, although there is some doubt about its effectiveness below eighty metres (265 ft).

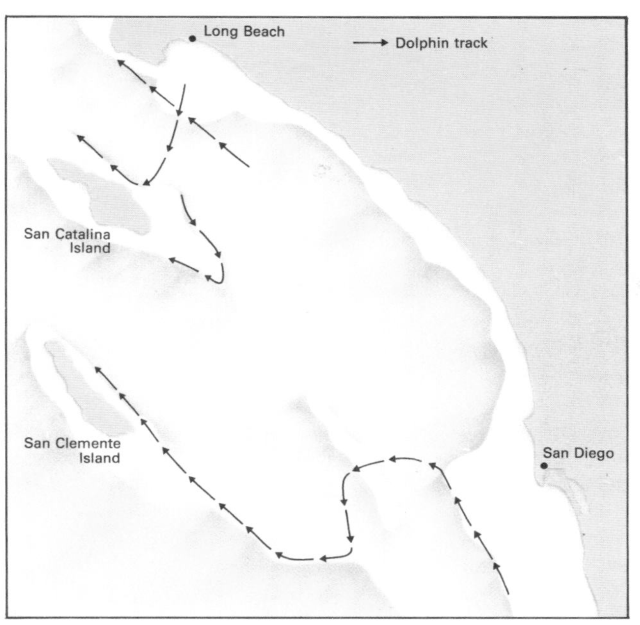

Humpback whales, *Megaptera novaeangliae*, are found typically in coastal waters. The females bear their young in the tropical seas after a twelve-month period of gestation. The calves are usually about four metres (13 ft) long at birth and are suckled by their mother for eleven months. On their migrations to feed in polar waters the females, calves and immature adults leave first followed by the males.

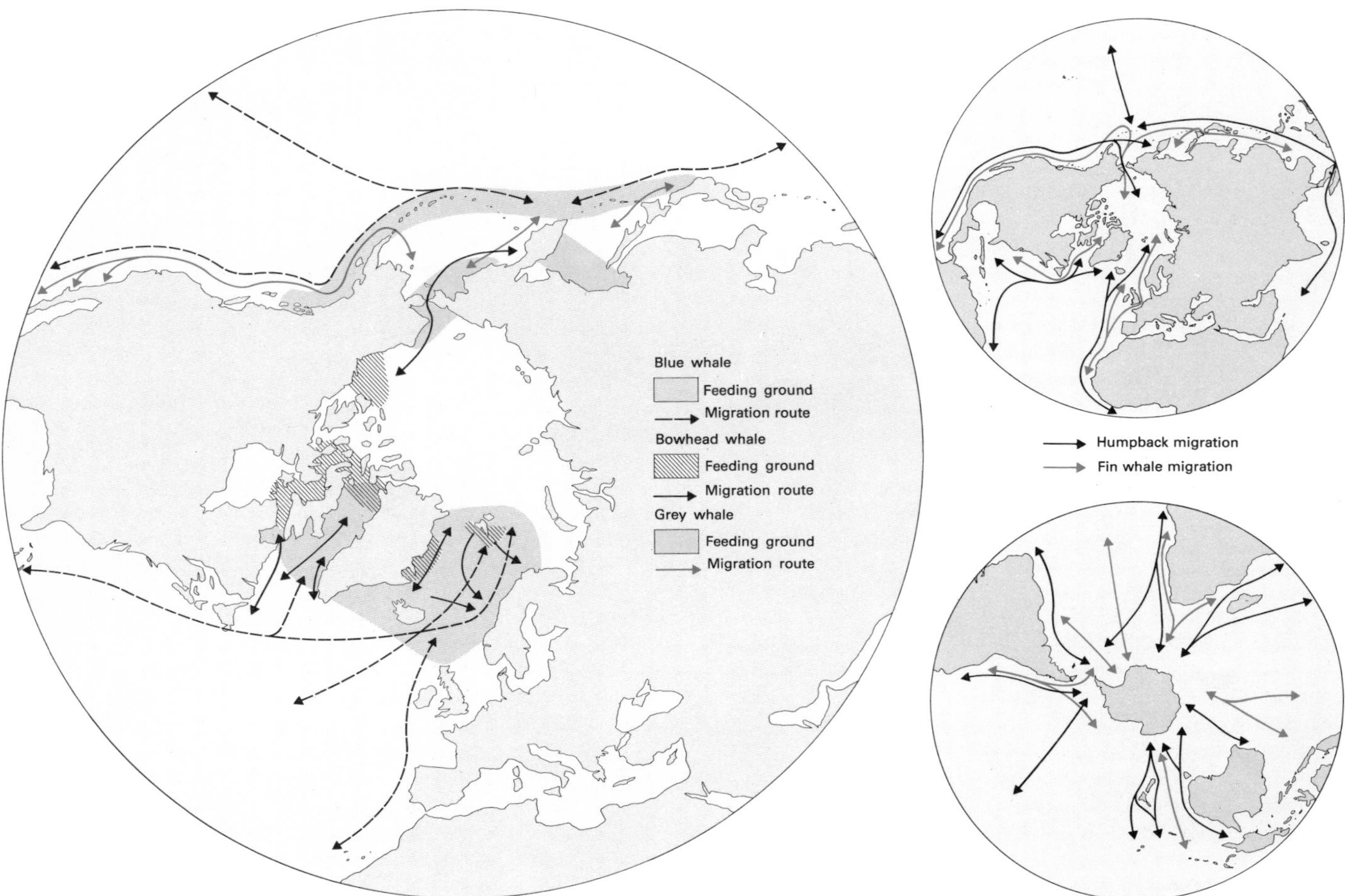

Most species of baleen whale travel immense distances. The humpback whales' migration from the North Pacific into the Indian Ocean is more than 16,000 kilometres (10,000 miles) long. This species, like the fin and blue whale, is divided into separate Northern and Southern Hemisphere populations. Although both populations winter in tropical waters they rarely meet as their winters are six months apart.

The first whale-tagging programme was started in the 1920s. Initially, marking a fifty-ton whale permanently and without injury was a problem. At first the whales were tagged with copper darts, but it was found that these easily fell out of the thick blubber and sometimes caused infection. Today stainless steel tubes are shot into the whale from a special harpoon gun so that they penetrate the blubber just sufficiently to stay in place. The darts are coated with antibiotic to stop infection and seem to cause the whale no discomfort. Scarcely ten per cent are recovered, since in order to reclaim the tag the scientist has to rely on the whale being caught and the dart being noticed as the whale is cut up. However, when taken with other observations, this rate of return has been sufficient to map out the routes of most whales.

Whales migrate so that they will be in favourable places for feeding and calving at particular times of the year. As the best places for each of these activities are sometimes thousands of kilometres apart, baleen whales must make huge seasonal migrations. In the Antarctic, baleen whales' principal food is the small crustacean *Euphausia superba*, known as "krill". It is found in the highest concentrations in upwelling sub-polar waters, which bring plenty of nutrients to the surface. The whales feed here during the summer months, but are forced by the spread of pack-ice in autumn to move north to winter in warmer tropical waters. The plankton concentration in these warmer waters may be only one per cent of that found in cold seas. The whales therefore spend most of the winter with only a minimum of food, living for the most part off the layer of blubber built up during the summer. Warm water, however, does have the advantage of being favourable for calving. The young are fed by their mothers and so are not dependent on plankton. In warm water the calves need less food to keep up their body temperature and as a result can turn a greater proportion of food into blubber, which they will need as insulation against the cold waters in which they are to spend the summer.

The global migrants

One of the best-documented whale migrations is that of the humpback, *Megaptera novaeangliae*. These large whales, weighing up to forty tons, are found in both the Northern and the Southern Hemisphere. There are some five or six separate populations in the Antarctic and another three in the North Atlantic and Pacific oceans. In winter each population migrates towards the tropics by a different route, but always keeping close to the continents. The population found in Norwegian waters during summer moves south past British coasts to winter and breed off northwest Africa. The summer population found off the Newfoundland coast winters in the Caribbean. The Pacific stocks summering in the northwest move down to Japan in winter and those in the northeast Pacific travel down to winter along the coast of Mexico. Humpbacks migrate in small herds, travelling at a leisurely rate of about 350 kilometres (220 miles) per month. Sometimes the pace is faster. One individual is known to have travelled 800 kilometres (500 miles) in six days. Humpback whales are occasionally seen around river estuaries. It is thought that they enter less saline water to rid themselves of barnacles.

The blue whale, *Balaenoptera musculus*, also migrates in ones and twos, but this whale and its close relation the fin whale, *Balaenoptera physalus*, are found widely dispersed throughout the oceans in winter and not just in coastal areas. Some individuals travel enormous distances. The blue whales and fin whales that summer in the northern Pacific may visit the Indian Ocean in the course of their winter migrations and are commonly found off the Gulf of Aden. Others spend the winter in the South Atlantic and off the coast of northwest Africa.

There was a time when the bowhead whale, *Balaena mysticetus*, was a harbinger of spring for the Eskimos of Alaska. Entering the Arctic Ocean in early spring it migrated around the coast, reaching its most northerly tip in June. These whales were an extremely useful resource. They provided oil for fuel, blubber and meat for food and bone for tools and ornaments. However, by the early twentieth century commercial whaling fleets – 200 to 300 ships from British ports alone – had almost exterminated the species. As the species is protected by international agreement and has not been commercially hunted for over fifty years, it may now be on the increase.

Some whale species, notably the grey whale, *Eschrichtius gibbosus*, were already in decline before the introduction of the cannon-fired harpoon in the 1860s. These harpoons enabled the larger whales to be caught.

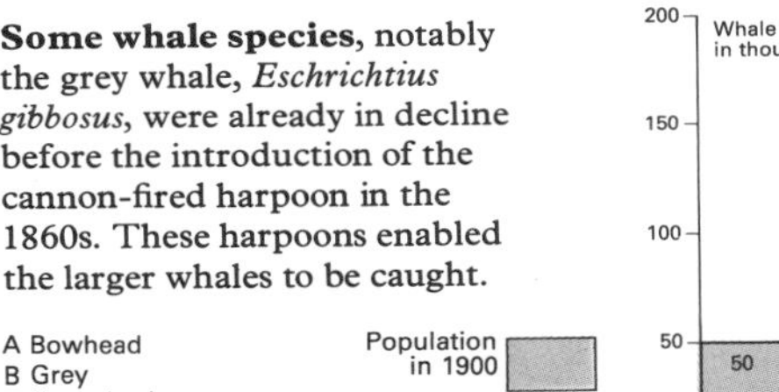

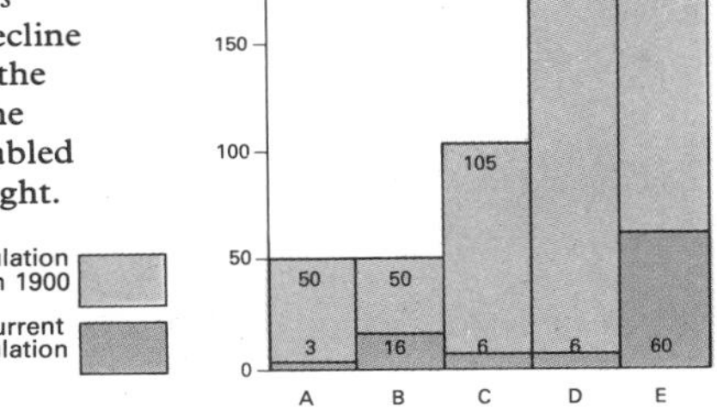

The grey whale, *Eschrichtius gibbosus*, is another species which was once abundant and is now on the verge of extinction. The comparatively small number remaining spend the summer in the Arctic Ocean and northern Pacific. In winter a tiny number, often travelling in pairs, move down the coast of eastern Asia to breed off the Korean shore. The majority, however, swim down the western American coast to winter along the coast of California and Mexico. The pregnant females are always the first to come south and the last to return north with their new-born calves. The whales swim within a few miles of the shore and can sometimes be seen from land. Their numbers are greatest as they pass San Diego in December and January and are often seen from there as they head south. The return journey to the feeding grounds, a distance of around 10,000 kilometres (6000 miles), takes them about ninety days.

The curiously equipped platypus has evolved to fit an odd niche in nature. Its sensitive rubbery bill is ideal for foraging in muddy river bottoms and its strong front legs for digging burrows.

In water the beaver's blade-like tail serves primarily as a rudder. Its hind feet are webbed and provide most of the forward propulsion. A beaver can remain under water for up to fifteen minutes at a time.

The diversity of aquatic migrants

Pinnipeds and whales are the only major groups of mammals in which all members are aquatic. With the exception of the dugongs and the manatees, all other aquatic mammals belong to groups in which the majority of species are terrestrial. The duck-billed platypus, *Ornithorhynchus anatinus*, for instance, a relation of the spiny anteaters, is the only aquatic member of the primitive egg-laying group of mammals, the monotremes.

The platypus lives mainly in the highlands of eastern Australia. It is found both in rapid-running water and in lakes, and prefers clean, clear water. The adults live alone in territories that do not alter with the seasons, although the females may occupy a different territory or home range for feeding, nest-building and egg-laying. Most of their life is spent in or near water. Platypus that have been caught and then released up to two kilometres (1.2 miles) from water have usually headed directly back to their home stream. Young platypus may venture further on their exploratory migrations and have been known to travel up to eight kilometres (5 miles) from one river to another across intervening high land.

The beaver, *Castor canadensis*, like the platypus, occupies a home range that is seasonally static. Their main migratory movements occur when the supply of bark, the beavers' main food, runs out. Although beavers form pairs that often last for life the male leaves the female each summer and does not return again until early autumn. It is thought that the males spend part of this time looking for a new home range to which the family will move if food supplies are running low. Most migrations occur in the autumn when the males return.

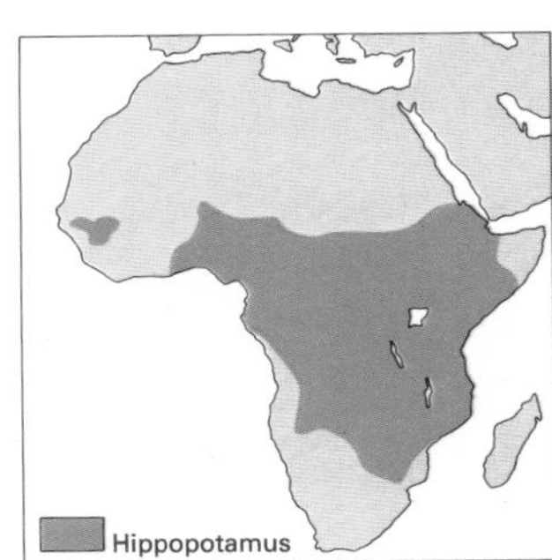

Weighing as much as three tons, the hippopotamus, *Hippopotamus amphibius*, is the largest freshwater animal in existence. It spends most of the day resting and keeping cool in rivers or muddy wallows, and only comes on to land to feed at night. It is entirely herbivorous and lives largely on a diet of grasses. Hippos are widely distributed throughout the rivers and lakes of tropical and equatorial Africa.

Compared with the beaver, the river otter, *Lutra canadensis*, of North America has a huge familiar area covering between 80 and 160 kilometres (50 and 100 miles) of river bank. However in any one season a family may use only five to sixteen kilometres (3 to 10 miles) of the total range. The way in which young otters build up such large familiar areas has been studied recently in Scotland using a novel technique. A young male European otter, *Lutra lutra*, was captured and labelled by feeding it small quantities of a harmless trace element. Otters mark out their home range with faeces and therefore always deposit them in conspicuous positions. As the trace element continued to appear in the otter's faeces for the next nine months, it was possible to track it on its pre-reproductive period of exploration.

The otter was labelled in October when four months old. For the next three or four months it stayed exclusively at the loch-side where it was caught and where it had almost certainly been born the previous summer. When it was seven or eight months old it began to move further afield and in particular began to explore a tributary river. The otter explored new territory at night, always returning to the loch during the day. During the course of the following spring the otter explored the river more extensively and eventually ceased to return to the loch each day. The otter was finally recorded forty kilometres (25 miles) upstream away from its probable birth place and is known to have visited places seventy kilometres (43 miles) apart. When it was about one year old it finally left the study area altogether.

This is probably the best description available of how a young mammal builds up a familiar area by exploration and it seems that all, except the females of some herd-living mammals, establish their familiar area in this way.

One of these land mammals is the hippopotamus, *Hippopotamus amphibius*, found in most African lakes south of the Sahara Desert. Hippos rest in water during the day, emerging at night to graze on land.

Groups of hippos found at resting sites consist mainly of females and young. Males tend to have individual resting sites situated around the main area.

With the rains hippos migrate to a wet season home range. Hippos migrate along waterways at night, resting in the water during the day. Females prefer to rest in lakes in the river system, whereas males prefer inland wallows that are cut off from rivers and lakes. These wallows can only be found, in the first place, by overland migration, suggesting that hippos travel considerable distances across land. Hippo tracks have been followed on land for distances up to thirty kilometres (19 miles).

Dugongs and manatees, sometimes called sea cows or sirens, spend their entire lives in the water, feeding on submerged vegetation. Many are marine, living in coastal waters, while others migrate between the sea and fresh water. One such group of manatee, *Trichechus manatus*, living in St John's River, on the east coast of Florida, has been cut off in the lower reaches of the river by a dam. This group, now entirely confined to fresh water, migrates between upriver feeding sites and a wintering range 300 kilometres (185 miles) downstream, where the water remains at a constant temperature of 23°C (73°F).

Marine migrants

The sea otter, *Enhydra lutris*, is the only fully marine otter species. It is found in the northern Pacific from California in the east to the Kuril Islands in the west. It inhabits water that is no more than sixty metres (200 feet) deep and feeds on a variety of fish and bottom-living invertebrates. It has the engaging habit of floating on its back, balancing a stone on its stomach; this stone is used to smash open shellfish. Sea otters have large home ranges, encompassing up to seventeen kilometres (11 miles) of shore line and normally extending about 2 kilometres (1.2 miles) from the shore. Continual hunting over the past 200 years has reduced the sea otter nearly to extinction and as a result there are many unoccupied but favourable habitats within its geographical range. This state of affairs has made it possible to study the way in which sea otters migrate when colonizing a new area. Unoccupied areas adjacent to sea otter populations are visited frequently by exploring migrants, but are not colonized until the density of otters in the nearby habitat has reached about sixteen individuals per square kilometre (41 per square mile). This seems to be a critical figure, for at this density sea otters are prepared to swim across water deeper than sixty metres (200 feet), which they would normally be reluctant to enter. Some individuals have crossed deep water barriers as much as 100 kilometres (60 miles) wide. It could be said that these journeys are not strictly speaking exploratory, for they are made with little opportunity of returning – the behaviour is probably more akin to that of the lemmings when making their famous exodus migrations in Scandinavia.

In the icy wastes of the Arctic lives one of the world's largest carnivores, the polar bear, *Ursus maritimus*. At one time it was thought that polar bears circumnavigated the Arctic Ocean by drifting on ice-floes, but recent

Dugongs and manatees are never seen on land. Their bone structure is very weak and they would have difficulty in breathing if unsupported by water. They prefer sheltered bays and coves with lush vegetation.

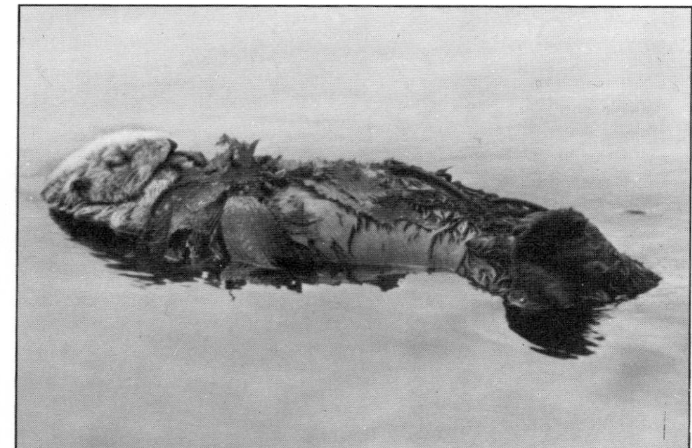

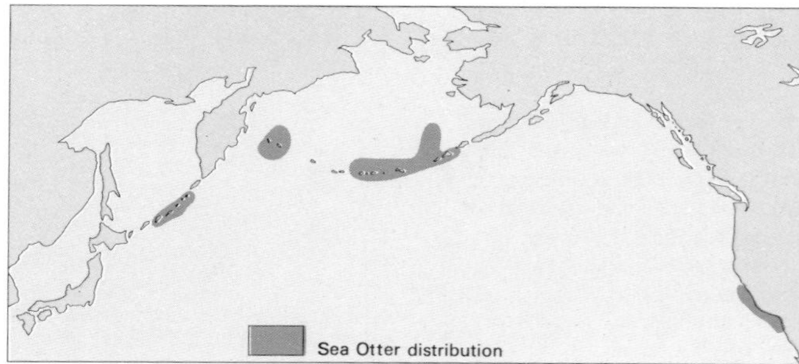

The sea otter, *Enhydra lutris*, is found along the island chains of the North Pacific. Among carnivores it is unique in having four incisors in the lower jaw. These teeth are used to crack open shell fish.

studies of the wind and current patterns have shown that this is unlikely. Like any other mammal, polar bears spend their lives within a familiar area, even though this area is probably larger than that of any other species of bear. The polar bear is probably more nomadic and opportunistic than other bears and whenever possible it will take advantage of floating ice to exploit hunting grounds that would otherwise be inaccessible.

As yet there is no detailed information about the movements of individual bears, but in recent years the species has become a favourite subject for long-range radio-tracking experiments. In some cases the radio receivers have been mounted in satellites, which track the animals' movements from space.

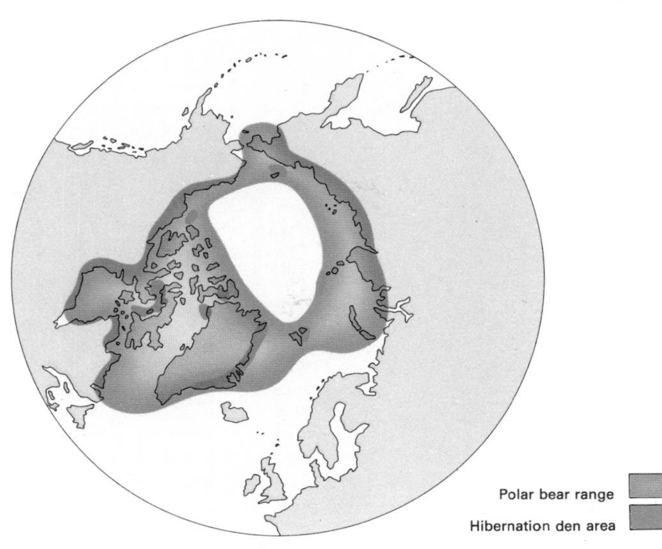

Polar bears, *Ursus maritimus*, are found along the southern edge of the Arctic pack-ice with a distribution that embraces the entire polar ocean. In spring they are carried south by the drift-ice, returning northward as the ice begins to break up in summer.

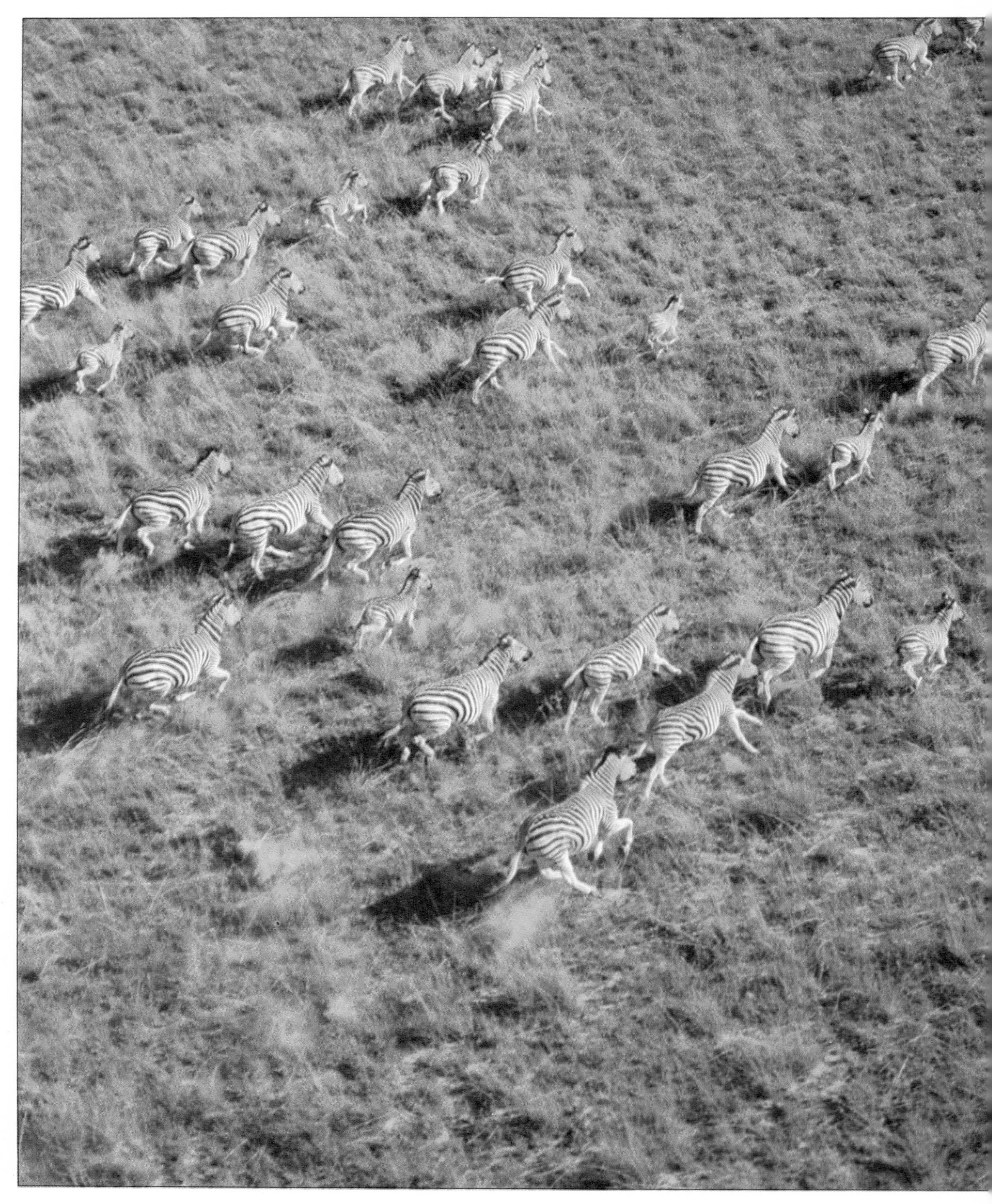

Land Mammals

Mammals are highly diverse. The land-living members range in size from the mouse to the elephant, in diet from vegetarian to carnivorous, and in life style from burrowing to tree dwelling. Within the mammal class almost all known ways of sexual reproduction are found. The most primitive members lay eggs like reptiles. Others give birth to immature young which are confined for the first months of life to a special pouch on the females' abdomens. At the opposite extreme the young of hoofed mammals are so well developed that they can run and keep up with their parents moments after birth. Almost the only thing that all mammals have in common is the females' ability to feed their young through mammary glands.

As mammals are so different from one another, it is hardly surprising that their migration patterns are so diverse. Their migrations may be one-way, to-and-fro or in the form of a circuit, and cover distances of anything up to thousands of kilometres. Nevertheless there are some basic similarities. Like other vertebrates all mammals establish a familiar area by exploration when young and from this area eventually extract a home range consisting of the places that provide them with everything necessary for life. However, the size of the home range does vary greatly from one species to another. The home range of small mammals such as badgers and rabbits are usually less than a square kilometre (0.4 square mile) in area, whereas in dry areas, those of elephants can be more than 100 square kilometres (40 square miles). Also the home ranges of many mammals are not static but change with the seasons, sometimes expanding during winter.

Some mammals have separate winter and summer, or wet and dry season, home ranges. This characteristic is not dependent on the species, and in some parts of the world the same mammals may live all year round in a single area. Those mammals that do migrate between separate home ranges, such as the wildebeeste and caribou, are among the best known of all animal migrants. Although the underlying reasons for migration are the same, the variety of mammals and their worldwide distribution in so many different environments, has provided a wide range of migration patterns.

Zebra are typical of seasonally migrant hoofed mammals. As they feed entirely on vegetation, they are compelled, in semi-arid areas, to migrate long distances to ensure a constant supply of food.

Mammals are essentially reptiles with the ability to control their body temperature. They have elongated scales (hair) and, most importantly, specially modified sweat glands through which they feed their young. These animals evolved from the reptiles about 200 million years ago. They made their first appearance shortly after the reptiles had evolved from the amphibians and just before the dinosaurs dominated the land. During their early evolution mammals were exclusively small nocturnal, insectivorous creatures not dissimilar from present-day shrews.

Evolution

It is thought that, about 200 million years ago, the continents were joined together as one land-mass. Shortly after the first mammals appeared this mass split into two halves, forming one continental area in the Northern Hemisphere – Laurasia – and another in the Southern Hemisphere – Gondwanaland. This split terrestrial life into two separately evolving communities.

At the outset mammals laid eggs like reptiles. They fed their young from modified sweat glands over large areas of their body and not just from specialized nipples. Mammals of this type, known as monotremes, are still in existence. They are represented by two groups of Australian animals, the spiny anteaters, family Tachyglossidae, and the duckbilled platypus, *Ornithorhynchus anatinus*. From this primitive form mammals evolved to give birth to live young instead of eggs. But the mode of

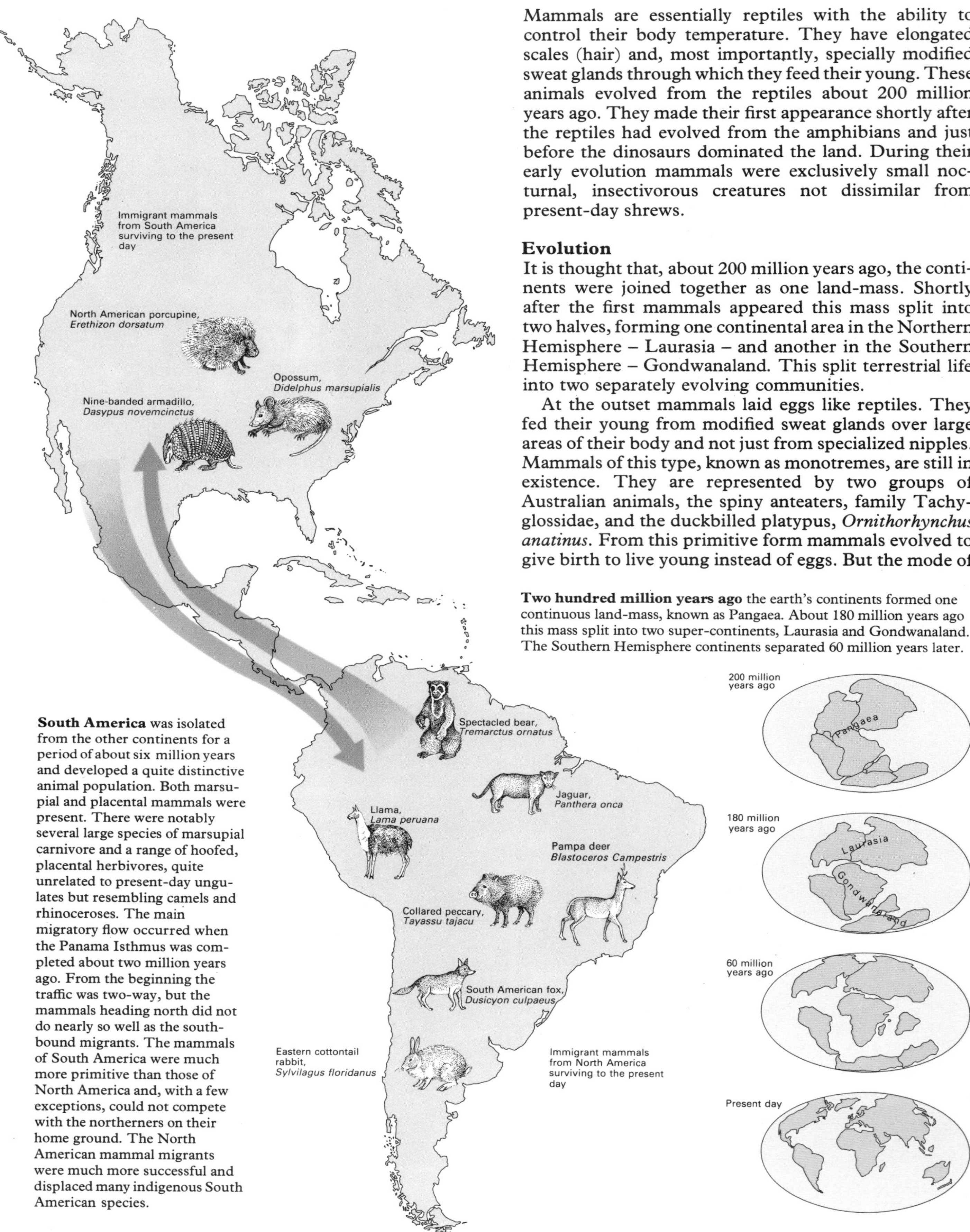

Two hundred million years ago the earth's continents formed one continuous land-mass, known as Pangaea. About 180 million years ago this mass split into two super-continents, Laurasia and Gondwanaland. The Southern Hemisphere continents separated 60 million years later.

South America was isolated from the other continents for a period of about six million years and developed a quite distinctive animal population. Both marsupial and placental mammals were present. There were notably several large species of marsupial carnivore and a range of hoofed, placental herbivores, quite unrelated to present-day ungulates but resembling camels and rhinoceroses. The main migratory flow occurred when the Panama Isthmus was completed about two million years ago. From the beginning the traffic was two-way, but the mammals heading north did not do nearly so well as the southbound migrants. The mammals of South America were much more primitive than those of North America and, with a few exceptions, could not compete with the northerners on their home ground. The North American mammal migrants were much more successful and displaced many indigenous South American species.

birth and, in particular, the way in which the young are cared for after the birth evolved differently in each continental area. In the northern area the young were retained within the womb and fed through a placenta until they achieved an advanced stage of development. The placental mammals, as they are called, are the most numerous and most advanced group. They account for nineteen out of twenty-one orders of existing mammals. In the southern area, except for that part which is now Africa, the females gave birth when their young were barely formed and nursed them in special pouches on the abdomen. These mammals were the ancestors of present-day marsupials, such as kangaroos and opossums. No marsupials appeared in Africa, for at about the time they were evolving, Africa separated from the rest of Gondwanaland and drifted north towards the part of Laurasia which is now Europe.

Although marsupials evolved in what were to become three of the earth's southern continents, today they are commonly found in only one of them – Australia. At the break-up of Gondwanaland, Antarctica drifted south over the South Pole and became a desert of snow and ice, totally hostile to land mammals. South America drifted north and became united with North America. The placental mammals that came south over the Panama Isthmus after the union of the two continents were in direct competition with their marsupial equivalents and were on the whole more successful. They displaced all except one group – the opossums.

Mammal diversity

About sixty-five million years ago the dinosaurs disappeared from the earth leaving a vacuum. The mammals were in a position to fill the gap and have dominated the earth ever since. From their small shrew-like ancestors, mammals evolved to fill every conceivable niche in nature. On land some, like rats and mice, have remained small, not unlike their forebears. Others have become highly specialized grazers. The existence of herbivores stimulated the evolution of the carnivores that prey on them and as the herbivores became larger so did the carnivores, giving rise to present-day lions and tigers.

Some mammals developed special attributes to enable them to live in the trees. They evolved grasping hands to hold on to the branches and binocular vision so that they could judge distances and jump accurately from tree to tree. These mammals are the primates, the order to which lemurs, monkeys and man belong.

By and large the marsupials evolved in parallel to the placentals and in many cases placentals have direct marsupial equivalents. There are marsupial versions of rats, shrews, moles and cats. The large grazing placental mammals such as deer have their marsupial equivalent in the kangaroos. Until relatively recently there were marsupial tigers, and the primates have marsupial equivalents in koalas and opossums.

Ranging from the mouse to the elephant the diversity of mammal form and behaviour is enormous and goes hand in hand with a corresponding diversity in migration

Kangaroos can be thought of as the marsupial equivalents of hoofed grazing mammals. As the young of both groups are mobile, or carried at birth, the adults superficially have similar migratory patterns. However, Australia's unreliable rainfall makes kangaroo migration much more irregular. During drought kangaroos converge on areas of permanent water, and disperse again when the rains return.

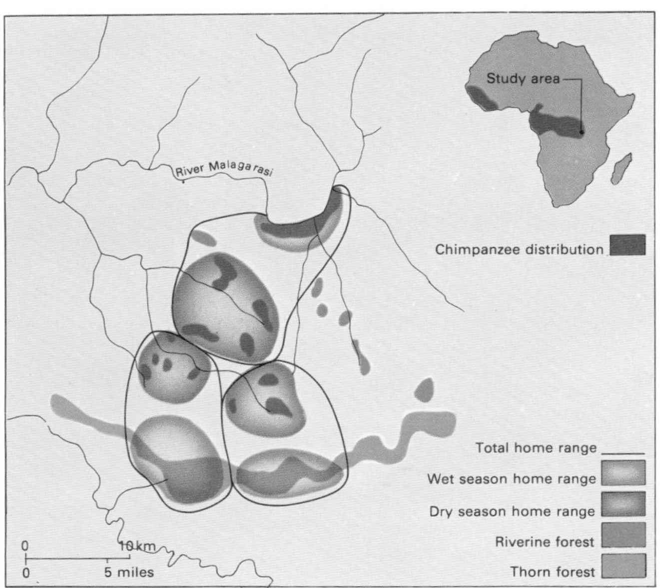

A study of chimpanzees, *Pan troglodytes*, living in the highlands of western Tanzania showed that, in the dry conditions prevailing, the chimpanzees had separate home ranges for the wet and dry seasons.

Moose, *Alces alces*, love water. Found throughout Alaska and Canada, their favourite habitat is the lush woodland pasture found near lakes and rivers. They frequently wade into the water to feed, and are said to be especially fond of water lilies. In summer they may immerse themselves totally to evade the ever-present mosquitoes.

MOOSE MIGRATION

In the mountains moose move downhill with the change in season. In summer they are found at the upper limit of the coniferous forest. They move down through the deciduous forest in autumn, reaching the valley floor in winter. Moose migrate primarily in response to snowfall. They have difficulty feeding when the depth is greater than seventy-five centimetres (30 in). Their broad hoofs, designed to prevent them sinking into soft ground, are also used in defence against predators.

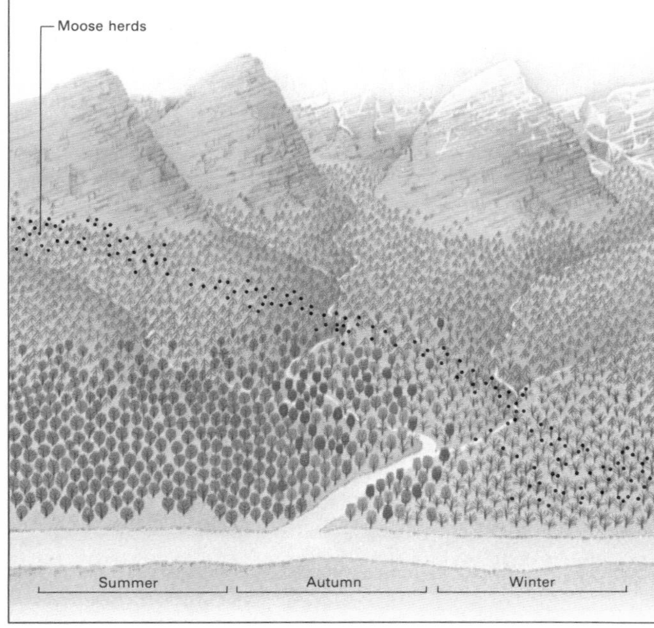

pattern. One important factor affecting mammal migration is the extent to which a young animal can travel immediately after birth. Excepting for the young of hoofed animals, the young of placental mammals are totally helpless at birth and are incapable of walking. The female placental mammal must leave her young in a nest while she forages for food, and so makes a series of return migrations between the nest and the feeding grounds until the young are old enough to travel with her. This pattern is absent from the lives of marsupials and primates, which can move around carrying their young in pouches in the case of marsupials or clinging to their backs in the case of primates.

The migrations of all terrestrial mammals take place within a familiar area. The area contains all the animal's feeding, breeding and wintering needs and is established by exploration when the animal is young. In many cases, there may be no clear pattern of movement within the familiar area. Forest animals such as deer and monkeys move within relatively small home ranges, in which their needs are met at all times of year. In a minority of cases an animal's needs may be met in different parts of its home range at different times of the year and it must therefore migrate seasonally between two or more areas.

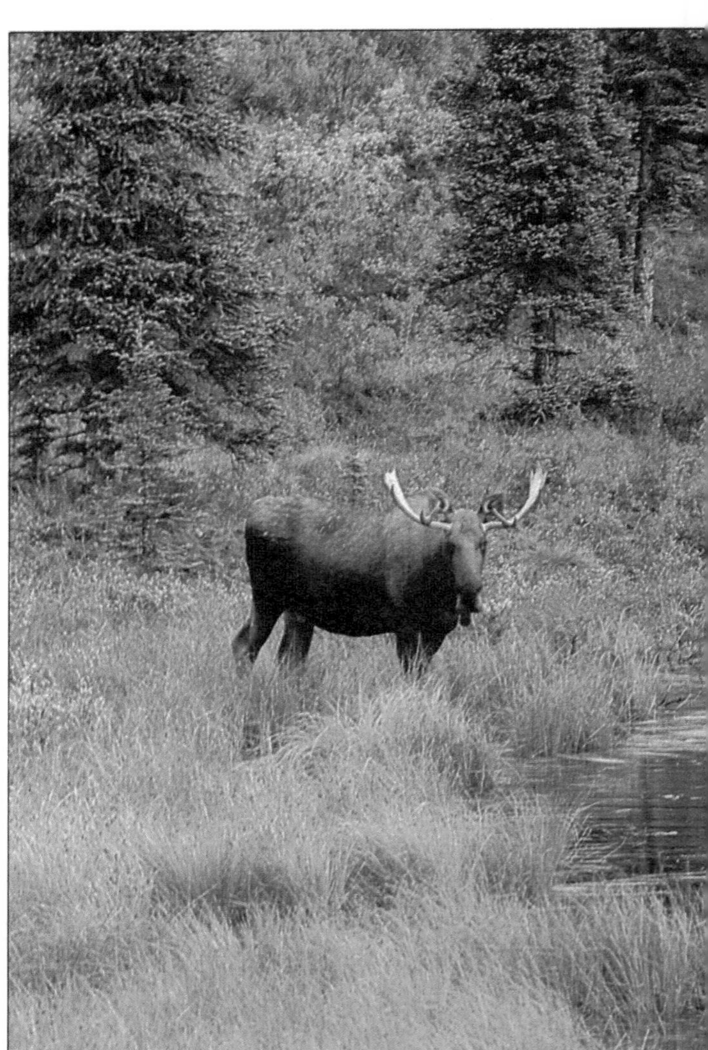

Most chimpanzees, *Pan troglodytes*, live in parts of the world where food is easily found at different times of the year. They move around nomadically within their home range taking advantage of the fruit of different trees as it comes into season. However, in dry areas, such as western Tanzania, chimpanzees make distinct return migrations between wet and dry season home ranges. During the latter part of the wet season and the early part of the dry season the chimpanzees feed mainly on the beans of the *Brachystegia bussei* in the open thorn woodlands. As the dry season progresses the chimpanzees migrate about ten kilometres (7 miles) to feed in the wetter riverine forests, where they remain until the vegetation in the thorn woodland has recovered sufficiently to provide new browsing.

Seasonal migration in highland areas

Seasonal return migrations between different home ranges occur in areas that are habitable only at certain times of the year and are typical of animals living on mountainsides anywhere on the globe.

The moose, *Alces alces*, of the Canadian Rockies spends the summer months among the high coniferous forest. They prefer open areas near a stream or lake, where they can browse on water plants. When the snows appear in autumn the moose head downhill, keeping just ahead of the deep snow coverage. By December the herds reach the upper valley areas and continue moving down towards the lowlands during the winter. Uphill migration begins in March or April at the start of the warm weather. A cold spell in spring may halt migration and may even cause the moose to travel temporarily downhill.

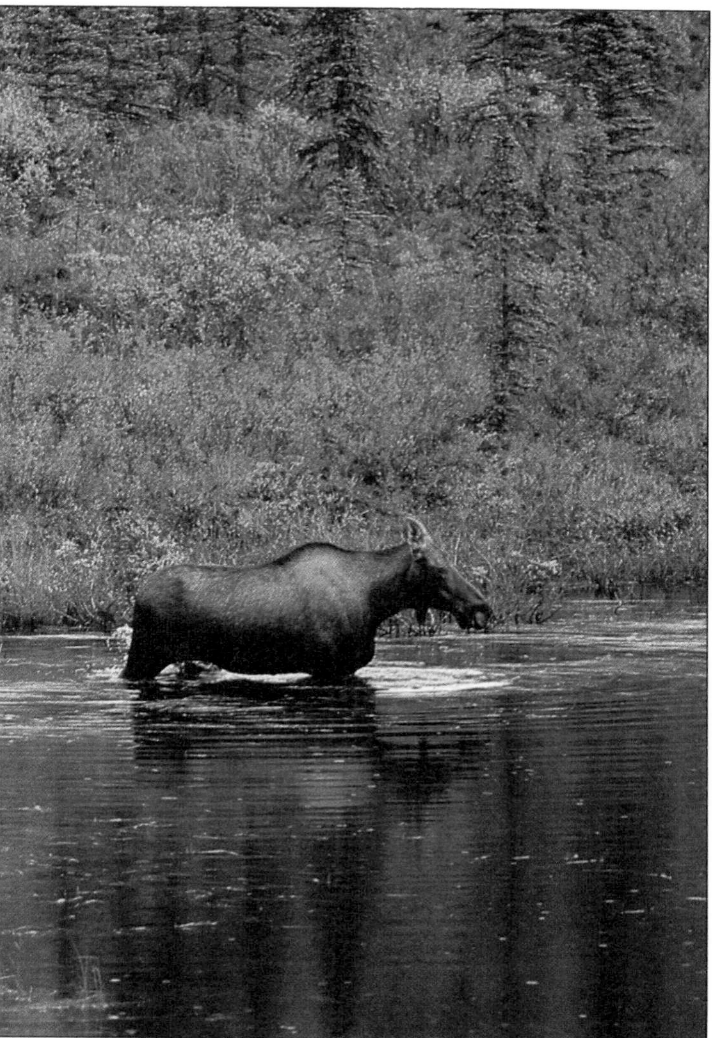

A similar pattern is seen in East Africa, where the elephants, *Loxodonta africana*, living on the slopes of Mount Kenya migrate up the mountain during the dry season and down again in the wet season.

Altitudinal migrations are not always so clear-cut. In Scotland, red deer, *Cervus elaphus*, are generally found at altitudes from sea level up to 520 metres (1900 feet) in winter and at altitudes above 520 metres in summer. Overlying the broad seasonal pattern of movement is the deer's need for shelter during the breeding season and in bad weather. In early summer, females migrate to lower altitudes to give birth, and both males and females migrate downhill to mate in the autumn. At any time of the year during bad weather the deer will move to lower levels. The return migration uphill in spring occurs in a series of steps. The deer move up during the day and return part way down at night.

Many factors are involved in the production of this pattern. The scarcity of food and its successive reappearance at high altitude in spring are probably most important. The lower levels also give more protection from storms in winter and the higher pastures are freer from blood-sucking parasites in summer.

The East African herds

The concept of an animal migrating within a familiar area holds true for hoofed mammals such as zebra, *Equus quagga*, and saiga, *Saiga tatarica*, that migrate over thousands of kilometres. The migratory track becomes an extended familiar area, learned by the young animals as they follow the herd in successive seasons.

Long-distance seasonal return migrations by land mammals have developed in only three major habitat types, tundra, desert and grassland. All are regions in

At the driest extremity of its range, the African elephant, *Loxodonta africana*, in common with other mammals living in normally humid conditions, migrates seasonally between wet and dry season home ranges.

BIGHORN SHEEP

In North America there are two separate species of bighorn sheep: *Ovis canadensis*, found in western North America, and *Ovis dalli*, found in Alaska and northwest Canada. They inhabit the high inaccessible country found above the treeline. Because the mountain pasture is so poor, both species have annual ranges consisting of several seasonal feeding home ranges in addition to mating and lambing sites. These home ranges are visited in turn by the sheep along clearly defined routes. Females may use up to four and males may use as many as seven separate home ranges each year. Often the ranges are on the opposite sides of a valley and the sheep must travel through extensive tracts of woodland to reach the next home range. Wolves, the sheep's main predators, are often found in these wooded valleys and, before crossing, the sheep will sit together on rocky outcrops for several hours, days or even weeks, surveying the valley floor. When the sheep have discovered the wolves' whereabouts and judge the time to be right, they travel down the mountainside, crossing the woodland as quickly as possible. However, despite their earlier vigilance many still fall prey to the wolves.

which the availability of food is highly seasonal or erratic, either because of drought or snowfall or both.

The influence of climate and vegetation on the availability of food and water is seen particularly clearly in and around the African plains. Most of the larger African mammals live in the savannah areas that form the transition zone between tropical grassland and equatorial forest. Although the number of different species is high in these transition zones, large concentrations of animals are rare and migration takes place over relatively short distances. Many animals, such as the black rhinoceros, *Diceros bicornis*, and the giraffe, *Giraffa camelopardalis*, migrate within the limits of a single continuous home range and most elephant movement is confined to single areas. They will normally only migrate outside it when forced to by a shortage of food or overpopulation. Where a mammal does have separate home ranges for wet and dry seasons, as is the case with the white rhinoceros, *Ceratotherium simum*, the two areas are close together.

In the grassland proper, migration is much more pronounced. Although there are fewer species the numbers involved are much greater and the distances travelled much further. With the approach of the wet season large herds of wildebeeste, *Connochaetes taurinus*, zebra and Thomson's gazelle, *Gazella thomsoni*, migrate from the scrubby woodland around Lake Victoria into the Serengeti. The migrant herds spend the dry season feeding in the more moist open woodlands. In December, when the first storms appear, the herds move off south-east into the central plains, where there are fresh pastures and where they can escape the worst ravages of the tsetse fly. The zebra are the first to arrive, feeding on the stems and leaves of the taller grasses. As they feed and trample over the new pasture they expose the lower layers of vegetation and prepare it for the later arrivals. The wildebeeste eat mainly the leaves of grasses and the gazelles eat the smaller, low-growing plants.

In the wet season from January to March the herds migrate in a predominantly counterclockwise direction. Their migration is entirely opportunistic, being directed, particularly early in the season, to any area where rain can be seen or heard to be falling. The herds may migrate towards thunder or storm clouds even when these are 100 kilometres (60 miles) distant. In June the plains dry out and the herds migrate back northwestward to their dry season home range, where food and water remain plentiful. The migrant females give birth in December and January during the migration to the wet season home range. Non-migrant inhabitants of the Serengeti Plain, such as the impala, *Aepyceros melampus*, and the giraffe, give birth in October while the herds are still present. In this way the non-migrants produce their young when the resident predators have a surfeit of prey available to them.

The movement of the migrant herds affects the behaviour of the predatory carnivores. These animals follow one of three patterns of migration. They may travel with the herd or commute between their home site and the place where the herd is grazing, or they may switch to an alternative prey. The first two modes of behaviour can be seen in hyenas. The spotted hyena, *Crocuta crocuta*, follows the herds northwestward across the Serengeti at the beginning of the dry season. Some hyenas, usually females with relatively immobile young, stop short of the thorn woodland and establish dens on the edges of the plains, from where they conduct hunting expeditions into their prey's dry season territory. The younger and more mobile hyenas follow the herds into the woodland and remain with them throughout the whole of their migration.

Lions, *Panthera leo*, normally remain in the same home range all year. They prey on the herds only when they pass through their territory and attack non-migrants such as impala at other times.

In common with large land animals in other parts of the world the Serengeti herds' migration is in the form of a circuit rather than a to-and-fro movement. Although in the case of zebra and wildebeeste the circuit's general form remains constant, it varies considerably in detail from year to year and depends largely on rainfall.

SERENGETI MIGRANTS

Herds of zebra, wildebeeste and Thomson's gazelle spend the dry season in the thorn forests to the northwest and the wet season in the open plains to the southeast of the Serengeti. The Serengeti National Park, founded in 1929, was established primarily to protect the herds' migration route.

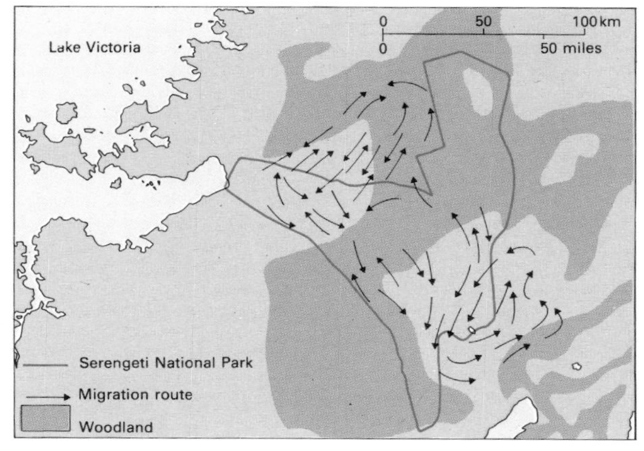

Vast herds of hoofed animals can still be seen on the plains of East Africa. However, their numbers are gradually falling due to the combined pressures of hunting and agriculture.

Most herd animals found in the true grasslands of Africa migrate between wet and dry season home ranges. As the transitional savannah is more humid most of its residents are able to remain in the same locality all the year round.

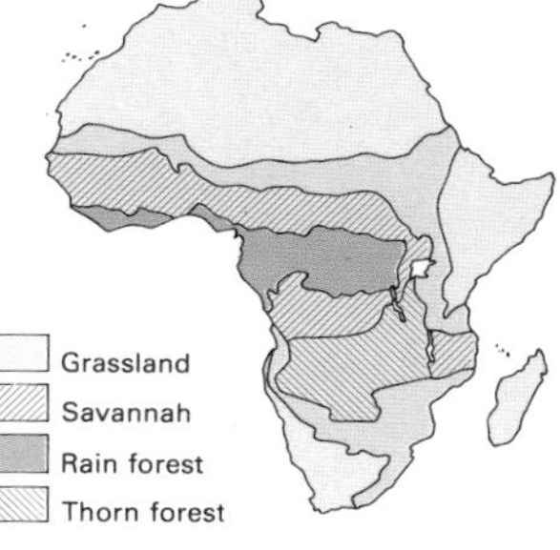

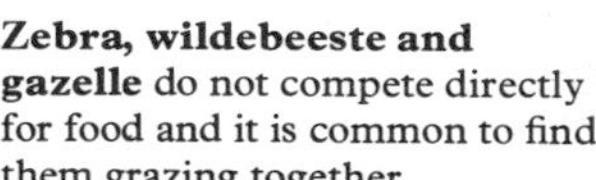

Zebra, wildebeeste and gazelle do not compete directly for food and it is common to find them grazing together.

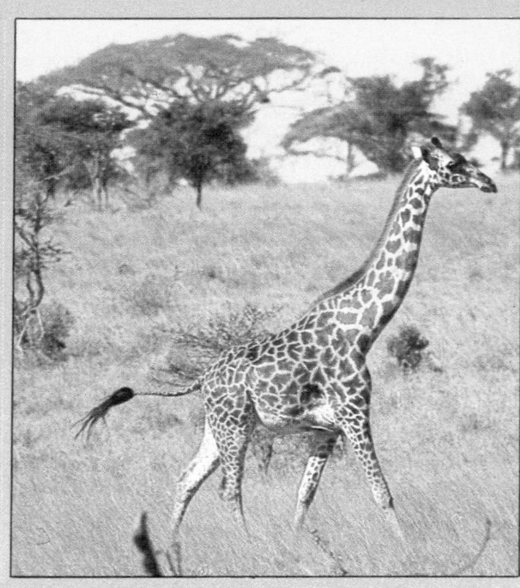

Giraffes, *Giraffa camelopardalis*, prefer more open areas among the savannah woodland.

Thomson's gazelle, *Gazella thomsoni*, are found mainly in the Serengeti and are the most numerous species of mammal in East Africa.

Hyenas, *Crocuta crocuta*, have a reputation as scavengers, but they are also highly effective hunters. They probably kill more grazing animals in East Africa than any other carnivore.

Lionesses normally do most of the hunting, but here a male has brought down a zebra that has passed through his territory.

The great savannah grasslands are the last refuge of migrant herd animals outside the Arctic. Lying both to the north and south of the equatorial forests, they account for more than one-third of Africa's total area. The immense expanses of rust-brown grasses are dotted with flat-topped acacia and baobab trees, and provide grazing for over forty species of herbivore. Water, or rather the lack of it, is the key factor. It governs all living things and is responsible for the annual migrations of the herds of zebra and wildebeeste.

Reindeer and caribou

The world's most numerous herd animals in existence outside the tropics are the reindeer and caribou. Both are sub-species of *Rangifer tarandus*, reindeer being found throughout Europe and Asia and caribou in North America. They are essentially grazers and eat only the leaves of plants, ignoring their stems and woody parts. They are, however, not particularly fussy about which plants they eat, and do not, as is often thought, feed exclusively on lichens. These are important in their diet, but make up only between thirty and fifty per cent of their intake, even in winter. The caribou and reindeer live in predominantly two types of habitat – coniferous forest and tundra. Those herds living exclusively in one or other habitat only migrate over relatively short distances, usually no more than a few tens of kilometres. The reindeer and caribou living in the transition zones between the forest and tundra embark on much longer migrations, up to 1000 kilometres (620 miles) in each direction. The best known of these populations is the barren-ground caribou of arctic Canada to the west of Hudson Bay.

As winter approaches, the snow cover on the tundra becomes deep and compacted. Repeated thawing and freezing of the surface creates a layer of ice over the snow and prevents the caribou from scraping it aside to reach the underlying vegetation. At this time the barren-ground caribou move from the tundra into the forests, where the snow, particularly in the interior, may be even deeper, but as it is shielded from the sun and the more severe frosts by trees, it remains light and fluffy. The caribou, using their front hoofs, are able to make feeding craters through the soft snow, allowing them to get at the lichens and sedges lying protected beneath. The adult females and the younger animals remain at the forest edge where the snow is shallower. Only the more powerful adult males venture into the deep snow of the forest to feed.

In spring, sometime between February and April, the herds move north towards the calving grounds, converging at the treeline about the first week in May. From there to the nearest calving ground is between 400 and 500 kilometres (250 and 300 miles), a distance which the herds complete at an average speed of between twenty-five and fifty kilometres (15 and 30 miles) a day. The first females arrive at about the end of May. Caribou migrate along lines of least resistance – across frozen lakes and rivers and over open snow-free uplands and ridges. The pregnant females lead the migration, with the males and immature animals gradually lagging further and further behind. A migrating herd may be as much as 300 kilometres (185 miles) in length; herds of caribou, in some instances, have been known to take several weeks to pass one particular point.

The calving grounds, situated around the Arctic Circle, to the northwest of Hudson Bay, are usually in rugged inhospitable uplands, well away from wolves and other predators. Within a few hours of birth the calves are able to run with their mothers and keep within the protection of the herd. In a matter of a few weeks they are able to forage for themselves. Suckling usually ceases around the first week in July. With the calves able to fend

for themselves the herds move on, 200 kilometres (125 miles) or so, to lower, greener pastures where the feeding is better. During early summer the caribou are plagued by swarms of warble flies and mosquitoes, and are compelled to move from place to place to avoid them. It is not uncommon at this time to find emaciated individuals, separated from the herd and utterly exhausted from their constant persecution. In July the herds disperse at the start of the return migration to the forest. They travel south during August in small groups of two or three individuals. At the end of the month the herds converge once more and by late September arrive, fat and in good condition, at the treeline. Being fitter and with no pregnant females to slow them down the caribou are able to travel faster in the autumn – at speeds of up to sixty-four kilometres (40 miles) a day – over the same distance that they covered during the spring migration.

In Europe and Asia, reindeer migration is mainly altitudinal or takes place to and from the coast. In the past the herds were accompanied by nomadic hunters, who depended on the deer for food and clothing. Today only the Norwegian Laplanders follow the herds from the winter home range in the sheltered forests of the interior to their summer home along the coast of the Arctic Ocean. Their northward trek, lasting between twelve and fourteen days, starts at the end of April near the Finnish border, along a route which has been in existence since the Ice Age.

Saiga

Until recently the grasslands of Eurasia were inhabited by herds of grazing animals that migrated in much the same way as those of the Serengeti. But because of man's

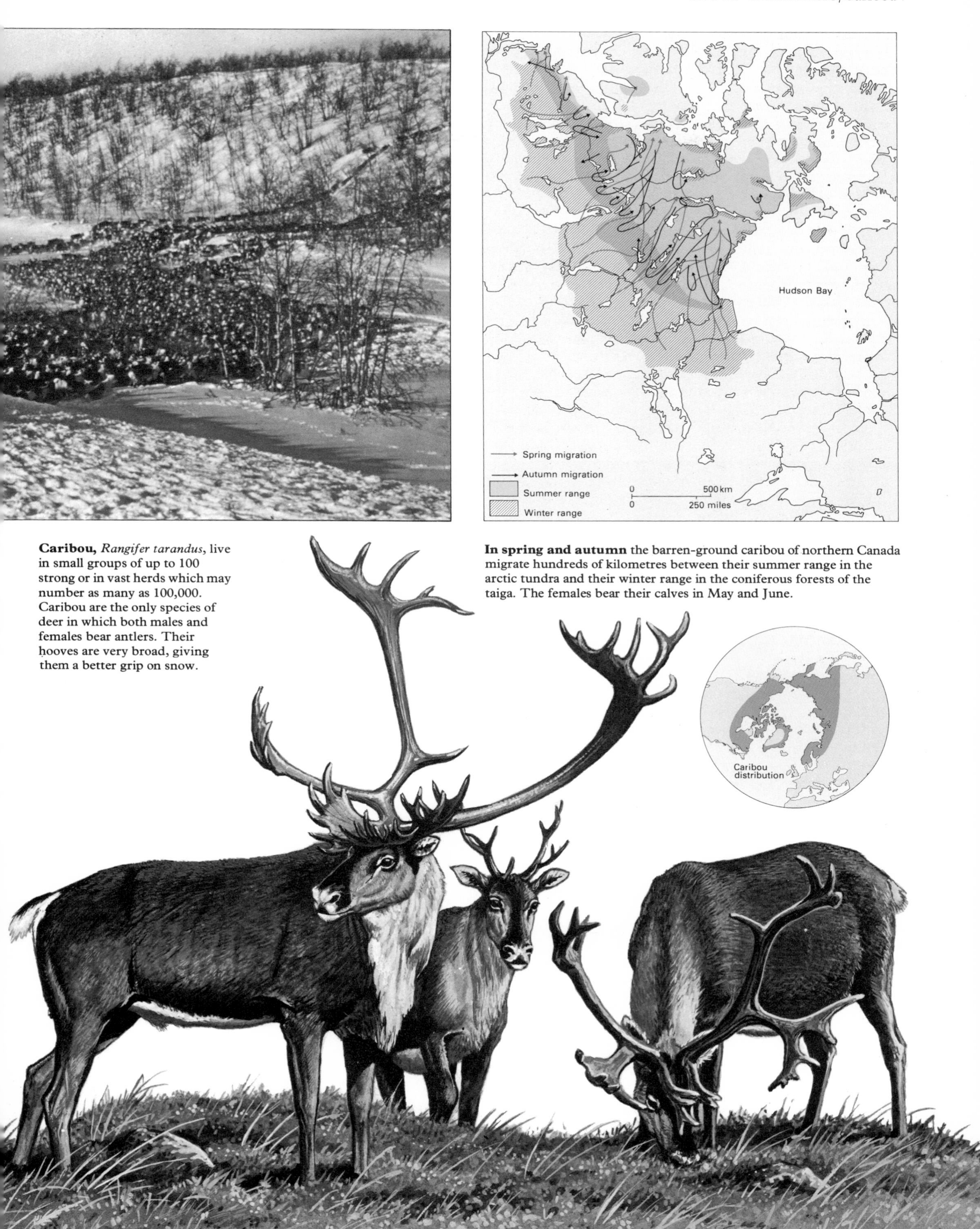

Caribou, *Rangifer tarandus*, live in small groups of up to 100 strong or in vast herds which may number as many as 100,000. Caribou are the only species of deer in which both males and females bear antlers. Their hooves are very broad, giving them a better grip on snow.

In spring and autumn the barren-ground caribou of northern Canada migrate hundreds of kilometres between their summer range in the arctic tundra and their winter range in the coniferous forests of the taiga. The females bear their calves in May and June.

interference many species such as the European bison, *Bison bonasus*, and Przewalski's horse, *Equus przewalskii*, have come dangerously near extinction. The only sizeable herds left are those of the saiga, *Saiga tatarica*, found on the southern Asiatic steppes, stretching from the Caspian Sea into Mongolia. In spring the saiga migrate from the Caspian region northward to their parturition grounds 300 to 350 kilometres (185 to 220 miles) away, where the females give birth. This leg of their migration takes about fourteen days, depending on weather conditions; extensive snow cover and frequent storms slow down their progress. They travel either in small groups or in herds up to 60,000 or 100,000 strong, moving across the plains in columns one to one and a half kilometres (0.6 to 1 mile) wide.

After the breeding season the herds migrate 200 to 250 kilometres (125 to 155 miles) southwest to the summer feeding grounds. The males and the non-breeding females leave first, followed by those with the young that were born that season. During summer the herds migrate continuously in search of food and water. In drier years the saiga travel further west, where the rainfall is higher. Between the end of August and the beginning of October the herds migrate eastward back to the Caspian lowlands. With the arrival of the snows at the end of November they head south to their winter quarters. The timing of the autumn migration varies widely between individuals and its extent differs from year to year according to the weather.

For centuries man has hunted the saiga without serious consequences. Only since the introduction of the firearm and the discovery of a lucrative market for saiga horns in China have their numbers dropped to dangerously low levels. In the late nineteenth century they were hunted with such vigour that from herds that had previously numbered millions there were scarcely 1,000 saiga left in 1918. Legislation to control hunting has thankfully saved the species from extinction. In 1960 the saiga were estimated to number 1.3 million and their numbers are now thought to be well over the two million mark.

In other parts of the world the fate of migrant herd animals is in doubt. In East Africa the designation of conservation areas spanning international boundaries has largely kept their populations and traditional migration routes intact. It remains to be seen how well these areas resist pressure of future development, particularly if the

The strange-looking saiga, *Saiga tatarica*, with its long neck and bulbous nostrils, has, thanks to a hunting prohibition, re-established itself on the Asiatic steppes. Its ancestry is obscure and, although classified as an antelope, it has many characteristics in common with sheep and goats. The almost trunk-like nose is designed to exclude dust and to warm the air before it reaches the lungs. Saiga are unable to withstand extreme cold or to feed with more than twenty centimetres (8 in) of snow on the ground. They spend the winter feeding in the lowlands around the Caspian Sea. During the climatic optimum that occurred 10,000 years ago, when temperatures were a degree or two higher, saiga were found across the Eurasian plains as far east as Lake Baikal. Hunting and climatic deterioration has reduced their distribution to its present size.

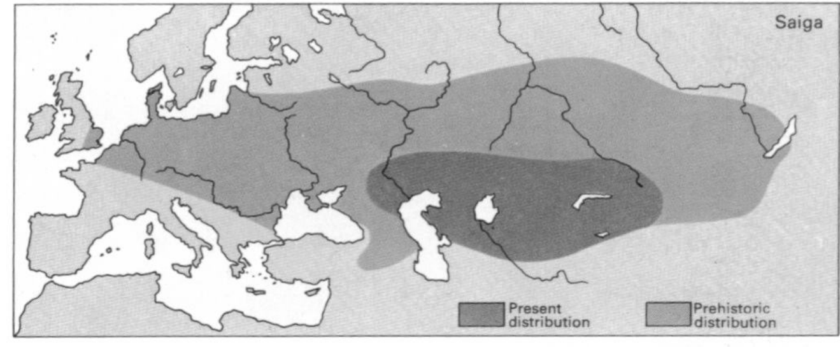

SPRINGBOK

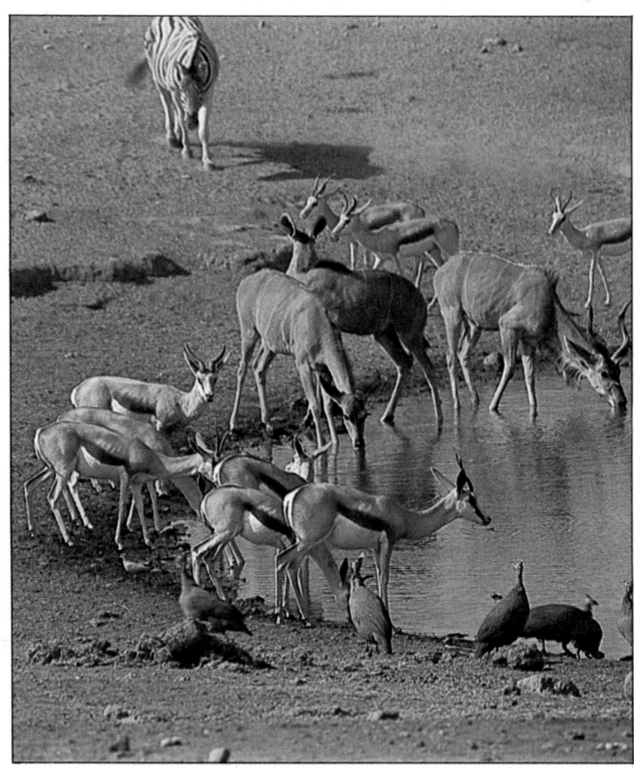

Until the late nineteenth century springbok, *Antidorcas marsupialis*, were found in herds numbering hundreds of thousands in many parts of South Africa. These small graceful antelopes unfortunately competed directly with the settlers' domestic grazing animals and were ruthlessly persecuted. Before human settlement the springbok migrated between humid upland areas in the southwest of the country and the semi-arid grasslands in the northeast. Apart from this seasonal pattern, mass migrations occurred every three or four years in response to drought or population pressures. Herds of springbok all moving in the same direction merged into massive hordes, thousands strong, trampling everything in their path. One such horde, witnessed in 1896, took several days to pass an observer. It was 220 kilometres (135 miles) long, twenty kilometres (12 miles) wide and estimated to contain about a million animals. During these episodes, the damage to crops was so extensive that at times the South African government issued firearms to the local population with instructions to shoot as many springbok as possible. The tiny surviving population is now confined almost entirely to nature reserves in the southwestern part of this country.

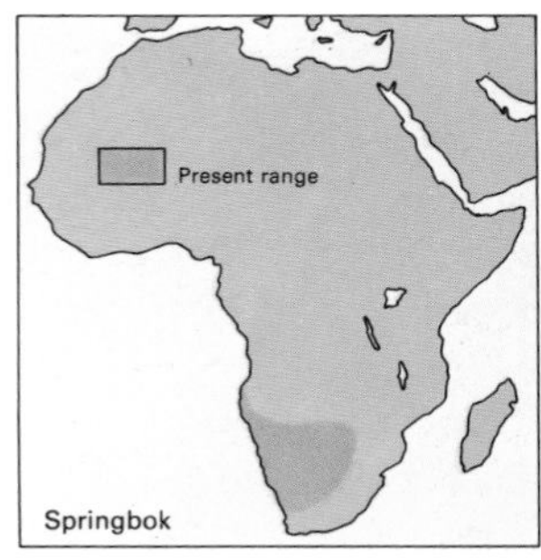

NORTH AMERICAN BISON

Before the Europeans arrived in North America, American bison, *Bison bison*, were found over an area stretching from southern Canada to northern Mexico and were estimated to number more than sixty million. They migrated up to 500 kilometres (310 miles) between summer and winter ranges along roughly circular routes. Early eyewitness accounts of migrating bison describe vast herds, millions strong, covering hundreds of square miles. A mass of bison eighty kilometres (50 miles) long, and forty kilometres (25 miles) wide was witnessed crossing the Arkansas River in 1871. From the middle of the nineteenth century bison were slaughtered by European settlers in quite staggering proportions. Between 1870 and 1875 alone, more than twelve and a half million animals were shot. Sometimes they were killed just for the tongue, which was considered a delicacy, and at other times purely to deprive the local Indians of their sole means of support. By 1880 there were no herds left south of the Arkansas River and a census conducted in 1889 could find only 1091 individuals remaining from the vast herds that had previously existed. From this pathetic remnant the current population of 30,000 has been re-established within the protection of the national parks.

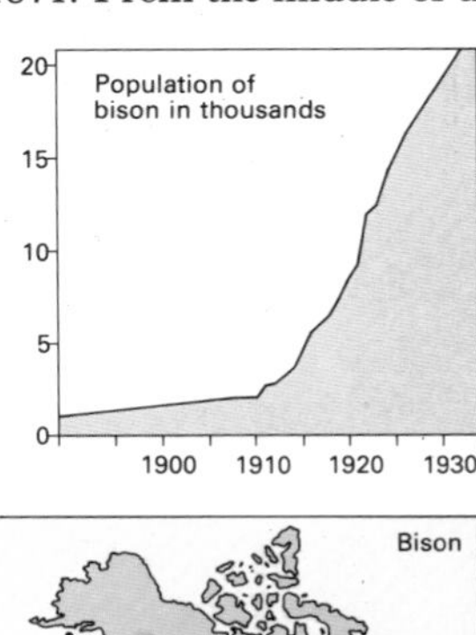

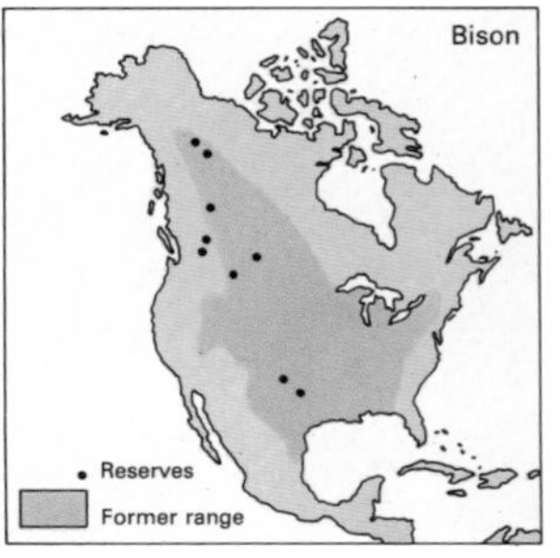

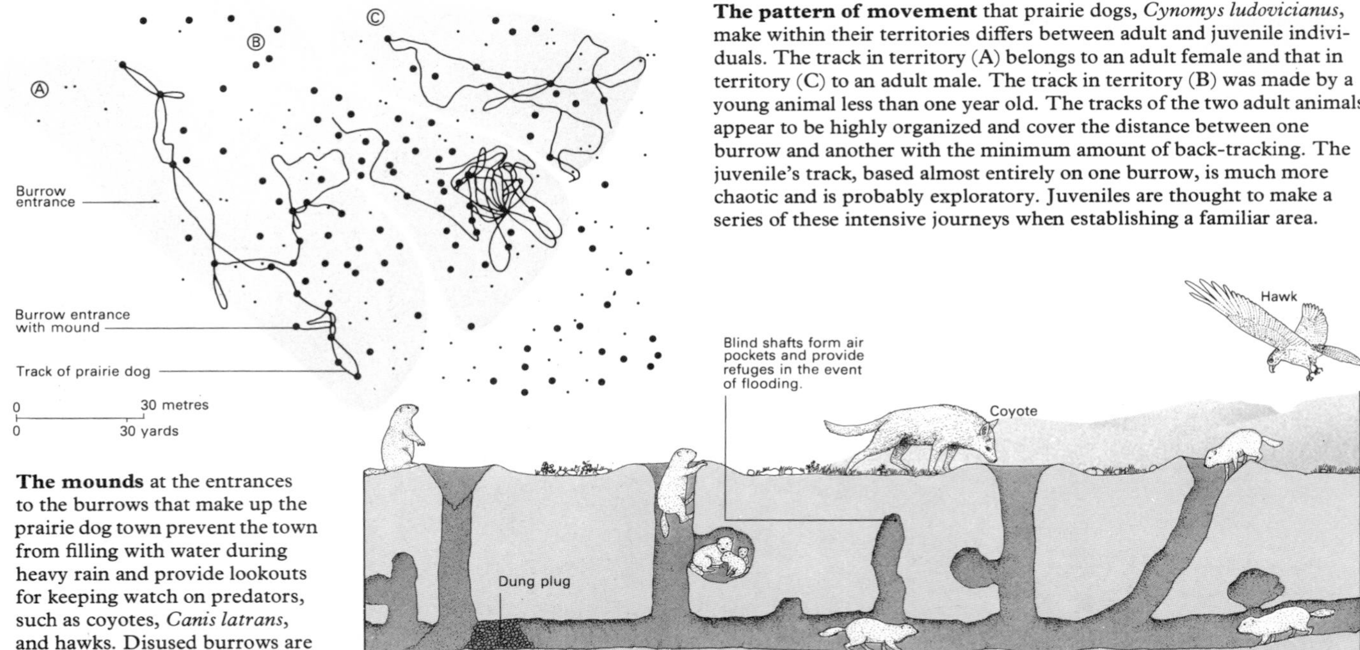

The pattern of movement that prairie dogs, *Cynomys ludovicianus*, make within their territories differs between adult and juvenile individuals. The track in territory (A) belongs to an adult female and that in territory (C) to an adult male. The track in territory (B) was made by a young animal less than one year old. The tracks of the two adult animals appear to be highly organized and cover the distance between one burrow and another with the minimum amount of back-tracking. The juvenile's track, based almost entirely on one burrow, is much more chaotic and is probably exploratory. Juveniles are thought to make a series of these intensive journeys when establishing a familiar area.

The mounds at the entrances to the burrows that make up the prairie dog town prevent the town from filling with water during heavy rain and provide lookouts for keeping watch on predators, such as coyotes, *Canis latrans*, and hawks. Disused burrows are plugged with dung or soil.

tsetse fly is brought under further control and cattle ranching becomes firmly established on the plains.

Wholesale hunting and agricultural pressure have largely wiped out the once enormous populations of springbok in South Africa and bison in North America. The remnants are confined to small reserves and the migrant herds are no more.

The home range

Apart from the mammals that make long-distance seasonal journeys between different feeding areas or between feeding and breeding areas, there are many species which spend all their adult life within a comparatively limited home range.

For some animals, living within a home range that is totally familiar is essential for survival. It is not only important to know where to find food and water but also where to take refuge from predators.

The black-tailed prairie dog, *Cynomys ludovicianus*, a ground squirrel found throughout North America, lives in vast colonies or "towns" occupying areas from three to thirty hectares (7 to 75 acres). The prairie dog is socially highly organized. Each town is divided into a number of wards and each ward into a number of territories, or coteries, occupied by individual prairie dog families. Each territory has a network of burrows with numerous entrances down which the animal escapes at the first sign of danger. The prairie dog's chance of survival is improved if it confines its movements to the part of the town it knows best.

Because the home range is so important, an animal must establish one as early in life as possible. As is the case for most animals, a mammal's home range is extracted from a familiar area, established by exploration when the animal is very young. After the familiar area has been established an animal may still visit places outside the home range that provide particular needs. The Norway rat, *Rattus norvegicus*, normally remains within a relatively small home range, but individual rats may sometimes travel distances up to a kilometre (0.6 mile) from the nest to feed at some particular site discovered during exploration.

The home ranges of many species fluctuate seasonally. The female American badger, *Taxidea taxus*, has a home range of approximately 750 hectares (1850 acres) in summer and about fifty-two hectares (128 acres) in autumn. In winter the same animal's home range may be only two hectares (5 acres). The female American red fox, *Vulpes vulpes fulva*, on the other hand, expands her home range in winter from three kilometres (2 miles) to between eight and sixteen kilometres (5 and 10 miles) across.

The American black bear, *Ursus americanus*, frequently migrates outside its usual home range. It is omnivorous, feeding on vegetation in spring, berries in autumn and flesh and insects when the opportunity arises. Its home range, which is small by carnivore standards, is no more than two and a half kilometres (1.5 miles) across for females and six kilometres (4 miles) across for males. When food is scarce in early spring the bears are commonly found foraging on rubbish dumps. To reach one they have been known to travel up to fifteen kilometres (10 miles) from their home range.

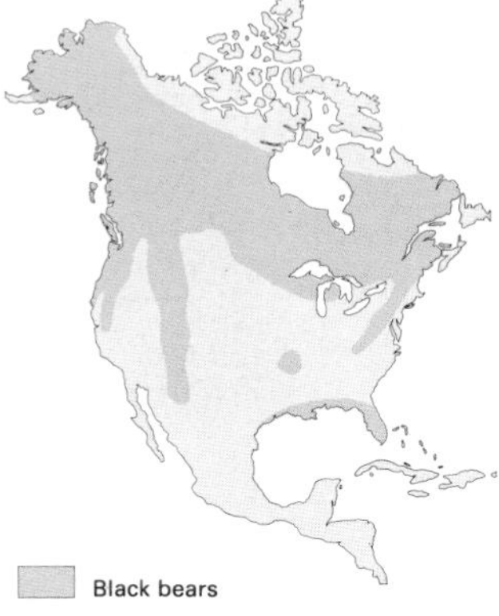

The black bear, *Ursus americanus*, is often found close to human settlements. Feeding on all manner of vegetation and almost any animal it can catch, it is truly omnivorous. Man's casual attitude to his own refuse has provided the bears with an additional source of food. Because there are so many rubbish dumps and the bears have such large familiar areas in relation to the size of their home ranges, the bears are more than likely to come across such a dump during exploratory migration.

Exploration

Apart from pre-reproductive periods of exploration, some mammals, such as the European rabbit, *Oryctolagus cuniculus*, make exploratory migrations during periods of food shortage or overpopulation. Rabbits live mainly in grassland in small social groups. Adults occupy well-defined home ranges of 150 to 200 metres (165 to 220 yards) around the burrows. Studies in Australia have shown that when food is scarce, rabbits may sometimes venture beyond the limits of the home range, doubtless in search of new food supplies. By exploration the animal is able to assess the rabbit population in neighbouring areas and decide whether it would be better to migrate than to remain where it is.

Tracking mammals

Building up a picture of an animal's movements takes some considerable time and patience, and several different techniques are used. Many field studies still rely heavily on conventional trapping and marking methods. Individual animals are caught, marked and then released. This technique yields information only about where and when particular animals were captured, and up to thirty captures of an individual may be needed to form an impression of its migration pattern and the size of its home range.

More recently radio transmitters have been used to monitor animal movements. Attached to the animal a tiny transmitter emits a signal that can be received and interpreted by a researcher. If separate transmitters are attached to several animals of different ages and sexes it is possible to form a picture of movement over a cross-section of the population. By tuning the receiver to different frequencies it is possible for one researcher to monitor several animals at once.

Bait marking has been used successfully in mapping the limit of an animal's territory. The European badger, *Meles meles*, uses dung as a territorial marker. If bait is marked with coloured glass beads or a trace element, the animal's dung can be recognized and the boundary of its territory distinguished. This technique unfortunately gives little information about how often an animal visits a particular place.

No field technique tried so far has proved particularly successful in studying a mammal's phase of exploration. The exploratory phase is one of the most important parts, but from the researcher's point of view one of the most elusive features of a mammal's lifetime track. Before an animal's period of exploratory migration can be recognized in the field it will be necessary to collect a complete record of its movements from birth so that it will be possible to tell when the animal moves beyond its familiar area.

Laboratory experiments

On the assumption that periods of exploration relate directly to periods of high physical activity the problem has been investigated by experimenting with caged animals. In the laboratory, golden hamsters, *Mesocricetus auratus*, and Mongolian gerbils, *Meriones unguiculatus*, have been kept under constant conditions in cages fitted with exercise wheels and their periods of wheel running monitored. Contrary to popular belief wheel running does not occur randomly or only when an animal is bored or has been deprived of exercise for some time. It takes place at the particular periods in its life and under the same conditions that one would expect the animal to make exploratory migrations in the wild. The captive animal seems to redirect its exploratory drive into wheel running and as far as we can tell seems to find it a satisfactory substitute.

These periods involve more than just the simple act of running round the wheel. Continual bouts of wheel running rarely last for more than a few minutes at a time. Sometimes the animal may leave the wheel and move around in its cage listening and sniffing before continuing wheel running.

All the animal's movements are automatically recorded. The wheel is linked to a pen recorder that traces out its periods of activity on paper tape. The recorder measures the period between each wheel-running episode and the length of time the animal runs. By controlling conditions such as food supply, temperature and the hours of light and darkness, it is possible to get some idea of how these conditions affect exploratory activity in the wild.

Shortage of food affects the amount of wheel running in different ways. Hamsters, rats and guinea pigs wheel run more when food is scarce. The Mongolian gerbil on the other hand wheel runs less overall but increases activity just before and after its normal feeding time. Experiments conducted throughout an animal's life have shown that wheel running first appears immediately after weaning and increases to a peak around sexual maturity, when the animal would normally be establishing its own home range. This corresponds to the pattern of exploration we would expect to see in nature. Work with lemmings has shown that animals lower down the social hierarchy wheel run more than the more dominant members. In the wild the less dominant individuals compete less successfully for food and territory, and have therefore more stimulus to explore new areas.

Moving home

Under certain conditions mammals abandon their home range altogether. Sometimes they migrate to avoid some temporary hazard, such as bad weather. The European mole, *Talpa europaea*, for example, migrates from its home range when the soil becomes either too wet or too dry. The evacuation is usually temporary and the moles return when things return to normal.

EXPLORATORY MIGRATION

Automatically recording an animal's pattern of wheel running on paper tape, in response to different conditions, provides useful information about its exploratory behaviour. For example, when a rat is denied food, its activity increases even though its weight falls. In the wild we would expect the rat to spend more of its time in exploration if it could not find enough to eat.

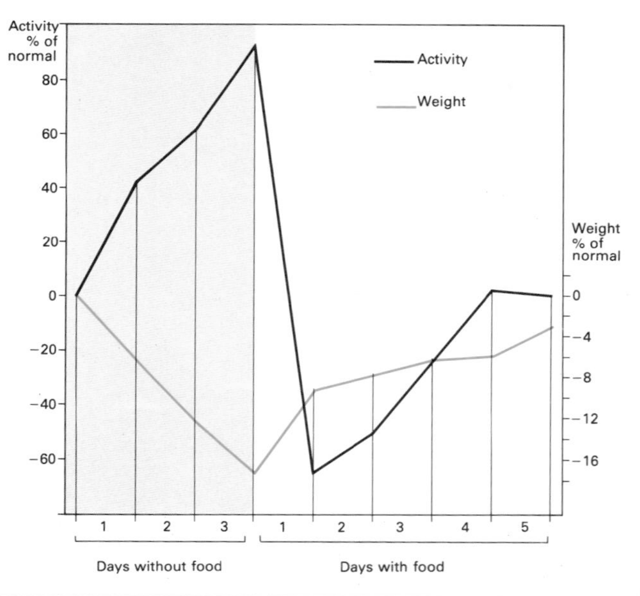

Woodchucks, *Marmota monax*, are reputedly able to forecast the weather and it is said to be possible to foretell the duration of winter from their behaviour when they awake from hibernation. In many ways the woodchuck is similar to a prairie dog; both are burrow-digging ground squirrels and members of the family Sciuridae. However, the migratory pattern of the woodchuck is much more conventional than that of the prairie dog. When about three months old they migrate to establish their own home range. Adult prairie dogs, however, migrate themselves to dig a fresh burrow.

The original habitat of the European mole, *Talpa europea*, lay beneath woodland, but, as the forests shrank, the moles moved extensively into agricultural land. Moles are highly sensitive to the humidity of the soil. They cannot burrow through dry earth, and worms, which form their basic diet, cannot survive in dry conditions or when the soil is waterlogged.

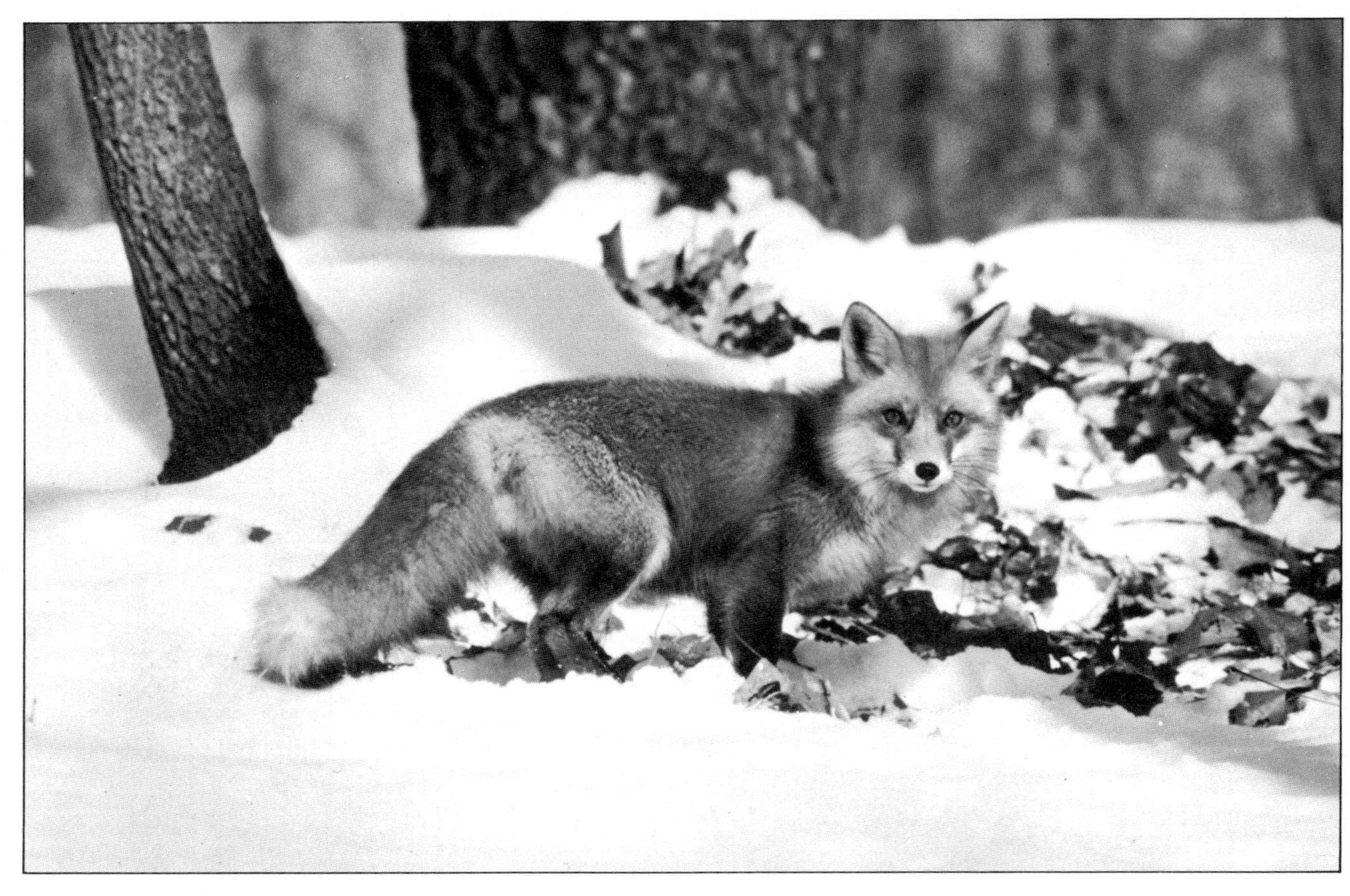

Many mammals move away from the home range to establish a new one at a particular time in their life. In most cases the mammals migrate before they become sexually mature. The woodchuck, *Marmota monax*, a North American ground squirrel, is found in woods and farmland. It lives in burrows usually dug among trees at the edge of meadowland, but, unlike the prairie dog, it is a solitary animal. Young woodchucks leave the parental burrow during midsummer, at the age of approximately three months, and dig temporary burrows within the home range. Later they migrate to establish their own more permanent burrow. In the same way the prairie deer mouse, *Peromyscus maniculatus*, leaves the parental home range to establish its own when it becomes sexually mature.

Except during the breeding season, the American black bear, *Ursus americanus*, lives alone. Each bear has its own home range and after mating each of the sexes returns to their respective territories. Black bears become sexually mature at between five and six years old. Adult females mate only every other year. The young bears are weaned at seven months and leave their mother at any time between one and five years old. For a few months the young bears are likely to remain within the mother's home range, not moving away entirely until at least their second summer. Migration normally coincides with the arrival of a new male to copulate with the mother. If the young remained it would be difficult for each member of the group, the mother, two offspring and the male, to find enough food. Their migration occurs in autumn, when berries, which bears normally eat at that time of year, are plentiful, and the young bears have no difficulty in fending for themselves while looking for a new territory.

The movement of young animals away from the parental home range is a common pattern. The young of the American red fox, *Vulpes vulpes fulva*, migrates from the home range in autumn, usually in September. For about a month or so they remain within about a kilometre (0.6 mile) of the natal den before moving right away.

The European badger, *Meles meles*, lives in groups in well-defined areas of about forty hectares (100 acres). Members of a particular social group may inhabit the same set or lair or, at particular seasons, neighbouring ones within the same home range. The social group's basic unit is the sow and her cubs. The cubs, which are born between mid-January and mid-March, remain with the mother until the autumn or the spring of the following year. Year-old badgers are often isolated from their own social group and inhabit outlying areas of the home range. This is especially true in winter during the breeding season, when the set is occupied by mature adults in preparation for the next litter.

In spring, when a new litter is born, the young badgers begin to explore the area around the set, in preparation

RED FOX MIGRATION

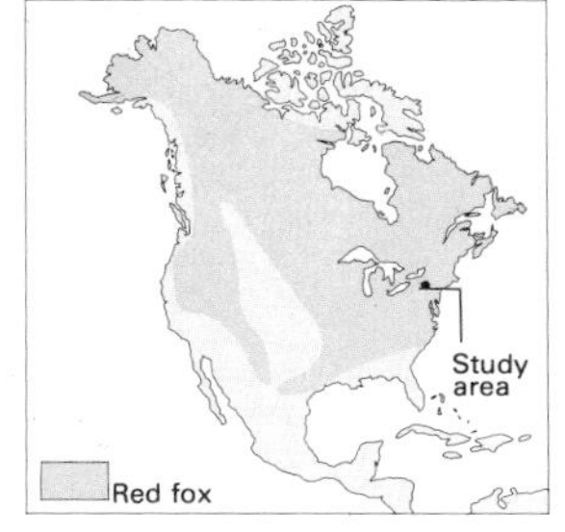

The red fox, *Vulpes vulpes fulva*, is found throughout most of the United States and Canada. In the autumn the young of both sexes leave the parental den. This may be an exploratory migration, but ultimately at least some individuals leave the den altogether. Once adult, the migratory pattern of both males and females becomes quite different. The females remain near the den all year, although they may travel a little further in winter when food is scarce. Males on the other hand migrate considerable distances away from the den in late autumn. Often their departure is permanent.

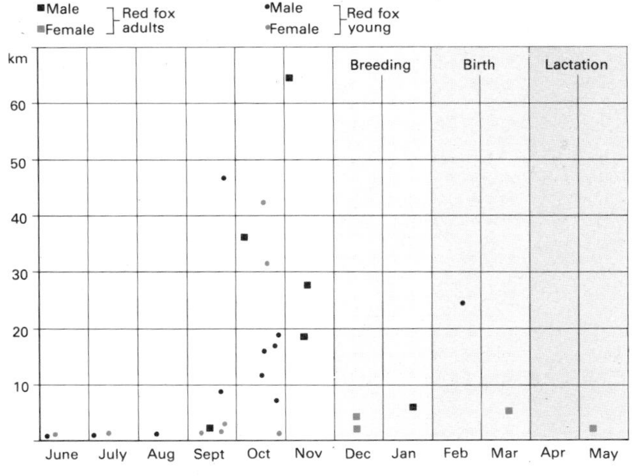

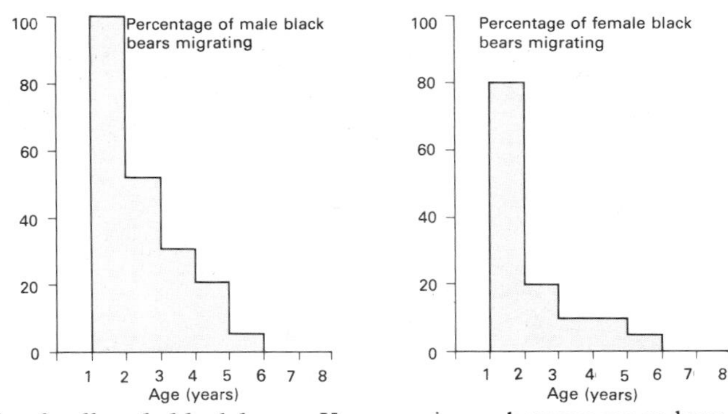

Nearly all male black bears, *Ursus americanus*, between one and two years old migrate away from the parental home range. Young bears, moving in from neighbouring areas, preserve the population balance.

The set of a European badger, *Meles meles*, can be distinguished from the dens and burrows of foxes and rabbits in other ways apart from size. The badger is a creature of habit and there are frequently several well-trodden paths leading from the set towards its foraging grounds.

for the time when they will leave the parental area altogether. Male badgers reach sexual maturity when they are about two years old and are not tolerated within the parental territory after that. When they are between one and two years of age immature males normally leave the natal home range to establish their own or join a nearby badger group. Females often leave at about the same age, but if the population density of the home range is low they may remain and become permanent members of the social group and bear a litter of cubs in the following year.

The migration of young animals away from the parental site before becoming sexually mature is a general characteristic of mammals living within a restricted home range. A notable exception is the black-tailed prairie dog, *Cynomys ludovicianus*. When young prairie dogs become independent, the adults migrate to new territories, leaving their offspring behind. This normally occurs in June or July, when the young are between three and four months old. Often the parents migrate to a territory that is already occupied and some time elapses before the newcomers are accepted and established in the new area. If the chosen territory is uninhabited the adults will make a preliminary exploration and dig new burrows before permanently moving into the area.

Other factors besides age affect the timing of migration. It can vary with the time of year, the animal's sex or its position in a social hierarchy.

The woodmouse, *Apodemus sylvaticus*, is found throughout Europe, North Africa and parts of Asia. It is largely nocturnal and lives in woods, fields, hedgerows, gardens, almost anywhere that it can be sure of a reliable supply of the seeds, nuts and insects that form the bulk of its diet. The mice dig extensive tunnel systems, sometimes marking the entrances with tiny stone cairns.

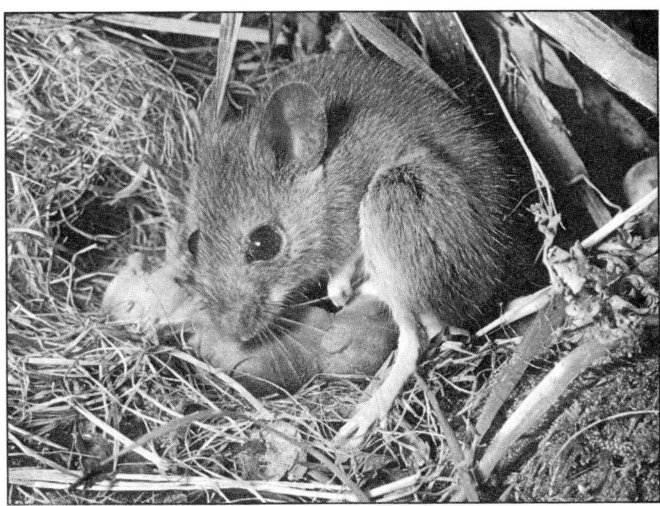

In areas, particularly in eastern Europe, where vast expanses of cereal crops are grown, the population of meadow voles, *Microtus agrestis*, periodically explodes. As population outstrips food supply many thousands migrate like lemmings into the surrounding countryside in search of food.

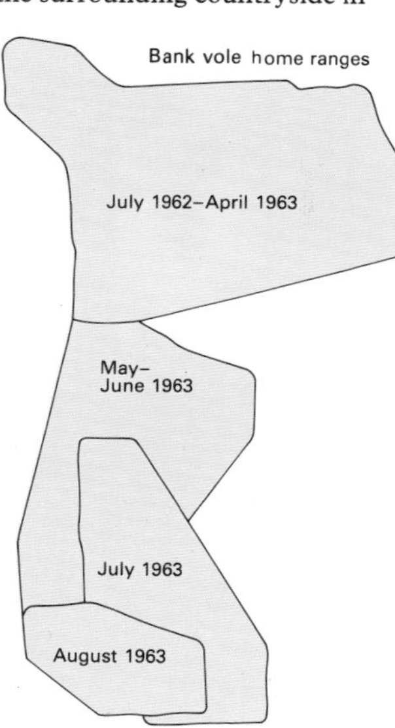

Bank voles, *Clethrionomys glareolus*, like many other small mammals, migrate outside their familiar areas at certain times of year. In the case of the female bank vole, migration occurs just before the breeding season. One female, observed on Skomer Island, Wales, lived within a particular area for ten months of the year. At the start of the breeding season in May she migrated to a new home range which she had probably explored earlier. During the remainder of the season she migrated successively to establish two more home ranges.

The wood mouse, *Apodemus sylvaticus*, is a nocturnal rodent living in colonies and has a home range of around two hectares (5 acres). Males normally have larger home ranges than females and migrate over greater distances. During the annual breeding seasons in spring and autumn the adult males spread over a wider range than normal, probably in search of mates. After the spring breeding season the dominant adults become more aggressive and force many of the population, usually the juveniles and young adults, to migrate to a new territory.

Sometimes, as in the case of the wood mouse, migration to a new territory takes place within the familiar area that the animal built up during its explorations when young, in other cases there may be no suitable territory within the familiar area and the animal has to migrate beyond it. Male eastern fox squirrels, *Sciurus niger*, migrate like this. They have been found at distances up to sixty-four kilometres (40 miles) from their home range, which must be well outside their original familiar area. However, the best-known example of this sort of behaviour and perhaps one of the most famous migration feats of all is the legendary mass migration of the Scandinavian lemmings.

Lemmings

Few migration phenomena have made a greater impact on people's minds than the lemmings' mythical headlong rush to death. The concept has become lodged in the English language as a powerful metaphor of mindless behaviour. But this is little more than a figment of the human imagination. The real story is much less bizarre but just as dramatic and much more believable.

The Scandinavian lemming, *Lemmus lemmus*, found throughout Norway, Sweden and Finland, is, unlike its relatives in Asia and America, primarily a montane animal. Its preferred habitat is the birch and willow woodland that lies between the coniferous forests and the snow-line of the high Scandinavian plateaux. In summer it feeds on the mosses and sedges that are typically found on the peatlands around the lower parts of its range. In winter, when the peat bogs freeze over and the sedges wither and die, the lemmings migrate to the upper slopes, where the vegetation is protected from frost by the snow. The lemmings burrow under the snow, constructing a system of lairs and interconnecting tunnels allowing them to get at the plants beneath. When in spring the snow melts, filling their burrows with water and rendering them useless, the lemmings return to the lower slopes. This pattern of seasonal migration persists as long as the population density does not become excessive.

For reasons that are not fully understood, lemming numbers fluctuate violently. Population explosions occur simultaneously over a wide area, whole mountainsides experiencing the phenomenon together. When their numbers increase beyond what the habitat can support, the young adults, in the course of their exploratory migrations, are compelled to investigate less favourable areas lower down in the margins of the coniferous forest. The lower the lemmings go the less attractive the territory becomes. There comes a point when the only habitat available is so inhospitable that they are forced to migrate to a completely new area. This seems to happen every three or four years.

Lemmings are naturally very aggressive and fight fiercely for their territorial and reproductive rights. It follows that, in a population explosion, the migrants are likely to be those that are less aggressive and have had less reproductive success. The resulting migration may involve thousands of individuals. *En masse* the migrants sweep down the mountainside into the valleys, travelling across the lowland, in a straight line wherever possible. They run directly across open fields, risking the attraction of predators. They swarm through villages, entering houses rather than running round them. Their conspicuous straight-line track across unsuitable territory implies that the time and energy spent in migration is more critical than the risk of predation. Because, like other rodents, their lives are short, they must waste no time in reaching a new habitat suitable for breeding. However, they are not entirely reckless and do avoid obvious risks by usually migrating at night and by evading predators wherever possible.

Lemmings are excellent swimmers, and rivers and lakes present them with little difficulty. However, they try to avoid a long water crossing and will not usually enter a lake unless they can see the opposite shore. If there is fog or the conditions are stormy they will pause, feed and rest some distance from the water's edge before continuing when conditions become more favourable. Once in the water they swim straight across towards the highest peaks on the opposite skyline. Lemmings are not primarily guided by either magnetic or celestial features but head straight towards the highest ground in sight. Their preference for a straight-line path is so strong that they have been reported scaling small boats rather than swimming round them.

When they reach land they normally start climbing straightaway. But if the mountain they are climbing is also experiencing a lemming population boom and the ascending migrants encounter others rushing down in the opposite direction, the climbers will turn at right angles along the valley bottom until the numbers of emigrating lemmings decrease.

The risk of death from predation or starvation is very high during migration. But even so the chances of survival must be better than remaining at the original site. Migration is the behaviour that gives them the best chance of reproduction in a desperate situation.

There are twelve species of lemming found throughout northern Europe, Asia and North America. The largest lemming and the one featured in most mass-migration stories is the Scandinavian lemming, *Lemmus lemmus*. Mass migration occurs during population booms, which probably have their root in the ability of the female to produce several litters of three to nine young each year. The precise timing of a population boom may be related to the climate. If a summer is abnormally long there will be more food available and conditions will be more favourable for breeding than they would be otherwise. Secondly if the winters are neither so mild that the snow melts, spoiling the lemmings' feeding tunnels beneath, or so severe that many of the young die, the lemming population is likely to be greater in the following summer. When both these conditions prevail there is the risk of a population explosion.

All lemmings

Scandinavian lemmings

Primates

Primates are the order of mammals comprising lemurs, monkeys, apes and man. Although some primates, such as the orang-utan, *Pongo pygmaeus*, are solitary, most live in social groups within a single home range. The general pattern of youthful exploration, followed by migration, away from the parental home range seen in other mammals is typical of primates.

The young of both the South American titi monkey, *Callicebus moloch*, and white-handed gibbon, *Hylobates lar*, move further out onto the periphery of the parental territory as they approach adulthood. Unless there is a vacant niche within their own or in a nearby territory the young monkeys eventually move away to establish their own home range.

Social bonds between members of primate groups are very strong and in many species females do not explore away from the home range by themselves. By leaving the family unit, the young female would forfeit the benefits of communal food gathering and protection found within the primate group. It is usual for young females to remain in the same social group as their mother. This is true of young female chimpanzees, *Pan troglodytes*, and Japanese macaques, *Macaca fuscata*.

The mountain gorilla, *Gorilla gorilla*, is found in the lowland equatorial rain forests of Africa at altitudes of between 500 and 1700 metres (1640 and 5600 ft). They feed on a variety of plants and usually live in areas that have been recently cleared, where there is plenty of regrowth. Up to six different groups may use the same area of forest at a time, in overlapping home ranges of between twenty-five and forty square kilometres (9.7 and 15.4 square miles) in size. Gorilla groups move around their home range nomadically, remaining in particular areas from two to twenty-six days.

The pattern of gorilla migration differs widely between the sexes. Males make exploratory migrations, spending as much as six years at a time away from their own social

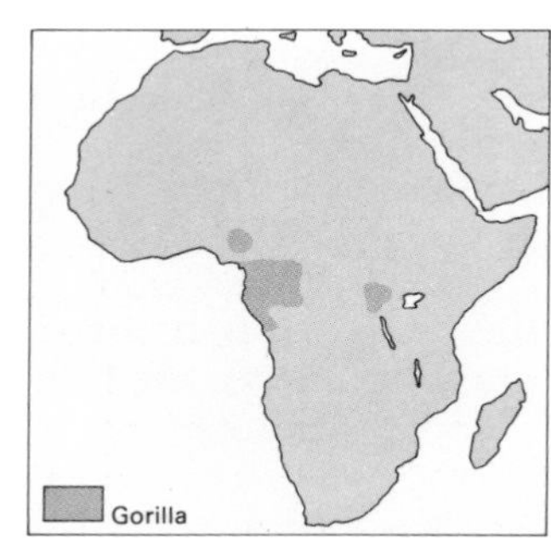

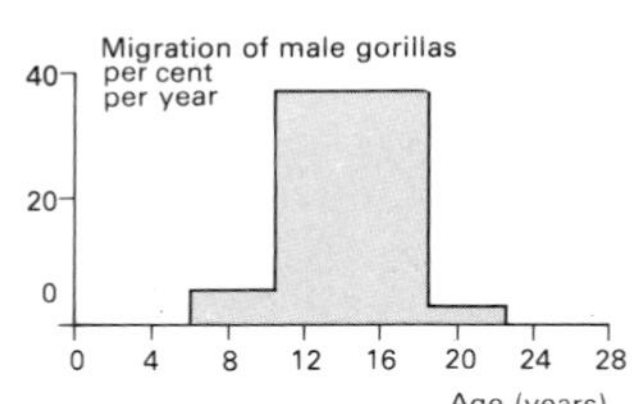

Gorillas, *Gorilla gorilla*, are confined to the equatorial forests of Africa above an altitude of 500 metres (1600 ft). They live in groups consisting of one mature male and two or three females and their young. The dominant male, known as a silver back, is distinguished by the bony crest on top of his skull and the white hairs along his back. Living within the family group, there may also be one or two immature black-backed males. These males must leave the group on maturity unless one of them is successful in displacing the dominant male. Males may leave a social group to live alone at almost any time, but usually solitary males are young silver backs attempting to establish their own family groups.

As many as six separate gorilla families may live in the same area of forest. Their home ranges, measuring between twenty-five and forty square kilometres (9.7 to 15.4 sq miles), usually overlap to a greater or lesser extent. In the region north of Lake Tanganyika, the home ranges of three separate gorilla families were investigated. The extent of each area was discovered by plotting the position of every gorilla encountered and drawing a boundary around the distribution. Although two of the areas share a large amount of common territory there is little aggression or interchange of individuals between the groups.

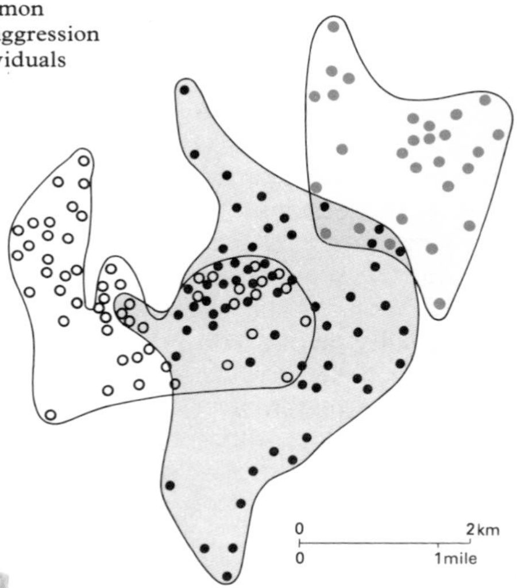

group. They range over a wide area that encompasses the home ranges of several family groups. During this period the young males extend their familiar areas by exploration and also, it is thought, by communication between one another. A male gorilla's exploratory phase ends when he succeeds in displacing the dominant male in a family group or when he succeeds in attracting females away from a group and creating a new one.

Young female gorillas do not make comparable exploratory migrations. Their movements are confined to short-distance migrations between nearby social groups.

The youthful exploratory phase is a common characteristic of male primate behaviour and occurs in many species, such as the chimpanzee, *Pan troglodytes*, the vervet monkey, *Cercopithecus aethiops*, and the Japanese macaque, *Macaca fuscata*. In some species, groups comprising both sexes make exploratory migrations.

Chimpanzees usually live in loose social groups numbering between twenty and forty individuals. These large groups are divided into sub-groups again with no fixed composition of individuals. When food is scarce the sub-groups disperse but remain close enough together for their members to keep in contact by calling to one another. It is common to find small units consisting of one or two adult males with a few females and their young wandering through the home ranges of several large-size groups. These units have no home range of their own and it is thought that they are searching for a vacant area in which to establish their own home range.

The same thing happens in rhesus macaques, *Macaca mulatta*. Small groups of monkeys outside the main population are found foraging in areas not much visited by other monkeys. These groups lack permanence and often rejoin the main population during the mating season. However, eventually the new group becomes stabilized and forms an identity of its own. In rhesus monkeys the new groups are often centred on females with an unfavourable social position in the old group. By leaving, the females are trying to increase their standing and consequently better their chances of reproduction.

Although primate groups live in overlapping home ranges they normally remain independent of each other and usually avoid contact. Sometimes neighbouring groups meet and mingle for a short period, and on these occasions some females may transfer from one group to another. In close contact it is possible for individuals to compare the composition of their own group with neighbouring groups. In the case of gorillas the amount of protection received by the female is an important factor. Gorillas live in family units of normally one mature silver-backed male, one or two immature black-backed males and two or three females with infants. The females look towards the silver-backed male for protection. When there happens to be too many females or too many black-backed males or infants in a particular group, the females will feel insecure and some – the less favoured ones – are likely to move to another group.

The migratory behaviour of apes and monkeys, particularly the gorillas, has a familiar feel to it. Their movements are undoubtedly closer to those of humans than any other animal.

Grooming is an important activity in the life of a chimpanzee, *Pan troglodytes*. It is not only a method of getting rid of parasites but an essential social activity. An adult's social status can be distinguished from how often he or she is groomed and by whom.

Both male and female Japanese macaques, *Macaca fuscata*, migrate short distances between social groups that are in contact with each other. Only the males migrate long distances, up to twenty-three kilometres (14 miles) from one group to another.

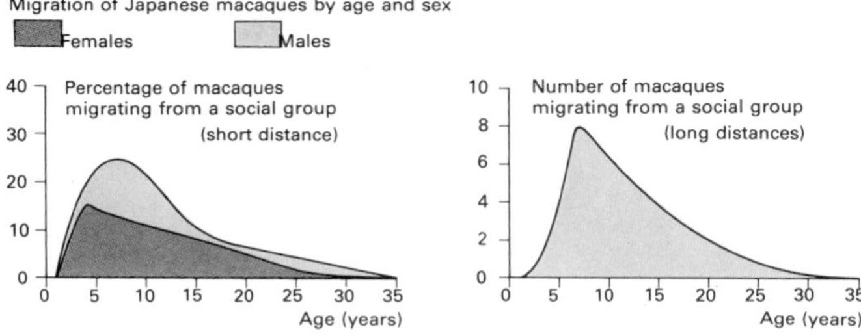

Man

Few of us think of ourselves as migrants. Yet we all take our mobility for granted; we go from home to work and back again; drive from city to city; fly from country to country. Individuals have been to the moon and returned to earth. Mobile, but not migratory, some would say. But if we study man's movements closely, we find that he follows virtually all of the patterns to be seen in the other members of the animal kingdom. Moreover, this similarity is not just an interesting, but superficial, analogy. The migrations of man and other animals are the same.

Man first evolved several million years ago on the savannah grasslands of Africa. Since that time he has spread out, migrating across land and sea, colonizing almost every habitable corner of earth. This migration took place over many thousands of years while man was a hunter-gatherer, living off animals and plants that he caught and collected. By the time the techniques of animal husbandry and agriculture were being established, in the Middle East and elsewhere, our species had already occupied all the continents save Antarctica.

Agriculture brought with it a settled existence and a different pattern of movement; a daily to-and-fro return migration cycle. This has persisted through the centuries and even exists in non-agricultural areas, for example the present-day industrial commuter.

In areas not suited to agriculture, pastoralists retain a nomadic existence, travelling with their herds of animals on annual migration circuits hundreds or thousands of kilometres in length. Such migrations are indistinguishable from those performed by many birds and, of course, from those of the large mammals with which humans share their lives.

From all over Rajasthan, northwestern India, in October nomadic tribes with their herds migrate great distances to Pushkar, near Jaipur, to trade and to celebrate an important Hindu festival.

Man belongs to the mammal order of Primates and the super–family Hominoidae consisting of the families Pongidae and Hominidae. Our own species, *Homo sapiens*, is the only surviving member of the Hominidae family. However, this was not always the case.

Hominids share a common ancestry with the apes (Pongidae), of which gibbons, orang-utans, chimpanzees and gorillas are the present-day representatives. Between ten and twelve million years ago the two lineages first began to separate. Discoveries made only a few decades ago indicate that the earliest hominids lived around the developing grasslands of Africa. Many scientists believe that it was the different requirements of living in forests on the one hand, and more open country on the other, that led to the evolutionary divergence of the two groups. In the forest, a wide range of primates can live side by side, each concentrating on a different food source and places to live and sleep. Life in open country, however, offers fewer varying ways of life and favours animals with an ability to run or to defend themselves and to see danger coming from some distance. In the case of the early hominids, this last feature was enhanced by an ability to stand erect.

Another characteristic of primates that move out into more open country is that they consume more animal food. Most primates have a diet of fruit, leaves and vegetables, which they augment with insect larvae, birds' eggs and small animals. On the savannah, however, baboons, *Papio* spp., will catch much larger, more mobile animals, even forming co-operative groups to hunt and kill relatively large mammals such as small antelope. Even chimpanzees, *Pan troglodytes*, when they live at the forest edge or in woodland savannah, will hunt other monkeys. The same would almost certainly have been true for the first hominids. There was probably another similarity between the behaviour of these early hominids and other such hunting primates: as the females of the species concerned tended to be smaller than the males and to be carrying young, whenever primates took to hunting it was invariably a male occupation.

The first hunter-gatherers

The fossil record of the hominid lineage is lamentably incomplete. It is, to all intents and purposes, one long blank peppered here and there with occasional bone fragments. But what is fairly certain is that about six million years ago there were present in southern and eastern Africa members of a type of hominid known as the australopithecines, the "southern apes". By two million years ago this group had evolved into three clearly recognizable species: *Australopithecus africanus*, *A. robustus*, and *A. boisei*, or "nutcracker man". There are indications that the latter two species were vegetarians, but *A. africanus* was clearly a hunter of the relatively large mammals that lived on the grasslands at that time.

Australopithecus certainly used naturally occurring objects as tools for killing and dismembering their prey. However, it is arguable whether or not they themselves manufactured tools for such purposes. This uncertainty revolves around the real identity of another hominid species that first appeared in Africa about three million years ago. These hominids were contemporary with the australopithecines, but differed from them in that they were undoubtedly tool-makers. Some authorities consider that these were the first members of the genus *Homo*, and have named the species *H. habilis*. Others consider them still to be members of the genus *Australopithecus*. Whatever we name this hominid, he was certainly a tool-making, co-operative hunter that lived on a com-

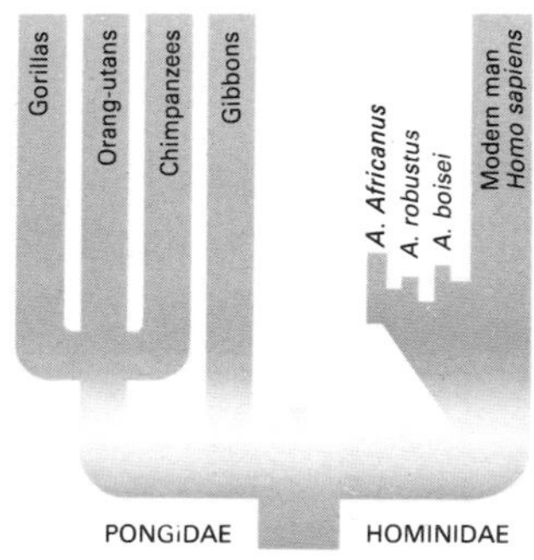

The human lineage, which, based on fossil evidence, commenced some thirty-five million years ago but on chemical evidence some ten million years ago, shows that man evolved as a hunter-gatherer. The hunter-gatherer pattern of migration in fact forms the basis of the movements of even present-day man.

Cuiva tribesmen inhabiting the Meta River area in Colombia, South America, are modern hunter-gatherers who live on the forest edge and hunt monkeys and occasionally snakes and birds.

bination of large and small animals and a variety of plants such as fruit, seeds, roots and some leaves. By nature he was a hunter-gatherer. So, too, was the first undoubted member of the genus *Homo*, *H. erectus*, which appeared some two million years ago.

Migration from the African cradle

Homo erectus was the first hominid to migrate out of Africa. By the time, some 300,000 years ago, that *H. erectus* gave way to modern man, *H. sapiens*, the genus *Homo* had spread over most of Africa and southern, western and central Europe as well as across southern Asia to central China and Indonesia. This spread took place at the same time as periods of glacial advance and bitter cold occurred in northern Europe and Asia. It is likely that *H. erectus* used fire; perhaps it was because of this that the species could spread as far as, and live at, the very edge of the frost line.

Remains of the earliest *H. sapiens* are found in Britain, Germany and North Africa. Like their predecessors, these were hunter-gatherers, and it was as a hunter-gatherer that man spread over the rest of the world. Australia was first reached about 32,000 years ago, probably via land bridges or by island-hopping southward from southeastern Asia along the archipelago of the East Indies. (There is scattered fossil evidence for the influx to Australia of light-boned people from China as well as the more robust people from southeastern Asia, implying that Australian Aborigines evolved from the interbreeding of these ancestral forms.) Twelve thousand years later virtually the entire Australian continent had been colonized. During that same period, man reached and colonized the Americas. The migration route to America was almost certainly across Beringia, the now-submerged land-mass that for about 15,000 years joined Siberia to Alaska. Beringia was not a narrow bridge, but wide, perhaps 1000 kilometres (620 miles) from north to south, and during most of its existence it would have supported tundra vegetation and a variety of animals such as mammoth, mastodon, caribou and muskox, all of which man is known to have hunted. Man lived on Beringia throughout its existence in settled hunter-gatherer communities and only incidentally would some have found their way into North America and a huge continent.

There seems to have been two major phases of migration into North America. During the period from about 30,000 to 19,000 years ago most of North America east of the Rocky Mountains was under ice and snow. Hunter-gatherers from northeast Siberia entered North America and spread rapidly southward, either down the west coast or via the valleys of the Yukon and Mackenzie rivers, reaching Central America about 20,000 years ago. Northern South America may have been infiltrated either by a gradual spread overland through Central America or by island-hopping along the Caribbean chain. Whatever the route, western and southern South America were reached by about 12,000 years ago.

The second phase came later and involved a different type of hunter-gatherer, a people that had previously become specially adapted for life along the coasts of the northern part of the western Pacific. These people, ancestors of present-day Eskimos and Aleuts, probably spread around the southern coast of Beringia and reached southwestern Alaska and the Aleutian Islands between 8000 and 10,000 years ago. They then migrated round the newly formed Alaskan coast and eastward along the northern coasts and islands of Canada, arriving at the eastern Canadian Arctic about 5000 years ago and northern Greenland about 4000 years ago.

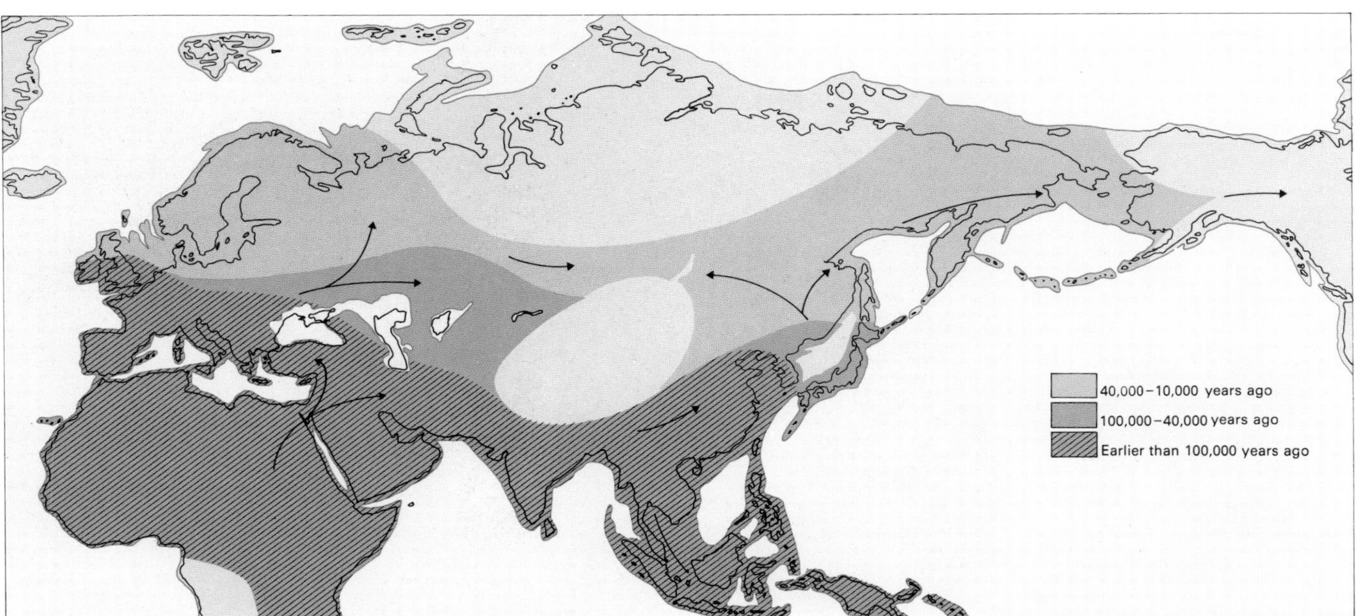

Colonization of the world by *Homo sapiens* was influenced by climatic conditions. Until about 100,000 years ago man was confined to southern Europe and Asia, land to the north being inhospitable on account of glaciation. With the development of clothes and fire to heat dwellings man was able to migrate further northward, almost as far as the Arctic Circle. But it was only with the end of the last ice age, some 10,000 years ago, that man was able to migrate into arctic America and northern Asia. (The map indicates the coastline as it existed during the last ice age.)

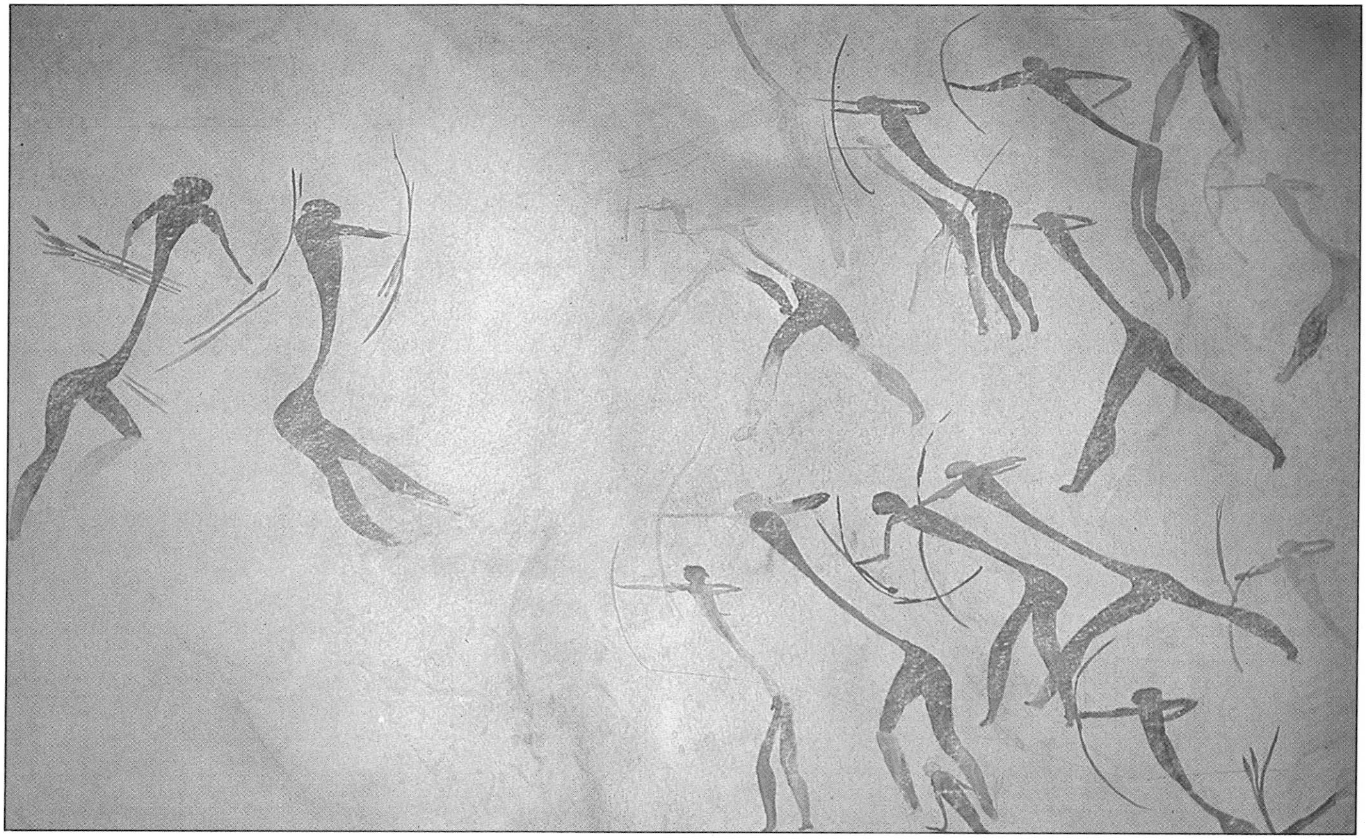

Cave paintings produced by early hunter-gatherer communities invariably portray hunting groups, migratory animals and animal herds. This hunting scene from a cave in southwestern Spain dates from about 8000 years ago. It is clear from the repetitive subject matter of these paintings that the way of life of these people was closely linked to that of the animals they preyed upon.

MALES HUNT WHILE THE FEMALES GATHER

Division of labour in terms of the males being responsible for group defence and the females for care of the young can be traced back through man's ancestory about sixty million years to when the primate group first evolved. The division into males as hunters and females as gatherers, however, appears to have evolved only some ten to twenty million years ago to about the time when the first hominids left the forests of Africa and invaded the savannah, searching for food in open country.

Female Amerindians gather fruits, seeds, insect grubs and vegetables.

Male Amerindians hunt mammals and also kill birds for food.

The lifetime track of hunter-gatherers

In various parts of the world people still live as hunter-gatherers, though their numbers are decreasing each year. Among them are the Bushmen of Africa and the Australian Aborigines, and studies of their behaviour can teach us much about the hunter-gatherer way of life. A great deal is known also about the social structure, ecology and migration patterns of Amerindians, Eskimos and the other hunter-gatherer tribes that were scattered across South America and Asia before they became assimilated into other civilizations. From these peoples and from the evidence of cave paintings and the bones and artefacts present in ancient human settlements, we can piece together a great deal concerning the form of the hunter-gatherer's lifetime track and our remote ancestors' way of life.

Among hunter-gatherers there is, and probably always has been, a universal division of labour for collecting the different foods: the males hunt large and small animals and the women and children gather vegetables, fruits, grains and insects. The relative importance to the population's diet of food collected by either hunting or gathering differs from area to area. In general, the importance of hunting decreases towards the equator and increases towards the poles. Around the Arctic Circle Eskimos are almost entirely hunters, living primarily on animal protein and fat. In contrast, the Pygmies of the African rain forests live mainly as gatherers; only about one-third of their diet consists of animal protein. Where rainfall is seasonal in the tropics, hunter-gatherers often live primarily as gatherers in the wet season and as hunters in the dry season. This emphasis on gathering in tropical regions means that the females make the major contribution towards collecting food. Among Bushmen, almost eighty per cent of the food eaten by a family is provided by the females. Among some Eskimos, the opposite is true, almost all of the food being obtained by the males, the females only collecting seafood such as seaweed and mussels where this can be found on unfrozen shores.

The division of labour between males and females of hunter-gatherer societies has a bearing on their social organization. Hunter-gatherers are almost invariably monogamous. The major exception is found in some Australian Aborigines, who, in desert regions, are often polygamous. Although monogamy is the rule, this does not mean that a pair is likely to stay together for their entire life. "Sequential monogamy", in which male and female may separate and each member of the pair finds a new partner, is more common. Such "divorce" may happen several times in a lifetime.

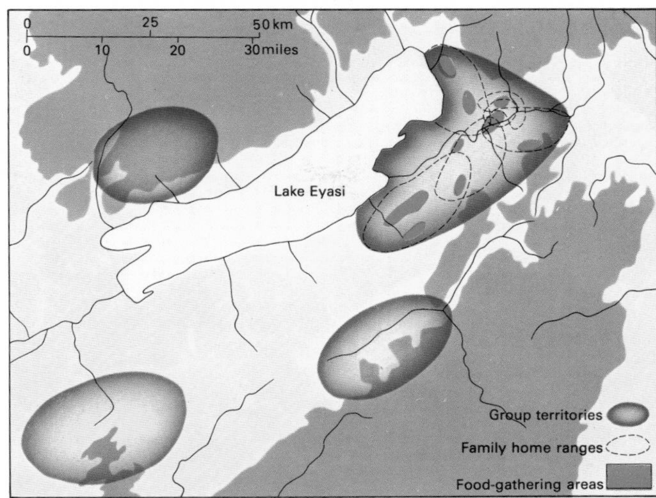

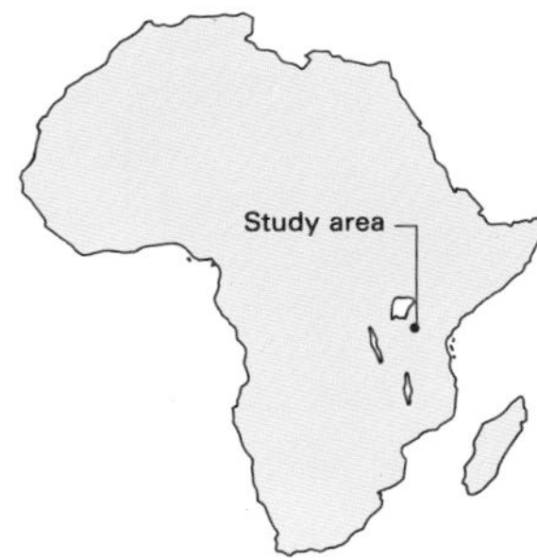

The Hadza of East Africa are modern hunter-gatherers. Around Lake Eyasi there are four large Hadza populations. The northeastern territorial group is divided into six smaller groups. During the wet season the sub-groups tend to aggregate in the lowlands. In the dry season the sub-groups split up into families which disperse into the surrounding mountains.

Territorial groups

Modern hunter-gatherers live in groups of, on average, about 350 individuals. Rarely does the number exceed 700. Each group lives within a large territory that is often between about 2500 and 7000 square kilometres (950 to 2700 square miles) in area. It has been calculated that the whole of England, before the introduction of agriculture between 5000 and 6000 years ago, supported only about 250 individuals. The density at which hunter-gatherers live is low, less than one individual in ten square kilometres (4 square miles). In the past, this meant that people could travel long distances before meeting another person. In certain places, however, such as along streams, the edges of lakes and sea coasts, the density was almost ten times as great. Food was more reliable and the population could specialize on sources such as fish and other seafood. Everywhere hunter-gatherers seemed to be limited by the availability of food. Studies of Australian Aborigines and of Great Basin Amerindians have shown that the density at which these people lived was related directly to the annual rainfall in the different parts of their range.

Although hunter-gatherers live, and lived, in these territorial groups, the members of each group spend little time together. Instead they split into smaller groups that scatter themselves throughout the territory. The size of these sub-groups again depends on the availability of food and water. Indeed, in places such as East Africa and the monsoon forests of Thailand, the entire territorial group may migrate to a base camp in those seasons when food is plentiful. Conversely, in times of drought they may converge on permanent water sources even though the result of living together may put food in short supply. The smallest sub-groups tend to form when food is scarce but water is available, even if only from succulent plants or the blood, intestines or bladders of animals. At such times, the large territorial group splits into family units. In the deserts of Australia, polygamous families of a man, his wives and their children wander from place to place within their tribe's territory, finding food and water where they can, joining with other families only briefly or when food and water

Hunter-gatherers live in temporary dwellings, abandoning them when they move on. The Nambicuara of Brazil build small shelters of branches, twigs and leaves which they inhabit for up to about ten days. Hunting tapir, monkeys and occasionally bats – they are one of the few people who do so – as well as collecting birds' eggs, they eke out an existence on the edge of forests.

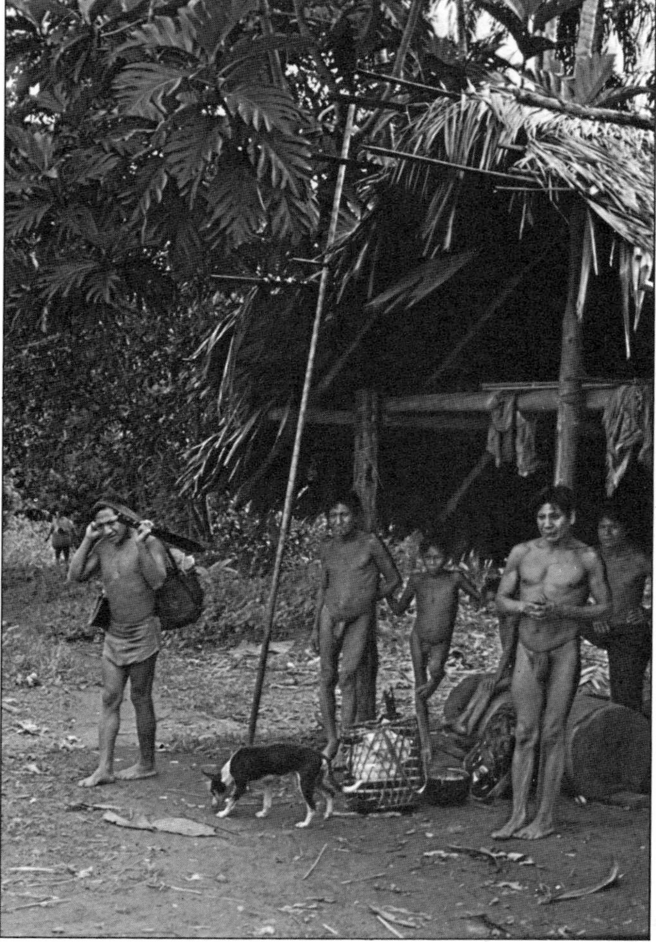

The Maku are hunter-gatherers living in Amazonian forests near the Colombian border who, for ceremonial occasions, build large huts in which they regularly congregate throughout a period of several weeks.

become temporarily plentiful following occasional rain.

Hunter-gatherers defend their territories against neighbouring groups and intruders. However, the territories are frequently so large and the tribe so scattered in its search for food, that communication and mobilization are difficult. As a result, territorial wars are rare and less conspicuous than among agriculturalists and industrialists. Whether visitors from other territories are discouraged and, if so, how forcibly, seems to depend primarily on whether food and water are scarce or abundant at the time.

The nomadic way of life

Most hunter-gatherer families are clearly nomadic, wandering within the tribal territory seeking food and water. As they have no domesticated animals except the dog, they carry very little with them by way of possessions. Roaming in desert regions of Africa and Australia they may sleep with no more than a windbreak for shelter, and although every form of building is found, even recognizable huts, these are used for no more than a few nights at most and are rarely substantial. Elsewhere, in areas where the group remains in one place, at least for certain favourable seasons, more permanent buildings are constructed. Before the last ice age, on their seasonal migrations the European nomadic hunter-gatherers used both caves and shelters consisting of animal hides stretched over holes dug in the ground. Along streams and coasts, fish-eating hunter-gatherers built permanent settlements. But the majority of hunter-gatherers seem always to have lived without a fixed home to which to return each night.

Establishing a familiar area

The fact that hunter-gatherers are nomadic does not mean that they wander at random or have no sense of location. On the contrary, each day's move to a new site is calculated, aimed at a place with which the group is familiar and which is expected to provide food. Each place will be visited again and again, even if weeks, months or even years elapse between each visit. Some places will be visited more often than others.

Familiarity with one's surroundings has to be acquired. This may be aided by discussing the merits of different sites with other individuals, but in the final analysis each place can only really be judged by visiting it. Just like so many other animals, hunter-gatherers build up their familiar area by a process of exploration. Most, if not all, of this exploration is done by the males. It is performed mainly during adolescence and early adulthood, before the male pairs off with or marries a female and begins to raise a family. This is logical since, until the male hunter-gatherer has built up a large enough familiar area to know the best places to find food and water, shelter and so on, he is unlikely to be capable of supporting a wife and children. This is probably why in environments such as the deserts of Australia, where it is difficult to build up a familiar area, a male may not be able to start a family until he is quite old, perhaps in his thirties. Once such an area has been built up, a male might be able to maintain more than one wife.

Australian Aborigines provide the best-known

example of exploration by adolescent males. This is the "walk-about", in which young males spend several years wandering within the Australian bush, familiarizing themselves with routes and places, learning the skill of finding food, water and of staying alive. All hunter-gatherer males travel extensively during adolescence, often visiting neighbouring territorial groups as they do so. Evidence for this lies in the presence in all territories of a relatively high number of young males and wives not born into the group; on their travels, adolescent males often meet and pair with a female and return with her to the area in which the male was born.

Whereas adolescent males may explore widely, females rarely do so. Most often a young girl remains and travels with her mother or other relatives within her group until such time as she pairs with a male and accompanies him instead. This sexual difference is the same as found in almost all other primates. In apes and monkeys, adolescent males become solitary and travel widely, associating temporarily with other groups until finding one with which to settle permanently. Females, on the other hand, either remain for their entire lives in the same group as their mother or, if they do migrate to join a new group, wait until the groups come into contact and then simply move across from one to the other.

Pastoral nomads – following the herds

In the tropics, hunter-gatherers have always had a variety of animal prey available to them, switching from one to another according to availability. In other places a single type of prey may live in such abundance that it is available the year round. By and large, such places are the grasslands and tundras, where huge herds of just one or a few species of animals, such as horses, cattle, bison or reindeer, may be found. In fewer numbers the same is true of sheep, goats and antelopes in hilly or mountainous regions. It is not surprising that in such areas early hunter-gatherers eventually specialized on one or other

In Arnhemland, Australia, surviving Aborigines still live as hunter-gatherers. Adolescent males spend several years exploring (and hunting) within the outback in order to build up a large familiar area.

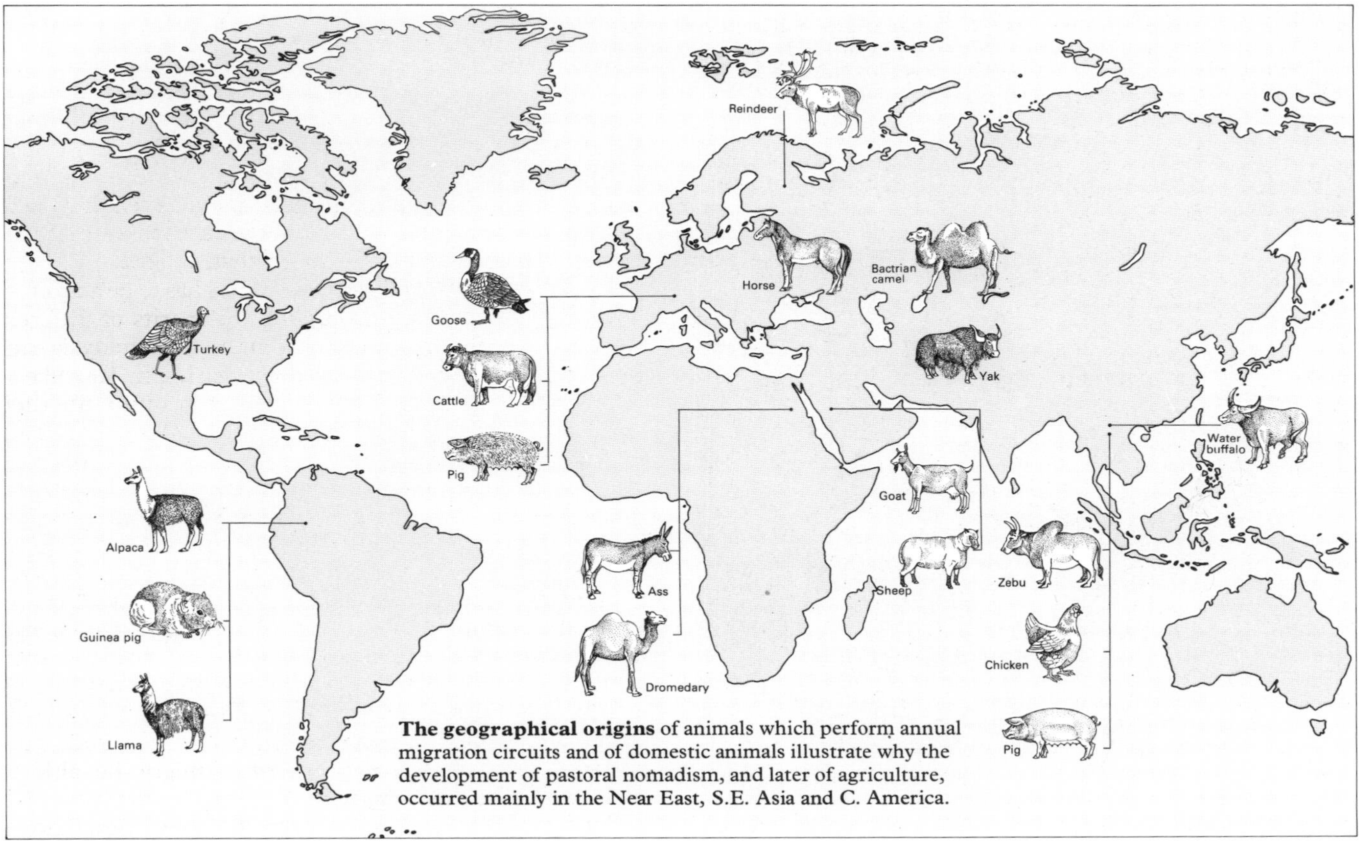

Reindeer
Horse
Bactrian camel
Goose
Turkey
Cattle
Yak
Pig
Water buffalo
Goat
Alpaca
Ass
Zebu
Sheep
Guinea pig
Chicken
Dromedary
Llama
Pig

The geographical origins of animals which perform annual migration circuits and of domestic animals illustrate why the development of pastoral nomadism, and later of agriculture, occurred mainly in the Near East, S.E. Asia and C. America.

The Dinka are pastoral nomads who inhabit savannah country around the Nile basin in southern Sudan. They raise herds of cattle which they move between wet- and dry-season camps.

Nomadic tribes in Kirgiz, southern USSR, raise mixed herds of sheep, goats and yaks. Moving in groups of about twenty families, these nomads follow traditional routes on a huge annual migration circuit.

of these abundant species of animals.

Wherever such animals form large herds, they often carry out huge annual migration circuits, hundreds or even thousands of kilometres in length. Specialization to subsist on one of these species involves the hunter-gatherers staying with their prey throughout the animals' yearly cycle and therefore adopting the animals' lifetime track. Such people are known as pastoral nomads.

The herds with which pastoral nomads are associated can be divided into two types: those consisting of a single species, and those "complex" herds made up of more than one species. Examples of single-species herds are the reindeer of the Lapps and other northern peoples and the cattle raised by the Masai and Hottentots of Africa. Among the complex herds are those of the pastoralists that live in the great arid grassland and desert belt of the Old World. This belt stretches from the Atlantic Ocean across northern Africa to southwestern Asia as far as Tibet and western Manchuria.

The major difference between hunter-gatherers and pastoral nomads is that the latter do not simply kill their animals. Instead, they concentrate primarily on keeping their herds alive, protecting them from predators and assisting them with giving birth, suckling and in finding new pastures. In general, only replenishable items are taken: milk, blood, wool and dung.

The home range of the Bedouin

The home range of pastoral nomads is huge, reflecting that of the animals with which they associate. The Bedouin of the Arabian Peninsula herd camel and sheep and live in an annual home range that averages about 55,000 square kilometres (21,200 square miles). The size of the range varies, depending on how much and where the rain falls each year. During the summer months, from June to mid-October, groups of Bedouin are concentrated around the permanent oases and water holes, living in the tents which they carry with them on their migrations. At this season, camels, sheep and horses have to drink daily. In Kuwait the groups begin their preparations to leave the water holes soon after 10 September, using as their cue the observation of the first appearance of the star Canopus at dawn. Final departure is often possible within a month of first preparation, though the actual date is governed by the arrival of rain. Whether or not rain has fallen, the seasonal migration begins by the end of October. At first, from time to time, the herds may have to return to the water holes, but once the rains have really started, the last contact with the summer home range is broken.

From November to May the Bedouin and their herds move round their huge migration circuit. Although broadly similar each year, the precise grazing and watering sites that are used vary according to the local distribution of rainfall. At each stage the decision of where next to migrate is made according to the direction of cloud banks seen the previous evening or of lightning seen during the night. Tents are shifted every ten days or so. In part this is for sanitary reasons and in part because the herds have consumed the vegetation available in the vicinity. Each shift of camp involves a migration of on average between sixteen and twenty kilometres (10 and 13 miles). Before the camp is moved, the intended destination has usually been visited by one of the male members of the group. Whereas in summer, camps are usually within one kilometre (0.6 mile) of water, in winter they may be as far as fifty kilometres (30 miles) away. During winter camels are not watered at all and sheep and horses have only to drink once every three or four days. The total length of the Bedouins' annual winter and early spring migration circuit may be as much as 1000 kilometres (620 miles).

Changing routes – the migration of the Fulani

Over a period of time, year-to-year changes in a migration circuit may lead to a gradual shift in the area used, particularly where there have been long-term changes in climate. This was the case with the Fulani, a group of people that first appeared in Senegal, in western Africa, about 1300 years ago and gradually spread eastward. Within the savannah region of the Inundation Zone they adopted a pastoral nomad life based largely on herds of cattle. Unlike the Bedouin, the present-day Fulani have a more or less to-and-fro seasonal migration circuit on an axis that runs roughly from north to south.

One group of Fulani that has been extensively studied comprised fourteen families, of which the head males shared common ancestry. At the peak of the wet season in August and September, the families gathered together at the northernmost point of their migration circuit. At the beginning of the dry season, which begins earlier in the north than the south, the southward migration began. Standing water persisted along the route taken until January, by which time the group had travelled some 120 kilometres (75 miles) from their wet-season camp. The group then began to disperse, eventually splitting into units of between one and three families.

Pastoral nomads that migrate within the border districts of the USSR, India, Pakistan, Iran and Turkey raise mixed herds. These they keep to provide wool for clothing, as a source of milk, meat and of dung, which they use for fires. They are also used as pack animals and to provide hides, which the nomads use as an outer covering for their temporary homes, or yurts. At the same time, the nomads assist the animals with the birth of their young. On their migrations between lowland winter pastures and upland or riverain summer residences, which in places are as far apart as 400 kilometres (250 miles), these people invariably ride and carry their possessions on donkeys or camels.

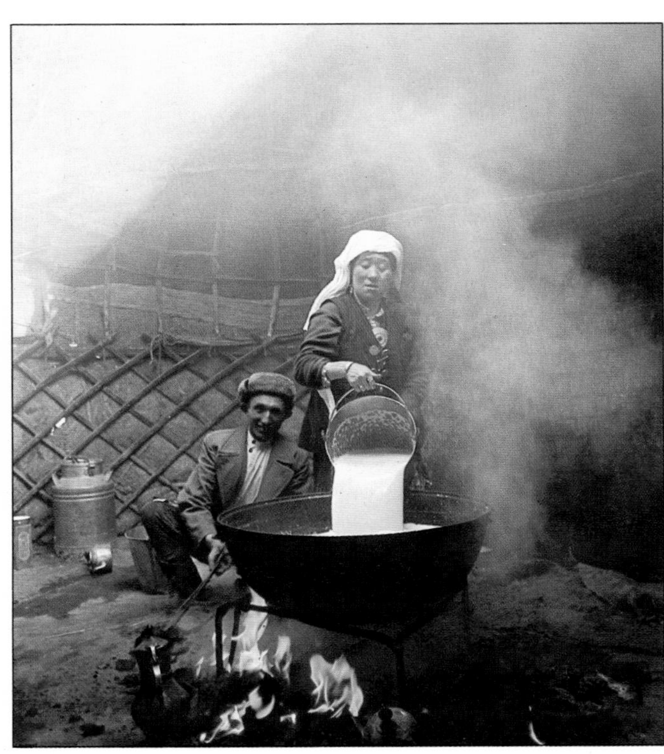

(Each family consisted of between two and fifteen individuals.) Each unit continued its migration to its particular dry-season home range, avoiding those places infested with tsetse flies where the people would be at risk. Some units eventually travelled more than 200 kilometres (125 miles) from where they had begun. At the beginning of April the rains reached the southernmost families, and the return migration to the north began, again trying to avoid the spreading area of the flourishing tsetse fly.

For one Fulani lineage, information is available on the annual migration circuits that have been travelled since about 1880. Each year the dry-season range has been extended slightly further to the south and has been accompanied by a retraction of the wet-season range. In about 1904, the original group divided into two, each of which adopted its own migration circuit. One group soon colonized a nearby plateau. At first, only the dry-season range was on the plateau. However, the higher region was better watered than the surrounding lowlands and was free of tsetse fly. Within four years the entire annual migration circuit took place on the plateau. Nevertheless, the southward drift continued. The second group did not permanently move on to the plateau until three years after the first.

By way of contrast to this shifting migrating route of cattle herders along the edge of a hot desert, the migration circuit of Norwegian Lapps and their herds of reindeer has remained unchanged for almost 400 years. These Lapps have a winter home range among sheltered inland forests near the Finnish border. At the end of April they begin a northward trek to a summer home range along the coast of the Arctic Ocean. The traditional route is about 400 kilometres (250 miles) long and is covered in ten to twelve days. The return southward migration takes place at the end of September or beginning of October.

Within the savannah of West Africa; on their southward dry-season migration Fulani families disperse, and when returning north in the wet season they recombine (below, left). They shift their migration circuits as new pastures and areas free from tsetse flies are found. The migration circuits of a large group that divided into two sub-groups shifted continuously over a period of fifty years (dashed and dotted lines, below right).

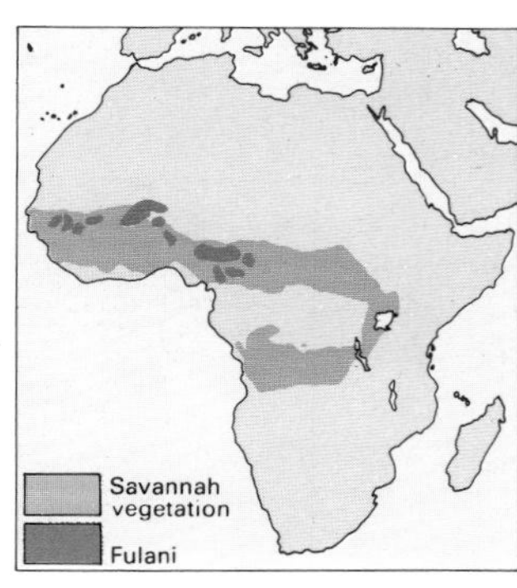

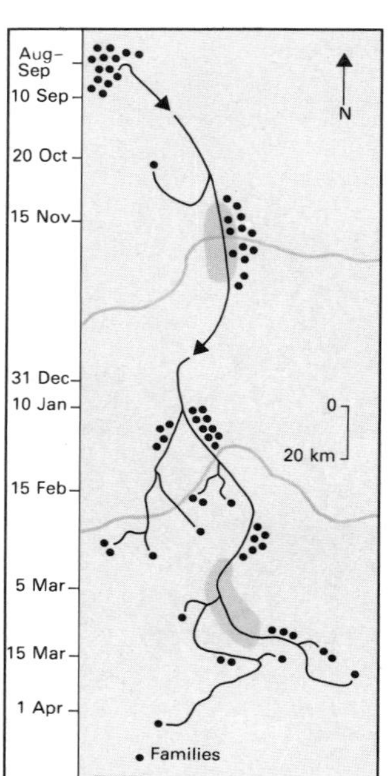

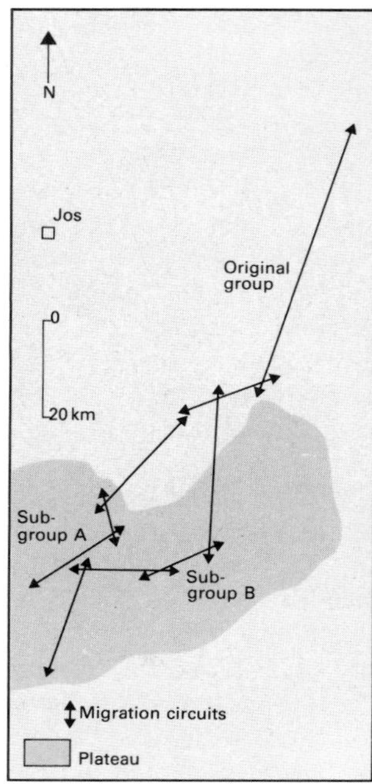

Similarity to hunter-gatherers

Although their yearly migration patterns may differ, the lifetime tracks of pastoral nomads share many similarities with those of hunter-gatherers. Young pastoral nomads establish a basic familiar area by association with their parents. Adolescent males then build on this basic area by a succession of explorations. Today many visit and explore cities and decide to abandon seasonal movement for the more sedentary life of a wage-earning industrialist. Others, as in the past, find new grazing, wintering and camping sites away from those used by the group in which they were born and raised. Information collected during their explorations may well be used to change existing migration routes over the years in the same way as the Fulani did. Alternatively, the information may merely serve to reaffirm that the routes used by their parents really are the best. Either way, the maturing males eventually settle down, each having found and paired with a female during his explorations. Usually, but not always, he returns to the group to which his father belongs. A female, on the other hand, is much less likely to explore independently over any distance until she pairs with or marries a male.

The information gathered by the males during their explorations is subsequently used when they are finding their way from one part of their migration circuit to another. There is no mystery to this navigation process. Pastoral nomads, like all other humans, learn the positions and directions of landmarks and routes, using when necessary the sun, moon and stars as compasses. All of this information is stored in some form of spatial memory and can be used at any time to find the way from one familiar place to another.

The beginnings of a more settled way of life

It was in the Near East, about 10,000 to 12,000 years ago, that man first began to cultivate plants instead of simply gathering them. The first plants to be cultivated were wheat and barley. At about the same time, the identical process was taking place in China, but using millet. The idea quickly spread, partly by word of mouth but probably also as a result of males travelling widely during their explorations. As agricultural practice spread to other areas, the resident people searched for local foodplants that could also be cultivated. We still do not know for certain whether the agricultural centres that arose in western North Africa about 7000 years ago, which were based on pearl millet and rice, or in Central and South America about 3000 years ago based on maize

The Bororo are pastoral Fulani who depend on cattle for their livelihood, exchanging surplus milk for other foods. Tending the herds is predominantly a male occupation, while care of the young and domestic duties are the sole responsibilities of the females.

and potato, were independent discoveries or modifications of an introduced practice.

The advent of agriculture in the Near East more or less coincided with the parallel transition in some nearby regions from simply hunting animals to pastoral nomadism. In other places, where the host animals were less mobile, it was possible to tend them without having to travel great distances and to combine animal husbandry

Traditionally, the Lapps migrated in pack and sled caravans.

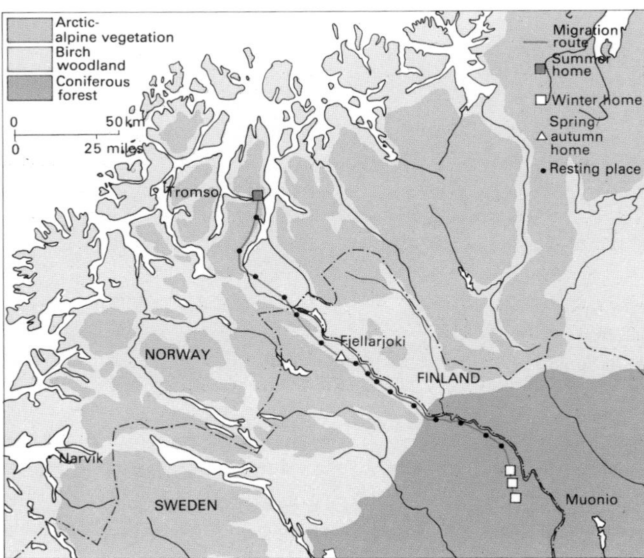

Lapps migrate with herds of reindeer. At each extremity of their migration circuit the Lapps establish fixed residences, where they spend several months. Along the circuit there is usually only one fixed point. Here, in spring, the reindeer are calved, and in autumn the migration halts for a month or two for the reindeer's rutting season.

with agriculture. Cattle, sheep, goats and pigs were first domesticated for food, followed by the use of the horse, ass, ox and camel for transport and traction, some 5000 to 6000 years ago. This was at about the time of the development of the plough and, in some places, the wheel. The use of sheep's wool for clothing, which arose about 4000 years ago, and dairy farming, which first developed about 3000 years ago, also seem to have originated in Mesopotamia.

It was no accident that agriculture first developed in the valley of the "fertile crescent" of Syria and Mesopotamia, areas that during the ice ages were subject to a much greater rainfall than now. Because hunter-gatherers once formed relatively permanent settlements along rivers and streams due to the abundance of food sources, cultivation of plants could not have begun until people stayed in more or less the same place during the yearly cycle. It was only in the alluvial beds of river valleys, where new soil was laid down by flood water year after year, that it was possible to grow crops in the same place over long successions of years. It was along major river systems such as those in northwestern Iran, the Indus, the African Nile, the Danube in central Europe and the Yangtse in China, that agricultural practice first developed on a large scale and spread most rapidly. Clearly, the development of a new culture and way of life is linked to man's patterns of movement and these then influence the spread of that development.

Away from major rivers, soil rapidly loses its fertility if the same crop is grown year after year. In such areas agriculture of the "slash and burn" type developed, with frequent clearance and use of new land as the old lost its productivity. Such agricultural practice is still found in many tropical areas. In the New Guinea highlands, cultivation involves first the clearance and burning of vegetation, then the seedlings are planted in holes made with sticks. No attempt is made to fertilize the soil and the land is allowed to continue bearing until the yield decreases. It is then left fallow to regain its fertility. An area may be cultivated for between four and ten years and then left fallow for the next five to twenty years. The result is that the distance between the village and its fields gradually increases as fresh land is sought and cultivated. Eventually the distances become too great and the entire village has to move and settle nearer to the fields currently being cultivated.

Despite the adoption of agriculture and animal husbandry, man did not give up hunting and gathering. Indeed, even in industrial Europe, the USA, Australia and Japan, at least until the last few decades, the

The development of irrigation and land drainage was the greatest boost to the spread of agriculture. In Southeast Asia rice is grown in paddy-fields, where rainwater is retained by low mud walls.

Along the Nile in Egypt farmers use a variety of methods for drawing water up from the river. The sakia, right, is operated by oxen and comprises buckets fixed to a rotating vertical wheel.

gathering of wild fruits, seeds and nuts was a notable, although small, part of the rural economy. Similarly, in these places hunting has survived to the present day, even though it is associated primarily with specially reared and protected game birds and fish. In other parts of the world, however, hunting and gathering still makes an important contribution to an otherwise agricultural economy. In central Zambia, for example, the Bantu gain forty per cent of their food from agriculture, twenty per cent from animal husbandry and as much as forty per cent from hunting and fishing.

The repercussions of agricultural practice

Among the effects of agriculture two immediate ones were that it made food easier to obtain and its availability more reliable. On the other hand, it led to an increase in the carbohydrate, and decrease in the protein, content of the diet and a corresponding decrease in resistance to disease. This was particularly unfortunate because of the other major effect of agriculture; namely that on the distribution of individuals. Man no longer had to travel great distances to find food. In consequence, territory size shrank from the thousands of square kilometres characteristic of hunter-gatherers to only the few tens of square kilometres found in agriculturalists such as the New Guinea Highlanders. Yet the amount of food that could be produced in this small area was much greater, with the result that the number of people in a territorial group increased. Whereas the larger territory of hunter-gatherers supported between 20 and 700 individuals, that of the more confined agriculturalists supported 2000 to 4000.

As a result of the increase in population density, diseases could be transmitted more rapidly among agriculturalists. In their lifetime, hunter-gatherer females gave birth to relatively few children – between four and six being usual – and there was a relatively good chance that at least half of these would survive to adulthood. Female agriculturalists, on the other hand, tended to produce many offspring, often into double figures, few of which survived childhood. Entire families of agriculturalists could be wiped out by disease, virtually overnight.

Agricultural practice has had another influence on reproduction. Based on possession of land and/or animals, there is a great opportunity for division into the "haves" and the "have nots". Such a dichotomy cannot easily arise among hunter-gatherers. The result is that some agriculturalist males are better able to provide for a large family than others, and so polygamy is common.

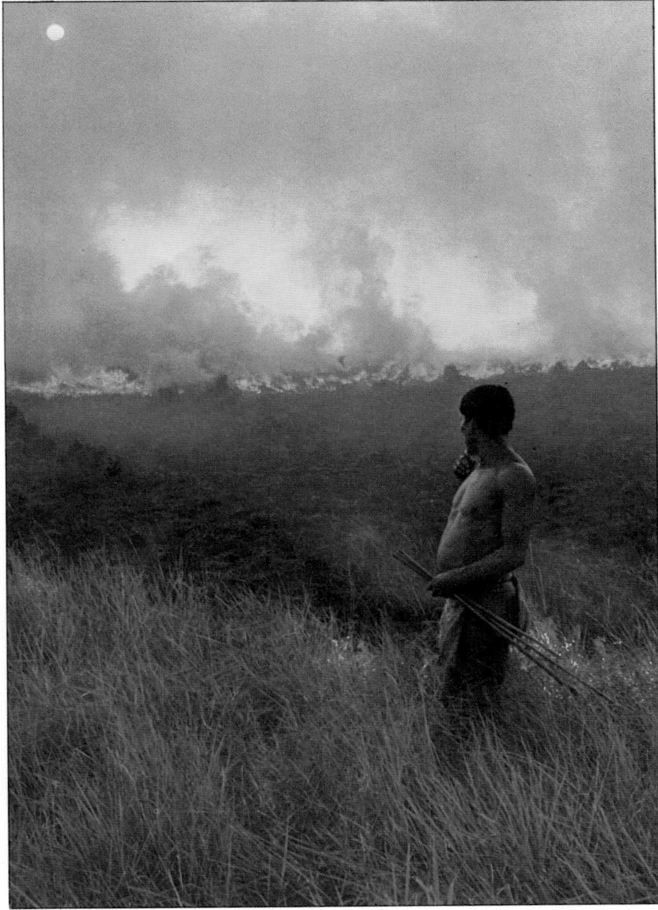

Slash and burn agriculture is practised by primitive farmers in tropical forests throughout the world. The burnt ground is cleared then cultivated, usually with root crops.

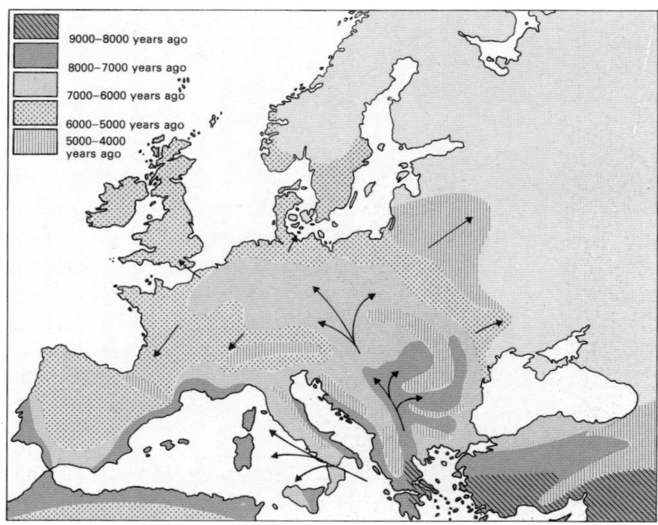

The spread of agricultural practice through Europe took more than 4000 years and occurred along two major routes: the lowland corridor through central Europe and along the Mediterranean coast.

The social structure within agriculturalist groups comprises a number of sub-groups, each with its own village and fields. The sub-groups are scattered through a relatively small area and so can communicate with one another and mobilize themselves for territorial defence or attack much faster and more easily than hunter-gatherers. In the past this gave agriculturalists a tremendous advantage over hunter-gatherers whenever the two came into conflict. In part this would be through sheer weight of numbers, but in part, also, because young hunter-gatherer males, during their explorations, would encounter villages of agriculturalists and would perhaps recognize the territorial advantages of living within a larger group. They would be more likely to settle within such a group than within the hunter-gatherer group into which they were born. Moreover, female hunter-gatherers, recognizing the same advantages, may have been inclined, when they had a choice, to pair with or marry exploratory males from agricultural groups in preference to males from their own hunter-gatherer groups. The net result could have been a wholesale migration, particularly of young people, from groups of

ANCIENT VOYAGERS

In 1969, Thor Heyerdahl, a Norwegian anthropologist, set out to prove that ancient Egyptians or other North Africans with a similar culture could have sailed across the Atlantic and established communities in South America. Sailing a ship of papyrus reeds lashed together with rope and fitted with single square sail – a design both illustrated in ancient Egyptian tomb reliefs and in use in South America at the time of Spanish conquest in the 1490s – Heyerdahl came within a few hundred kilometres of the West Indies before his boat, *Ra I*, was irreparably damaged in a storm. However, in the following year, in *Ra II*, he successfully sailed from Morocco to Barbados, some 5200 kilometres (3250 miles). Throughout the fifty-seven-day journey the crew lived on a diet of dried and salted meat and fish, fruit, eggs, dried vegetables and bread.

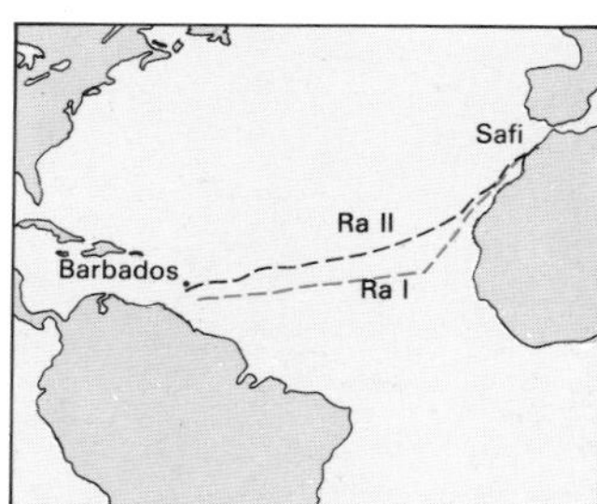

Both *Ra I* and *Ra II* sailed westward from Safi on the coast of Morocco.

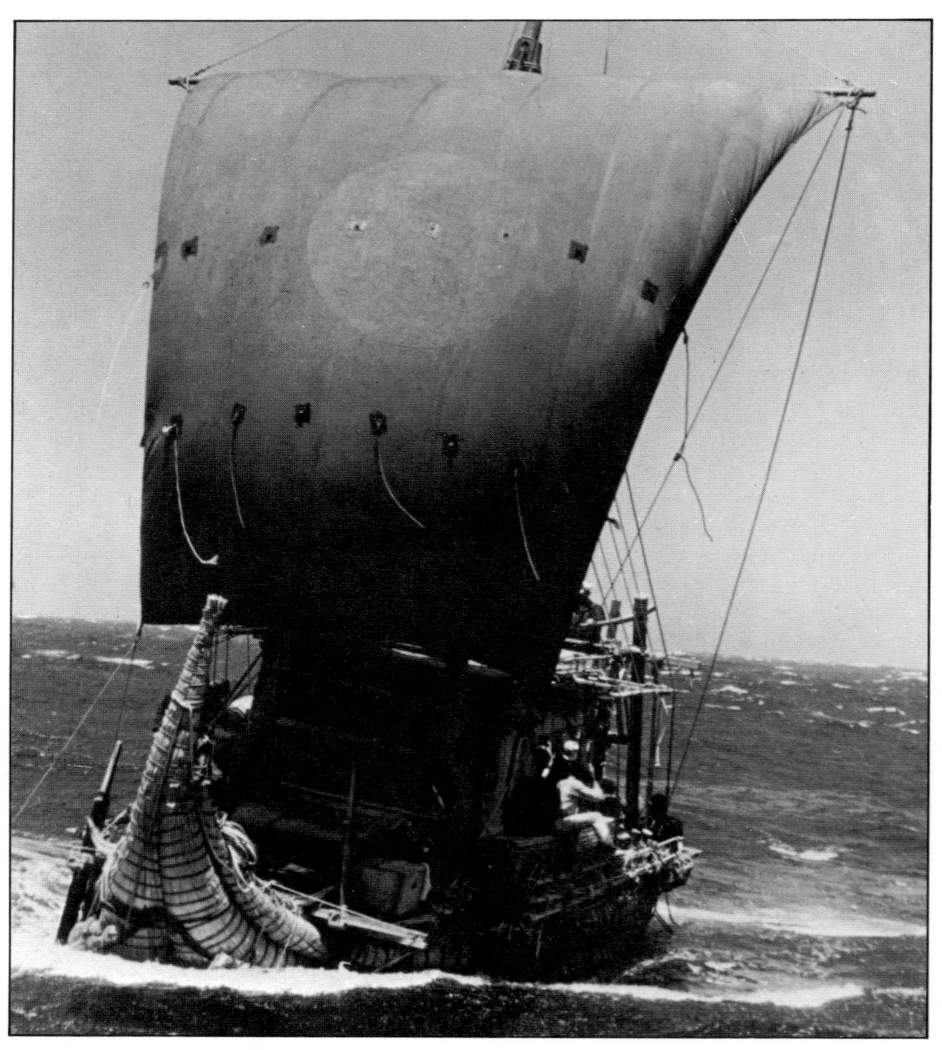

hunter-gatherers to groups of agriculturalists, further swelling the numbers of the latter. This migration stream must have made a major contribution to the speed with which agricultural practice spread across the world. It could also have rivalled in size and importance the migration stream from rural areas to towns and cities that came with the advent of industrialization some 200 to 300 years ago.

Whatever the details of the process, there is no doubt that agricultural practice, and the change in life-style that went with it, spread rapidly across the world. From the Near East it spread south into Africa and east into Asia and west and north through Europe. A similar spread took place, centred on China, in which agricultural practice and peoples moved north and south and across to the islands of the Pacific Ocean. Some authorities believe that the practice arrived in Central and Southern America as a result of migrants crossing the Atlantic from the Mediterranean region. These migrants may have been explorers or they may have been individuals who drifted westward accidentally on rafts or boats with broken steering. Other authorities maintain that agriculture arose in America independently. Either way, it did not really spread across the American continent until the final influx of Europeans, beginning in the late fifteenth century.

The subsequent development of agriculture

In some places, the spread of agricultural practice came to a temporary or even permanent halt because of a barrier of climate or vegetation. When agricultural practice first appeared in western North Africa about 6000 years ago, for example, its southward progress ceased at the edge of the tropical rain forest. This was because both the crops on which it was based were suited only to the savannah conditions further to the north and none of the local cereals, vegetables and fruits were suitable for cultivation in forest conditions. Negroid agriculturalists from the north did establish agricultural communities at the edge of the rain forest, but the forest itself remained the domain of its hunter-gatherer Pygmy inhabitants.

About 3500 years later, plants such as rice, yams and bananas, which had originated in the rain forests of Malaysia, arrived on the East African coast. They had been transported by exploratory individuals, particularly males, who had crossed the Indian Ocean. From the coast, cultivation of these introduced plants spread gradually westward across North Africa, arriving about 2000 years ago along the northern edge of the African rain forest. Adoption of these plants by the local agriculturalists eventually led to the establishment of agriculture within the rain forest, and throughout the region the advancing Negroids encountered the hunter-gatherer Pygmies. However, even with the new plants not all of the rain forest was suitable for cultivation. In such places Pygmies retained a hunter-gatherer economy, their territories existing as pockets among those of the agriculturalists. Where this happened, the two cultures entered into a symbiotic relationship: the hunters caught animals which they traded with the agriculturalists for fruit, grain and vegetables.

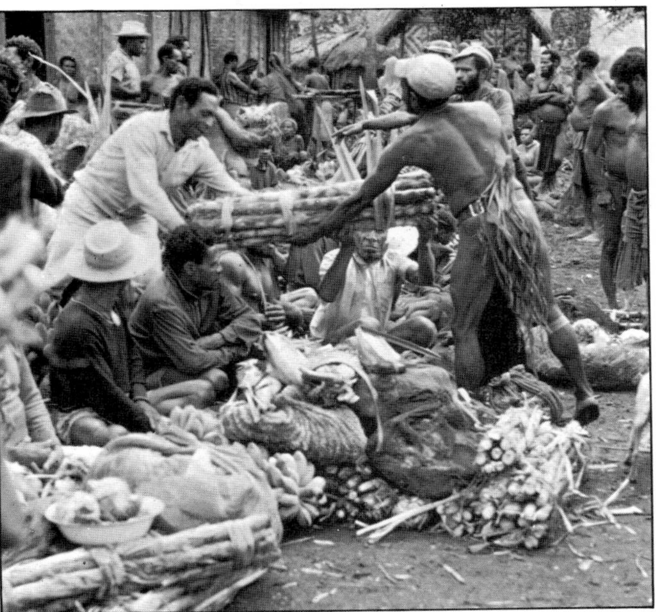

In rural areas of West Africa agricultural communities regularly trade with one another. Here members of a village are receiving food from a family of a neighbouring village as a gift for a bride.

The Negroid agriculturalists, on their slow migration to the south and east, finally emerged from the rain forest about 1200 years ago. Here they contacted, and spread at the expense of, another human race, the Bushmanoids. Previously these hunter-gatherers had occupied all of Africa south of latitude about 10° South. Eventually, the agriculturalists spread over all of Africa, displacing and absorbing the hunter-gatherer Bushmen as they went. Only in the most arid regions of east and southwest Africa, such as the Kalahari Desert, where agriculture was impossible, did the advance of agriculture cease, leaving pockets of the old culture to continue their hunter-gatherer existence.

The spread of agricultural Europeans across North America at the expense of the hunter-gatherer Amerindians and the fate of the hunter-gatherers of Southeast Asia and Australasia is a similar story.

Exploration – its relevance to man's migrations

The spread of people and of their life-styles such as we have been discussing occurs gradually, generation by generation. No matter how large scale the movements may appear on maps and graphs, they are carried out by individuals. Each shift is due to an individual or group at some point travelling into an area for the first time and deciding that this is a better area in which to live than the place in which they were born. In other words, it is the result of exploration. Whether an explorer then simply settles or whether he returns to his "home" and persuades others to come with him probably varies from occasion to occasion, but it is to the explorers that we must look to find the mechanism by which the spread of people occurs.

By the term "explorer", we do not mean only those individuals, few and far between, that travel vast distances and return with descriptions of exotic and distant lands,

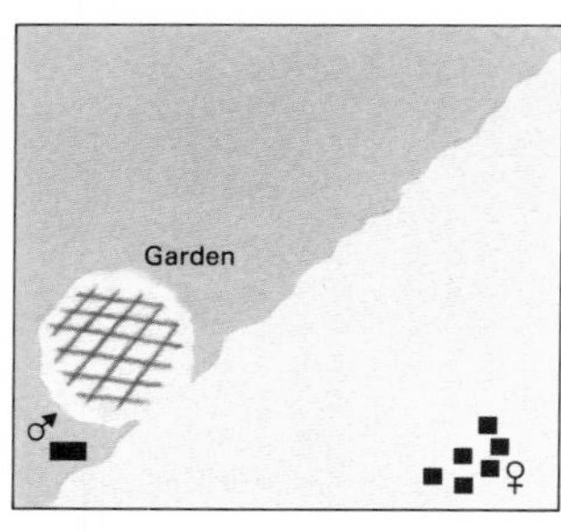

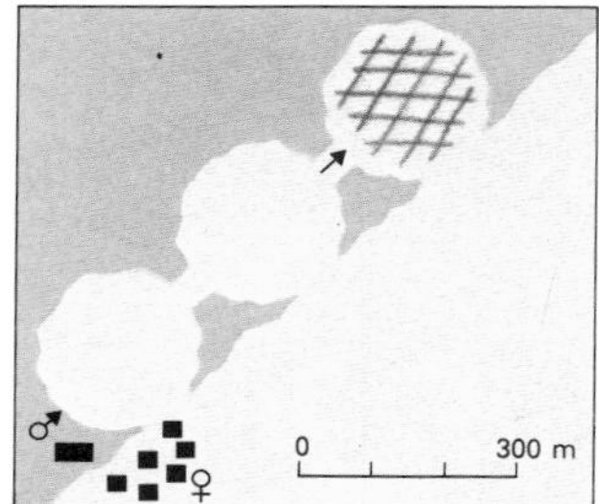

New Guinea Highlanders shift their food-growing area as the soil loses its fertility. At the same time, the huts inhabited by the males or the females and children are moved to keep the community together.

The "pig ceremony" is a remnant of the territorial conflicts that used to take place between groups of Highlanders.

but also those individuals that, during the normal course of building up their familiar area, visit new (to them), but not necessarily distant, places. Exploration is a normal part of the lifetime track of male hunter-gatherers, pastoral nomads, agriculturalists and, as we shall see, of modern industrialists. To illustrate the ubiquity of exploration we can look at the lifetime track of a New Guinea Highlander, who, while being classed as a modern agriculturalist, follows a way of life not unlike that of those early agriculturalists responsible for the ousting of the hunter-gatherers and for paving the way for the development of industrialization.

When the first studies were made in the 1960s, New Guinea Highlanders employed a type of shifting agriculture in which areas of land were cleared, cultivated and then left fallow, the entire village shifting to a new site when the distance to the fields became too great. New Guinea Highlanders subsist largely on cultivation of the sweet potato, which in places provides more than ninety per cent of their calories. Hunting, though important, makes only a small contribution to the diet as a whole. Animal husbandry makes even less. Pigs only are reared, but their growth and reproduction are so slow that they can be killed at only irregular intervals and large numbers are killed only every five to ten years. Pigs are grazed in the uncultivated no man's land between the territories of neighbouring groups.

Each territorial group consists of up to 4000 individuals and occupies an area of up to ninety square kilometres (35 square miles). Most of the conflicts between neighbouring groups seem to arise over pigs, and occasionally small-scale raiding parties are organized to make incursions into a neighbouring territory. These raiding parties attempt either to obtain a few of the neighbouring group's pigs; to regain pigs previously owned but which were lost in an earlier confrontation; or to restore the balance if a fellow male has been killed in, or by, a raiding party. Friction caused by these raiding parties can sometimes cause larger-scale, more open, battles. These are often shows of strength, taking the form of displays rather than actual fighting, but escalation can occur. On average, territorial skirmishes result in the death of between ten and twenty males each year from each territorial group. On other occasions, however, they can lead to wholesale eviction of one group by another.

Against this background of agriculture and territorial conflict, the young males build up their familiar areas by exploration during adolescence and early adulthood. Despite the aggressive atmosphere that exists between neighbouring groups, exploratory solitary males do travel within neighbouring territories and may live with these groups for a short time before moving on. In one count, eleven per cent of all males in a village had been born elsewhere. Of these, sixty per cent had moved on within sixteen months.

Further testimony to the extent of this exploration by young males is given by the fact that fifty per cent of all marriages are between males and females from different territories. This compares with a rate of only twenty-one per cent maximum reported for Australian hunter-gatherers. As with most hunter-gatherers and pastoral nomads, the pair most commonly return to settle in the territorial group into which the male was born. Among the Bundi Highlanders of New Guinea, eighty-seven per cent of all marriages in which one of the partners moved to a new group settled within the male's original territory. This compares with only five per cent that settled within the female's original territory. Eight per cent settled in an area to which neither of them originally belonged.

It seems, therefore, that despite their wide-ranging exploration when adolescent, most male New Guinea Highlanders eventually decide to return to their original area. It is those that decide that somewhere else is better that are the individuals who gradually produce the large-scale population movements that have been such a feature of human history.

The birth and spread of industrialization

Cities first appeared in the valleys of the Nile, Tigris and Euphrates (5000 years ago), along the Indus (4000 years ago) and perhaps independently in the valley of the Yangtse in China and along major rivers in Central and South America (about 3000 years ago). They were originally centres for trading and as such attracted

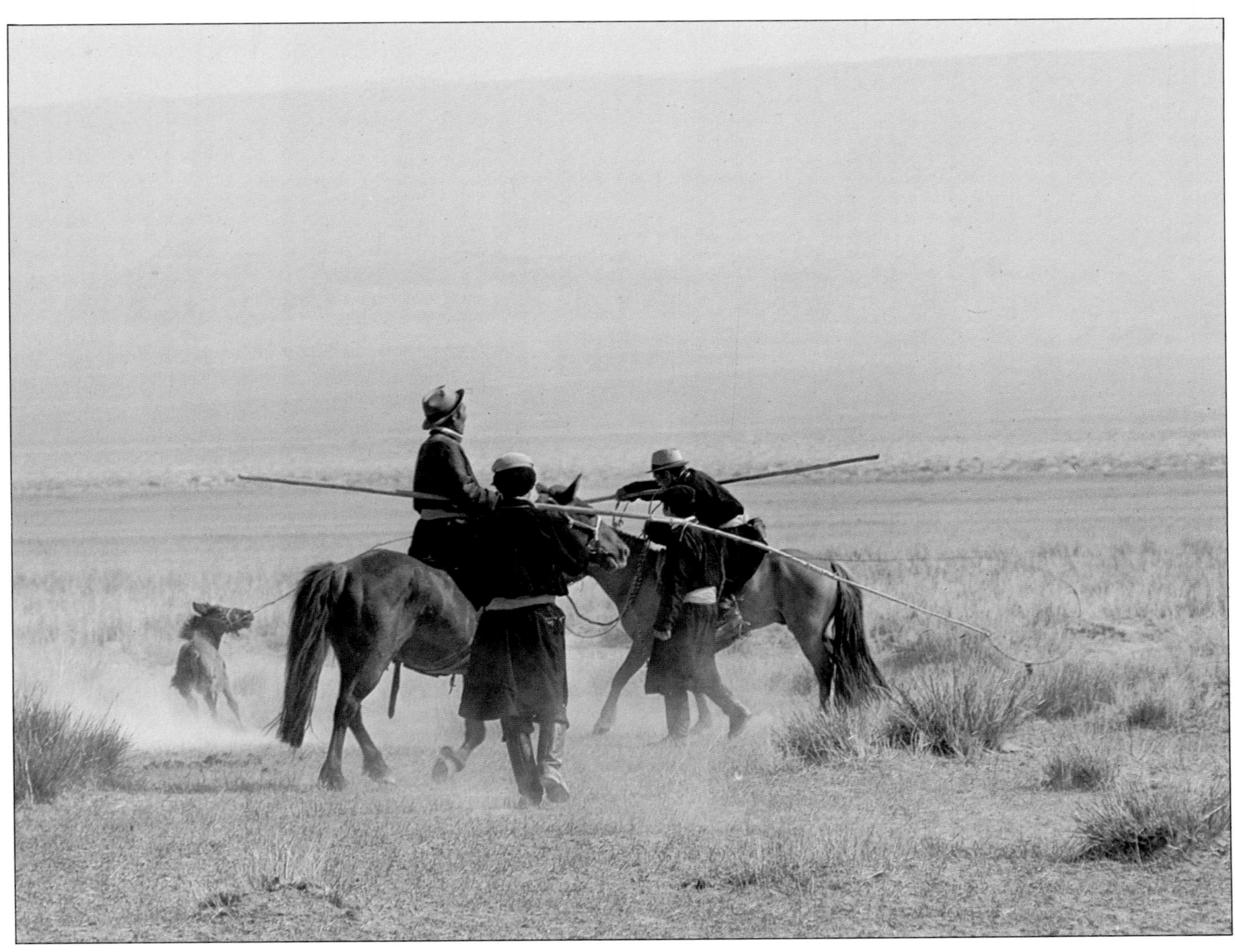

The steppe nomads of eastern Asia in the past exploited the horse for war, but today these herdsmen use the horse primarily as a domestic animal. The nomads' contests of horsemanship are relics from their past.

raiders as well as traders. About 4000 years ago the nomadic pastoralists of the Eurasian steppes developed the art of horse-riding. This no doubt evolved in response to the distances that such people had to travel each year to keep up with their herds of horses and bison. Horse-riding, however, for a time gave the pastoral nomads a distinct advantage in territorial conflict and in raids on the settled farmers and inhabitants of the first cities. This threat gave impetus to the development of the city as a walled, defendable area. Thereafter, the evolution of cities was slow and gradual. Not until the last 200 to 300 years in western Europe or the last 100 years or less elsewhere did cities receive the major impetus of a massive rural-urban migration. This came in the wake of industrialization and led to the birth of the modern city.

Industrialization is the new agriculture. From its birthplace in western Europe it has spread throughout the world, carried largely by European explorers. Early agricultural Europeans had settled and established colonies in places as far apart as North and South America and southern Africa. Not until industrialization had diffused from Europe to these expatriates did the colonists spread extensively at the expense of the indigenous agriculturalists, pastoralists and hunter-gatherers in the Americas, Africa, India and Australasia. The reason for the success of industrialists in these early territorial conflicts was once again that more people were concentrated in larger groups in a smaller space. The increased manpower and more efficient communication and mobilization of people and resources that resulted, not to mention the improved weaponry that was, and is, a special feature of industrialization, proved to be an unconquerable force.

The lifetime track of industrialists

The cities of industrialists, like the villages of agriculturalists, are made up largely of people's homes. These are fixed structures. In consequence, the daily pattern for the lifetime track of male agriculturalists and industrialists is a daily return migration cycle: out from the home in the morning and back again later, usually in the evening. Females have a similar pattern, but usually travel less far from the home and often repeat the pattern several times a day.

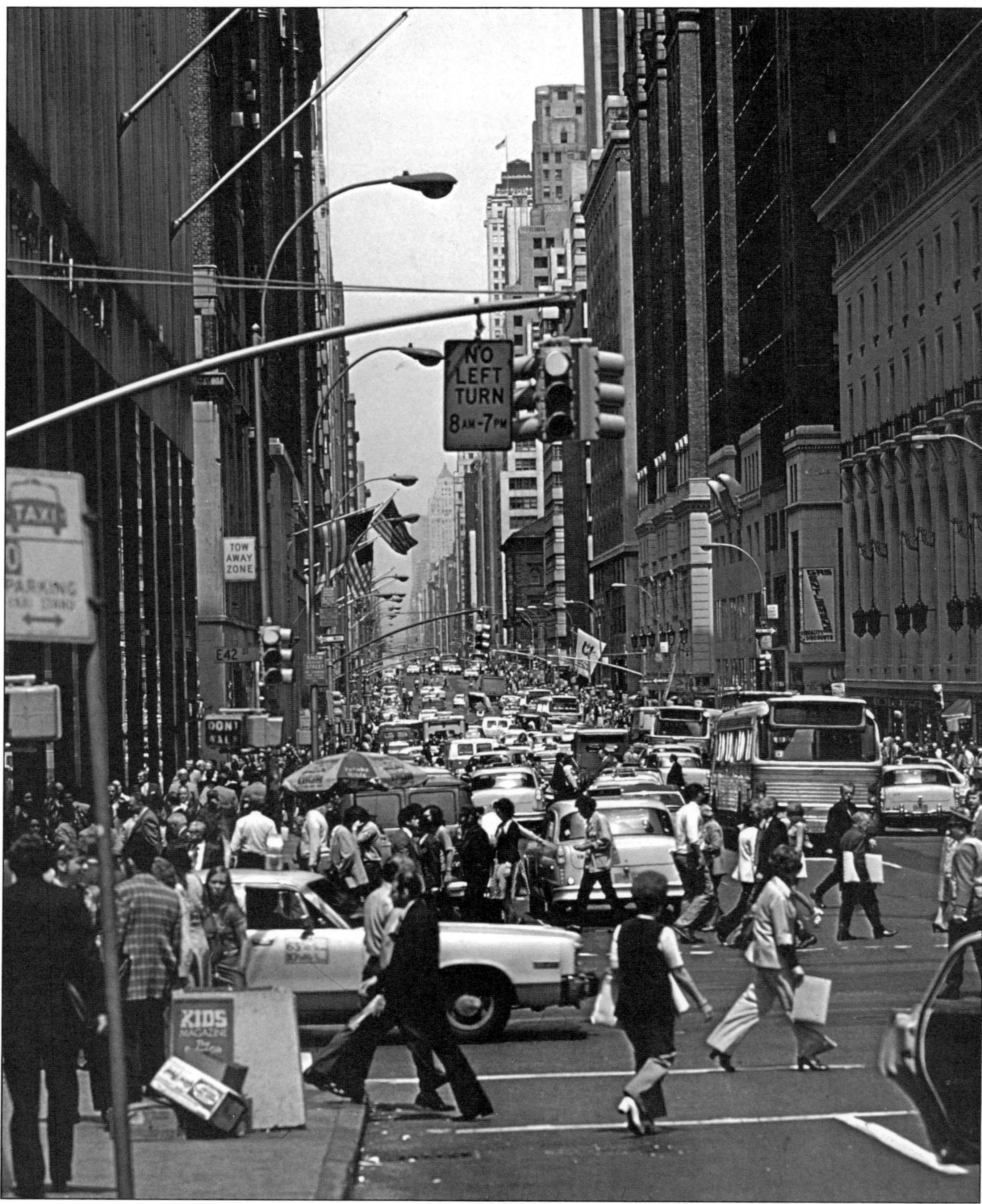

The world over, commuting forms the basis of a city-dweller's daily return migrations. Furthermore, all our other seemingly unimportant movements also form an essential part of our lifetime track. Going on holiday, for example, can be thought of as an exploratory migration or, if revisiting a location, as a migration to reassess a site within one's familiar area.

The furthest distance that is reached from the home during the course of the day obviously varies considerably from individual to individual. It also varies from place to place, culture to culture and with the passage of time. Most agriculturalists are limited to the distance they can cover by walking. When their fields reach this limit, slash and burn agriculturalists shift their home. As an inhabitant of a pre-industrial city, man travelled up to one kilometre (0.6 mile) from home during his daily migration cycle. In the USA in the late 1960s, the equivalent average distance was nine kilometres (6 miles) and was increasing at the rate of about 120 metres (130 yards) a year. The inhabitants of large modern cities, with access to modes of transport such as cars, trains and aeroplanes, can travel at least 1000 kilometres (630 miles) from home and still return in the course of a day. Most often, however, for modern city-dwellers as for agriculturalists, longer return journeys involve spending the night or many nights somewhere other than at the home.

From population studies in India, central and eastern Africa, Japan, the USA and western Europe, a picture has been built up of the movements of modern industrialists both between cities and rural areas and within cities. It is evident from these studies that the lifetime track of a modern industrialist is similar to that of a pre-industrial city-dweller and an agriculturalist. The following is a description of the basic pattern of the track.

During childhood, an individual accompanies its parents or other adults and by puberty has built up a sizeable familiar area. The area covered by this, however, reflects more the movements and interests of the parents than it does the predilections of the child. At about puberty, the young industrialist begins a phase of independent exploration. At first, this involves longer and longer return migrations from the parental home, perhaps involving staying overnight elsewhere with relatives or friends. Many eventually leave the parental home and sleep elsewhere, returning only at intervals. The first such removal migration away from the parental home is usually short-distance. If others follow, they become of increasingly long distance and visits back to the parental home become less frequent.

Rural/urban migration is a feature of the industrial world. The migration pattern in France between 1962 and 1968, for example, showed a net emigration from old industrial regions to the north and southeast and a net immigration into large cities such as Paris.

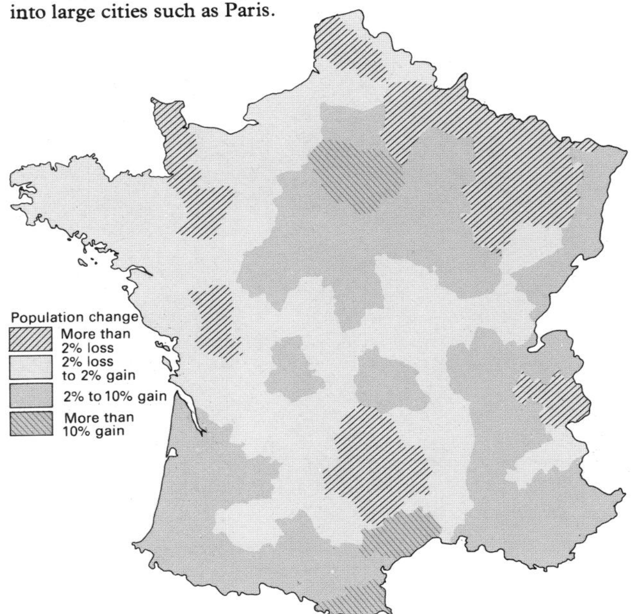

Adolescence is clearly a time of heightened restlessness; of an urge to visit new places and perhaps to travel; of an urge to explore. The rate at which the modern industrialist moves from home to home reaches a peak in his or her early twenties, females reaching their peak a year or so earlier. Whether or not a male marries, this rate remains unchanged up to the age of about twenty-four years. After that time married men move house less frequently. Single men, however, continue to move at a high rate, travelling gradually further and further, until they are about forty years old. The most common category of applicants wishing to emigrate from Europe to Australia and New Zealand, for example, is that of unmarried males approaching thirty years of age and with a history of shorter-distance movements.

During this major exploratory phase of their lives, males travel more frequently, and much further, than females. They also travel more solitarily. Unlike most primates, however, and unlike female hunter-gatherers, pastoral nomads and, to a lesser extent, female agriculturalists, female industrialists do perform some independent exploration during adolescence. It is also evident that adolescents and young adults visit a much wider range of places than their elders, and they are much less selective as to where they go. If, and when, a male and female marry, they most often settle in a place familiar to the male through earlier exploration and which they have probably previously visited as a pair. As with hunter-gatherers and agriculturalists, this is often close to the male's parental home. Even those young, single males that migrate from one continent to another on the final, most distant, phase of their exploration are quite likely to return to their native country, bringing with them a female met in the distant land.

Migration into cities and to foreign lands

One of the features of industrialization has been a massive migration from country to town. This has not been a local phenomenon. In places such as Britain it may have been aggravated by government legislation over the partitioning of land and the availability of work for people in rural areas, but it has occurred everywhere that industrialization has taken place. It implies that as a result of their explorations, during which they are as likely to visit remote rural areas as overpopulated conurbations, young industrialists decide that cities are the best places in which to settle down and raise a family. But nothing could be further from the truth. Now, just as in the early years of industrialization, life expectancy is statistically less for city-dwellers than for inhabitants of more rural areas. Furthermore, city-dwellers produce fewer children and these are more likely to die in infancy.

In the middle to late nineteenth century, when rural-urban migration in Europe was reaching flood proportions, a second major stream of human migration was in

WORLD MIGRATIONS SINCE THE EIGHTEENTH CENTURY

Modern population movements have generally been the result of political, cultural, religious and economic pressures. Famines, however, were the main reason for emigration from Ireland in 1847, from India in 1866 and 1877, from China in 1878 and from Russia in 1891. The largest migration in recent times and, in fact, in man's history, occurred in the latter half of the nineteenth century. During this period North America alone experienced an influx of some twenty million individuals (below, left). Most of these came from Europe, where trade slumps in the industrialized nations brought unemployment, where population growth led to scarcity of land and where upheaval due to war was commonplace. The emigrants were attracted to North America by the prospects for employment, cheap land suitable for agriculture and even the discovery of gold. Similar prospects attracted English people to Australia and New Zealand and Chinese and Japanese people to the west coast of the Americas. Transportation of convicts from Britain to Australia and later, in Russia, of political prisoners to Siberia, has been another significant migration. At about the turn of the nineteenth century there was also a large movement of people to the colonies of the major European countries.

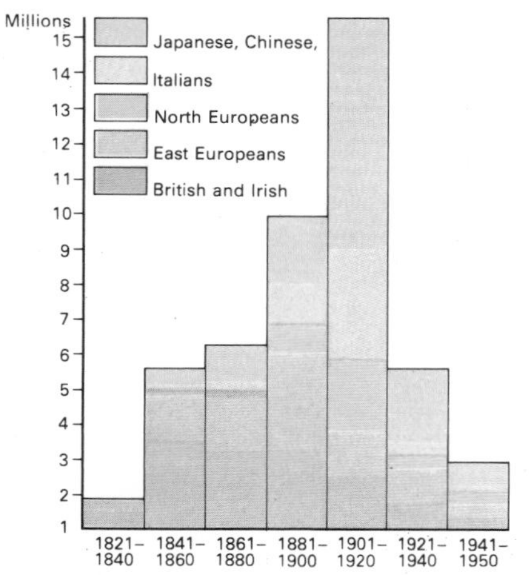

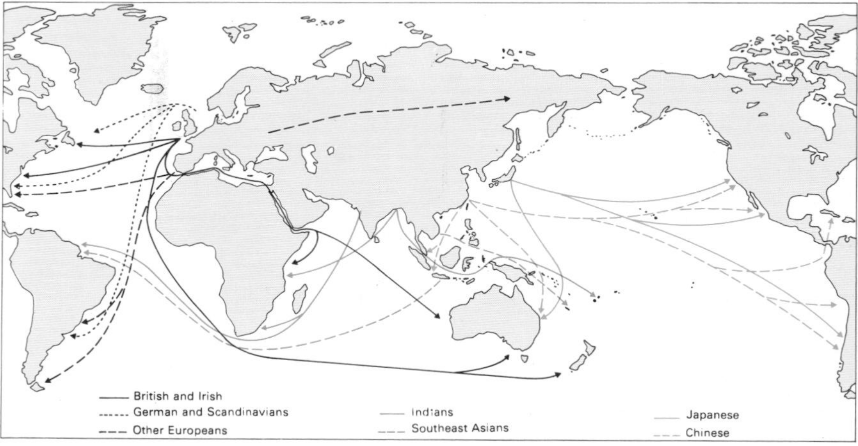

During the gold rush of 1851 in Victoria, southeastern Australia, many thousands of immigrants flocked to the area in the hope of making a fortune either from prospecting or by establishing themselves as shopkeepers in the towns or villages that rapidly grew up. The pioneers' only link with their homeland, and often with their family, was the occasional letter.

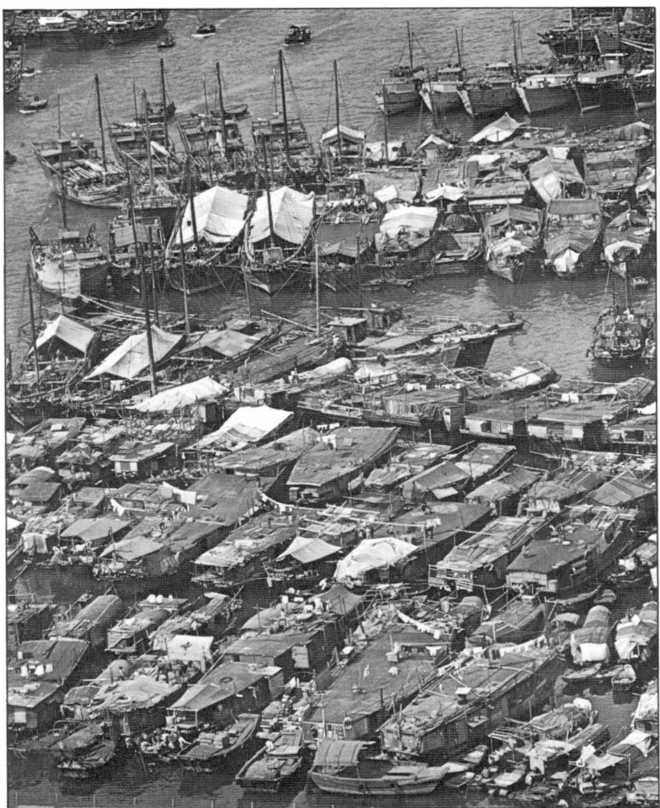

In Hong Kong, a large, rapid, and therefore unmanageable, influx of immigrants and people from rural areas has resulted in many families having to live permanently on boats in the harbour.

progress. This was the international migration of people, mainly from Europe, but also from China and other parts of Asia, to the new, exciting lands of North America, Australia and New Zealand. In many ways, these international migrations were the opposite of rural-urban migration; they were aimed at places with an image of wide open spaces. Of course, many of the migrants eventually opted to settle in one of the major, developing cities of their adopted homeland. It is doubtful, however, whether the promise of crowded city life was the vision that first attracted these migrants to the new lands.

The stimulus for migration

If there is a pattern to the migrations that came with industrialization it is that, faced with increasing food supply, wealth and opportunity – the benefits of industrialization – young people decided to settle among the crowds of the cities, to become part of the rural-urban flood. Faced with famine and repression, as were the people of Ireland and eastern Europe at various times in the nineteenth and early twentieth centuries, they opted for international migration.

Looking back through human history we find indications that such a pattern is not new. Whether hunter-gatherers, pastoral nomads or agriculturalists, there will always have been an advantage in settling within a large group. More people means greater manpower to hunt game, herd animals or to tend and clear fields. Most important of all, it means being better able to defend the territory against neighbouring groups. This holds true only for as long as food is plentiful and the risk of disease associated with crowded conditions is not too great. This logic should always have paid dividends. So much so, that it may even have become instinctive rather than rational. It will always have paid dividends; always, that is, until industrialization. The instinct to go where there are fewer people when conditions become harsh is still a good one; nineteenth-century international migrants probably gained a great advantage from their behaviour. In contrast, the instinct to join large groups because conditions were improving, leading as it did to rural-urban migration, as we have seen, sent many people to premature death and reduced health and fertility.

Human navigation

All animals that explore need to be able to navigate; humans are no exception. Having explored a particular place, an individual has to be able to find his way back to his previous familiar area. Places found during exploration then become part of the familiar area. This is true whether the explorer is finding his way back from the South Pole or trying to return home after visiting an unknown part of town.

Our modern way of life is such that we are surrounded by aids to navigation. Street names, and numbers, sign-posts, maps and magnetic compasses are all great assets when exploring new areas. Against the backdrop of human history, however, it is only extremely recently that people have had access to such aids. Indeed, in large parts of the world such aids still are unavailable. Certainly, they did not exist during those periods of thousands of years when all humans were hunter-gatherers or agriculturalists. How, then, do humans manage to navigate without these aids?

If we place pigeons in a van and transport them to some unknown release site, we now know that even before they are taken out of the van they know in which direction to fly to return home. They know this because they have used route-based navigation. They have monitored their outward journey, either by watching their surroundings as they travel or, if they cannot see out of the van, by noting familiar smells or by checking their direction against the earth's magnetic field. If we do the same experiment with blindfolded humans we find that they too know the direction of home before they get out of the van. How do they do it?

The subjects of these experiments cannot describe how they performed route-based navigation. Indeed, more often than not they are amazed when their "guess" turns out to be so near to the home direction. Of course, some of them chose the completely wrong direction, but the results obtained, as for pigeons, are statistically significant. We still do not know how individuals navigated. The simple answers have been ruled out. They did not follow a memorized map. Nor did they detect the heat of the sun through the windows of the van. And their route-based navigation was just as accurate on completely overcast days as on sunny days. In one such displacement experiment half the subjects had a bar magnet placed against the back of their head and tucked into the elastic of their blindfold. The other half were fitted similarly with a dummy magnet made out of brass. All of the subjects thought they were wearing a real magnet. When asked to indicate their homeward direction, only those people wearing the dummy magnets could carry out route-based navigation. Those wearing real magnets were disorientated!

Is it possible that humans have a subconscious sense of direction based on detection of the earth's magnetic field? Certainly pigeons have a sense organ, located between the brain and the skull, which contains magnetite, a chemical that aligns itself along the lines of the earth's magnetic field. It is thought that this organ detects geomagnetic direction. Perhaps humans have the same organ? However, pigeons have to learn how to use and improve their sense of direction relative to the magnetic field. If humans have such a sense, we should expect them also to have to learn how to use it effectively. Most people, because of the modern way of life and the many aids to navigation with which they are surrounded, have little cause to make use of a geomagnetic sense.

Experiments further to determine if humans possess this sixth sense, and to what degree of accuracy it can be trained, have been based on modifications of the above. When subjects were displaced blindfolded to an unfamiliar site and the blindfolds then removed, they were able to point in the direction of home as accurately as pigeons fly towards home when they are released. Like pigeons, they were able to do this because they followed the outward journey. Analysis of the subjects' method of navigation showed that if they knew they were south of home, they simply checked the position of the sun or wind direction, determined north, and set off in that direction. The question then was: did the subjects improve on their route-based estimate of home direction by seeing their surroundings? This was difficult to answer. Because the subjects were so good at route-based navigation there was little room for improvement. Nevertheless, in some circumstances they did improve. If they had visited the release site before, their new "visual" estimate tended to be better than their route-based estimate. Even if they had not visited the site before, as long as they could see familiar landmarks such as hills on the horizon and as long as either the sun was shining or the wind blowing, they could improve on their original estimate. None of the people involved in the experiments, however, could describe how they used this additional information.

By the combination of route-based navigation and a familiar area map, a human need never get lost during exploration. If the direction of the outward journey is known, this direction can be reversed until the familiar area map is encountered. The chances of getting lost therefore increase the more inaccurately the outward direction is noted and reversed and the more limited is the person's familiar area. There is clearly an advantage in building up the familiar area gradually, building it large and leaving longer-distance explorations until it is large.

Such a navigation system is adequate for most humans and other animals during their everyday lives. It is, of course, too imprecise for mariners and other long-distance travellers. For this reason, man has given great emphasis to the development of navigational aids as he explores further and further across the earth and into space. For an individual exploring the surrounding countryside, a city may be a sufficiently large target to which to return, but even earth itself is a small target to a person exploring the solar system. As man pushes his explorations further and further into space, we can expect greater and greater refinement of the mechanical navigation systems we have devised. As individuals, however, it seems that we may still have to depend on the navigational mechanisms that we share with birds and other animals.

Our migration knows no boundaries. In the past our familiar area was restricted to planet earth. When, on 20 July, 1969, the Apollo 11 astronauts Neil Armstrong and Buzz Aldrin landed on the moon it was indeed, certainly in terms of migration, "one big step for mankind". To where next will our inborn exploratory urge take us?

Helmets carried electric coils which produced a magnetic field.

HUMAN NAVIGATION

Having been displaced southward and then asked to point in the direction of travel, those people subjected to a shift in the magnetic field either to the left or right of normal pointed in a direction different to, and either side of, that of the control group.

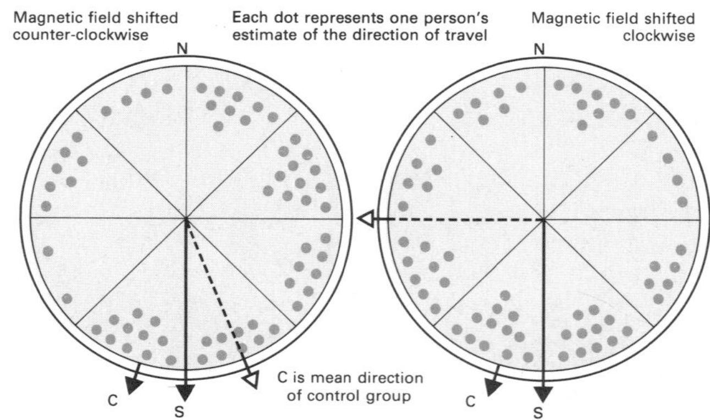

Glossary

Aerial plankton Wind-borne animals and plants.
Amphipod Aquatic crustacean with narrow body, rounded appendages and lacking a tough casing over the head and thorax.
Asexual reproduction Reproduction without male and female sex cells (gametes).
Banding Method of marking an animal using a metal band attached usually to the animal's leg or, in the case of bats, the wing. Also known as ringing.
Bivalve mollusc Member of the group of invertebrates including snails and mussels which bears a shell with two halves hinged together.
Bract Modified leaf sheathing a flower.
Copepod Aquatic crustacean with a reduced number of body segments and which lacks a tough casing over the head and thorax.
Crustacea Mostly aquatic invertebrates with a segmented body, an external skeleton and paired, jointed appendages. Examples include crabs, lobsters, shrimps, barnacles and water-fleas.
Decapod Aquatic crustacean with ten legs.
Displacement Usually passive movement of an animal, plant or its offspring from one place to another by, for example, wind or water currents.
Dispersal Scattering in all directions.
Echolocation Determining the position of objects by reflected sounds.
Emigration Act of leaving an area.
Exploratory migration Movement beyond the familiar area with the intention of extending its limits while retaining the ability to return.
Familiar area Region within which an animal knows, by means of exploration or social communication, the best places to feed, sleep and breed and within which it can navigate from one place to another.
Gastrotriche Flattened, spiny, aquatic invertebrate.
Home range That part of an animal's familiar area within which it moves in the course of a given interval such as a day, season or year.
Homing Returning to a place of capture from a distant release point.
Hydrozoan Aquatic invertebrate of simple form.
Immigration Act of entering and settling in a place.
Invertebrate Animal lacking a backbone.
Isopod Crustacean, usually aquatic, with flattened body and appendages and lacking a tough casing over the head and thorax.
Larva Usually sexually immature form of an animal which hatches from an egg and feeds and grows rapidly prior to transforming into an adult.
Lifetime track Path traced out in space by an individual between birth and death.
Loop migration To-and-fro movement using a different route for the outward and return journeys.
Marsupial Mammal in which the young are born in an underdeveloped state and are usually reared within a pouch.
Metabolism Chemical processes that take place within an animal or plant.
Migration Movement from one place to another.
Migratory divide Migration in which individuals either side of an imaginary mid-line move in different directions to the same destination.
Mysid Shrimp-like crustacean which carries its young in a pouch under the thorax.
Nauplial larva Oval, unsegmented pre-adult form of many crustacea.
Navigation Sensory mechanism by which an animal determines the position of a given point in space.
Nomadism Migration with no fixed pattern.
Nymph Young of many species of insects which differs from the adult in being sexually immature and bearing underdeveloped wings.
Orientation Sensory mechanism by which an animal determines and maintains movement in a given direction.
Parasite Organism living in or on another organism from which it obtains food.
Partial migration Movement involving only part of a population.
Parturition Birth of young.
Peak direction Most common direction of movement of individuals within a given population.
Photosynthesis Process driven by sunlight by which plants manufacture food from carbon dioxide and water.
Phytoplankton *See* Plankton.
Plankton Animals and plants which float or drift almost passively in seas, oceans and lakes. Known as zooplankton and phytoplankton respectively.
Polychaete worm Invertebrate, usually marine, which bears bristles along the length of its body.
Re-migration Return journey cycle completed only by virtue of the movements of different generations of a population.
Removal migration One-way movement from one place to another.
Return migration Movement from one place to another and back again.
Ringing *See* Banding.
Roosting Resting or sleeping.
Sexual reproduction Reproduction involving the fusion of egg- and sperm-like cells (gametes).
Spawning Liberation of eggs and sperm.
Spore Usually single-celled reproductive body of a plant or simple animal that gives rise to a new individual.
Sonar System for underwater detection of objects using reflected sounds.
Symbiosis Association of two dissimilar organisms for mutual benefit.
Tagging Method of marking an animal using a metal, coloured plastic or rubber label attached to the animal's body.
Vertebrate Animal with a backbone.
Vertical migration To-and-fro movement in the vertical plane.
Zooplankton *See* Plankton.

Index

The index is alphabetized word by word. References to the text are in roman type; references to captions and illustrations are in *italics*

G

H

O

P

U

V

W

Y

Z

Acknowledgements

Harrow House Editions would like to thank Hodder and Stoughton Limited for their kind permission to use *The Evolutionary Ecology of Animal Migration* by Dr Robin Baker, published in 1978, as a source for maps and diagrams. The editors would also like to thank the following people for their assistance: Theresa Alexis, Dr Clive Bagshaw, Martyn Bramwell, Sue Brown, Dougal Dixon, Trevor Dolby, Harding Dunnit and John Sitworthy.

Artists

All maps by **Eugene Fleury,** excepting
pages 20, 23, 171, 175, 186, 190, 194, 239 by Arka Cartographics Ltd.
pages 223, 227, 230, 231, 234 by Clyde Surveys Ltd.
relief map on page 137 by Product Support (Graphics) Ltd.

All diagrams by **Richard Lewis**

All major illustration by **Hilary Burn,** excepting
pages 42/43, 66, 67 by Andrew Farmer
pages 69, 74, 76, 77, 81 by John Barber
page 174 by Colin Newman (Linden Artists)

All line illustration by **Vana Haggerty,** excepting
page 103 by David Ashby

Picture Credits

Photographs are credited by descending order of the base line of each photograph. Where two or more photographs lie on the same base line, credits read left to right. Oxford Scientific Films has been abbreviated to OSF, Natural History Photographic Agency Ltd. to NHPA and Natural Science Photos to NSP.

2 Bruce Coleman Ltd/Rod Williams; **6–7** Bruce Coleman Ltd/Jen & Des Bartlett; **9** British Library, Private Collection; **10** Private Collection; **11** British Library; **12** British Library; **13** Ralph Morse; **14** Susan Griggs Agency/Jonathan Blair; **16** Bruce Coleman Ltd/Stephen Dalton; **17** Bruce Coleman Ltd/ Ronald Thompson, Bruce Coleman Ltd/ Rob & Clara Calhoun; **18** D.P. Wilson; **19** Australian News & Info. Service, Bruce Coleman Ltd/Norman Tomalin; **20–21** Bruce Coleman Ltd/ J.T. Wright; **22** Courtesy S.T. Emlen Cornell University; **23** Bruce Coleman Ltd/D & K Utty; **25** The Ramblers' Association; **26** Bruce Coleman Ltd/Nicholas Devere; **28** Bridlington Free Press; **30** Eric Hosking; **31** Bruce Coleman Ltd/Jeff Foott, NASA/Cornell University, Courtesy S.T. Emlen Cornell University; **32** Heather Angel; **33** Hans Dossenbach; **34** Bruce Coleman Ltd/Jane Burton; **36** Heather Angel; **37** M.J.D. Hirons; **38** Heather Angel; **39** Heather Angel; **40** Heather Angel; **43** Bruce Coleman Ltd/Hans Reinhard; **44** Heather Angel; **46** D.P. Wilson; **48** OSF; **50** Jacana/Fred Winner, Bruce Coleman Ltd/ Kim Taylor, Bruce Coleman Ltd/John Shaw; **51** OSF; **53** Bruce Coleman Ltd/Bill Wood, Heather Angel; **54** Herve Chaumeton, Bruce Coleman Ltd/Jane Burton; **55** Bruce Coleman Ltd/M.P. Kahl, Herve Chaumeton; **56** Donald Smetzer; **57** Heather Angel, NHPA/Peter Johnson; **58** Bruce Coleman Ltd/C.B. Frith; **59** Bruce Coleman Ltd/ Jane Burton; **60** Bruce Coleman Ltd/ Robert Schroeder; **61** BBC Educational Publications; **62** R.W. Martin, Severn Trent Water Authority; **63** Bruce Coleman Ltd/Peter Ward, R.W. Martin, Severn Trent Water Authority, Ardea/J.L. Mason; **64** George D. Lepp; **68** Sdeuard Bisserot; **71** Sdeuard Bisserot; **72** Bruce Coleman Ltd/Stephen Dalton; **73** Bruce Coleman Ltd/Stephen Dalton; **75** George D. Lepp; **77** NHPA/A. Bannister; **78** Prema Photos/K. Preston-Mafham; **79** OSF/J.A.L. Cooke; **80** Prema Photos/K. Preston-Mafham; **81** NHPA/Stephen Dalton; **82–83** Gianni Tortoli; **84** NHPA/A. Bannister, Gianni Tortoli; **87** NHPA/ A. Bannister; **89** OSF; **90** OSF; **91** G.R. Roberts; **92** Seaphot/Richard Chester; **94** Jacana, Bruce Coleman Ltd/Jane Burton; **95** D.P. Wilson, Heather Angel; **96** Bruce Coleman Ltd/Jeff Foott; **97** Jacana; **98** Frank Lane/W.T. Davidson; **99** Bruce Coleman Ltd/Jane Burton; **100** Bruce Coleman Ltd/Hans Reinhard; **103** Bruce Coleman Ltd/Jeff Foott; **105** Bruce Coleman Ltd/Harold Schultz; **106** Bruce Coleman Ltd/Jeff Foott; **107** NHPA/I. Polunin; **109** Seaphot/Dick Clarke; **111** Zefa, Seaphot/J. N. Perez; **113** G.R. Roberts; **114** Bruce Coleman Ltd/Jeff Foott; **115** Seaphot/Dick Clarke; **116** Bruce Coleman Ltd/Stephen Dalton; **120** Bruce Coleman Ltd/J. Burnley, OSF/Animals Animals/ Paul Benson; **121** Bruce Coleman Ltd/Peter Jackson, NHPA/F. Greenaway; **122** Bruce Coleman Ltd/Jane Burton, OSF/Animals Animals/Michael Gadomski; **124** OSF/Animals Animals/Leszczynski; **125** Heather Angel; **126** OSF/Animals Animals/Leszczynski, OSF; **128** Eric Hosking; **130** Ardea/Richard Vaughn; **131** NHPA; **132** Bruce Coleman Ltd/Udo Hirsch, Studies in Bird migration by William E. Clarke; **134** Bruce Coleman Ltd/Jen & Des Bartlett; **135** Radar Ornithology by Sir Eric Eastwood Marconi Research Labs; **136–7** Ardea; **138** Brian Hawkes; **139** Ardea/Andre Fatras; **141** Frank Lane/F. Merlet; **143** Ardea/C.R. Knights; **146** OSF/J.A.L. Cooke; **147** Ardea/Jean-Paul Ferrero; **151** Susan Griggs Agency/Jonathan Blair; **152** Bruce Coleman Inc/Laura Riley; **153** Bruce Coleman Ltd/Clara Calhoun, OSF; **154** Heather Angel; **155** Bruce Coleman Ltd/Francisco Erize; **157** Bruce Coleman Ltd/Jen & Des Bartlett; **161** Bruce Coleman Ltd/Jen & Des Bartlett; **162** Frank Lane/Signal Corps; **165** Susan Griggs Agency/ Jonathan Blair; **166** Ardea/Il Beames, Ardea/M.E. Gore, Ardea/Ake Lindau; **167** Brian Hawkes; **168** OSF; **170** Sdeuard Bisserot; **173** OSF/ Animals Animals/Robert Mitchell; **174** OSF/Animals Animals/Robert Mitchell; **175** Bruce Coleman Ltd/Graham Pizzey, Ardea/Jean-Paul Ferrero; **176** OSF; **177** Sdeuard Bisserot, Bruce Coleman Ltd/Sdeuard Bisserot; **178–9** Dr. M.D. Tuttle; **180** William Curtsinger; **183** Bruce Coleman Ltd/Christian Zubor; **184–185** Bruce Coleman Ltd/Al Gidding, Bruce Coleman Ltd/N.R. Lightfoot; **186** Frank Lane/Leonard Lee Rue III; **188** Jacana/Jean-Phillipe; **189** William Curtsinger; **191** Mary Evans Picture Library; **192** Bruce Coleman Ltd/Simon Trevor; **193** Australian News & Info. Service, OSF/Animals Animals/Harry Engles; **194** Bruce Coleman Ltd/Jeff Foott, Ardea/Kenneth Fink; **195** Seaphot/Rod Salm; **196** NHPA/Peter Johnson; **199** Frank Lane/Len Robinson; **200–1** Bruce Coleman Ltd/C.J. Ott, Frank Lane/Peter Davey; **202** Bruce Coleman Ltd/C.J. Ott; **203** Bruce Coleman Ltd/R.M. Campbell, Bruce Coleman Ltd/M. Pearson; **204** Eric Hosking; **204–5** NSP/MS Price, Hans Dossenbach, Ardea/John Wrightman; **206–7** Jacana/Massart; **208** NHPA/Peter Johnson, OSF/Animals Animals/Harry Engles; **209** Bruce Coleman Ltd/Jane Burton; **210** OSF/Animals Animals/Leonard Lee Rue III; **211** Ardea/S. Roberts; **212** Janice G. Mather; **213** Bruce Coleman Ltd/Leonard Lee Rue III, NSP/G. Kinns; **214** Bruce Coleman Ltd/Leonard Lee Rue III; **215** OSF Animals Animals/Stefan Meyers, NSP/G. Kinns; **216** Bruce Coleman Ltd/Jane Burton; **217** Eric Hosking; **219** NHPA/John Sparks, OSF/Animals Animals/Kojo Tanaka; **220** Alan Hutchison; **222** Alan Hutchison Library/Brian Moser; **224** Ronald Sheridan, Alan Hutchison, Alan Hutchison Library/J.V. Puttkamer; **226** Alan Hutchison Library/J.V. Puttkamer, Alan Hutchison Library/Brian Moser; **227** Axel Poignant; **228** Alan Hutchison Library/Sarah Errington, Alan Hutchison Library/Andre Singer; **229** Alan Hutchison Library/Andre Singer, Alan Hutchison; **231** Susan Griggs Agency/Victor Englebert, B. & C. Alexander; **232** Alan Hutchison; **233** Alan Hutchison Library/Brian Moser; **234** Camera Press; **235** Axel Poignant; **236** Steve Shaw; **237** Alan Hutchison Library/Brian Moser; **238** Bruce Coleman Ltd/Norman Tomalin; **240** Axel Poignant; **241** Zefa; **242** Les Lockey; **243** Aspect Picture Library.

Bibliography

Amphibians and Reptiles by Čihař and Čepická (Octopus); *Animal Marking* ed. Bernard Stonehouse (Macmillan); *Animal Migration* by Otto von Frisch (Collins); *Animal Migration, Navigation and Homing* by Schmidt-Koenig and Keeton (Springer); *Atlas of the Oceans* (Mitchell Beazley); *Bird Navigation* by G. V. T. Matthews (Cambridge University Press); *The Book of Birds* by A.M. Lysaght (Phaidon); *The Book of British Birds* (Mitchell Beazley); *Collins Guide to Butterflies of Britain and Europe/Freshwater Fishes of Britain and Europe/ Seabirds* (Collins); *Fish Migration* by Harden-Jones (Arnold); *The International Wildlife Encyclopaedia* eds. Dr M. & R. Burton (BPC); *Introduction to Biogeography* by Brian Seddon (Duckworth); *Larousse Encyclopaedia of Animal Life* (Hamlyn); *Life in the Sea* by Gunnar Thorson (Weidenfeld and Nicolson); *Life Nature Library* (Time Life); *The Lives of Bats* by Yalden and Morris (David and Charles); *The Living World of Animals* (Reader's Digest); *Mammals of the World* Vol. I & II by Walker (John Hopkins); *The Migrations of Birds* by Jean Dorst (Heinemann); *The Mystery of Animal Migration* by Matthieu Ricard (Constable); *The Times Atlas of World History* (Times Books); *World Atlas of Birds* (Mitchell Beazley); *The World of Amphibians and Reptiles / Birds / Fish / Insects / Mammals* (Sampson Low Guides).